I0822997

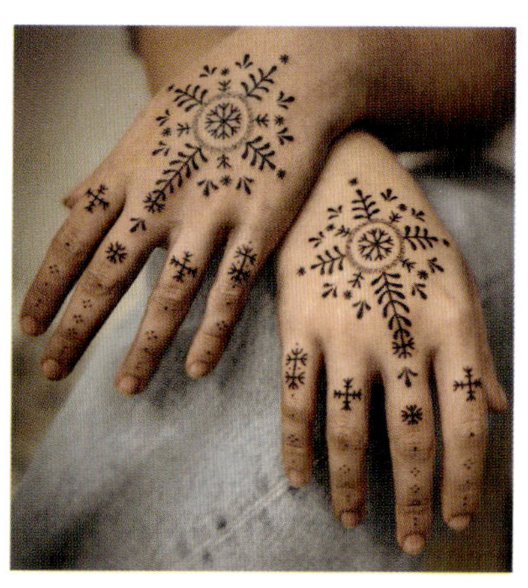

INDIGENOUS TATTOO TRADITIONS

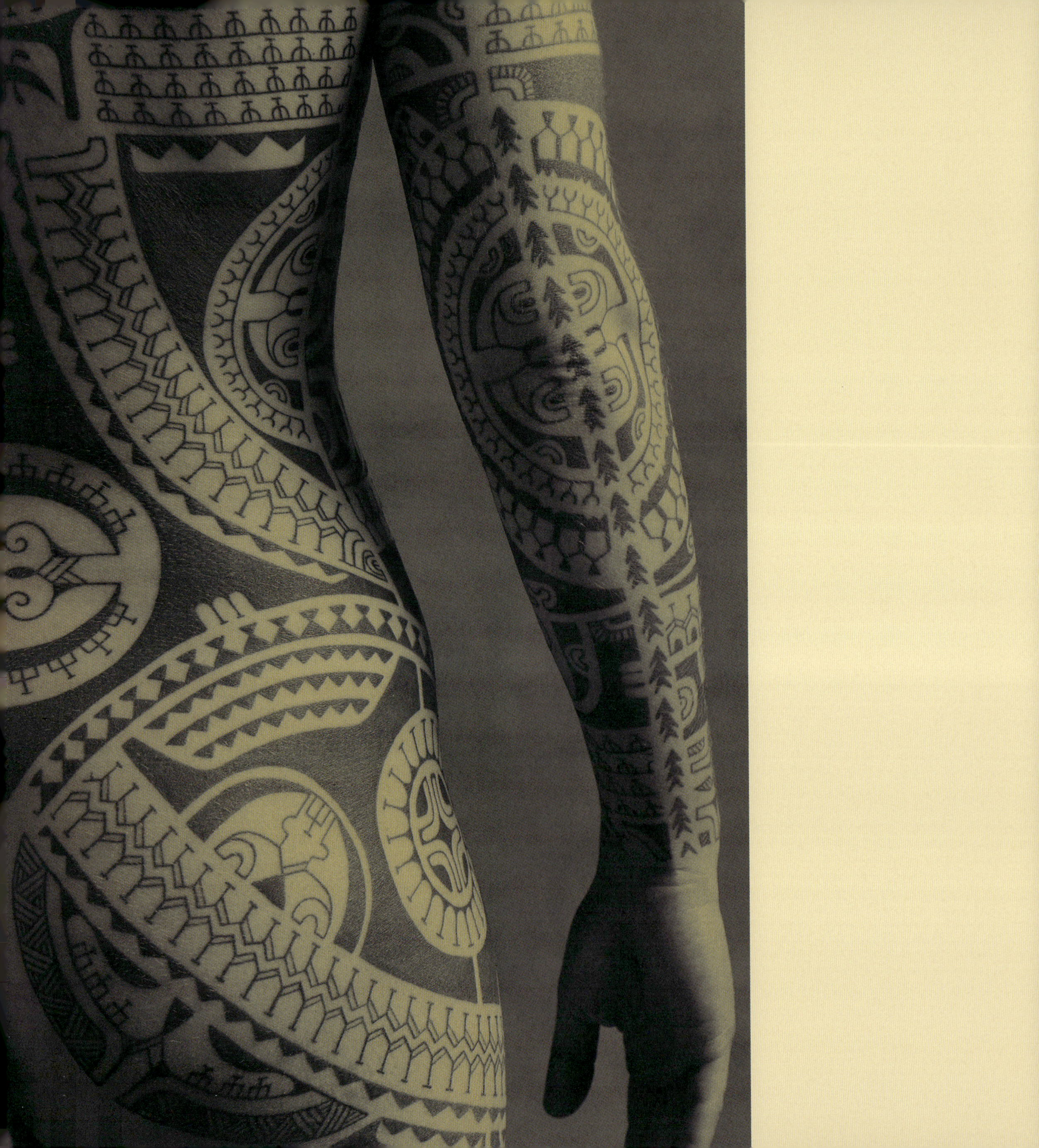

LARS KRUTAK

INDIGENOUS TATTOO TRADITIONS

Humanity through Skin and Ink

PRINCETON UNIVERSITY PRESS
PRINCETON & OXFORD

Published by
Princeton University Press
41 William Street
Princeton, New Jersey 08540

99 Banbury Road,
Oxford OX2 6JX

press.princeton.edu

ISBN: 978-0-691-25539-2
Ebook ISBN: 978-0-691-27117-0

Library of Congress Control Number: 2024939852

British Library Cataloging-in-Publication Data
is available.

This book was conceived, designed, and produced by
Quintessence, an imprint of The Quarto Group
1 Triptych Place, Second Floor
London SE1 9SH
www.quarto.com

For Quintessence:
Senior Commissioning Editor: Eszter Karpati
Managing Editor: Emma Harverson
Senior Editor: Kath Stathers
Copyeditor: Victoria Lympus
Design: Eoghan O' Brien with Tony Seddon
Senior Designer: Rachel Cross
Art Director: Gemma Wilson
Picture Research: Sarah Bell
Production Manager: David Hearn
Associate Publisher: Eszter Karpati
Publisher: Lorraine Dickey

For Princeton University Press:
Publisher, Art & Architecture: Michelle Komie
Senior Art Book Publications Coordinator: Annie Miller
Copublications Specialist: Ruthie Rosenstock
Senior Publicists: Jodi Price and Kathryn Stevens

Front cover image: Tattooed Rabari woman, Junaghad, India, 2016. © Shatabdi Chakrabarti

Back cover images: Fulani girl in Kouande, Benin, 2012. © Jordi Zaragozà Anglès; Jōmon Project bodysuit tattoos by Taku Oshima, Japan, 2022. © Ryoichi Keroppy Maeda

Printed in Malaysia

10 9 8 7 6 5 4 3 2 1

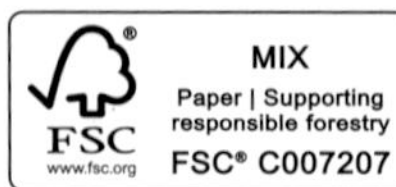

Contents

Foreword

For thousands of years, tattooing or permanently marking the body has allowed people to convey their individual or group identities, mark important life transitions and journeys, or express their creativity. Historically and across cultures tattooing has accounted for "ways of being in the world."

In this book, anthropologist Lars Krutak introduces the great diversity of tattooing practices among Indigenous peoples. He sheds light on the histories and aesthetics of the art form over time, ranging geographically from Africa and the Americas to Japan, and Southeast Asia, Papua New Guinea, the Pacific Islands, the Indian subcontinent, China, and Siberia. He highlights the cultural significance of tattooing as a permanent record of a wearer's "memories, life stories, rites of passage, ancestral ties, spiritual values, and communal and personal achievements." He reveals how Indigenous tattooing represents a spectrum of cultural activity, encapsulating the making of tools and pigments, the design of individual motifs, the composition of tattooed works to complement the body, and the maintenance or creation of appropriate rites and rituals.

This book is a celebration of cultural persistence and the survival of Indigenous peoples' tattooing practices, and also marks their remarkable innovation, creativity, and healing in the face of cultural loss. Historically, tattooing is one of many Indigenous cultural practices affected by processes of colonization, the influence of foreign religions, literacy, disaster, disease, and conflict. These were processes experienced by Indigenous peoples differently and with varying consequences. While they were very often destructive, they could also elicit creative responses. Some tattooing practices kept going, others waned, and some ceased altogether. In the twenty-first century, globalization and the intensity of the global cultural flows would appear to be a looming threat, potentially homogenizing cultures. However, scholars of globalization argue that these same flows set conditions for people to resist and hold onto cultural forms and practices that make them distinctive and different. It is against this background of cultural loss, persistence, and rapid change that contemporary Indigenous tattooists reconstruct and reproduce their practices in new and ingenious ways to suit the conditions of their clients' lives.

One feature of this book is a series of interviews in which Krutak highlights the agency of Indigenous tattoo artists and their clients in how they have initiated revivals of their ancestral tattooing practices while innovating with an eye to the present and future. He shares insights from tattooists such as Julia Mage'au Gray (Papua New Guinea) from her work among women in the Pacific; Dion Kaszas (Native North America) on rediscovering the tattooing of his Nlaka'pamux ancestors and helping other First Nations peoples to do the same; and Taku Oshima (Japan), a tattooist deeply influenced by the tattooing practices of the past and yet powerfully inspired by the creative possibilities of the future.

Krutak is well placed to bring a reference book of this kind together. He is an experienced researcher, writer, traveler, and an active contributor to the global network of tattooing practitioners and researchers. In *Indigenous Tattoo Traditions*, he has assembled a valuable reference informed by more than twenty years of archival research in libraries and museums across the world. He draws upon long-term field work and hundreds of relationships and conversations in places among people who make tattoos and wear them.

This book is one of several that have been published in the last decade with a focus on Indigenous tattooing. They have accompanied survey exhibitions in museums such as *Tattoo* at the Musée du quai Branly (2014) and the artist-led exhibition and publication *Tatau: Marks of Polynesia* at the Japanese American National Museum (2016–17). Other books such as *Ancient Ink: The Archaeology of Tattooing* (2017) survey the long history of tattooing, and there are global and regional surveys: *Body Art* (2014) and *Tattoo Traditions of Asia: Ancient and Contemporary Expressions of Identity* (2024).

The addition of *Indigenous Tattoo Traditions* to this list is a reminder that Indigenous tattooing has a history, as does the writing about this history. This timely book helps move the conversation forward. It offers the reader a glimpse both of our Indigenous tattooed histories and our tattooed futures.

Sean Mallon (Sāmoa/Ireland/Aotearoa-New Zealand)

Preface

I have been fascinated with Indigenous tattooing practices since I encountered them in Alaska more than twenty years ago. At that time, I was a graduate student in anthropology, and within weeks of arriving on campus at the University of Alaska Fairbanks I walked past a Gwich'in elder with three tattooed lines on her chin. Wanting to know more, I began exploring the vast archives at the university library and soon learned that, not too long ago, nearly every Indigenous community of the Arctic practiced some form of tattooing.

As I acquired more knowledge, I sought and obtained written consent from Indigenous leaders, families, and tattoo bearers to conduct field research (interviews and photography) on St. Lawrence Island in the north Bering Sea. I decided to focus my master's thesis research on the tattooing traditions of the St. Lawrence Island Yupik people. In the mid-1990s, there were more traditionally tattooed elders—all women—living on this remote volcanic island than anywhere else in Alaska; the custom of male tattooing had disappeared many decades before. Most of these women were in their eighties and nineties, including one traditional tattoo artist, Alice Yaavgaghsiq, who was ninety-seven years of age.

With the arrival of missionaries in the 1890s, most of the formerly animistic St. Lawrence Island Yupiget, who were led by shamans, had become Christian and were compelled to leave behind their tattooing traditions in the 1920s. Indeed, of the dozen or so tattooed women I interviewed, all of them received their tattoos around this time. In the first decade of the new millennium, this final generation of tattooed elders passed away, and so too did a 2,000-year-old tradition of tattooing on the island until it was reborn there and across the Arctic more recently through various revival movements.

Sensing that this unique and seemingly unrecognized cultural heritage was vanishing in Alaska and around the globe, over the course of two decades I largely self-funded numerous international research trips to travel to other Indigenous communities to document the meanings and functions behind this ancient form of human expression. I had no model to follow in these pursuits because I was unaware of any other researchers who were actively conducting multi-sited fieldwork on preserving the global heritage of Indigenous tattooing, especially in the remoter parts of our planet. Along these journeys I often encountered individuals who were the last bearers of specific Indigenous tattoos and the gatekeepers of associated cultural knowledge that unfortunately are no longer living today. Thus, photography was essential so that I could permanently record these important cultural and artistic traditions for future generations.

Documenting the rarest tattoos on earth through word and imagery comes with a great responsibility, and I always strive to give voice to the elders who bear these ancient marks because they too wanted to have this vanishing traditional knowledge shared with future generations. Without exception, every tattooed elder who invited me to interview them and take their portrait was extremely proud of their hard-earned body markings and they wanted others to appreciate these unique and culturally rooted expressions that were closely tied to Indigenous concepts of individual and community identity. This collaborative work would never have been possible without the consent and support of the hundreds of tattooed elders who are featured throughout the pages of this book. As a non-Indigenous scholar, I am indebted to many other local collaborators, translators, and Native knowledge experts who helped guide and cross-check my efforts to ensure that the oral histories and voices I recorded were accurately represented. Over the years many of these individuals have become close friends because I continue to revisit their Indigenous communities to deepen my understanding of local tattooing practices and the various roles that tattoos played in the making of the people who wear them.

In many Indigenous languages the performance of tattooing was likened to a form of "writing." What was being written upon the skin varied cross-culturally, but for most people, tattoos identified the specific tribal group of the wearer vis-à-vis other Indigenous communities and were associated with coming-of-age ceremonies that permanently marked significant rites of passage from one life stage to the next, among other significant aspects of local culture including personal histories, life accomplishments, and spiritual ties to one's ancestors. In essence, tattoos were essential in the making and marking of "ideal" men and women in the eyes of the local community and especially the ancestors, because tattooing was enmeshed in a system of Indigenous values and rules that organized social and spiritual life. As many Indigenous elders have told me, if you were not tattooed like your ancestors you were not considered to be a properly socialized human being and it was quite possible you would not be recognized by them in the afterlife.

Introduction

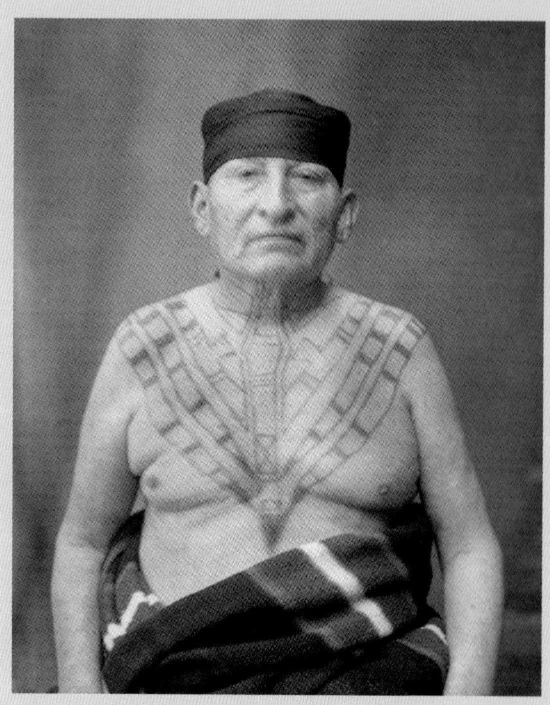

Tattooed Osage elder, Oklahoma (USA), *ca.* 1910. Osage tattoos were created by a priestly class of men, and tattooing was believed to combat old age and disease, increase fertility, and help maintain the strength of the Osage people.

In the 1980s, non-Indigenous writers coined the term "New Tribalism" to describe an emergent tattoo movement inspired by Indigenous Polynesian and Borneo tattooing motifs. This neo-tribal tattooing style was driven by tattoo publications such as tattoo artist Don Ed Hardy's *TattooTime: New Tribalism* (1982), legendary tattoo artist Lyle Tuttle's *The Tattoo Historian* magazine,[1] and later by RE/Search's *Modern Primitives* (1989). New Tribalism gained worldwide popularity in tattoo circles and exposed the rich cultural diversity of Indigenous tattooing to the masses.

Even though publications like these sparked global interest in tribal tattoos over forty years ago, the Indigenous contributions to the origins, art, history, performance, and perpetuation of tattooing over the millennia have largely remained unrecognized. Furthermore, many Indigenous tattoo artists depicted in historical images remain anonymous because, ethnographically, tattooing—like numerous other Indigenous art forms—was seen as a craft, a collective and repetitive practice, rather than an individualized art created by renowned master artisans. Consequently, the names of most tattooists in this book are unknown, though they were almost certainly recognized locally and sometimes regionally for their exceptional works. *Indigenous Tattoo Traditions* seeks to expose this neglected history by showcasing the artistic achievements of past and present Indigenous tattoo artists and the cultural beliefs that support ancestral skin-marking practices. Celebrated in their time, these artists have left behind remarkable legacies of art and performance that continue to inspire new generations.

For more than 5,000 years, Indigenous or tribal tattoos have chronicled human history, one painful mark at a time. Spanning numerous ancestral lands, cultures, and continents, tattooing has adorned ancient Europeans, Native Americans, Polynesians, Southeast Asians, Africans, and seemingly everyone in between.

But these tattooing traditions were far more than mere adornment or decoration. Indigenous tattoos served as a powerful visual language of the skin, permanently recording the memories, life stories, rites of passage, ancestral ties, spiritual values, and communal and personal achievements of their owners for all to see and read.

Right Jody Potts-Joseph, a Hän Gwich'in tattoo artist from Stevens Village, Alaska, hand-poking a *Yidįįłtoo*, or chin tattoo, on her daughter Quannah Chasinghorse, an Indigenous model who is redefining notions of beauty.

Far right Quannah Chasinghorse tattooing her cousin Lorena Village-Center-Simon, who said, "It was important for me to get my chin tattoo because I wanted to represent my people and connect with our ancestors."

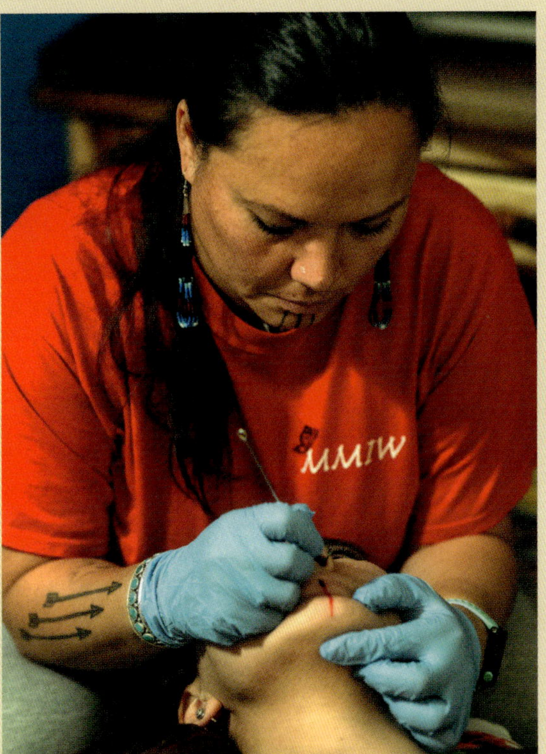

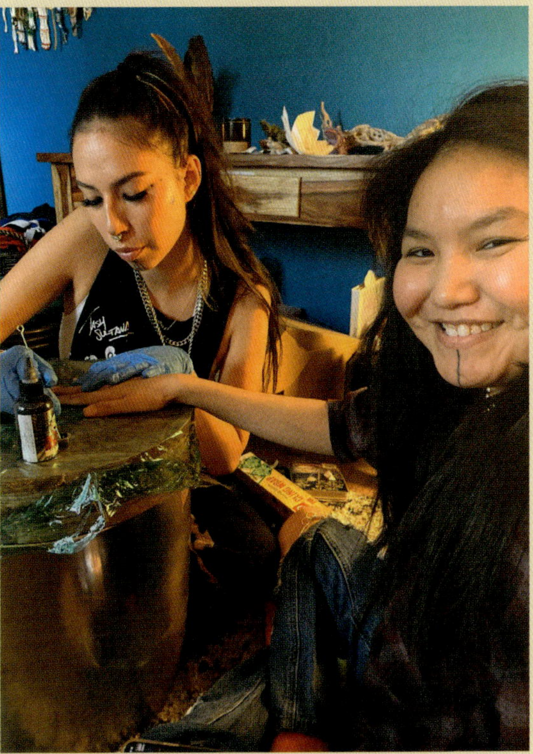

Indigenous tattooing, the process of inserting pigment into the skin to create permanent designs and iconography,[2] functioned like writing and conveyed stories that left behind their traces. Like texts, tattoos were composed of signs that related to an awareness of concepts such as identity, genealogy, status, achievement, and medicine, as well as ontological relations with ancestors, spirits, and animals.[3]

The textuality of tattooing is often acknowledged in Indigenous languages, which have predominantly been described as "unwritten" in scientific literature. In North America, the performance of Omaha women's tattooing on the Great Plains was textual in its syntax and literally served as an act of writing. These *xthexe*,[4] or "Marks of Honor," were rich with cosmic meaning and embodied oral historical teachings. They also conferred life-giving and life-prolonging powers to the tattoo recipient(s).

In the Gran Chaco of South America, the 'Weenhayek (Mataco-Noctenes) people of Argentina referred to tattooing as *'nootshànek*, a general term for "sign" or "letter" related to the verb *tshàneh*, meaning "to inject" (literally, inject signs/letters into the skin). Today, *'nootshànek* also denotes "writing," and *'nootshànekkya* (tattooing tools) refers to any kind of "writing instrument."[5]

In Polynesia, the terms for tattooing (e.g., *tatau* in Sāmoa and *kakau* in Hawai'i) are derived from the roots *tau* and *kau*, which convey activities such as "to strike," "to mark," and "to write."[6] Among the Māori of New Zealand, the patterns of men's *tā moko* (facial tattoos) were unique to each individual. Leaders sometimes drew their facial tattoos on early settlement documents and treaties, since they were regarded as personal signatures.[7]

The Ainu of northern Japan originally used the term *nuye* for tattooing, which encompassed several meanings: "to carve," "to tattoo," and "to write."[8] For the Ainu, tattooing was associated with medicinal therapy, protective power, amuletic properties, cosmic relations with specific deities, and the afterworld.[9]

For the Paiwan people of southern Taiwan, the word for tattooing is *vecik*, meaning "writing."[10] Before its near-disappearance in the mid-twentieth century, Paiwan tattooing was closely linked to social status, leadership, accomplishments, and ancestral ties to specific deities and spirits.[11]

In the Chinese lexicon, the modern term for tattoo is derived from the ancient Han character *wen*, 文 dating to about the first millennium BCE, which also means "to write." Today, *wen* signifies literacy, cultural refinement, and civilization,[12] but the original character 文 is believed to have originated from a tattooed person, possibly a northern Indigenous "barbarian" with a marked chest.[13]

What this short ethnographic review demonstrates is that Indigenous skin marking communicated a variety of cultural meanings and concepts that could be read by others.

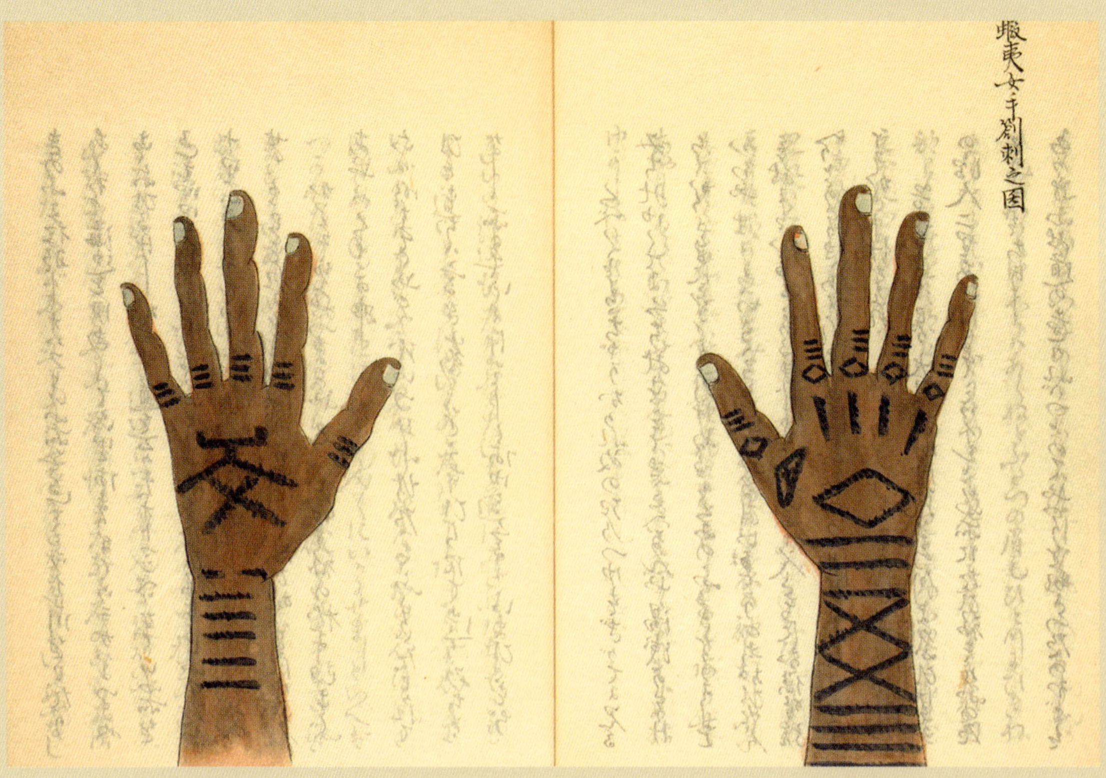

Ainu woman's hand and arm tattooing, *ca.* 1810.

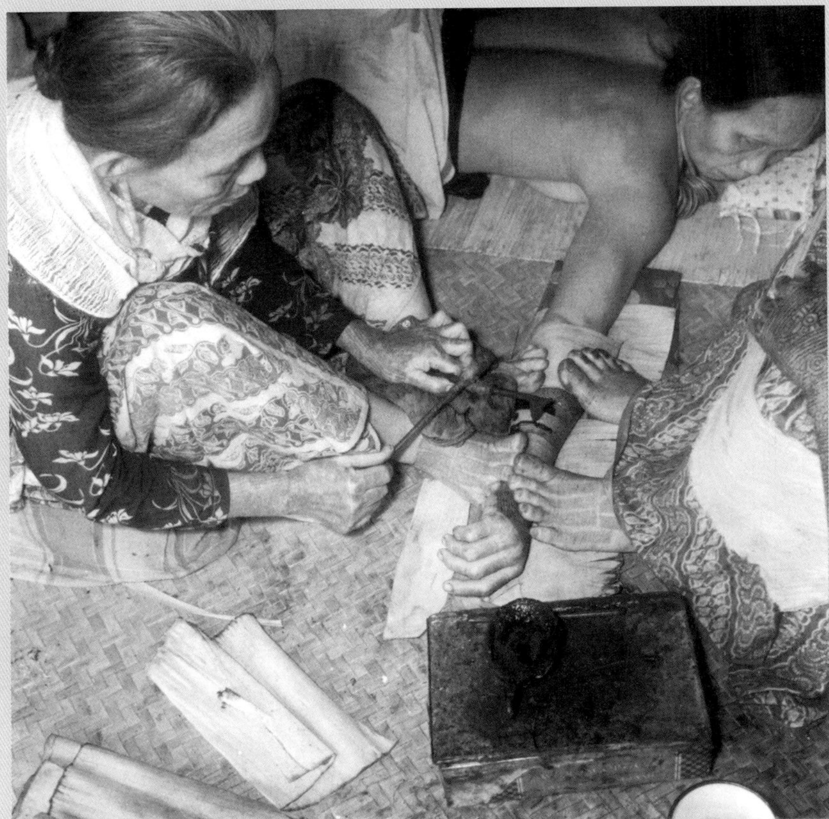

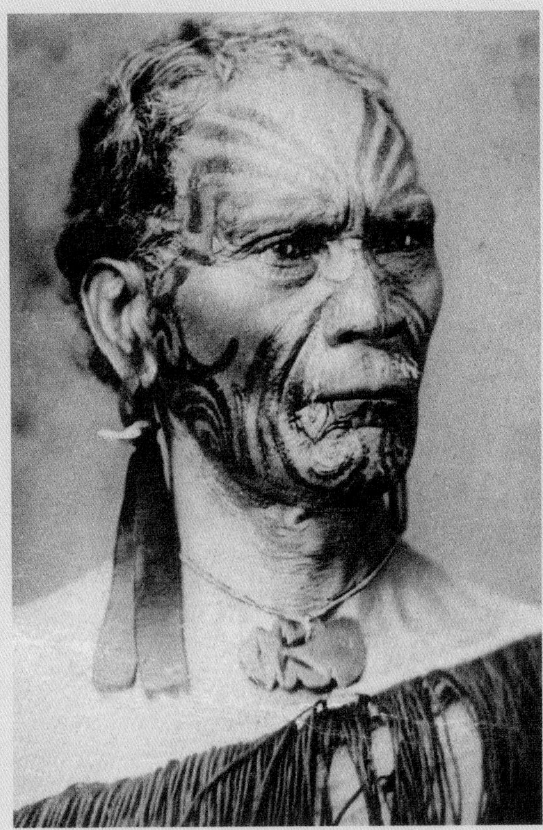

Above Kayan tattooing session at Long Jegan, Sarawak, Borneo, 1956.

Above right Photo postcard of Māori Chief Kamariera Te Hau Takiri Wharepapa (d. 1920), *ca.* 1915. His *tā moko* (facial tattoo) is over painted to accentuate his tattoos which were chiseled into the skin.

Tattooing, as a medium of traditional knowledge transmission, broadcast essential Indigenous values and ontological concerns "in a cohesive, coherent visual language that spoke to [one's] ancestral world view and everyday realities."[14] Moreover, the bodily performance of Indigenous tattooing, which was almost universally ritualized, bound the tattoo recipient to a deeply felt collective history. In turn, tattooing traced a pathway through the world that individuals navigated in their attempts to acquire new knowledge of themselves and their positions in the world.

Tattoo Techniques and Taboo

Indigenous tattooists used locally available materials (such as citrus thorns, cactus spines, stone lancets, human and animal bones)[15] to create tattoos through various traditional methods: hand-tapping, hand-poking or pricking, incision tattooing, and subdermal skin-stitching. Tattoo pigments were typically carbon-based and sometimes infused with magical ingredients, or charmed amulets were dipped into the resinous liquid to imbue it with certain powers and cures.

Receiving a tattoo was a serious undertaking in most cultures, not only due to the considerable pain and risk of infection, but also because of the elaborate ceremonies involved. For example, female Kayan tattooists in Borneo worked under the tutelage

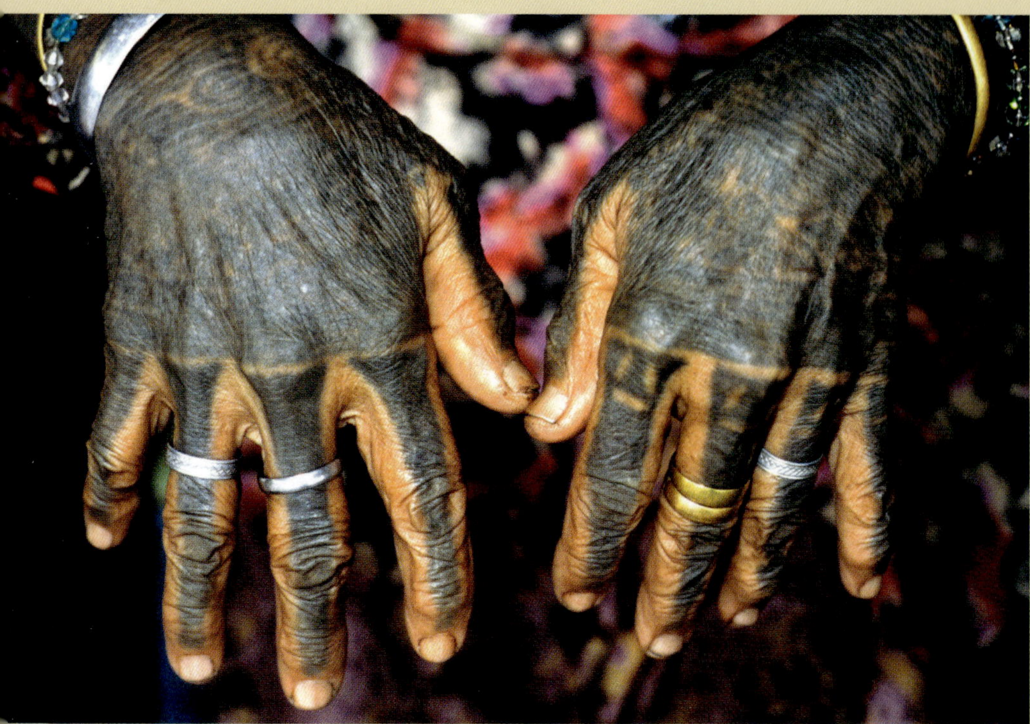

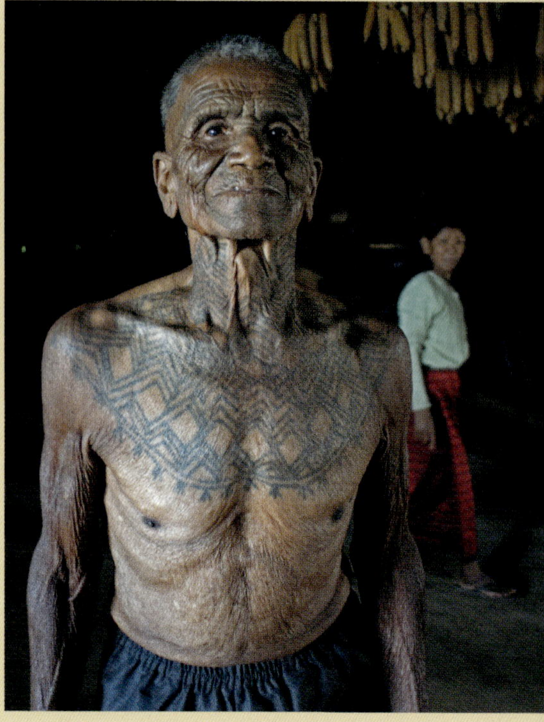

Above Kayan elder Ado Ngo displays her bold hand tattoos, Sarawak, Borneo, 2011. *Song irang*, the black spikes along her fingers, represent bamboo shoots, a fertility symbol.

Above right Chingkei Sokompa of Chen Loisho village, Nagaland, 2019. Due to headhunting bans in the 1950s, he was allowed to earn the right to the warrior's *ring tu pu* (neck tattoos) for beheading a wooden effigy placed behind enemy territory.

and protection of two spirits. They were invoked before any new tattoo pattern was initiated. The prayer asked for the tattoo recipient to feel little pain and the tattooist to make beautiful designs, and a blood sacrifice (usually a chicken) was offered.[16]

Ritual restrictions and taboos abounded for tattoo artists and tattoo recipients. Among the Wancho Naga of India, it was taboo for men to witness the tattooing act, otherwise it was believed they would have bad luck in hunting and fishing for the remainder of their lives.[17]

After a Māori chief received his *tā moko* or facial tattooing, it was taboo for anyone or anything to touch his inflamed skin. The head was regarded as having great *tapu* (holiness or sacredness), and even contact with cooked food could remove or diminish this personal power. Therefore, elaborately carved *kōrere* (funnels) with apotropaic motifs were used to feed chiefs until they healed (see Chapter 4).[18]

Stories on Skin

The ensuing volume is organized into eight chapters, corresponding to the global distribution of Indigenous tattooing where body-marking traditions and technologies once existed prehistorically and continue into the present day. Chapter 1 discusses preserved tattoos on ancient Egyptian and other mummies from North Africa, and also explores the resilience of tattooing among several contemporary Indigenous peoples, including the Amazigh (also known as the Berber in older literature), Bedouin, and other peoples of Eurasia whose repertoire of tattooing motifs are seemingly related.

Chapter 2 explores the astonishingly rich and diverse forms of tattooing in Native North America. Prior to its near erasure by colonial powers and missionaries of various denominations, tattooing here was a time-honored traditional practice that expressed the patterns of tribal social organization and religion, while also channeling worlds inhabited by deities, spirits, and the ancestors.

For thousands of years many Indigenous peoples of South America practiced tattooing and other permanent forms of body modification. Anciently preserved mummies and burial objects made from precious metals attest to the great antiquity of tattooing here. Chapter 3 investigates the enduring legacy of these.

Just as tattoos were closely linked to identity in South America, today they testify to the resilience of the Indigenous cultures and peoples of Oceania. Chapter 4 investigates the tattooing traditions of Papua New Guinea and portions of Polynesia where tattoo revival efforts are underway.

Among the Indigenous peoples of Japan and Southeast Asia, the tattooing tradition constituted a significant aspect of customary laws, taboos, and religious beliefs focused on the propitiation of spirits and deities. Chapters 5 and 6 elaborate on these meanings and discuss how body marking here served as a marker of identity as well as an emblem of personal achievement and being.

Although tattooing has been practiced for millennia by cultures around the world, until recently there have been relatively few studies of tattooing across the Indian subcontinent. This lack of research is due to various factors, including the suppression of Indigenous tattoo practices under colonial rule and the migration of Indigenous peoples into urban centers where "tribal" tattoos are perceived as "old fashioned" and unmodern. Chapter 7 provides an overview of Indigenous tattooing across India to reveal what tattooing can tell us about culture change and migration.

The final chapter focuses on the antiquity and practice of Indigenous tattooing in China and Siberia, where some of the oldest tattooed human mummies have been unearthed. In these discussions, the study of tattooing has an important role to play in reconstructing the spiritual and cultural beliefs of ancient peoples, not to mention contemporary Indigenous groups who continue to possess the tattoos of their ancestors.

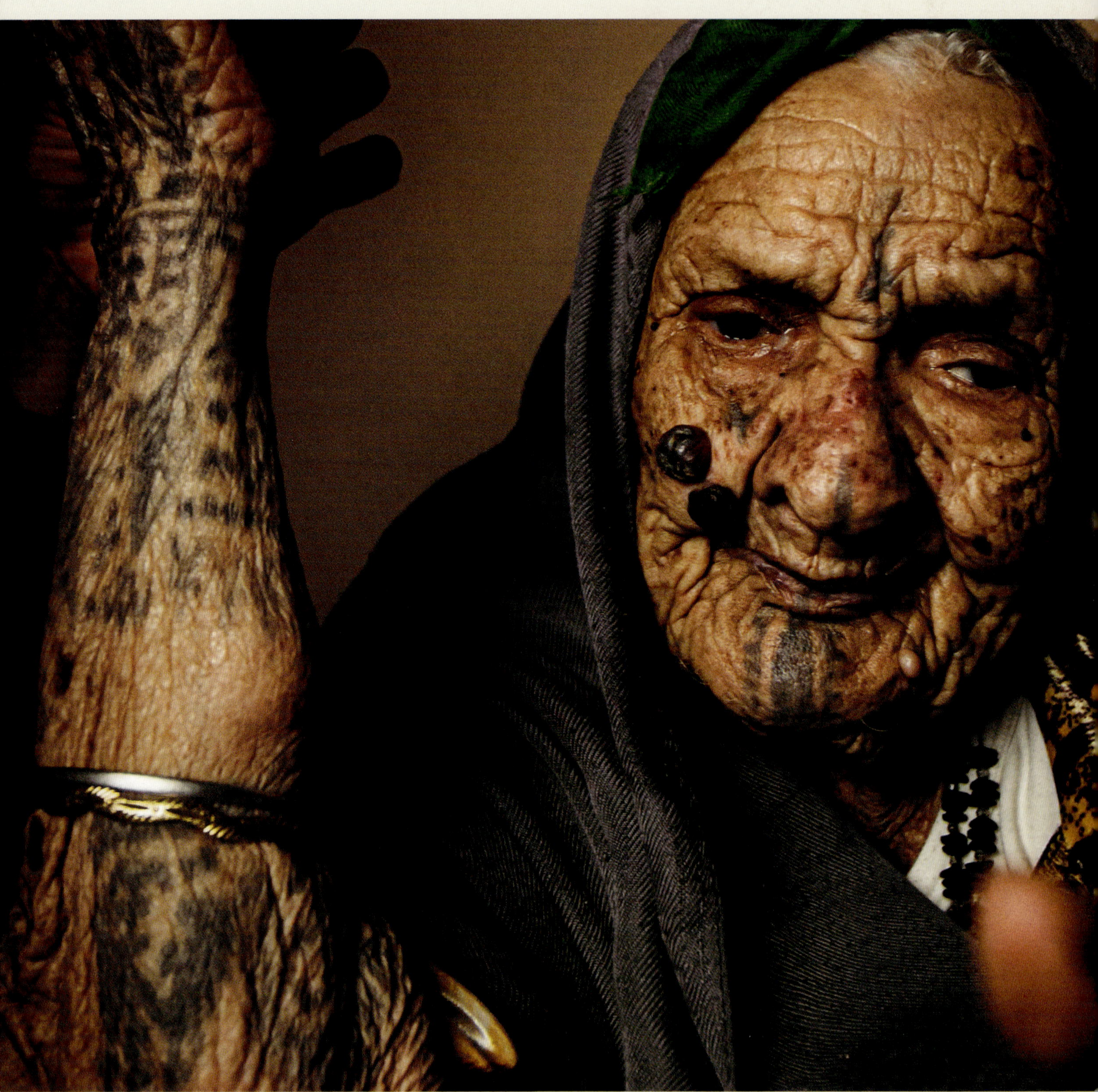

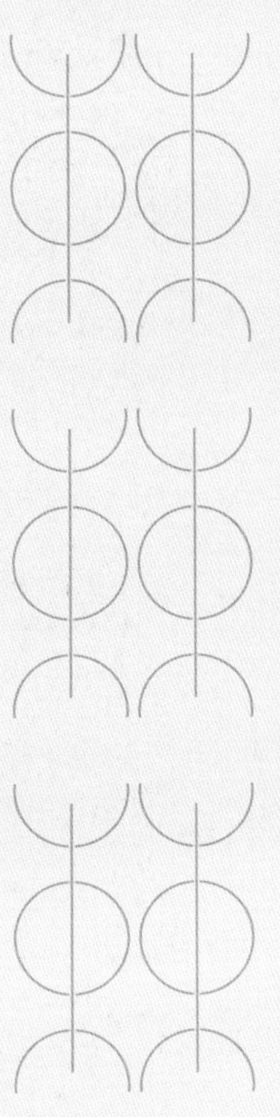

1 TATTOOS OF AFRICA, THE MIDDLE EAST, AND BEYOND

During the age of exploration in the fifteenth through sixteenth centuries, Europeans first became aware of the relatively extreme forms of body art practiced across Africa, the Middle East, and neighboring regions. One of these was scarification, a body modification procedure that offered a sculptural quality to the skin. Sometimes a colored pigment was added to the incisions forming a kind of tattoo, sometimes not. Tattooing was also very common and was practiced as early as the predynastic period of ancient Egypt.

Khamsa, a tattooed Amazigh woman of Matmata village, Tunisia, 2022. *Nahla*, or palm tree motifs, often in the form of *siyâla* (chin markings), were thought to induce fertility. The origin of the symbol is identified with the ancient Carthaginian goddess Tanit.

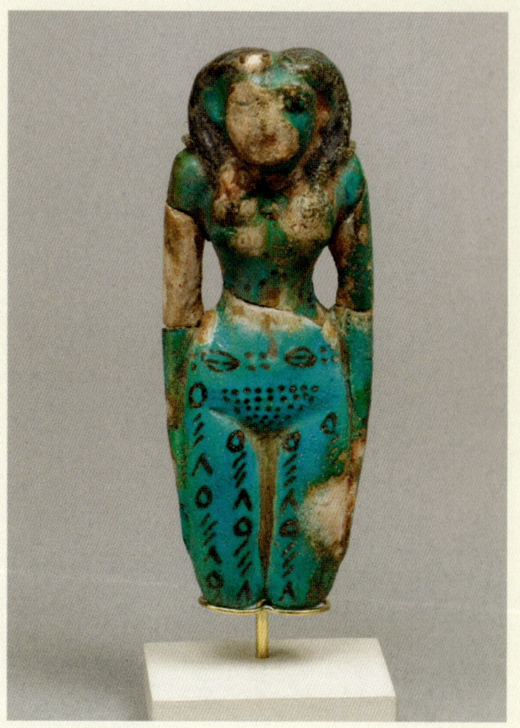

Egyptian faience figurine with decoration possibly representing tattoos on truncated thighs, *ca*. 1850–1750 BCE.

As noted, tattooing has been practiced in North Africa for thousands of years. Two predynastic Egyptian mummies dating to 3350–3000 BCE exhibit the oldest evidence of tattooing from this region, and both have figurative tattoos (the woman, a staff; the male, two horned animals) on their well-preserved bodies.[1] Roughly contemporary with the European Alpine mummy known as Ötzi,[2] these mummies are the second-oldest tattooed mummies in the world and may point to earlier traditions that await discovery.

While tattooing was performed during later periods in ancient Egypt and is preserved on objects of material culture and mummies,[3] other forms of tattooing in North Africa have survived on the bodies of tribal elders until the present day. Although these tattooing customs

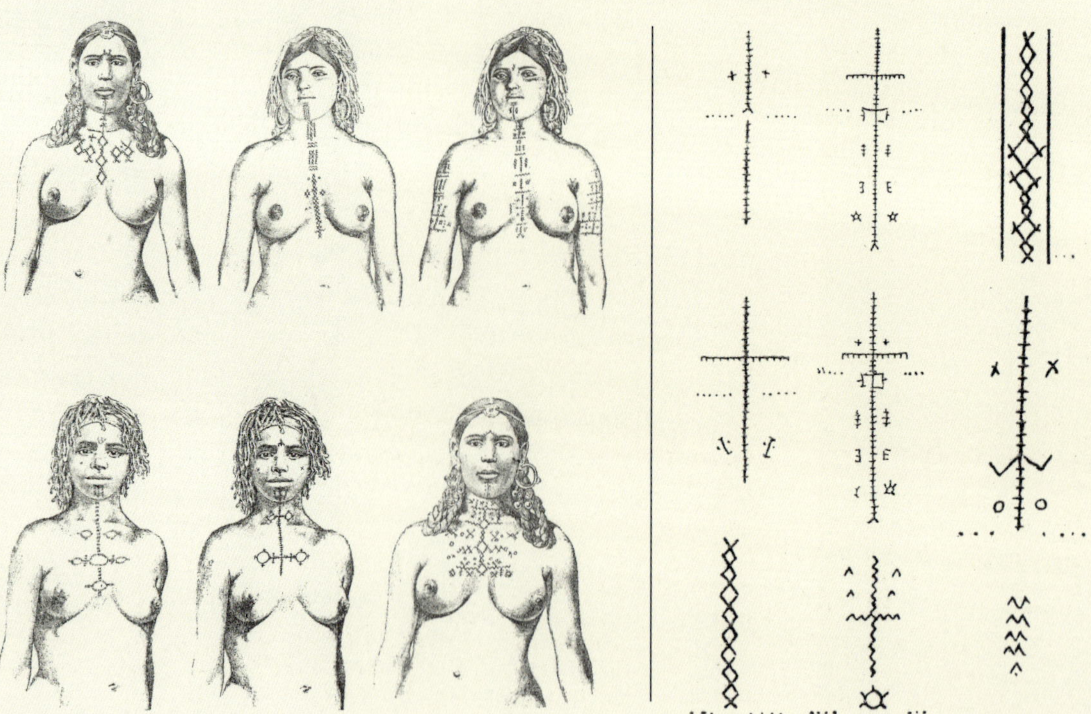

Amazigh tattoos, *ca*. 1920. Most Amazigh tattoos employ the same motifs, although many symbols are difficult to classify by name because various tribes interpret each motif differently. Pictured here are tattooed Shilha, Chaouian, and Beni Ouarain Amazigh women.

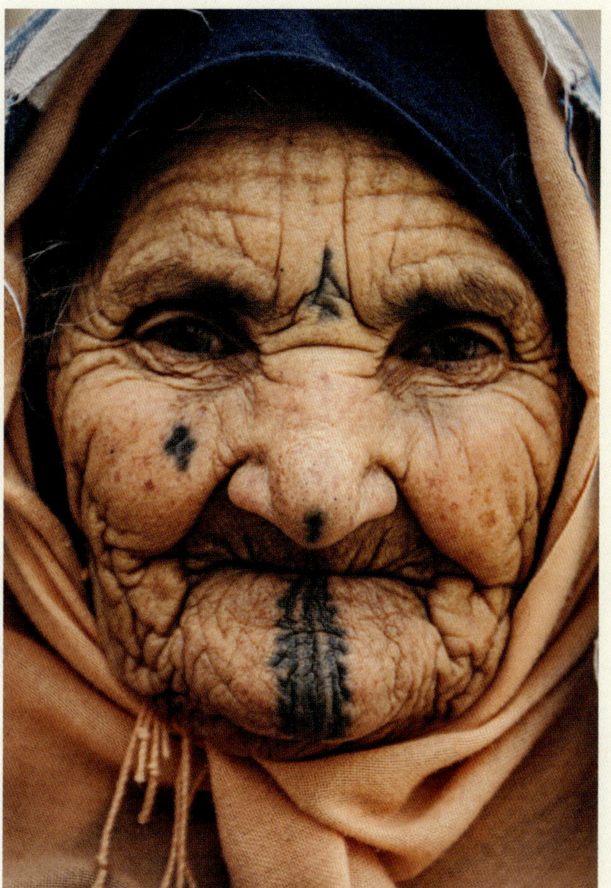

Salma, a tattooed Amazigh elder of Taoujout village, Tunisia, 2022.

are no longer practiced, these traditions are associated with the Indigenous Amazigh (also known as Berber) people. Living in Morocco, Algeria, Libya, Tunisia, and Egypt, the Amazigh are Muslims who follow a specialized branch of that religion, one that retains elements of atavistic animism: a belief that *baraka* (supernatural energy) resides in all things.[4]

Amazigh tattoo designs hold the sacred energy of *baraka*, which can be used to deal with the darker forces of life, to cure illnesses and joint pain, and to protect oneself against *jnoun* (spirits).[5] Oftentimes Amazigh tattoos were placed near body orifices (eyes, mouth, nose, navel, vagina) or surfaces believed to be vulnerable to the machinations of these evil entities.[6] For example, tattoos usually marked the feet to protect women from *jnoun* who attempted to enter their body through the earth. Other designs on the ankles, hands, and face were believed to protect individuals from the evil eye. Thus, it is not surprising that many Amazigh tattoos carried the tag of *jedwel* or "talisman."[7]

The Amazigh method of tattoo application was largely a form of hand-poking and pigment was created from lampblack mixed with juice squeezed from the leaves of broad (fava) beans.[8] The natural products chosen to heal the tattoo wounds were diverse and varied: ashes of watermelon rinds, saffron, henna, crushed belladonna, cabbage leaves, barley, ivy, spittle, and mint among other things.[9] Sometimes these substances enhanced the color of the tattoos, sometimes not, or they were believed to contain *baraka* that added curative power.

Nearly all Amazigh tattooists were women, praised for their knowledge of healing substances and their skill in epidermic artistry. In the High Atlas Mountains of Morocco, excerpts from the late 1920s Amazigh poem "Chants de la Tessaout" reveal that a tattooist named Lalla Taouchamt, "The Madame Tattooer," was divinely blessed, demonstrating that tattooists were locally recognized and often remembered by their community histories.[10]

Hand tattooing of Amazigh elder Khadija of Taoujout village, Tunisia, 2022.

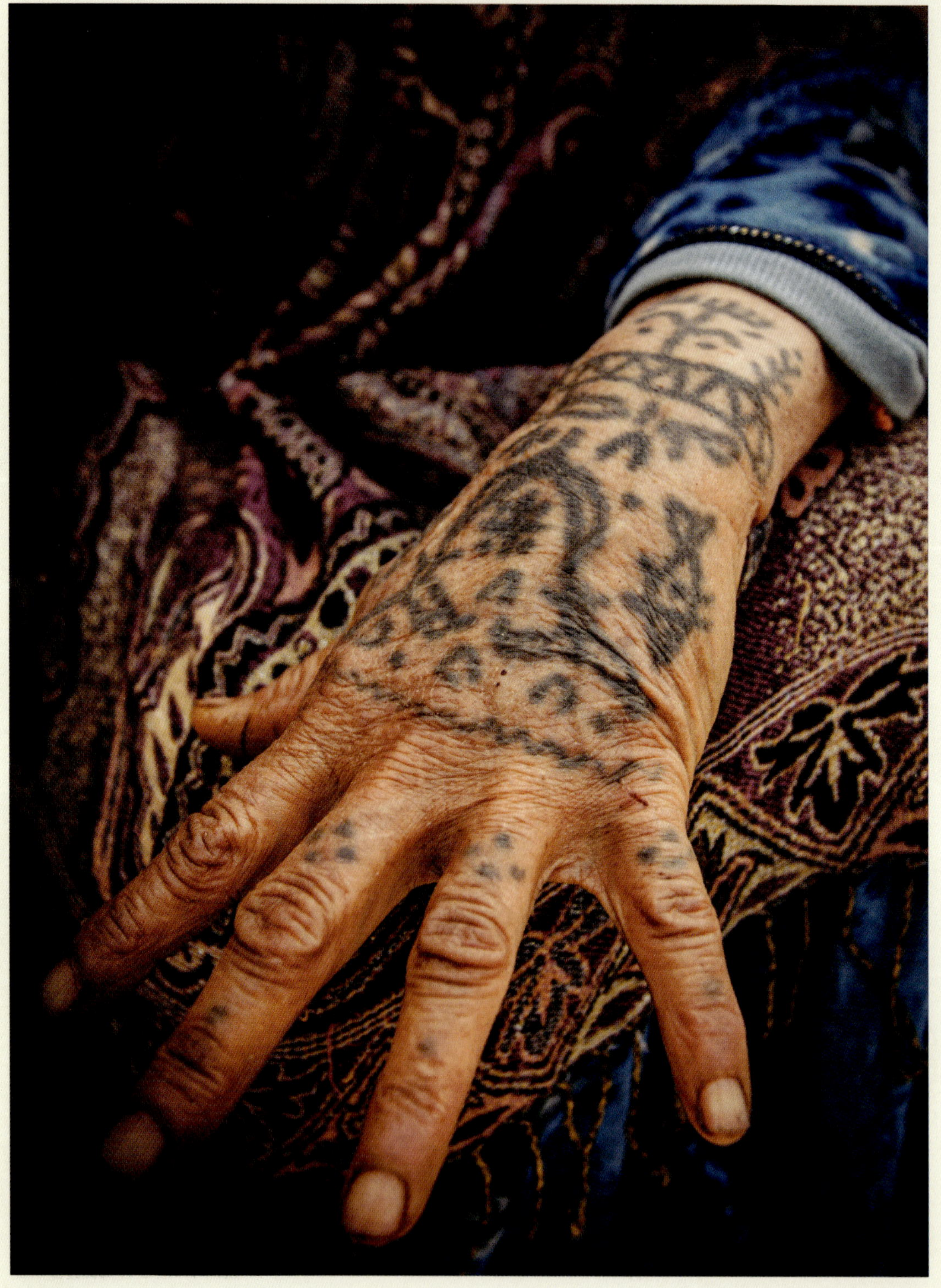

Arab Tattooing

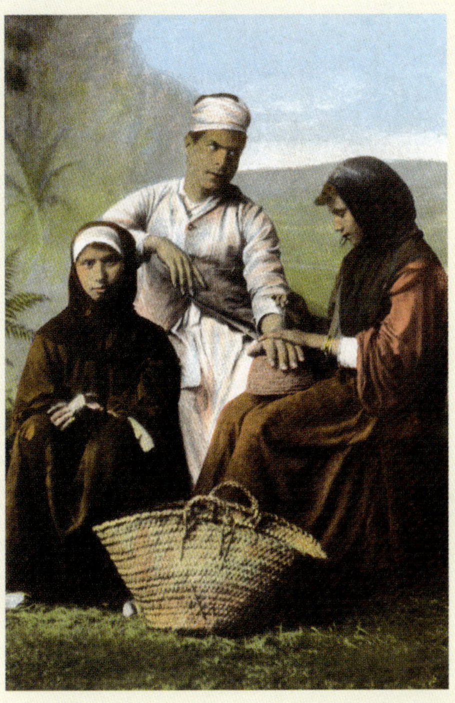

Postcard of Bedouin tattooing in Egypt using a hand-poking technique, *ca*. 1920.

While the Amazigh have retained a distinct culture and language over the centuries, Arab peoples across North Africa, Turkey, and the Middle East shared many beliefs, including the evil eye, *jnoun*, and the therapeutic power of tattooing. As with the Amazigh, Arab tattooing practices are no longer part of an active tradition, but in the early twentieth century Arabs in Iraq placed tattoos over a region of pain to cure rheumatism, wounds, bruises, or sprains.[11] More complex and beautiful designs were applied to women for purposes of ornamentation and as enhancements to physical beauty. Arab proverbs praise the beautifully tattooed woman: "the limb of such a person was worth more than an entire woman."[12] Other forms of more "magical" tattooing existed: to guard children against death, to induce pregnancy in women, and to create potent love charms.

Women performed nearly all the tattooing among the Arabs of Iraq. This was not a hereditary profession, and any woman who had the skill and inclination could become a *daggagah* or tattooer. There were various methods of making the tattoo pigment, which was known as *kohl* or *basmah*, but the principle was the same. The chief ingredient was always carbon in the form of lampblack. Sometimes indigo was added, or bile from the gallbladder of an ox, which set the dye. But the commonest method was to gather the soot from the bottom of a cooking pot or dish held over a kerosene lamp to make a pigment paste. The residual soot was then moistened with the milk of a woman nursing a daughter, which had magical properties.[13]

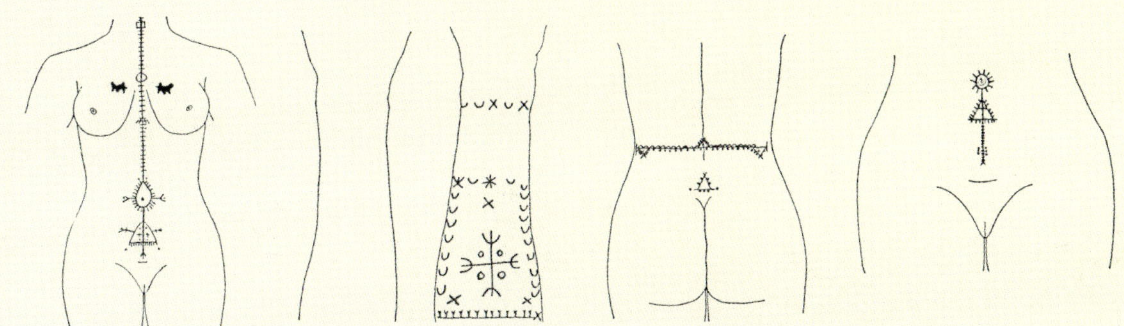

Arab women's body tattooing, Iraq, *ca*. 1930. Cross motifs were considered "powerful" fertility designs.

Tattooing instruments were ordinary sewing needles of a varying number according to their size and the technique of the operator: two to four needles were bound together for at least half their length. The design, which in most cases depended on the taste and skill of the operator, was drawn on the skin with the needles dipped in the dye, and then pricked through.

Some Arab women had three to five large dots irregularly placed on the lower abdomen, below or around their navel, or on the lower back. The dots were marked upon the skin to ensure the bearer would have children, and this form of magical tattooing was performed on the third day of her menstruation.[14]

Other forms of tattooing were sympathetic "love magic," and were aided by having someone read the Koran while the tattoo was being applied. One woman from Baghdad noted she had three dots tattooed in a triangle on the palm of her right hand to ensure she kept her husband's love. A similar design on the left hand would mean that the woman no longer wanted her husband's devotion.

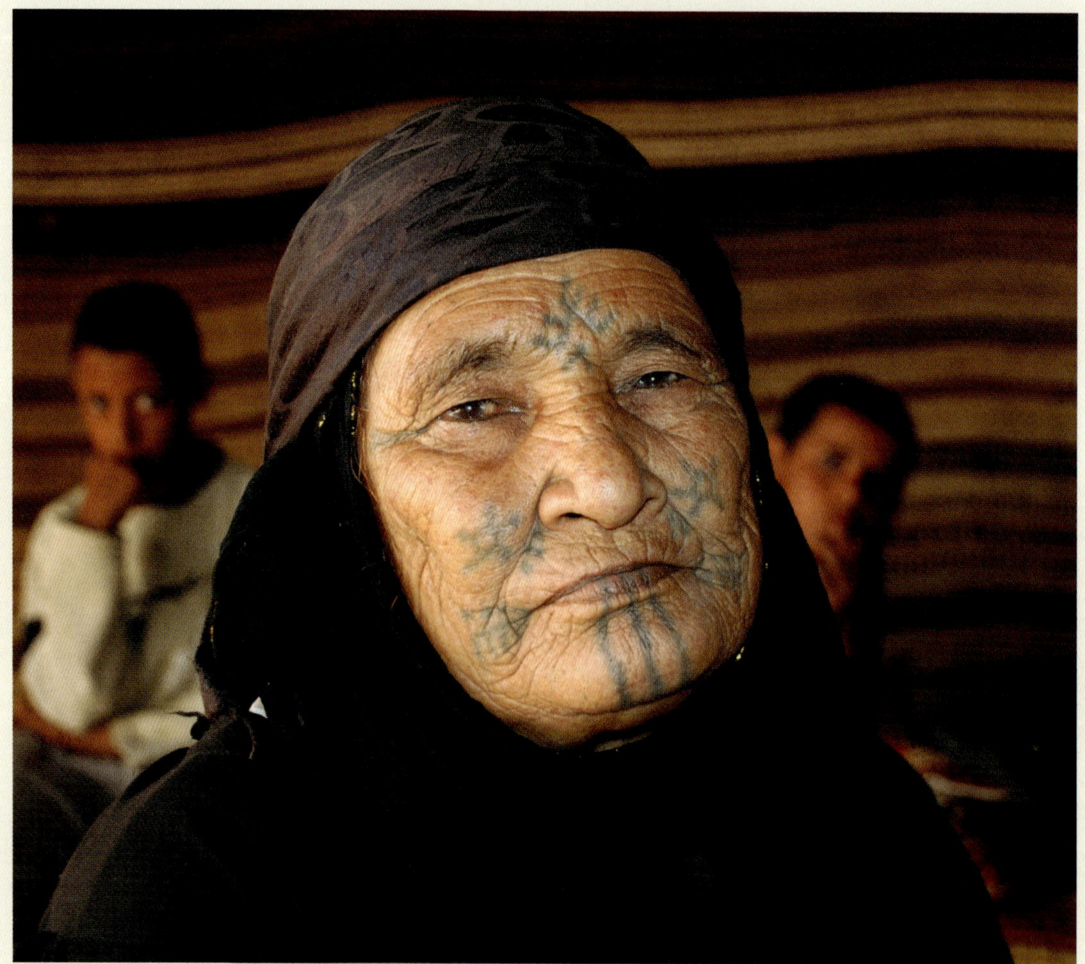

Bedouin elder from the Arab Twaiseh tribe (Al Zawaideh), Ad Dīsah, Jordan, 2007. Solar motifs appear on her cheeks and clusters of three dots near the nostrils protect her from the evil eye.

Kurdish Tattooing

Zekiye Yıldız, a Kurdish woman living in Viranşehir, Turkey. Her tattoos tell the story of a migrating tribe.

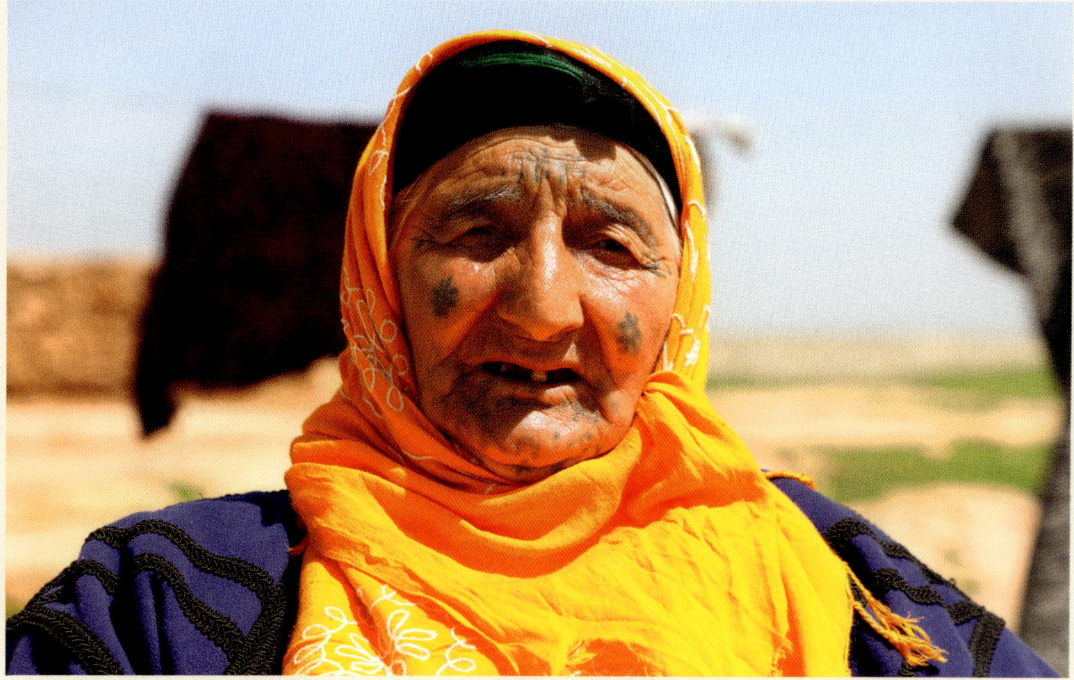

The Kurds, who inhabit Syria, Turkey,[15] Iraq, and Iran also practiced tattooing through the early to mid-twentieth century.[16] Although there are many groups of Kurds, the Yezidi (also Yazidi or Ezidi) have preserved their ancient tattooing practices as well as many of their secretive religious ceremonies, like the "Jam." Held at the sacred shrine in modern Lalish, Iraq, Jam coincides with the great Aryan festival of Mithrakan, which celebrated the act of world creation by the sun god Mithras, who has been worshipped by various peoples for more than 3,500 years.

Elderly Yezidi men and women still wear *kutra'i* (tattoos) associated with Mithras, and some of these motifs are found adorning the outer walls of the Yezidi shrine at Lalish.[17] They were frequently tattooed with a *misht* or *meshed* (comb design), and a rayed circle or "sun disk" with a varying number of rays and sometimes a circular *kawi* (branded scar) in the center.[18] Among the Amazigh of Morocco, similar tattoo

Yezidi Kurd women's ankle tattoos from Iraq, *ca*. 1930.

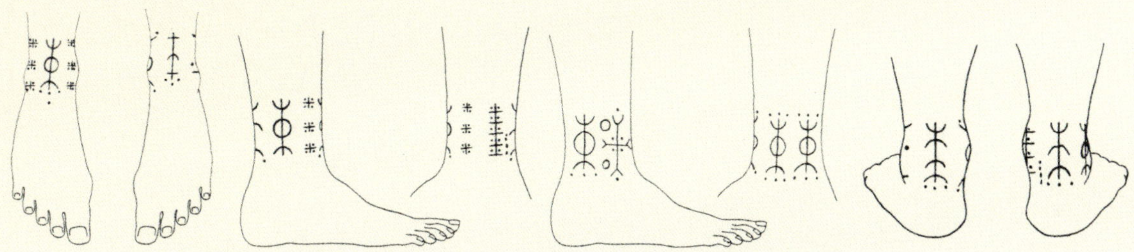

Top right Kurdish elder Gemra Yavuklu of Viranşehir, Turkey. She has tattoos that tell the ancient love story of Leylā and Mecnun: the attraction of the human spirit to divine beauty.

Far right Idi Ayaz of Viranşehir, Turkey. The motifs in her tattoos represent the sun, stars and beauty.

Bottom right Tattooed Kochi woman, 2023. The Kochi people, a nomadic Pashtun society of Afghanistan, continue to wear tattoos that are believed to enhance the beauty of the possessor as well as other markings that embody apotropaic power. They closely resemble the tattooing motifs worn by the Amazigh, Arabs, and Kurds.

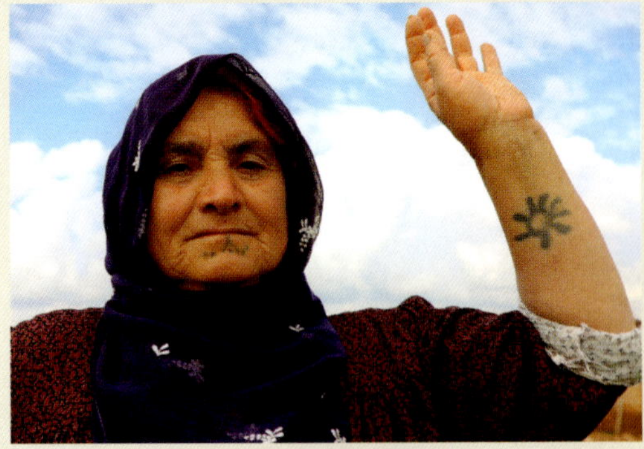

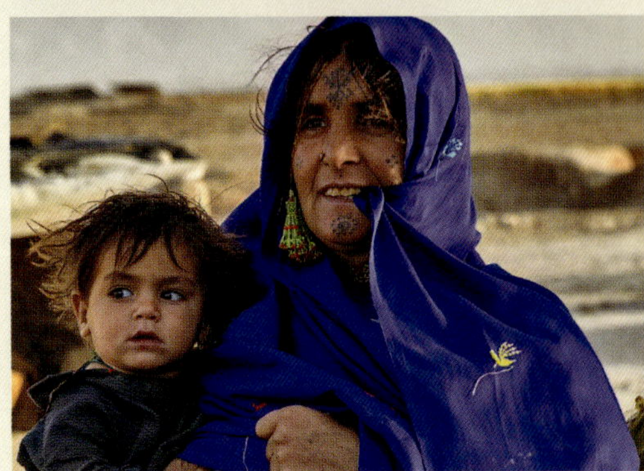

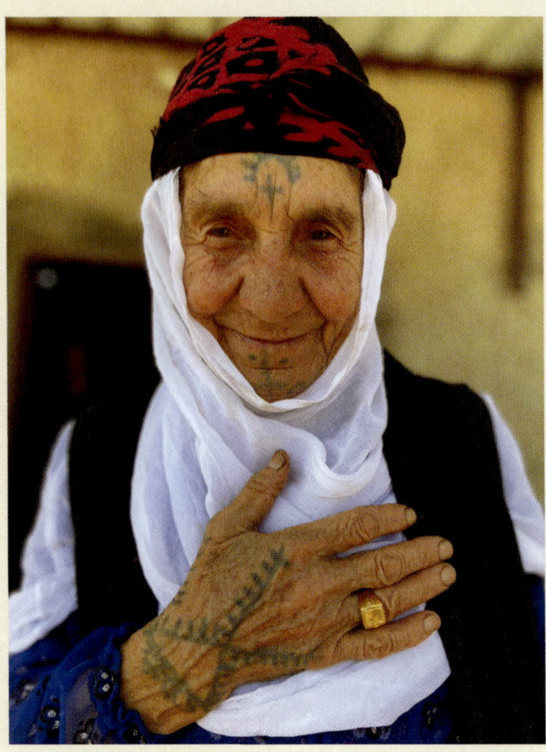

motifs were called *mechta* (iron carding comb); these were considered to be "fire symbols" because of their association with the blacksmith who made combs of this type. Rayed crosses were also tattooed among the Amazigh and have been documented as the remnants of an ancient solar cult.[19] However, both symbols (fire and sun) embodied properties of purification, and hence protection, because of their association with heat.

Rayed semicircles enclosing a star and two dots were worn by Yezidi women to ward off the evil eye, while other tattoos were therapeutic and used to cure rheumatism and headaches because of their perceived healing properties.[20]

Kurdish women's tattoo designs from Iraq, *ca.* 1930.

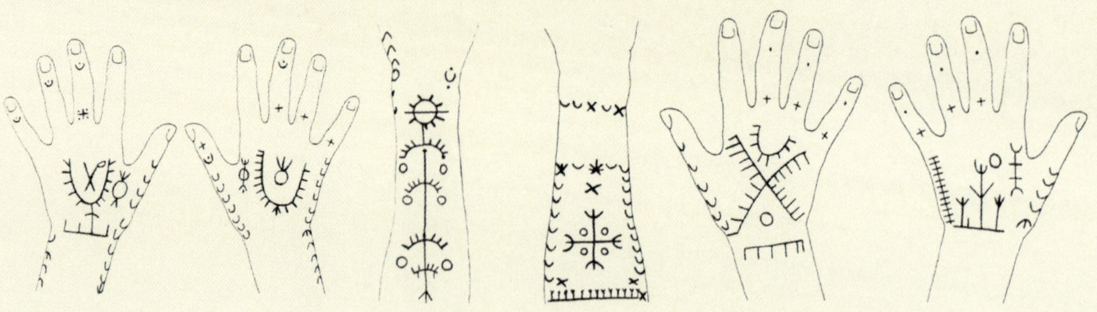

Balkan Tattooing

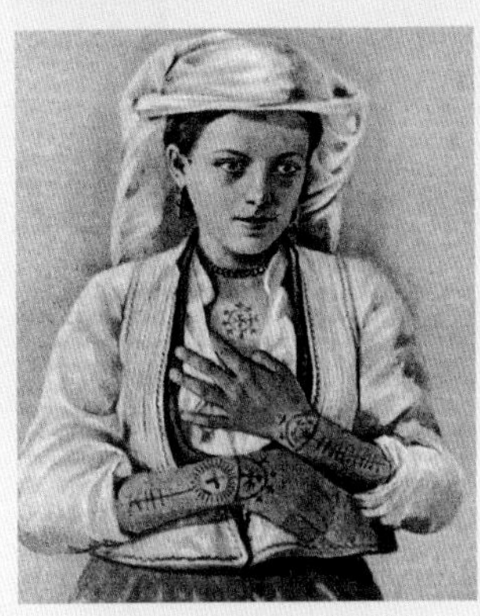

Above Catholic women illustrated in Bosnia and Herzegovina with tattooed forearms and sternum, late nineteenth century.

Interestingly, many Amazigh and Kurdish tattoo motifs occur in varying degrees among several Indigenous peoples living in the Balkan countries of Albania, Bosnia and Herzegovina, Croatia, and Greece,[21] with the latter practices representing Europe's oldest tattooing tradition.[22] Among Muslim communities in Albania, tattooing was once commonplace in the early twentieth century. Men and women were marked with a triangle—which forms a star and is the substitute for the rayed sun.

Catholics living in Albania, most of whom had migrated to the area from Bosnia and Herzegovina to evade the Ottoman Turks in the fifteenth century, were also heavily tattooed through the early-twentieth century to reaffirm their Christian faith, among other things. Both men and women were marked on the back of the hand, the forearm, or the breast with a cross. These cruciforms also displayed a crescent above and below it, or the arms terminated in small circles, to resemble a form of "sun-wheel."

Today, traces of these ancient tattoos continue to be found among a small number of Catholic men and women living in Croatia and Bosnia and Herzegovina. In Bosnia, the tattooing process is called *sharati* (to color) and many patterns are as follows: *kolo* (the circle), named after the traditional dance of the region, *klas* (ear of corn), *ograda* (ring-fence), *narukvotza* (bracelet), *grancica* (small pine twig), *eliza* (fir tree), *krizh* or *krizhevi* (cross, crosses), and sun, moon, and star.[23]

Old women who knew the tattoo patterns worked as tattoo artists. Tattoo pigment consisted of the soot of resinous pinesap collected on a plate, combined with honey and water, saliva, and mother's milk.[24] However, many other substances could also be combined with soot to produce tattoo ink, including milk from a black sheep, horse milk, egg yolk, juniper berry juice, holy water, or sugar.[25] Sometimes tattoo designs were carved into a piece of willow bark and stenciled on the skin as a guide.

Certain days of the year were considered better for tattooing than others. Annunciation Day (March 25) and Palm Sunday were tattooing days, but March 19 (St. Joseph's Day) was the most common. According to tattooed elders interviewed in the early twentieth century, tattooing was connected to fertility, springtime, new life, religion, and the position of the sun.[26]

A selection of tattoo designs seen on hands and lower forearms of Catholic women of Bosnia and Herzegovina, late nineteenth century.

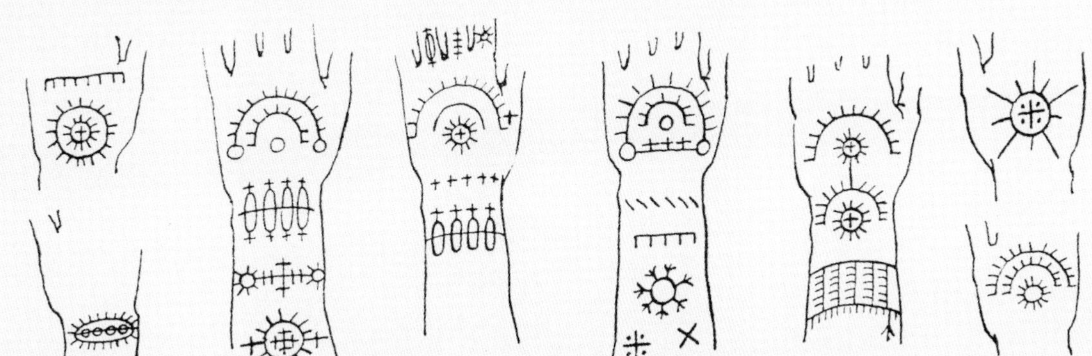

Tattooed Catholic women seen in Bosnia and Herzegovina with traditional arm and hand patterns, late nineteenth century.

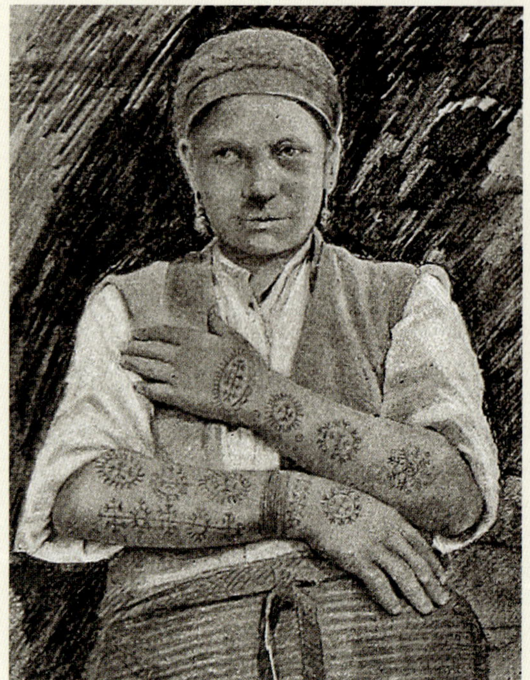

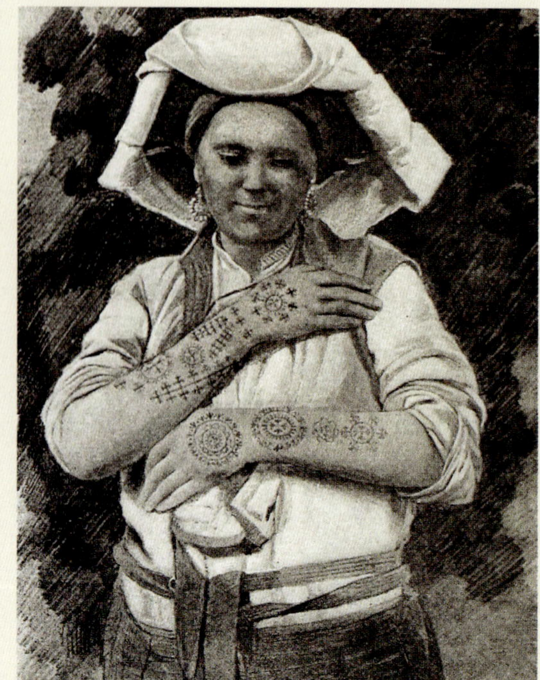

Right Tattooed Bosnian elder Jela Sivonjíc, Zubovići village, 2012.

Far right Hand and arm tattoos of Croatian Catholic woman Anđa Jakovljević from Cvitović, Bosnia. She received the tattoos when she was about fifteen years old, on St. Joseph's Day (March 19). The female tattooist used chicken feathers and matches to stencil the patterns, then she tattooed them with a needle and pigment of honey mixed with soot.

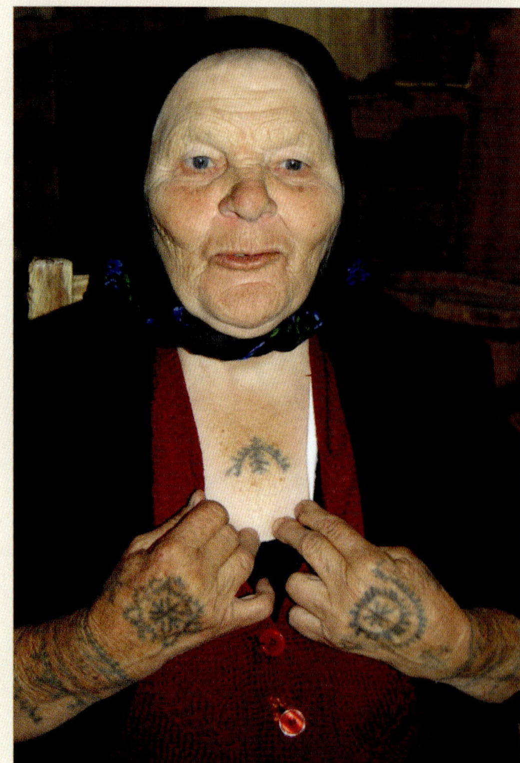

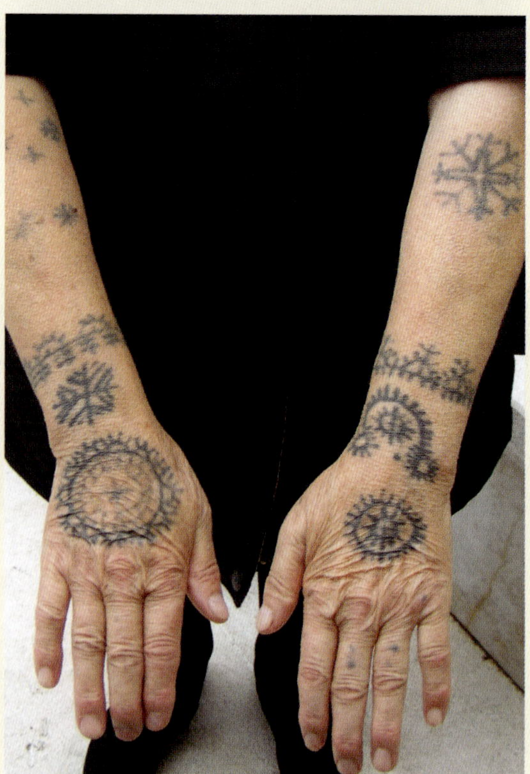

Tattoos of Sub-Saharan Africa

Traditionally in many African cultures, the words used to communicate “to scarify” and “to tattoo” had other meanings, such as “to draw” or “to paint.” In other locations, these definitions extended toward other verbs, including “to design,” “to inscribe,” and even “to succeed” and “to reach a goal.” Because there was a plethora of meanings that were embodied within the sacred art forms of the skin, African body art moved far beyond the Western construct of “art” itself. For it represented a much wider corpus of knowledge and expression encompassing identity, rites of passage, medicinal treatment, and esoteric beliefs.

In the Sahel, which is an ecoregion or climatic zone located between the Sahara Desert in the north and the savanna grasslands to the south, many groups continue to practice tattooing, including the Fulani, who are also known as the Peul, Fula, Fulbe, or Felaata. These nomadic herders inhabit the western Sahel region (from Senegal to Chad) and are devout Muslims. Perhaps the most heavily tattooed of all Fulani subgroups are the Wodaabe.

In the Fulfilde language spoken by all Fulani tribes, Wodaabe means “people of the taboo.” This moniker is appropriate because the Wodaabe are governed by a series of customary laws and behaviors passed down by their ancestors that emphasize humbleness and modesty, patience and fortitude, hospitality, and physical beauty. Men also seek to repel bad luck using many forms of talisman worn in pouches or

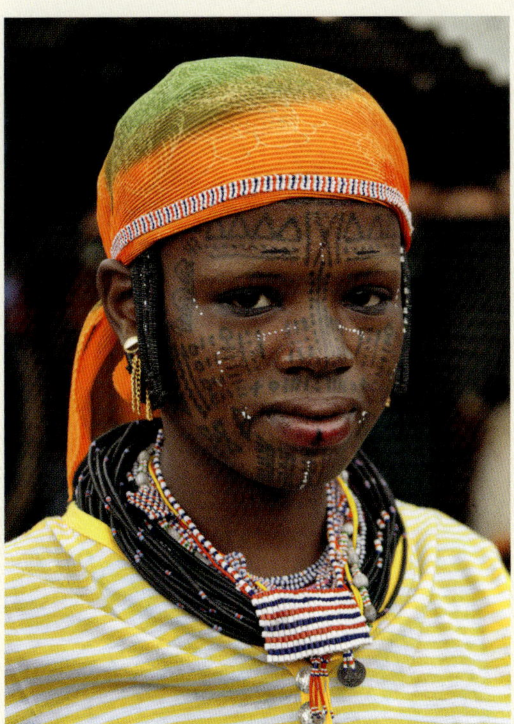

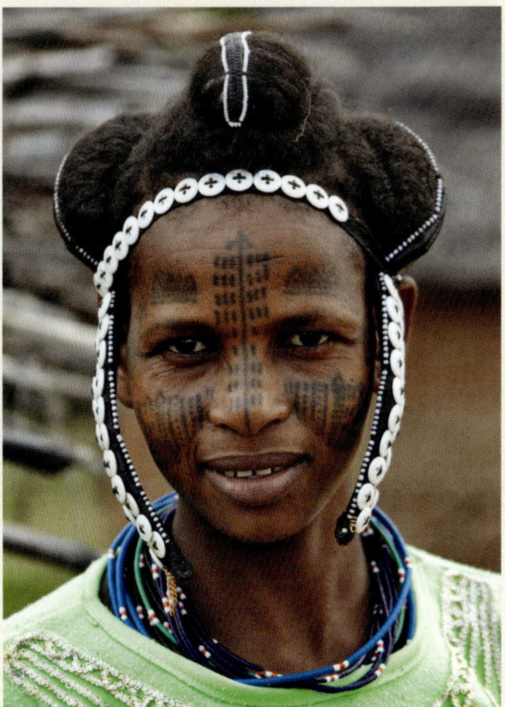

Peul (Fulani) of Benin, 2012. The Peul are nomadic cattle herders who cover great distances in the dry season in search of water for their herds. They are intricately tattooed for apotropaic reasons and also so they might impress the individuals they meet during their long journeys through Benin, Burkina Faso, and Niger.

Young Wodaabe men with facial and torso tattoos, Abouza, Zinder-Tanout region, Niger, 1970.

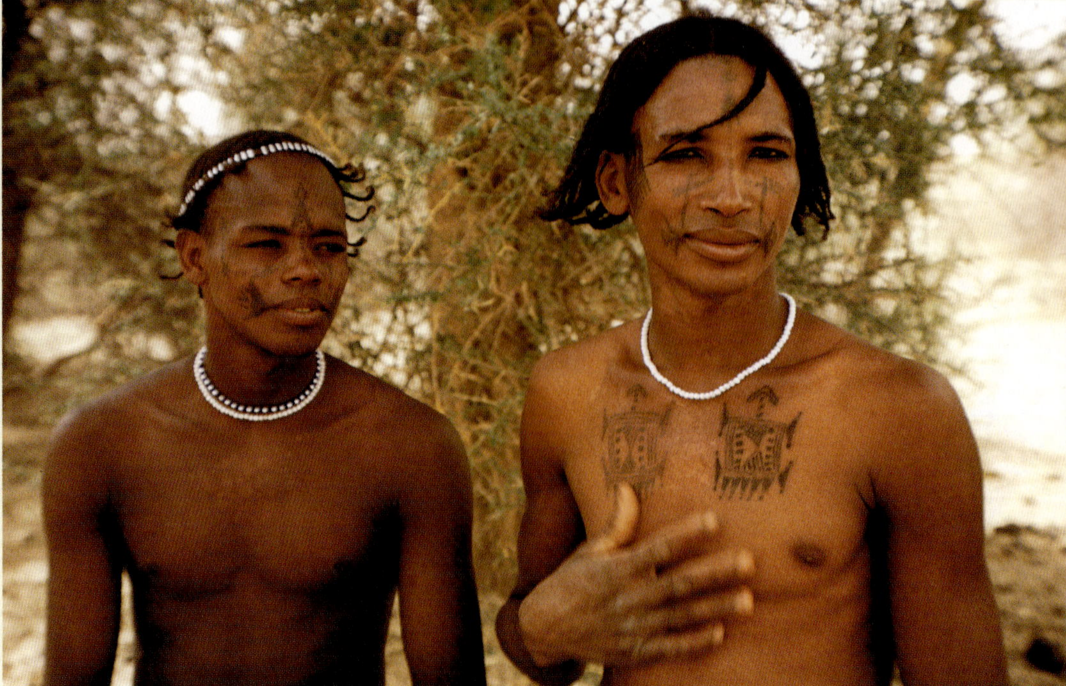

Tattooed Fulani woman of Cameroon, 2013. Fulani tattoo artists can be male or female and the motifs are cut into the skin and a sooty pigment rubbed into the wounds to make them indelible.

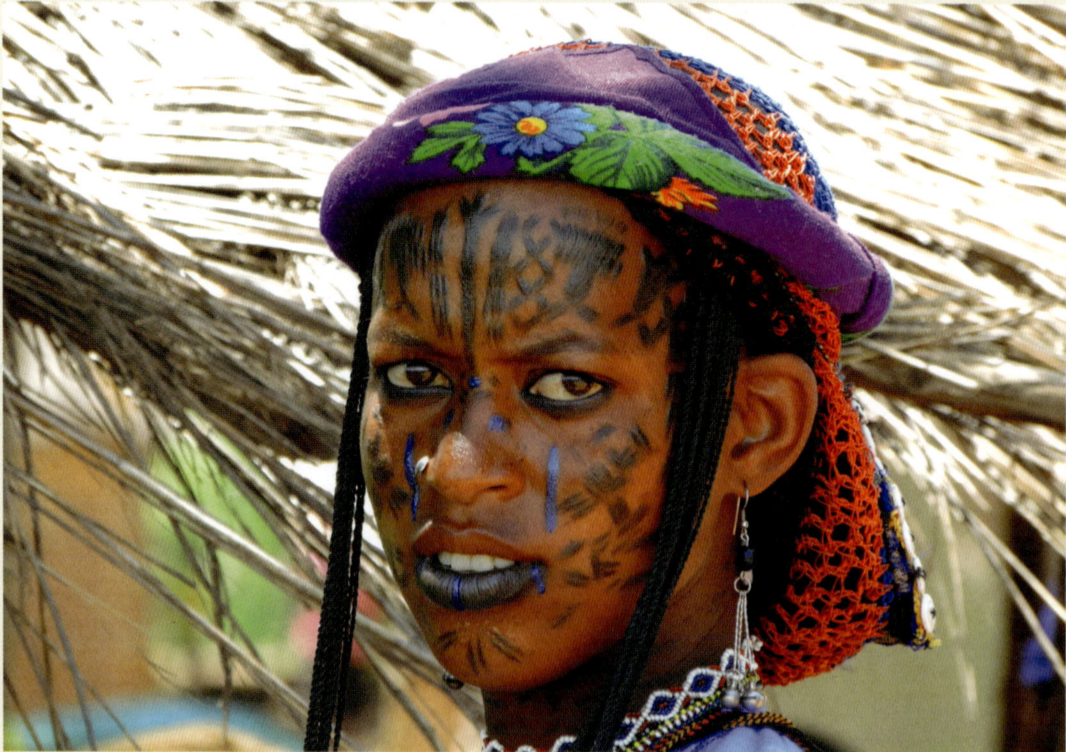

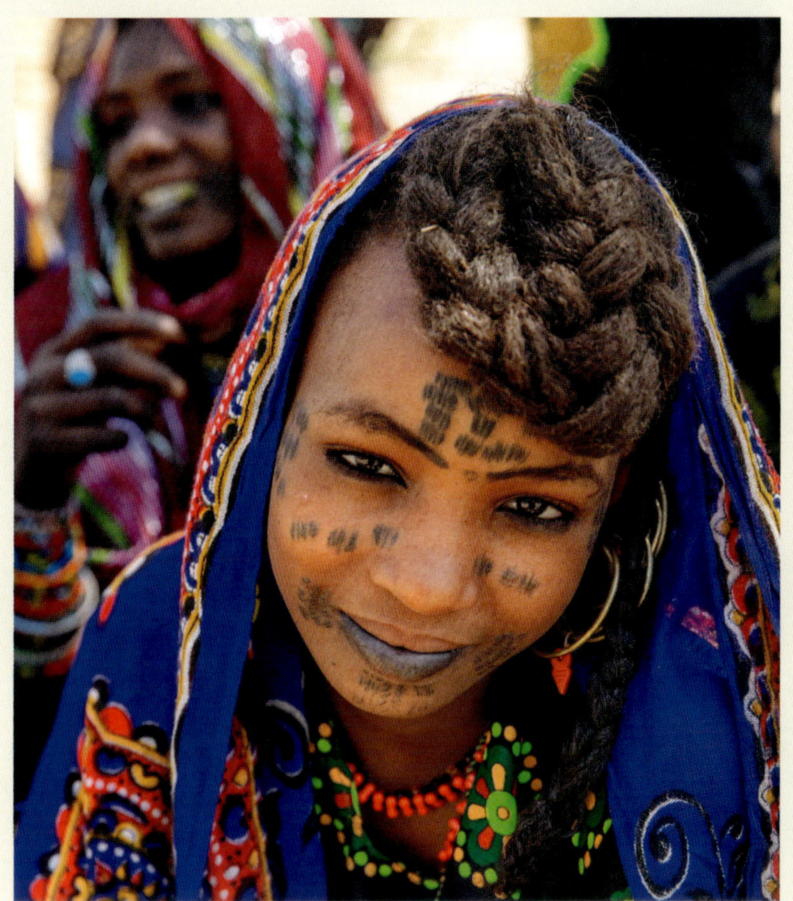

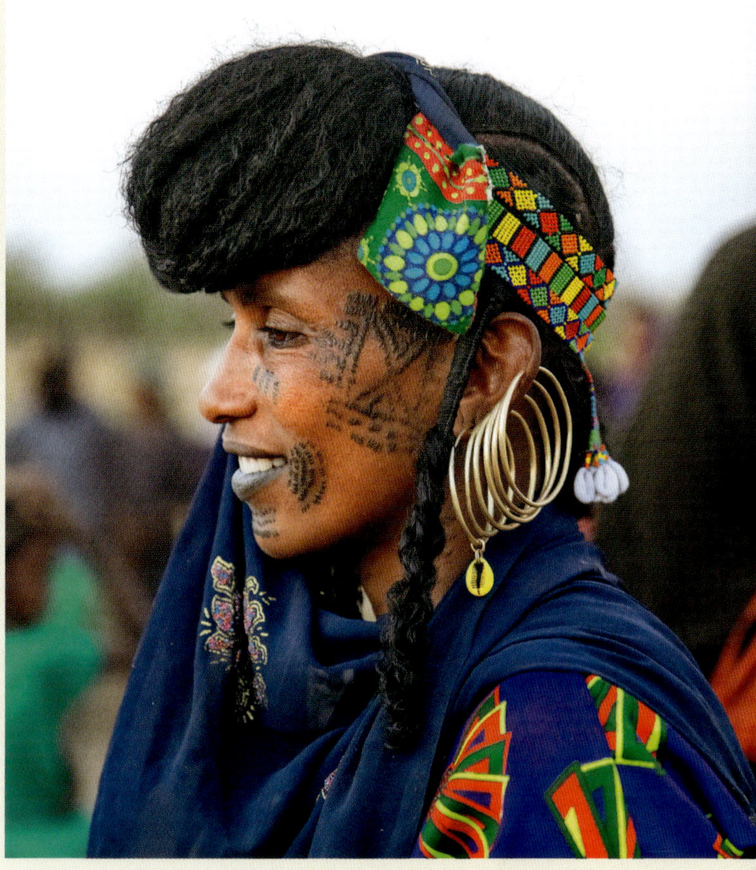

Magical facial markings of Wodaabe women, Chad, 2020.

placed in their turbans.[27] Powdered tree bark, seeds, and leaves are believed to ward off evil words, enemies, or attract women and it is not surprising that throughout West Africa the Wodaabe are famous for their knowledge of *maagani*, secret cures both real and magical.[28]

Wodaabe tattoos also reflect this magic because many symbols are associated with fertility or are employed as *toggu* (charms) to increase a man's or woman's beauty.[29] Other marks are believed to hold medicinal cures; a practice that was widespread across Sub-Saharan Africa.[30]

Nomadic peoples of the great African savannas of Tanzania, Uganda, and Namibia also possess tattoos and these markings are produced in relief and resemble colored scars. For example, men and women of the Barabaig and Datooga of Tanzania and Karamajong of Uganda display pigmented "goggle" tattoos surrounding their eye sockets. The tattooist picks up a fold of skin and cuts the tip, removing the skin from the body. A charcoal pigment mixed with cow urine is rubbed into the incisions, resulting in small bumps that delicately encircle the face over time. Bantu-speaking Chowke women and their linguistic relatives living in Namibia and Angola possess similar designs.[31]

Right Barabaig woman, Tanzania, 2020.

Far right Datooga woman, Tanzania, 2009.

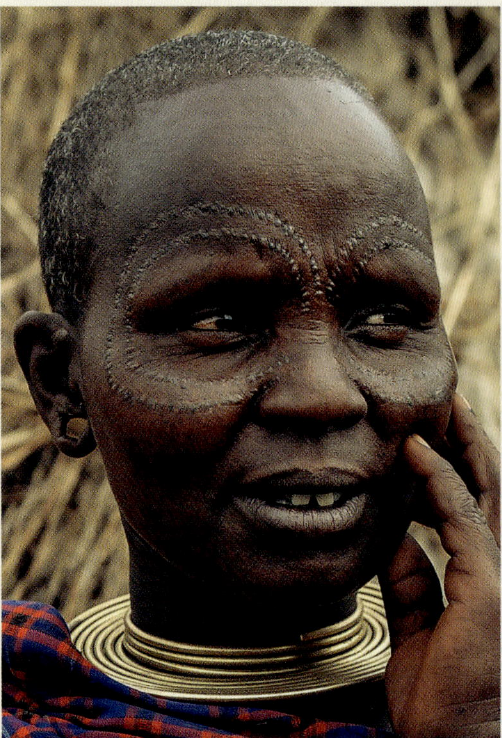

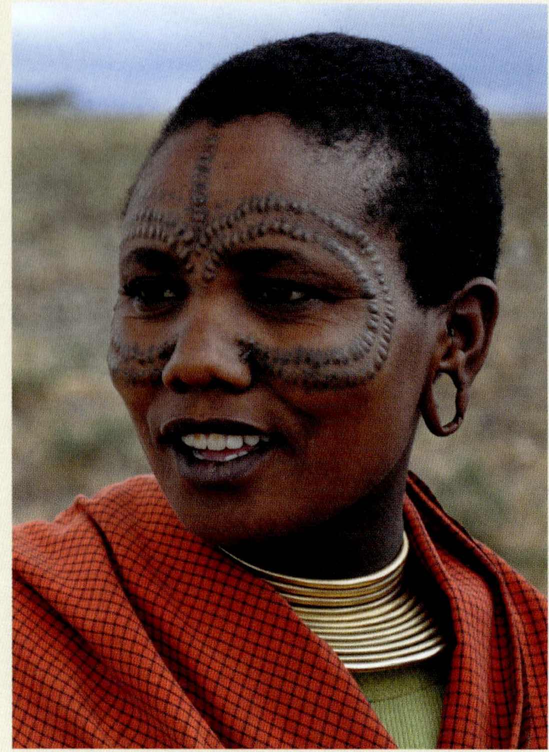

Further south, many Bushmen tribes of Namibia and southern Angola cut the skin during initiation or when setting out on a hunt for large game. Using a stone knife or sharp arrowhead, an elder medicine man makes a cut between the eyes of the patient and inserts into it a carbonized pigment with magical ingredients that may include the pulverized remains of specific animals believed to enhance human abilities. For example, the infusion might be introduced into the wounds to give the bearer better sight, stamina, or strength when thrusting a hunting spear.[32]

The Kwengo Bushmen placed additional tattoos on important muscles. Special substances were rubbed into the cuts to make the owner more successful on the hunt. For example, the fat from the lower reaches of a slain deer or eland provided the hunter with speed and endurance and were rubbed into cuts placed on the thighs. If these substances were introduced into marks on the right arm, they strengthened the force of the arm while it tensioned the hunter's bow.[43] The Nharo placed such incisions between the shoulder blades. Among the Sekele of Namibia, old men tattooed a successful hunter in return for an offering of game in order to give him good luck in finding the next buck. A piece of the foreleg biceps of the animal was burnt, and the ash was daubed into the incision.[34]

Among the Zul and Kambari of Nigeria, the Lokele of the Democratic Republic of the Congo, and among many other African ethnic groups, permanent body markings are still worn by the last generation of tattooed elders. Traditionally, these marks

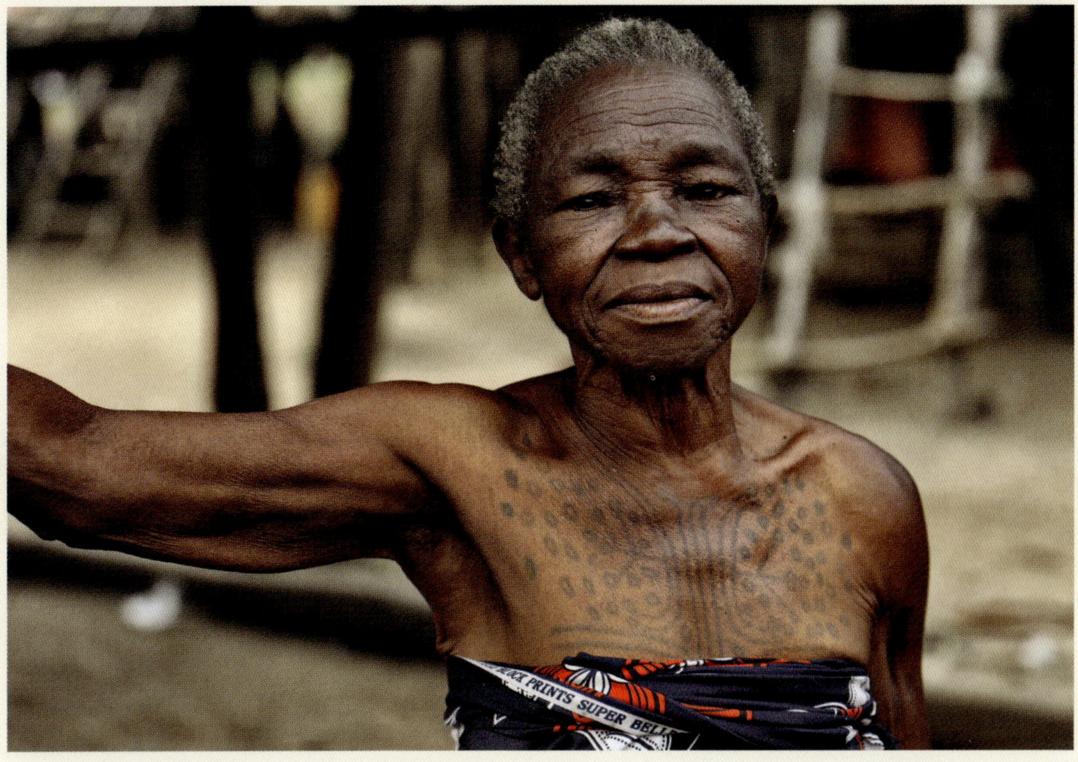

Lokele elder Mrs. Gumba bearing intricate tribal initiation markings on her chest, Democratic Republic of the Congo, 2021.

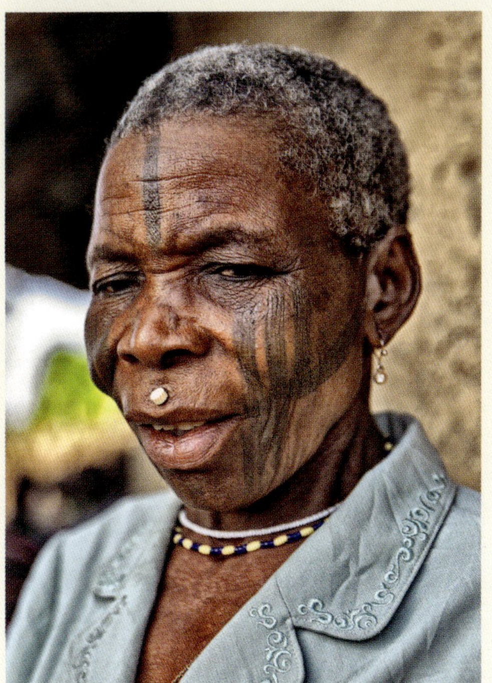

Zul woman with distinctive tribal markings, Nigeria, 2019.

were considered as tribal indicators of identity, with each group preferring specific motifs that were laid down in a variety of set patterns across the body and face.[35] Sometimes tattoo artists doubled as traditional healers who specialized in treating specific medical disorders with small incisions placed on various parts of their patients' bodies. Medicinal plants, which were sometimes charred, were then rubbed into these wounds to relieve such ailments as head pain, respiratory complaints, arthritis, boils, and eye problems. These linear cuts resemble tiny scarifications or even pigmented tattoos.

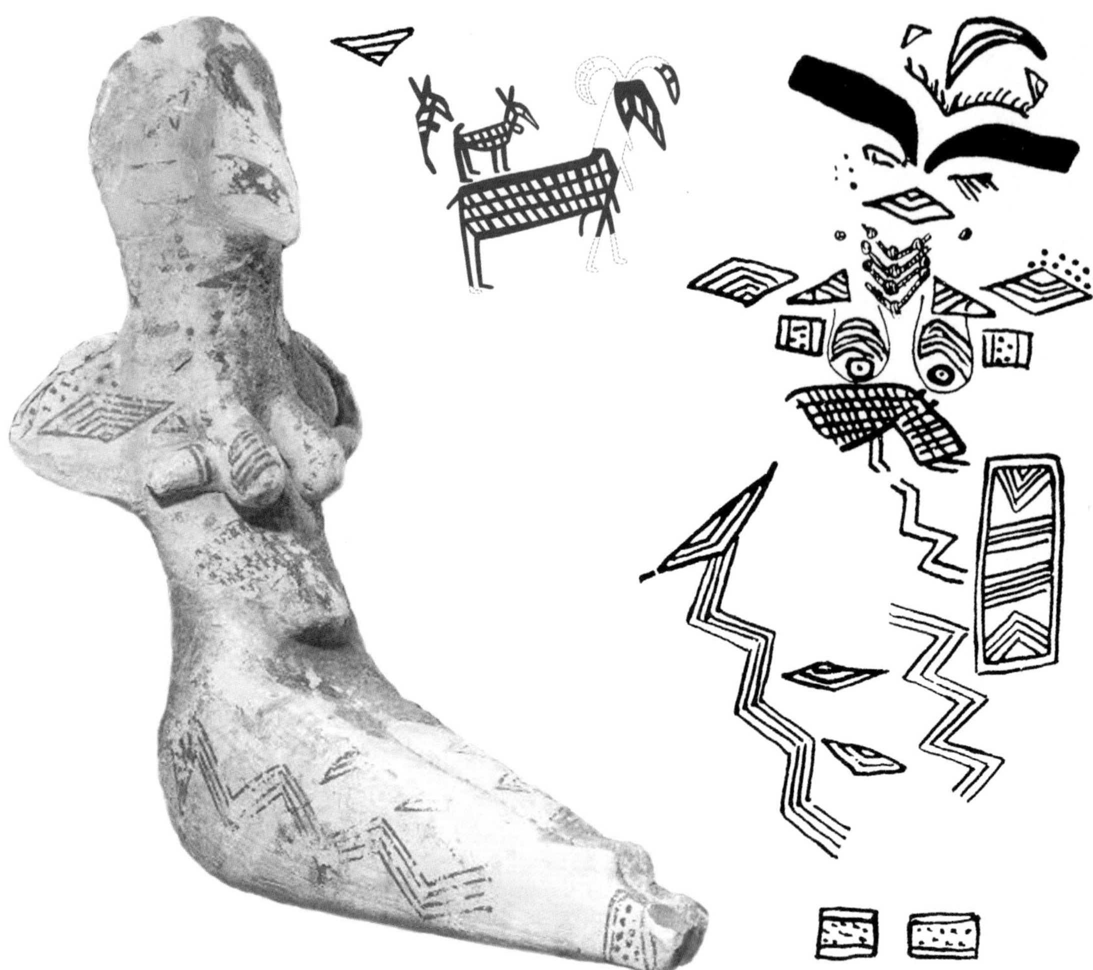

Predynastic Egyptian female ceramic figurine (*ca.* 3700–3500 BCE) with painted designs covering the body. Several of these markings correspond to figural tattoos (i.e., mammals) recently discovered on mummies of the same era.

Tattooed Mummies and Figurines of Ancient Egypt

Tattoos marking the bodies of ceramic figurines and mummies made their first appearance during the predynastic period of ancient Egypt (fourth millennium BCE). These were often composed of geometric patterns and animal motifs.

Right Egyptian faience figurine (*ca*. 2000–1850 BCE) on truncated legs with dotted, diamond-shaped markings corresponding to tattoos seen on ancient female mummies.

Far right Middle Kingdom Egyptian paddle doll (*ca*. 2030–1802 BCE) with dotted, diamond-shaped markings on buttocks resembling tattoos found on mummies.

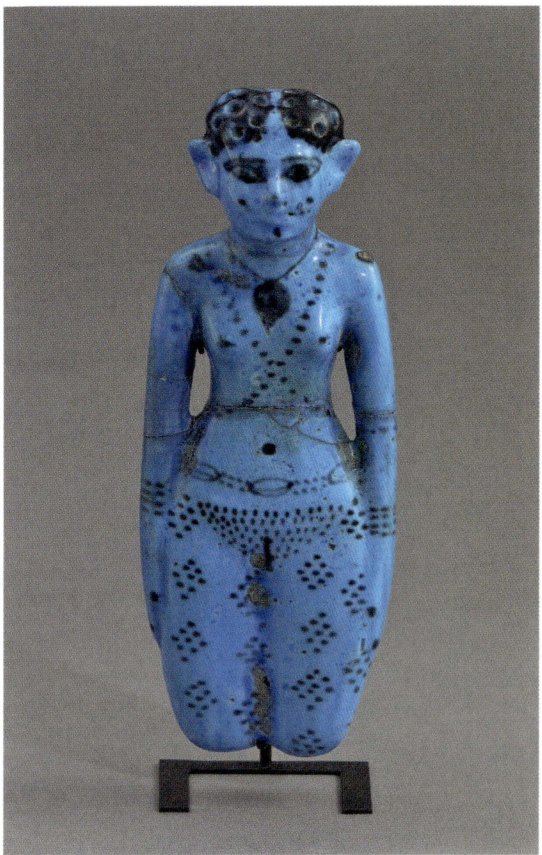

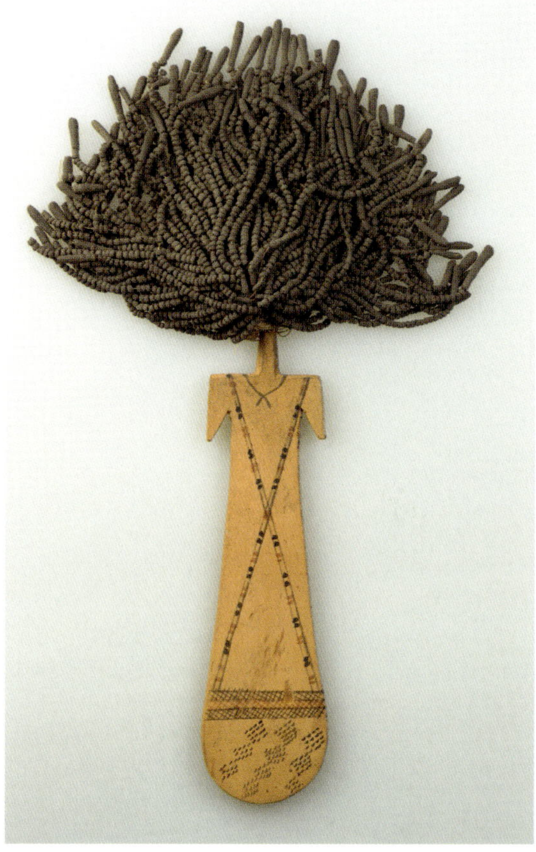

These sculptures are quite rare but are somewhat consistent regarding the placement of the painted ornamentation: geometric patterns occur on the legs, shoulders, abdomen, and across the breasts, and horned animal figures (sheep or antelope) are typically placed in pairs on the small of the back.

Were it not for the recent discovery of similar tattoos on mummified human remains[36] from the same era, it would not have been possible to corroborate these ancient markings with actual tattooing traditions. More specifically, two approximately 5,000-year-old mummies from the site of Gebelein possess, to date, the second-oldest tattoos in the world. The man and woman have been at the British Museum for more than one hundred years, but it was only when scientists recently reexamined their apparently tattoo-less bodies with infrared photography that their tattoos emerged.[37] On the right shoulder of the woman appears to be a crooked staff, perhaps a symbol of authority that may have been related to her social position or her role in ceremonial, ritual, or cult activities. She also bears a band of four "S-like" tattoos on her upper right arm, which have not yet been deciphered. On the man's upper right arm appears what is believed to be a horned Barbary sheep and a horned auroch (an extinct form of wild cattle), animals that may have been associated with strength or virility.

In the later Middle Kingdom evidence for tattooing is manifest in both art and human remains. Specifically, truncated ceramic

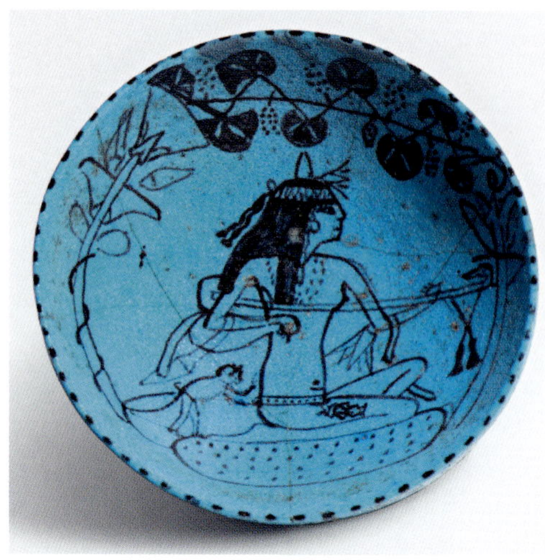

Above Blue faience bowl (fourteenth century BCE) showing a female lute player with a Bes tattoo on her thigh.

faience female figurines and wooden so-called "paddle dolls," particularly devoted to the cult of Hathor, were sometimes decorated with geometrically patterned dots on the arms, thighs, abdomen, and buttocks, and figurative (avian) motifs on the dorsal and frontal aspect of their bodies. The geometric markings, especially dotted patterns forming diamond or lozenge shapes, closely resemble tattoos identified on female Middle Kingdom mummies (2055–2004 BCE) from the Deir el-Bahari site, as well as at least one twelfth-dynasty (2025–1700 BCE) tomb mural from Qua, depicting an acrobatic dancer with linked diamond tattoos on her hips.[38] Another coterminous mummy from the Asasif site (*ca.* 2030–1981 BCE), which is very near to Deir el-Bahari, displays two avian tattoos located halfway between its right shoulder and elbow, tattoos that bear a striking resemblance to those seen on paddle dolls excavated at the same site.[39] The tattooed Deir el-Bahari women also possess geometric tattoos (lines, strokes, and dots, often arranged in the form of rhombuses) located on the hips, chest, shoulders, arms, stomach, and feet. One of these tattooed women was Amunet, known as the priestess of Hathor and described as the "King's Favorite Ornament," while the others likely functioned in a lesser ritual capacity.

Hathor was a celestial deity associated with the sky and daughter of the Egyptian sun god Ra. Her agency was related to cults associated with fertility, love, maternal care, and funerary rites. Hathor was also the patron of music and dance and assumed the status of a "mother goddess" who facilitated rebirth and resurrection.[40] Through these Hathoric associations, ceramic and wooden paddle dolls presumably formed elements of women's domestic and other sacred rituals associated with conception, birth, the health of newborns and their mothers, and/or mortuary rituals.[41] Because most of the aforementioned body markings (i.e., tattoos) observed on female Middle Kingdom ceramic and wooden figurines and human remains were located on the chest, abdomen, and hips, it can be suggested they

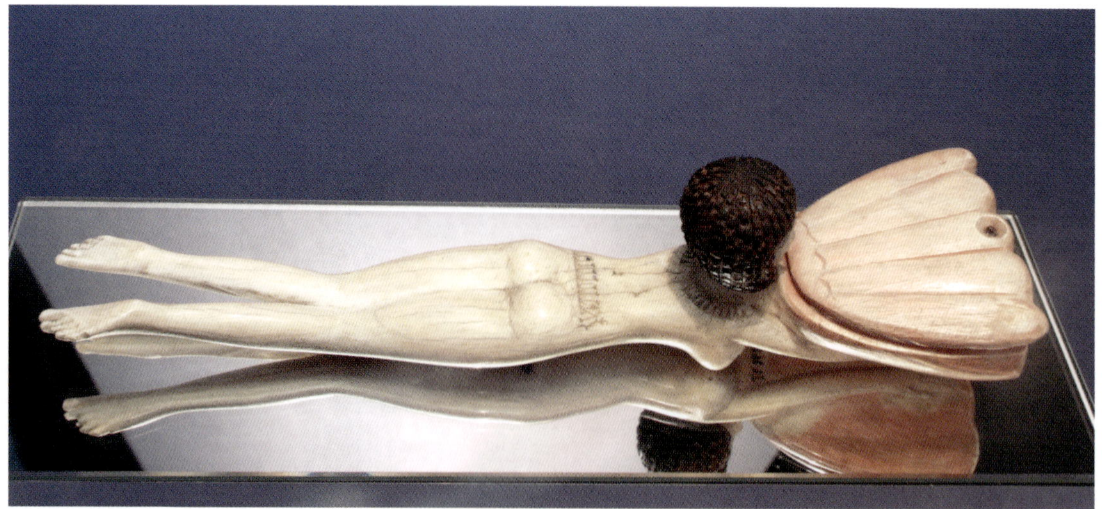

Right New Kingdom Egyptian ivory spoon (fourteenth century BCE) in the form of a swimming girl with a large lotus flower in her hands. She possesses a tattooed waist belt on her back composed of papyri buds flanked by two mammals, possibly gazelles (as well as a pair of unseen Bes tattoos on the front of her thighs).

Ancient Egyptian tattoo motifs in the form of Bes.

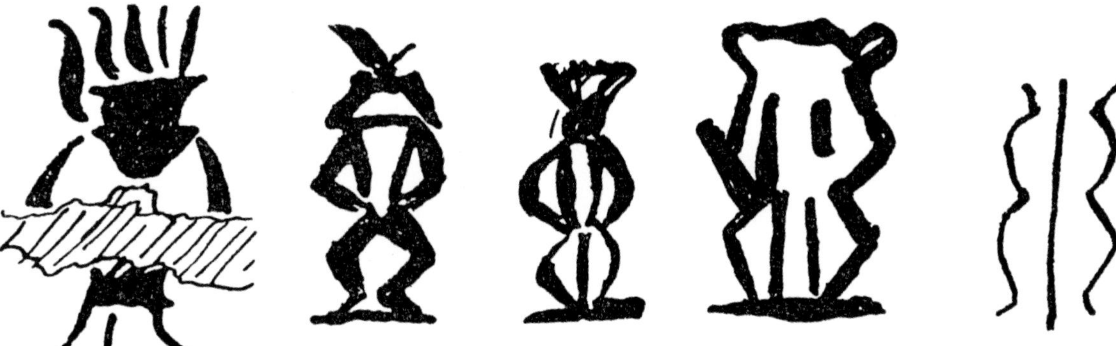

Below Dot-work and dotted, diamond-shaped tattoos on the mummified body of a Middle Kingdom woman from Deir el-Bahari (2055–2004 BCE).

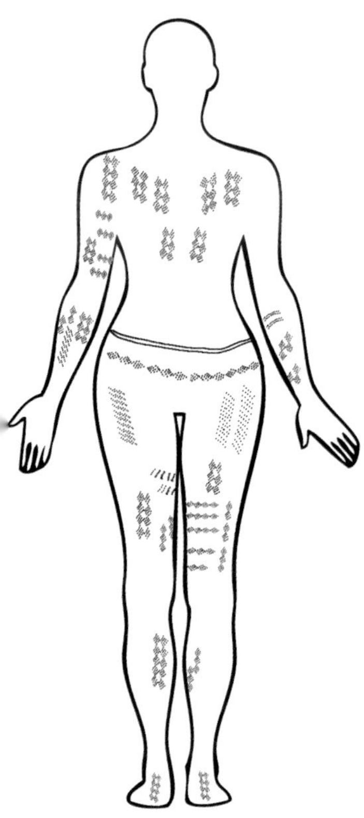

were connected with beliefs associated with fertility and enhanced sexuality that were carried into the afterlife.

Given these cultural correlations, it should not be surprising that certain human figurines of the New Kingdom continue to embody these religious patterns. A so-called ivory "cosmetic spoon" (*ca.* 1388–1351 BCE), in the form of a swimming nude girl holding a pink lotus flower in her hands, brings such ideas into bold relief. This ornately shaped and beautiful vessel, which is housed in the collections of the Pushkin State Museum of Fine Arts, Moscow, likely held cosmetic paints, aromatic oils, or incense, but it may have contained sacrificial substances used in religious rituals.[42]

Upon close examination of the girl's back is seen a delicately carved row of papyri with buds bent upward, flanked at each side by two figural images, perhaps gazelles.[43] Because these inscribed motifs do not continue around the waist to form a belt, it is likely they are tattoos. This idea is reinforced by a similar tattooed band discovered on the lower back of a heavily tattooed (neck, shoulders, back, arms) female religious practitioner of the New Kingdom from Deir el-Medina, which consists of a dotted line flanked by two large lotus flowers bending up and outward.[44] Papyri symbols were related to the creation of the world, fertility, regenerative power, eternal life, and associated with Hathor; and gazelles, especially those used to decorate specific sistrum rattles, wands, or crowns worn by women, can also be associated with this deity.[45]

As well as an engraved necklace and emphasized pubic area, the ivory woman features two Bes deity figures atop its upper thighs. These are likely tattoos, not body paint, and correspond to Bes figures appearing on women's thighs in frescoes[46] and other forms of New Kingdom objects of material culture, including clay figurines,[47] a blue faience bowl (*ca.* 1375 BCE) depicting a nude female lute player,[48] and a bronze mirror handle (*ca.* 1400–1292 BCE) in the form of a nude woman.[49] The god Bes, who resembles a bow-legged dwarf with a lion's mane or adorned in lion's skin, was associated with the cult of Hathor. He was the patron of music, dance, warfare, and the hearth, and also associated with eroticism, sexuality, and the protection of newborns, women, and the household.[50] He watched over health and beauty and was featured on many types of female toiletry items, such as boxes, hairpins, mirrors, and cosmetic spoons.

Tattoos of Nigeria

Nigeria's diverse peoples boast a dynamic blend of permanent body markings, with many adorned by striking, pigmented tattoos that swell into bold, elevated keloid patterns.

Until the mid- to late twentieth century, the Yoruba, Dukkawa, Kamberi, and Ije of neighboring Benin employed lasting designs for a variety of purposes, including initiation, beautification, and especially to proclaim the courage of those individuals who bore them.

Women were the primary recipients of many of these markings and female Yoruba elders have stated their highly visible *kolo* (tattoos) were a "test" of physical and inner strength because only the brave could endure the painful skin-cut tattoos. The patterns, which were applied in stages, were acquired before marriage, and prepared women for childbirth. The qualities of courage and fortitude were widely respected and parallel those of the patron of body artists, Ogun, the god of iron.[51]

Yoruba tattoo masters were highly sought after and were held in great regard. They were called *oniisonon* or "skilled designer" or "one who creates art." Renowned tattooists were praised for their speed, skill, dexterity, and technique. Some were quite famous since "200 faces [i.e., clients] know [them]."[52]

Skin artists of the highest caliber mastered a repertoire of many kinds of cuts, from *ko ture* (long and bold facial incisions), to broad *keke* (slashing cuts), and *bu abaja* (short, shallow and faint designs), among others.[53]

Most Yoruba motifs were derived from nature and featured cowrie *esa* (shells), *alangba* (lizards), *igi ope* (palm trees), *ofa*

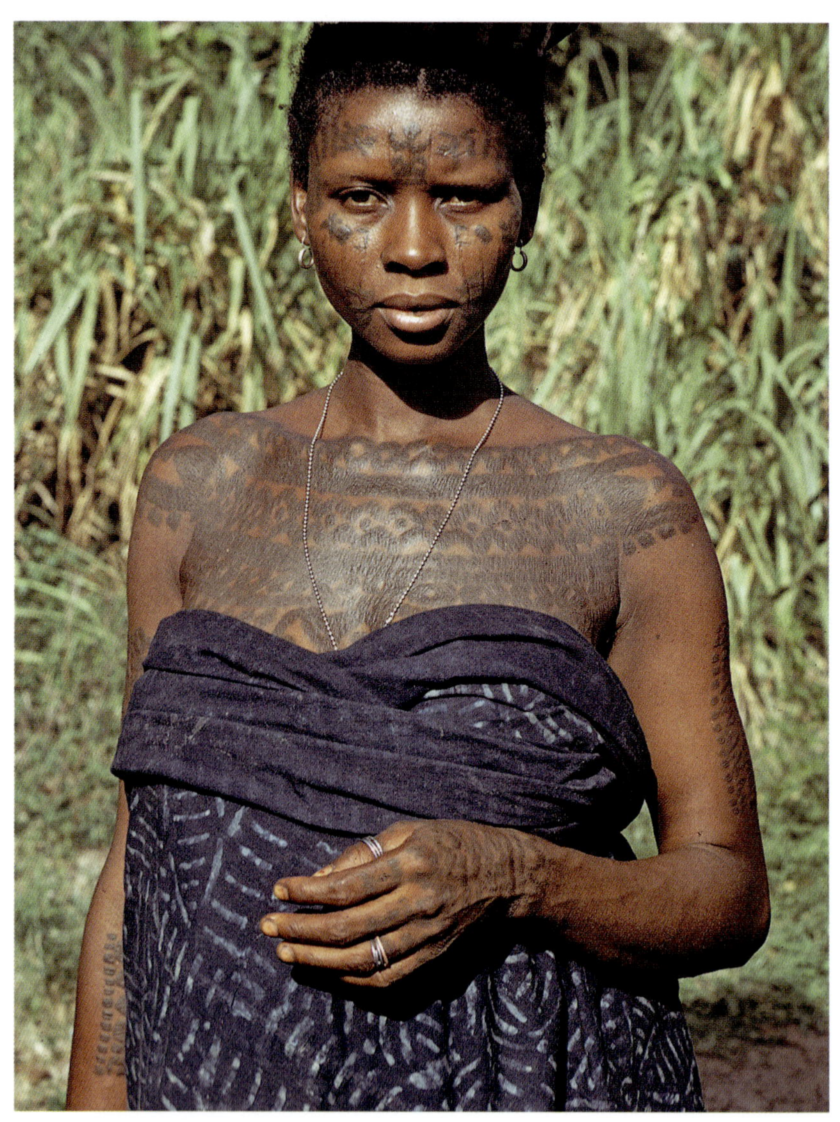

Right Heavily tattooed Ije woman, 2023. The Ije of Benin formerly marked the body with extensive scar tattoos that resemble those of the Yoruba. They were a form of beautification and proclaimed the courage of the bearer.

Far right Tattooed Dukkawa woman, 2019. The Dukkawa of central Nigeria once practiced extensive body tattooing but little documentation exists on their traditional tattooing customs.

Opposite Yoruba woman with extensive *kolo* markings, *ca*. 1970.

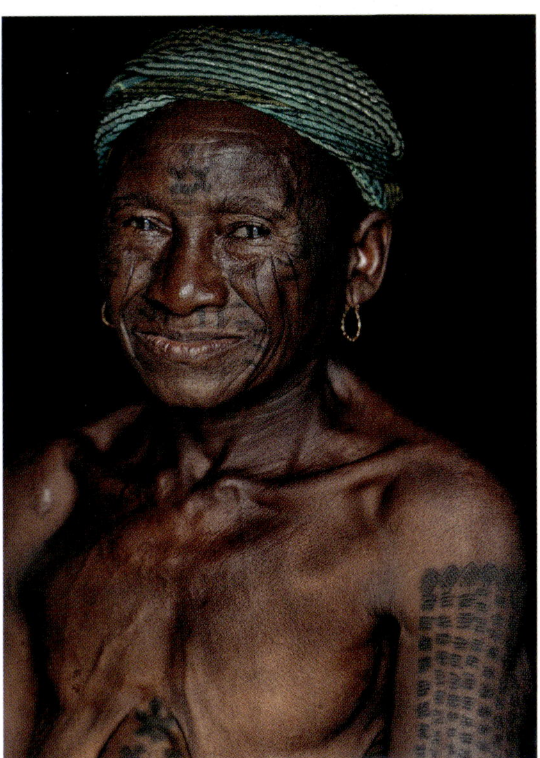

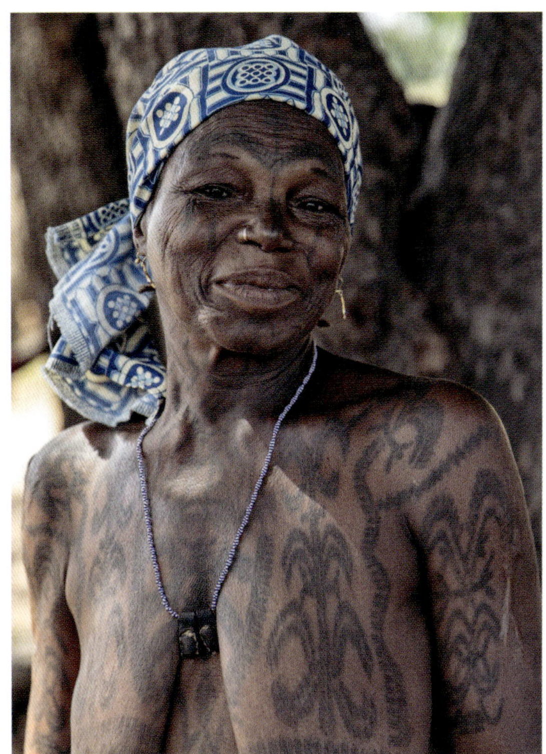

(arrows), *ogongo* (ostrich), *igun* (vultures), *adaba* (doves), *agemo* (chameleons), and *okun* (centipedes). Other motifs were taken from the material world and encompassed *ose* (dance wands) of the thunder god Sango, *walaa* (Islamic writing boards), *apa tira* (arm amulets), *opon ayo* (game boards), and even scissors, airplanes, wristwatches, and personal names in recent times.[54]

Other Yoruba incisions were medicinal in nature, but instead of inserting soot or lampblack into these wounds, body artists, priests, and village healers administered a variety of herbal remedies. Typically speaking, the location of such treatments corresponded to local ailments so, for example, short vertical marks placed beneath the eyes of children were incised to prevent them from trembling, a condition believed to have been brought to the living by spirits.[55] Incisions infused with herbs near the mouth might add to a hunter's courage and increase his memory. While medicines rubbed into cuts below the lip may have enhanced an individual's curses against another since, "when the individual wishes to curse he licks his lower lip and whatever he says will come to pass."[56]

Finally, these potent substances were also employed to attract specific deities or their spiritual familiars into the bodies of the initiated. To accomplish such goals, small cuts were made on the crown of the devotee's head and special herbs were then applied to "activate" the vital essence of the god.[57]

The Fang of Central Africa

The Fang are an enigmatic forest-dwelling people who inhabit a vast region that transcends the international borders of Cameroon, Gabon, Congo, and Equatorial Guinea.

Their once vibrant body-marking traditions embodied a shared cultural legacy that was as deep and enduring as the ancient forests that surrounded them.

In the 1950s, the eminent Catalan primatologist Jordi Sabater Pi began documenting the tattooing practices of the Fang, but by that time Fang tattooing was already in decline and the meanings behind most motifs had been largely forgotten. Thankfully, Sabater recorded many ancient patterns that could only be seen on the faces and bodies of the very old and speculated that originally the tattoos of the Fang were possibly created "as a response to the need for identification or totemic protection."[58]

Prior to the influx of missionaries in the late nineteenth and early twentieth centuries, the Fang believed that the dense forests of their homeland were "full of dangers and the temporary residence of good or evil spirits of ancestors incarnated in certain trees and animals."[59] But just as the wilderness could be dangerous, it also served as the primary source of aesthetic inspiration in the tattooing arts of the Fang people.

The Fang practiced two types of tattooing: *mamvam* (relief tattoos), which were a form of pigmented scarification, and *mevale* (flat tattoos), which were pricked with a comb-like tool into the skin. The former variety of adornment was already quite rare

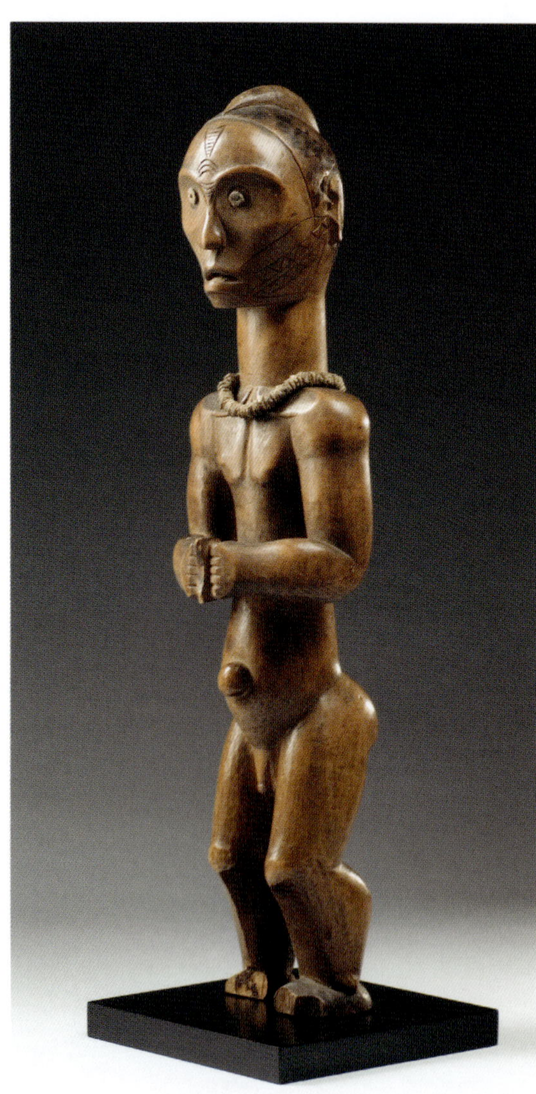

Fang male reliquary guardian figure from Cameroon, late nineteenth century. It has *efà ngon* (moon crescents) on the forehead, *king-koro* (spearhead) patterns on the jawline, as well as other tattoos.

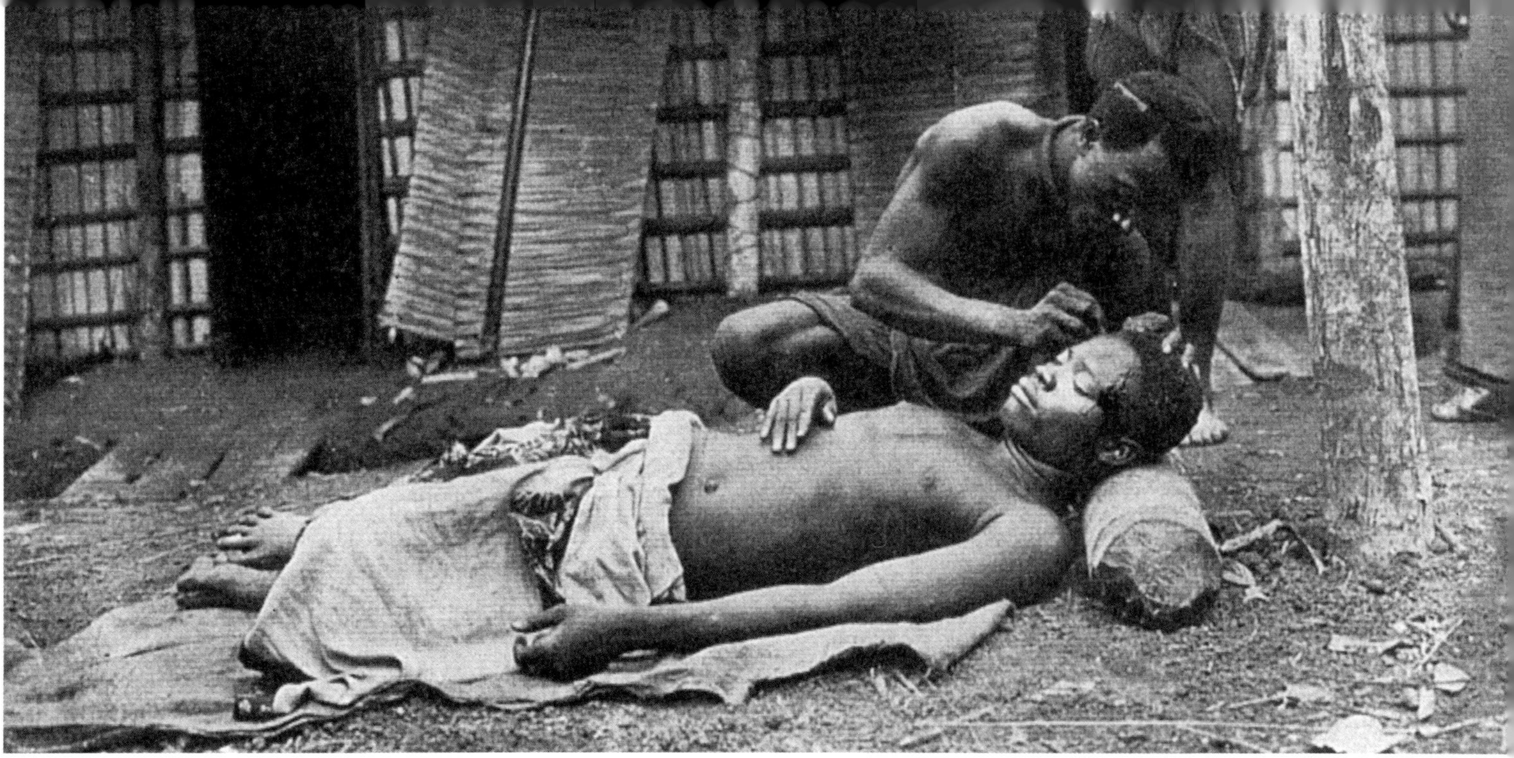

Above Fang tattooing scene, *ca*. 1906.

Right and below Tattooed Ntum Fang man, 1956. He bears *efà ngon* (moon crescents) on the forehead, *ekob kueiny* (monkey design) on the nose, and *king-koro* (spearhead) patterns on the neck. The Fang maintained several secret societies. Specific tattoos placed at the nape of the neck indicated an individual's membership to these organizations.

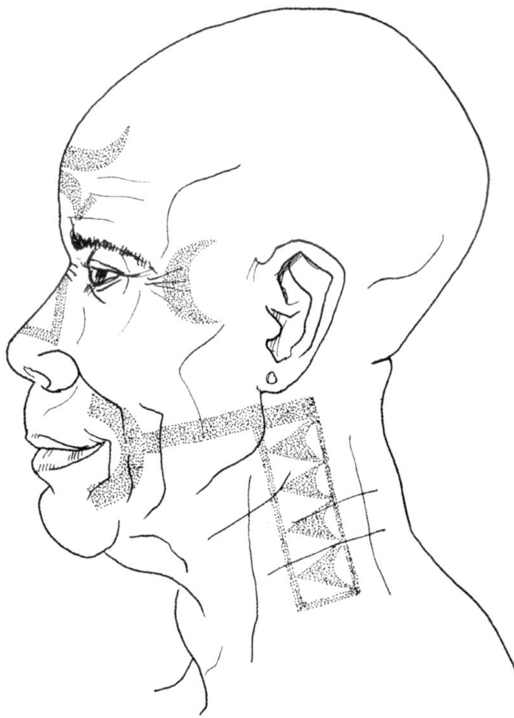

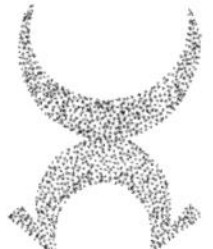

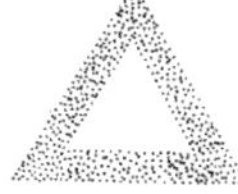

in Fang territory when Sabater began his investigations, but he was able to study old reliquary sculptures that were decorated on the chest, abdomen, and face with special tattoos dedicated to ancestor worship. These forms of statuary were used as guardians to protect the baskets containing the bones and skulls of venerated ancestors and have always been amongst the most admired and sought-after genres of African art among collectors.

Between 1907 and 1909, the German ethnologist Günther Tessmann witnessed several tattooing sessions among the Fang. He wrote that specific clans specialized in tattooing and that "perhaps only one in a hundred men" were skilled enough to perform it.[60] Many of these men were long remembered as masters of their art decades after they had died.

The operation of knife-cut tattooing was performed in the village meeting house without ceremony. The *otu* (pigment) was obtained by burning wood and collecting the soot on

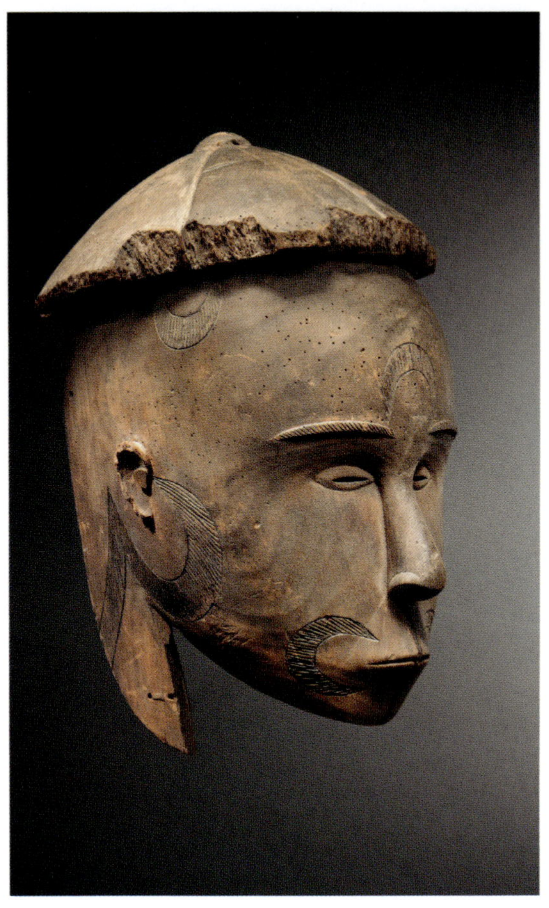

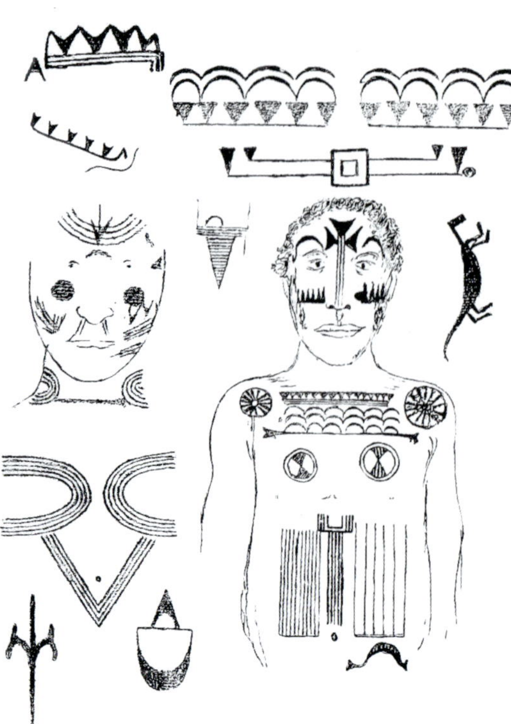

Far left Tattooed Fang mask, Gabon, before 1914. This rare mask portrays a man with a series of *efà ngon* (moon crescents) on the forehead, temple, and beside the mouth, a pair of linear tattoos running down the nose to the chin, and a hooked motif on the neck. The latter may signify the bells placed on the necks of hunting dogs, although its curved shape also resembles Fang throwing knifes.

Left Fang tattooing motifs, ca. 1907–09. Fang tattoo designs were derived from the surrounding environment. Basic motifs included: diamonds, lozenges, parallel lines, ribbons of palm, sticks, birds, fish, arrows, basketry designs, full moons, spear barbs, scorpions, monkeys, tear drops, spiders, frog's legs, rattles, knives, chameleons, and pipes.

a pot shard placed over the smoking fire. The artist drew a stencil on the part of the body to be tattooed with a wet, curved piece of local grass – leaf stems of the *musanga* (umbrella tree) – or he dipped his finger in the soot and carefully delineated the desired motif.[61]

Before dawn, the tattooist began puncturing his client by making short, small crosscutting and transverse incisions with an *endolo* or handleless iron knife. The artist wiped away any excess blood and rubbed in more *otu* pigment with his thumb or forefinger. In other instances, a powder made from the seeds of the *Xylopia aethiopica* was vigorously rubbed into the wounds.[62] This tree is a tropical evergreen bearing pungent, aromatic seeds and is still used today as a food condiment and folk medicine in West Africa. After the cutting was complete, the body was washed to remove residual blood and soot. Then, another layer of pigment was rubbed into the clean wounds to make the color darker.

According to Sabater, these kinds of tattoos were applied to boys and girls aged five to ten years of age. Family members would bring their children to the village tattooist where they often requested specific designs (half-moons, circles, leopard spots, or whiskers, etc.) because of their association with protective magic and/or clan unity.[63]

The missionary Father R. P. Trilles, who traveled throughout Fang country in the

Right Mvai Fang woman with *efà ngon* (moon crescents) on the forehead, *ngama akong* (spearpoints) on the temples and cheeks, and *mendgim mendjà* ("splashes of cassava leaf soup") on the chin, 1956.

Below Okak Fang man with *nguem obam* (dovetail) on abdomen and geometric motifs on the neck, chest, and upper left forearm, 1954. Father Trilles noted that Fang men without tattooing "were of inferior quality" because they had not dared to face the pain and difficulties associated with the ancestral rite.

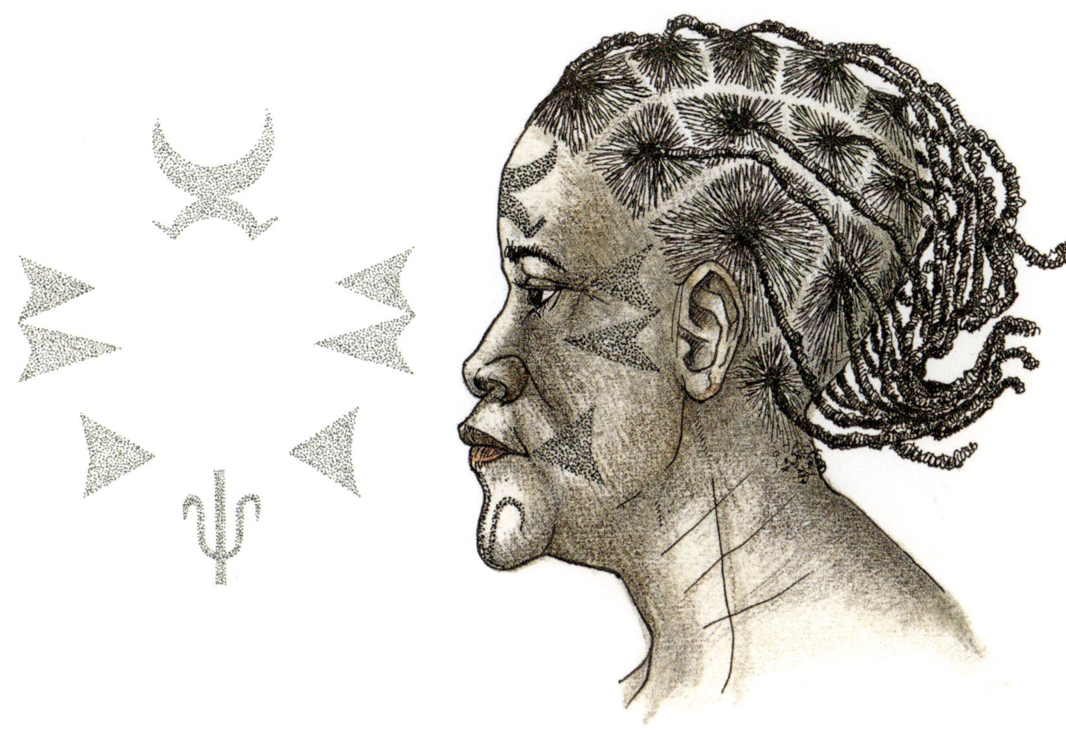

early twentieth century, recorded intriguing information regarding the spiritual and medicinal ramifications of tattoo. He wrote that small linear cuts at the temples or on the arms of children with a fine powder of red pal wood were therapeutic and eliminated "afflictions."[64] *Nsam* or *nsilé* (totemic or clan identification) tattoos symbolized a spirit protector. Thus, members of the Amvom clan placed the figure of the *mvom* (python) on their temple, while members of the Iemvi clan utilized a *mvi* (flower) in the form of two concentric circles with a center point.[65] These designs not only identified clan members, but also reconciled the bearer with the animal (or plant) protector of the group.

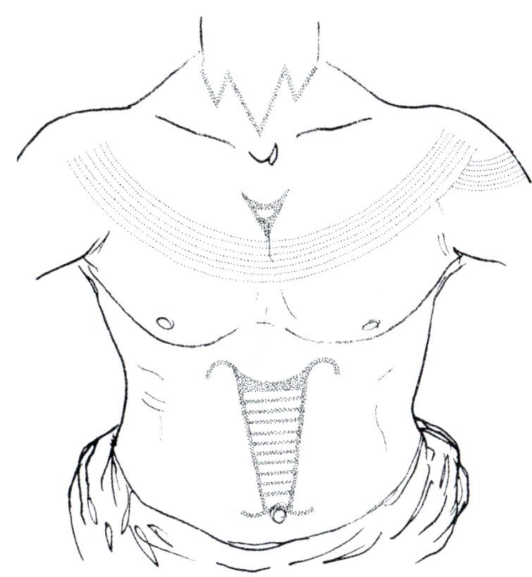

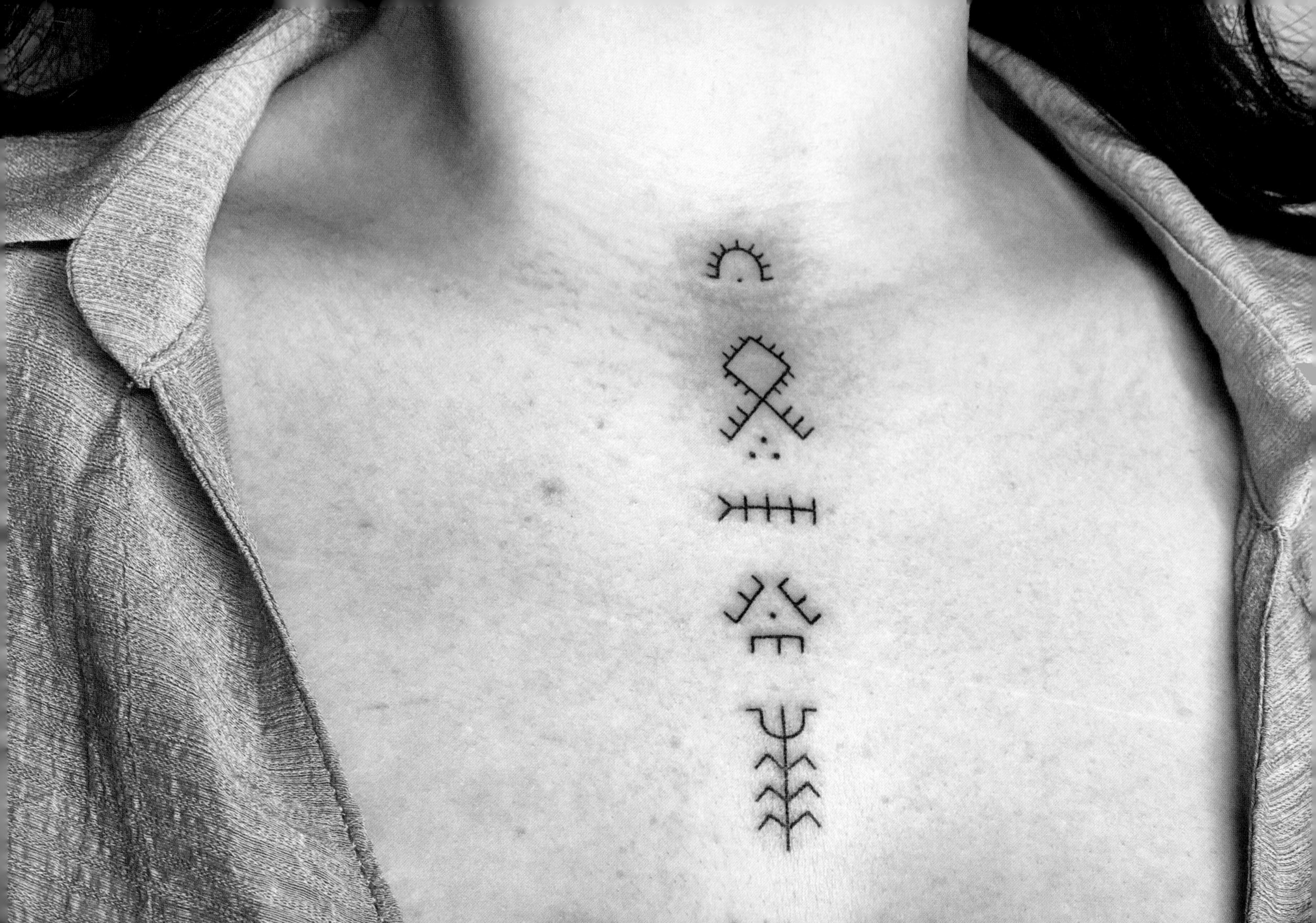

The *Deq* Maker: Elu

Opposite Traditional Kurdish tattooing motifs marking the upper chest and throats of women were derived from the Tree of Life and were believed to enhance one's well-being, longevity, fertility, and wisdom, 2023.

Right Elu at work with a Kurdish woman in Barcelona, Spain, 2023.

Far right A client displays various constellations representing their path through life, lineage, and connections to the land through various animal, plant, and tribal symbols, 2023.

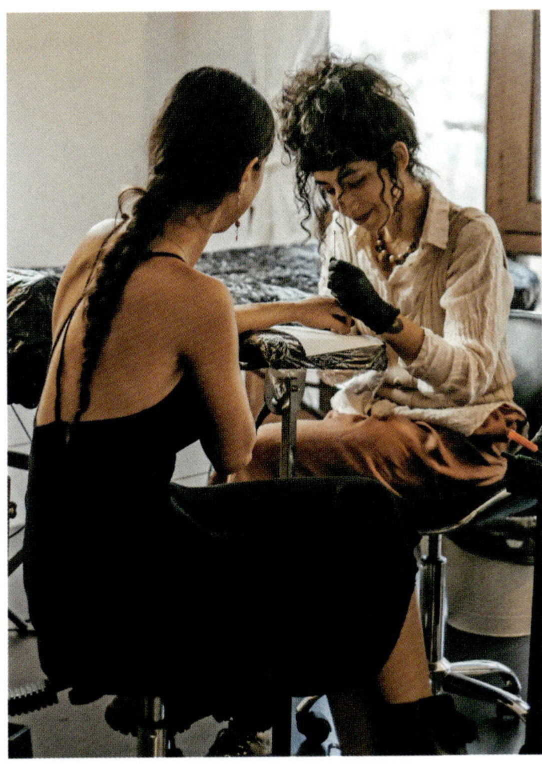

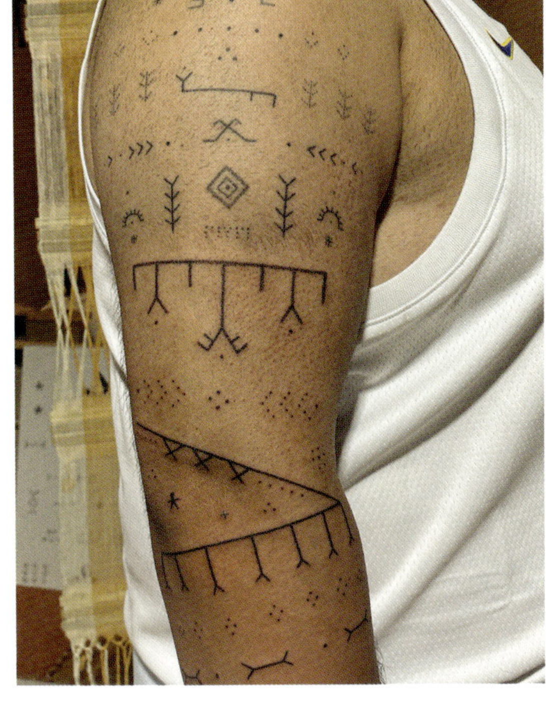

> *Now is the time to remember our roots again.*
> *It's time to connect with the story of the* deq *(tattoo), the art of expression.*
> *It's time to absorb the diversity, texture, spirit of our common values, our past, and the ancientness of our land.*
> *Now is the time to remember, tell, convey and blend with today's spirit in the footsteps of those who caravanned beyond the soul.*
> *(Ömer Dereci)*[66]

Portugal-based Elu is a tattoo artist of Zaza (Kirmançki) Alevi Kurdish descent who has been working via the traditional method of hand-poking for nearly a decade to help revive her people's ancient tattooing traditions. In her Native Zaza language, skin marking (tattooing) was called *kutêne*, or *kut* for short, but today it is more popularly known as *deq* (also *daq* or *xal*). Although she always felt connected to her Kurdish roots, Elu's family was displaced from their ancestral homelands in the Dêrsim region of eastern Turkey more than two decades ago. There they faced constant persecution and eventually settled in Germany, where Elu was born.

Kurdish tattooing, which today is worn on the bodies of elderly men and women in Turkey, Syria, Iraq, and western Iran, is gradually fading from view and has not been regularly practiced in decades. Elu hopes to change this by liberating *deq* from the negative connotations that Islamic societies across the Middle East have attached to it over many generations, a movement that compelled many Kurds and other ethnic minorities who tattooed to feel ashamed of their ancestral marks.

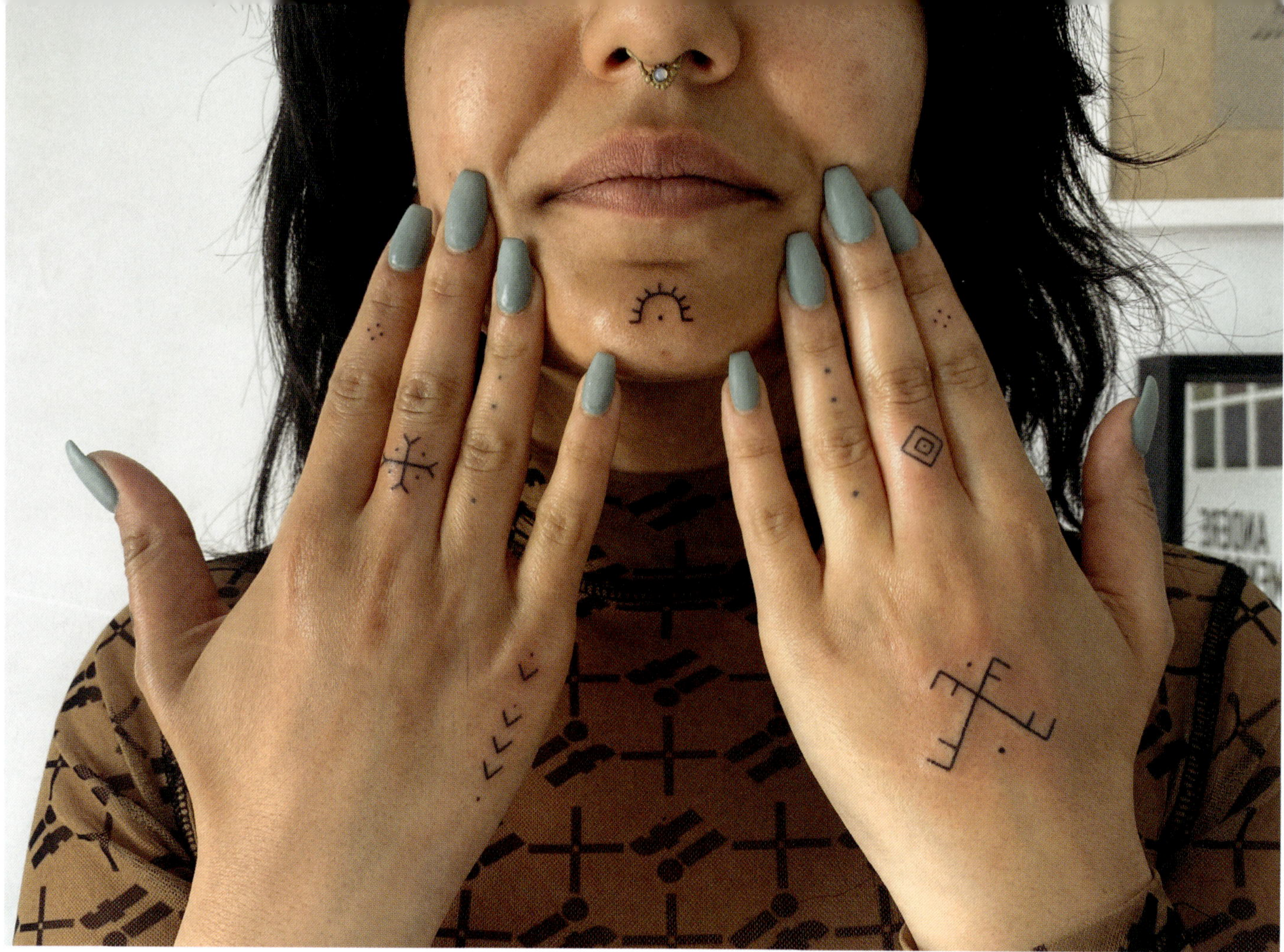

"My great-grandmother was the last person in my family to have *deq*, and she marked her face herself, but sadly I never met her or saw a picture of her. In the following generations, *deq* quickly vanished from the faces of our mothers and grandmothers, and I grew up learning that tattoos were *haram* [forbidden] because of the assimilating forces of Islamization," she explained.[67]

Kurdish tattoos were originally derived from natural phenomena that were not only believed to provide the body with spiritual protection, but also to enhance a woman's fertility and beauty and provide medicinal benefits, among other more esoteric beliefs.

"All my life, I felt uprooted, because I have always lived somewhere other than where my ancestors were from," Elu said. "And because there are virtually no books or other sources on *deq*, I have been drawn to each individual motif as if it were an element of a visual language of the skin; one that relates to nature, the cosmos, our people, and humanity itself," she shared. "I firmly believe that *deq* is ancestral to language, and was the medium we used to communicate before language was born."

With each *deq* she creates, Elu is inspired to help reinvigorate the ancient tattooing practices of her Kurdish ancestors. "It is

Above Elu's client has a crescent-sun tattoo on her chin and symbols for protection and connectivity to the land and Kurdish people on her hands, 2023.

Opposite right Crescent and eye tattoos representing the moon, sun, or eye are traditional Kurdish motifs of spiritual connectivity, 2023.

Opposite far right Motifs representing mountains, tents, trees, and flowers are symbols of belonging, protection, and connectivity to nature, 2023.

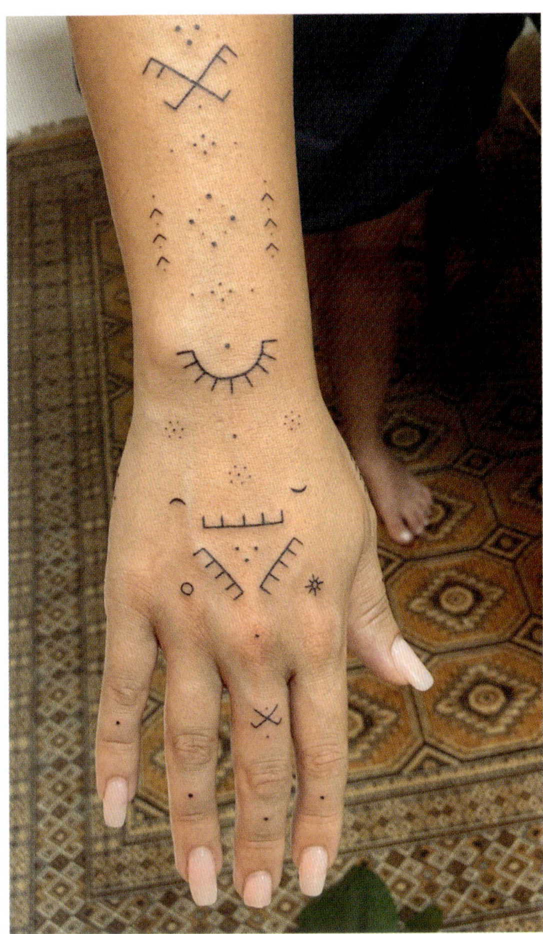

a personal choice to reclaim your body and wear our *deq* forever on your skin. As a *deq* maker, I totally respect that thought process, but I also want to encourage others from the diaspora to think openly about their personal journey and to reconnect with their cultural heritage and ancestral ties. For me, this a lifelong journey to discover and never forget what these symbols mean."

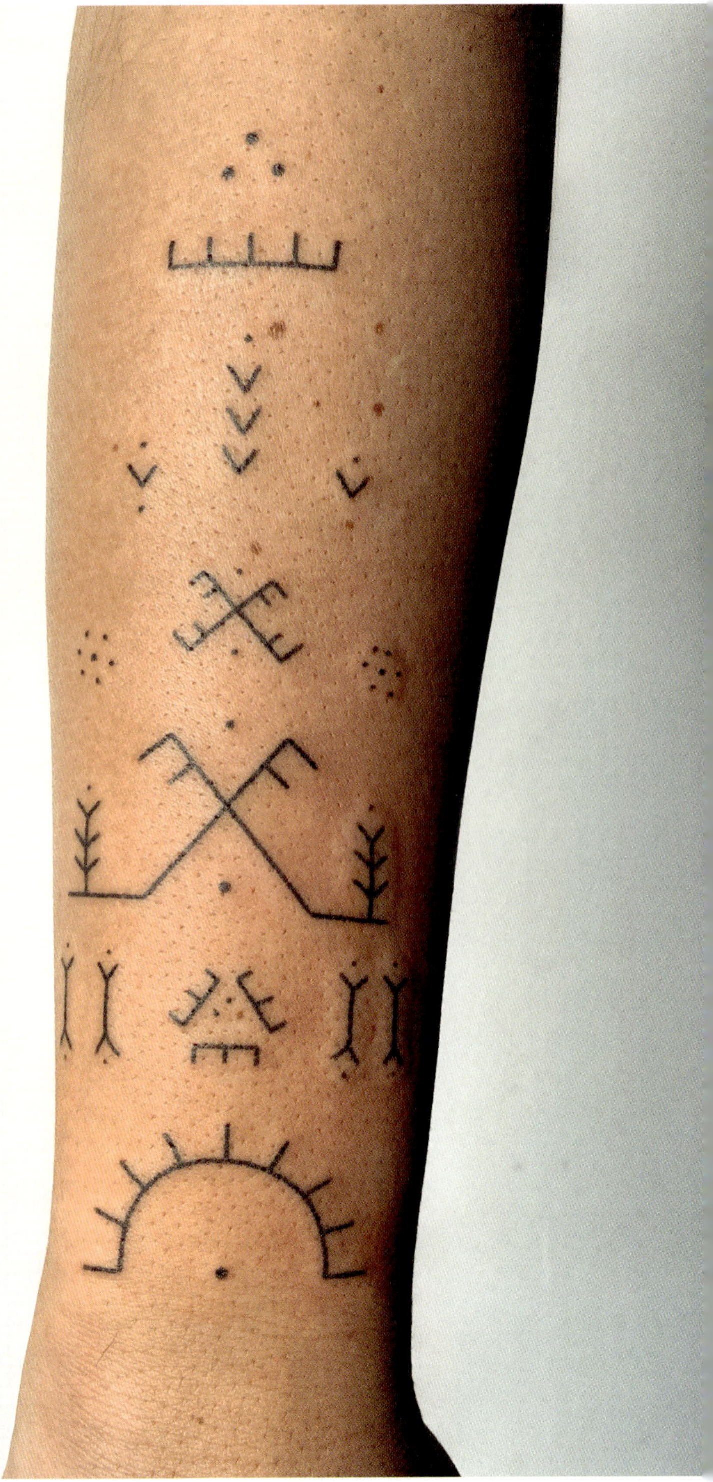

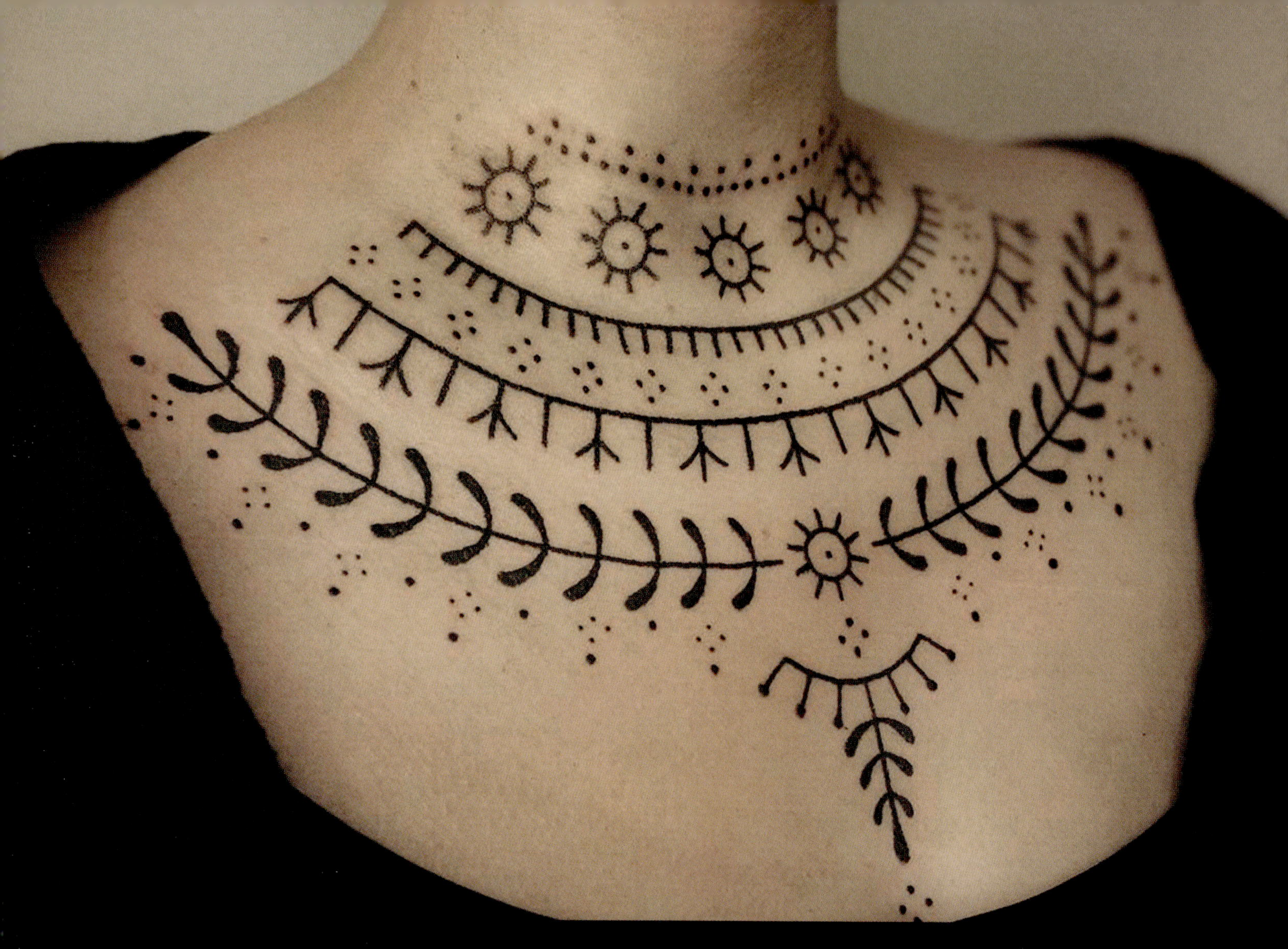

Marked by Tradition: Mélissa Pizović

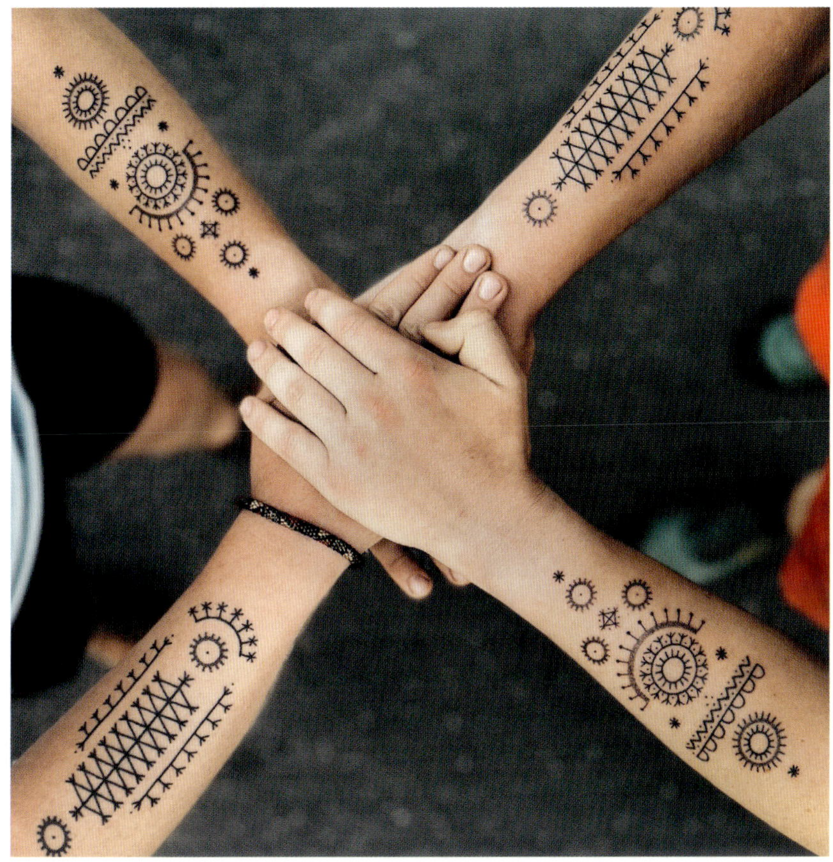

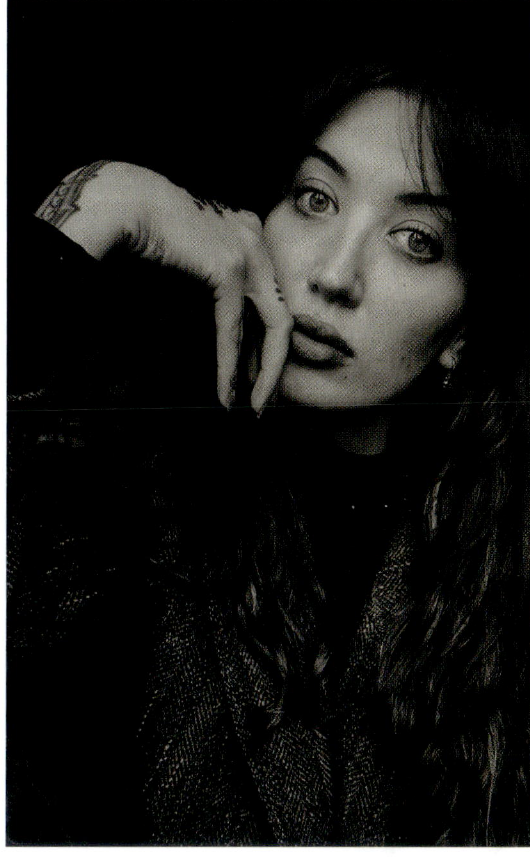

Opposite Neck and upper chest composition composed of *kolo* (circle), *ograda* (fence), and *jelica* (pine tree) motifs, 2022.

Above Matching *sicanje* compositions for two brothers, 2023.

Above right Portrait of Mélissa Pizović, 2023.

Mélissa Pizović (Mel) is a tattoo artist based in France whose father is an ethnic Bosnian born in Croatia. After studying and working as an architect in Montréal and Paris, she turned to tattooing in 2020 to integrate part of her life story and family roots into her artwork.

"Professionally, I was unfulfilled working in architecture and wanted to find a way to express myself and be more connected with my father's culture, and that is why I choose to create symbols inspired by traditional designs derived from my own graphic identity as an artist," she said. "I began to do more research about traditional tattoos from Bosnia and Croatia to really understand what each shape and symbol means or what it refers to in order to share this heritage with others."[68]

Mel perfected her hand-poking technique, which was the original method for applying Bosnian-Croatian tattoos, by practicing on herself. "For me, hand-poking was very intuitive. I already had a few tattoos via this technique, and I really enjoyed the experience of receiving them because they are less painful and heal more quickly than a machined tattoo."

In 2021, Mel opened Melrose Studio Tattoo in Paris. She also began tattooing as a guest artist in studios in Croatia. "One of the best parts of my job is meeting people with the same cultural heritage and connecting with one another through our tattooing traditions, even though we live in different countries and speak different languages," she explained.

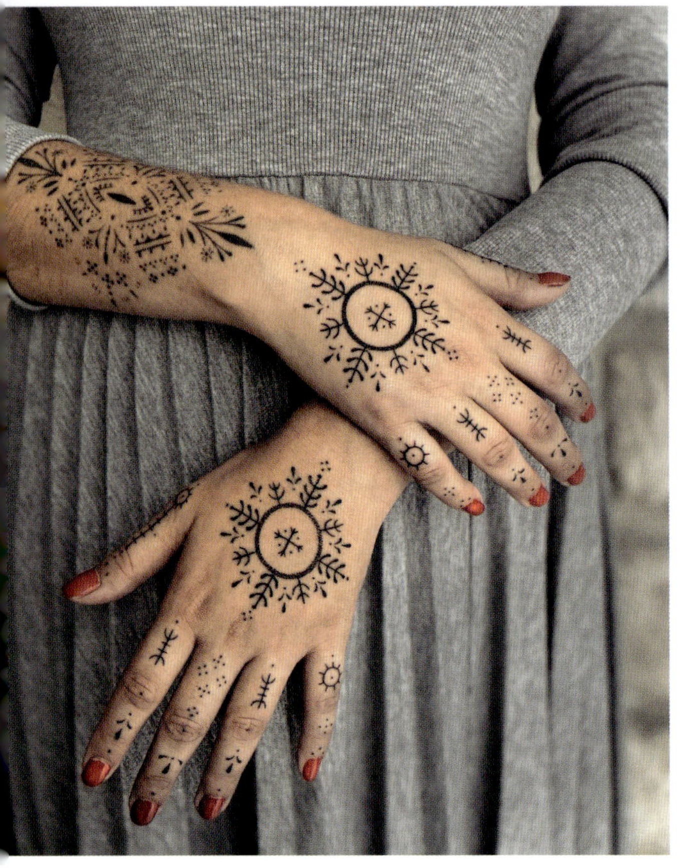

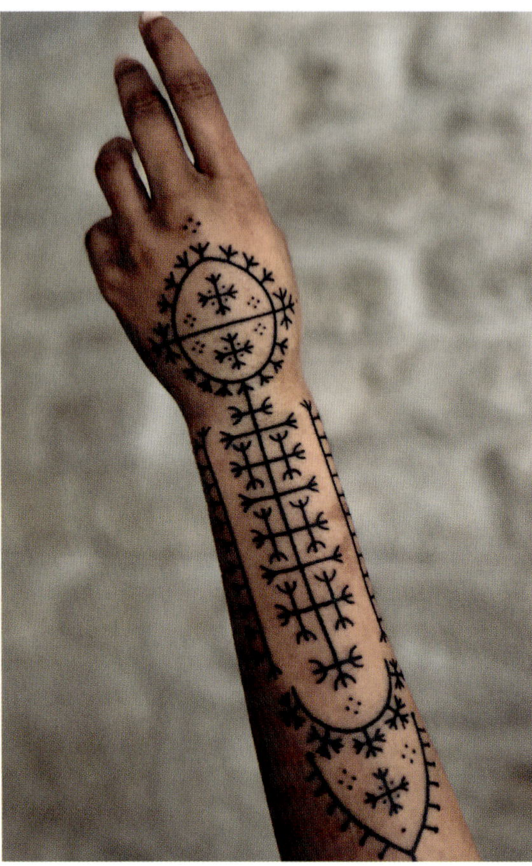

Far left Women's hand, arm, and finger tattoos based on traditional Bosnian-Croatian tattoo motifs and embroidery designs, 2021.

Left Female hand and forearm tattoo featuring *križ* (cross), *kolo* (circle), *klas* (ear of corn), and *ograda* (fence), 2023. For Mel, the *kolo* symbolizes family and community, *klas* personal growth, and *ograda* is a protective symbol.

Opposite Female torso tattoo composed of *križ* (cross), *jelica* (pine tree), *kolo* (circle), and *zvijezda* (star) motifs, 2023.

"And because our tattoos were created by women, I feel a deep connection to this sorority of female practitioners."

It is not known when or where the practice of tattooing originated among early Christian peoples of the Balkan Peninsula. However, it has been demonstrated that it was an Indigenous tradition of Thraco-Illyrian cultures that inhabited the Balkans prior to 300 BCE.[69] Moreover, Croatian anthropologists Ćiro Truhelka and Mario Petrić, among others, wrote that the combinations of cruciform, celestial bodies, and other natural symbols that comprise the graphic tradition predated Christianity.[70]

As Mel continues to integrate her family's cultural heritage into her art, she is very aware of cultural appropriation. "I continue to see tattooists without any Balkan roots apply *sicanje*-style tattoos rarely mentioning their origins, functions, or meanings," she exclaimed. "I do not mix our symbols with foreign figurative elements, because my goal is to keep this tradition alive in a respectful and ethical manner and to highlight the cultural legacy of our tattooing heritage. I feel it is very important to educate the new generation of tattoo artists about cultural appropriation, because it is offensive for others to steal a tradition, use it as a mainstream ornament, and turn it into a trend."

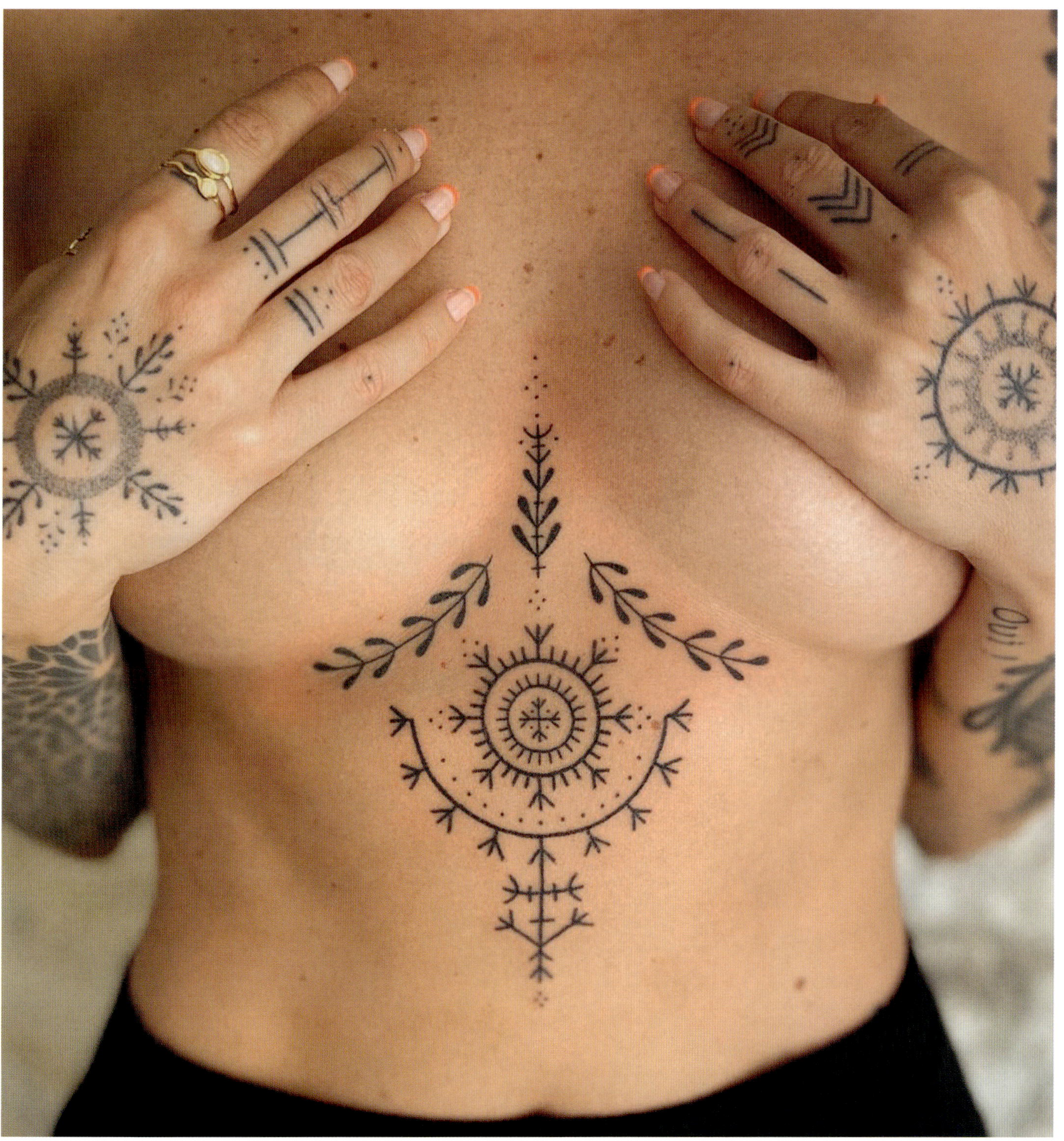

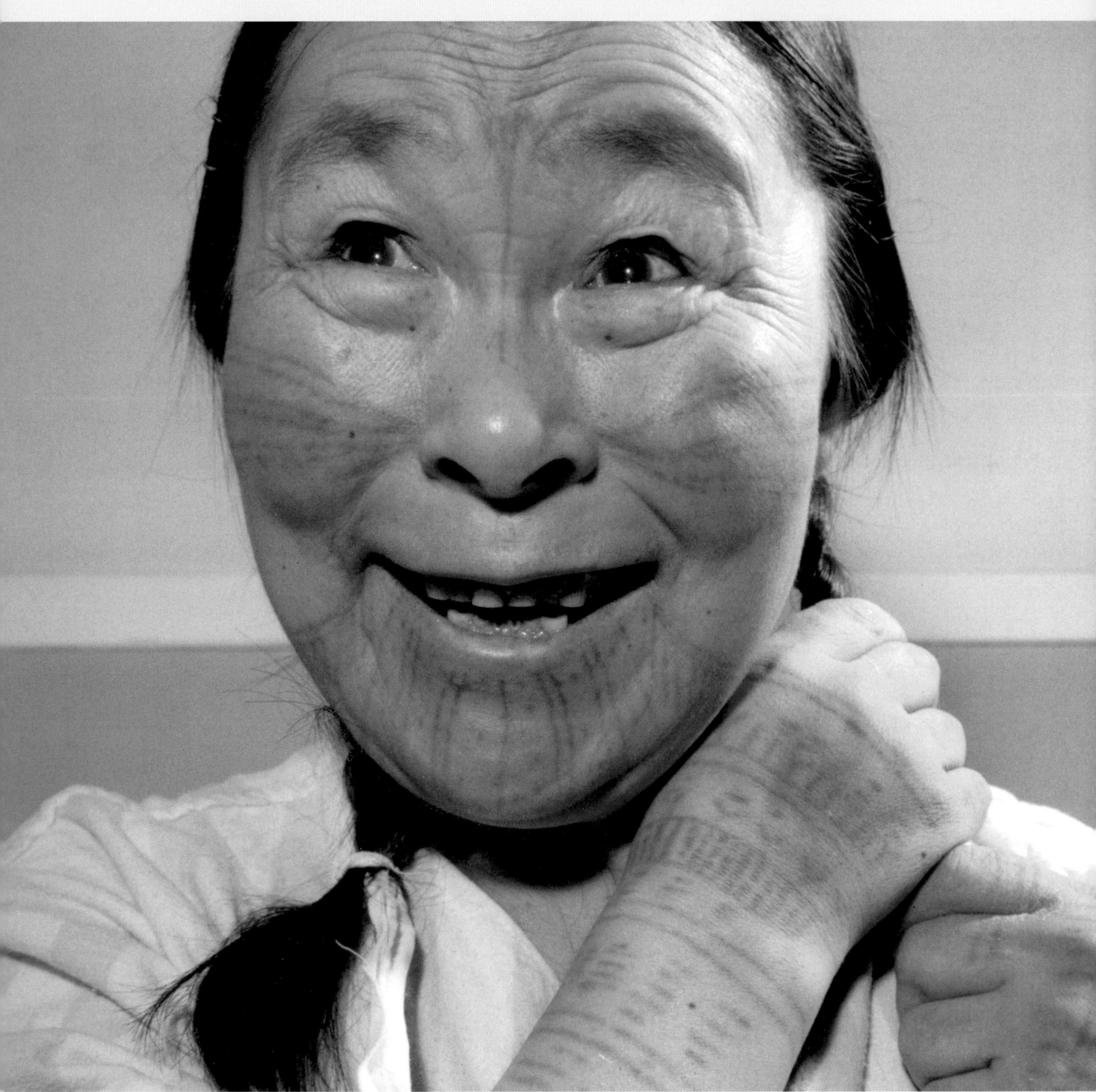

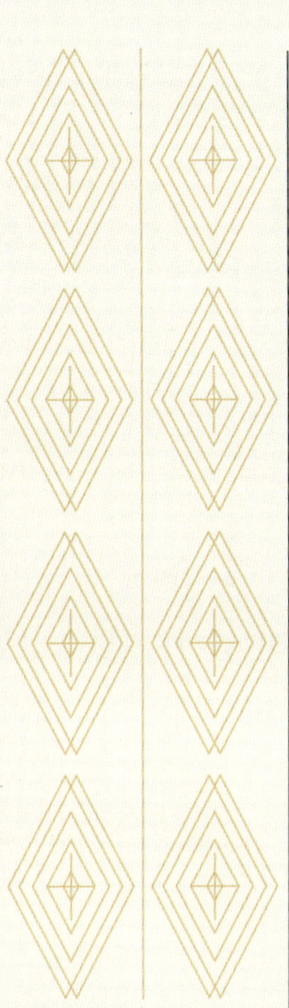

2

TATTOOS OF NATIVE NORTH AMERICA

Tattooing was once practiced by almost every Indigenous Tribal Nation across Canada, the circumpolar north, and the United States. Despite centuries of colonialism and forced assimilation that fractured their lands, altered their cultures, and reshaped their identities, the ancient tattoo traditions of Indigenous Native North Americans and Arctic First Peoples persist. These enduring marks tell powerful stories of cultural identity and resilience.[1]

Netsilingmiut elder Mary Edetoak from Taloyoak (Spence Bay), Nunavut, *ca.* 1958, with subdermal skin-stitched tattoos on her face, arms, and hands.

Right Various styles of Inuit facial tattooing, 1905. **Top row:** Netsilingmiut, Qairnirmiut, and Aivilingmiut tattooing. **Bottom row:** Kitlinermiut, Iglulingmiut, and Southampton Island tattooing.

Below Prehistoric Old Bering Sea culture ivory doll head, probably from St. Lawrence Island, Alaska, *ca.* 100–300 CE. This female portrait shows extensive facial tattooing, a style that continued into the historic period among the Inuit.

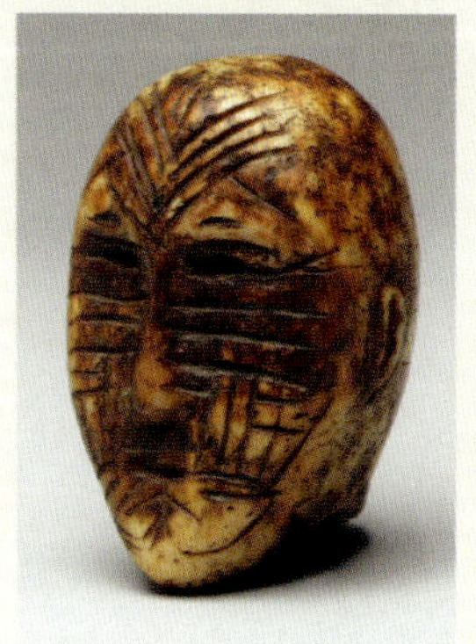

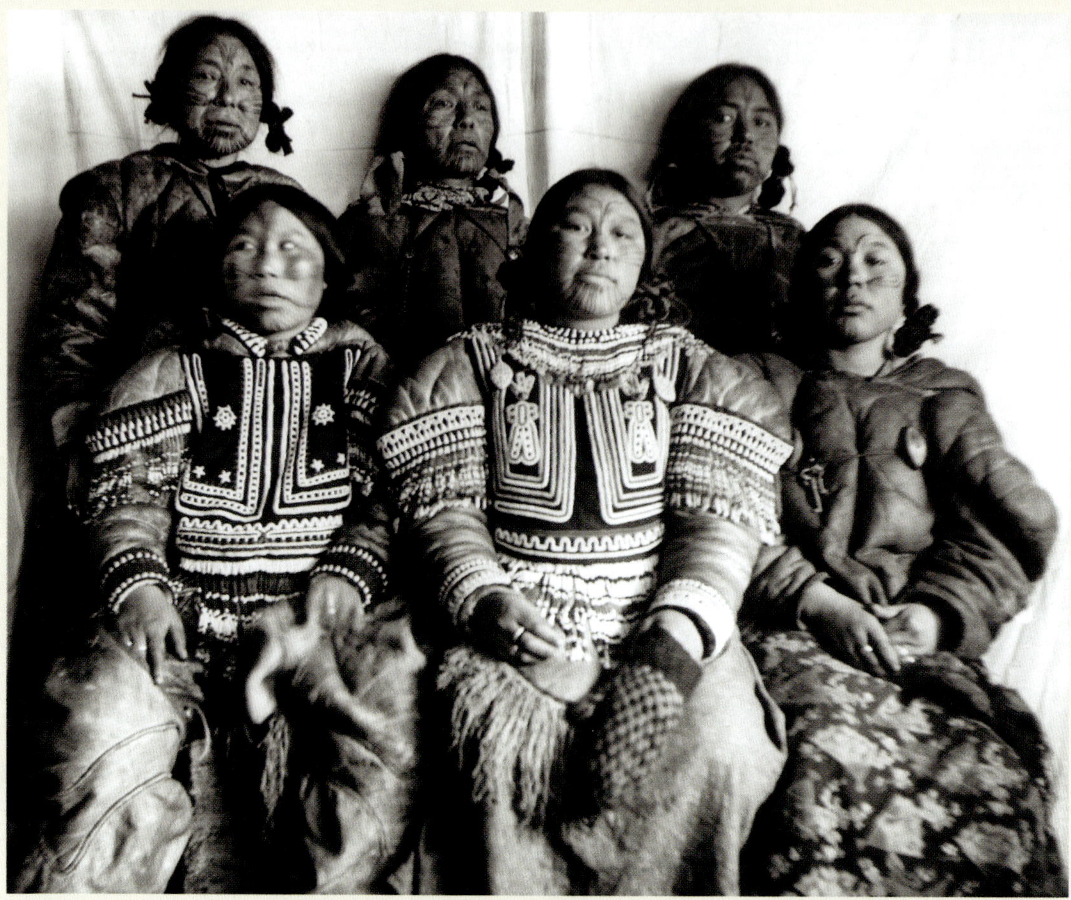

Perhaps the oldest archaeological evidence for tattooing in North America is a 3,500-year-old Palaeo-Eskimo maskette from Devon Island, Nunavut. The naturalistically carved face of this ancient woman displays numerous linear tattoos that are remarkably similar to those worn by various Inuit peoples of the historic era in the Canadian Arctic and Alaska. Here in the far north, and prior to the early twentieth century, women were tattooed with specific symbols to identify their tribe and/or clan and to mark life stages (e.g., puberty to marriageable age). Other female tattoos were medicinal,[2] marked hunting tallies or significant life accomplishments, or helped carry the body safely into the afterlife. Male markings carried similar meanings.[3]

In the American Southwest, Cocopah women were tattooed with linear designs on their chins with mesquite or cactus thorns. These markings were necessary because they enabled the soul to pass safely and comfortably into the afterlife. More specifically, in Cocopah belief untattooed women who traveled to the next world were forced to sit on a road with their backs bent over, so that other (tattooed) souls could use them as steps.[4] The neighboring Mohave shared a similar tradition, because "a man or woman without marks on the face would be refused entrance to the 'land of the dead.'"[5]

Facial tattoos of Mohave woman, O Che Che, southern California, 1903.

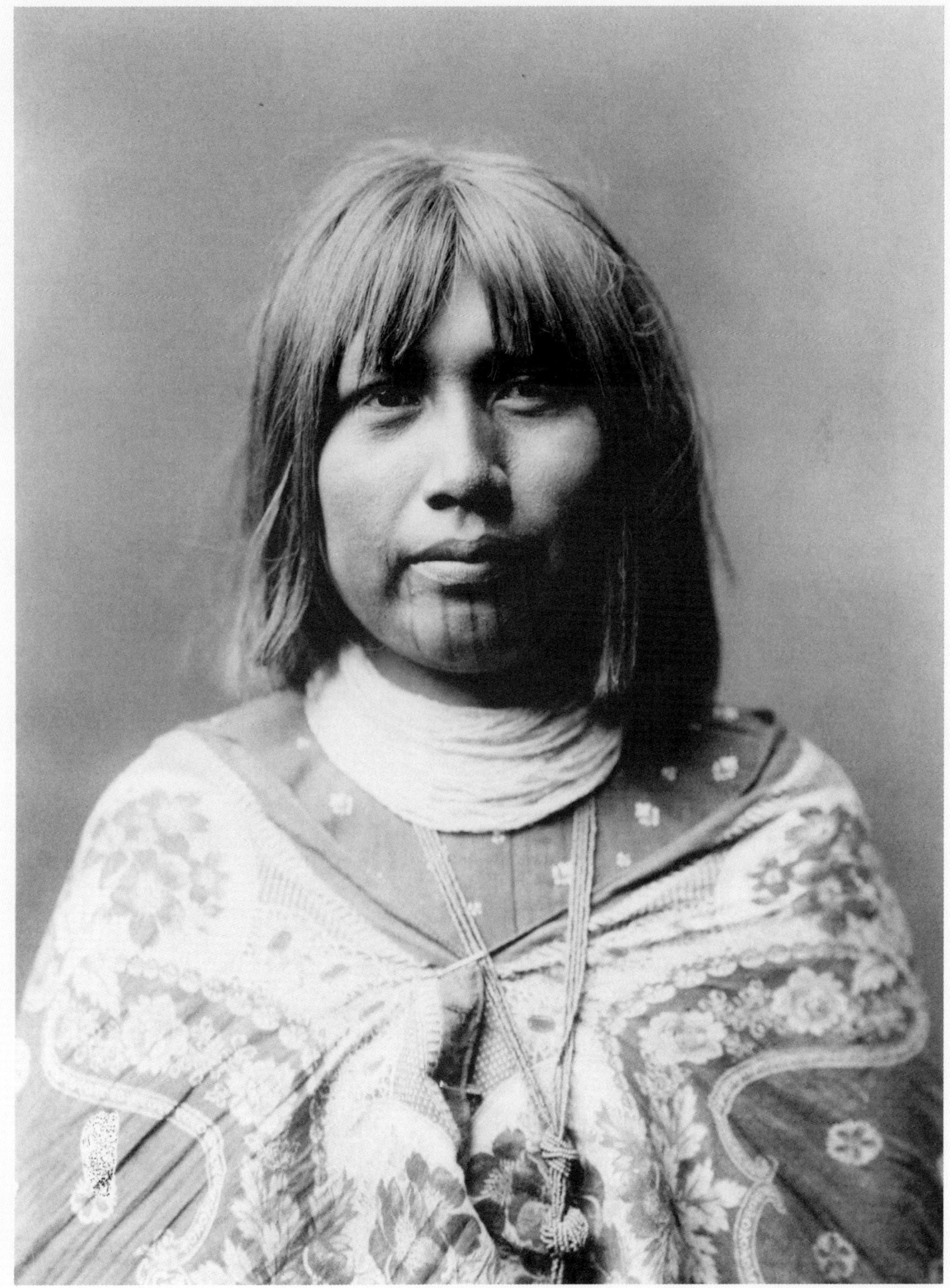

Mohave women's chin tattooing, southern California, *ca*. 1930.

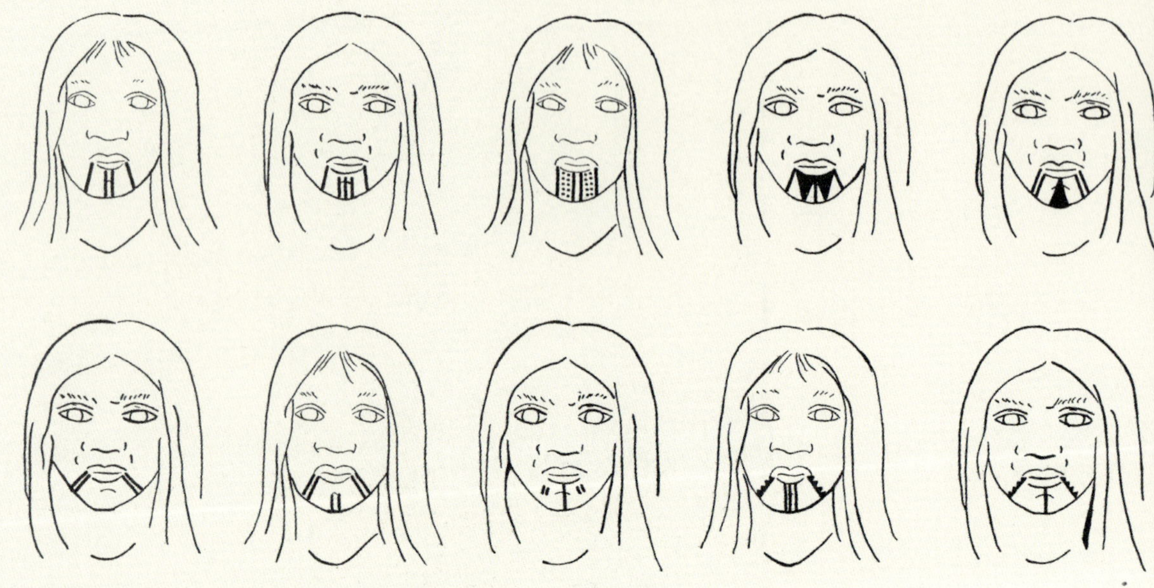

Akimel O'otham (Pima) tattooing kit from Arizona, *ca*. 1900. Tattoos were made using cactus spines tied together with cotton. Creosote and mesquite charcoal were rubbed into the wounds to create a permanent color.

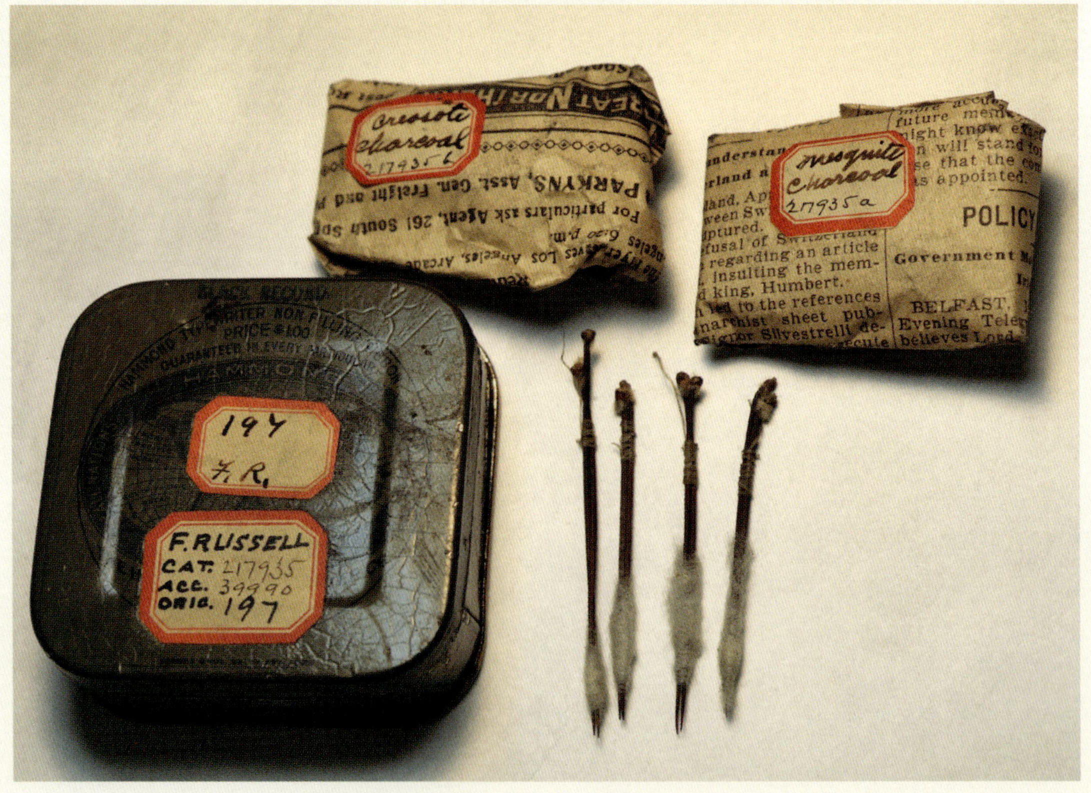

Tolowa (Dee-ni') man measuring shell money based on the tattoo marks on his arms, northern California, *ca*. 1920.

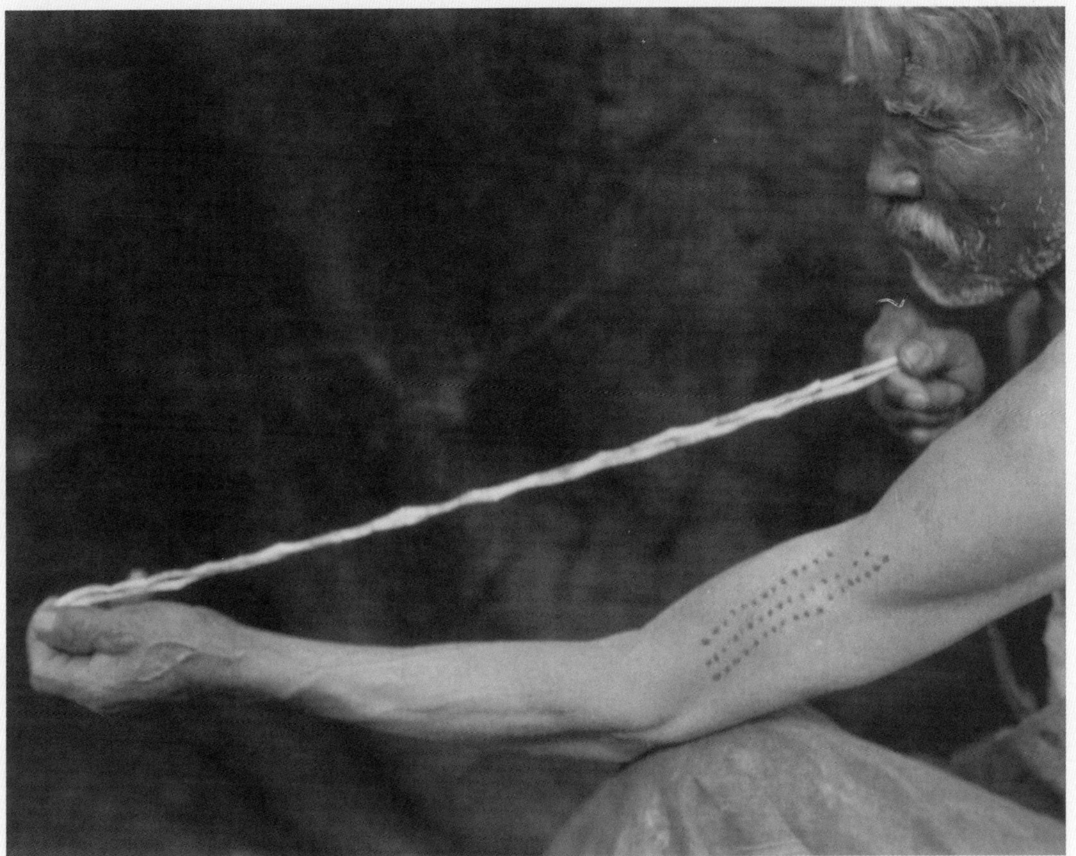

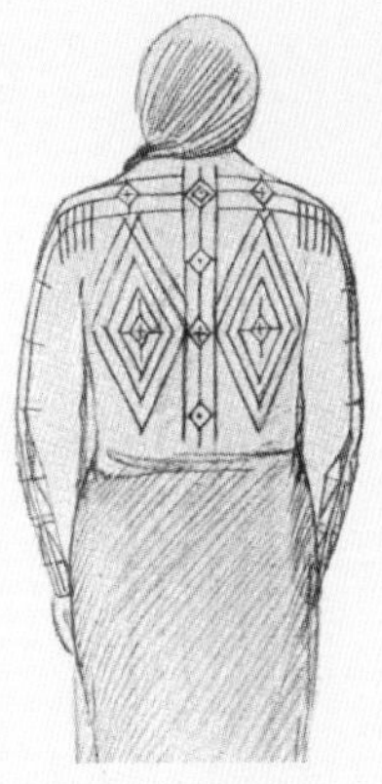

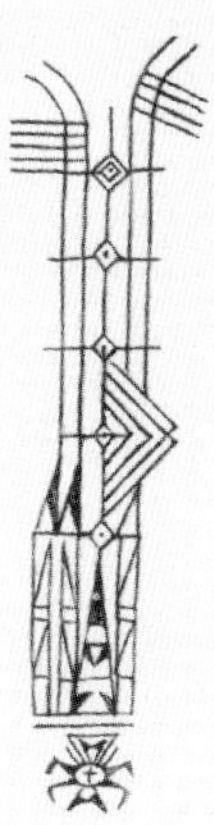

Tattooed Osage woman with tattoos marking the "Path of Life," Oklahoma, *ca*. 1910. Her tattoos were believed to channel various life forces from the cosmos resulting in the birth of children and reaching old age.

On the Great Plains prior to the twentieth century, women of several Dhegihan and Chiwere Sioux tribes received "honor markings" on their foreheads that were believed to be imbued with "life-giving" powers.[6] These single or double blue circles represented celestial bodies, and among the Osage people the two-dot motif depicted the double stars of theta and iota of the constellation Orion. This star cluster was called "Stars-strung-together" and addressed as "grandmother" who symbolized the procreative force.[7] "Blue Spot" women of the Omaha Night Blessed Society and Ponca women of the *Ni kagahi EshonGa* ("Chief's Daughters Dance Society") were adorned with a solar (male) symbol on their forehead and a four-pointed star (female) symbol on their chest.[8] Omaha and Ponca women stated that the star was emblematic of night, the great mother force of creation, and that its four points represented the "life giving winds."[9]

But these incredibly powerful tattoos came at a high price and could not be worn by just anyone. Omaha men who wished to have their daughters tattooed had to present a *wathin'ethe* ("long count") of gifts or respectable actions to earn membership into the order of honorary chieftainship in the Night Blessed Society.[10] It was believed these sacred gifts or personal sacrifices related "to the welfare of the tribe by promoting internal order and peace."[11]

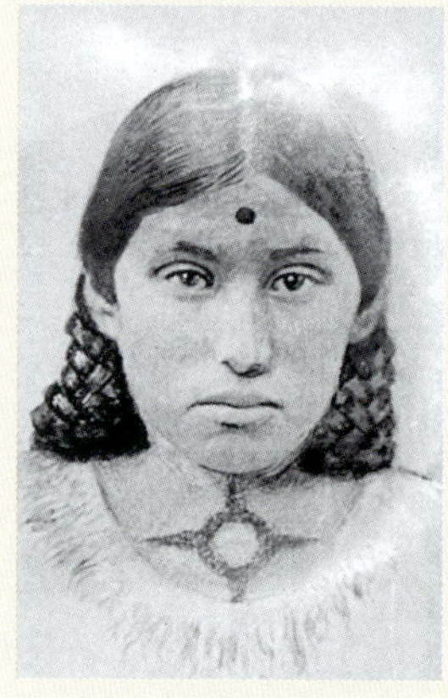

Above Omaha woman with "Mark of Honor" tattoo on forehead and "Star" motif on sternum, Nebraska, *ca.* 1900. The forehead tattoo symbolized the sun, representing day, and, when combined with the forces of night (star), it was believed supernatural power was channeled into the body, ensuring the perpetuation of life.

Right Hee-láh-dee (Pure Fountain), a Ponca woman, Missouri, 1832. Star and solar tattoos were placed on her body for fertility and long life.

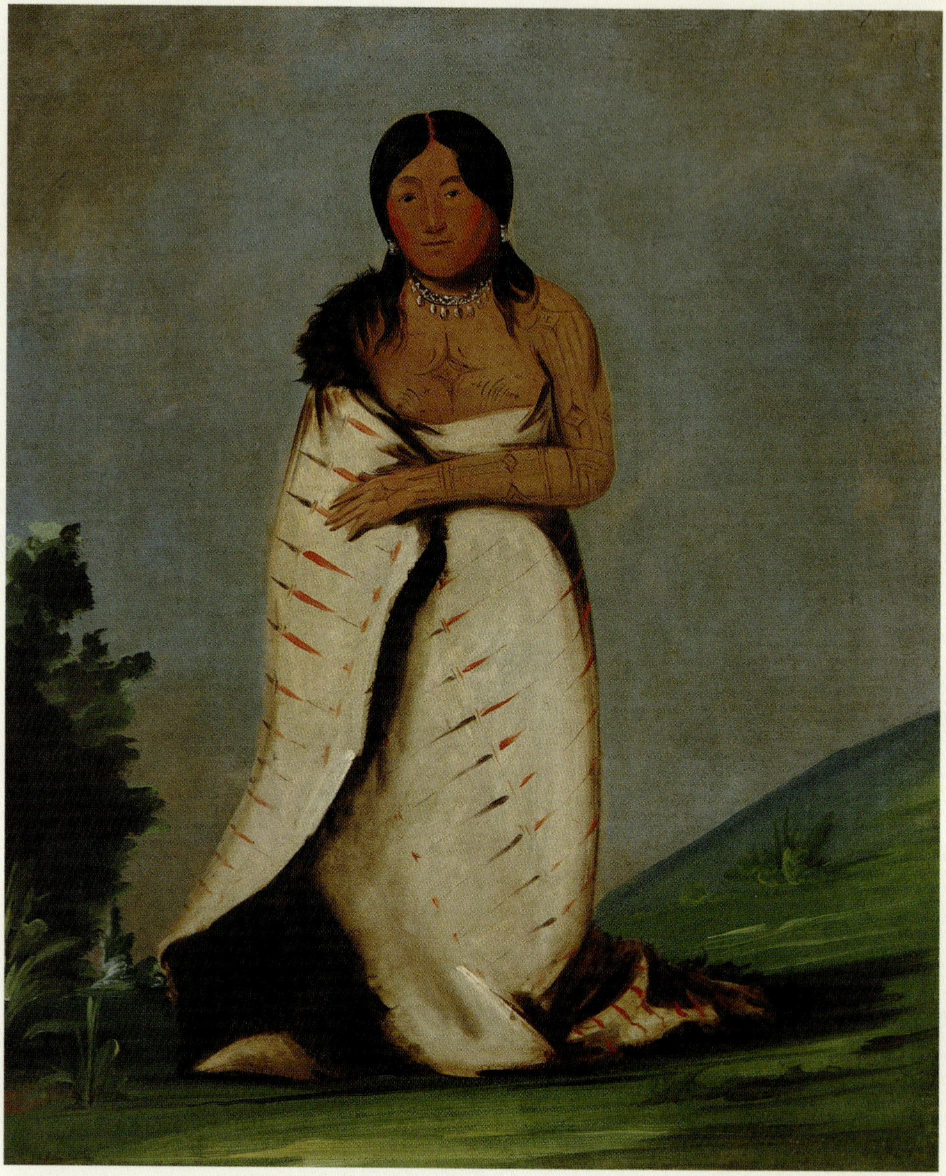

Regarding the Otoe tribe, only the eldest daughter of a chief was tattooed.[12] These markings were directly associated with her father's prowess in battle, because, as one Otoe informant stated, "in the old days, war deeds, recited by the father, validated the right to be tattooed. Later the pattern changed to recitation of benevolent acts: how many people a man had helped; how much money he had given away."[13] Among the Ponca and Osage, men who had acquired great military merit were also allowed the privilege of having their wives and daughters tattooed with marks of honor in a public ceremony that was very costly.[14]

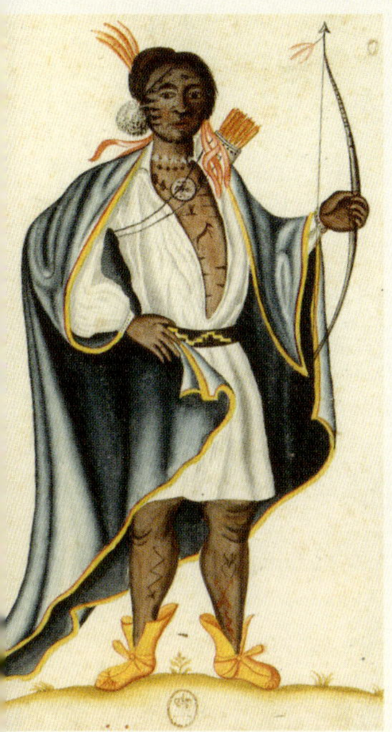

Guardian Tattoos

From the Pacific Northwest across to the Great Lakes and Eastern Woodlands of the United States, "guardian" tattooing was another form of facial marking in the historic period. This specific type of body modification harnessed particular physical, spiritual, and elemental powers, and was typically associated with what has been called a *manitou* (or *manito*)—a personal protective and helping spirit. Although guardian tattoos were possessed by both men and women, they were more typically associated with male warrior culture and shamanism.

Once a young man attained manhood, he was encouraged to fast and wander the wilderness until he made contact with a tutelary spirit (through a dream or vision) that

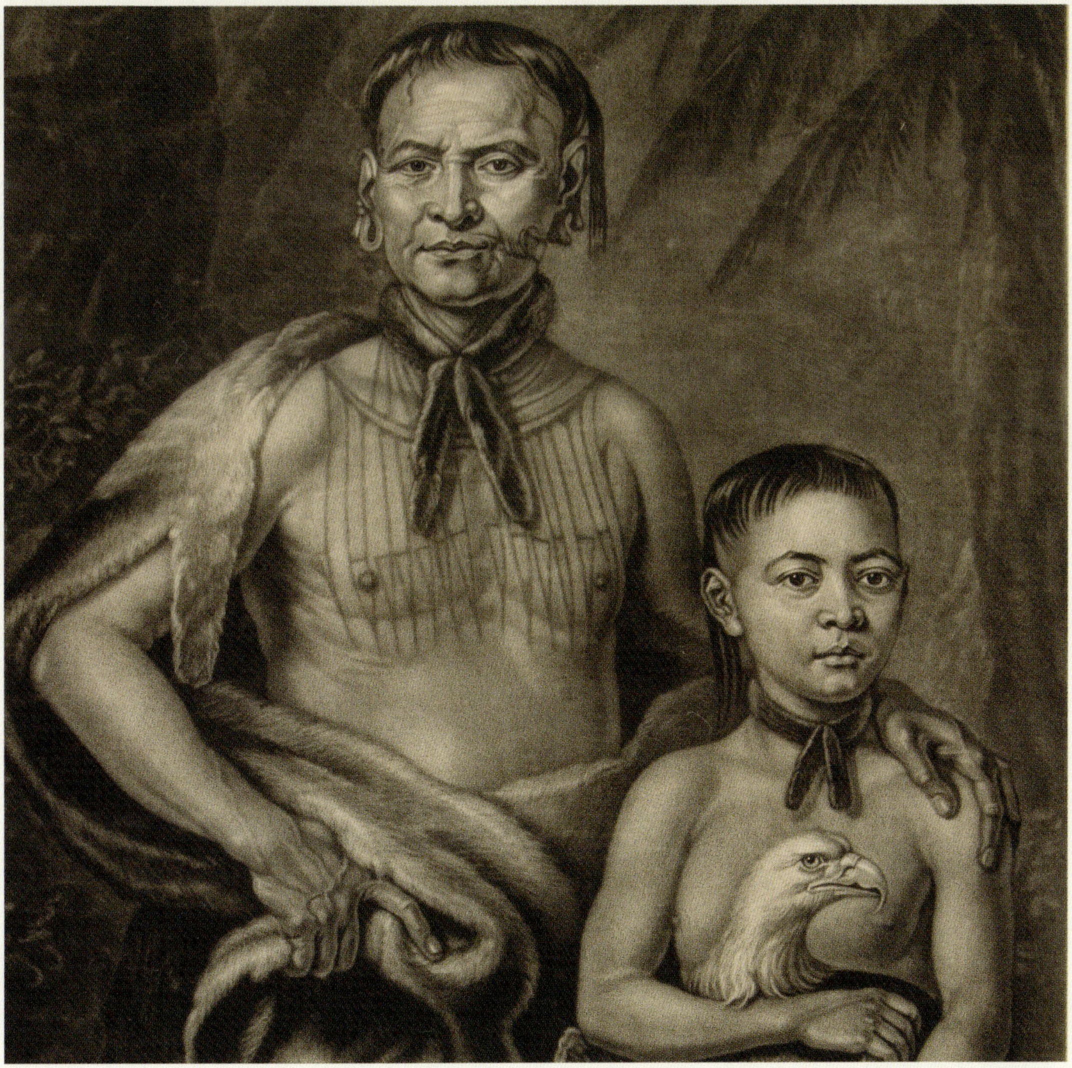

Above Tattooed Nipissing warrior of Canada, 1717. His tattoos are related to achievements in battle as well as protective omen creatures (*manitou*).

Right Yamacraw-Creek leader and warrior, Tomochichi, and his nephew, Georgia, 1739. His tattoos are related to omen creatures and marks of honor earned for combat.

Tattooing of the great Mohawk war leader, Brant Saquainquaragton, 1710. His tattoos are related to omen creatures called *manitou* and marks of merit earned on the battlefield.

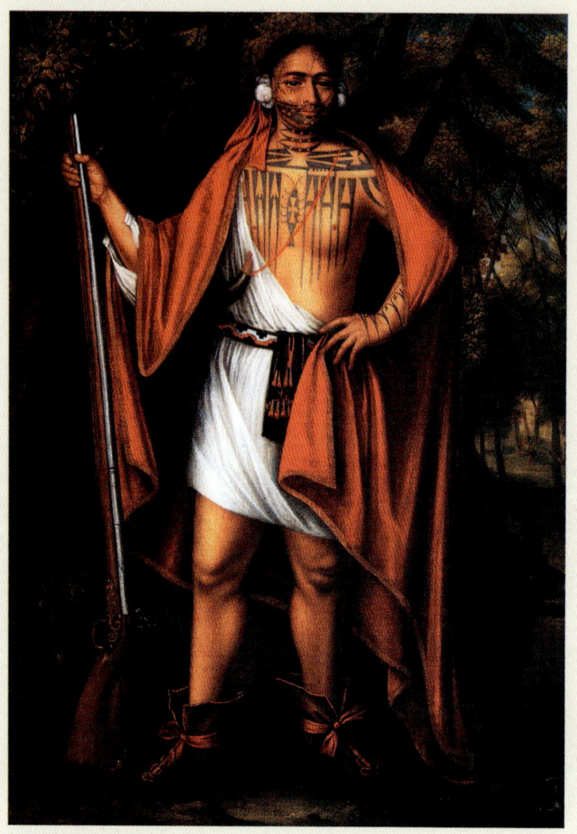

would protect and assist him for the rest of his life, provided he appeased it with the necessary sacrifices.[15] Sometimes a man's *manitou* was the sun or another celestial object. But if it was an animal, then its skin, or its plumage if it was a bird, was often carried by the man on his journeys and especially on the warpath, because it was believed to confer its attributes to the *manitou* holder.[16] Warriors and male shamans may have had more than one helping *manitou* spirit.

Men "had the utmost confidence in their *manitos* because they believed that these spirits gave them ideas which came [directly] from the superior being, and that it was he who showed them in their dreams the animals which they took for their *manitos*, because he wished to use these animals to lead them," wrote the eighteenth-century Quebecois merchant Francois Pachot.[17] And because a man's personal relationship with his *manitou* was essentially linked to his overall sense of personhood, *manitous* were often tattooed upon the face to permanently reinforce these sacred bonds of affinity.[18]

In 1710, four Native American "Indian Kings" of the Haudenosaunee Confederacy and Mahican tribes visited Queen Anne's court in England. Two of these men were Mohawk tribal warriors, including the famous leader Brant Saquainquaragton (1673–1710), and they sported facial tattoos comprised of *manitou* motifs, scalp tally marks, and other designs that probably denoted the number of times they were wounded in battle.[19] The Mahican warrior was adorned with three avian tattoos on his forehead, symbols that may have represented thunderbird *manitous* or those of other predatorial birds.

Nearly all Haudenosaunee men's tattoos were distinct to them. According to the account book of an early seventeenth-century Dutch trader, financial transactions were completed by drawing the facial and body tattoos of Native American clients; because these body ornaments were equivalent to personal signatures.[20] Not surprisingly, Woodlands warriors also carved their facial tattoo patterns into their war clubs. And once a man had built up his name through military success, he eventually deposited his inscribed war club next to the body of a slain enemy as a "calling card" for others to meet him in battle.[21]

Right Tattooed Haida Chief Xa'na, Queen Charlotte Islands, Canada, *ca.* 1895. He wears a grizzly bear crest on his chest, seated bears on his shoulders, and possibly a killer whale crest on his forearm.

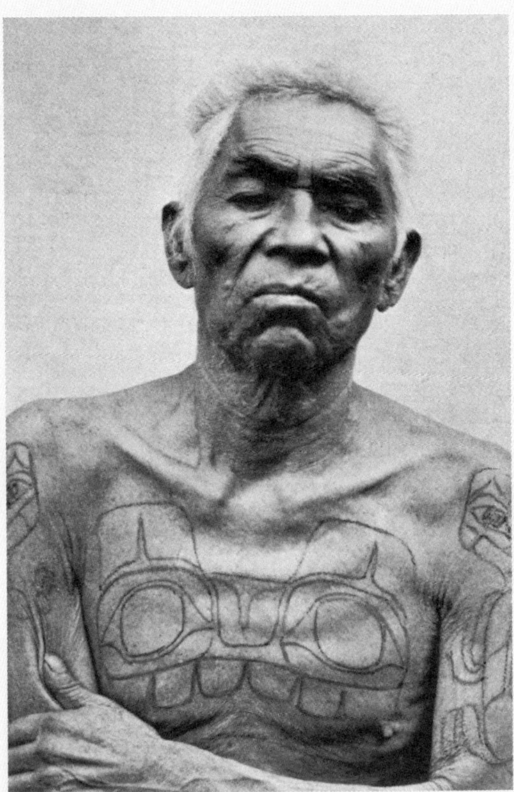

Haida tattoo designs by tattoo artist Geneskelos, 1873.

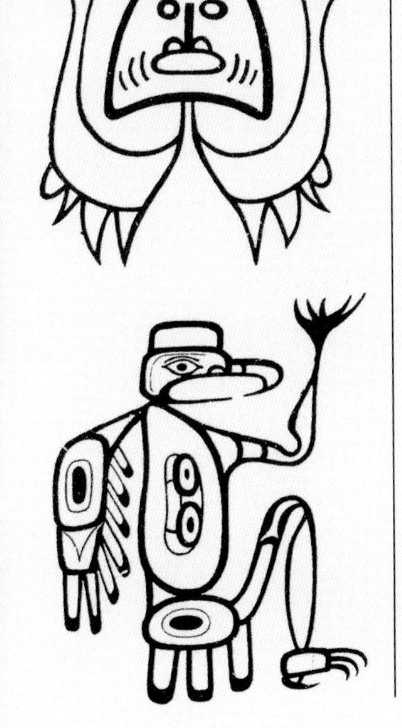

Tattooed Bodies of Meaning

Prior to the twentieth century, one of the best known Native North American tattooing traditions was found on the Northwest Coast. Here among the Haida and Tlingit peoples,[22] bold form-line chest and body tattoos depicting clan crests were hand-poked[23] into the body with blue/black and red mineral pigments. Crests, which could portray animals, trees, objects, or celestial bodies, were drawn from the legendary past, and represented embodied symbols of a clan's origin, history, and identity that set them apart from other clans.

The social functions that crest tattoos served, however, are inseparable in Haida and Tlingit thought from their role as sacred subjects. That is because crest tattoos were considered to be animate, since they embodied the spiritual essence of the being that was marked upon human skin. Tattooed crests also symbolized kinship relations, because as spiritual bonds they united tattooed individuals to their ancestors who, over the generations, either earned or maintained the right to use the crest with their deeds and accomplishments.[24]

As crests served to unify the Haida and Tlingit people to their ancestors and to the (super)natural forces[25] around them, they were treated with great respect and reverence. Although the Haida and Tlingit did not worship crests or the creatures (or spirits) they portrayed, crests certainly had spiritual meaning to the people. Traditionally they were represented on a wide variety of a clan's objects, including blankets, tools or weapons, rock art, hats, crest (totem) poles, and tattooing kits.[26] At the first potlatch or ceremonial party where the crests were displayed, the public witnessing of the crest by the potlatch attendees imparted great value to it. The guests were appropriately compensated for their attendance because it validated the prestige and importance of the crest, especially if it were the newly tattooed body of the potlatch host's son or daughter.

Tattoo artists, who created tattoos at potlatches, were likewise compensated for their services, since tattooing was highly ritualized and very expensive by local standards. Among the Tlingit, "An average would be fifty blankets for tattooing the hands, [and] one hundred blankets for a chest tattoo."[27]

Marks of Honor: Tattoos of the Great Plains

Prior to their abandonment in the late nineteenth century, on the Great Plains of North America the right to wear tattoos had to be earned through the performance of a series of ritually mandated acts or "war honors."[28]

Mähsette-Kuuiuab, Chief of the Cree Indians, with tattooed honor markings for exploits in battle, *ca.* 1840.

These acts of bravery differed amongst each tribe, and because men had to confront death every time, they attempted to distinguish themselves from their fellows; as a result "few persons ever attained the honor" of receiving a tattoo.[29]

Among the Kansa, men who had killed seven enemies, or who had captured or stolen six horses, would receive "the greatest honor that could befall a Kansa, that of being tattooed on the breast."[30] On the northern Plains, the Hidatsa and neighboring Mandan also earned tattoos for brave deeds on the battlefield. Striking a live enemy was considered a higher honor than striking one who had been killed; if a man made contact with an enemy he could have two hands tattooed on his chest.[31] Men of the Assiniboine tribe who struck their first enemy were said to have been tattooed across their entire chest and arms for accomplishing the great deed,[32] while other warriors wore additional tattoo designs related to their guardian spirits.

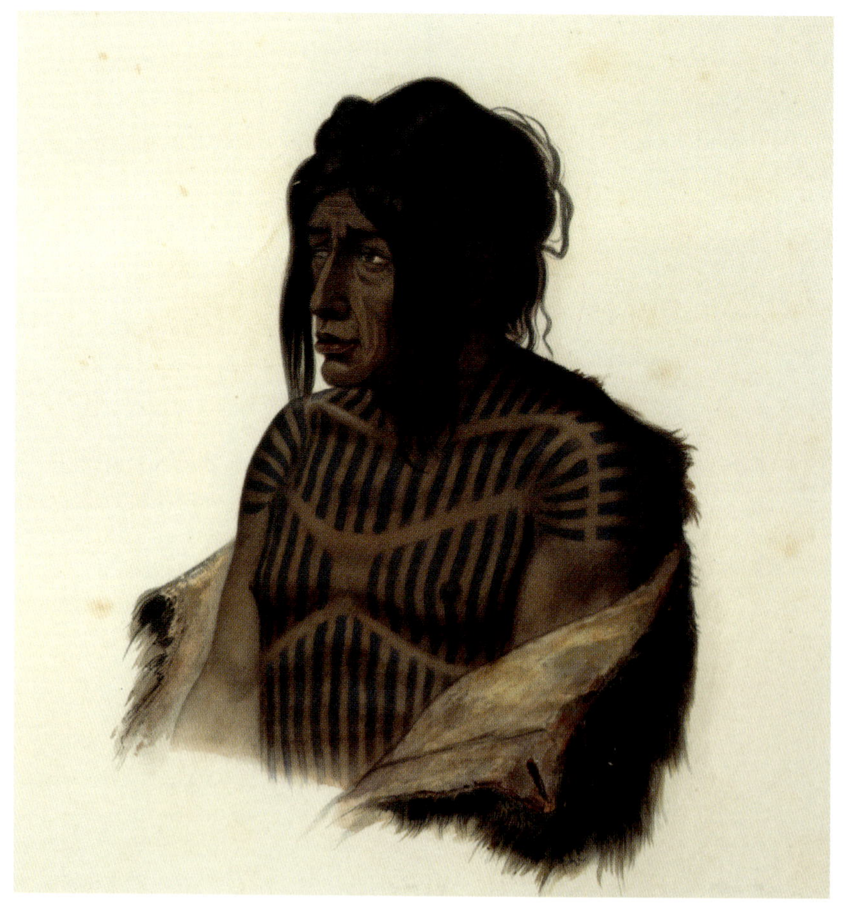

Further south among the Osage, the central component in men's chest tattooing was a weapon – the sacred flint knife. In oral

Right Hidatsa Chief and tattooist, Addíh-Hiddísch, or Road Maker, *ca.* 1840. He is tattooed with honor markings earned in combat and animals related to *manitou* or supernatural omen creatures.

Far right Bacon Rind (1860–1932), a tattooed Osage chief, Oklahoma, *ca.* 1910. Osage chest tattoos were earned for accomplishments on the battlefield, but warfare had ceased by the time Bacon Rind became a young man. Instead, he was tattooed with warrior markings "to make him faithful in keeping the [sacred] rites."

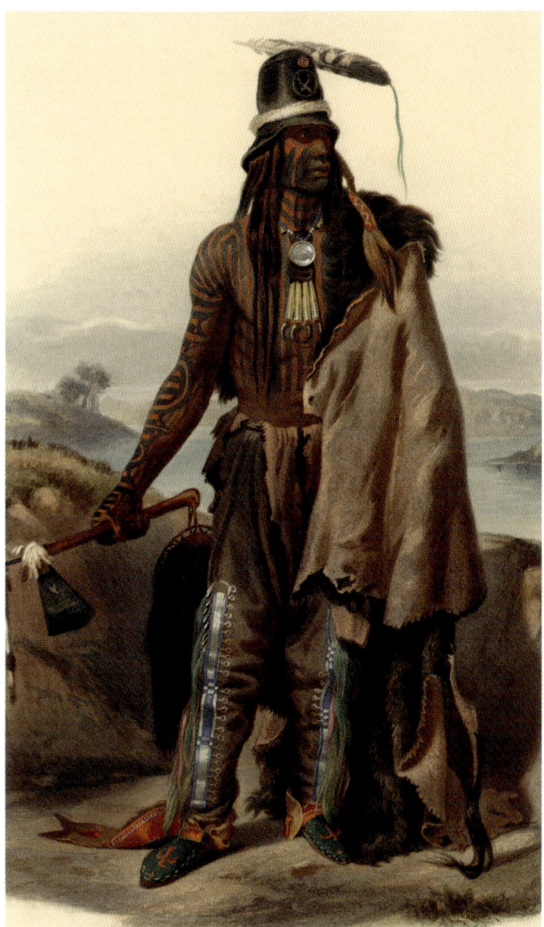

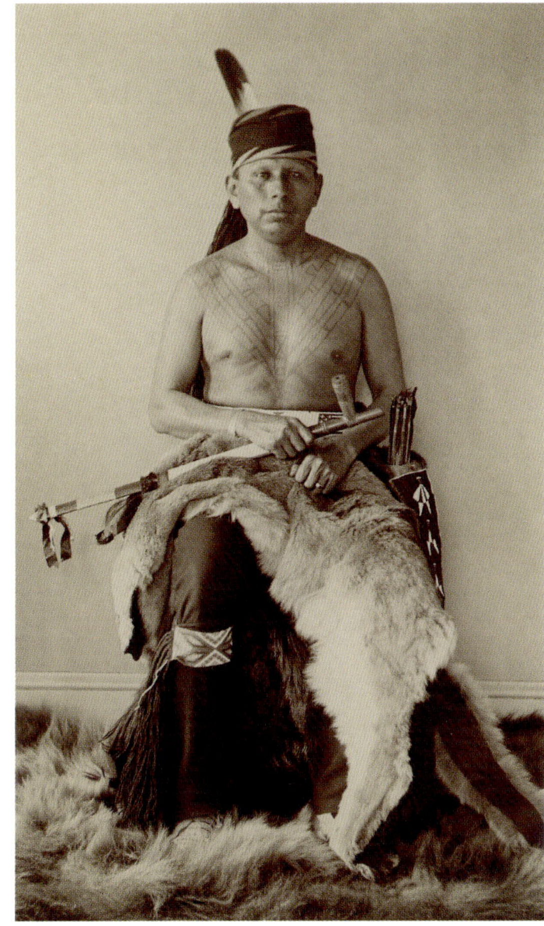

history, it is said that the flint knife "shall always" be used when the Osage "go forth toward the setting sun [i.e., West] against their enemies."[33] For Osage men, the honor of receiving a warrior tattoo had to be earned through feats of extraordinary courage, and only those men who had achieved all thirteen sacred war honors (*o-don'*) could ever hope to be tattooed. The tattooing ritual was deeply symbolic and considered greater than any other Osage ceremony.[34]

The knife motif was just one of many sacred Osage "life symbols" that were incorporated into the overall chest tattoo. Every element of this design, including the pigment, was stated in oral histories to have been derived from supernatural powers that were given and "belonged" to particular Osage clans. Because the sacred chest piece was a composite design drawn from clan symbols, primordial sources, and their creator himself, it was a unifying tribal symbol representing the Osage's ability to meet and overcome their enemies in order to perpetuate tribal existence.[35] This was because "the safety of the people as an aggregate body must always be regarded as of the first importance, [and] the perpetuity of tribal existence must depend upon the bodily strength and valor of the warrior," who was the ultimate protector of tribal life.[36]

Tattooing Tools of Native North America

When you receive a tattoo from an electric machine, your skin is pierced 50–3,000 times per minute with commercially manufactured needles. Conversely, among historic Native North American tattooists, who plied human skin with non-electrified tools (e.g., hand-poking, subdermal skin-stitching, and incision-tattooing instruments) with locally available materials (e.g., cactus thorns, animal bone needles, lithic lancets), the piercing rate is much less, usually 100–150 punctures a minute.

Some of these non-mechanized tools are quite ancient, and very recently two of the oldest-known tattooing implements have been identified: a 2,000-year-old cactus thorn tattooing tool from Utah, and a 3,600-year-old sharpened turkey-leg bone from Tennessee.[37]

While contemporary tattoo clients enjoy a plethora of aftercare products to help heal their tattoos, the specifics of Indigenous aftercare treatments are largely unknown. However, ethnographic records from the nineteenth through early twentieth century demonstrate that the peoples of Native North America used a variety of plants and natural substances to create tattoo pigments, which were almost invariably carbon-based, and many of these harnessed medicinal properties.[38] Some groups also employed sedatives or local anesthetics to deaden the pain associated with tattooing.[39]

A tattooist's tools might be embodied with ancestral, apotropaic, and/or supernatural power.[40] Some of the most powerful of these tattooing objects were used prior to the late nineteenth century across the Great Plains and stored in what have been described as "bundles" and "portable shrines."[41]

Bundles may be roughly defined as an object (or cadre of objects) that was stored in a woven container or skin cover and functioned as a repository for the transfer of supernatural power. These sacred objects had their origins in individual visions or tribal oral histories wherein ritual rules of use and care were stipulated by deities, spirits, and other personages.[42]

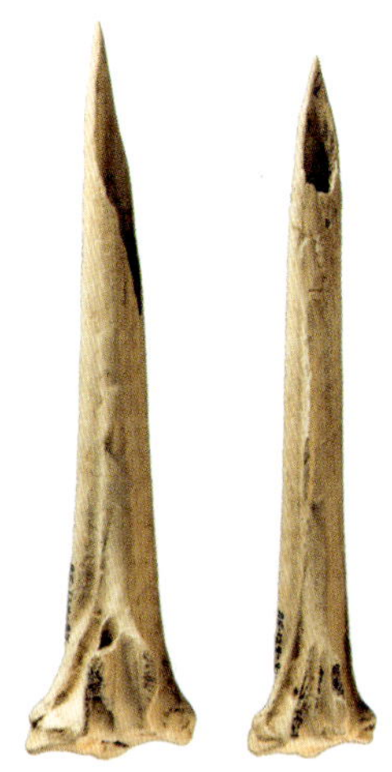

Sharpened turkey leg bones used for tattooing from the Fernvale site, Tennessee, *ca.* 1570 BCE. The two turkey leg bones with sharpened tips are, to date, the oldest known tattooing tools in the world. They were unearthed archaeologically in 1985 from a man's burial pit.

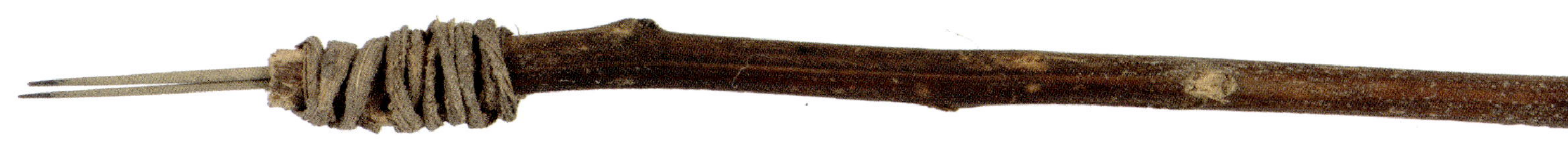

Above Tattooing implement from the Turkey Pen site in southeastern Utah, *ca*. 50 CE. It is constructed from a sumac stem, prickly pear cactus spines, and yucca leaf stems. It was excavated in 1972, but unidentified until 2018. It represents one of the oldest Indigenous North American tattooing tools yet found.

Right and far right Missouria tattoo bundle bag and implements, *ca*. 1905. Buffalo bone spatulas were used to rub the pigment into the punctures and sacred thunderbirds adorn the bundle bag.

Below Menominee medicinal tattooing kit collected in 1911. The paper packages hold the therapeutic pigments.

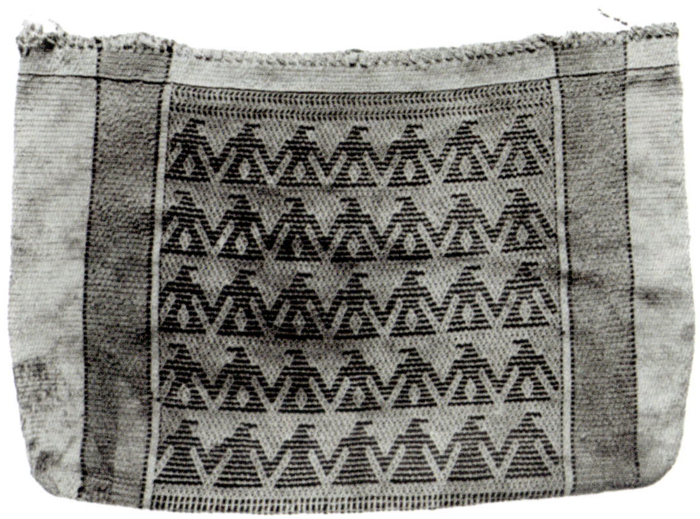

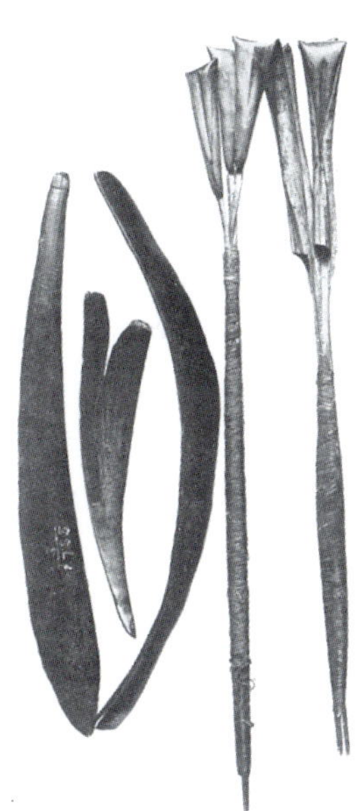

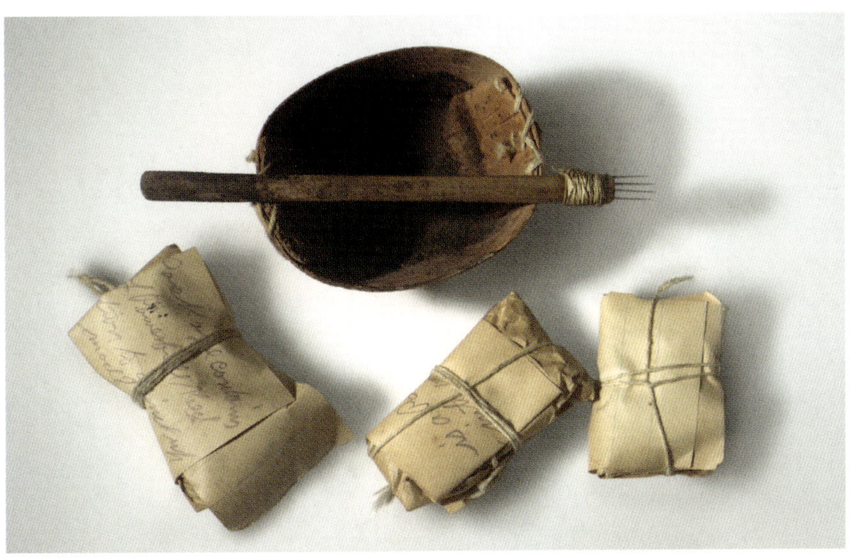

Ancient Faces from the Arctic: Ivory Figurines

In the Bering Strait, at the crossroads of the Asian and North American continents, ancient peoples produced tattooed anthropomorphic ivory figures that have survived into the present.

Members of the Old Bering Sea (*ca.* 250 BCE–800 CE), Punuk (*ca.* 400–1200 CE), and later prehistoric cultures inhabiting the coasts of the Chukotka Peninsula of Siberia and St. Lawrence Island, Alaska, carved realistic and sometimes abstract human figurines of walrus ivory. Based on historical analogies, these were likely employed[43] to please ancestral, elemental, animal, and other spiritual entities that were believed to control human destiny and the surrounding world.

One important class of these human-like bone, ivory, and wooden figurines were called *yugaaq* ("powerful" or "important person"), and they also took the form of anthropomorphic stick-like tattoos placed upon the face and body. *Yugaaq* were believed to be sentient and acted as "guardians" and/or helping spirits. Among the St. Lawrence Yupiget of Alaska these guardian objects were used until the twentieth century to protect households from wandering evil spirits or they were deployed as spiritual assistants to capture prey, among other things.[44] They were known as *tunghialkutat* or family fetishes, and were said to be permanent fixtures in the household, inherited from generation to generation in the male line.[45]

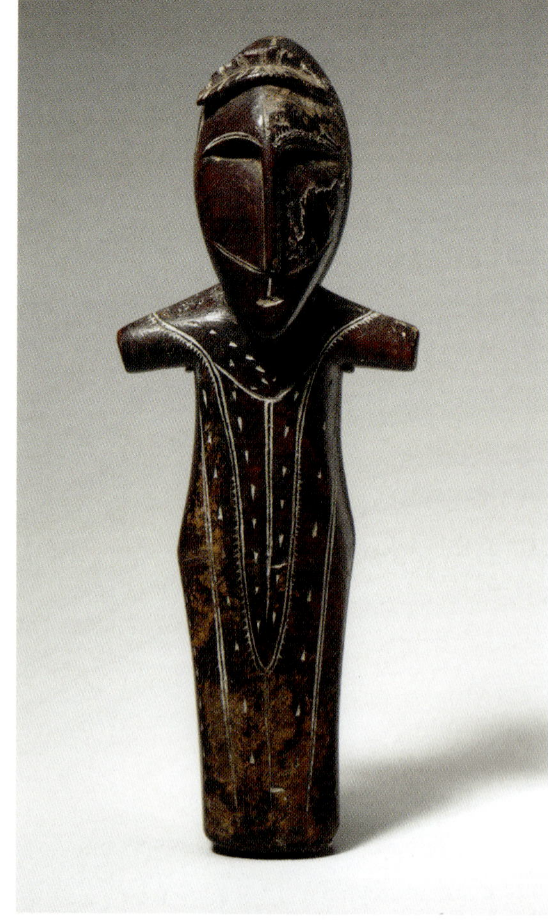

Tattooed Old Bering Sea culture male ivory figurine, St. Lawrence Island, Alaska, *ca.* 250–100 BCE. This portrait depicts a tattooed whaling captain dressed in a ceremonial garment and a hunting visor. The linear bands of tattooing flaring upward from his nostrils parallel those worn by successful whalemen of the historic period.

Like the ancient Old Bering Sea human figurines that predated them, historical St. Lawrence Island guardian figures displayed enlarged heads and mouths but typically lacked arms or legs. To keep their favor close to the living, the head of the household fed them small pieces of meat or tallow from freshly killed game, tobacco, and/or uttered incantations to them. It was taboo to destroy these figures because such an act was "equivalent to murder of one of the members of the patriclan or of a family member where the fetish was found."[46] Similar figures comprised of a simple head and torso were used on St. Lawrence Island before the twentieth century and hung from the center pole of the *mangteghapik* (winter house) or tied to the outer flap at the back of the house to "keep watch" and protect its inhabitants from disease-bearing spirits.[47] Others were hung on the walls and fed blubber during the whale hunting season to ensure a successful hunt.[48]

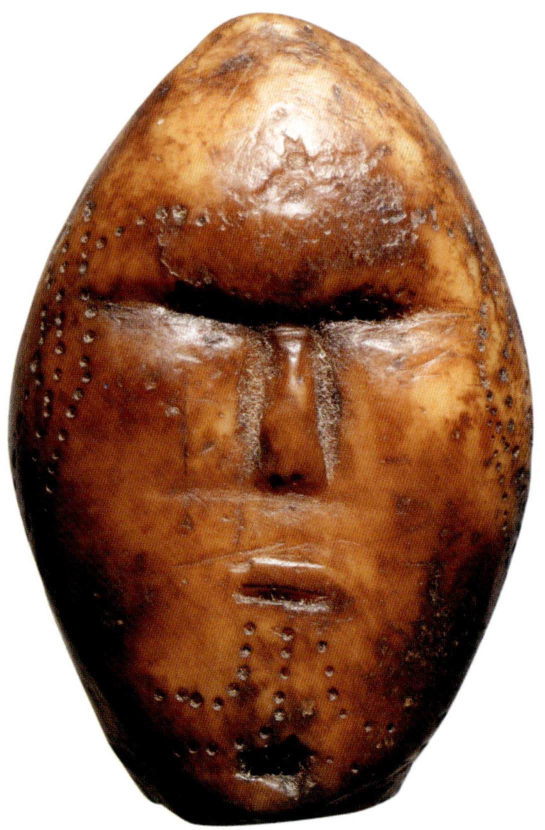

Portrait of a Punuk culture woman, St. Lawrence Island, Alaska, *ca*. 800–1000 CE. The cheek bands on this female figure, which were worn into the historic period, likely represent charms against infertility.

Another category of human figurines in use around Bering Strait was the shaman's doll or "helper." On St. Lawrence Island, *alignalghiit* or practicing shamans in the 1920s were freelance specialists and the carvers "of the many dolls, idols, [and] fetishes . . . found in many of the island homes."[49] A shaman usually had one or more helper or "tutelary" spirits, "who are men, bird, fish or animals of any kind [but] most are people [ancestors]" carved into human form.[50] St. Lawrence Island Yupik shamans "claimed that the [primary] helper was the spirit of some dead person."[51]

The special powers of a shaman's doll helper were derived from the spirit residing within the object, not from the item itself. Thus, it was very important to render these objects realistically through exquisite craftsmanship, and their finely carved nature suggests an extraordinary function. Facial features, personal tattoos, and ceremonial outer garments were carved with precision because ancestral spirits and deities, as well as the spirits of game animals, were attracted to and pleased by beautiful things. And if these ancient ancestral devices were individual representations of powerful ancestors or other spiritual beings, then it would have been extremely important to capture their unique portraits, and especially their facial tattoos, because they were essential equipment for the afterlife. I base this idea on the fact that Inuit peoples of the Arctic believed that women must be tattooed to enter the realm of the ancestors, which was presided over by female deities who were themselves tattooed and who brought tattooing to humankind.[52]

Another characteristic shared among Bering Strait anthropomorphic figurines is that most of them were purposefully dismembered by their owners once they fell out of personal or communal use, and later discarded or "buried."[53] Various theories have been proposed for this activity. Some scholars suggest the figurines were ceremonially "killed" to release potentially malignant powers embodied within them[54] or they were broken to forestall their reanimation by evil spirits after the death of their owner.[55] Other theories propose dismemberment was necessary to release the spirit of the object so that it could accompany the owner to the afterlife[56] or join its counterparts in the spirit world in an attempt to propagate itself and return to the human world anew. Regarding the latter theory, the destruction of these ancient dolls could be seen as a type of sacrifice or prayer to the spiritual realm for abundance, whether it be for new human life or communal fertility.

It is known that the heads of anthropomorphic dolls from Bering Strait were sometimes severed from their bodies and added to apotropaic cords that held a family's charms; heads were also attached to the charm belts of individuals, especially hunters, to promote success in their sometimes-dangerous endeavors.[57] Moreover, the production of household amulet strings featuring several attached charms, including various carved figures and human heads, was an Indigenous tradition of various Amur River Basin people inhabiting eastern Siberia that extended northward to Chukotka.[58]

Another perspective on breakage can be drawn from the ethnographic record. When an object of a dead person was broken, "it was thought to become whole again in the Other World," since in the land of the dead everything was reversed. For example, in the St. Lawrence Island Yupik afterlife, when it was daytime in the human world, it was nighttime in the afterworld. The deceased lived in villages with their dogs

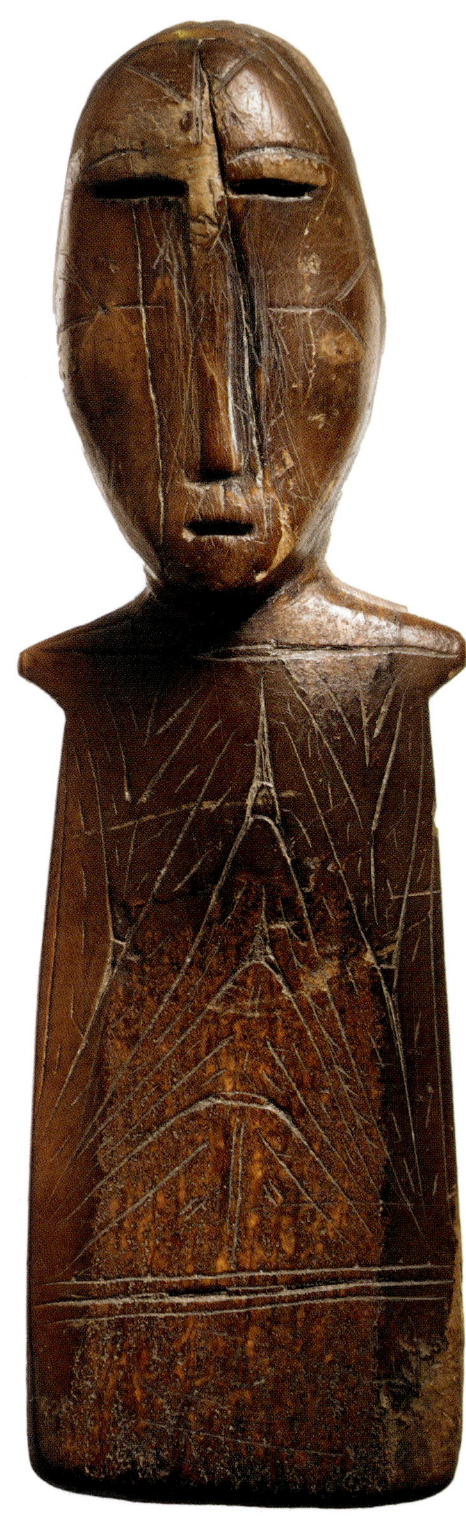

Old Bering Sea figure with tattooed fluke tails on cheeks, said to be from the Punuk Islands, Bering Strait, Alaska, *ca*. 100–400 CE. The spurred lines radiating across the torso may represent a ceremonial garment, or they might signify amulet straps, the waistband of an undergarment, and, perhaps, tattoos.

Right Portrait of an Old Bering Sea woman with extensive facial tattoos, including chin marks and lines near the eyes that were likely medicinal in function, St. Lawrence Island, Alaska, *ca*. 300–500 CE. Similar facial tattoos were worn by Inuit women into the historic period.

Below Old Bering Sea figure head with facial tattoos, said to be from the Punuk Islands, Bering Strait, Alaska, *ca*. 100–400 CE. The portrait probably represents a great hunter with tattoo tally marks running across the cheeks and under the nose. On the forehead, a series of lines marks the location of his hunting visor.

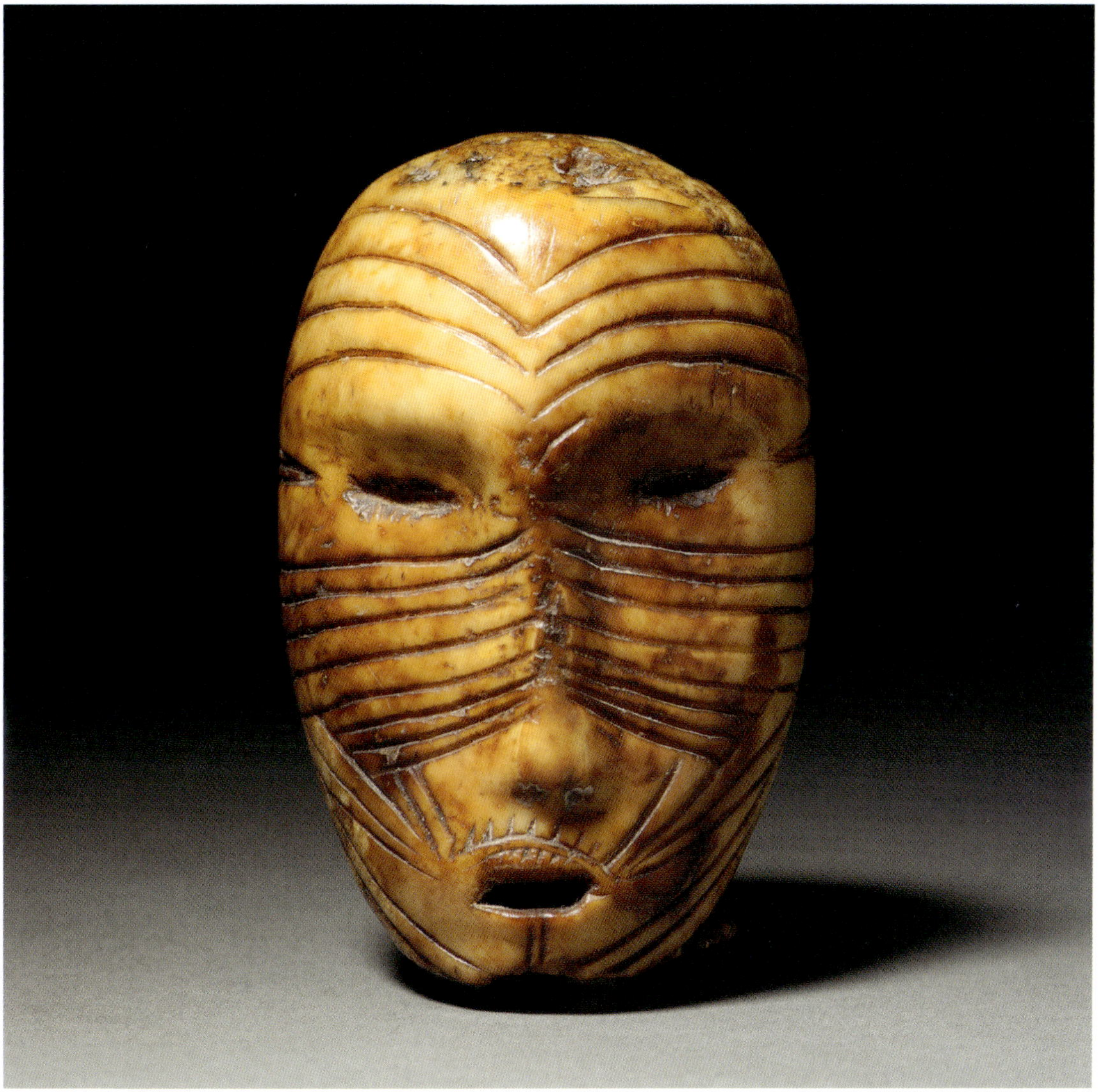

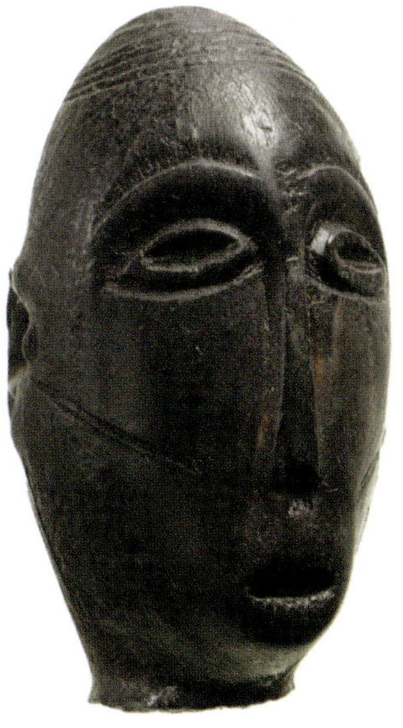

and their cemeteries contained dwellings instead of graves; when someone died the ancestors held a "festival" to celebrate, they did not mourn like humankind.[59] It was here in a world turned inside out and upside down that the figurine became resurrected and whole again to find renewed use in the world of ancestral spirits.

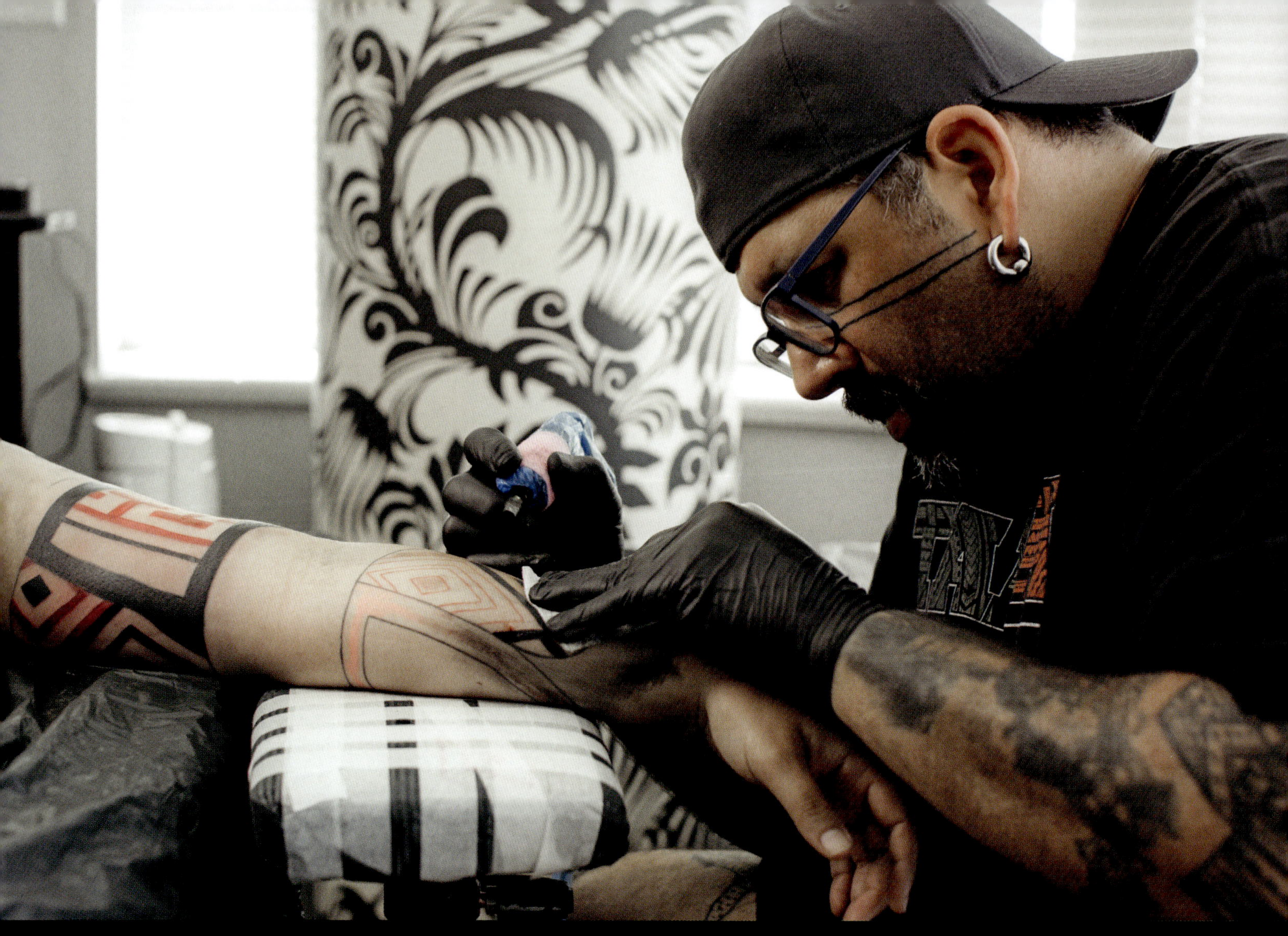

Dion Kaszas: Re-writing Indigenous Identity in Ink

Opposite Dion Kaszas working on Alison Cuffley's Nlaka'pamux blackwork sleeve, which includes patterns for protection and celebrates connection and protection of cedar trees, 2023.

Right Nlaka'pamux blackwork tattoos by Dion Kaszas, 2023. Torso suit on Toonasa Tscke, including pictograph of frog and patterns for protection and connection to the mountains, forests, and trees.

Far right Nlaka'pamux blackwork tattoos by Dion Kaszas, 2023. This tattoo was received following the Indigenous blockade of the Coastal Gaslink pipeline in 2021. The symbol down the spine represents the waterways that Indigenous people are fighting to protect. The half arrowhead patterns are a prayer for healing and wholeness.

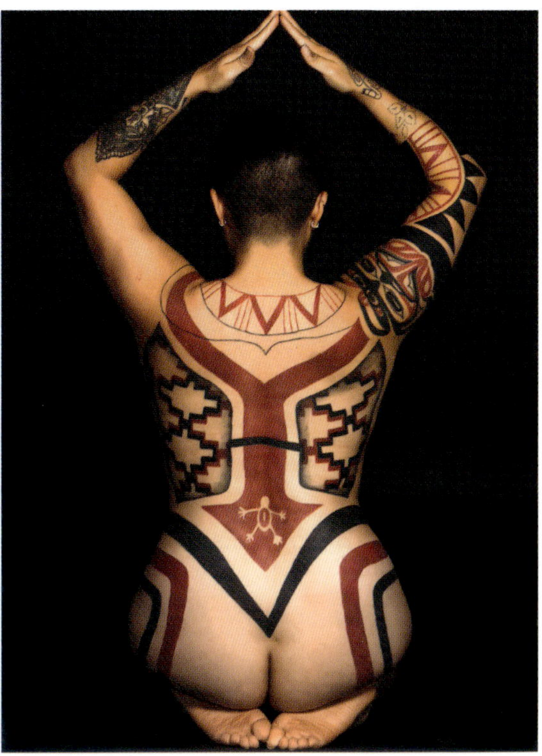

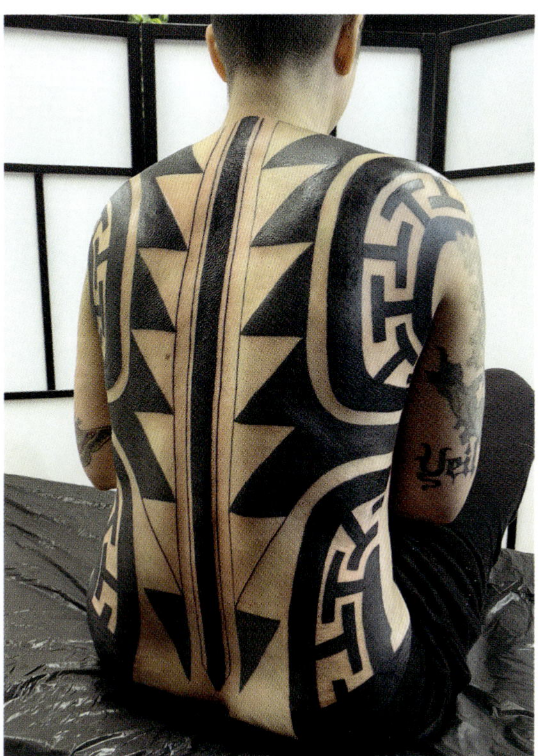

Tattooing was once practiced by almost every Indigenous Nation across Native North America. From the high Arctic to the desert Southwest and Eastern Woodlands, tattooing permanently imprinted unique cultural identities and Indigenous knowledge systems onto the surfaces of bodies that were deeply rooted to tribal homelands, clans, lineages, families, and ancestral communities.

After centuries of forced colonialism, missionization, and acculturation these widespread cultural practices nearly disappeared until tattoo revitalization efforts were launched a few decades ago in several Indigenous communities, a movement that continues to this day. For cultural tattoo practitioners and authors like Dion Kaszas, who is of Nlaka'pamux and Métis descent, "the revival of tattooing has become a medium of reclaiming our Indigenous identities and even our bodies from the colonial machinery which sought to divide us, control us, and wipe us out," he explains.[60] "Today our tattoos also contain the knowledge of the processes of colonization and our resistance and resilience to it."[61]

Kaszas, who is originally from Salmon Arm, British Columbia, Canada, has been tattooing for nearly fifteen years. He began as an electric machine artist but over the last decade he has relearned the ancestral tattooing techniques of his Nlaka'pamux ancestors – hand-poking and skin-stitching. He has not only reconnected fellow Nlaka'pamux clients with their cultural tattoos, but also those of many other First Nations, including Nêhiyaw (Cree), Sécwepemc, St'at'imc, Shuswap, Syilx, Métis, and many others.

Kaszas was first introduced to his people's ancestral tattooing traditions in 2006 when he

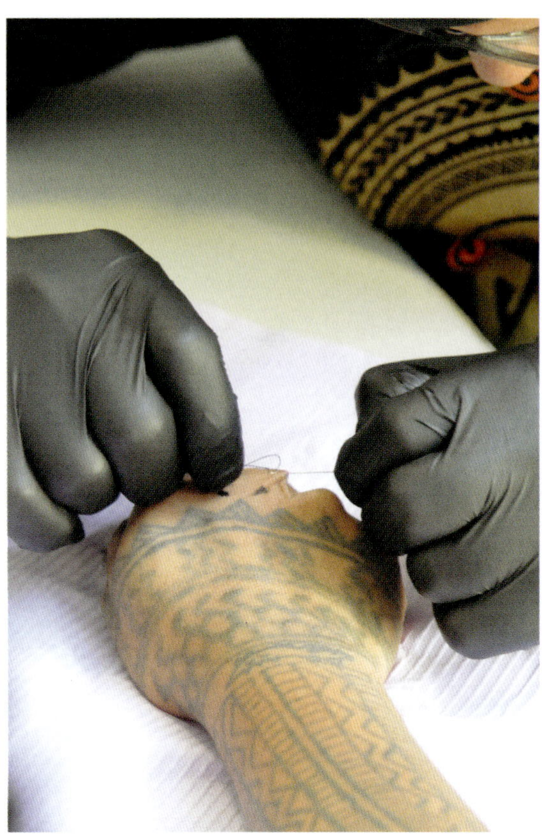

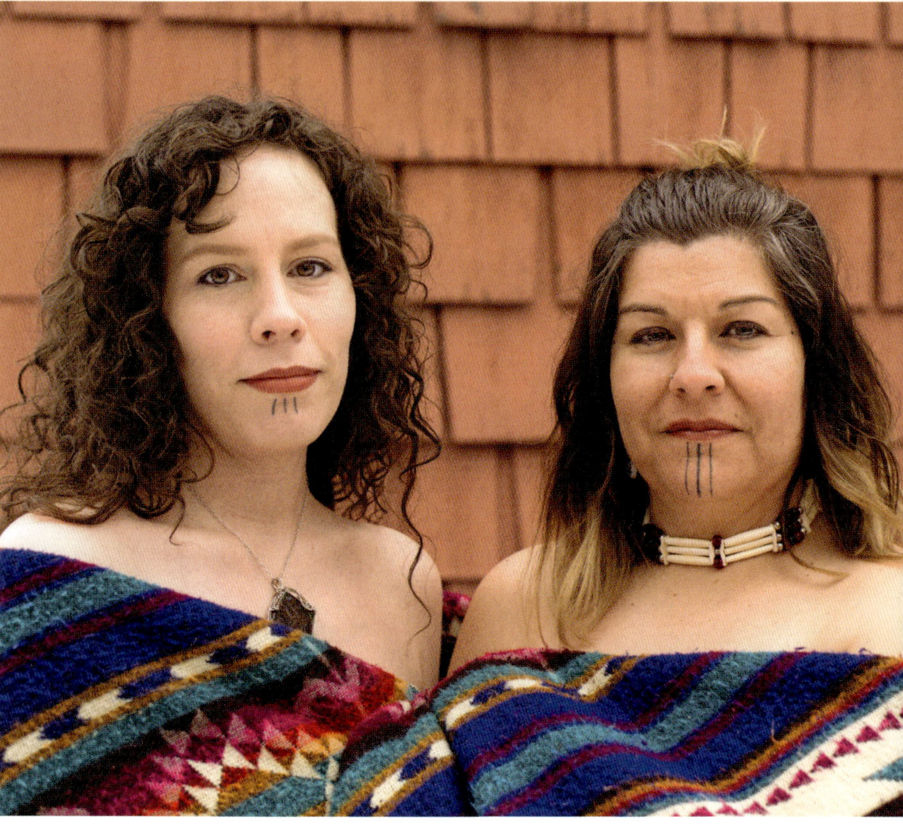

Above left Dion Kaszas skin-stitching fellow Indigenous cultural tattoo practitioner Cudjuy Patjidres of the Paiwan people (Taiwan), 2019. This tattooing technique was once widely performed among the Nlaka'pamux and other Native North American peoples.

Above Hand-poked Syilx and Cree facial tattoos by Dion Kaszas, 2017.

stumbled upon an obscure publication while waiting to be tattooed in a tattoo studio. From that point forward, he began collecting every ethnographic report and initiated interviews with family, friends, and community members. He also studied Nlaka'pamux visual material culture, including rock art, basketry, textile patterns, and carvings. In some cases, these carried patterns identical or similar to those used in traditional tattooing, and connected community members to their territories, ancestral lands, history, and identities.[62]

In today's world, cultural identity is a complicated issue for many Indigenous and non-Indigenous people, especially regarding contemporary tattoo revivals. Kaszas writes: "The revival of Indigenous tattooing is a process of re-Indigenization. We are using our traditional tattoo practices in a way that communicates who we are at the core of our being. Our ancestors never had to worry about who they were because they grew up in a community with story, culture, and language that affirmed who they were. [And] when we take on our traditional markings, we are resisting colonialism and affirming who we are in a way that makes us visible as Indigenous people to ourselves and to the world."[63]

But as a maker of permanent marks on other people's skin, Kaszas recognizes that his work comes with great responsibility, which is rooted to his community, family, ancestors, relationship to the *tmíx^w* (land), the community of Indigenous tattoo practitioners, as well as future generations of Indigenous tattoo recipients. His goal is to teach others how

Indigenous people experience their tattooing and ultimately what it means to them, because only then can we decolonize our thought and engage with Native epistemologies of knowing, thinking, and being through the act of tattooing.

One of the educational platforms he uses to further knowledge about the practices and meanings of Indigenous tattooing is the Earthline Tattoo Collective. Co-founded in 2015 with fellow First Nations artists Jordan Bennett (Mi'kmaq) and Amy Malbeuf (Métis), the group is a residency-style training program to help fulfill the need for skilled cultural tattoo artists who can safely serve their communities and Nations. The Collective includes coursework in traditional tattoo techniques and tool manufacture, cultural and spiritual safety, and a certificate program in blood-borne pathogens.[64]

A new endeavor is Kaszas's podcast, *Transformative Marks*, which journeys through the world of Indigenous tattooing, amplifying the voices of ancestral skin markers, Indigenous tattoo artists, cultural tattoo practitioners, and those who wear ancestral marks.

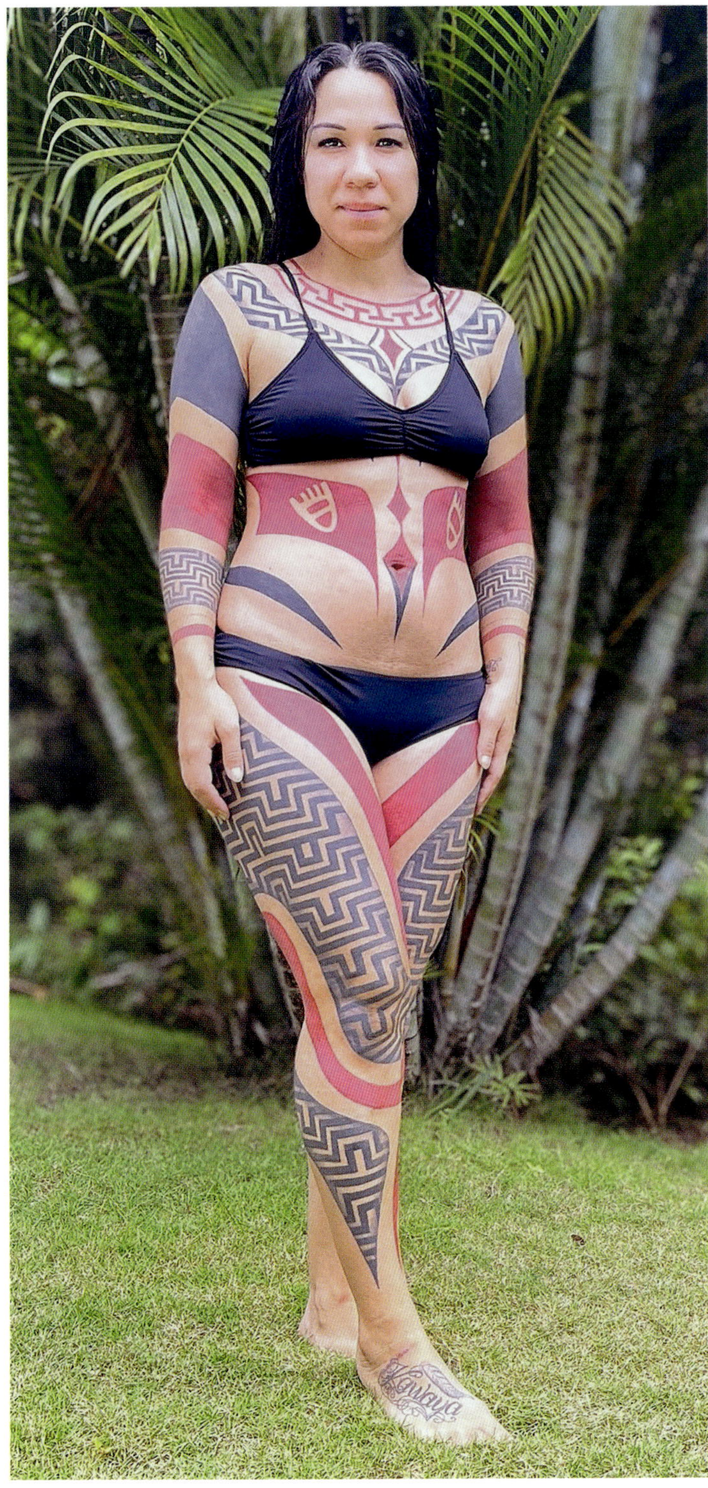

Nlaka'pamux blackwork tattoos by Dion Kaszas, 2023. Bodysuit tattoo on Ecko Aleck includes grizzly bear patterns on the ribs and basketry patterns across the thighs; the latter represent the ripples made by the bow of a canoe.

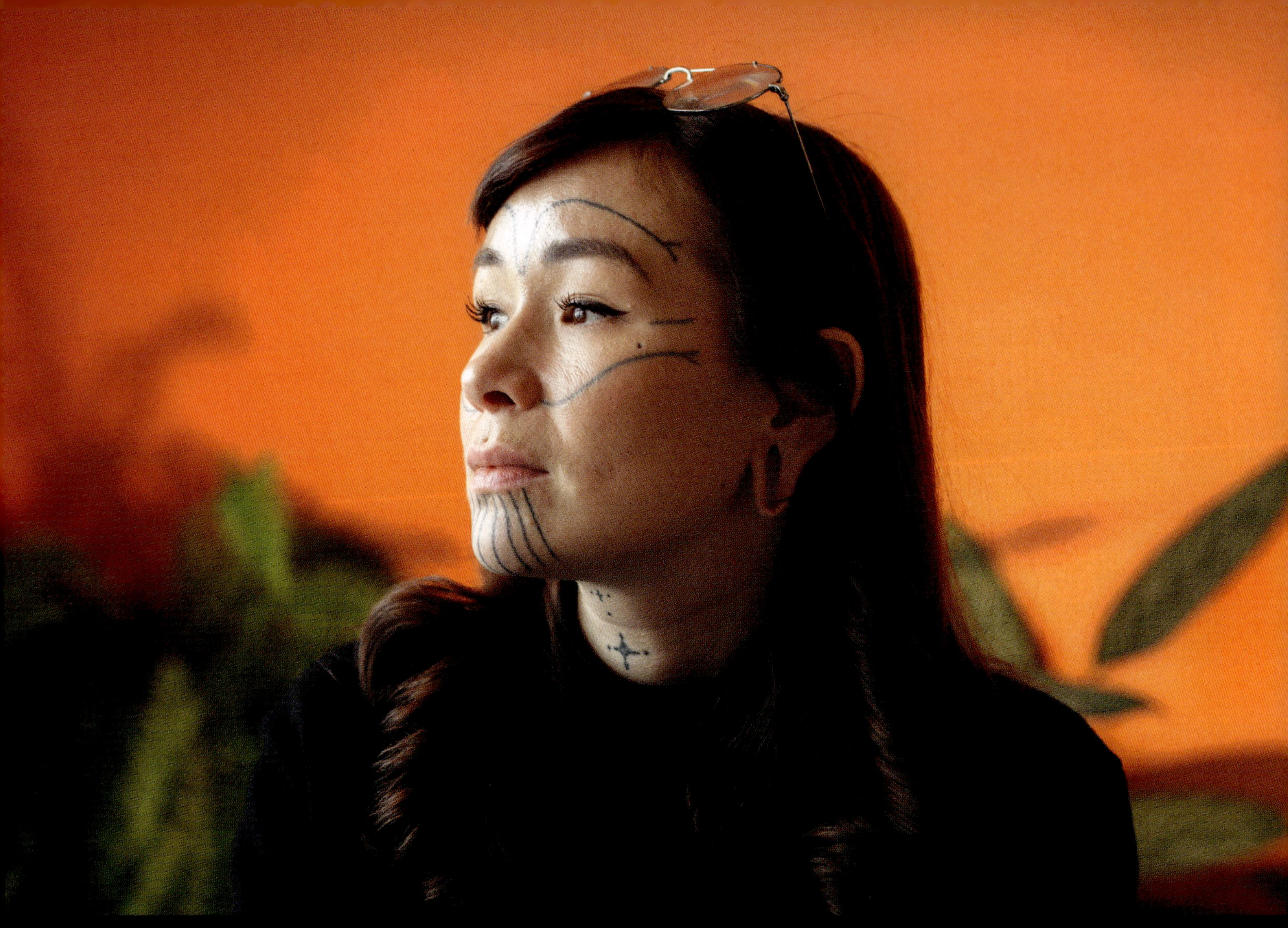

Paninnguaq Pikilak: *Kakiorneq* in Greenland

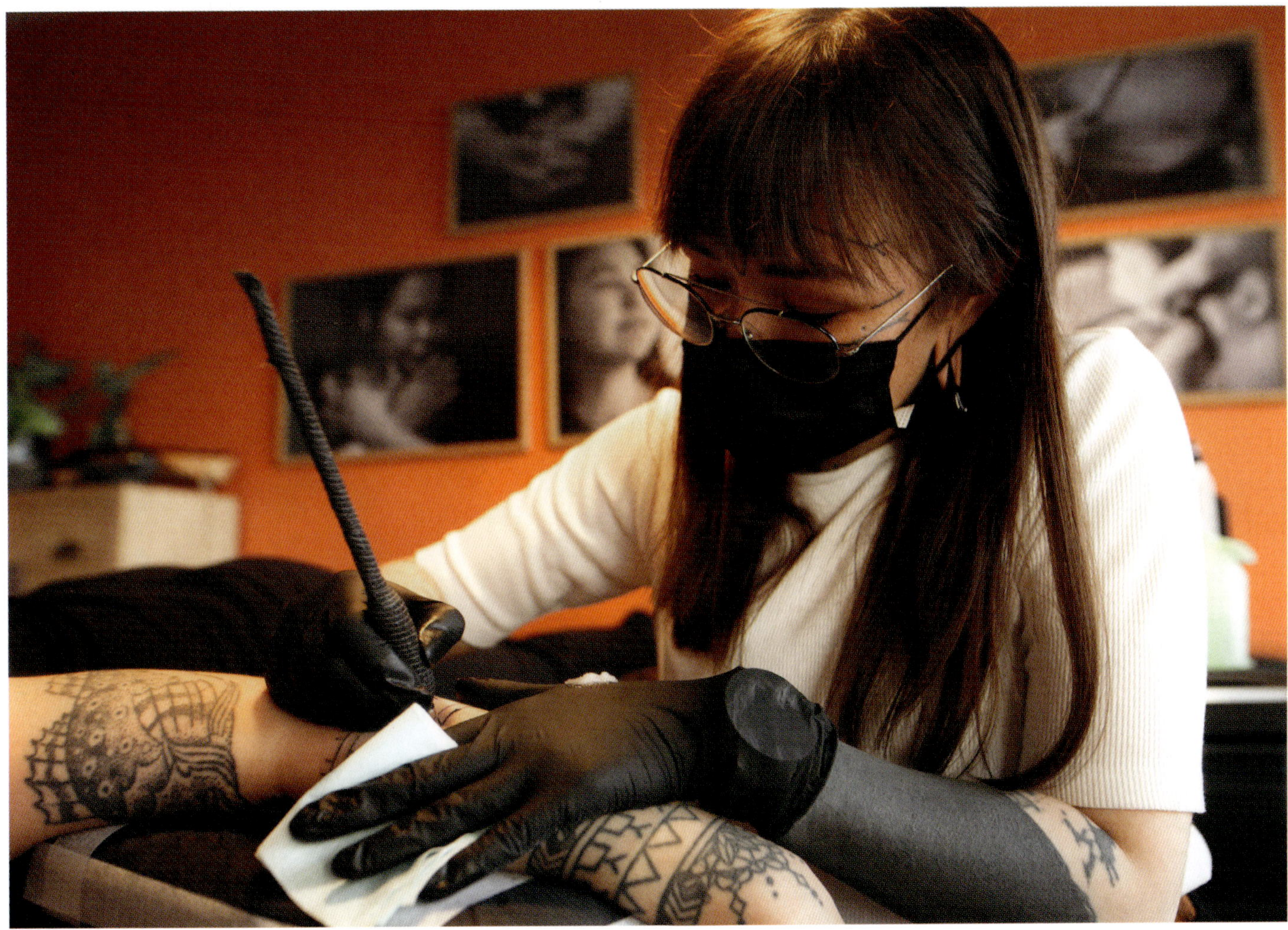

Opposite Portrait of Paninnguaq Pikilak, 2022.

Above *Tunniit* artist Paninnguaq Pikilak at work, 2022.

Across the Arctic, the tradition of tattooing has been invariably performed by female practitioners for more than 3,000 years.[65] Subdermal skin-stitching was the predominate method of tattooing although hand-poking was also practiced in Alaska, the Central Inuit region of Canada, and Greenland.[66]

With the arrival of missionaries and government agents as early as the eighteenth century in Greenland and Chukotka, and the early nineteenth century in other regions of the Arctic, Inuit and other Indigenous tattooing practices began to fade from view. Religious beliefs and cultural practices like tattooing that were inextricably linked to Indigenous concepts of identity and spirituality were suppressed, and by the end of the twentieth century only a handful of traditionally tattooed female elders in Alaska, Canada, and Nunavut remained.

Kakiorneq,[67] or tattooing, in Greenland vanished long before this era, but in the last decade there has been a resurgence of these practices by *Kalaallit* (Greenlandic Inuit) tattooists, including Paninnguaq Pikilak. Originally from Narsaq, South Greenland, Pikilak began tattooing in 2012, and just

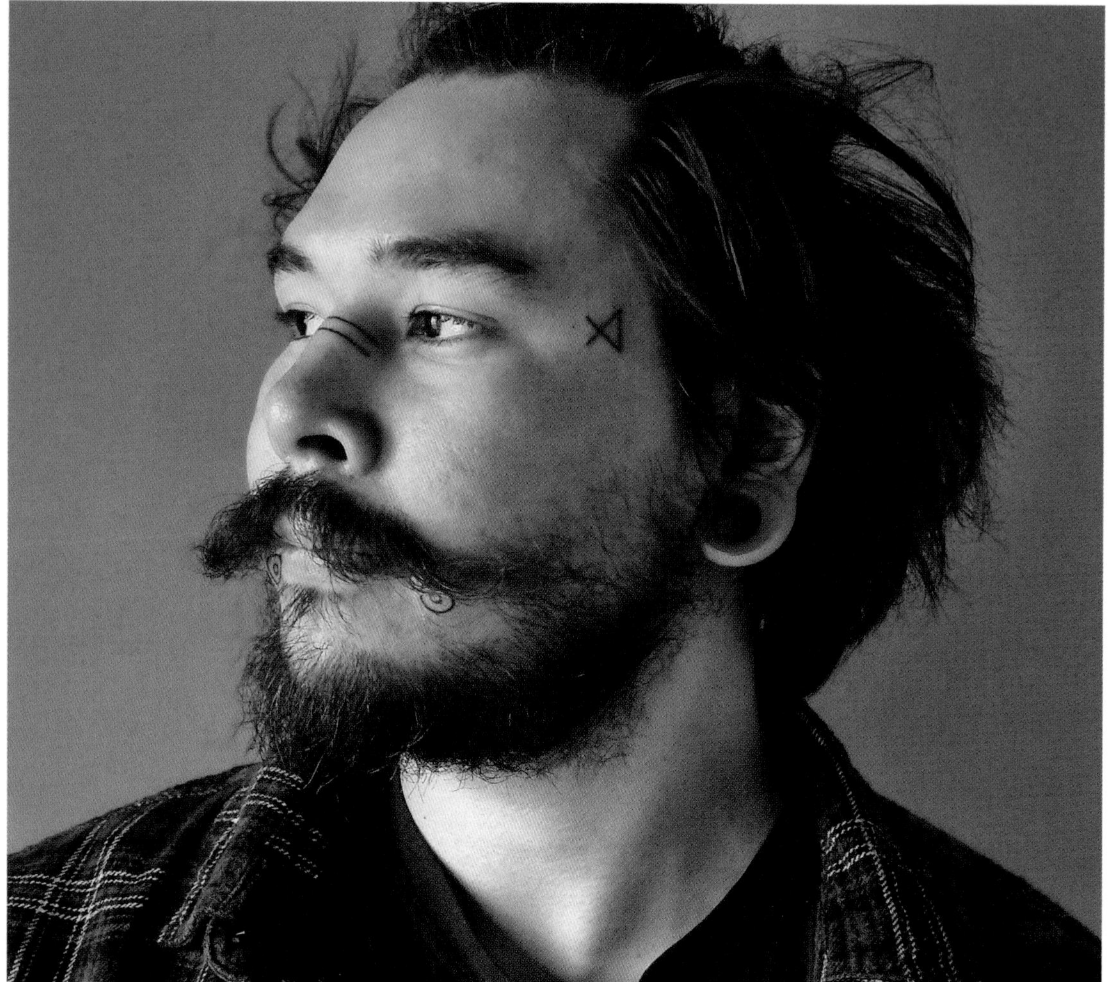

Tunniit of Dennis Møller, 2023. Among the Inuit of the Western Arctic, Tulugaq (Raven) appears in stories as a creator or trickster figure, while in the Central and Eastern Inuit regions Tulugaq appears as the bringer of light in memories of origin, enabling the People to see. The *tunniit* of Dennis Møller embody the latter tradition, and enhance his vision.

a few years ago she was one of only three Inuit women in Greenland to have facial tattoos; today there are now more than one hundred. "What was surprising to me was how quickly Inuit women embraced and reconnected with their markings, especially in a time where Western beauty standards dictate that tattooed female faces and hands are not necessarily becoming. But in our worldview, that is a part of being a woman," she explains.

Pikilak, who is also an author of the illustrated children's books *Talloqut* (2021) and *Pivik Learns from Takannaaluk* (2022), which share information about Inuit knowledge, culture, and tattooing, suggests that perhaps the most important Inuit markings or *tunniit* (patterns) are those worn on the face and hands of women.[68] A woman's first *tunneq* (pattern) is the *talloqut*, the chin mark she receives when her skills are good enough to help her fill a role and assume responsibility in her family and community.[69] The shape of the facial tattoos, especially on the forehead and cheeks, denote which group of Inuit the individual belonged to, and they

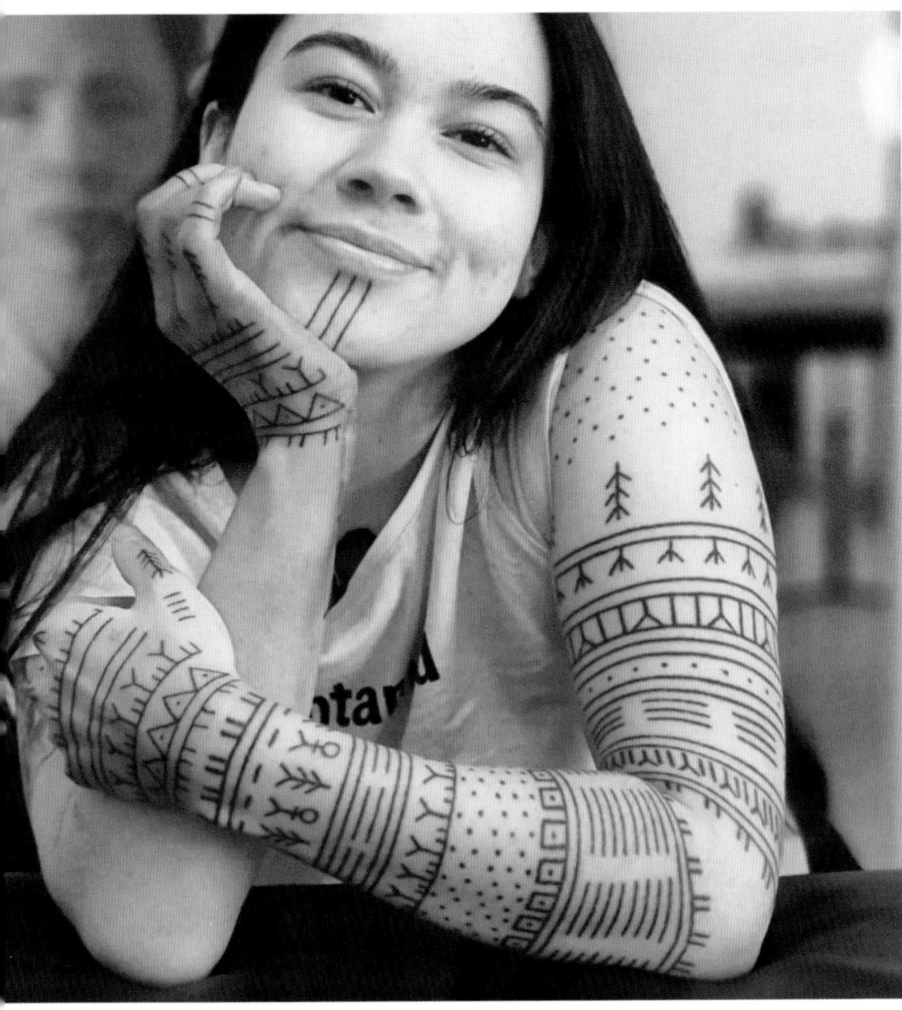

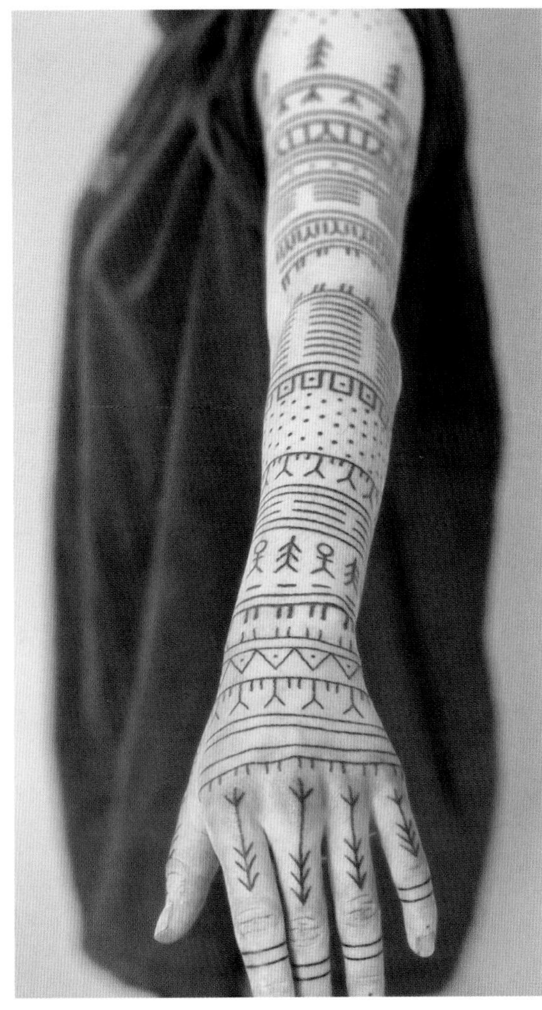

Above and above right
Tunniit of Sikkerninnguaq, 2022. Since the beginning of time, Inuit women have carried *tunniit* to maintain the cosmic order between the spiritual realm and the living world. In turn, a woman's *tunniit* secured the ancestral balance of body, mind, and spirit.

therefore vary in appearance among all Inuit groups. In Greenland, other parts of a woman's body might have been marked, including the shoulders, arms, legs, and breast, with amuletic and/or medicinal markings.

Although the revitalization of Greenlandic Inuit tattooing is no longer in doubt and patterns and designs are increasingly exchanged across social media, Pikilak has deep concerns about cultural (mis) appropriation. "Increasingly, there are many non-Inuit who seek to wear our patterns. But *tunniit* are part of our spiritual responsibility to our community, and they put women in a sacred space as we carry our ancestral markings on our faces and bodies. They are our heritage and ours to pass onto the next Inuit generations, just as they have been passed down to us through our ancestors. They are not a souvenir for non-Inuit to entitle themselves to," she says. "Cultural appropriation does not decorate very nicely, and we suggest non-Inuit to seek out their own ancestral heritage and belonging. They deserve that too."

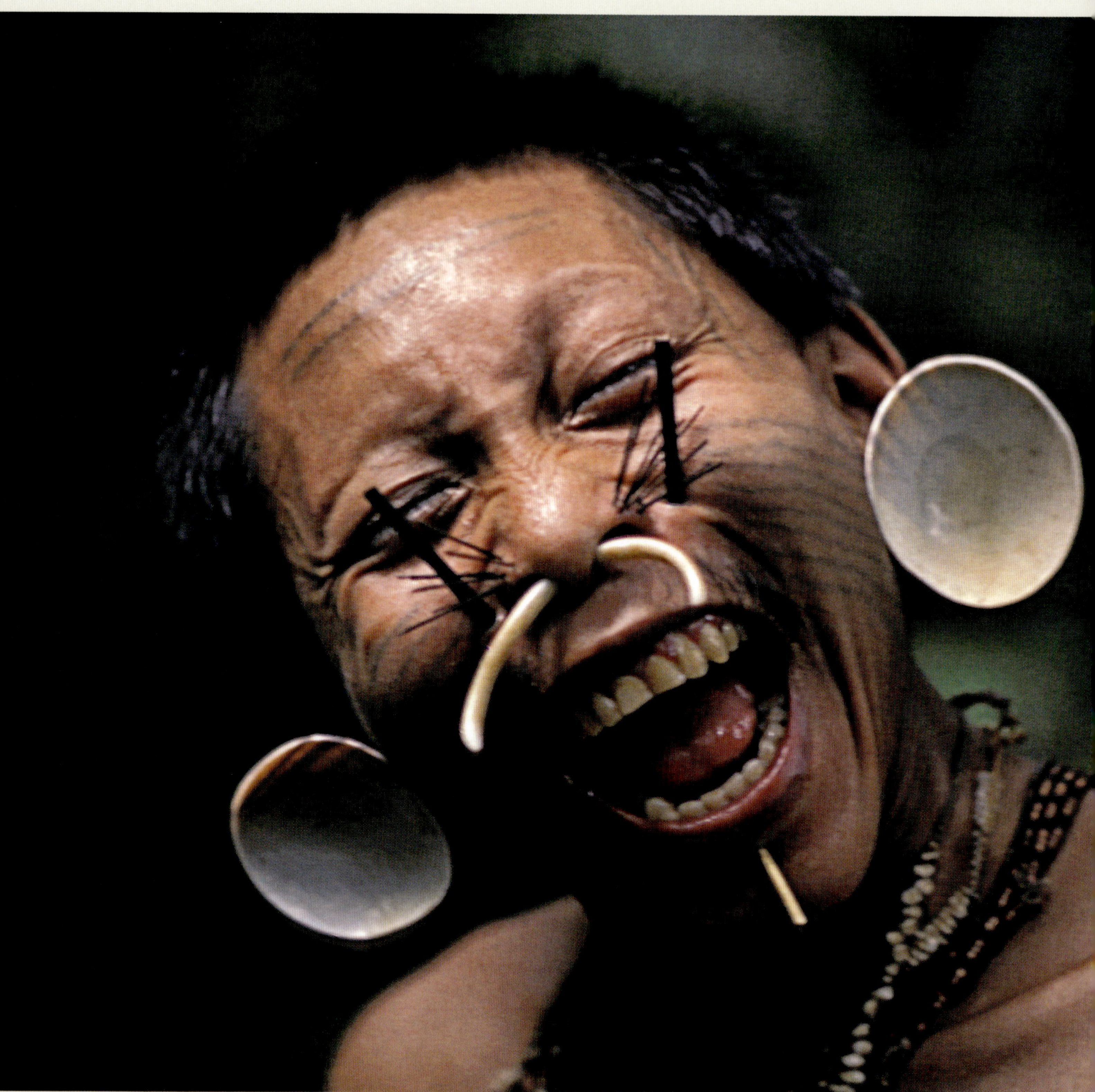

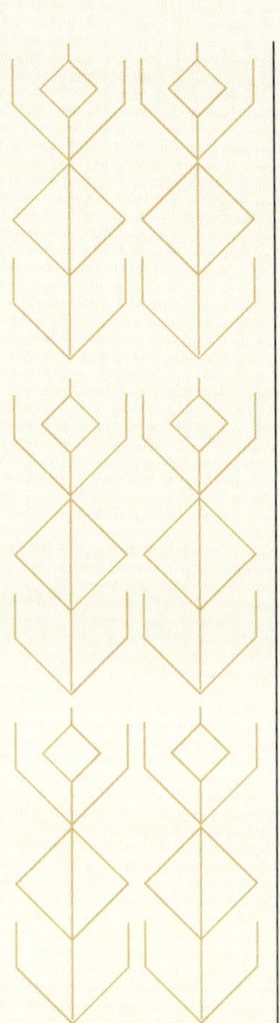

3

TATTOOS OF SOUTH AMERICA

In South America, tattoos have firmly anchored cultural identity, communal bonds, and cultural heritage for at least four millennia. These indelible marks have etched themselves into history, serving as symbols of deeply rooted values that transcend time. Archaeological discoveries reveal that the earliest tattoos in this region were statements of self-expression. More than 3,800 years ago, a mummified man from Chile's ancient Chinchorro culture bore one of the earliest known tattoos—a subtle design resembling a small mustache adorning his upper lip,[1] forever immortalizing his presence in the annals of history.

Matis tribal member Kwini mimicking a jaguar, Brazil, 1985. The Matis are one of a handful of Amazonian peoples that continue their ancestral practices of tattooing today.

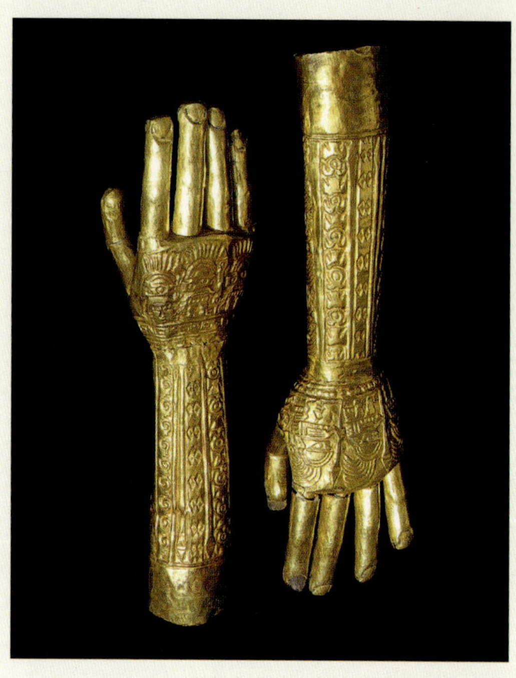

Embossed burial "gloves" with tattooing motifs, Peru, 800–1100 CE. Scholars believe pre-Columbian tattoos signified one's status, enhanced relationships with particularly deities, and perhaps offered protection against negative forces. Although the precise functions of burial objects like these remain unclear, it is likely they helped carry one's tattoos into the afterlife.

Hidden in shifting sands along the coastal valleys of Chile and Peru, prehistoric mummies have been discovered in the hundreds—some bearing intricate tattoos on their desiccated skins. Whether depicting stylized marine and terrestrial fauna, weapons used in war or in the hunt (harpoons, projectile points), highly abstract geometric designs representing features of the surrounding landscape (ocean waves and mountains), or anthropomorphic deities, the tattoos of the dead perhaps served as mediators between this world and the next.

Of Peru's many prehistoric cultures, the ancient Chimú (900–1450 CE) were perhaps the most heavily and elaborately tattooed of all.[2] The exquisite designs tattooed on living flesh, and carved into silver, gold, and wooden burial objects, suggest that the body's skin projected both personal power and identity across the plane of the living and the dead. Dressing oneself in a secondary skin of tattoos not only transformed the wearer visually; it established identity and reconstructed personhood.

Chimú tattooists applied their tattoo pigments with various types of fine needles (fish bone, parrot quill, spiny conch), each of which have been found in mummy burials.[3] The technical application of tattooing was likely a form of hand-poking or incision tattooing,[4] and it can be suggested that women were the primary tattoo artists. Their expert knowledge of working animal skins and hides would certainly have facilitated the precision needed for piercing the human epidermis with complex motifs.

Although no studies have attempted to identify the work of individual Chimú tattooists from others, it is certain that skin artisans were highly skilled, probably full-time craftspeople who enjoyed some degree of prestige in their communities. As in other Indigenous cultures, tattooists likely received high payments for their artistry, wages that perhaps only affluent or aristocratic individuals could afford.[5] In this context, tattooists were in a good position to acquire intimate knowledge of secular, political, and religious affairs over the course of tattooing their elite clients.

The tattoo artist was also a repository of ritual knowledge. Their occupation encompassed not only the inscription and patterning of supernatural or other figures on human skin, but also the ritual release and manipulation of human blood. In prehistoric South American cultures, human blood—the fertilizing essence of everything animate—was a highly revered sacred substance believed to appease spiritual powers that controlled the forces of nature.[6]

Blood Sacrifice in Ancient Peru

Ritual blood sacrifice has a long history in the coastal valleys of ancient Peru, and almost every major culture—Chimú, Moche, and others—practiced it, especially the tradition of taking human heads for ritual use.[7] Ritually prepared human heads were seen as potent sources of power to be harnessed and tapped in order to promote agricultural fertility and relations with the ancestral dead and deities.

The blood cult of the prehistoric Chimú, which has been widely documented, paled in comparison to its Moche (50–800 CE) antecedent. Indeed, many facets of Chimú culture largely grew out of older Moche traditions, including artistic iconography, architecture, technological innovations in ceramics and casting, and tattooing.[8] References to warfare, human sacrifice, and the drinking of human blood appear on Moche ceramics, textiles, ritual objects, and tattooed mummies.

One rare, remarkable example of such tattooing was discovered on the mummified skin of an eighteen-year-old Moche woman from the ancient city of Pacatnamu.[9] The figures on her arms depict anthropomorphic beings who might be deities or costumed priests practicing ritual blood sacrifices.

Other examples of tattooed Moche mummies have been found in recent years at the archaeological site of El Brujo. Here an elite Moche woman dubbed "The Lady of Cao" was unearthed in 2006 with intricate tattoos of supernatural creatures and geometric designs covering much of her forearms, hands, and knuckles.[10] Although similar tattoos have been found on mummies of the later Tiwanaku (600-1000 CE) and Chimú cultures of Peru, scientists are perplexed by the context of this woman's burial, which dates to

Right Designs etched into the skin of a tattooed eighteen-year-old Moche noblewoman showed anthropomorphic deities and zoomorphic designs, Pacatnamu site, Peru, 450–750 CE.

Far right Naturalistic and geometric markings found on a tattooed mummy of the Chimú culture of Peru, 1200 CE. The intricately patterned tattoos probably recorded significant events in the lifetime of the wearer.

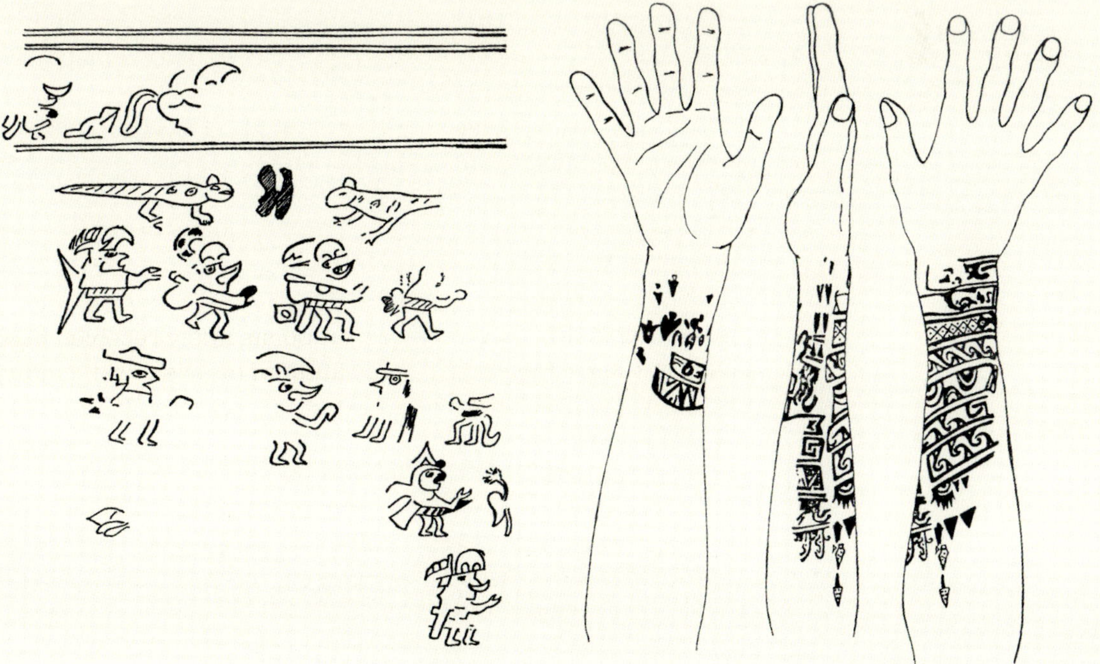

Right Tattoos of a female mummy, *ca*. 1000 CE. This female mummy was probably a member of the Tiwanaku culture. She has decorative tattoos (spider, bird, lizard, and floraform motifs) on her hands, arms, and legs, and circular tattoos on her neck. These partially overlapping circles were found to align with acupuncture points utilized today to relieve neck and head discomfort.

Below Tattoos of the Moche "Lady of Cao," Peru, 450 CE. She was buried with weaponry and opulent burial goods. It has been proposed she was a ruler, a healer, and/or a priestess.

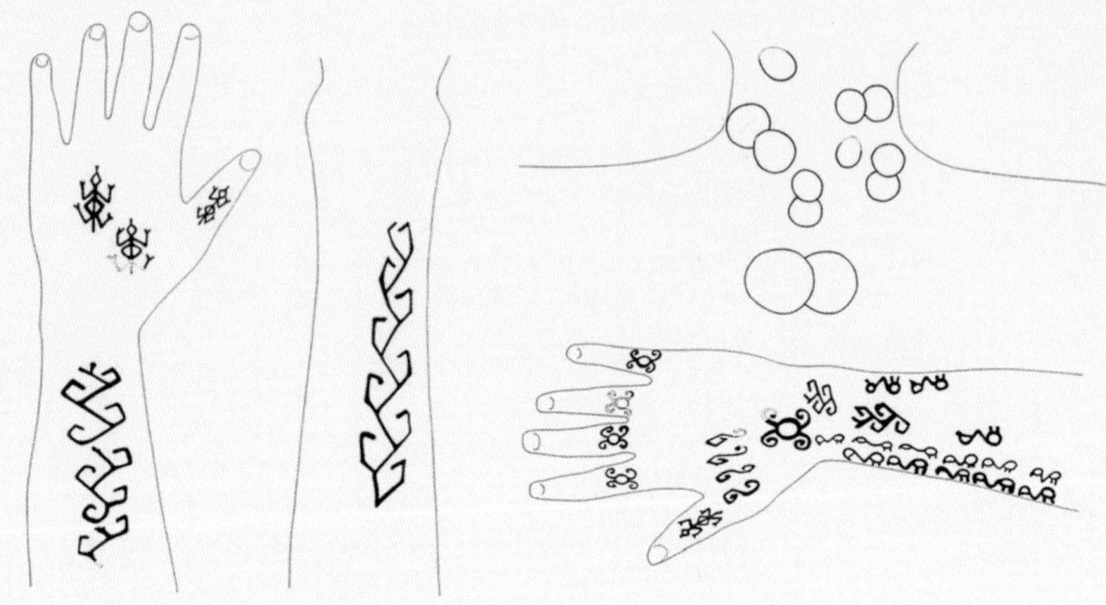

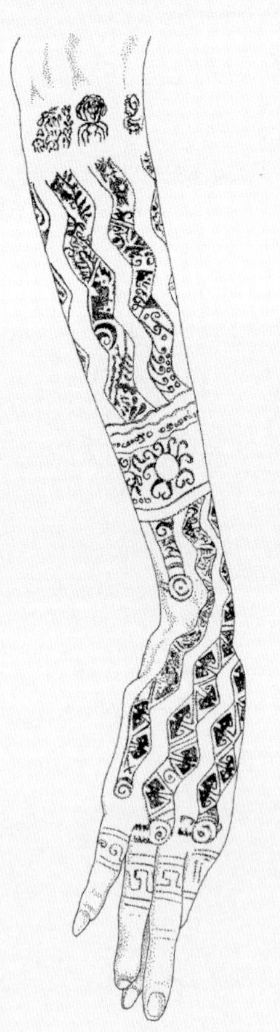

450 CE. Moche burials containing priestesses have been found before,[11] but never has a woman's burial been associated with weapons like war clubs and spear throwers—male objects par excellence. This suggests that some Moche women were perhaps revered for their martial abilities in combat and/or for their religious roles in warfare.

The Lady of Cao's skin shows extensive tattooing on her arms, hands, legs, and feet. Her tattooing pigment was rather superficial and consists mainly of ferrous oxide, which might have been partially extracted from *jagua* fruits (known in the Brazilian Amazon as *genipapo*), although it is more likely the pigment was carbon based and *jagua* was utilized as a diluent.[12]

The complex designs include representations of spiders, snakes, birds, lunar animals, geometric figures, and other motifs that have yet to be deciphered,[13] including a possible manifestation of the Moche creator god, Ai Apaec ("The Decapitator").

The tattoos undoubtedly formed part of the spiritual power that the Lady of Cao displayed in the Moche world. The figures tattooed on the Lady's forearms indicated the social position and power that she possessed, and they are seemingly charged with highly symbolic content. Scholars have suggested that spider forms are linked to rain-calling rituals, whereas the figures of snakes are perhaps associated with fertility rites focused on agricultural abundance. Other tattoo motifs might have been related to healing rites. The association between the Lady, her tattoos, and her assumed powers of agricultural and/or weather prognostication—through calling upon sacred beings to benefit her community—and healing undoubtedly support her hypothesized cultural position as a bearer of significant magical-religious powers.

Amazonian Tribes

Apart from the ancient societies discussed thus far, several contemporary Indigenous peoples living in the Amazon rainforest have practiced various forms of tattooing and body modification. Among the Matis, Munduruku, Apiaká, Kayabí, Matsés, Marubo, and others, body modification was utilized[14] to enhance human well-being, access supernatural power, and to please or seek protection from particular spirits or ancestors who inhabited their worlds.

The Matis of Brazil, who speak a Panoan language, are one of a few contemporary peoples of the Amazon who continue to practice tattooing today. The Matis "tattooing festival," as it has been called, typically occurs during the middle of the rainy season

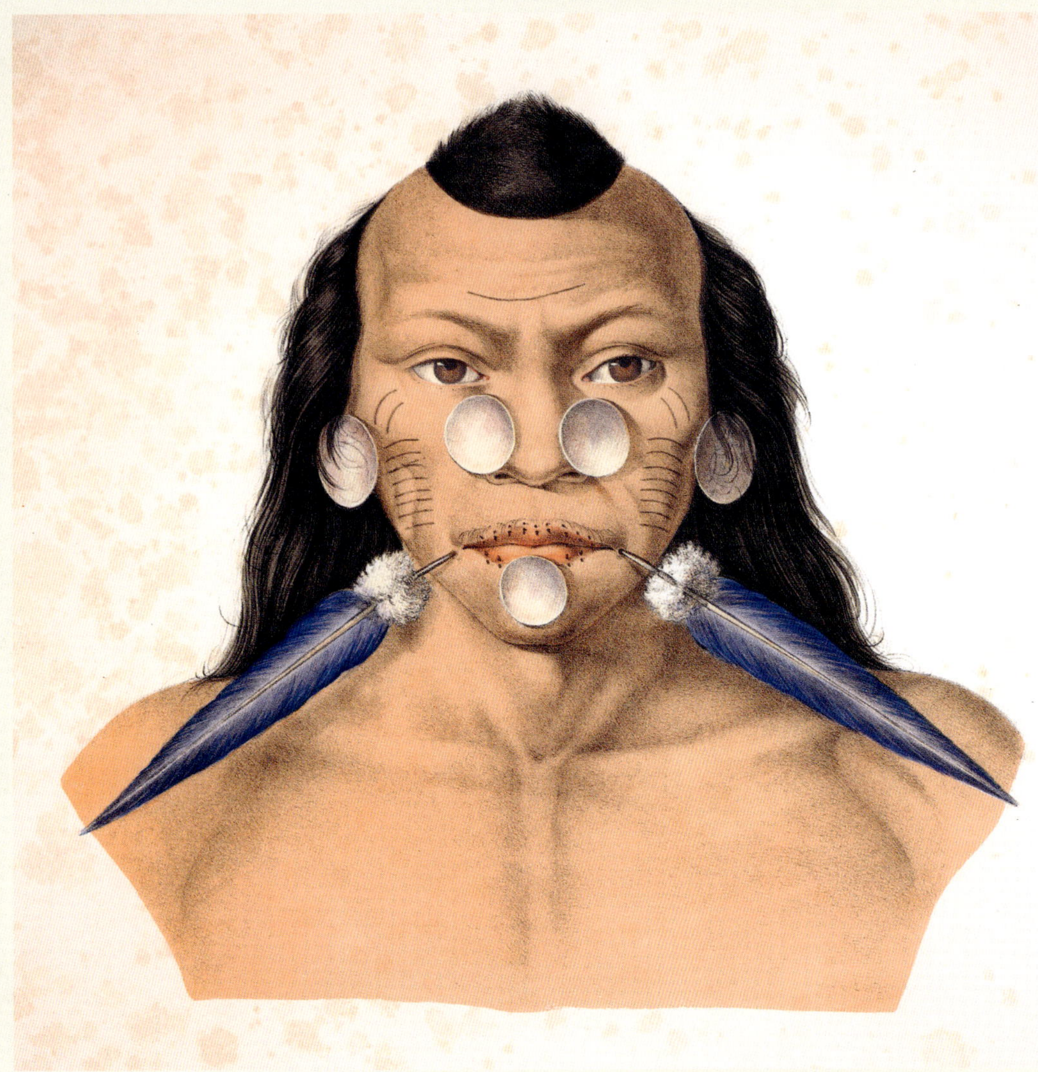

This is perhaps the first Western illustration of Matis tattooing drawn from life. The initiation tattoos of the male warrior are captured in vivid detail, Brazil, *ca*. 1820.

(November to December) when hunting is restricted due to bad weather and the annual corn crop is ready to be harvested.[15] The Matis state that their *mariwin* (ancestor spirits) come to visit them at this time of the year and that is why it is an appropriate time for male and female initiates to be tattooed. They also believe they acquire ancestral and other forms of mystical power through tattooing, especially that of the jaguar (their linear facial tattoos mimic its whiskers), which enhances the essence of their being.[16]

The patterns Matis initiates receive resemble fine lines tattooed on the temples and forehead. As they grow older, additional lines are added to adorn their cheeks. The procedure, which is said to be more painful on the forehead and temples, is experienced as a kind of dangerous and bloody test that proves the initiates' value in the eyes of the elders and particularly their ancestral spirits, the *mariwin*. According to the Matis, tattooing permits one to appear more like the ancestral spirits because it makes your face black, which is the color of prestige and of the dead. In turn, those individuals who are tattooed are believed to gain power, because the ancestors are pleased by those who are marked like them.

Once the tattooing has been completed the ancestor spirits leave and the newly tattooed are required to follow a set of taboos until their tattoos heal. These restrictions include not bathing and observing a prescribed diet while they remain secluded in the communal house where they were tattooed. After their tattoos have scabbed over, the initiates give away their belongings and receive equivalent items reserved for men and women. It is at this moment that they begin their new lives as adults in the Matis community.

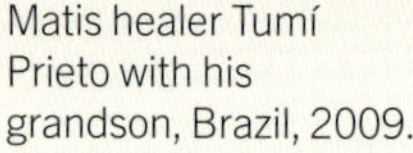

Matis healer Tumí Prieto with his grandson, Brazil, 2009.

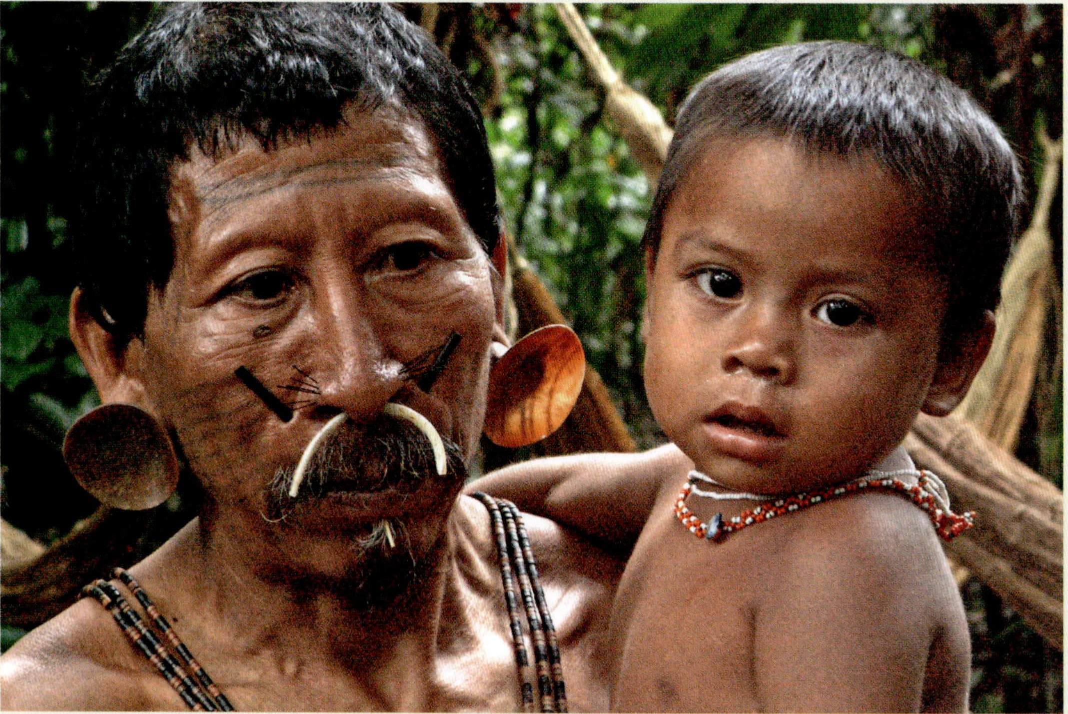

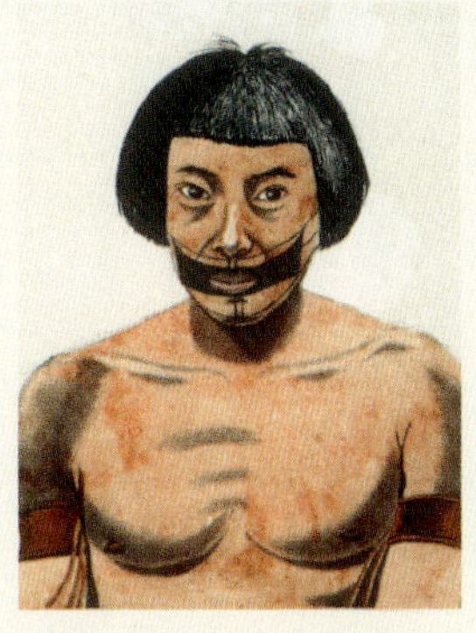

Above Apiaká warrior with facial tattooing, including a box-like square around his mouth denoting he had tasted human flesh, Brazil, 1828.

Right Tattooed Munduruku warrior in ceremonial attire, Santarém, Brazil, 1828.

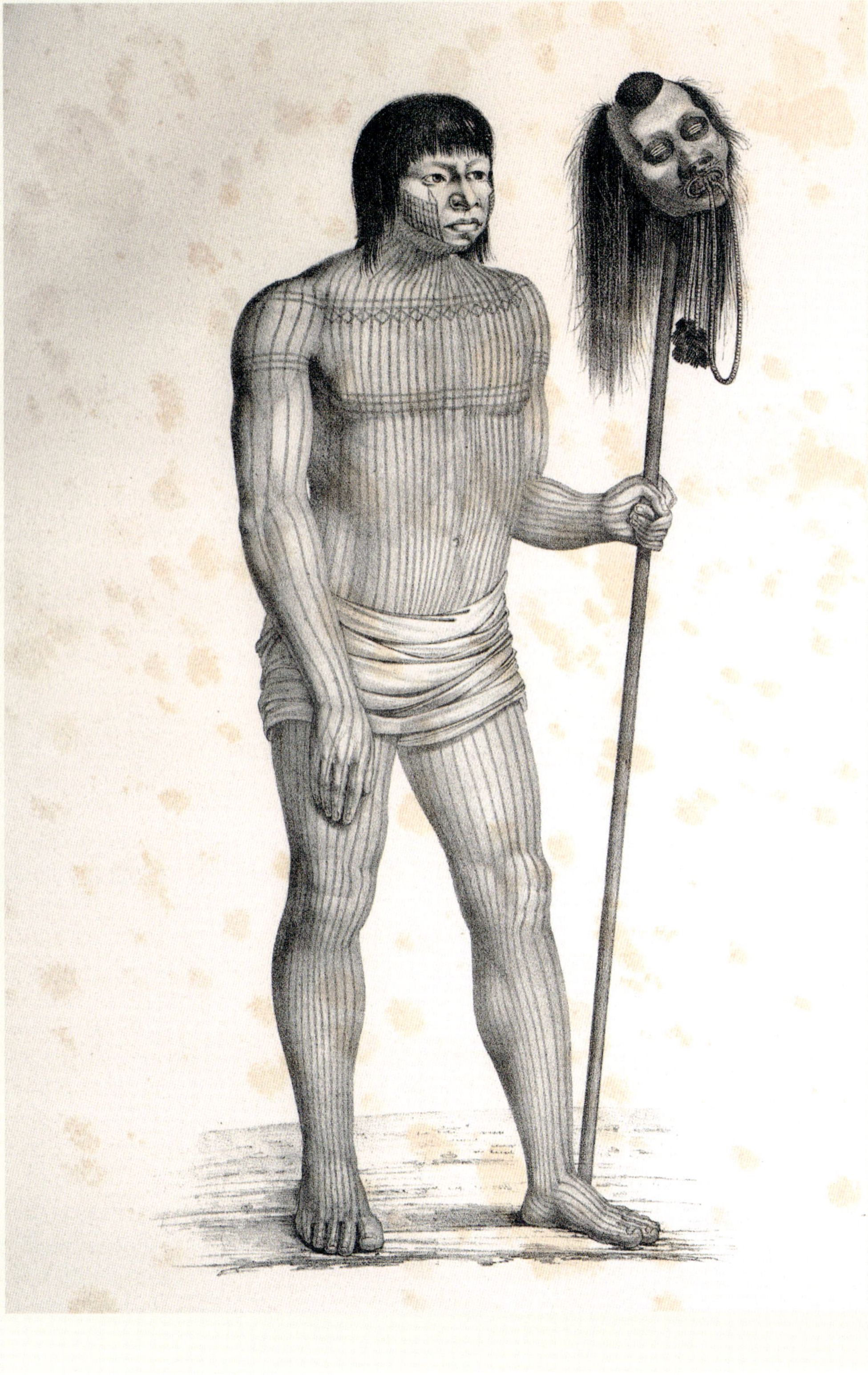

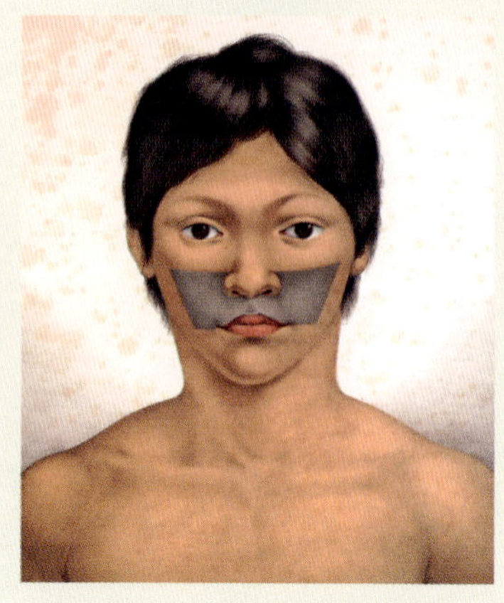

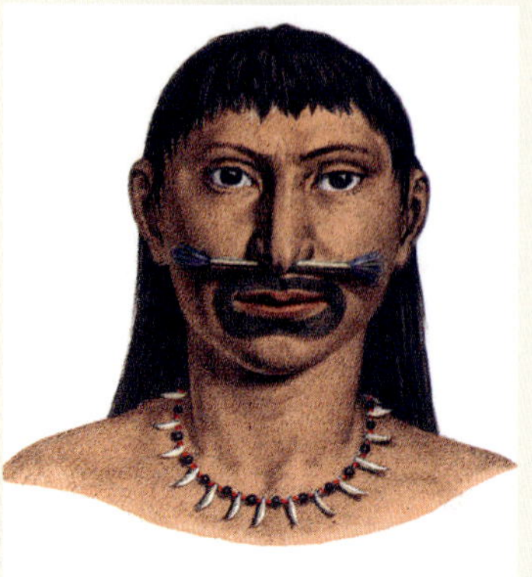

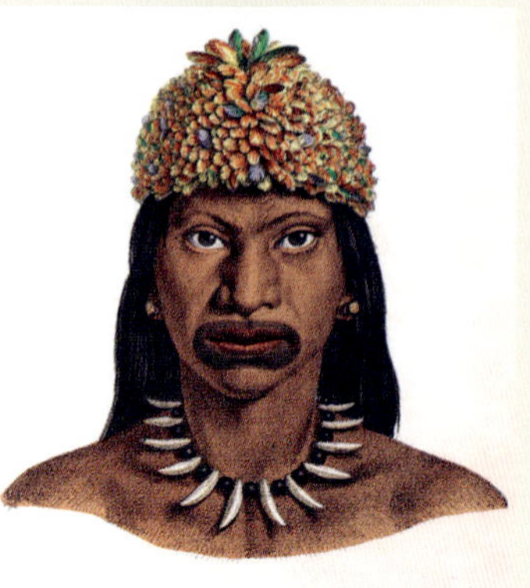

Near right Tattooed Yurí man, Brazil, *ca*. 1820. This Amazonian tribe no longer tattoos and is perhaps extinct.

Center right Tattooed Arara man, Brazil, *ca*. 1820. The Arara, who no longer tattoo, were the primary foe of the Munduruku of the Brazilian Amazon and were easily distinguished by the black circular tattoo placed around men's mouths.

Far right Tattooed Mawé man, Brazil, *ca*. 1820. The Mawé, who were formerly tattooed, were a traditional enemy of the Munduruku.

In the nineteenth century, perhaps the most famous Indigenous society in Amazonia was the Munduruku of central Brazil. Their notoriety stemmed from their prowess in headhunting and the embalming of trophy heads, which were avidly collected as curios by international museums.[17] The Munduruku, who speak a Tupian language, were also perhaps the most heavily tattooed Indigenous group of South America at that time. Oral histories indicate that their creator god and culture hero Karusakaibo originated the practice of tattooing as well as headhunting.[18] He set out to model his human representatives after himself, thus they were covered with linear arrangements of tattooed lines and other markings that were essentially bird plumes. Feathers were considered the "power centers" of birds and were especially charged with supernatural power. They were analogous to human hairs which, with their capacity for constant growth and renewal, were universally believed to be the point of concentration of the human spirit or soul.

The Suruí (also known as Paiter), who live on the Mato Grosso-Rondônia border of Brazil, are another Tupian-speaking people that practiced unique forms of tattooing until recent times. Face tattooing, however, abruptly stopped after sustained contact with outsiders around 1969, and elders have explained that the demise of the tradition was because the Suruí would now "live like Whites."[19] Traditionally, facial tattoos for men and women were received in public between the ages of twelve and twenty by one's mother's brother or grandfather and were part of coming-of-age ceremonies demarcating that the individual had achieved the capacities of his or her age (hunting, engaging in war or a ritual party, having sex, wearing certain adornments, drinking beer, etc.).[20] Since the tattooed person had now become a member of Suruí society, their *mixakoña*—a soul-like element—became fully activated. The *mixakoña* provided its owner with dream omens, and had the ability to act upon others, either on its own initiative or out of a shared (dreamt) decision between itself and its owner; for example, it could bring illness or cause accidents (snakebite, falling tree) to malicious people.[21]

Yet another Tupian-speaking tattoo group is the Apiaká. Prior to the twentieth century, they were the primary enemy of the Munduruku and were easily distinguished by the black rectangular tattoo placed around men's mouths after they had earned the

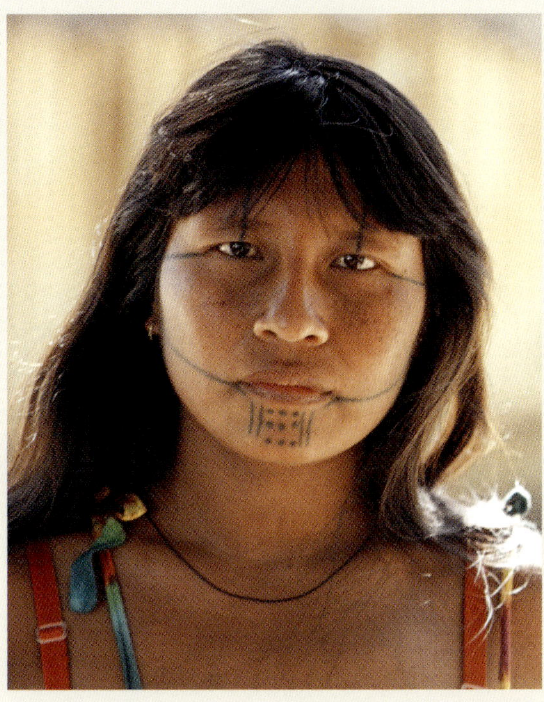

Tattooed Kayabí woman bearing a traditional facial design called *apejan*, Capivara village, Brazil, 2007.

right to eat human flesh, a practice that was meant to instill in them a spirit of courage.[22] Neighboring Indigenous men from other societies illustrated in the early eighteenth century also possessed similar mouth markings, but the functions of the markings have not been recorded in detail and these practices of tattooing became extinct toward the end of the nineteenth century.[23]

A related tribe to the Apiaká, the Urueu-wau-wau, continued their tattooing practices into the twentieth century and the facial tattoos worn by men today are very similar in their patterning. The facial tattoos of Urueu-wau-wau women resemble those of the Kayabí people of Brazil (i.e., single lines running above and beside the eyes) except for their chin patterning, which is geometric in form and was applied as part of marriage ceremonies. Apiaká men who had been initiated might have possessed name glyph tattoos on their arms or other body parts that were geometric, anthropomorphic, or zoomorphic and tied to an individual soul.

The Apiaká's linguistic relatives, the Kayabí, also consumed the boiled meat from trophy heads to give them spiritual strength. More details concerning Kayabí tattooing, which is an active tradition, are related later in this chapter (see page 98).[24]

In summary, the Indigenous Amazonian tattooing tradition focused upon permanently marking the transition from adolescence to adulthood and served as a tribal identifier, among other functions that are associated with the world of spirits and ancestors.

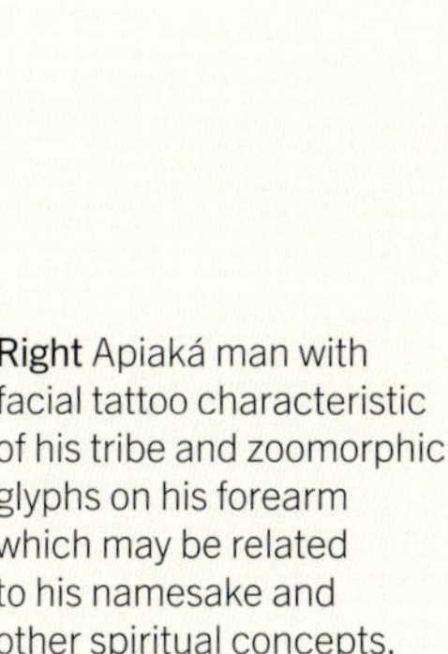

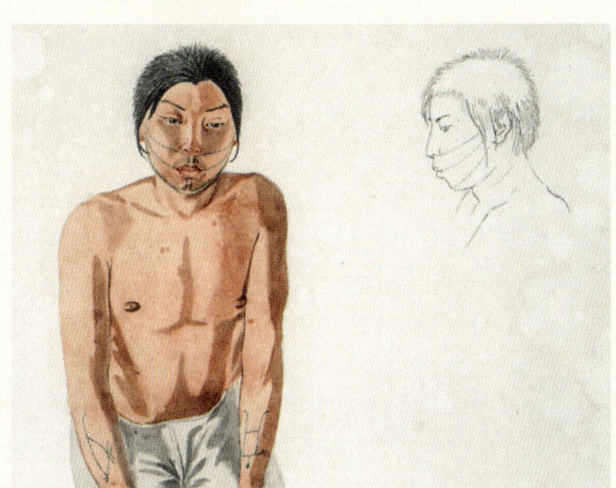

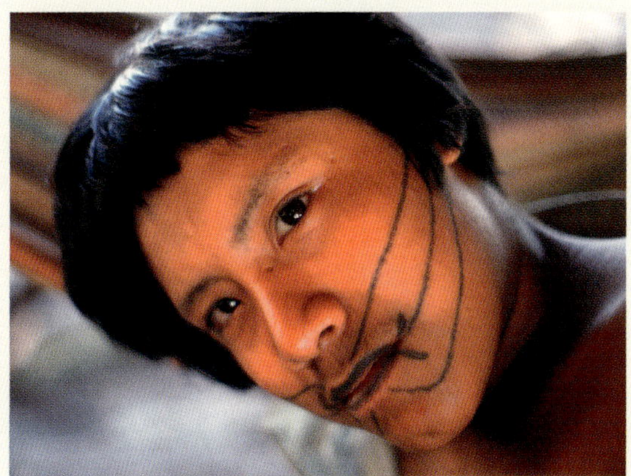

Right Apiaká man with facial tattoo characteristic of his tribe and zoomorphic glyphs on his forearm which may be related to his namesake and other spiritual concepts, Brazil, 1828.

Far right Man with facial tattooing, Rondônia state, Brazil, 1990. The Urueu-wau-wau recount in oral histories that they are descended from the blue-and-yellow macaw (*Ara ararauna*), and the characteristic facial tattoos of men represent the three facial lines that appear beneath the eyes of their avian ancestor.

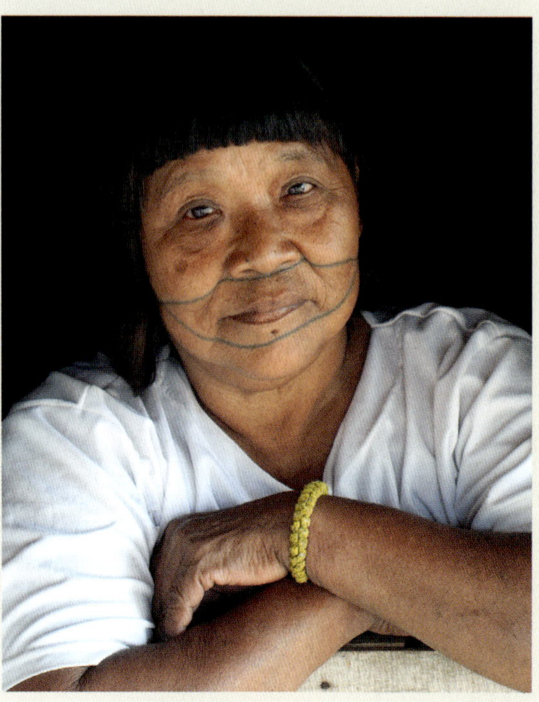

Tattooed Suruí woman displaying rite-of-passage tattoos, Brazil, 2010.

The Matsés and Other Tattooing Tribes

Compared to the Kayabí, far less has been written about the culture and especially the tattooing customs of the Panoan-speaking Matsés and Matis people of the Javari River valley, an isolated region that cuts an international border between Peru and Brazil. Until recently, both groups were collectively called "Mayoruna," a Quechua word meaning "water people," which was perhaps related to their custom of locating traditional settlements near rivers.

By most accounts, these tribes made "first contact" with the outside world around 1970, but pictorial evidence resulting from the German-sponsored von Spix and von Martius expedition to the region around 1820 indicates that the Matis may have been "discovered" much earlier (see illustration on page 81). Moreover, many Matsés have recorded in their oral tradition that they were forced to work as slave laborers by rubber tappers around 1900.

The Matsés are often referred to as the "jaguar people" due to the characteristic whisker-like labrets and tattoos that they wear on their faces. The Matsés revere the jaguar's strength and hunting prowess, and attempt to harness its power through body modifications they describe as "fearsome" and make them appear aggressive and formidable to other tribes in the region. The long stems worn underneath the lips of women have been said to symbolize prey hanging from the jaguar's mouth.

Although *chëshëcte* (tattooing) is no longer performed and today only seen on the faces and bodies of tribal elders, it was formerly closely associated with ethnic identity. For example, when warriors encountered a similarly facially tattooed individual while roaming the forest, they immediately knew they were of the same ethnic group and would not be killed.[25]

Matsés men also wore a band of teeth-like tattoos across their chests that some writers have misidentified as tally marks enumerating the number of human victims slain in battle. The Matsés have indicated that this was not the function of the tattoos, rather these types of tattoo represent feats of *ombo*, the Matsés word for "true bravery."

Although there are many tattooed Matsés living today and tattoo artists capable of creating the delicate designs, no one has received a traditional tattoo for several decades. Traditionally, tattoo pigments were created from the soot of burnt copal resin mixed with *genipapo* juice and pricked in the skin with a palm tree thorn, like

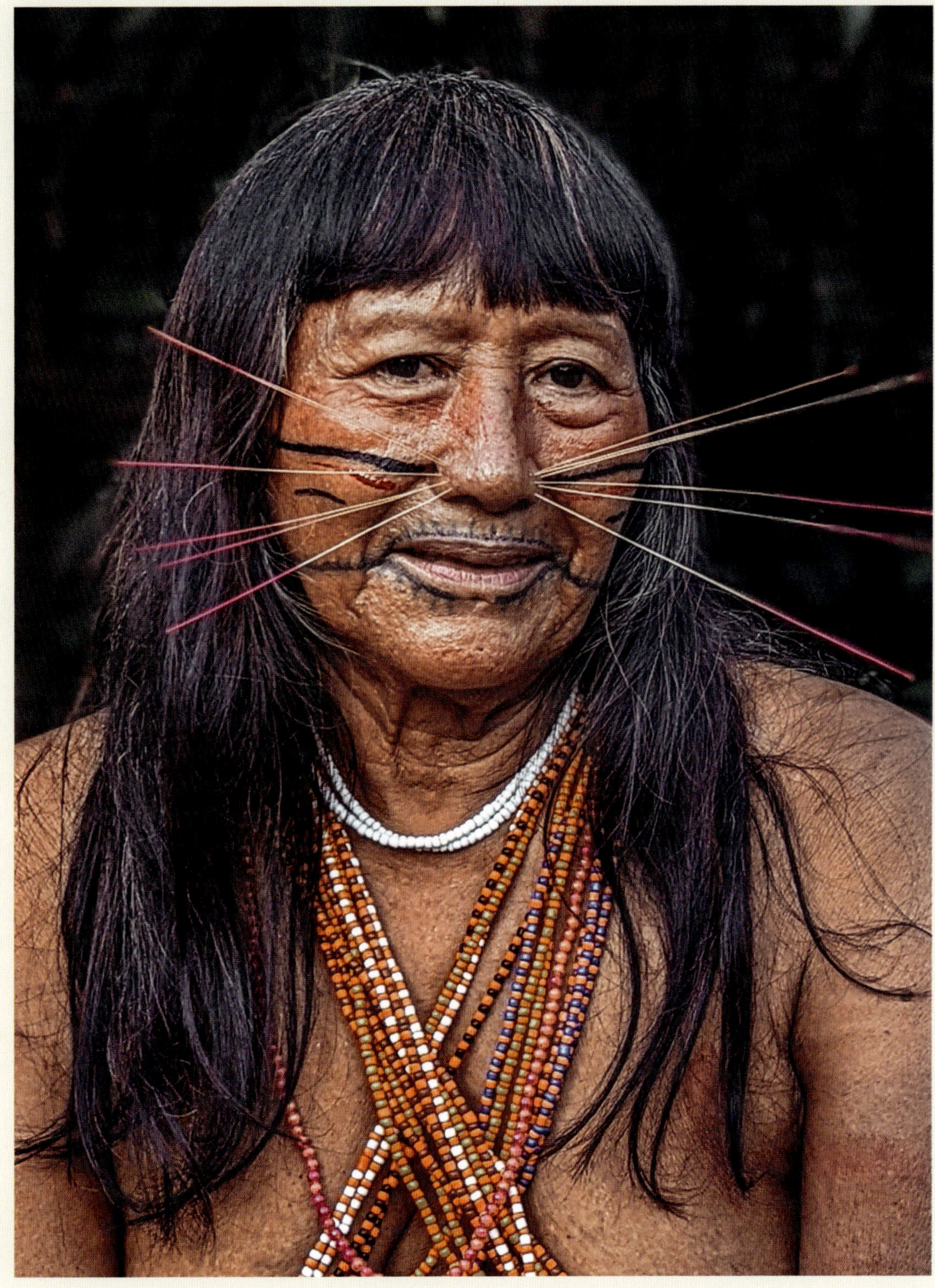

Tattooed Matsés woman,
Peru, 2021.

Matsés man with facial and chest tattoos, Peru, 2021.

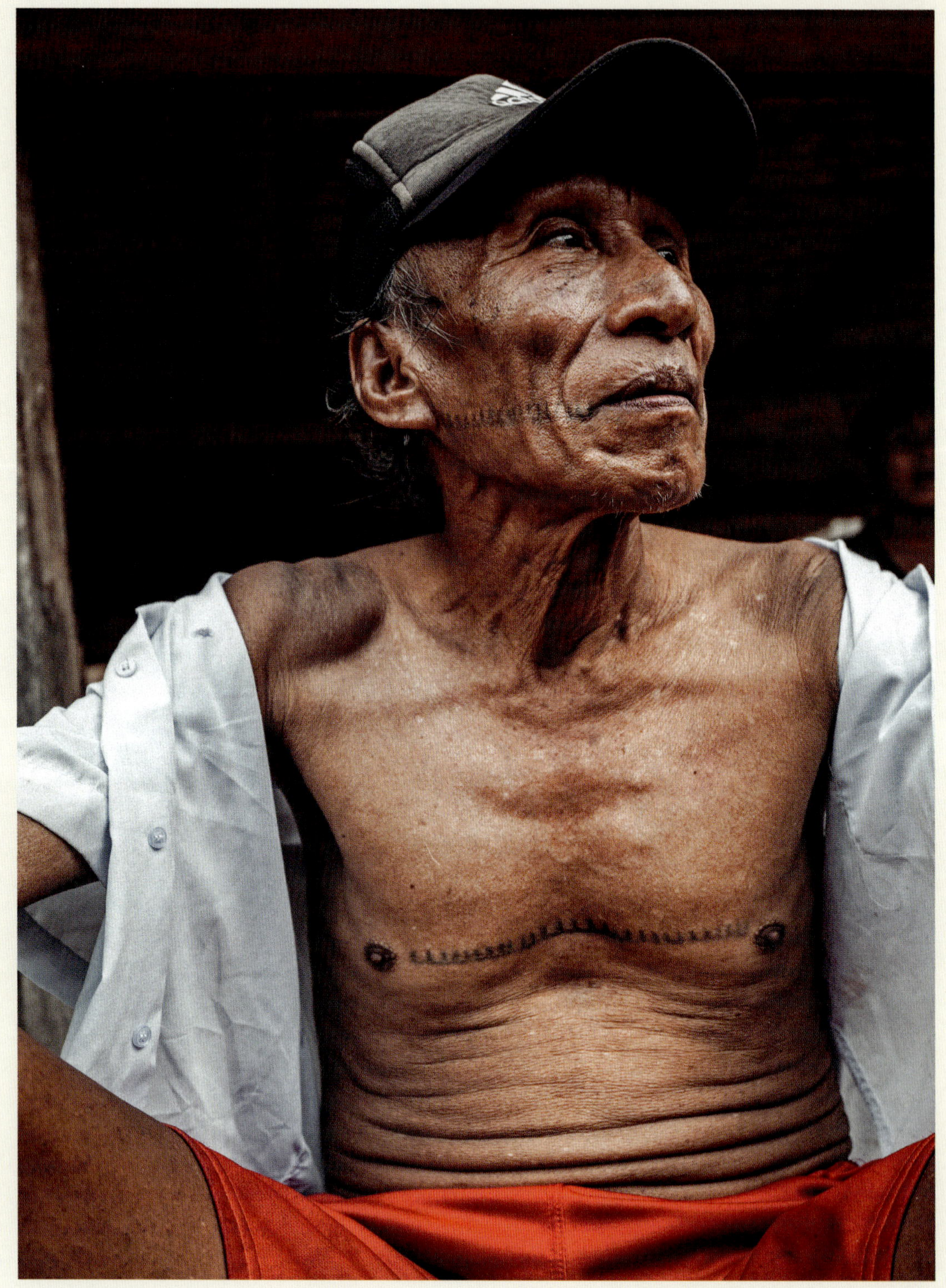

other Amazonian peoples who tattooed. Men worked as the tattooists and the freshly tattooed were not allowed to bathe until four days after they had received their permanent markings.

The neighboring Marubo people, who also speak a Panoan language related to Matsés and Matis, also used to practice tattooing, as did several other Panoan peoples. According to Brazilian anthropologist Elena Welper,[26] all of these peoples had facial tattoo variations, and although some of the patterns might look similar (e.g., Matsés and Marubo), there were subtle variations and these were recognized by each group as a distinct mark of tribal identity. Today, there are very few living tattooed Marubo, but at one time tattoos were considered to be a hallmark of what constituted a *yora koin* ("true person") in the eyes of the ancestors and acted as "cosmic passports," so that bearers could be recognized in the afterlife by departed family members.[27] Moreover, and speaking of their function as a mark of tribal identity, outside peoples who were not marked like the Marubo were considered *mokanawavo* ("people of poison"), a term used to primarily identify the Matsés and Matis.

Marubo tattoo was performed on young men and women between the ages of ten and fourteen years of age. The tattoos were created by two experienced women: while one pricked in the pigment, the other daubed the liquid pigment into the wound. Tattoo ink was created from a prepared mixture of a *mina* (local leaf), *twiwã* (local fruit), and *mei se* (pitch soot).[28] The Marubo used a kind of sedative to prepare for the pain of tattooing; this was made of *ape waka*—a fermented corn *caiçuma* (beverage)—which caused a drowsy state. Then, the pattern was stenciled onto the skin and piercing with a bundle of three to four peach palm or *mururumu* (*Astrocaryum murumuru*) thorns began. Once the tattoo was complete, the excess blood was wiped away and an herbal medicine was applied so that the fresh tattoo would heal quickly and not become infected.

There were other functions of Marubo facial tattooing. Like the Matis, Marubo elders have noted that the pain arising from piercing the skin enhanced one's strength and growth. Moreover, one of Welper's Marubo informants explained that facially tattooed women commanded *eseya* (respect), even when they traveled far away from their communities, because they had withstood the pain to look like and become an ideal member of the Marubo community.

Of Gold, Bone, and Wood: Prehistoric Tattooed Objects from Peru

South America boasts a rich tradition of tattooing practices among various prehistoric cultures as evinced by numerous mummified, tattooed human remains.[29] Moreover, thousands of ceramic portrait vessels produced by the Moche (50–800 CE) and other Andean civilizations likely depict tattooing traditions,but due to editorial considerations this section will focus on lesser-known tattooed human limbs from Peru handcrafted of bone, wood, and precious metals.[30]

Although the precise function of these enigmatic objects is not known, tattoos across the Indigenous universe outwardly anchored cultural identity, status, and genealogical ties.[31] In many cultures, tattoos transformed the human body into a ritual vessel that channeled spiritual and protective power across the planes of the living and the dead. Whether the prehistoric Andean peoples of Peru believed tattoos etched into manufactured bodily limbs helped carry their own bodies and tattoos safely into the afterlife is a matter of speculation. But as tattooed bodies recorded the experiences, abilities, achievements, and memories of human lives, they distinguished who a person was in the present world and presumably in the afterlife.

The iconography of pre-Columbian tattooed limbs parallels that found on mummies of the prehistoric Moche, Lambayeque (Sicán) (750–1375 CE), Chancay (1000–1476 CE), Chimú (1100–1470 CE), and other cultures of Peru. The visual compositions depicted on these objects of material culture are quite diverse,[32] consisting of geometric patterns featuring the step-fret motif, ocean waves,[33] avian forms, mountain peaks or stepped pyramids, as well as scenes of anthropomorphic and (possibly masked) zoomorphic personages carrying out rituals, oftentimes revolving around human sacrifice, the drinking of ritual substances, among other activities.[34] Indeed, images and archaeological evidence of human sacrifice are ubiquitous during the Moche and later Chimú periods, and it must be assumed that these practices were not rare or isolated occurrences; rather they must have formed a significant component of secular and religious life.[35]

References to these activities are especially prevalent on peculiar inlaid and

Hammered gold burial object in the form of a human hand with intricate tattoo motifs, Lambayeque (Sicán) culture, Peru, 800–1100 CE.

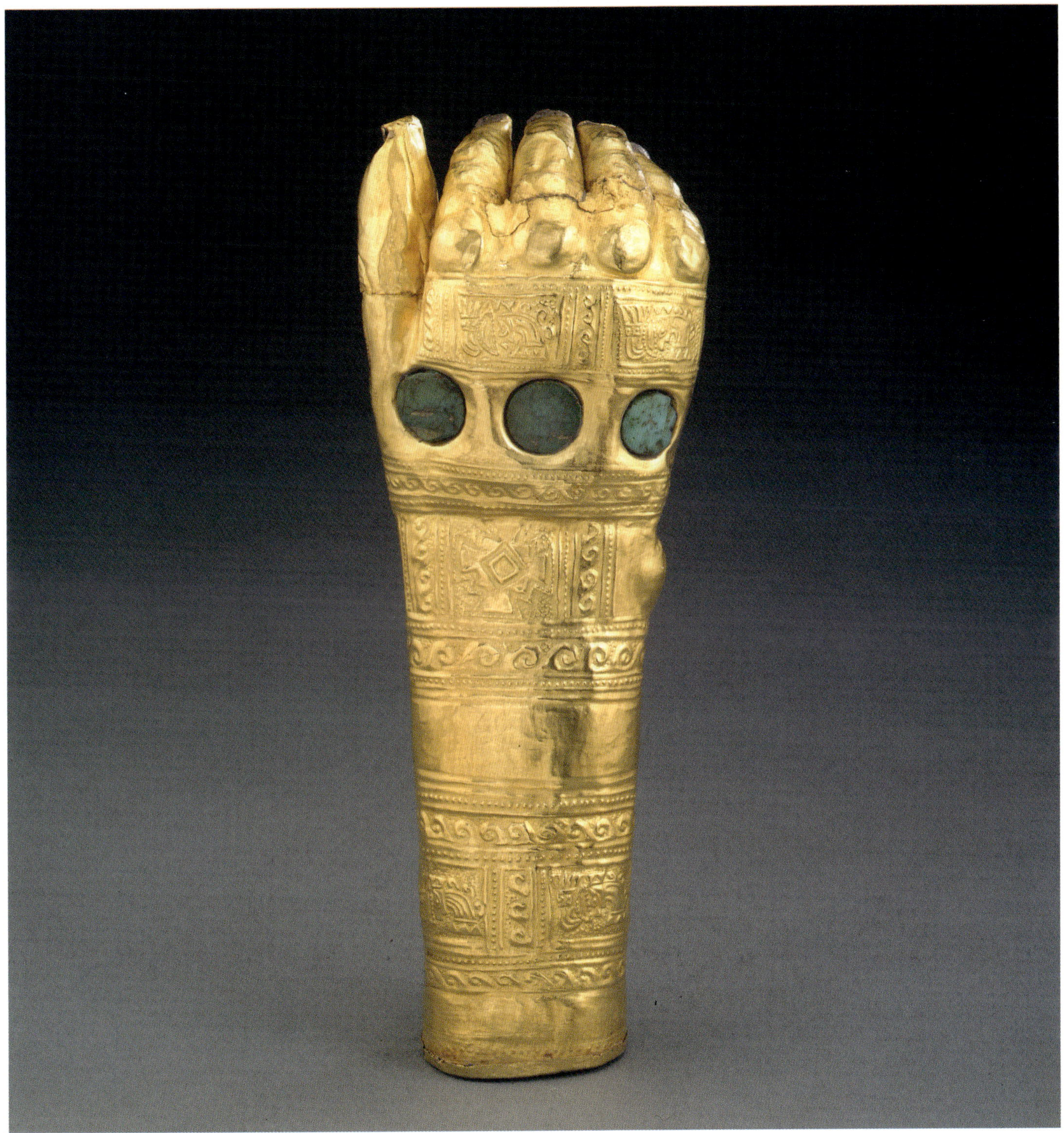

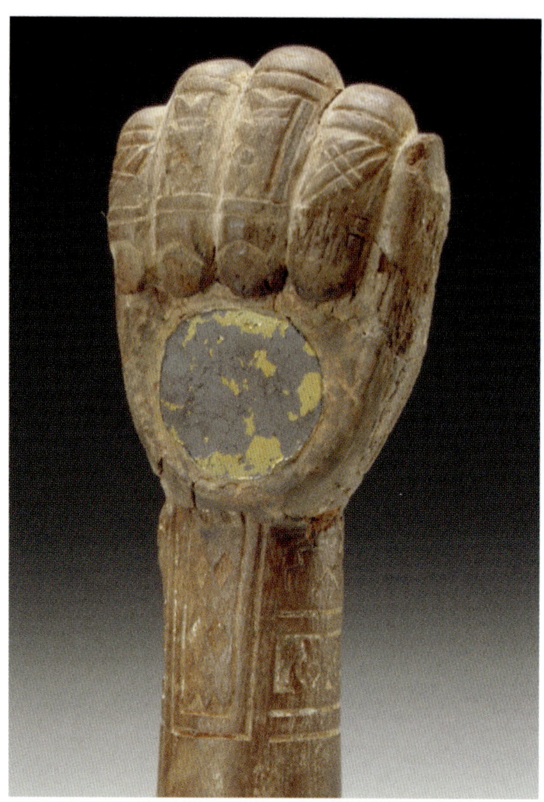

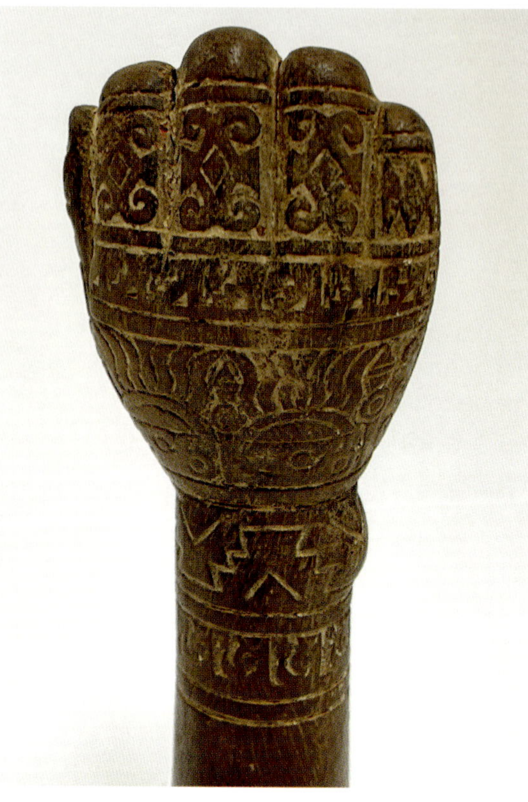

Far left and left Front and back of Chimú tattooed wooden hand with mirror, Peru, *ca.* 1100 CE.

Opposite Chimú silver panpiper vessel with malachite inlay and tattooed hands, Peru, *ca.* 1350 CE.

carved camelid (llama) bone Moche objects in the form of human arms. Of the eleven so-called "spatulas" held in museum and private collections worldwide, the designs carved into them replicate Moche tattoo designs found on mummies and include armed warriors, warclubs, supernatural figures, animals, and sometimes the hallucinogenic San Pedro cactus, as well as sacrificial victims.[36] Spatula handles resemble human fists, and in Moche art the "half-fist" – with protruding knuckle – symbolizes a mountain peak,[37] a geographical landmark that also appears as a tattoo on the hands (especially knuckles or mid-digits) of ancient Andean mummies and anthropomorphic vessels; sometimes these tattoos, which are generally comprised of five interconnected triangular elements, are accentuated with the head of a bird motif.[38]

The Moche, like the later Chimú and Inka, held complex rituals on mountaintops, often including human sacrifice. Although the function of these bone objects is not clear, they appear to have been used by priests, priestesses, or other sacred individuals in esoteric rites to transfer liquids, perhaps human blood or hallucinogenic substances, into the mouths of sacrificial victims or other individuals. To date, however, none of these spatulas have been tested for blood or hallucinogenic residues.

Chimú artisans also created wooden mirror handles in the form of carved human arms. One important example resides in the collections of the Minneapolis Museum of Art.[39] This object, dated to 1100 CE, is inscribed with tattoo iconography recurring on tattooed Chimú and Chancay mummies.[40] The lower wrist displays

Line drawing of Moche bone spatula.

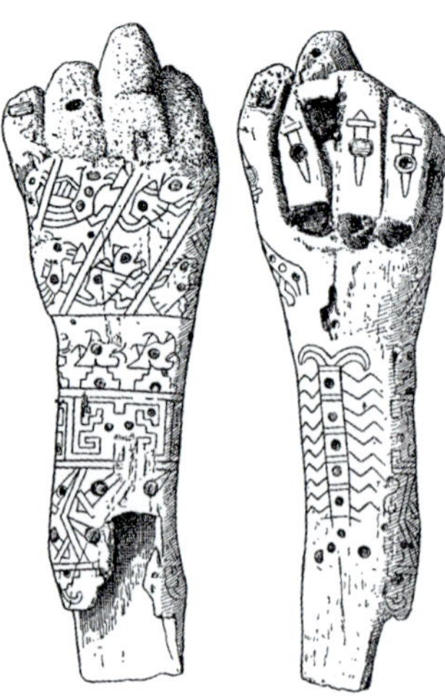

a banded series of birds, perhaps predatorial, looking upward in profile with beaks open and one wing outstretched above to render them in flight. The familiar five-stepped mountain or pyramid motif occurs as a band atop the avian series. Two plumed warriors holding warclubs are carefully carved into the base of the hand. Why they were carved into the hand is not known, but perhaps their inclusion was meant to offer some form of protection to the object's owner? A pair of horizontal lines separate the warriors from a narrow band of imagery depicting a series of stepped frets, some of which may feature curling waves: symbols of strength and possibly renewal. Two more horizontal lines of tattooing, which have been documented on mummies, divide the aforementioned band from three large tendril-like motifs with diamond centers and a fourth design on the mid-digit of the pinky. Certain Peruvian mummies display similar tattooed markings at this location,[41] and have been interpreted as spiders, which among Peru's ancient coastal peoples have been associated with rain (agricultural fertility), sacrifice, and regeneration.[42] The once-mirrored side of the hand shows other markings on the phalanges that have been documented as tattooing motifs among the Chimú, including pairs of tattooed horizontal lines, pairs of crossed lines, two one-eyed fish or shark designs with open mouths, and a vertically oriented band of geometric patterning with diamond shapes beginning on the lower forearm and running upward toward the now missing mirror.

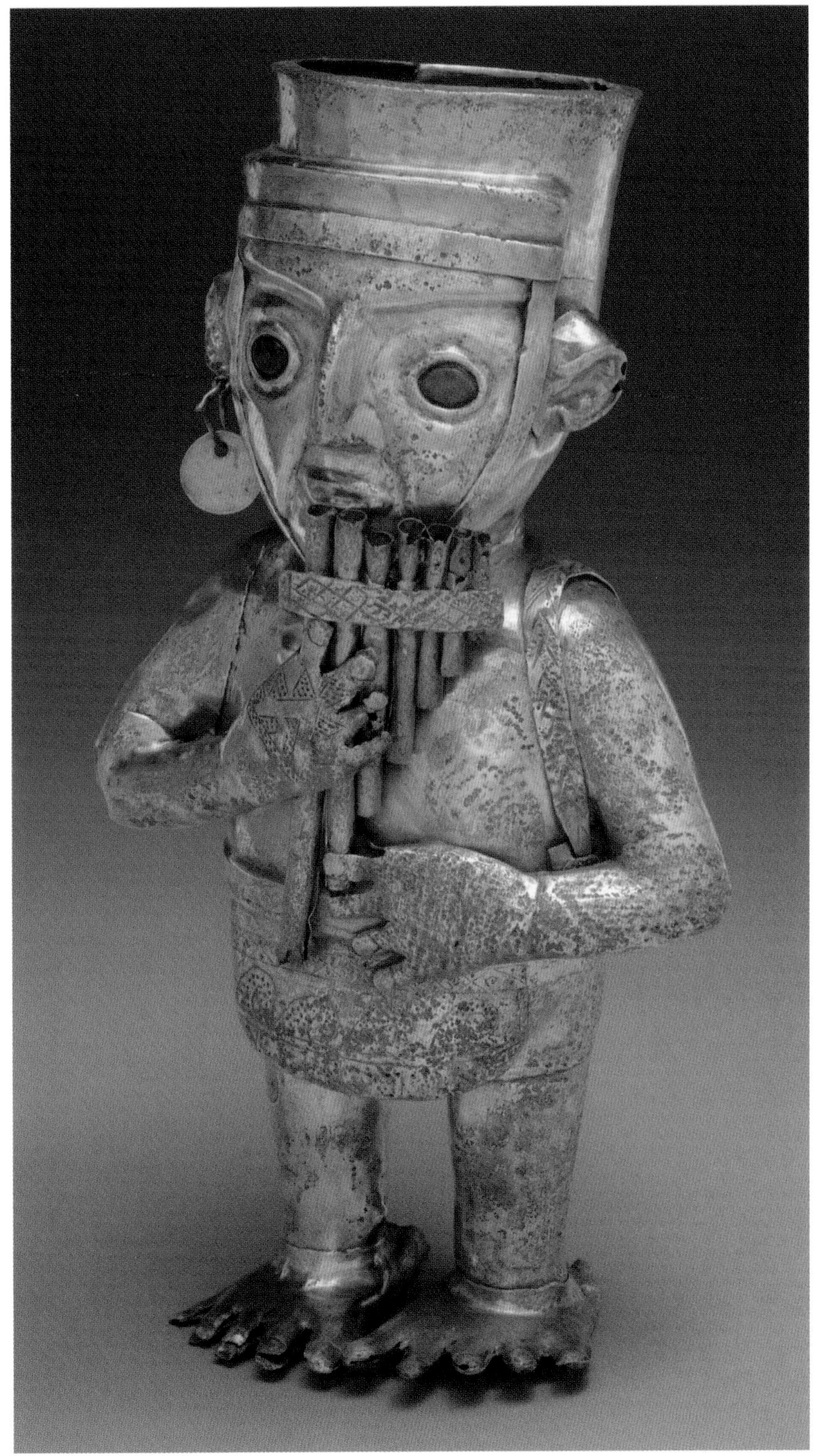

Tattooed Peoples of the Gran Chaco

Although tattooing in the Gran Chaco was replaced by less painful and infective forms of body painting in the early twentieth century,[43] its origins are tied to oral histories whereby deities instructed their people to be marked with tattoos to reaffirm their identity, morality, and devotion to the supreme being.

Lying 1,000 miles (1,600 km) to the south of the Amazon River, the Gran Chaco, which possibly derives its name from an Indigenous Quechua word meaning "hunting ground," is a vast arid plain located at the center of the South American continent. This very hot and semi-desertic lowland region covers portions of Argentina, Bolivia, and Paraguay, and is drained by several rivers. Overall, the entire region is barely suitable for human settlement, yet several groups of Indigenous people continue to live here despite the harsh climate and landscape. Although there are no reliable studies that delve into the meanings behind individual tattoo motifs and overall patterning, women generally displayed more abundant (facial) tattooing and it was truly exceptional to find men as profusely tattooed as women. However, in the 1960s, Swedish anthropologist Niels Fock, who worked among the Qom (Toba) people, maintained that tribal members could recognize an individual's *wikyi'* or family group and clan based on the tattoo patterns they wore.[44]

Prior to 1940, girls were first marked on their foreheads when five to seven years old, and with the passing of the years they received additional tattoos consisting of small circles, crosses, half-moons, and lines on their faces. By the time a girl reached maturity, her facial tattoos were finally completed, at which time she was eligible for marriage.

Tattoo artists were almost always older women. They first traced the outline of the design on their client's face (or other body part) with crushed charcoal obtained from *algarroba* (*Prosopis nigra*) or other sources, mixed with water.[45] Then the tattooist punctured the facial skin with a small bundle of cactus thorns or a single bone awl[46] dipped in the liquid pigment mixture, which also contained the artist's saliva and was believed to have apotropaic properties. Among the Qom (Toba) people, tattooing needles for hand-poking were procured from the *lagadik-leé* or *Stetsonia coryne* cactus,[47] tools that the 'Weenhayek (Mataco-Noctenes) call *nootshànekkya'*, a term used today for any kind of "writing instrument."[48] After a few pricks, the tattooist rubbed more pigment into the skin, which began to swell, and a steady stream of blood ran out of the wounds.

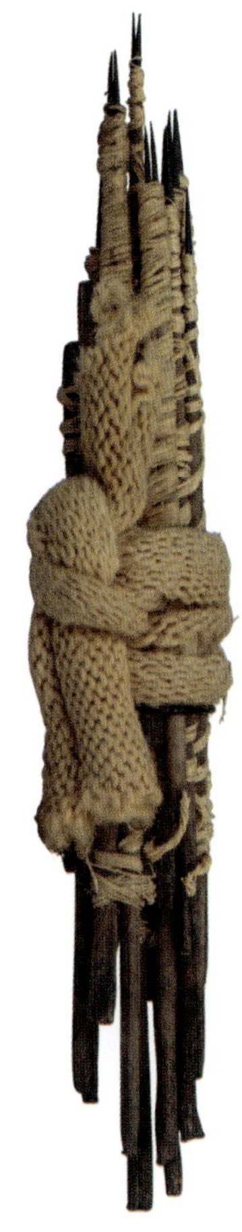

Opposite Qom tattooing needles, 2 in. (5 cm) in length, *ca*. 1930.

Right Qom woman of Argentina with facial tattooing, *ca*. 1905.

Far right Tattooed Pilagá woman of the Gran Chaco, *ca*. 1920.

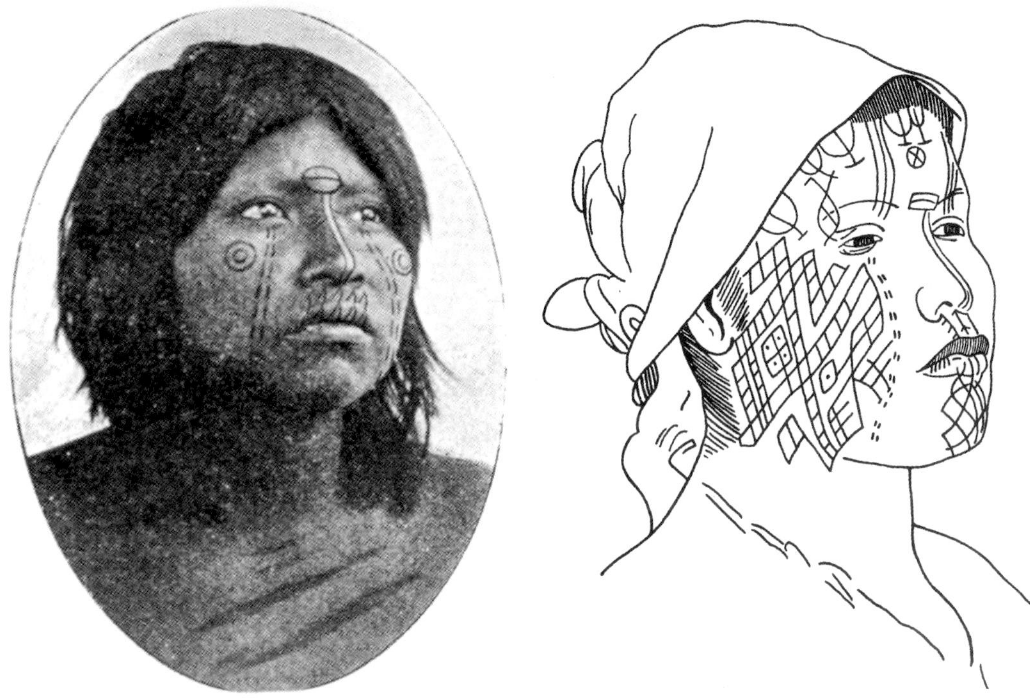

Among the Qom, 'Weenhayek, and Chorote of the Gran Chaco, prior to the tattooing rite, a young girl was kept secluded in her family's home for a period of four to five days and her face and entire body were carefully covered (or painted) to prevent lurking local spirits from harming her. The girl was obliged to fast strictly, ingesting only vegetable products. Sometimes she was permitted to uncover herself and exit the dwelling, but only if she moved to the center of a dance circle where a group of men (Qom) or women (Chorote) wielding deer hoof rattles attempted to shield her from the incorrigible spirits to whom she was exposed for the moment.

Food restrictions were tied to local Indigenous concepts. Particular foodstuffs, especially those that were associated with blood in their raw state (like meat and fish) and that were believed to attract evil spirits, were prohibited from being ingested due to the fear of a spirit entering into the body with the food itself, causing madness. Moreover, specific prey animals (armadillo, peccary, rhea, etc.) were associated with "spirit masters" that, if offended, could either bring illness to the community or cause the game animals to disappear. The meat of predatory animals was particularly forsaken, especially if that species performed a key symbolic role in oral history (e.g., jaguar, puma, hunting dogs, particular birds, etc.) or if the predatory or prey animal was one believed to "share immortality with men [and women]."[49]

In 1750, the Jesuit missionary Martin Dobrizhoffer provided a rare illustrated, first-hand account of the tattooing ritual among the now extinct Abipón. His observations follow the general Chacoan pattern, whereby the female initiate was secluded in her family's dwelling and compelled to abstain from eating meat, fish, and other sorts of food, and was only allowed to feed upon a small amount of fruit that grows on brambles and conduces much "toward cooling the blood."

The female client laid her head upon the artist's lap, generally an elder woman, and over the course of multiple tattooing sessions that lasted four to five days she shed much blood, sweat, and tears, returning every day until the face, arms, and breasts were full of tattoos. If the tattoo client moaned or complained too often, or attempted to escape from the tattooist's lap, she would be pinned down and told by the irritated old lady: "Enough of this cowardice, you are a disgrace to our Nation, just because I am tickling you with a few spines. Don't you know that you are the descendant of those who had their pleasures and glory in being wounded? You should be ashamed of yourself for being a timid little creature!"[50]

Dobrizhoffer's account is important because it illustrates that tattooing was a timeworn Indigenous practice central to local concepts

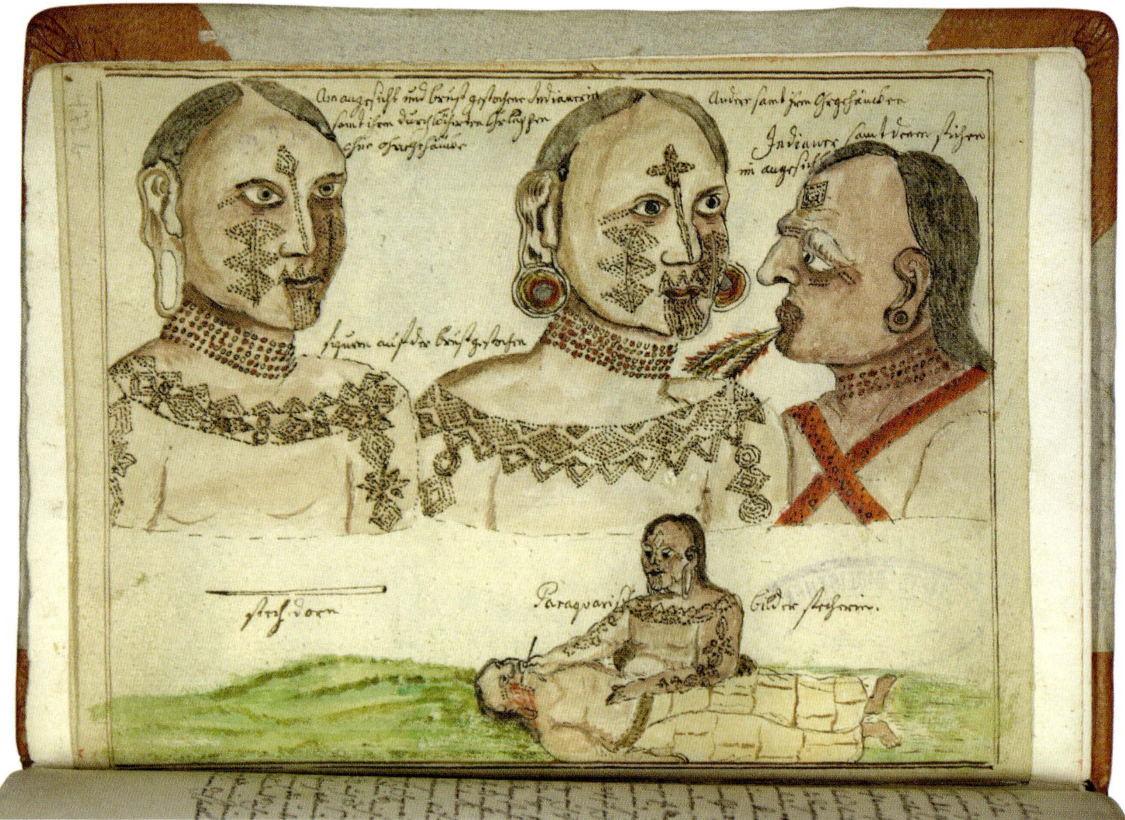

Mocoví tattoos and a female tattooist at work, *ca.* 1750.

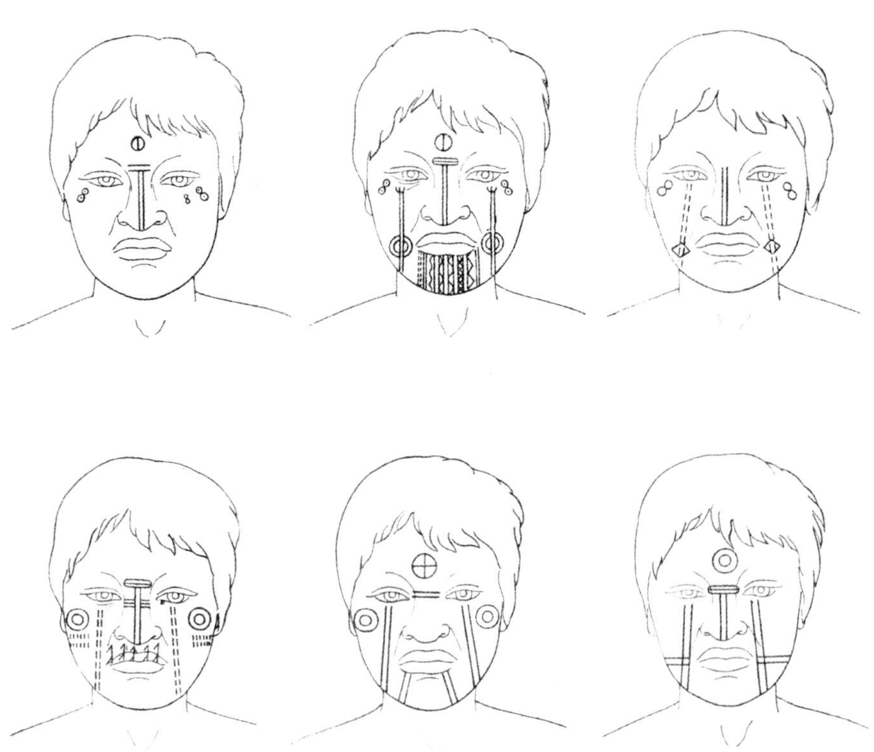

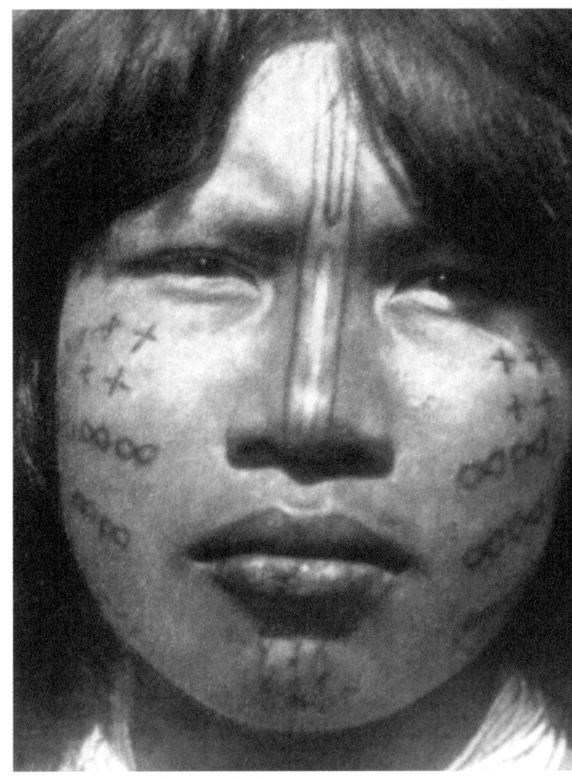

Above (top row) Chorote women's facial tattooing, Argentina, *ca.* 1900.

Above (bottom row) 'Weenhayek women's facial tattooing, Argentina, *ca.* 1900.

Above right Tattooed Lengua woman of the Gran Chaco, *ca.* 1930.

of ancestry, identity, and cultural pride. The oral histories of the Qom, who today speak a related language and possess community members with Abipón bloodlines, relate similar findings. Within Qom religious beliefs, tattooed marks on the body are inscribed as a sacred pact that affirms, on the one hand, social belonging and, on the other, friendship with the supreme being and creator Qad'ta'á. In a story about the Qom shaman and culture hero Patagon, the following was revealed: "The Supreme Being, with his finger, has tattooed you. And just as He tattooed you, you will tattoo all your children and all those who want to be faithful to Him. His face and his chest and his arms and his legs you will tattoo. And in this way, they will be the People of the Tattoo, the People of the Pact. And whoever does not get a tattoo will certainly not be counted among his children nor will they be part of my People."[51]

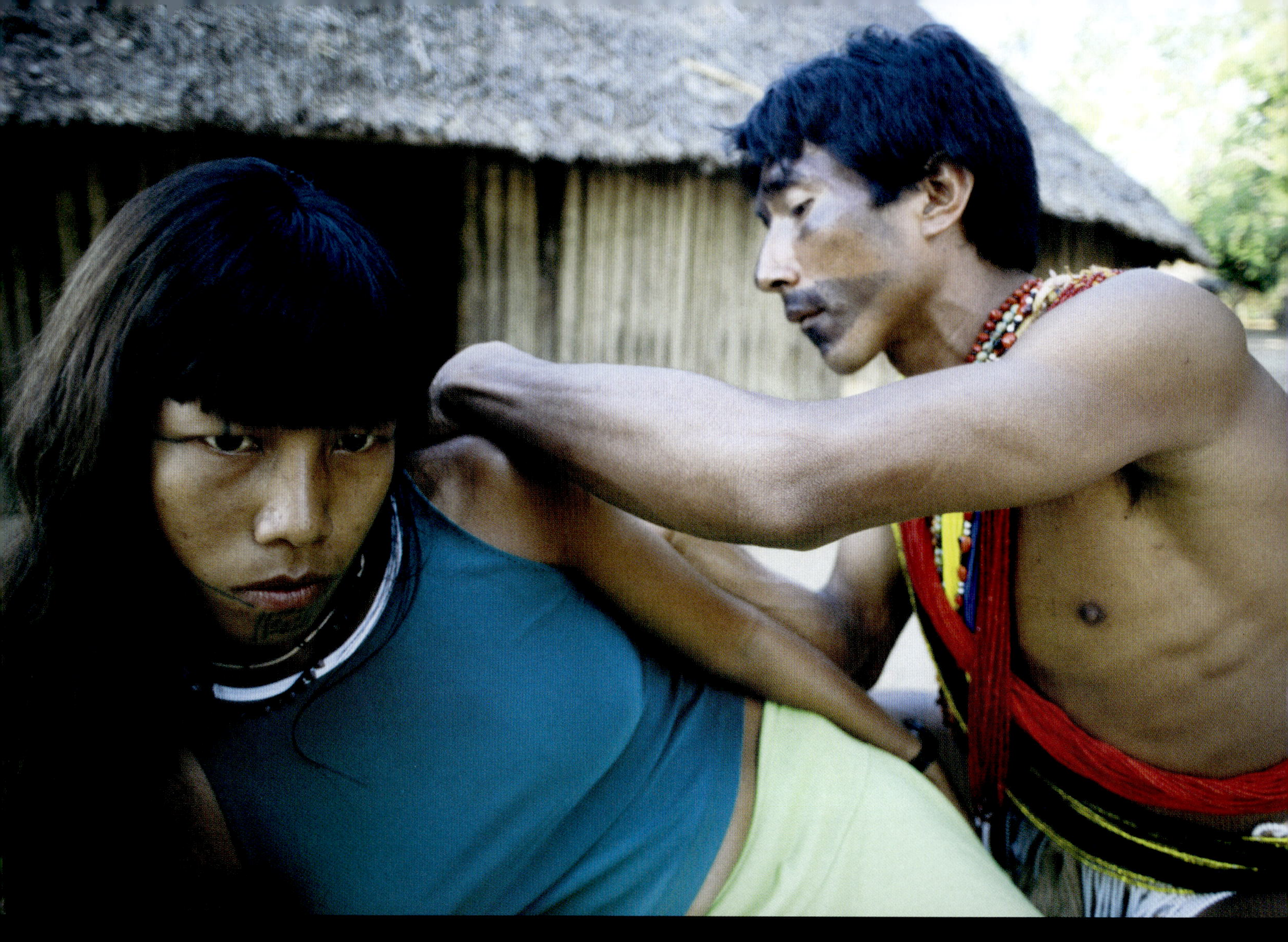

The Art of Kayabí Tattoo

Opposite Kayabí tattooist Jemy tattooing his client Silvana's arm, Capivara village, Brazil, 2007.

Right The wife of Kayabí tribal elder Javari, Brazil, 2007. She is one of only a handful of elder women in Capivara village who wears the facial tattoos of her ancestors. She was tattooed in the 1950s in the traditional homeland of the Kayabí, the Rio dos Peixes, before the tribe migrated to the Xingu Reserve.

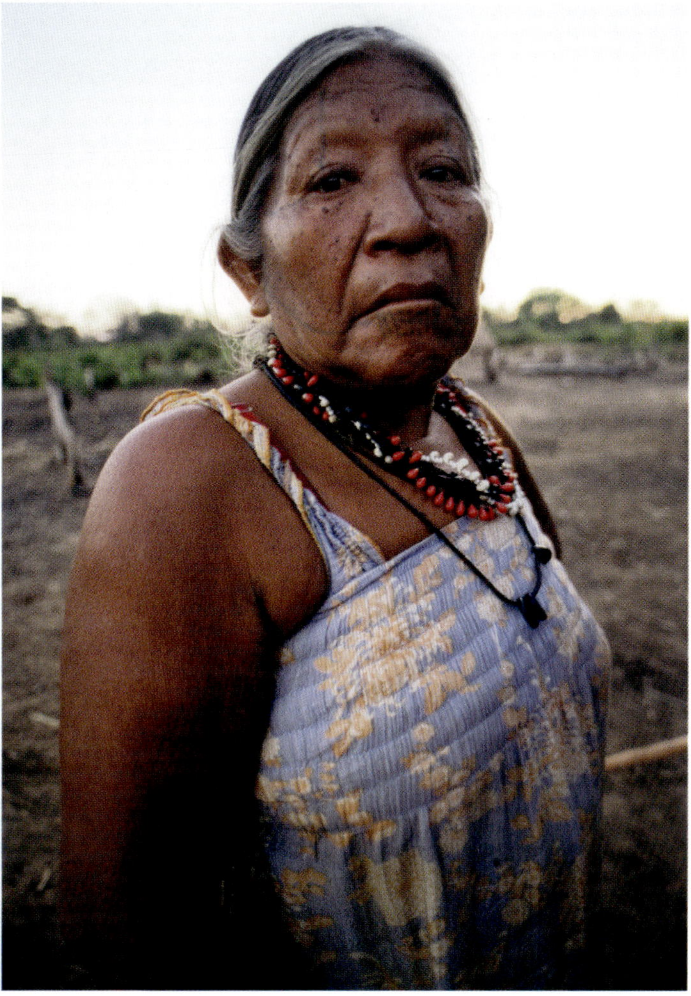

Numerous Indigenous peoples living in the dense Amazonian jungles of South America practiced tattooing. Some groups tattooed for medicinal purposes or to ward away evil spirits; others inserted designs into their bodies to show success in battle or to venerate or imitate the cultural heroes of the past.

Still more attempted to transform themselves into predatory animals or gain spiritual guardians with their ritual markings, while others believed that their ancestral marks transformed "girls" into "women" and "boys" into "men."

Today, however, there are perhaps less than twenty tribes that continue to tattoo or wear the marks of their ancestors, including the Matis, Matsés, Karajá, Ikpeng, Kayabí and presumably "uncontacted" peoples who live in remote and inaccessible parts of the Amazonian hinterlands.

Among the Kayabí, who today live in the Xingu Indigenous Reserve in the State of Mato Grosso, Brazil, two tattooists continue to ply *-jupot* (tattoos) to both men and women via the timeworn practice of hand-poking human skin. Aspiring Kayabí tattoo artists, who were

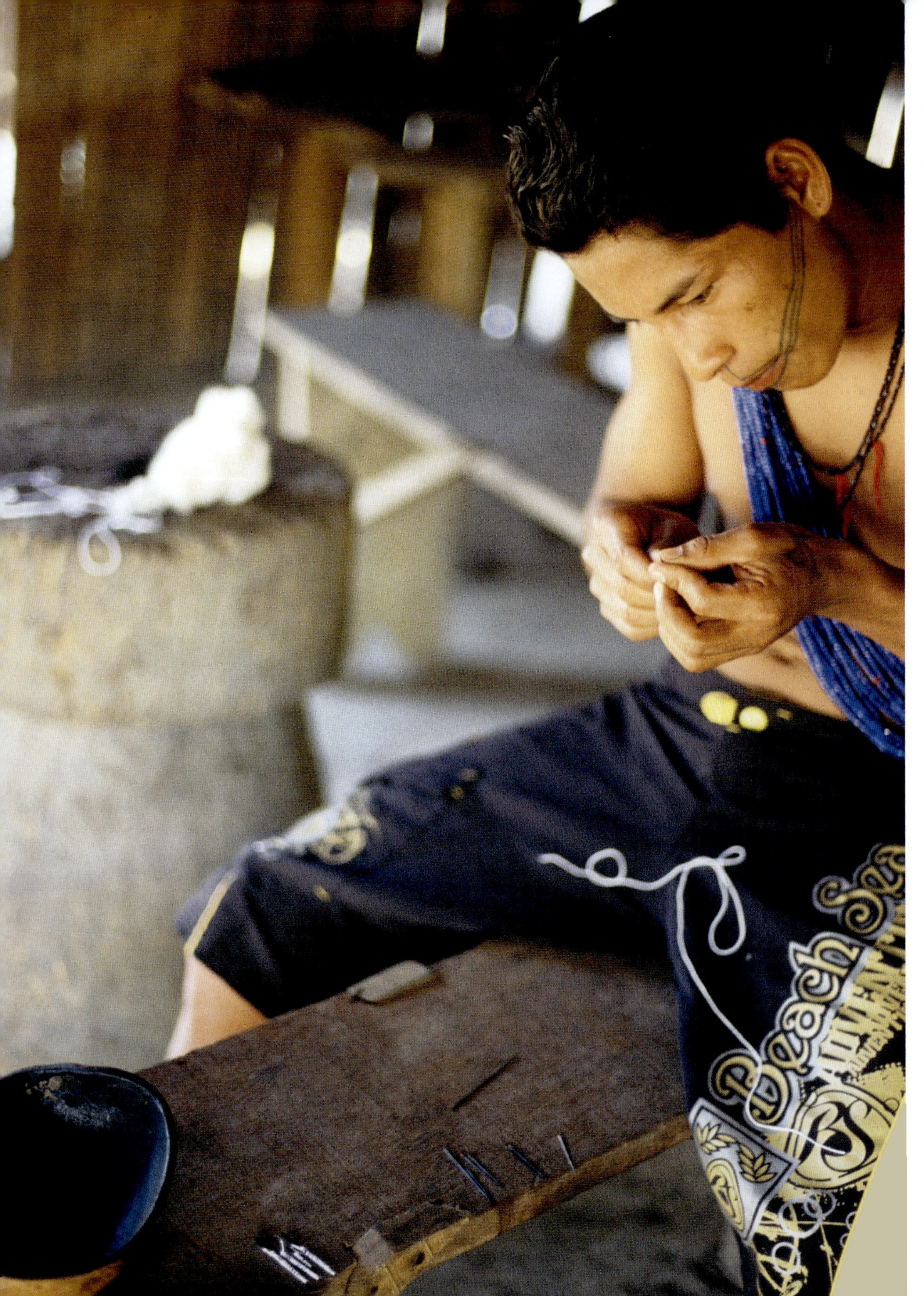

Kayabí tattooist Kurapi preparing his tools for an upcoming tattooing session, Capivara village, Brazil, 2007.

traditionally male, usually apprenticed under a tattoo master for months and even years learning the requisite skills and all about the raw materials needed to prepare the tattooing needles and pigments derived from various trees growing in the jungle. Tattoos were applied with the long thorns of the tucum (*Astrocaryum vulgare*). Two such thorns were wound together with a piece of homespun native cotton thread. The depth of the thorn pricking was controlled with another piece of cotton thread wound near the bottom of the thorn. The small reservoir that was created between the tips of the two needles held the tattoo pigment, which was a resinous material obtained from slicing the trunk of the *ipau-ip* tree, burning it, and mixing it with charcoal and water.[52] Because the *ipau-ip* tree is rare in some regions and difficult to identify, the sap from the rubber tree was often used as a substitute: although it only worked if mixed with the correct amount of water.

Jemy and his cousin Kurapi Kaiabi of Capivara village represent the new generation of Kayabí tattooists. Jemy was apprenticed by his uncle, the tattooist Yxyt, who was responsible for the revival of Kayabí tattooing in the late 1980s and early 1990s after his people moved to the Xingu Reserve from their traditional homelands on the Rio dos Peixes to escape the exploits of rubber tappers and farmers who were stealing their Indigenous lands.

According to Jemy, Yxyt was deeply fascinated by the tattooing traditions of his people at an early age. His father was a great warrior and he learned many of the traditional tattooing designs from him. Combining this knowledge with interviews of Kayabí elders who lived in several villages, Yxyt compiled a vast "directory" of names and designs which he kept locked away in his memory. As Jemy told the author, "He saw that our customs were disappearing before us when most Kayabí didn't seem to care. He was a visionary, and a role model. He then began to give traditional facial tattoos to some of the girls and boys in the Xingu. And around 1995, he tattooed Kurapi and some of the girls here in Capivara village – these were his last works of art. No one had been tattooed in the Kayabí style since the early 1950s, and this was a great achievement!"

But suddenly, the Kayabí tattoo renaissance came crashing to a standstill with the death of the master in 2003. "Yxyt was not an old person, he was forty years old, a young man when he was murdered by *blancos* [Brazilians]," Jemy said. "When he went back to our homeland in the Rio dos Peixes to urge our people to return to our traditional practices and to fight the people taking our ancestral lands, he disappeared after visiting a *blanco* bar one night. The white people killed him, and his body was never found. He didn't have enough time to pass on to his apprentices all of his secrets, so a lot of information was buried with him, including information on our traditional name-glyph tattoos, which have been replaced by Portuguese letters and names."

Traditionally, when Kayabí adolescents completed their initiation rites under the watchful eyes of their elders, they received a tattooed name glyph on their legs, arms, or chest which was embodied with a new soul. Interestingly, several early drawings of other Tupian speaking peoples of the Amazon (e.g., Tubinambá, Apiaká) are depicted with glyph-like markings closely resembling Kayabí glyph tattoos and perhaps speak to related, but as of yet unstudied, traditions and beliefs. Notwithstanding, this soul became permanently attached to the individual when he or she was tattooed with the corresponding glyph. The names and tattoo glyphs were provided by a *pajé* (shaman). The powerful Kayabí *pajé* Tuiarajup told me: "In my spiritual dreams,

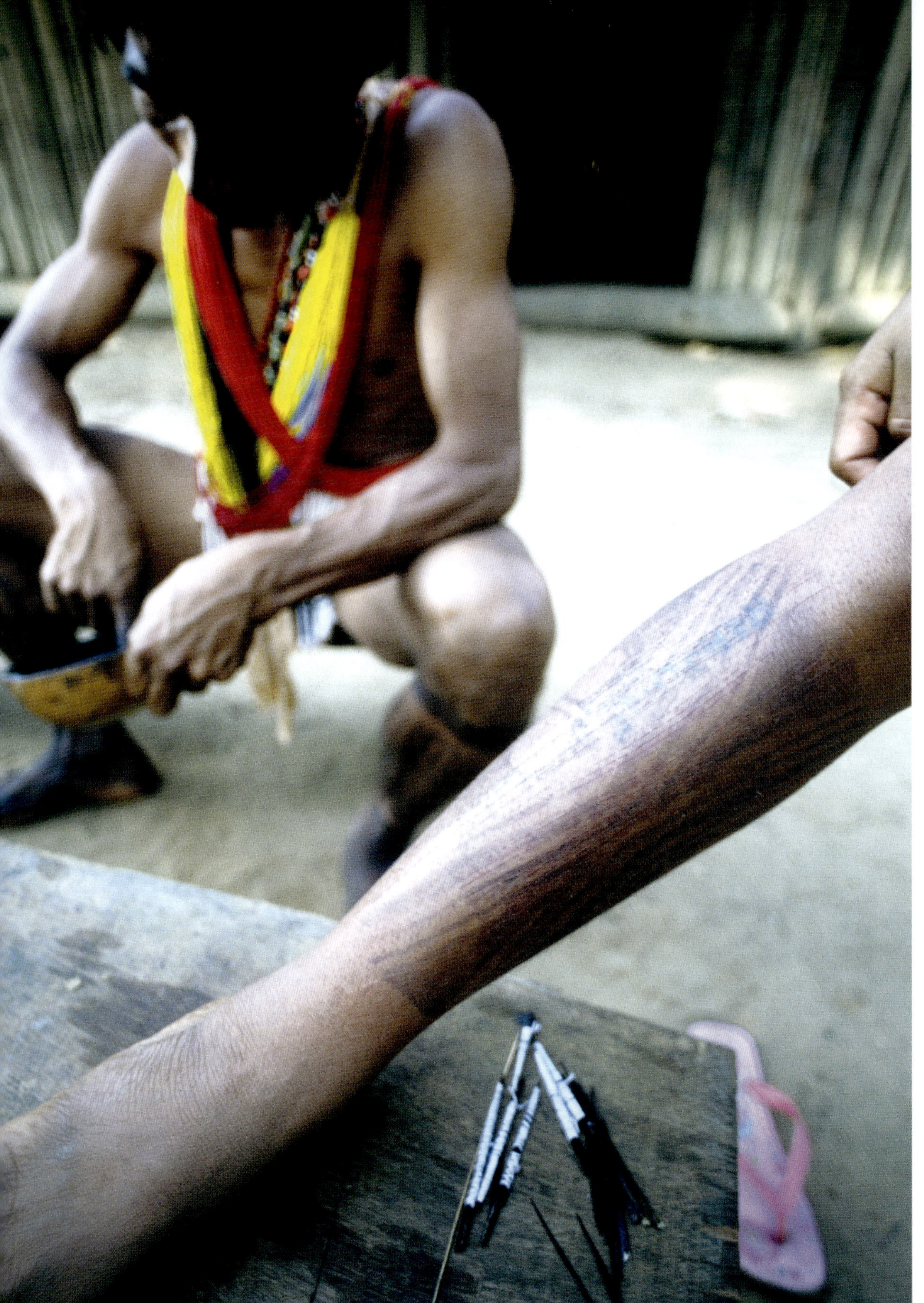

Tattooing needles, "scratch" marks, and name-glyph tattoo, Capivara village, 2007. Traditionally, the Kayabí used a cutia or agouti-tooth scratcher called a *paratsi* to release "bad blood" during ritual purification ceremonies.

Right Kayabí man with frog glyph tattooed on his arm, Capivara village, Brazil, 2007. The frog tattoo is related to a lineage of spirit helpers (*mait*) and is worn as a protective device.

each spirit, which could be ancestral or *mait* ('spirit master' of an animal), provides me with a different name symbol or glyph which will become the tattoo we place on the body. Each symbol has a spirit attached to it, and sometimes the spirit of the name even appears before me. You know, these spirits also have tattoos on their bodies, and the name and its associated design must be respected; otherwise, it will bring grave danger or even death to the wearer," he said.

After a Kayabí individual was initiated, that person was acknowledged as having the capacity to *-kwaap* (understand) the world more fully. In turn, that specific individual had learned how to interact with "Others" of various sorts: other ethnicities when traveling abroad, other spirits (sometimes ancestral), and even other families into which one might marry. Through these interactions with Others, personal knowledge of them grew to the point where the person began to assume some of their attributes, such as their ways of speaking, emotional states, or even their behaviors. In

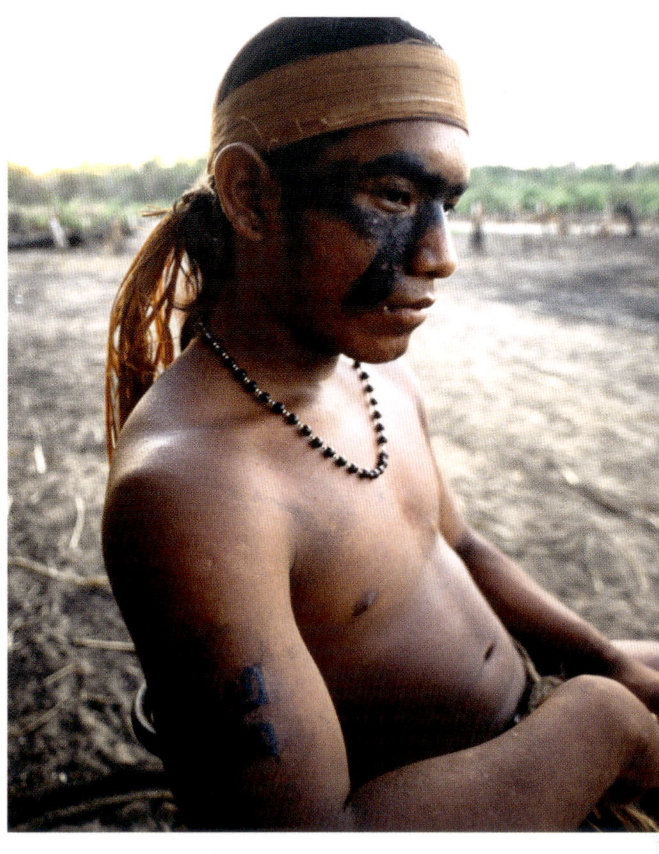

Far right Apiaká man with facial tattoo characteristic of his tribe and zoomorphic glyphs on his forearm which may be related to his namesake and other spiritual concepts, Brazil, 1828.

Right Early twentieth-century drawing depicting Kayabí name-glyph tattoos on forearm, obtained through the dreams of old shamans. Similar tattoos were also applied to the legs and chest.

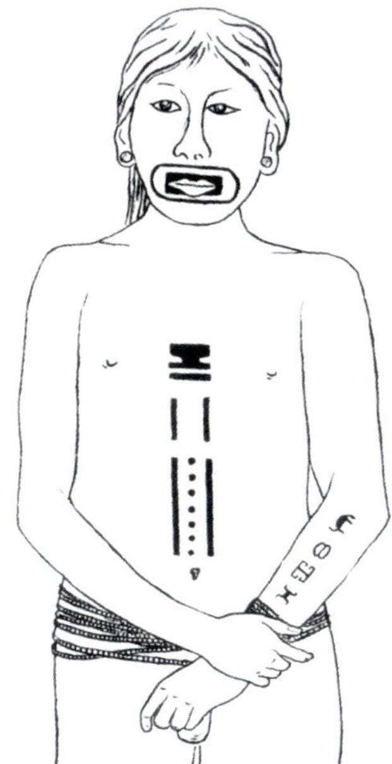

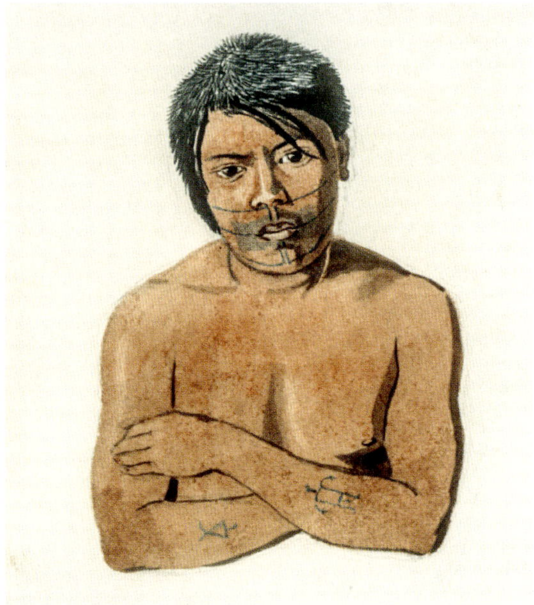

such cases, they were usually given another new name derived from an ancestor, an animal, or spirit being they resembled in thought, action, or appearance.

Jemy reflected: “Today, I believe that not all of the young people receive their soul because they are not tattooed. Therefore, I am worried that their souls will become confused, and if they are left untreated this soul-loss can cause death, sickness, or even trouble for the community. If we don’t tattoo anymore, we will be out of our tradition and that is unacceptable. That is why I am conducting a deep study to gather the glyph meanings from existing elders and to tattoo them again.”

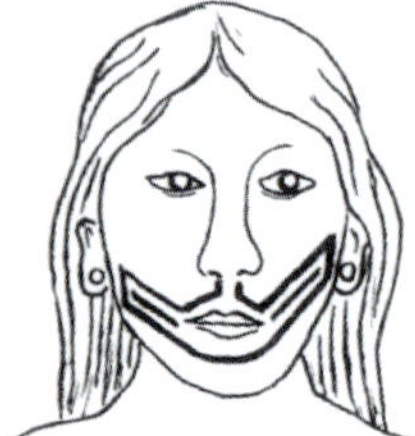

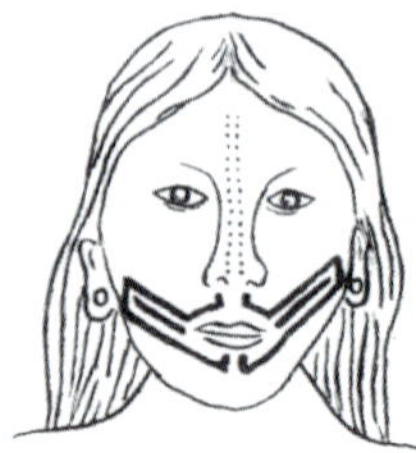

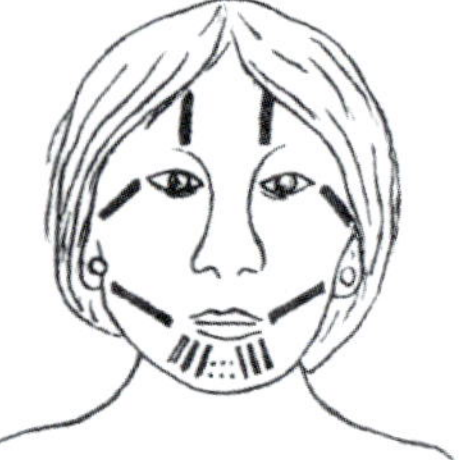

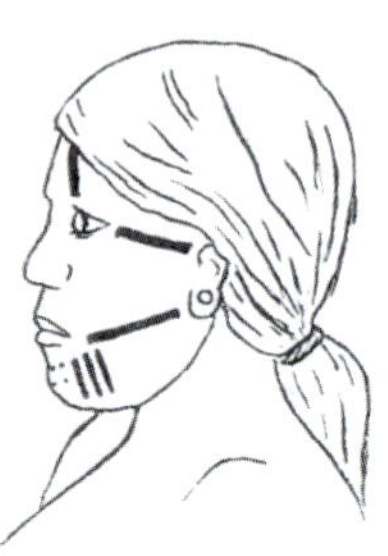

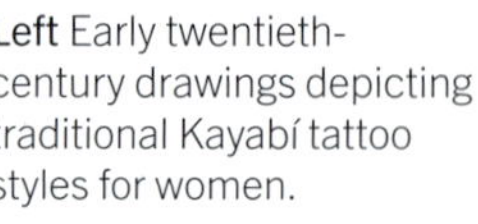

Left Early twentieth-century drawings depicting traditional Kayabí tattoo styles for women.

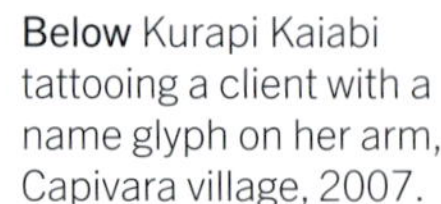

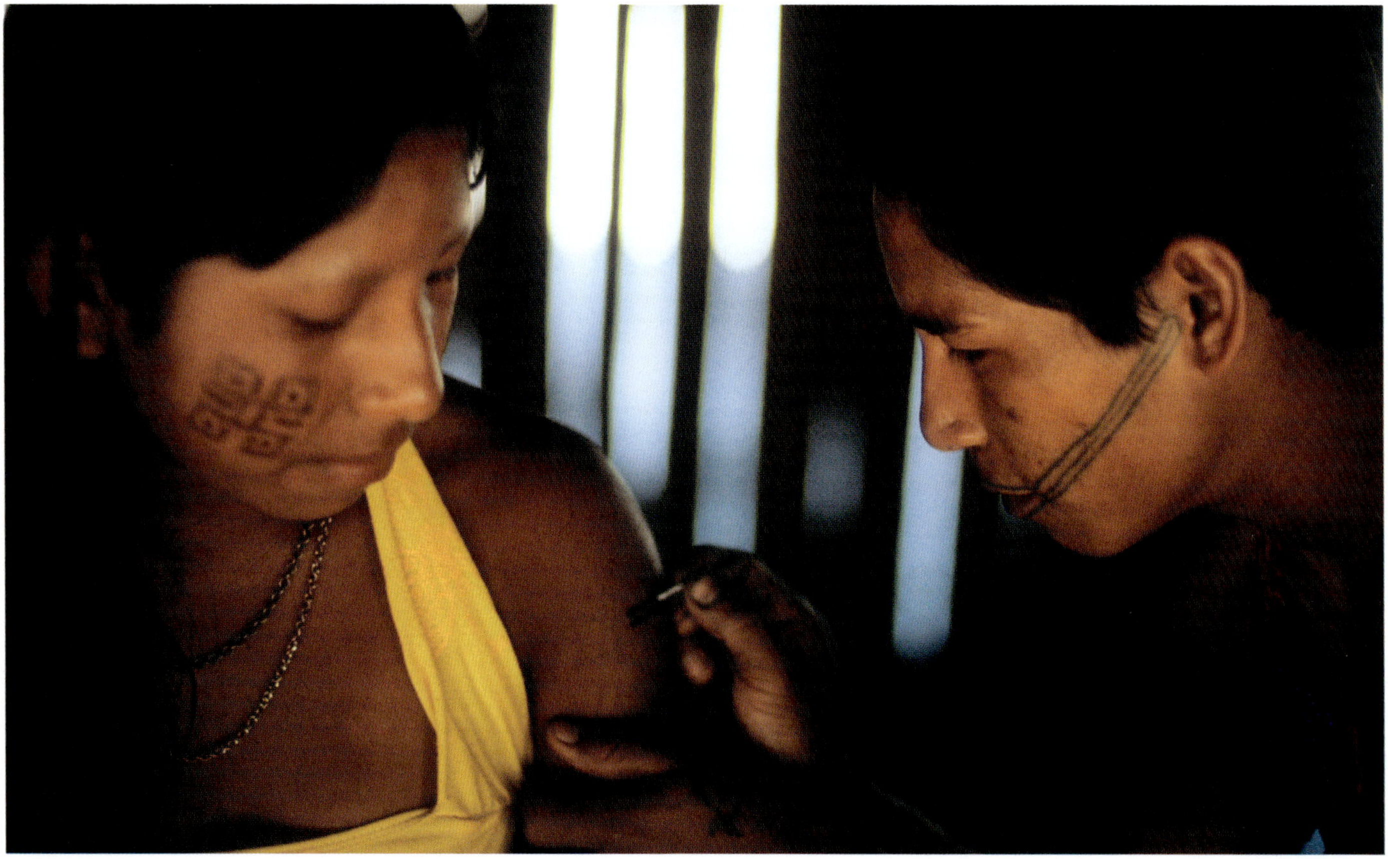

Below Kurapi Kaiabi tattooing a client with a name glyph on her arm, Capivara village, 2007.

Jemy practicing his tattoo stenciling skills on a family member, Capivara village, 2007.

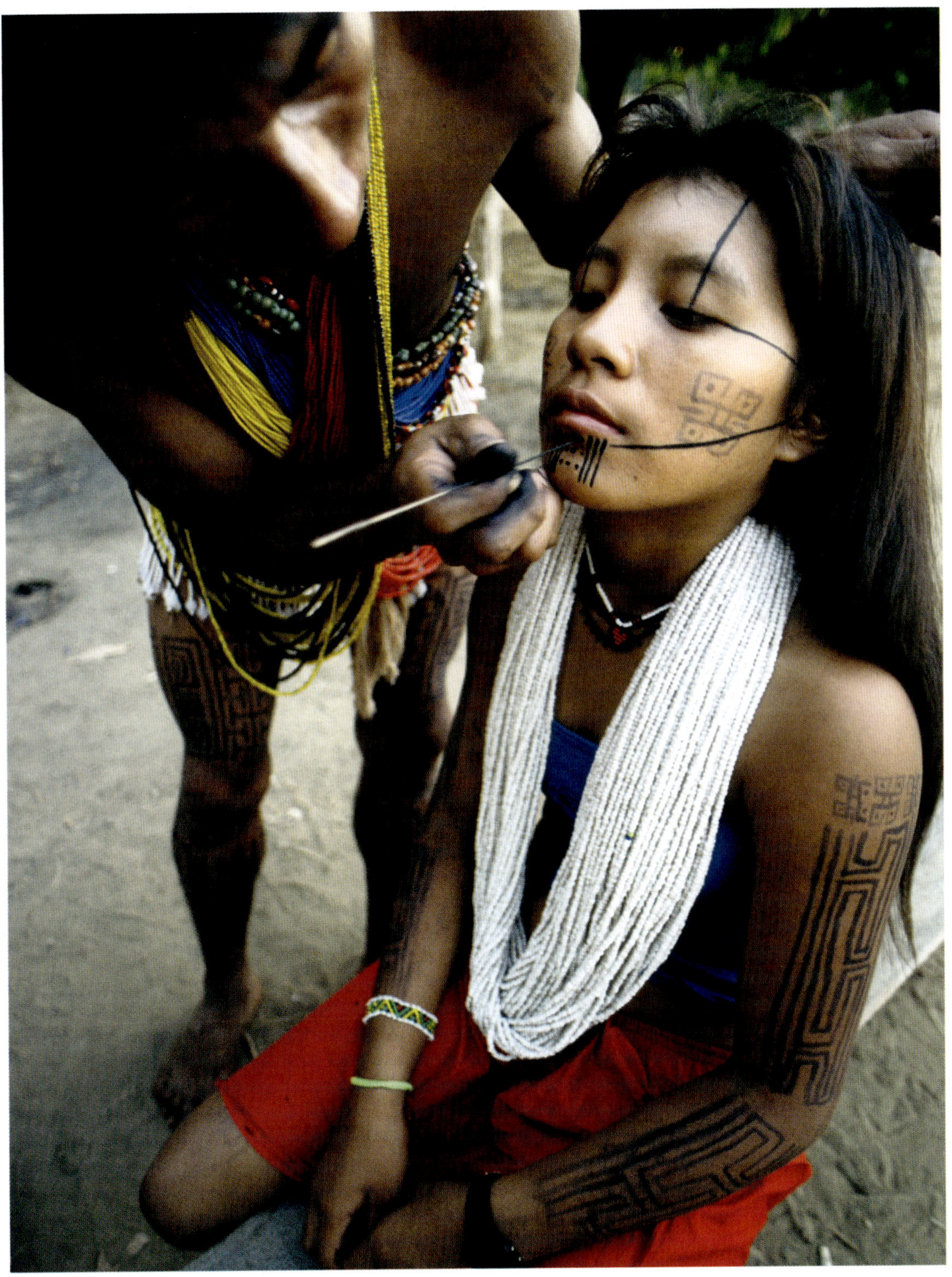

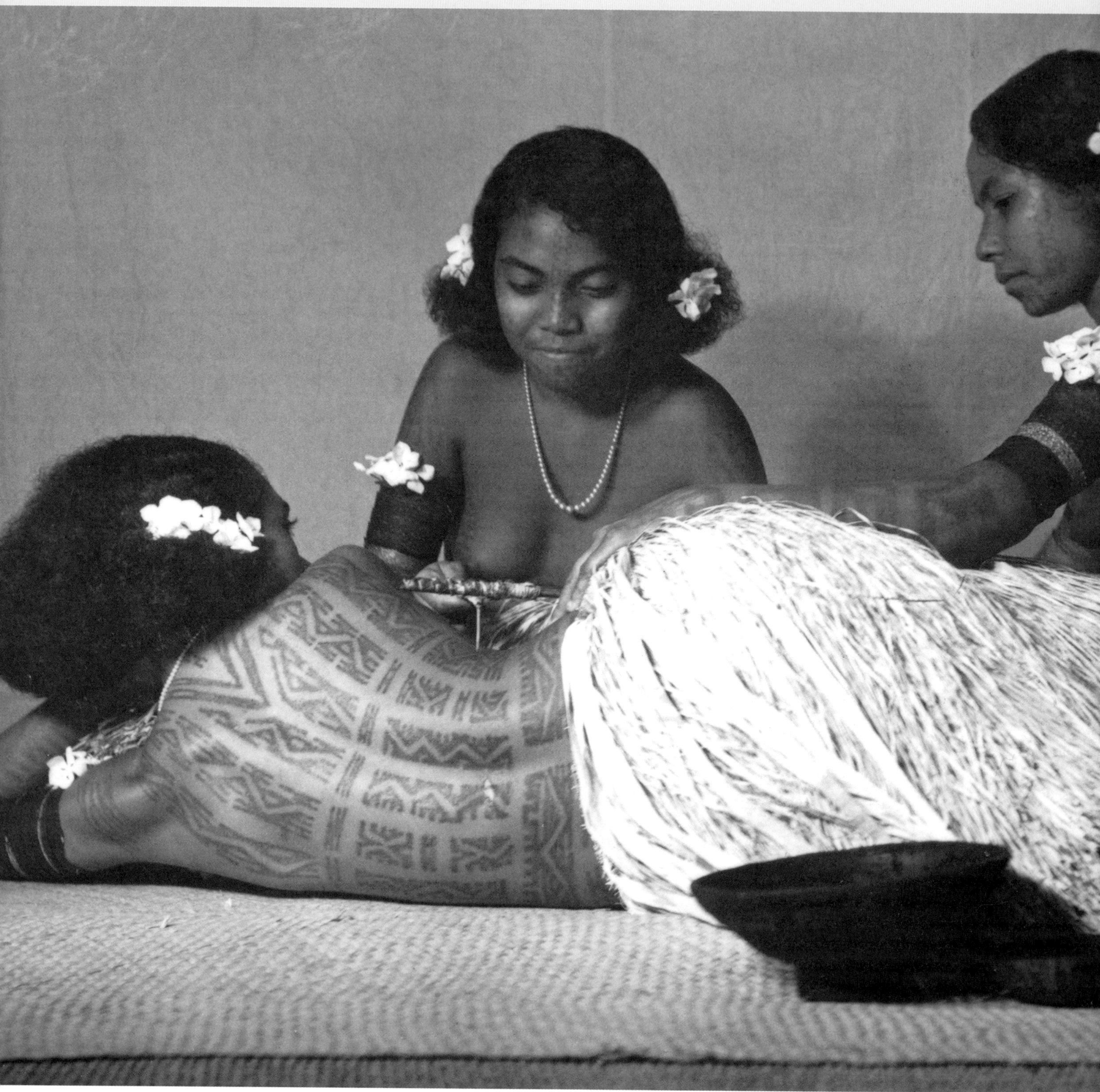

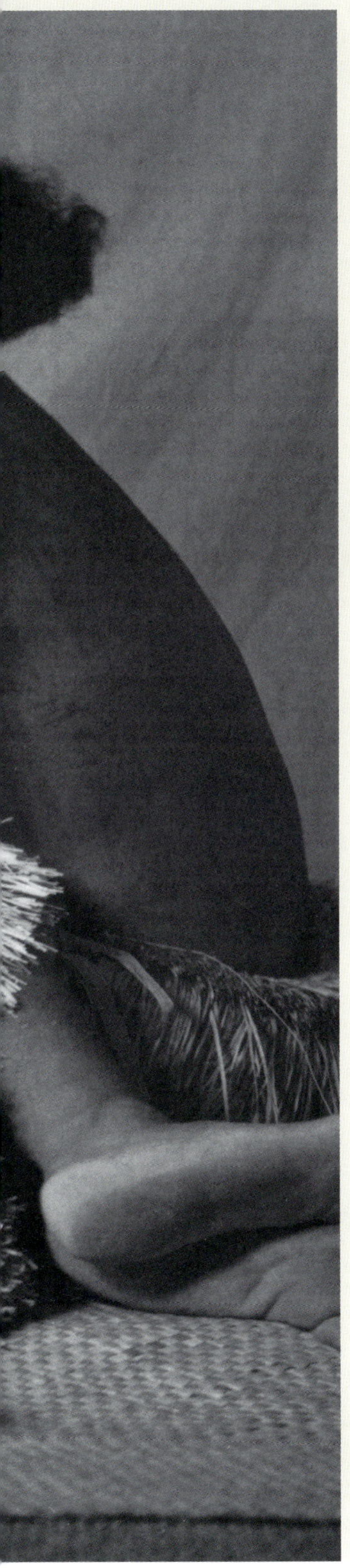

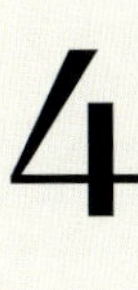

4

TATTOOS OF THE SOUTH SEAS

During late-eighteenth-century European voyages, Captain James Cook documented the practice of "tattow," or "tatau," in Tahiti. Phonetically, the word resembled the English word "tattoo," which referred to a drumbeat—an association perhaps strengthened by the rhythmic hand-tapping method of creating Indigenous tattoos across Oceania. The technique of hand-tapping is shared with several ethnic groups of Asia (in Taiwan, the Philippines, Indonesia, China) and its origins have been linked to the Indigenous peoples from the southeastern coasts of China and Taiwan who crossed the sea millennia ago.[1]

Motu women demonstrating the hand-tapping technique, *ca*. 1940.

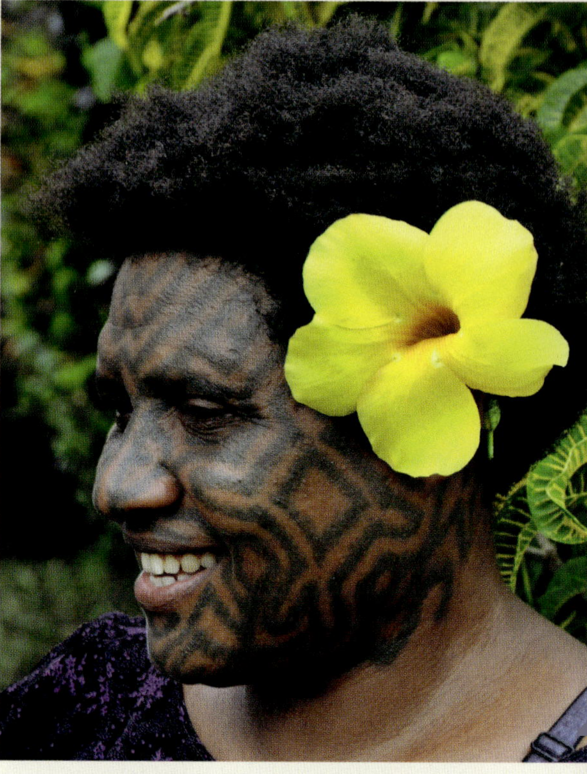

Edna Kareba, a Miniafia woman from Utukwaf Village, Papua New Guinea, 2011.

Around 2000 BCE ancient mariners speaking an Austronesian tongue arrived in the western islands of Micronesia from insular southern China and Taiwan. Several centuries later another linguistically related seafaring people, the Lapitas, sailed from the Philippines to the southwest, settling in Papua New Guinea (PNG) and Melanesia and eventually the islands of Polynesia, including Fiji, Tonga, and Sāmoa. The Lapitas traveled immense distances, sometimes over 2,000 miles (3,200 km) of ocean without landfall, navigating by the stars and without the aid of instruments.

For their new lives among the coral atolls and volcanic peaks, they transported seeds, domesticated animals, and agricultural implements. They told stories about the descent of chiefs from gods, the voyages of ancestral heroes, and oral histories of creation, and they also left behind tattooing tools and pottery fragments that broadly resemble tattooing designs.[2] Although the Lapitas populated these sun-drenched islands by 1100 BCE, it would be another 800 years before their descendants colonized other parts of Oceania, including the Marquesas, Rapa Nui (Easter Island), Hawai`i, Tahiti, and New Zealand.

However, across Oceania tattooing largely disappeared during the early to mid-nineteenth and early twentieth centuries for a variety of reasons: tribal warfare gradually ceased and so too did warrior tattooing culture, missionaries discouraged initiation and other ceremonies linked to tattooing, and marks once associated with denoting social classes were gradually abandoned as Indigenous peoples became assimilated into European culture.[3]

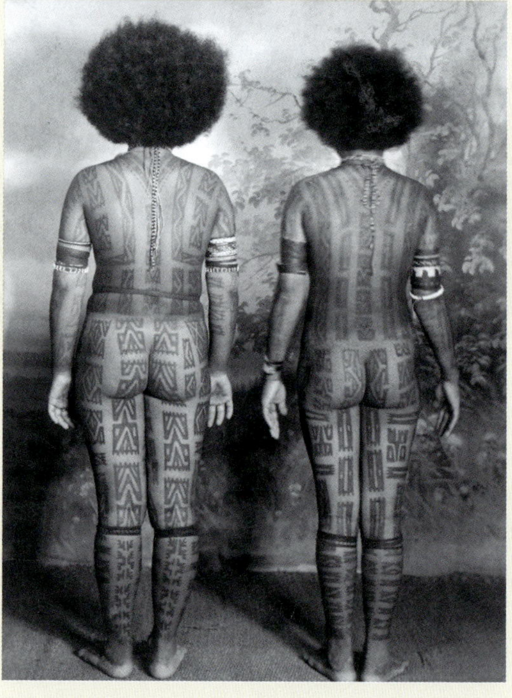

Photo postcard of Motu women's tattooing, *ca.* 1940. Traditionally, most Motu tattoo sessions were performed in relation to trading expeditions called *hiri* that were undertaken via *lakatoi* or sea-going canoes. During a *hiri*, the first-born daughters of the *lakatoi* owners were secluded in a house with ten to fifteen daughters of expedition members until the voyage had been completed; then they were tattooed.

Tattoos of Coastal Papua New Guinea

Today female tribal elders of the Motu, Waima, Aroma, Hula, and Mekeo people living on the coasts of PNG continue to possess some of the most complete forms of facial and body tattooing ever worn in the Indigenous world.[4] Prior to missionization at the turn of the twentieth century, these striking tattoos were applied by women experts via hand-tapping the surfaces of the skin at certain life stages, with the hands, arms, and face being tattooed at the age of five to seven; shortly thereafter, the abdomen, navel, vulva, and inner thighs were marked. At about the age of ten, the armpits down to the nipples, and throat were tattooed. When puberty was reached, the back, buttocks, outer thighs, and legs were inked, and when a girl reached marriageable age a large V-shaped design marked the chest.

On the northwest coast of PNG, Waima and Mekeo women possessed tattooing motifs that resembled those worn by women further south, including the *mairi mairi* or V-shaped tattoo extending from the shoulders to between the breasts signifying that a woman had reached marriageable age or had been betrothed. Among the Waima, however, there were other tattooing motifs that only occurred among this group. For example, the *ra'a ra'a*, or centipede design, covered a woman's abdomen and navel, and *areau,* or frigate-bird markings, were tattooed below the neck in between the V-shaped pattern.[5]

On the southeast coast of PNG, Korafe, Miniafia, and Maisin women continue to display bold facial tattooing, although the practice stopped in the 1980s. Here, tattooing was also female-focused and signified a girl's transition from childhood into a marriageable adult. The patterns were also worn as a marker of tribal identity and tattoo recipients were compelled to observe various taboos, such as remaining out of sight of men and not eating certain foodstuffs.[6]

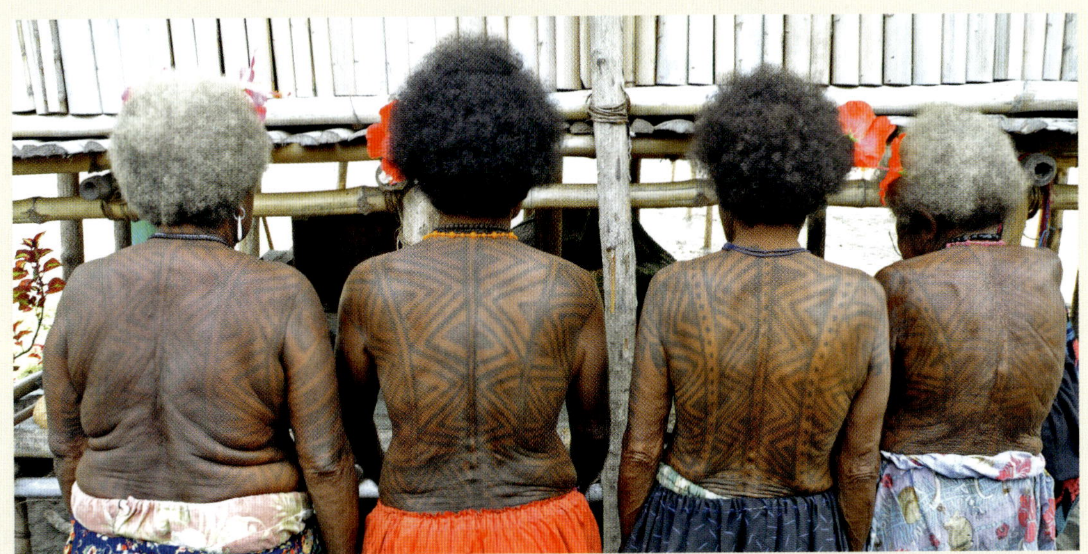

Waima elders Oa'ete Aihi, Madeleine Baeho Baki, Mary Avia Baki and her older sister waiting for a funeral procession in Waima village, PNG, 2011. All parts of a Waima woman's body were tattooed with a thorn implement, including the scalp, which was shaved before the hand-tapping.

Tattoos of Polynesia

The Pacific Ocean covers one-third of the planet and washes the shores of numerous island chains, including Polynesia, which literally means "many islands." Roughly speaking, the geographical area of Polynesia forms a nearly perfect triangle defined by Hawai`i at the northern tip supported by its two bases: New Zealand at the western edge and Easter Island at the eastern boundary.

Before the twentieth century, traditional Māori tattoo artists in New Zealand were called *tohunga tā moko*, or "tattoo specialists," and were men.[7] These experts were often craftsmen in other skills like wood carving, and their knowledge was transmitted through family lines—from grandfathers, mother's brothers, or fathers—although some artisans had natural abilities that were cultivated.

Tohunga tā moko used a range of hand-tapping tools, as well as *uhi* (chisels), made from albatross or whale bone, that were attached to a wooden handle and struck with a mallet. The chiseling technique was more distinct than other Oceanic forms of hand-tapped tattooing because the designs created grooves carved into the skin.

Māori tattooing marked the faces and bodies of chiefs and warriors, whereas women's tattoos were more commonly confined to the lips and chin. Until the late nineteenth century, however, a woman's thighs, hips, lower abdomen, neck, breasts, arms, forehead, and mons veneris might also be tattooed.[8] Obtaining Māori facial tattoos was a long and painful operation, especially for chiefs and other members of aristocratic families. After the lips had been tattooed and the patient was recuperating,

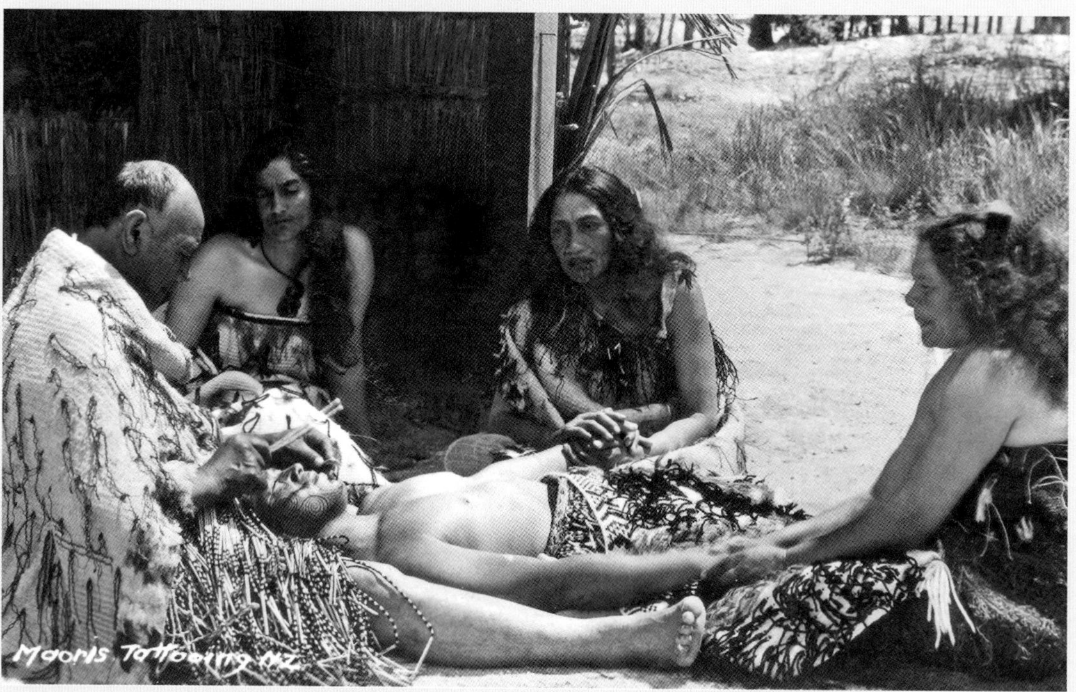

Photo postcard of a Māori tattooing demonstration, *ca*. 1910.

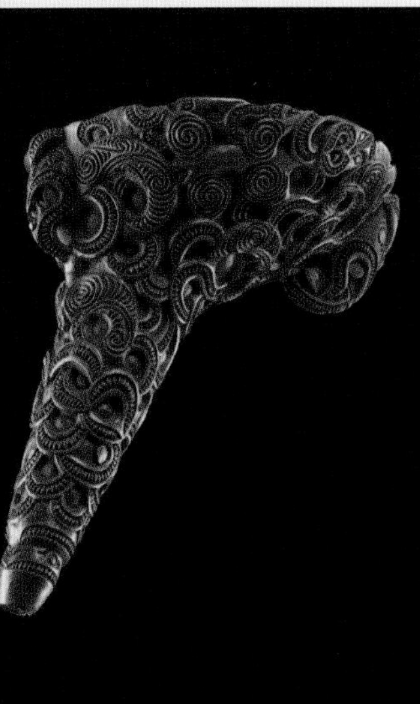

Above Māori *kōrere*, *ca*. 1700-1850. After male individuals received facial tattoos, their mouths swelled and *kōrere* (feeding funnels) were used to pass pureed foods to men of rank because it was taboo to touch their heads. *Kōrere* are thought to originate from the Hokianga-Northland region of New Zealand and generally attributed to the Ngāpuhi tribes.

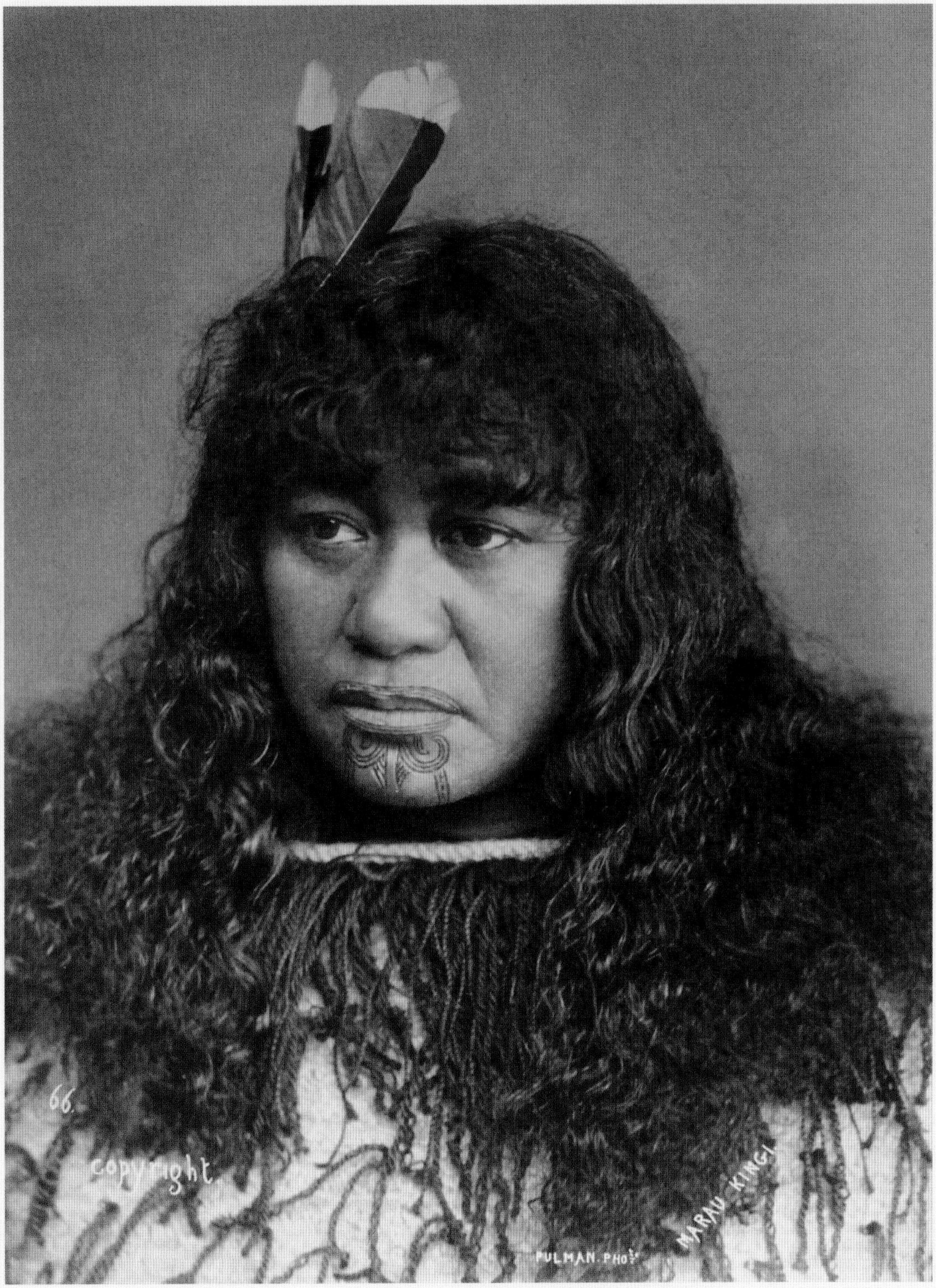

Right "Marau Kingi," a Māori woman with *kauae*, chiseled lip and chin markings, 1891.

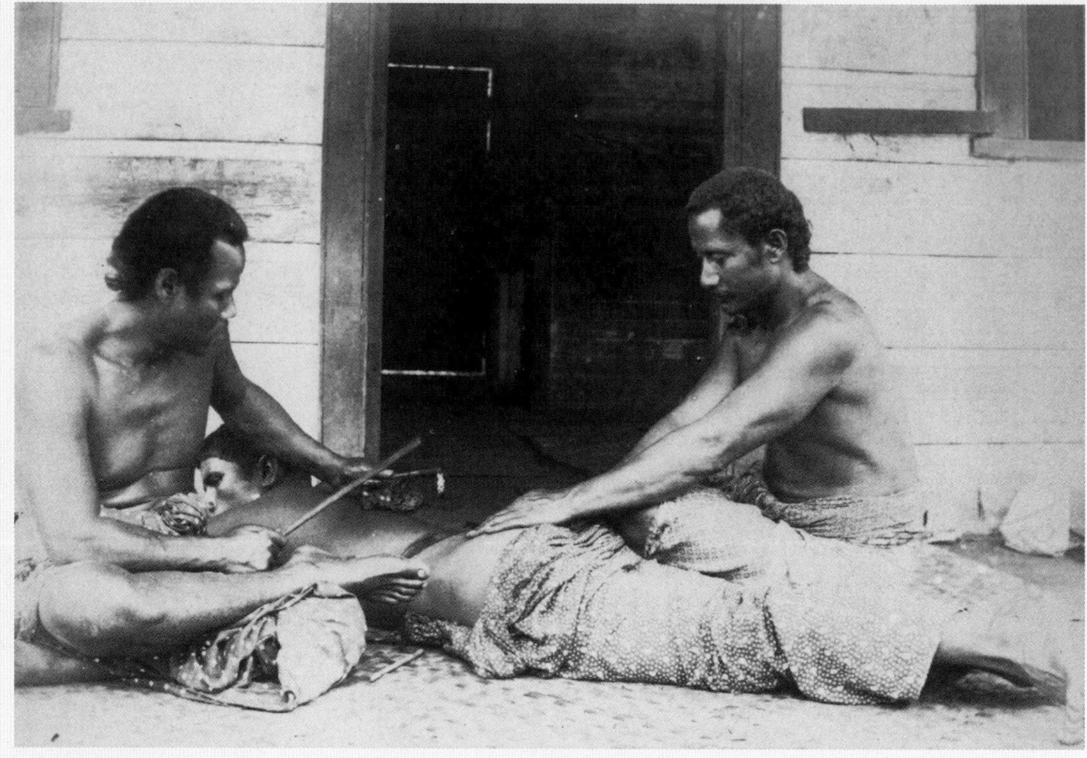

Sāmoan tattooing demonstration, *ca*. 1895. The artist worked with a set of six or more mallets. The handles were typically constructed of bamboo or another light wood, to which were lashed heads of tortoise-shell. These heads were attached to *au* (flat combs) of sharpened pig's teeth or human bone that pierced the skin with indelible designs.

it was taboo for anyone to touch their skin. The head was regarded as having great *tapu* (holiness or sacredness), and cooked food had the property of removing or diminishing the *tapu*. Thus, if any food touched the lips of a great chief after he had been tattooed, this would remove the *tapu* from the artwork and cause it "to fail."[9]

In Sāmoa, *tatau* (tattooing) was continuously practiced throughout the missionary period and today it is highly valued especially among individuals of high rank, although only *matai* (chiefs) and their sons and daughters were originally allowed to be tattooed.[10] The overall patterning of designs consists of a series of bounded zones that were created within a framework of abstract motifs derived from highly stylized designs taken from nature, like millipedes, shells, birds, and the flying fox or fruit bat.[11] Some of these animals were held to be sacred by some families because they embodied ancestral spirits; when worn as tattoos they enveloped the body in a sacred cloak of protection.

Sāmoan tattoo artists are called *tufuga tā tatau* (*tatau*,"correct, artfully done"), and tattooists with great *mana* (spiritual power) have always been recognized by the symmetrical designs and finely balanced compositions and linework they executed for their clients.[12] Certain linear arrangements referred to genealogies, adventures, and accomplishments, and because *'aso faaifo* (curved lines) encircled your being, they served as a visual testament to an individual's commitment to permanently incorporate their family's lineage into his or her life.

Profile view of Sāmoan *pe'a* tattoo as seen by American tattooist Lyle Tuttle during his trip to Sāmoa, 1973.

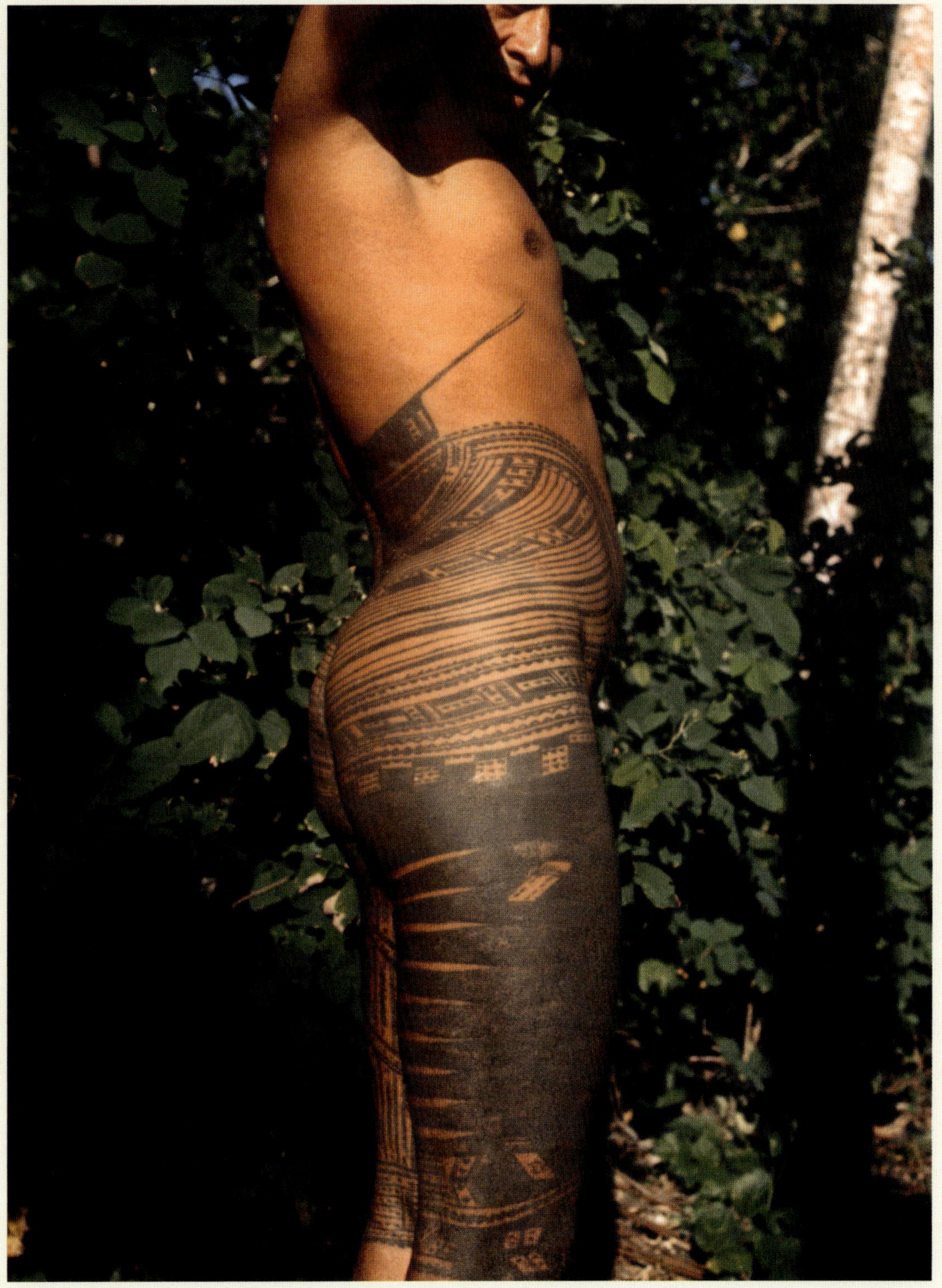

Right Albumen silver print by Eugène Maunoury (1830–1896) in his studio in Lima, Peru, of Hitoro, Marquesan Chief of Ua Pou Island, 1863.

Below Watercolor drawing of a tattooed Marquesan man, *ca.* 1838. This drawing is the work of Randon de Grolier, who was an officer on board the ship *L'Artemise* (1837–1840).

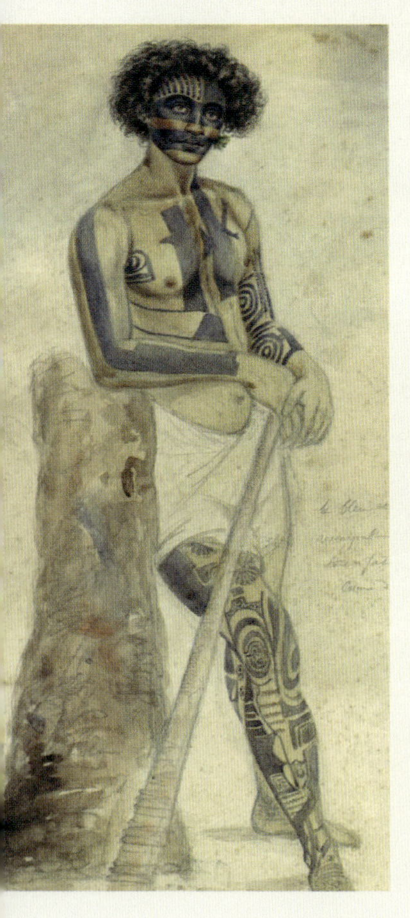

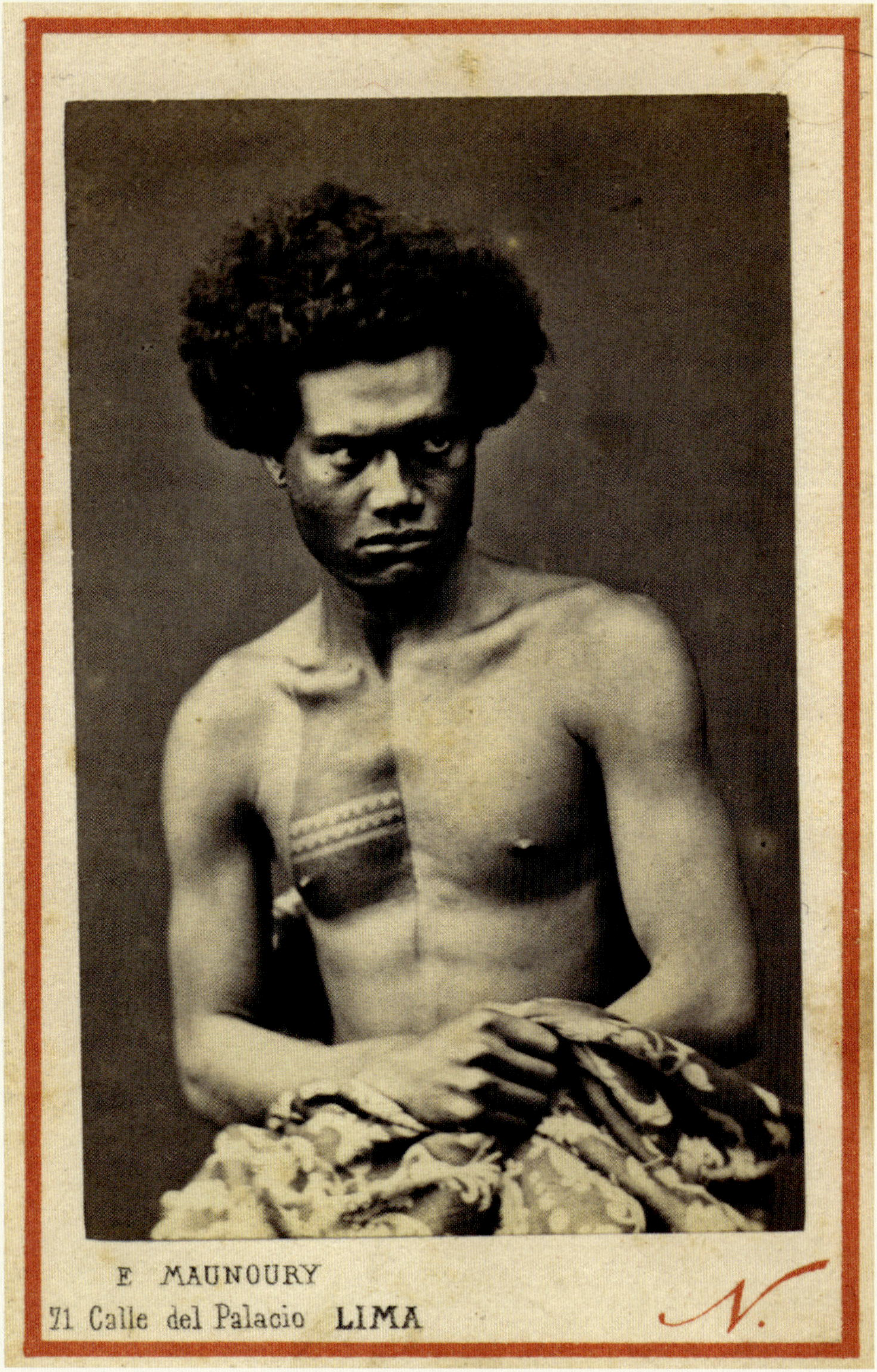

Right Tattooed Marquesan man, Puamau village, Hiva Oa, 1897.

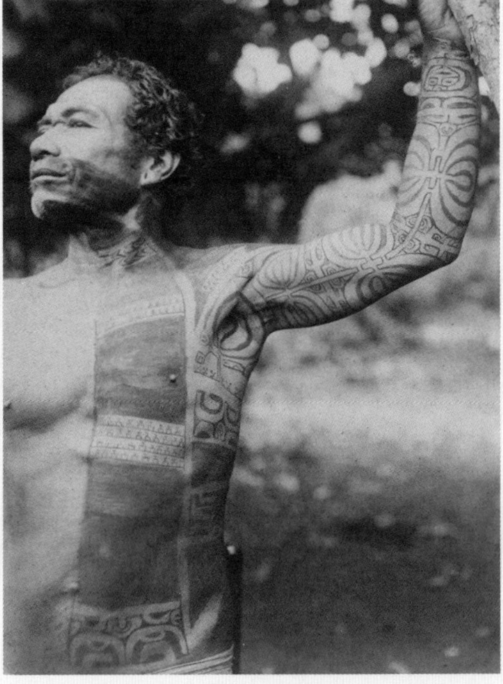

Prior to the mid-nineteenth century, tattooing in the Marquesas Islands was not confined to certain ranks, classes, or sexes. In fact, certain sacred chiefs of the highest rank were not tattooed at all. However, fine work was widely enjoyed by other chiefs, their warriors, and wealthy individuals who could afford to employ the best artists.

The German explorer and ethnologist Karl von den Steinen, who visited the isles in 1891, listed over 170 individually named tattooing motifs, which is remarkable since the tradition was "banned" by French officials approximately fifty years before that time.[13]

Male *tuhuna* (tattooists), or more appropriately *tuhuna patu tiki* ("one who strikes or marks designs"), worked under the protection of a patron deity whose contagious power also enveloped those who encountered him while he worked. One early-twentieth-century writer stated that the office of *tuhuna* was hereditary, and that each great family had its own stable of tattooists who were trained from generation to generation.

The *tuhuna* carried his instruments in a bamboo case that measured 7–8 in. (18–20 cm) long. He laid out his tools on a piece of tapa spread on the ground and prepared himself for work. These instruments were generally known as *ta* ("to strike").[14] Like in other parts of Polynesia, there was an assortment of these tools and the combs varied in fineness depending on the grade of work (linework or fill) that was to be performed. The flat instruments for straight lines and gradual curves were of human bone, sometimes acquired from the corpses of sacrificed enemies.[15] Each was about 3 in. (8 cm) long, flat, slightly wedge-shaped, and toothed or comb-like at the end. Tools for the smaller curves were made from the leg or wing bones of a booby or another avian species.

Below Marquesan leg patterns for men, 1897.

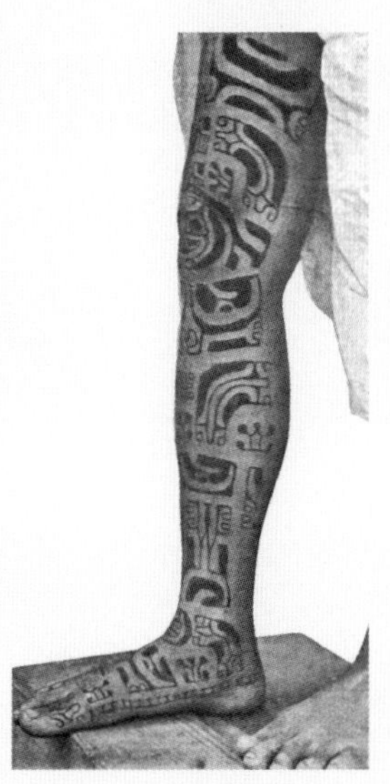

Marquesan warriors and certain chiefs were perhaps the most heavily tattooed of all individuals, and the epidermises of these men were covered with layers upon layers of ink until the body was nearly black with designs. At death, however, these markings were erased through ritual flaying.

The Marquesans believed in an afterworld divided into a melancholy realm occupied by past servants and common people, and an Eden ruled by the goddess Oupu into which the spirits of chiefs and other persons of status might be admitted.[16] However, Oupu forbade tattooing in her abode, and particularly violent deities lingered there to punish those people who possessed the tabooed body modifications.

Tattoo Myths: The "Painted Prince" Giolo (1691–92)

One of the longest-running myths about tribal, non-Western tattooing is that it was "brought" to Europe and the West by sailors associated with Captain Cook's voyages to Oceania.

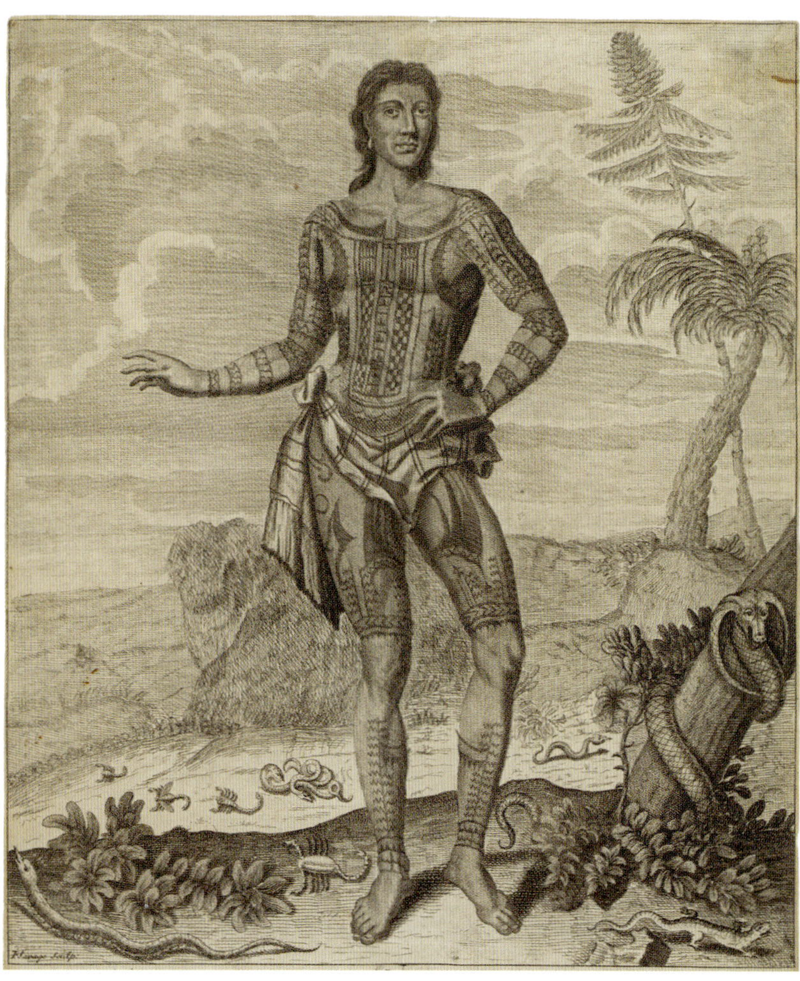

This is not true, of course, since there have been Indigenous forms of tattooing practiced in Europe since the Neolithic period (think Iceman) and onward (Catholics from Bosnia and Herzegovina, Christian pilgrims to the Holy Land, etc.) prior to Cook's return. Sadly, peer-reviewed "scholarly" tomes continue to perpetuate these "facts" and one of the most perplexing is this (mis)statement: "The first ever tattoo was reported by Captain Cook."[17] Although it is clear that Captain Cook did not re-introduce tattooing to Europe, he and his officers popularized the discussion of it through their writings, which were widely read.

Another longstanding myth that continues to be perpetuated in the popular press, academic literature, and recent academic conferences is that of the "Painted Prince" Giolo, real name Jeoly, who several authors have posited was the "first recorded tattooed person to be exhibited in England"[18] or the "first" in Europe.[19]

"Prince" Jeoly was purchased as a slave in India (via the Philippines) by colorful British explorer, navigator, pirate, and naturalist William Dampier in 1691 and brought to England for display as a sideshow attraction in a money-making venture. His home island was recorded as the Spice Island of "Meangis" (today's Miangas Island), located less than 100 miles (160 km) approximately due east of the southern coast of Mindanao, the Philippines.

But are these aforementioned facts legitimate or the stuff of legends?

In 1566, a tattooed Canadian Inuit woman and her unmarked child were kidnapped by

Opposite The "Painted Prince" Giolo, 1692. A portion of his tattooed skin was preserved and it hung in Oxford University's Bodleian Library for centuries until it was lost.

Right Merchandise wrapper for a pack of cards, with portrait of Prince Giolo standing in a landscape with palm tree, 1691.

Far right William Dampier, holding his book *A New Voyage Round the World*, *ca*. 1697–8.

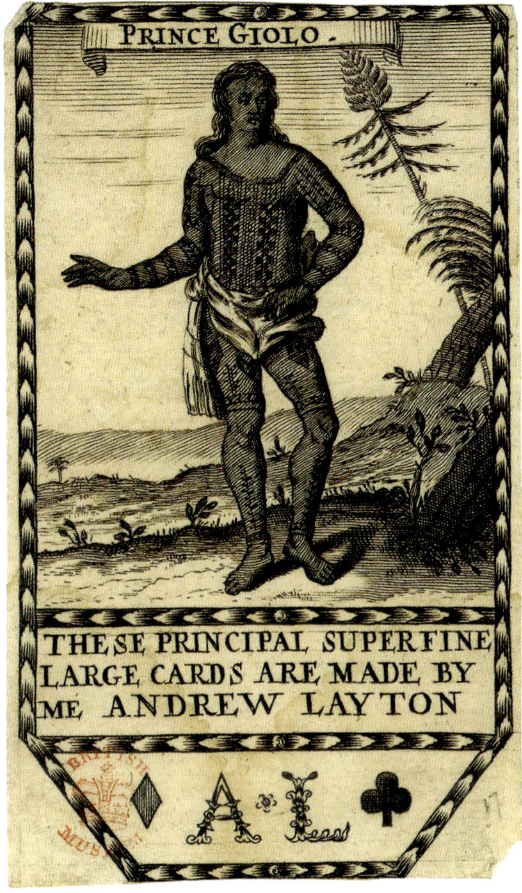

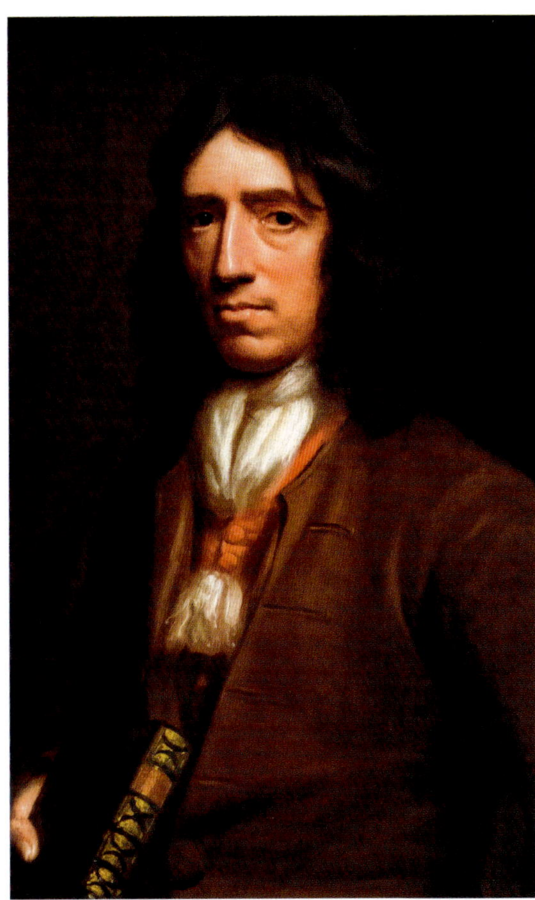

French sailors in Labrador and brought to Antwerp in Belgium. Here, they were put on display in 1567 for money at a local tavern and handbills survive documenting the sad event. This woman was the first tattooed Native North American drawn from life,[20] a fact that busts a widely perpetuated tattoo myth: Many past and contemporary writers have wrongly identified English colonial governor, explorer, and artist John White as the creator of the "earliest" portraits of tattooed Native North Americans (1590), Algonquian-speaking peoples he encountered in coastal North Carolina (USA) in the late sixteenth century.

Returning to the previous statement that Jeoly was the first tattooed person to be exhibited in England, it should be highlighted here that English sailor and privateer Sir Martin Frobisher captured two Canadian Inuit in 1577 and brought them to England for display. One of his captives was a tattooed woman from Baffin Island who was later illustrated by John White. Therefore, it seems that there were at least two Indigenous tattooed people exhibited in Europe prior to the Painted Prince's arrival in 1691.

Over the years, Jeoly has been described as a "Visayan" from the southern Philippines[21] and especially a "Marquesan,"[22] because his "pattern of tattooing is similar to designs recorded in the Marquesas Islands in the nineteenth century."[23]

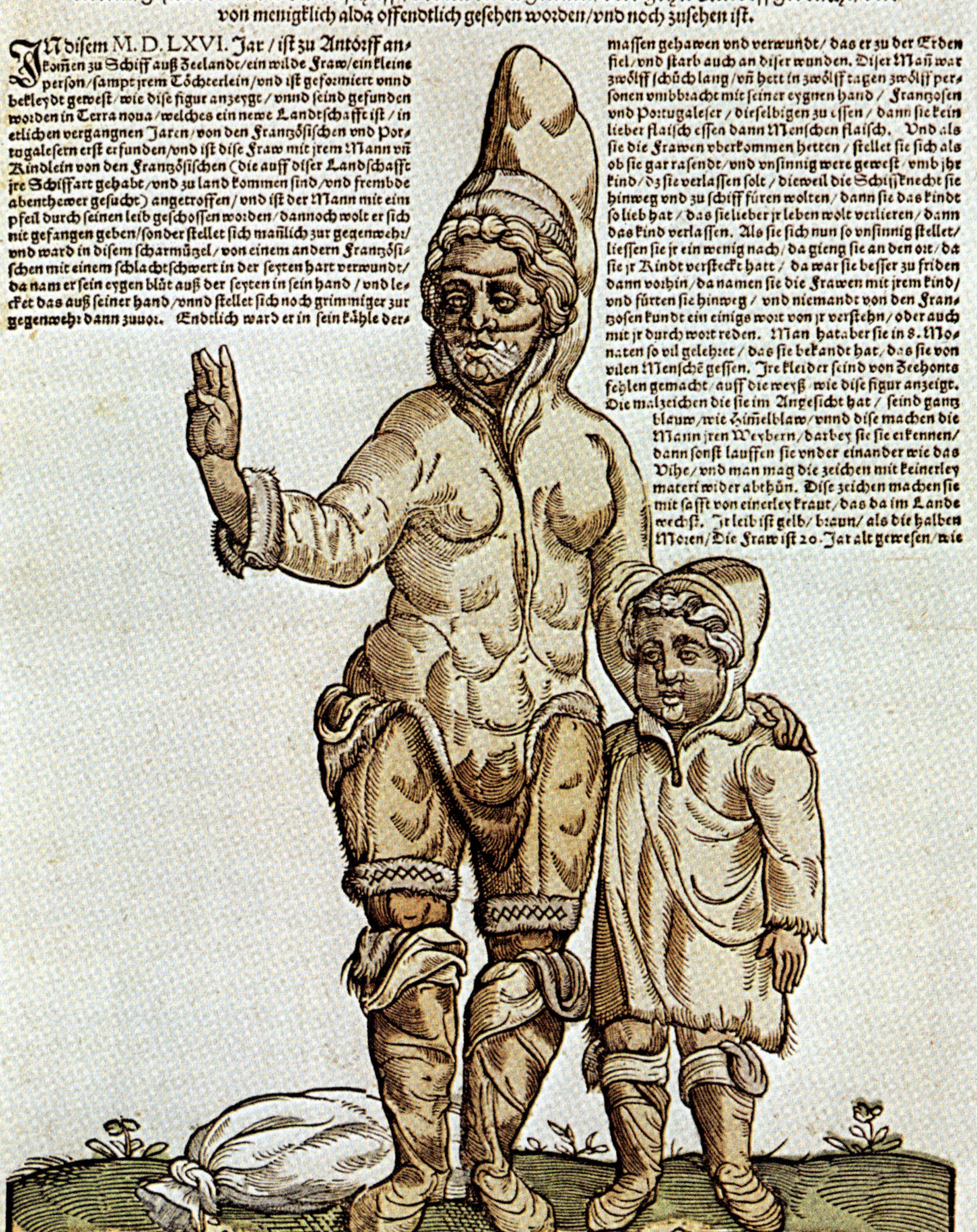

Illustrated handbill in German advertising the exhibition of a facially tattooed Canadian Inuit woman and her child, 1566. This woodblock print is the oldest known European depiction of a tattooed Indigenous person drawn from life.

Right Micronesian body tattoos from the island of Merir, Sonsorol group, Palau, 1927.

Far right Tattooed male *Pintados*, or Visayans, as illustrated in the Boxer Codex, Central Philippines, *ca*. 1595.

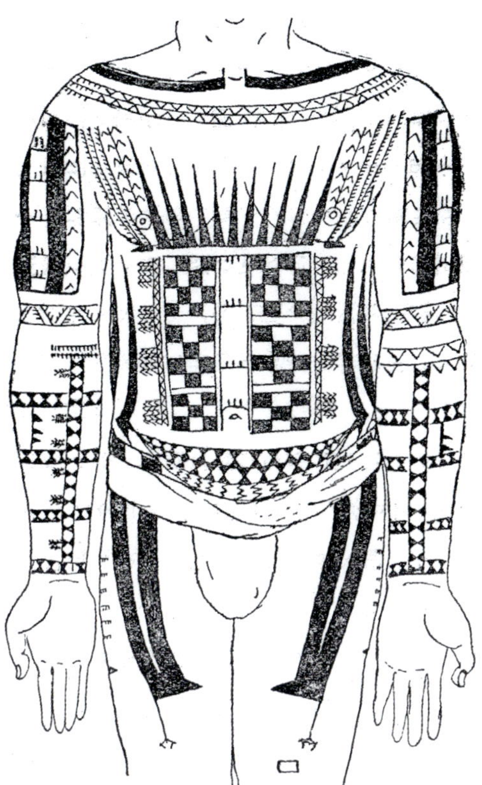

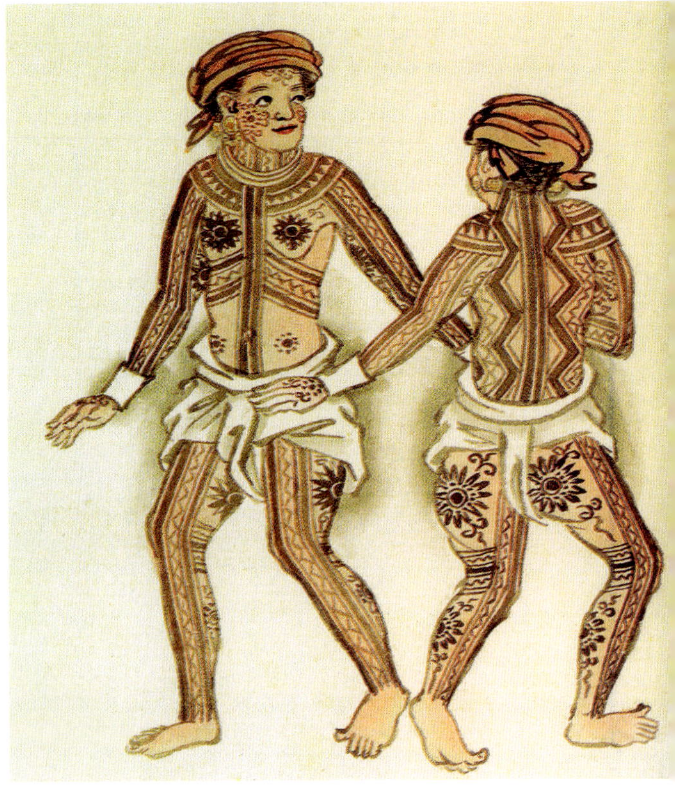

Of course, anyone with knowledge of Micronesian and Marquesan tattooing practices and styles would tell you that Jeoly wore Micronesian tattoos that closely resembled those from the Caroline Islands, not the Philippines. However, elements of Jeoly's tattoos closely match those documented for men inhabiting the Palauan island of Merir[24] and other isles in the Sonsorol group, islands that lie approximately 400 nautical miles (645 km) due east of Miangis where Dampier proclaimed Jeoly was born.

As evinced from illustrations in the sixteenth-century Spanish manuscript the Boxer Codex (*ca*. 1595), Visayan tattooing from the southern Philippines is quite dissimilar as compared to Jeoly's Micronesian bodysuit. Although little information survives regarding the tattooing practices of the so-called Visayan "Pintados" ("painted" or "tattooed people"), Visayan tattooists were male, unlike their predominately female counterparts working in Palau and the Carolines, and Jeoly told Dampier that "one of his wives painted [tattooed] him."

Concerning the "Marquesan" attribution of Jeoly's tattoos, I think the greatest fault does not lie with the scholars who first made this attribution. Rather, it lies with those subsequent researchers who, many years later, continue to cite the "primary source"–despite the data available to them–thereby failing to question the original analysis.

"Thorn Hit": Managalase Tattoos of Papua New Guinea

As far as books go, you will be hard pressed to find much information on the Managalase people of Papua New Guinea (PNG), let alone their tattooing practices.[25] This fact is probably due to the relative inaccessibility of their mountainous homeland, which is located on a plateau enclosed on all sides by rugged rain-soaked terrain that forms the Hydrographer range of Oro Province.

Benjamin, the last tattooed elder of Tabuane village, 2012.

One of the most striking features of Managalase culture is its body tattooing. Here, unlike most other parts of PNG, tattooing is largely male focused and associated with complex rite-of-passage ceremonies that have not been conducted since the 1950s. Missionaries and government authorities compelled the Managalase to abandon these puberty rituals and now the last vestiges of this painful art form are worn on the bodies of men in their eighties and nineties.

Managalase tattooing is called *kuije kanan* or "thorn hit" for the tool used to pierce the skin with natural pigment. The single bush thorn instrument was twined at a right angle to the end of a short stick about 8 in. (20 cm) long. This was hand-tapped by male artists who, like wood carvers and warriors, were highly respected men in their communities. Before a tattoo was applied, the design was stenciled on the skin with a sticky black tattoo pigment obtained by heating the gum of the local *sakira* tree.[26]

Managalase boys were ceremonially prepared for their painful initiation many years before they were actually tattooed. At about the age of ten or eleven, they were removed from their homes and began living in the village men's house, an act that separated them from their mothers and sisters. For a year or more, the boys lived here and were taught hunting, war, and agricultural "magic" while at the same time they were forbidden from having sexual relations with women or eating meat. During this period, male relatives began making arrangements for their marriages, which would occur only after they had been tattooed.

Once a young boy had mastered the knowledge of how to become a Managalase man, he was then allowed to participate in the tattooing ritual with six to twelve other boys; but first he had to undergo a lengthy period of

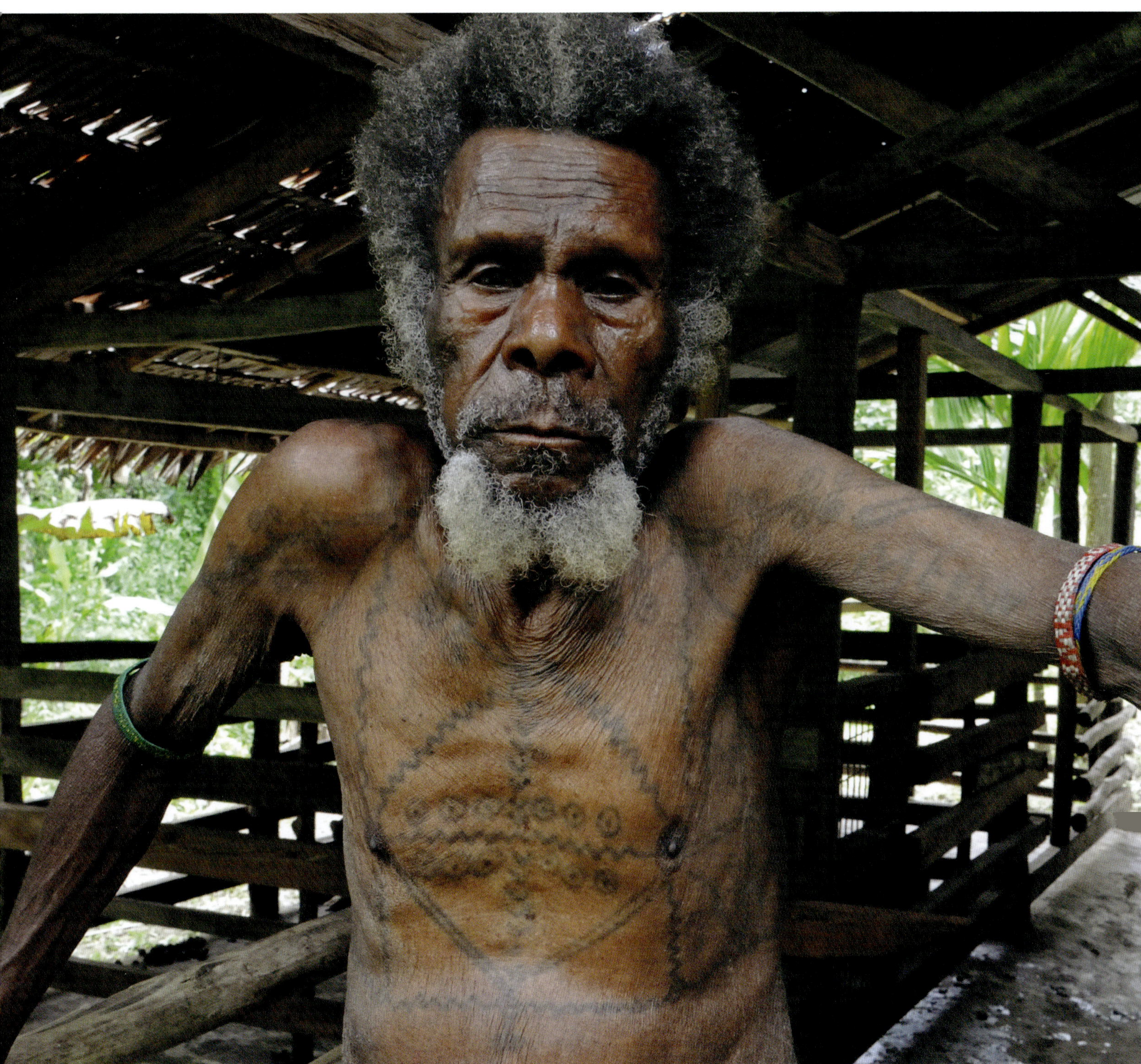

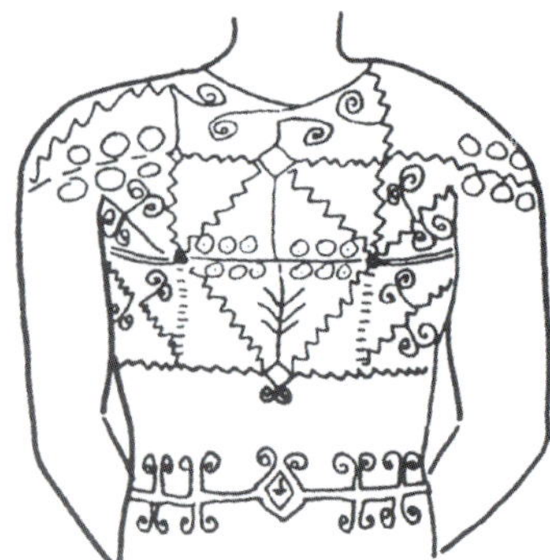

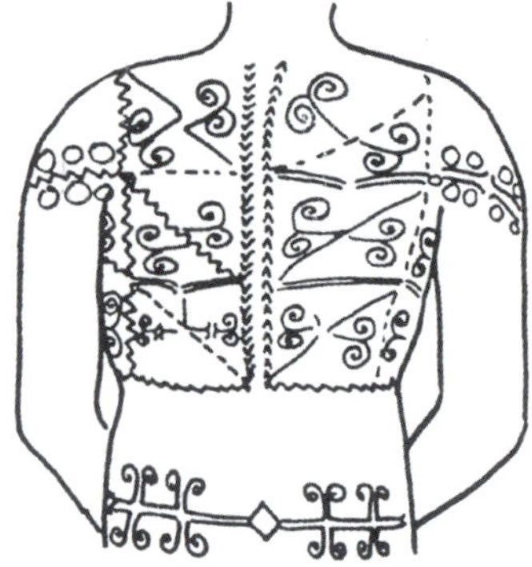

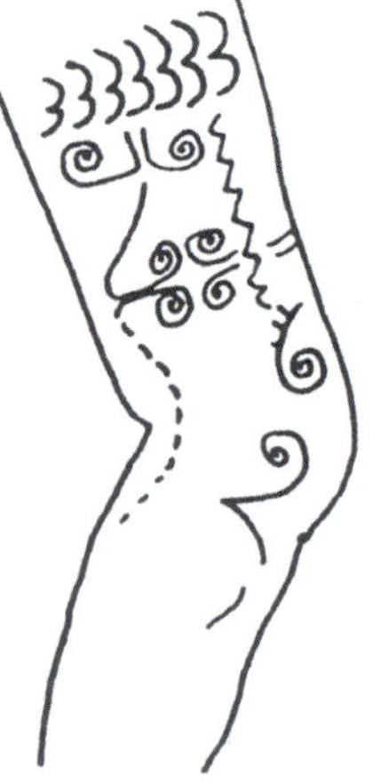

Lancelot of Sila village and drawings of his tattooing marks, 2012.

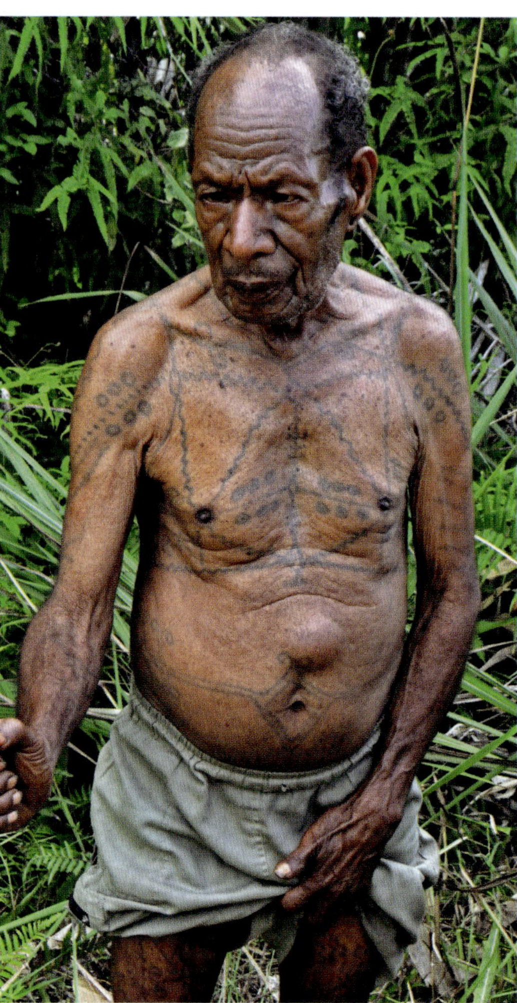

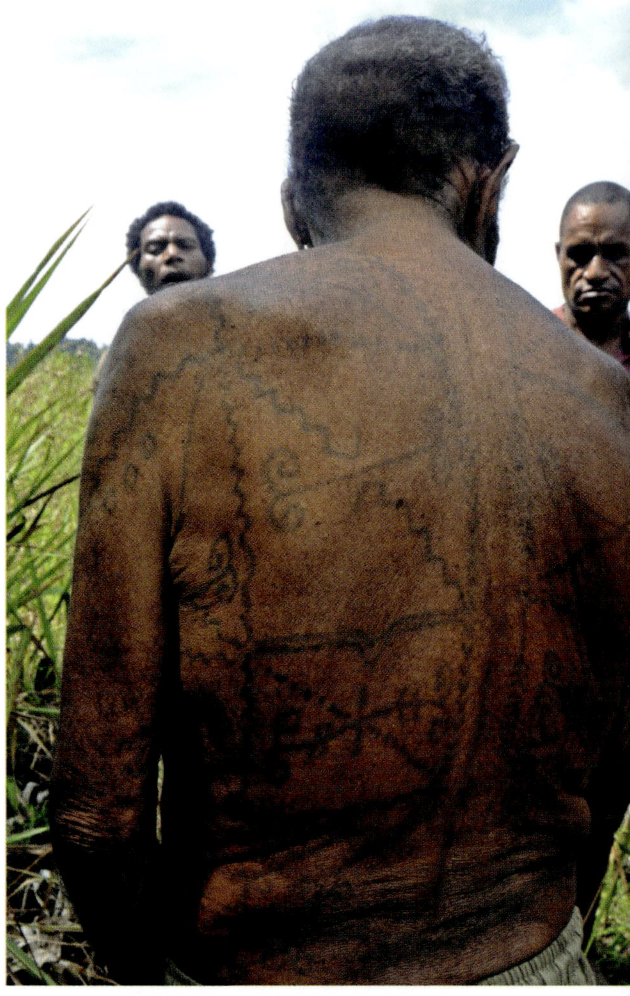

isolation in the *marakara* or seclusion hut to prepare his body for the transformation that would take place. If the boy lived in a village that was hosting a tattoo event, the seclusion period would last three months. If he had to travel to another village, the seclusion lasted six months.

Managalase tattooists usually began their sessions by tattooing a *tine* or sternum mark. From this central point zigzag lines, representing serrated feathers used in ceremonial clothing, radiated outward to form quadrants that divided the chest into distinct sections. Interestingly, the *tine* marked the seat of the body's soul, since the Managalase believe that the soul resides in this location.

Other tattoo motifs included the flying fox, circular motifs representing a *hikodi* (bamboo musical instrument), spiraling forms of a *yuki* (local fern), and zigzagging patterns derived from patterns seen in tree bark.

During the tattooing, male elders who gathered round each initiate sang war songs that were also performed when giving food at feasts or after killing an enemy.

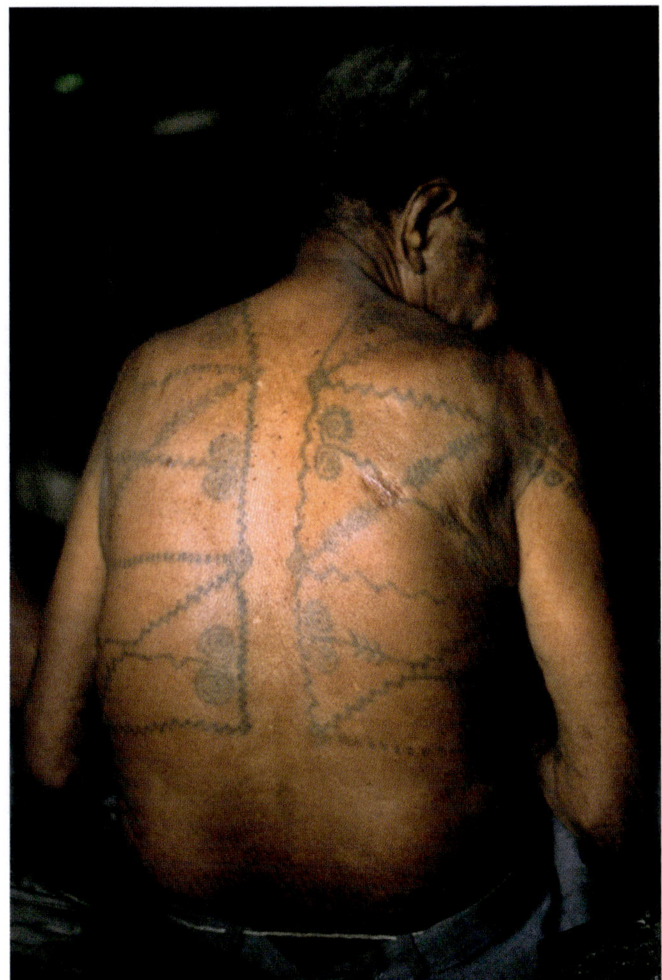

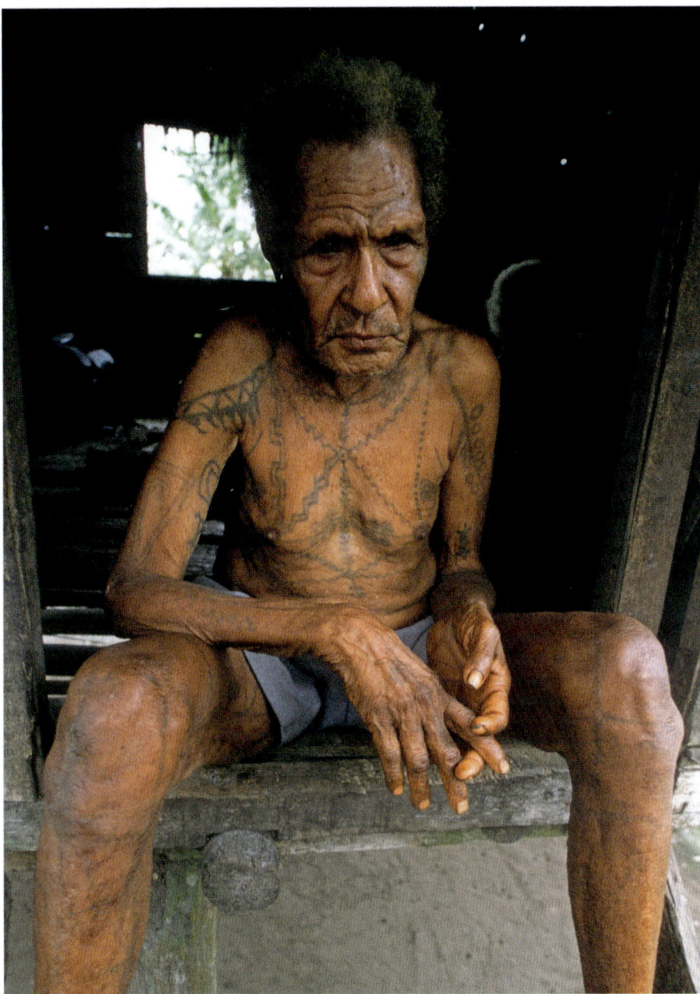

Lukas Arade, the last tattooed man of Uguma village, 2012.

At the end of the operation the newly marked men made mirrors out of bowls of water so they could admire their tattoos. Then they returned to the *marakara* for another month and reclined on their beds near the lengthy fire pit. A *susara* or jungle leaf was placed over the embers of the fire and then pressed onto the wounds to promote healing. Then the tattoos were cleansed with mountain spring water and the entire process was repeated until the men were ready to leave the smoky confines of the *marakara*.

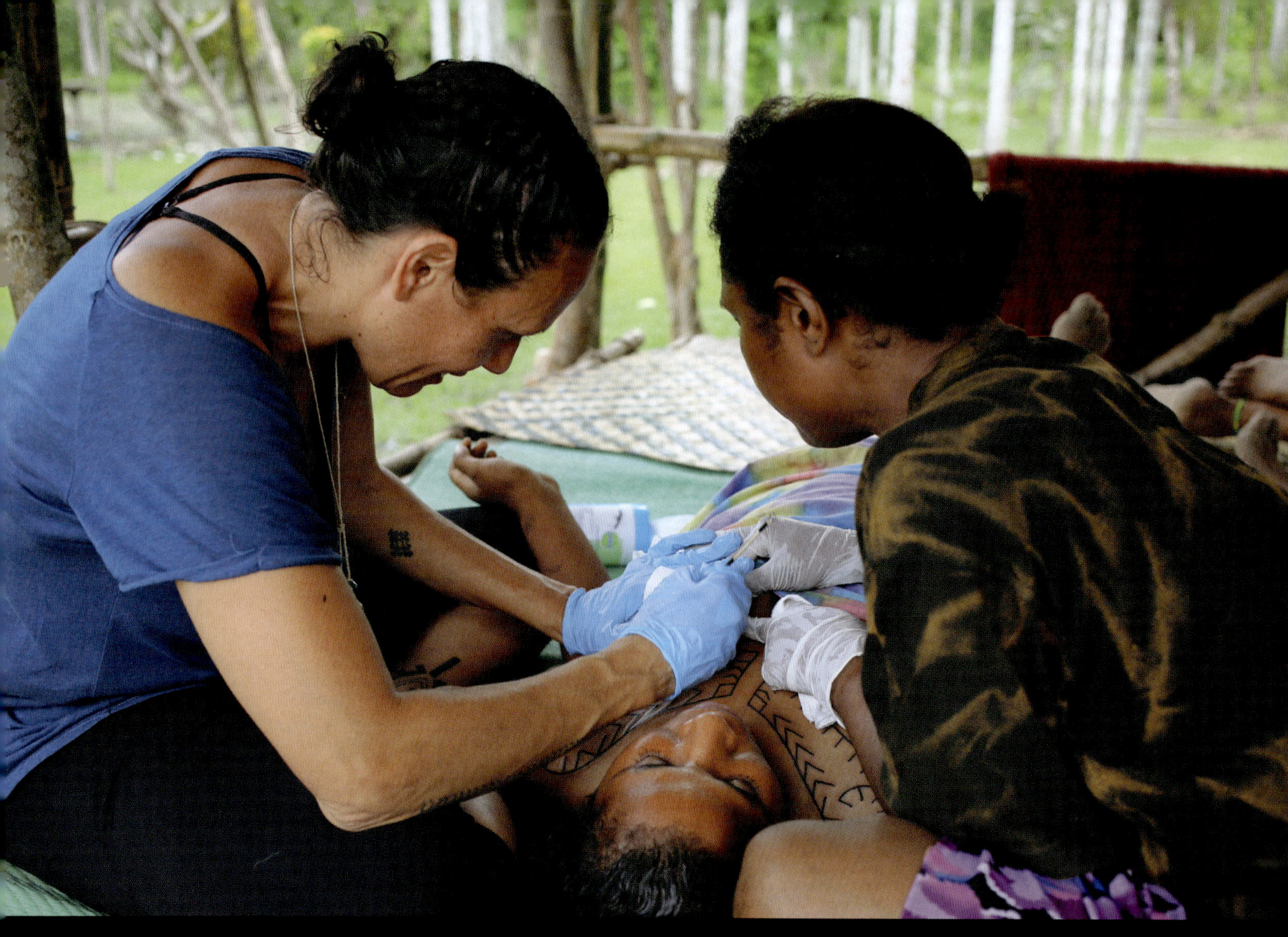

Julia Mage'au Gray: Stories Between the Lines

Opposite Julia Mage'au Gray tattooing Elaka, a Mekeo woman of Oaisaka village, PNG, 2014. She wears her grandmother's tattoos.

Right Magaiva Oini Opu and Ofoi Isoaimo Auki from Inawi Village, Mekeo, PNG, 2013. The bold markings relate to familial patterns and represent the first traditional tattoos given in Mekeo territory in some eighty years. Tattooing by Julia Mage'au Gray.

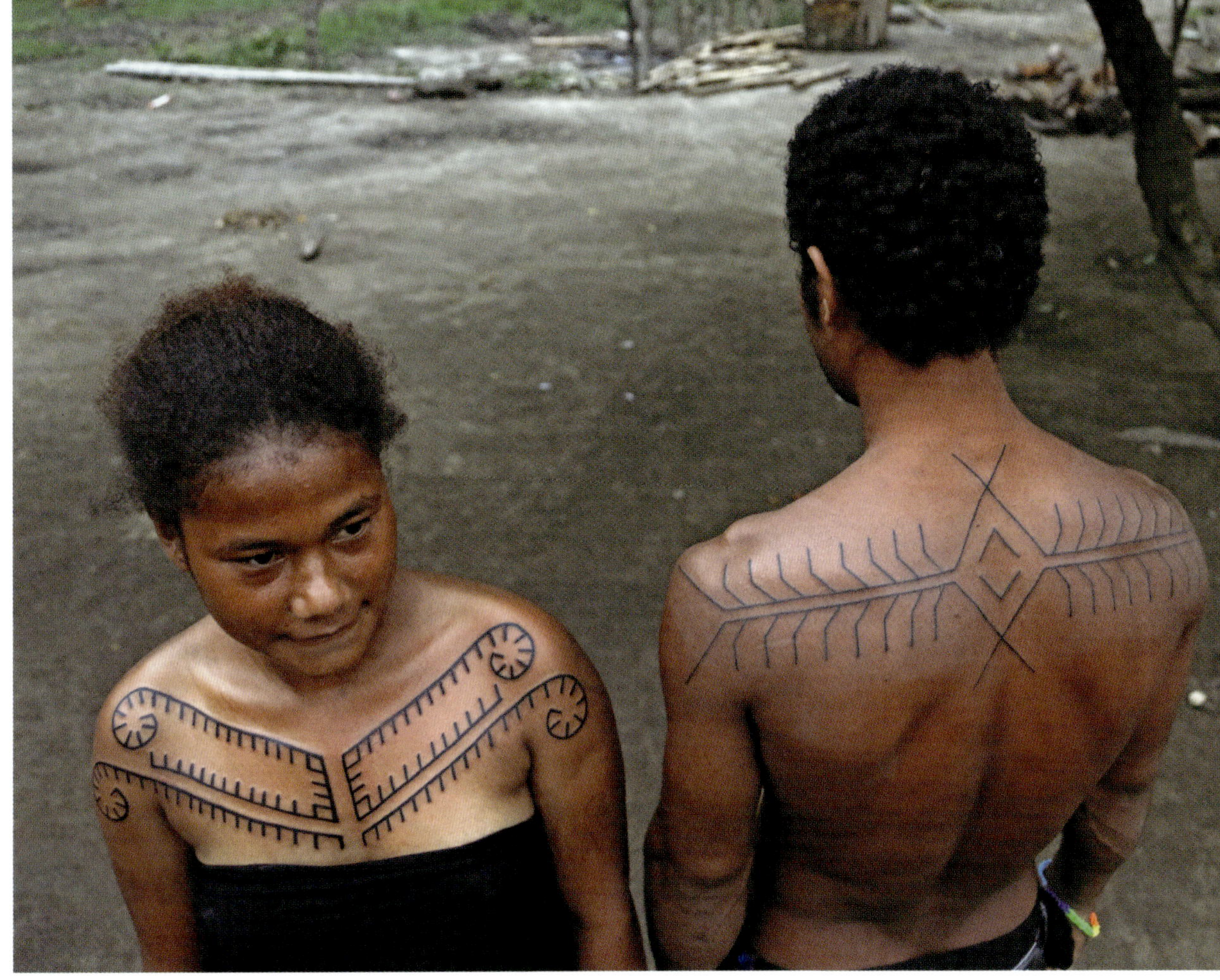

Julia Mage'au Gray, a dancer and choreographer by training, was born in the Indigenous Mekeo homelands of Papua New Guinea (PNG) and grew up in Australia. Despite this, she has always maintained strong ties to her Indigenous Mekeo community. Together with three PNG-Australian women, in 2013 she created the documentary project *Tep Tok: Reading Between Our Lines*, which was the culmination of several years of research with Mekeo and other Indigenous community members across PNG.

While interviewing some of the Mekeo women adorned with traditional skin markings, Gray grasped the full magnitude of her work. It was not merely about documenting a vanishing cultural practice to ensure it was remembered; for Gray, exploring tattooing – particularly within a PNG context – required fully immersing herself in the practice in order to revive it.[27]

She began tattooing in 2014 in New Zealand, apprenticing with a host of traditional tattooists, including Tahitian artist Tihoti Mataura. There she learned how to hand-tap and hand-poke tattoos and, shortly thereafter, she began tattooing family members back in the Mekeo heartland – the first traditional tattoos given there in some eighty years.

The demise of Mekeo tattooing traditions, as with nearly all other Indigenous tattooing traditions across PNG, can be attributed to

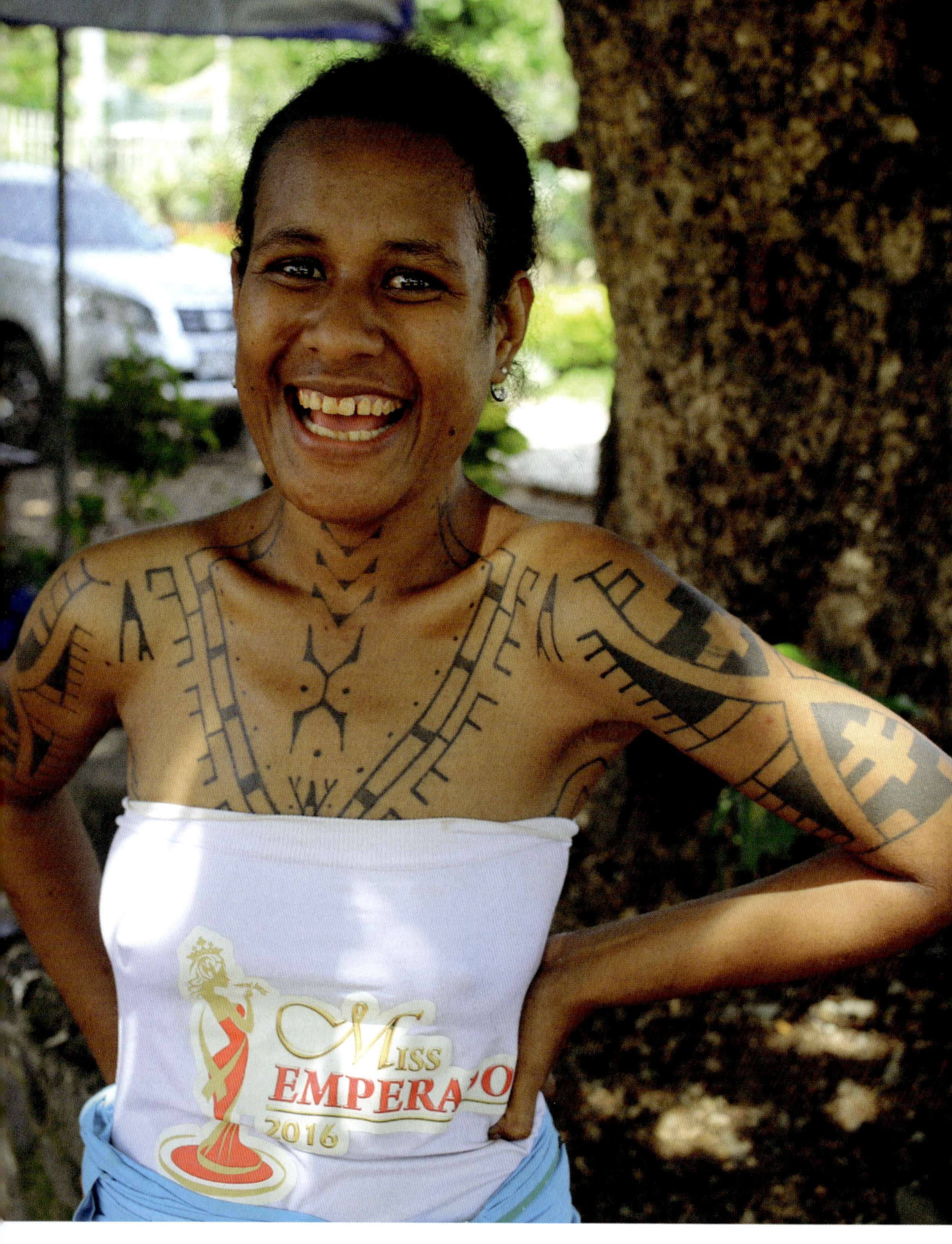

Terita Gamoga Toea with Motu *revareva* (tattoos) on her chest, 2019. Traditionally, these and other (facial) patterns would have been received after the completion of a successful *hiri* sailing expedition by her male relatives. Tattooing by Julia Mage'au Gray.

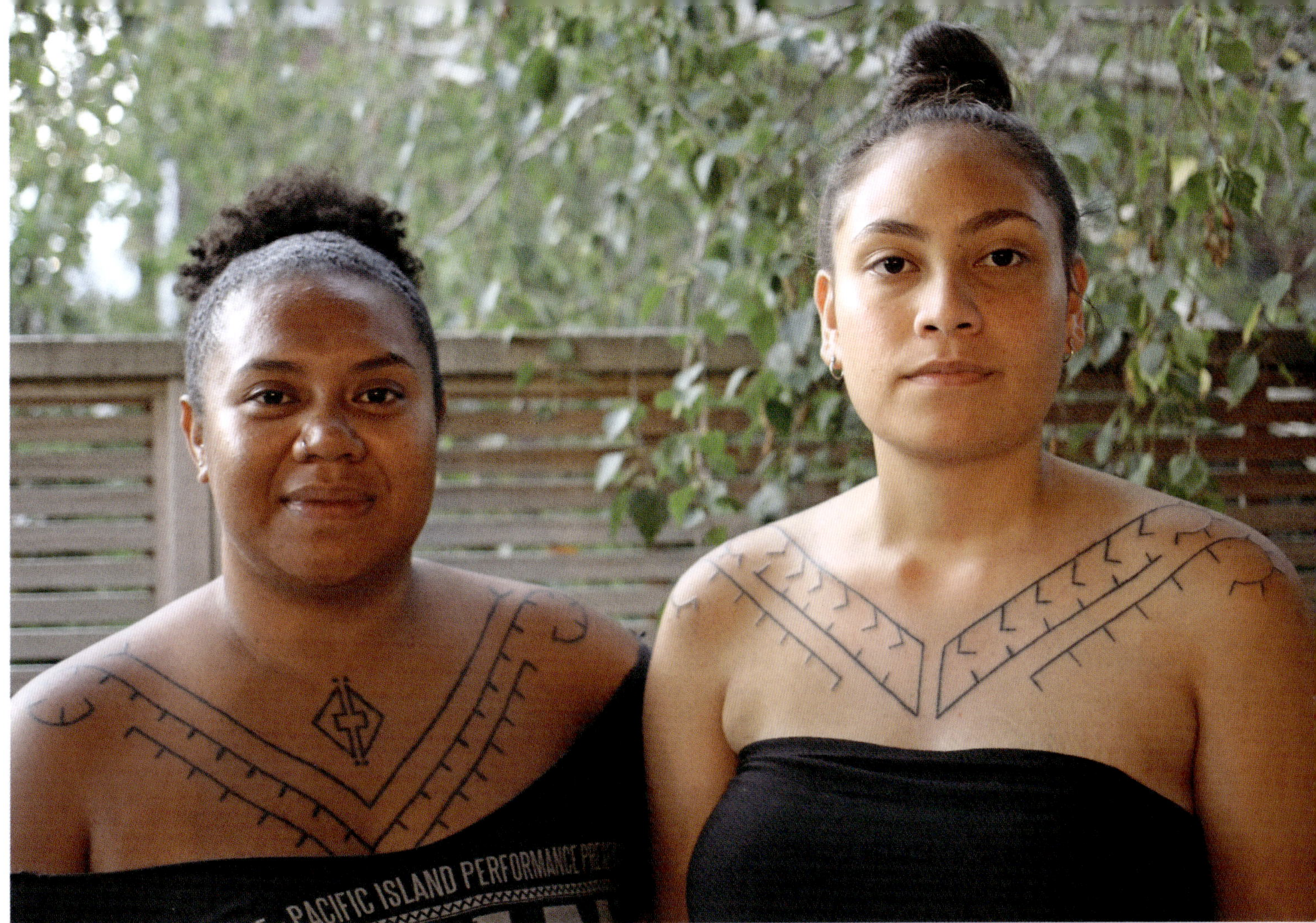

Gray's aunt Michaelyn Pokarop and niece Salevasa Gray display their newly acquired Mekeo *poapoa* or chest tattoos, 2020. Tattooing by Julia Mage'au Gray.

the arrival of Christian missionaries more than one hundred years ago. Losing these tattoos, which were once intimately associated with cultural rites of passage, identity, and social accomplishments, was unacceptable for Gray.

"We lost our elders' knowledge and vision, our connections to the past, and who we were as women," she explained. "And because we no longer had tattooists, we needed someone to imprint our stories on skin again and return this important role back to the community. After all, these signs on skin are not just pictures, they are stories about your life and your journey through it."[28]

"Marking our people's skin with the patterns that hold the visual language of our ancestors is work that is loaded with responsibility," Gray said. "I aim to recreate patterns that hold the integrity of the past, while still marking transitions for an individual (and their families) in today's context. Wearing our marks today empowers us to state an identity we are often asked to justify. Our marks reconnect us in a way that visually holds us to our heritage. The responsibility to inspire the next generation to continue to find the value in marking and wearing our old peoples' way of thinking on their skin is an honor for myself and my family."[29]

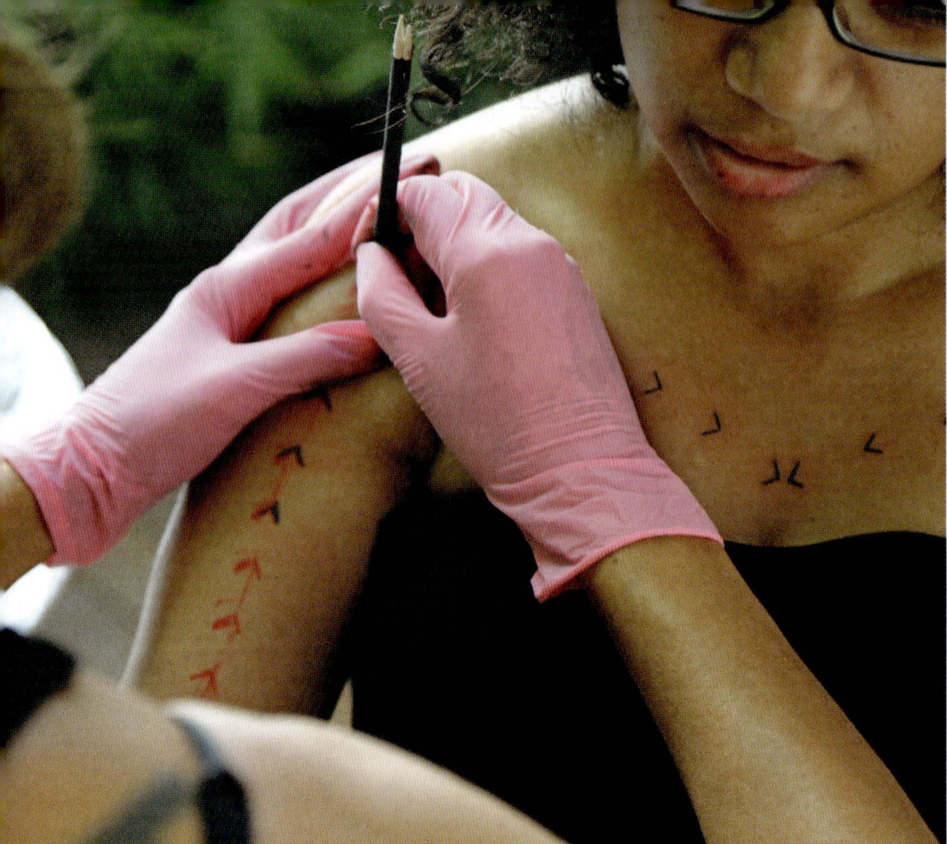

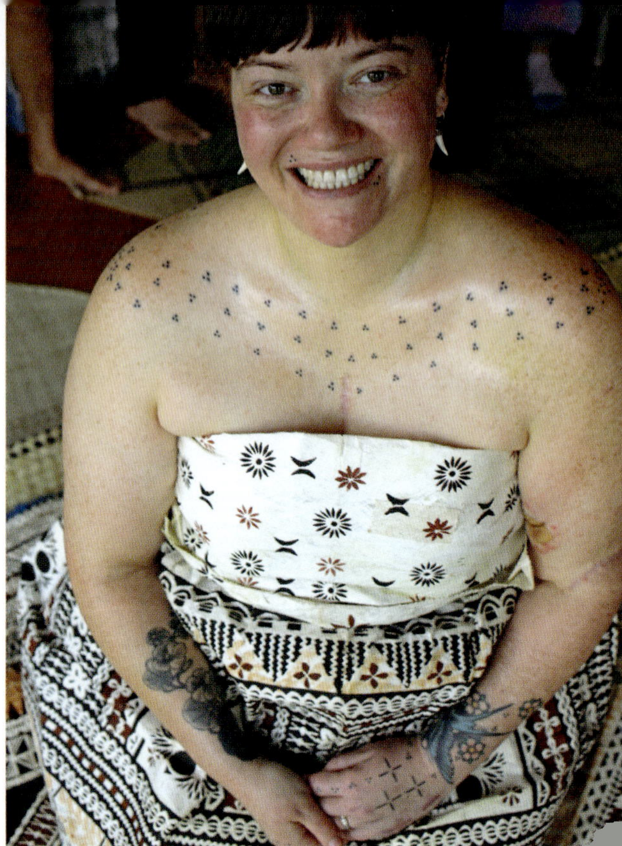

Gray has made great strides in re-instilling cultural pride into Mekeo and other Indigenous tattooing traditions in PNG, inking many Motu and Hula clients who seek to firmly re-root themselves to their ancestry through cultural tattoos.

"Polynesian cultures are tattooing again . . . they have had their renaissance," she shared. "They have brought it back, and we are only beginning to do so now. We need to remember what we have [in PNG] is incredible. We can keep it alive, and it is up to us. And if we don't do it, then we're being negligent and lazy," and, she believes, not fulfilling their potential.[30]

Gray is also part of the *Veiqia Project*, a creative research movement that engages ethnic Fijian artists and curators living in New Zealand and Australia to recover their traditional *veiqia* (tattooing) practices. "Fijian women used to have a very proud and ancient tradition of *veiqia*, where female children were tattooed when they reached puberty," explained *Veiqia Project* curator Ema Tavola. "But this tradition has been lost over time due to colonization, missionization, and other factors."[31]

Gray tattooed Tavola on her arms and hands with Fijian motifs through the ancient technique of hand-poking. Tavola, who bears other Indigenous-style tattoos, says her *veiqia* are the most important of all. "For me, the meaning of these marks is related to revival and memory, Fijian art history, and the power and prestige of an art form reserved exclusively for women and girls. These tattoos are part of my identity as a Fijian woman, as an artist, as a Melanesian. They challenge ideas about beauty and aesthetics, history and colonization, gender and power, and galvanize my love and loyalty for Fiji."

Above left Julia Mage'au Gray hand-pokes *qia* (tattoos) on Dulcie Stewart, 2015.

Above Cassandra Gibs-Low displays her new Fijian-style *qia* (tattoos), 2020. Tattooing by Julia Mage'au Gray.

Opposite *Veiqia Project* curator Vasemaca Tavola displays her new *qia* (tattoos) with Julia Mage'au Gray, 2015. Tattooing by Julia Mage'au Gray.

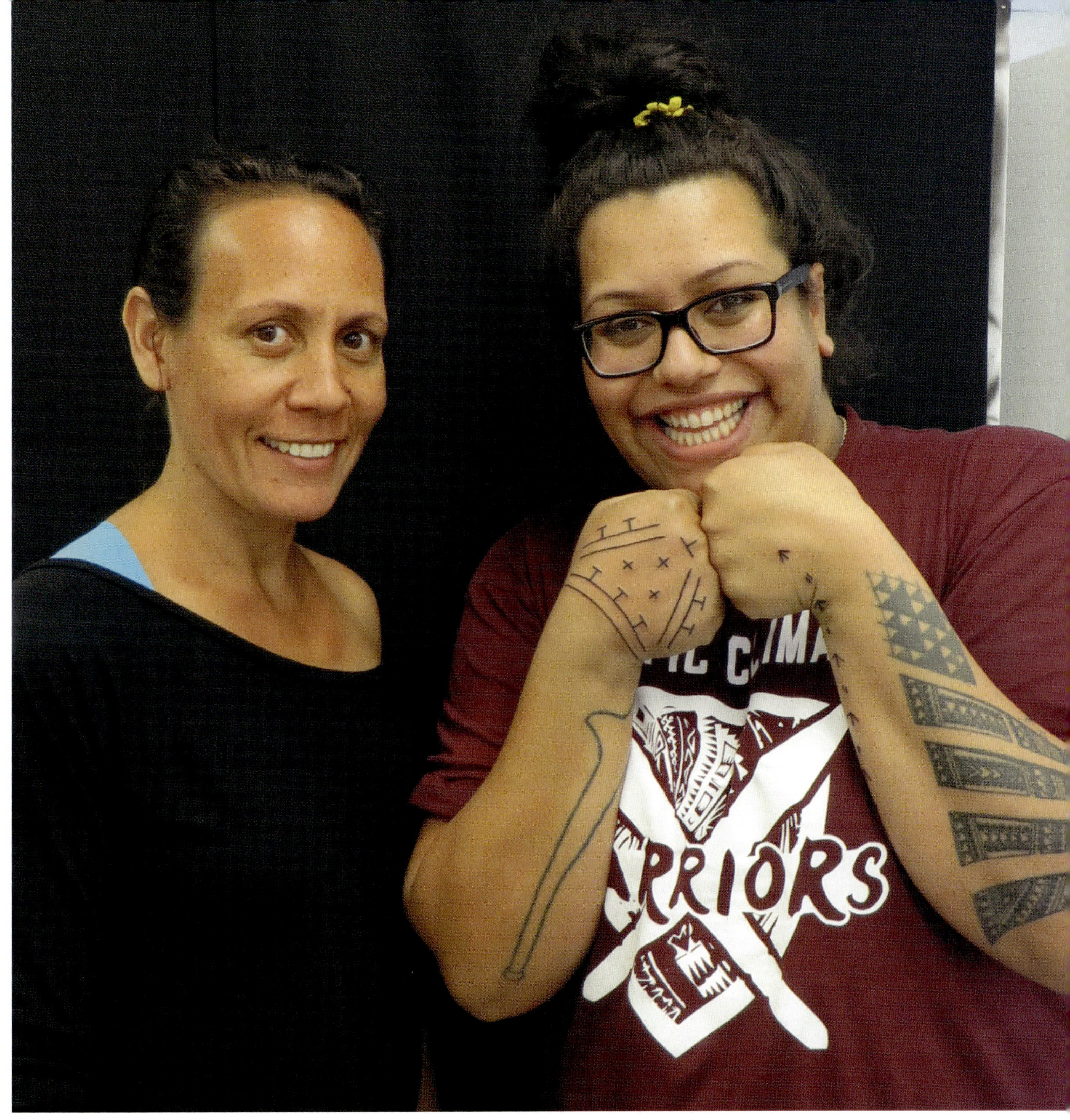

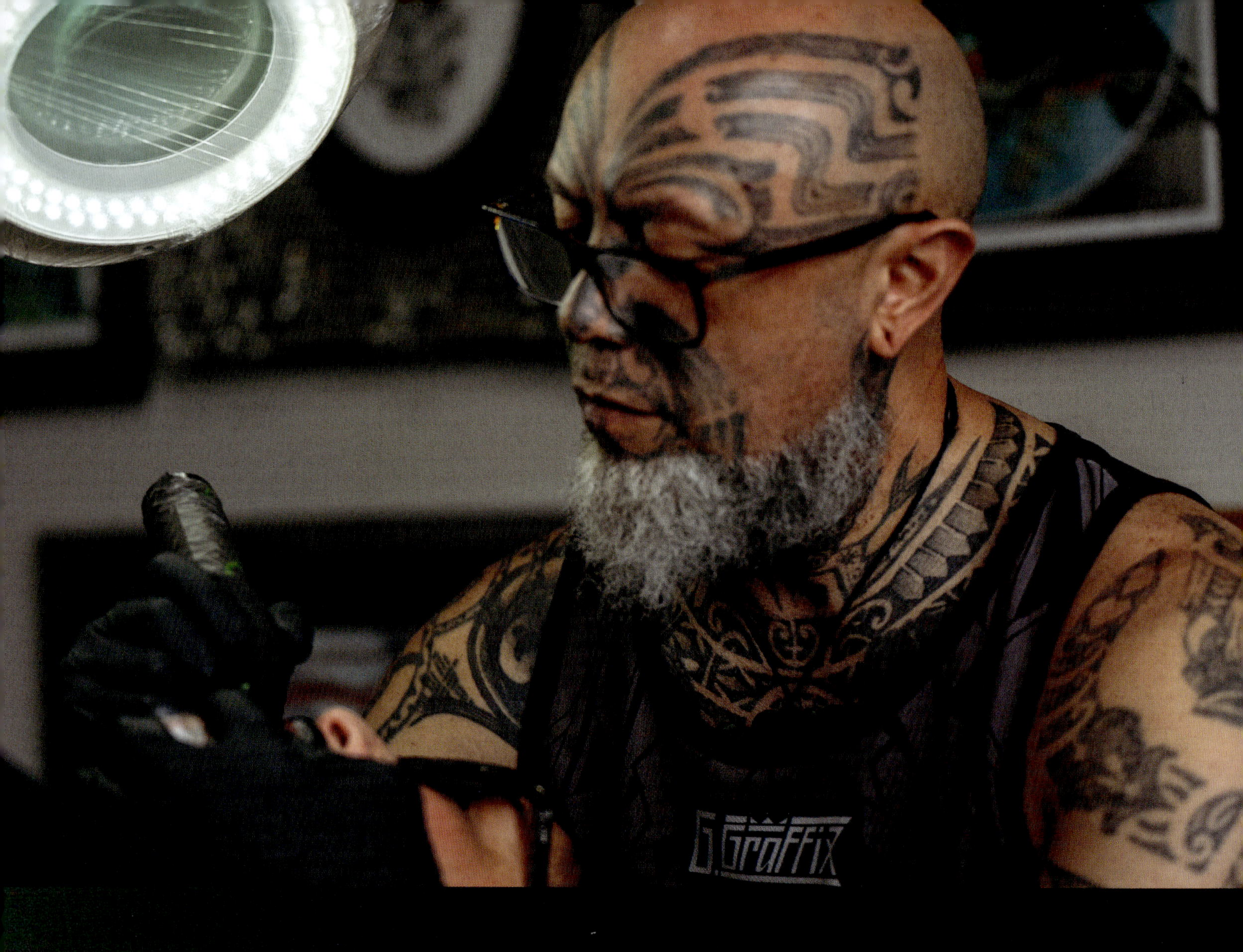

Turumakina Duley: Māori *Tohunga Tā Moko*

Opposite Turumakina Duley at work, 2023. He said, "Prior to the arrival of Europeans in New Zealand . . . The unique scarification/tattoo markings delineated information about the person from afar, so individuals did not have to get too close and risk a violent encounter."

Right Facial *tā moko* of Ngarino Te Waati by Turumakina Duley, 2020. As it was in the past, *tā moko* continues to be worn today as a mark of Māori cultural identity and pride.

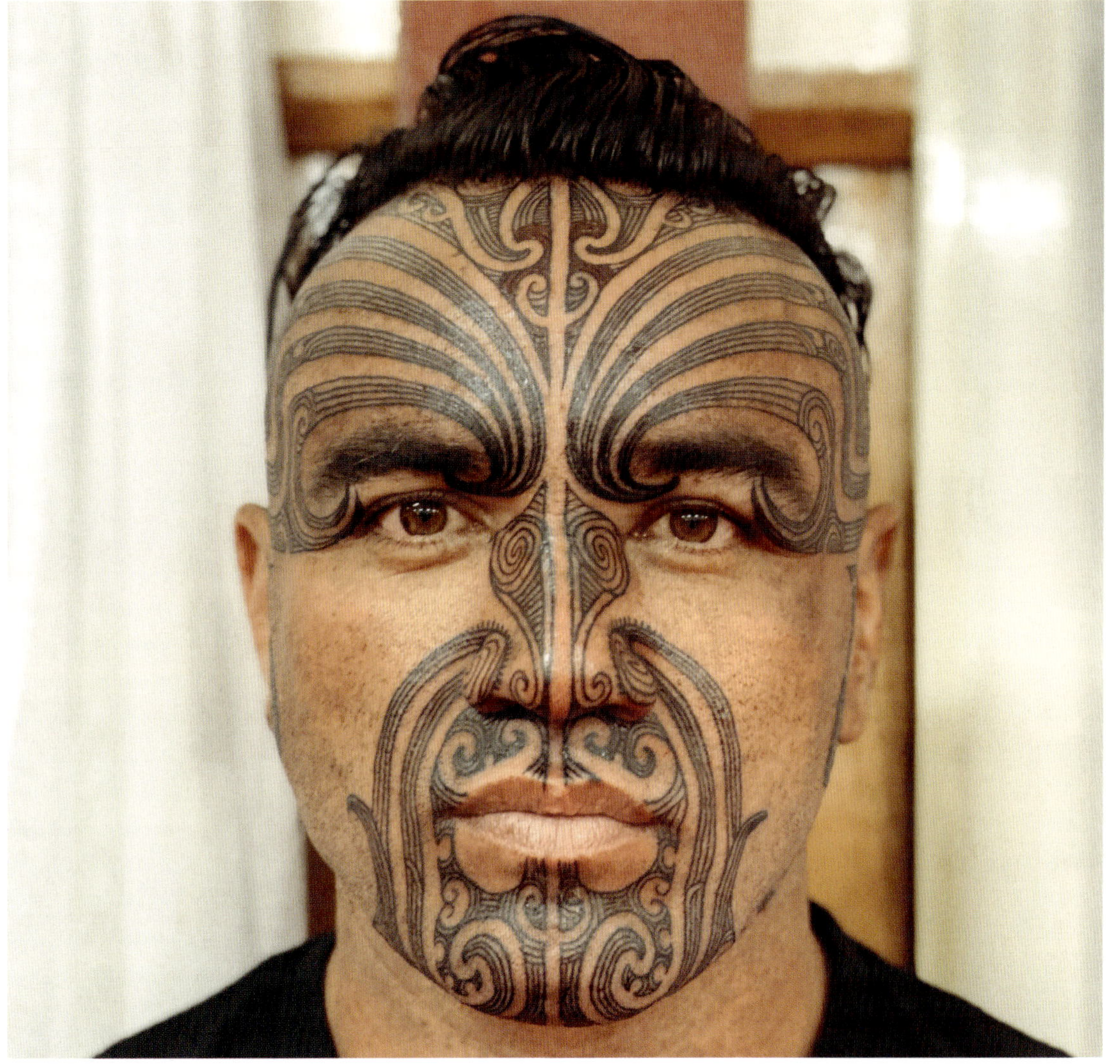

Born in Whakatāne in the Bay of Plenty region of northern New Zealand, Turumakina Duley has been tattooing for thirty years. He began reclaiming his Māori culture in his teenage years as a member of a traveling Pacific Island dance troupe where he began drawing Māori *tā moko* (tattoos) on the bodies of performers to accentuate their stage presence. Later, he began a tattoo apprenticeship under Mark Kopua, which initiated his career as a Māori *tohunga tā moko* (tattoo specialist).

Prior to settling on Australia's Gold Coast in 2009, where today he and his wife Ify-Refini operate Arts Elemental studio, Duley frequently traveled outside of New Zealand to tattoo diasporic Māori who were looking to more firmly connect with their cultural roots. Sometimes he would ink thirty or more *tā moko* on a trip.

"These *kaiwhiwhi* (recipients) may not have had a firm idea of where their family came from," he said. "Māori culture and *tā moko* are

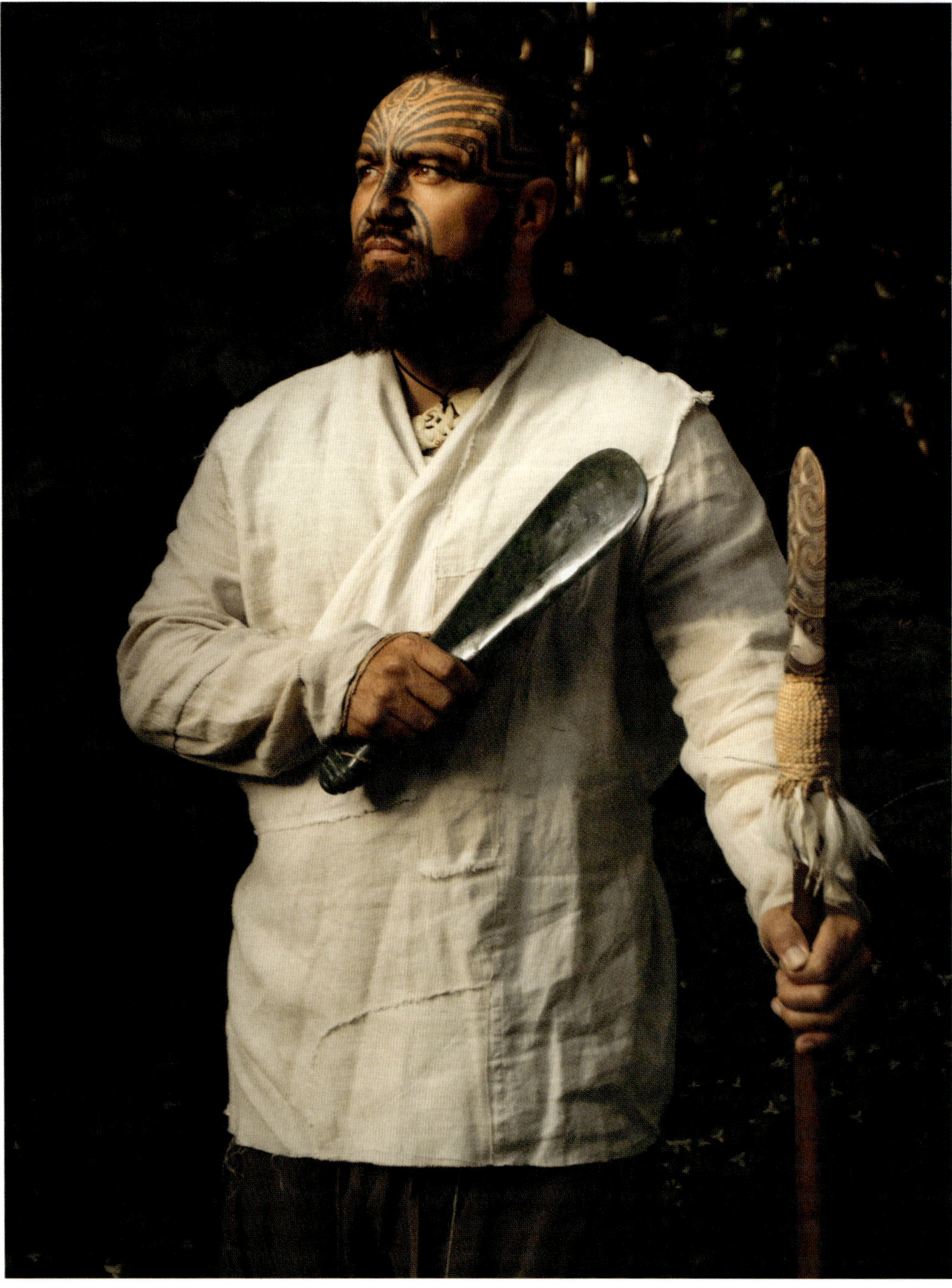

Portrait of Ngarino Te Waati, 2023. "*Moko* is a symbol of transformation of one's personal character and the responsibility one undertakes for his fellow human beings," Duley said. "In our modern world this sense of social contribution is becoming increasingly important." Tattooing by Turumakina Duley.

Facial *tā moko* of Arekatera "Katz" Maihi by Turumakina Duley, 2017.

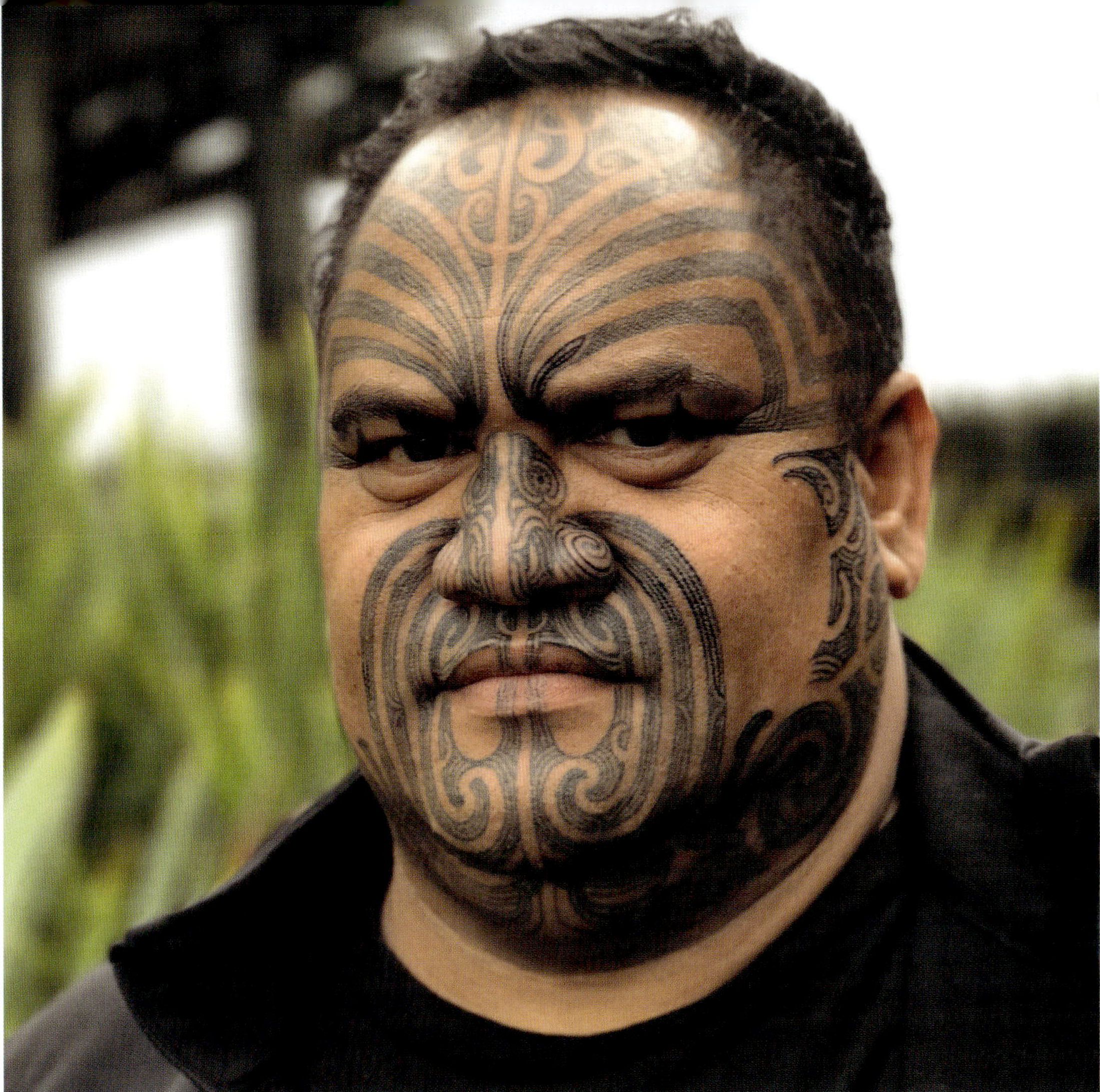

grounded in *Whakapapa* – genealogy – modern *tā moko* can therefore urge a person to seek their roots in order to carry the stories of their ancestors with integrity, this often sparks a journey of self-discovery for those disconnected from their roots through colonization."[32]

Prior to applying *tā moko*, Duley prepares spiritually, especially if he is tattooing a person's face or some other major work, like a *puhoro* (buttocks and thigh tattoo), because the shedding of blood is highly *tapu* (sacred/restricted) and the head is considered the most *tapu* part of a human being. He recites *karakia*, an invocation/incantation that Māori specialists (carvers, weavers, etc.) utter prior to many important activities. The *karakia* invokes the presence of the ancestors, acknowledges the *atua* Māori (deities) connected to any natural resources used, and asks for the safety of all involved. For Duley, the *karakia* also provides him with a sense of preparedness and well-being.

Duley does not normally utilize stencils and masterfully crafts each *tā moko* as he works the surfaces of the body. "*Moko* practitioners

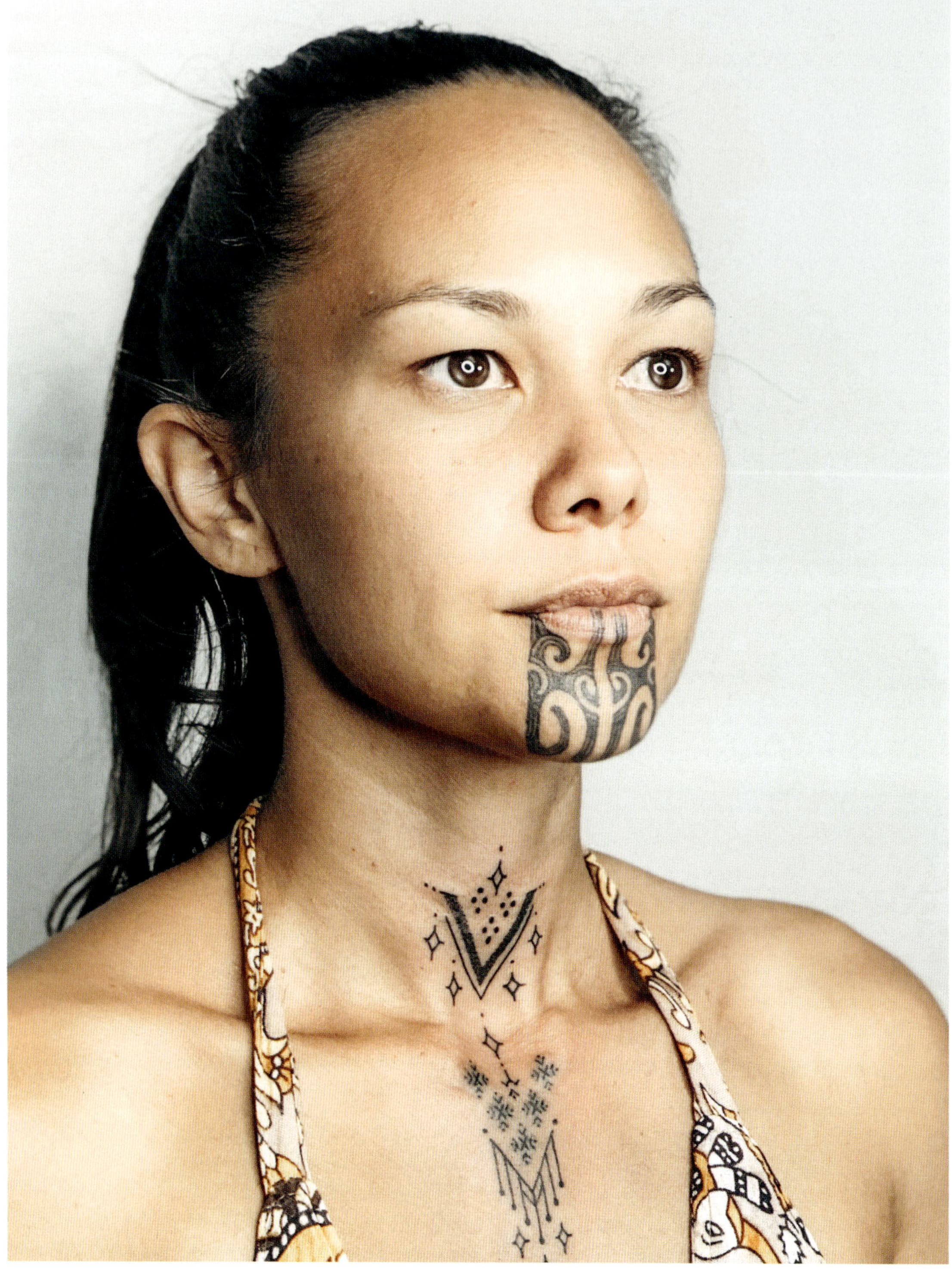

Facial *moko kauae* of Vanessa Voigt by Turumakina Duley, 2021.

Right Facial *moko kauae* of Oriini Kaipara by Turumakina Duley, 2019.

Far right Facial *tā moko* of James Peacock by Turumakina Duley, 2021.

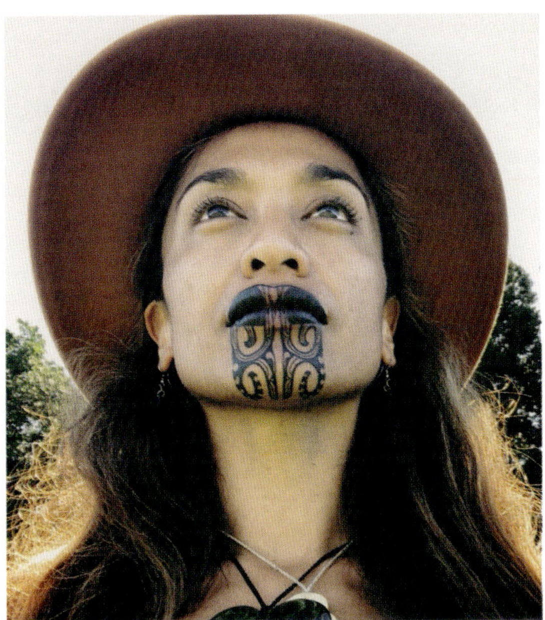

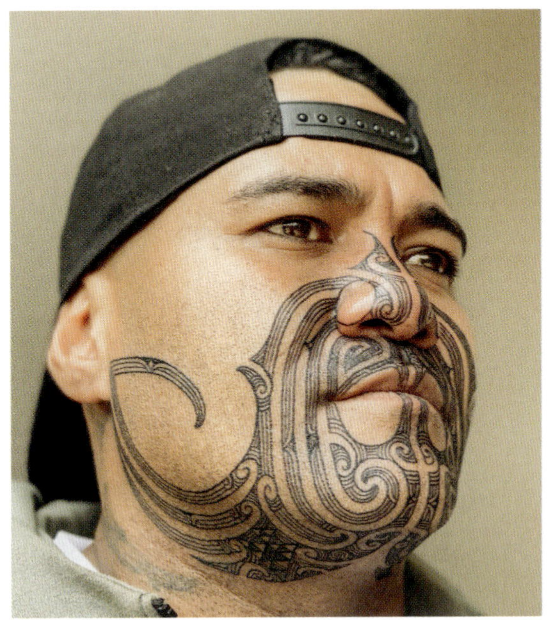

gather a 'repertoire' of patterns, arranging them on the body as we work," he explained. "This allows me to use the body's natural contours to delineate a natural flow as I go about interpreting their *Whakapapa* and intentions for the *moko*. Thus, the *tā mako* comes from the *kaiwhiwhi* in more ways than one."[33]

For the Māori, "the origins of *tā moko* or tattooing begin in the spirit world," Duley said. "Acquired from Rarohenga by our ancestor Mataora through the lineage of his wife Niwareka, it is a mark of transformation that mirrors his epic life journey of self-discovery and upholds the noble characteristics of the people of Rarohenga, where love and peace preside."[34]

"Although the tradition was nearly lost during the European colonial invasion into the Land of the Long White Cloud, today a new generation of *tā moko* practitioners work to revive the art form and modernize its practicability for Māori," Duley revealed.[35] This includes female practitioners such as Julie Paama-Pengelly, Pip Hartley, Christine Harvey, and Henriata Nicholas, among others. Moreover, the full-body tattoos of Māori women have resurfaced, featuring skin markings on the forehead, thighs, buttocks, shoulders, back, neck, arms, lower abdomen, and *kopu whakairo* (genital area).[36] "This *taonga* [cultural treasure or property] was [removed] away from us, and I am really proud of the fact that there are a lot of [tattooed] Māori people walking around now," because this signifies a reclamation of cultural identity and a peaceful resistance, despite the ongoing challenges of colonization.[37] Indeed, *tā moko* has been crucial to restoring Māori identity and is proudly worn by public figures such as former New Zealand foreign minister Nanaia Mahuta, prime-time television journalist Oriini Kaipara, and musician Ariana Tikao, among others. Nowadays, *tā moko* also serves as a healing tool, reestablishing the traditional balance among men, women, *takatāpui* (Māori with diverse genders), and the *tīpuna* (ancestors), while addressing the enduring historical trauma and violence of colonization.[38]

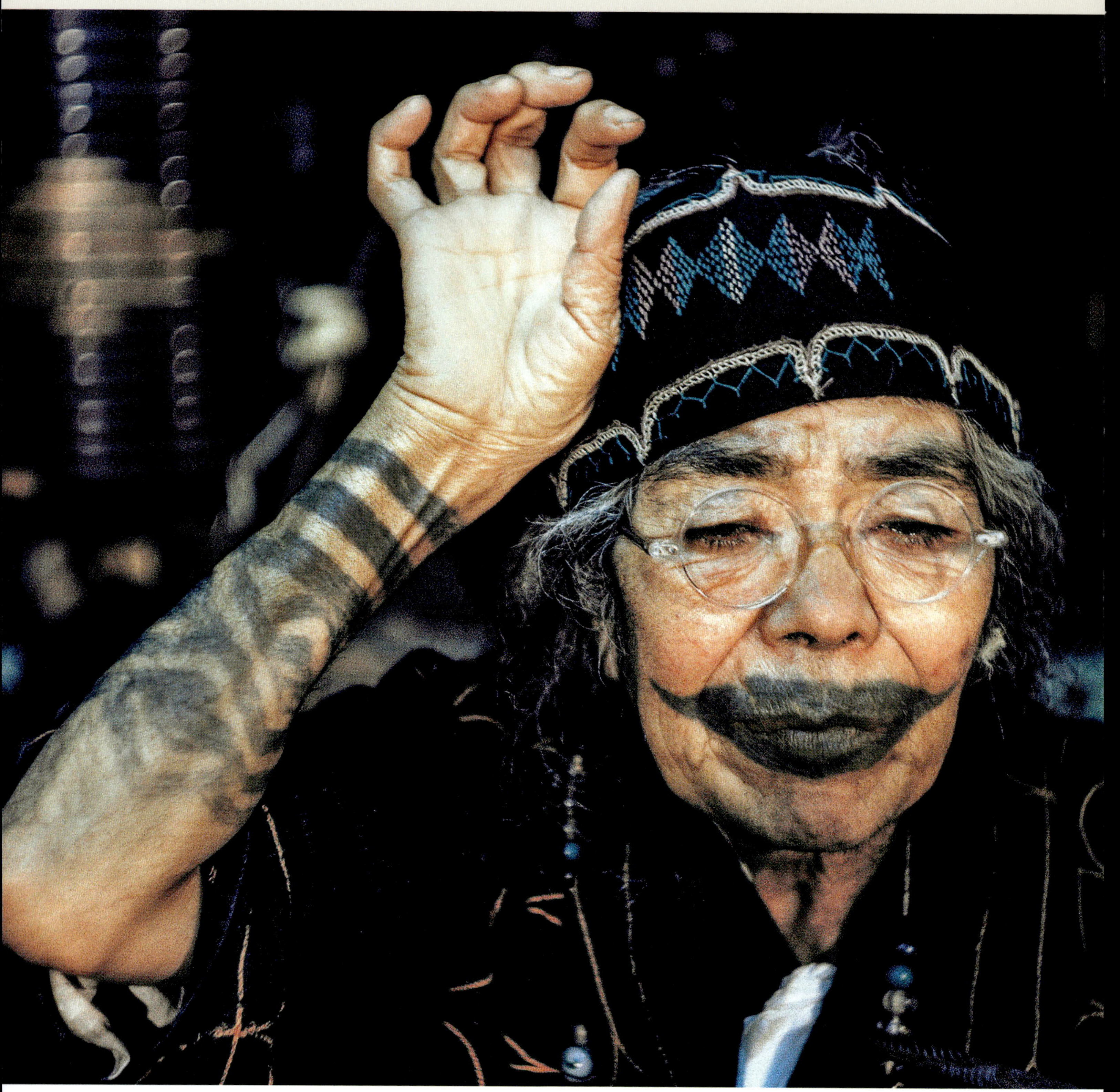

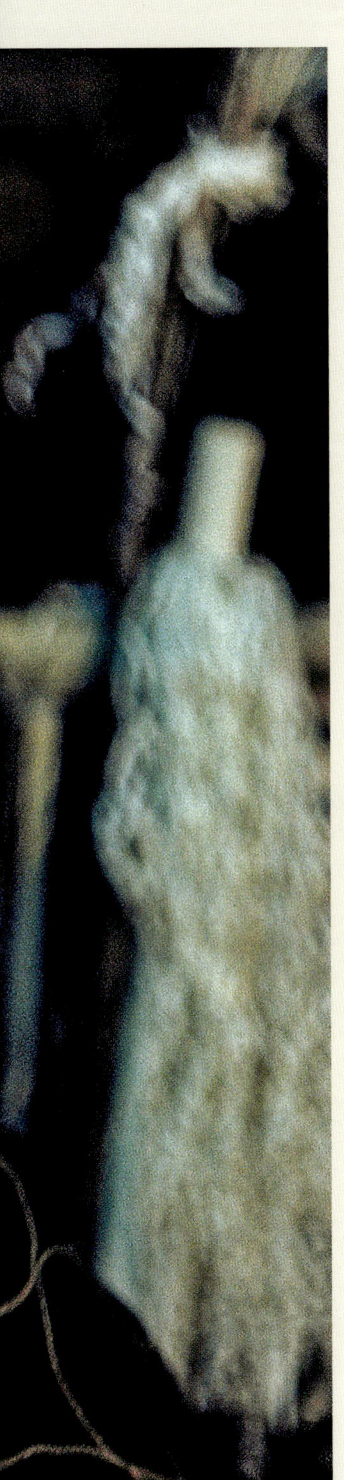

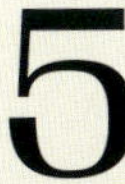

5 TRIBAL TATTOOS OF JAPAN

Japan has an ancient history of tattooing-practice spanning thousands of years and dozens of islands. The Indigenous Ryukyuan people from the Nantō (Southern Islands) and the Ainu of the northernmost island of Hokkaido each maintained distinctive tattooing traditions, yet similarities in their ceremonial beliefs and religious practices seemingly link them to one another in profound ways. DNA evidence and other biological traits demonstrate that these two peoples were direct descendants of the Prehistoric Jōmon people, who inhabited Japan as early as 16,000 years ago.[1] But exactly when the Ryukyuans and Ainu diverged from the ancestral Jōmon culture remains a mystery.

Ainu woman's facial and arm tattoos, 1962.

At the turn of the twentieth century, Ryukyuan and Ainu tattooing traditions faced a severe and relentless decline, driven by the Japanese government's harsh condemnation of these "primitive" and "backward" practices. The Japanese Empire, in its fervent quest to impose Western ideals, embarked on an aggressive campaign of *dōka*, or sociocultural assimilation, with the intent of eradicating Indigenous customs, including tattooing.[2]

In 1879, as the Japanese government annexed the Ryukyu Islands, they began to actively discourage the practice of *hajichi*, the deeply ingrained and culturally significant tradition of Ryukyuan tattooing. This marked the beginning of a systematic effort to erase these traditions altogether. By 1899, the Empire took a more draconian approach, officially banning all forms of tattooing. Those found guilty of either performing or receiving tattoos were not merely reprimanded; they faced severe penalties, including hefty fines and imprisonment.[3] To amplify the shame and deter others, the authorities took the extraordinary step of publicizing the names and addresses of tattooists and their clients in local newspapers, subjecting them to public humiliation and social ostracism.

The Ainu faced a similar fate under the Ezo Shogunate, which had partially banned *nuye* or *sinuye* (Ainu tattoos) as early as 1799. This prohibition was further expanded in 1871 when the government's Hokkaido Development Mission issued a more stringent tattoo ban.[4] The Mission, driven by a zealous determination to "modernize" the Ainu, systematically targeted and suppressed Ainu tattooing traditions, branding them as obstacles to progress and civilization.

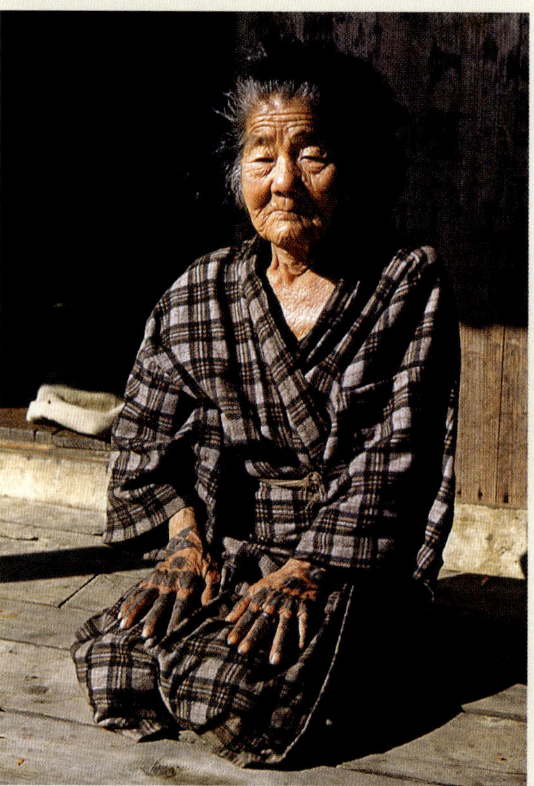

Tattooed Okinawan elder, Itoman district, *ca.* 1960s.

The Empire's relentless pursuit of *dōka* aimed not only to assimilate the Indigenous peoples of Japan but also to obliterate their cultural identities. Tattooing, once a profound expression of identity and cultural heritage among the Ryukyuans and Ainu, was reduced to a symbol of defiance against a regime obsessed with uniformity and Westernization.

Despite government bans on Ryukyuan and Ainu tattooing, some women rebelliously continued the practice well into the early twentieth century, as it was deeply woven into the fabric of their Indigenous culture. Tattooed elders from the Ryukyuan and Ainu communities, interviewed over the last century, often described their tattoo experiences as profoundly

Tattooed Ainu woman of Japan portrayed in the book *Ezotō kikan* by Awagimaru Hata (1764–1808), 1799.

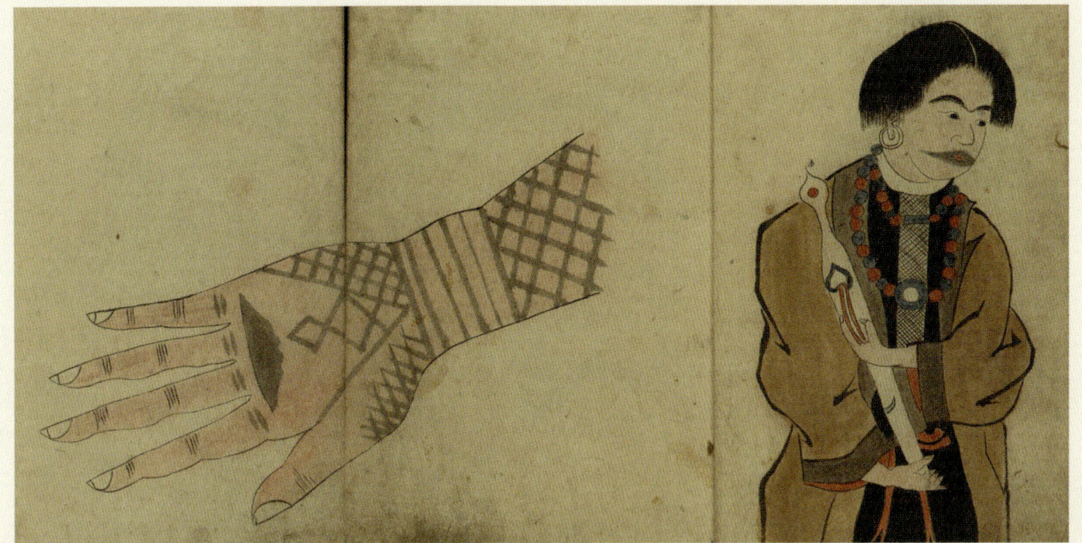

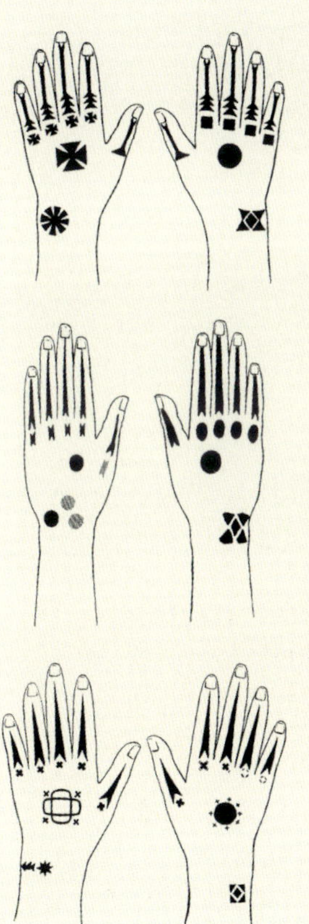

Tattoos of Yaeyama Island, Shuri district of Okinawa, and Tokunoshima Island, 1910.

spiritual. For them, these tattoos were not mere adornments but essential rites of passage for the afterlife.[5]

Various accounts reveal the torment Ryukyuan women believed they would face after death if they were not tattooed, including being condemned to perform arduous tasks in the afterlife. Kazuo Obara, a pioneering tattoo researcher, highlighted that untattooed Ryukyuan women were thought to be unable to enter paradise after death, with their souls destined to be lost forever without their sacred *hajichi* markings.[6]

American missionary and anthropologist M. Inez Hilger documented similar beliefs among the Ainu. According to her research, tattooed Ainu women were assured a life after death among their deceased ancestors.[7] Conversely, untattooed women who reached Kamui Moshir, the Ainu afterlife, were warned: "they'll tattoo you [there] with a bamboo knife, and that . . . will really be painful."[8]

These vivid narratives underscore the deep spiritual and cultural significance of tattooing for the Ryukyuan and Ainu people. Despite facing severe restrictions, the enduring commitment to these traditional practices reveals a resilient spirit and a profound connection to their ancestral beliefs. Tattoos were a sacred bond with the divine, a necessary passage to a serene and honorable afterlife, and a testament to their indomitable cultural identity.

Ryukyuan and Ainu tattooists were invariably female. Although tattooing was almost always carried out by women for female clients, men were also tattooed among both groups. All these markings, whether for men or women, were inserted into the skin either as an indicator of ethnic or regional identity, for apotropaic means, or as a medicinal treatment.

For the Ryukyuans, tattooing was steeped in tradition and spirituality. While they often used Chinese and India inks for tattoo pigments, they also relied on a more mundane yet sacred substance: soot from the hearth.[9] This soot, gathered from the very heart of their homes, carried with it the essence of the hearth spirit—a deity of immense significance in the Ryukyuan universe. The hearth spirit, intimately connected to all women, was one of the most crucial *kami*, or deities, serving as the messenger to higher *kami* and ancestor spirits.[10] As a female deity, the hearth goddess enjoyed exclusive worship from women, who were considered spiritually superior to men.

The Ainu people shared a similar reverence for the hearth, associating it with a powerful female deity. The soot from their sacred fires was used to create women's tattoos, imbuing them with protective properties. The Ainu fire goddess, Fuchi, believed to be adorned with tattoos herself, was invoked before all ceremonies. Communication with other *kamuy*, or deities, was deemed impossible without her divine intervention.[11] Fuchi stood as a guardian and guide, ensuring that the spiritual and everyday worlds remained interconnected.

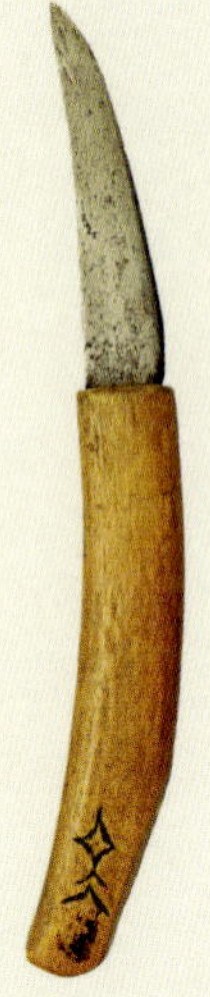

Above Ainu *makiri*, or tattooing knife, Piratori village, Hokkaido, 1888. An apotropaic symbol is carved into the handle.

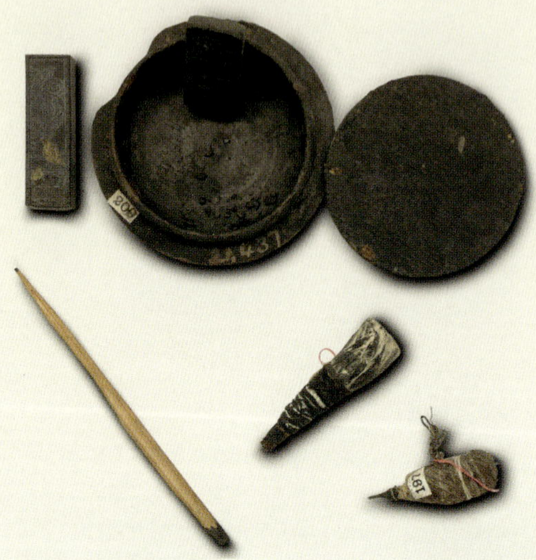

Above right Ryukyuan tattooing tools from Okinawa and Amami Ōshima, 1896. The implements consist of two needled devices, a stencil stick, an ink slab, and ceramic pigment pot. The twelve-needle tool is from Okinawa and the smaller three-needle tool, Amami Ōshima Island. The needles are cemented together in a row between two strips of bamboo, which are set in a bulbous handle of crumpled paper.

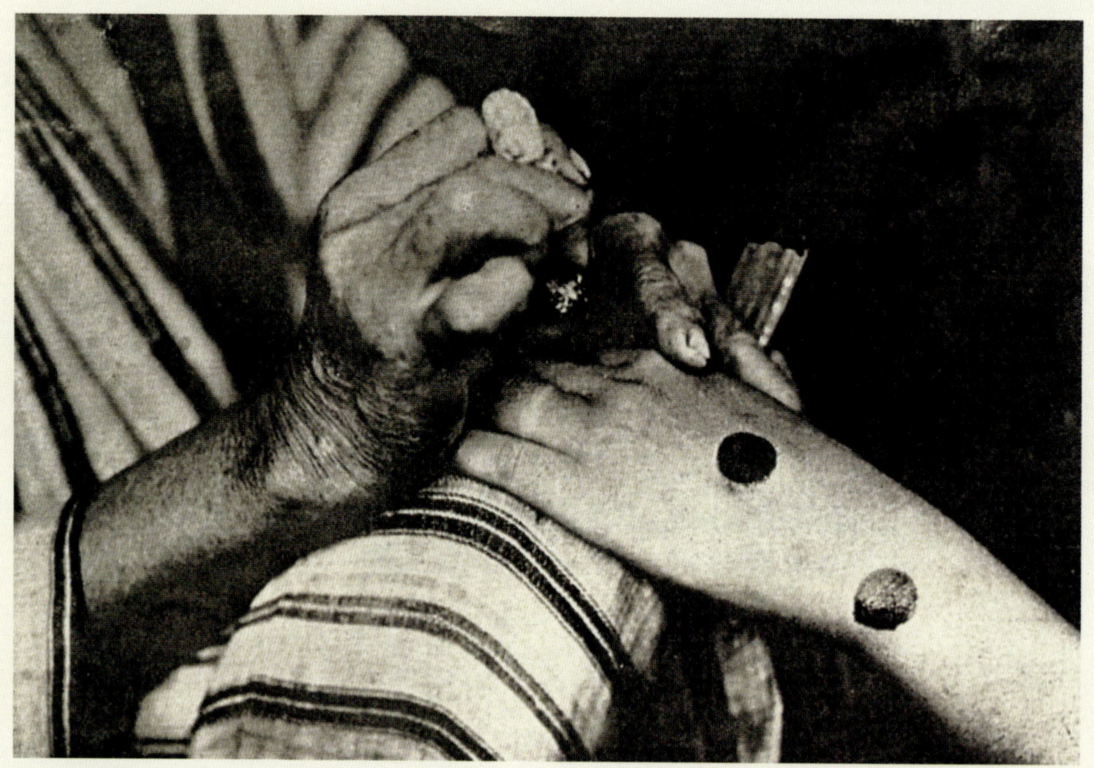

Right Ryukyuan tattooing demonstration, *ca.* 1930.

Ryukyuan tattooing demonstration, *ca.* 1930.

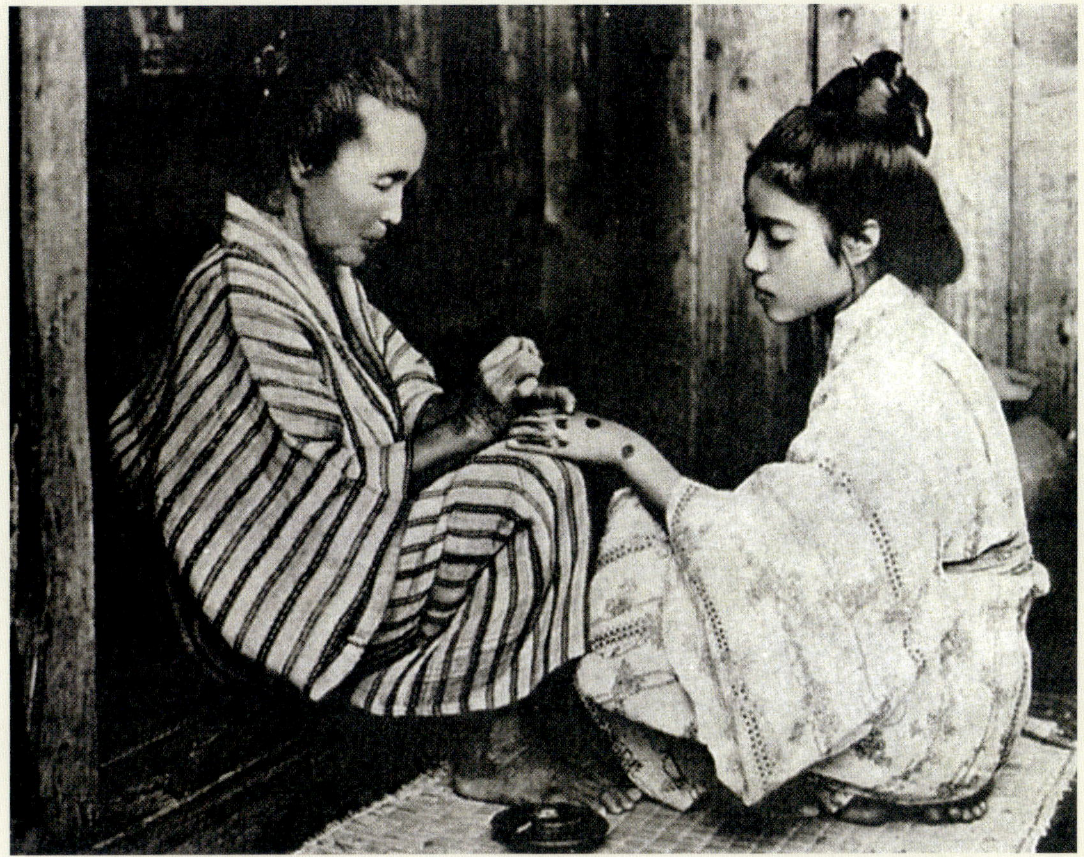

In both Ryukyuan and Ainu cultures, the hearth goddess played a pivotal role, safeguarding families and communities during times of uncertainty and danger. She was the essential messenger to higher powers, bridging the human and divine realms. The hearth, therefore, was not merely a place for warmth and cooking; it was a microcosm of the universe, a sacred space where rituals were performed and cosmic interventions took place.

These hearth deities exemplified the profound connection between women and spirituality in both cultures. Women, through their exclusive worship and use of hearth soot in tattooing, maintained a direct link to the divine. The tattoos themselves became symbols of this connection, protective emblems that carried the blessings of the hearth goddesses. Through the act of tattooing, women inscribed not just symbols but the very essence of their spiritual beliefs onto their bodies, creating living testaments to their faith and adherence to ancestral traditions.

A full set of Ryukyuan women's tattoos took several sessions and years to complete. The aesthetics and groupings of specific tattoo motifs appearing on a woman's arms and hands indicated her place of origin, because certain islands or local insular regions were distinguished by specific tattoo iconography.

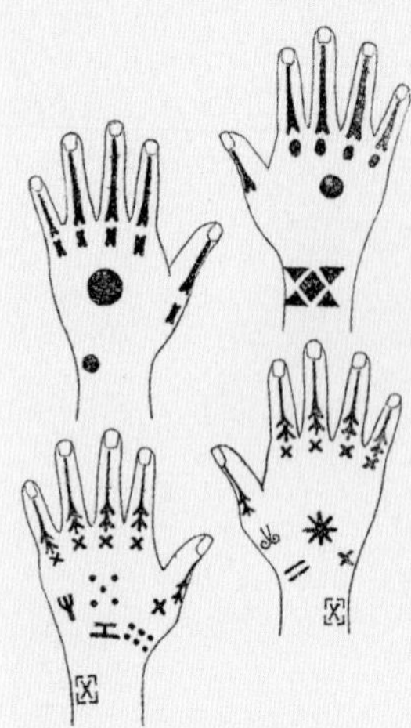

Above Hand tattoos of Okinawa, Miyako, and Amami Ōshima Islands, *ca*. 1898.

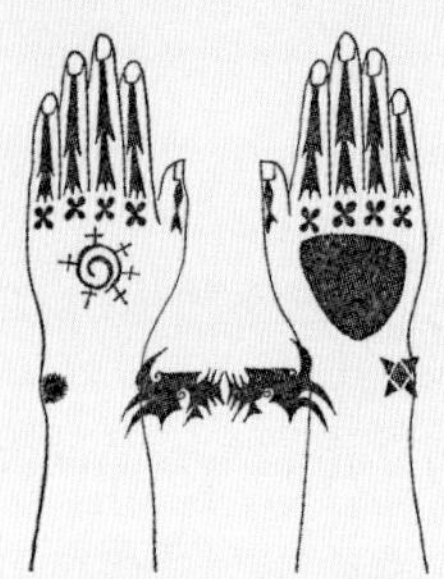

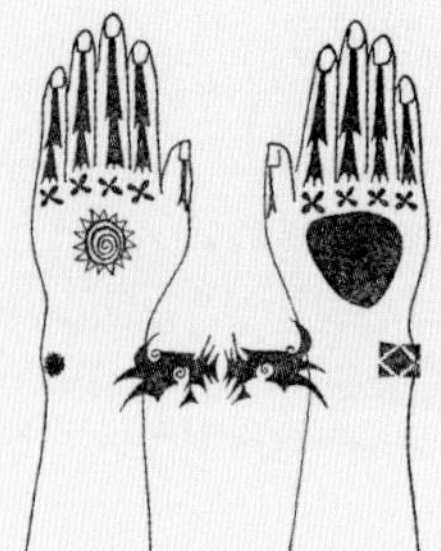

Above Women's tattoo patterns of Amami Ōshima Island, *ca*. 1930.

Across the Ryukyu Islands, a plethora of dialects gave rise to various local terms for "tattooist". One such term, *hajichyaa* (literally, "person who pokes with needles"),[12] was commonly used on Okinawa.[13] The intricate process of tattooing began at a young age for Ryukyuan girls, with their first tattoos being small—about the size of a kidney bean—and the sequence of their placement varying by region. As outlined by Obara, the general progression of the tattoos started on the right hand, beginning with the ring finger and moving through the middle finger, index finger, and thumb. This was followed by the side of the pinky finger, the first knuckle section, and then the stem-shaped protrusions on the side. Once the right hand was completed, the left hand was tattooed in the same meticulous order.[14]

Historical accounts suggest that this initiation into the world of tattoos began as early as age seven or eight, sometimes even before then.[15] As the girls matured, their tattoos were expanded and elaborated upon during significant life stages—first at puberty (between twelve and fifteen years) and again before marriage (at seventeen to eighteen years).[16] Each phase of life brought new layers to their ink, deepening the symbolism and significance of their body art.

The tools of the *hajichyaa* were as varied as the tattoos themselves. They used configurations ranging from single needles to groups of three, five, ten, twenty, or even forty-five sewing needles bound together. For larger patterns on the back of the hand, multiple needle groupings were employed, while finer work on the fingers and arms called for smaller clusters. In a testament to their ingenuity, some *hajichyaa* used natural implements such as the needle-like protective barbs from the leaf stems of Japanese sago palm (*Cycas revoluta*) or the thorns from the "tiger's claw" tree (*Erythrina variegata*).

The art of Ryukyuan tattooing was not merely about aesthetics; it was a deeply ingrained cultural practice that marked significant milestones in a woman's life. Each needle prick, each drop of ink, was a rite of passage, a symbol of growth and transformation. The *hajichyaa*, with their deft hands and keen eyes, were the custodians of this ancient tradition, preserving the stories and heritage of their people through the intricate designs etched onto the skin. In their skilled hands, the needles became more than tools—they were instruments of cultural continuity, weaving the past and present into a vibrant mosaic of living art.

The Ainu practiced a unique form of tattooing, characterized by an incision or cutting technique. Traditional tattoo instruments, known as *makiri*, were reminiscent of small knives, complete with sheaths and handles often intricately carved with zoomorphic or apotropaic motifs meant to ward off evil.[17] Long before the introduction of iron-tipped *makiri* or razor blades, the Ainu relied on razor-sharp obsidian points to make their incisions. These tools, wrapped with fibers near their tips, allowed precise control over the depth of each cut.

Before any skin-cutting began, a sacred ritual unfolded. A greenish antiseptic liquid called *nire* was meticulously prepared. This mixture, essential for both sanitizing the skin and controlling blood flow, also played a role in setting the tattoo pigment.[18] The process began with a clean pot strung above the hearth. Bark from a specific species

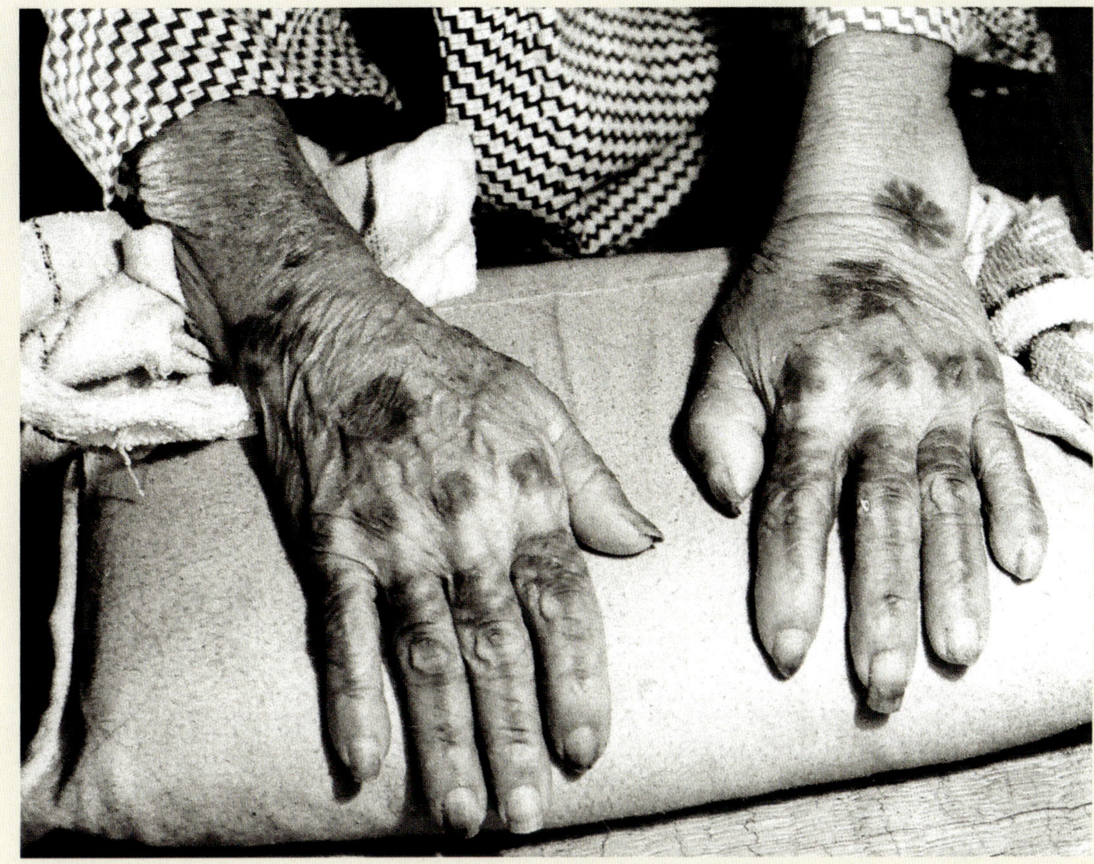

Hajichi of Yaeyama Island elder Matsuru Uema (b. 1874), 1971.

of ash tree was soaked and boiled within it, and *noya*, or mugwort leaves (*Artemisia vulgaris* L. var. *yezoana* Kedo), were added, along with water. The hearth was then kindled with white birch bark, which created a layer of *pash* or soot. The Ainu believed that *noya* leaves had the power to repel evil spirits, and the white birch, deeply associated with women, was often used to create charms and ritual objects for female deities, including the revered fire goddess Fuchi.[19]

Once the antiseptic solution and soot were ready, the tattoo artist dipped a black cloth into the mixture and wiped down the area of the girl's body to be tattooed. Using her fingers, she drew the patterns she would soon cut into the skin. As the incising began, the flowing blood was wiped away with the black cloth, and soot was meticulously rubbed into the *makiri* cuts, embedding the ink into the skin. During this process, female relatives often restrained the girl if she struggled, holding her hands behind her back to prevent resistance.[20]

The tattooing journey for Ainu girls typically began at the tender age of seven or eight with their first lip cuts, although in some regions this initiation started later, around fourteen or fifteen. By eleven or twelve, their hands and arms were tattooed in stages, building up the intricate designs over time. By the time a girl reached seventeen

Women's tattoo patterns of the Kamara district, Okinawa, *ca.* 2001.

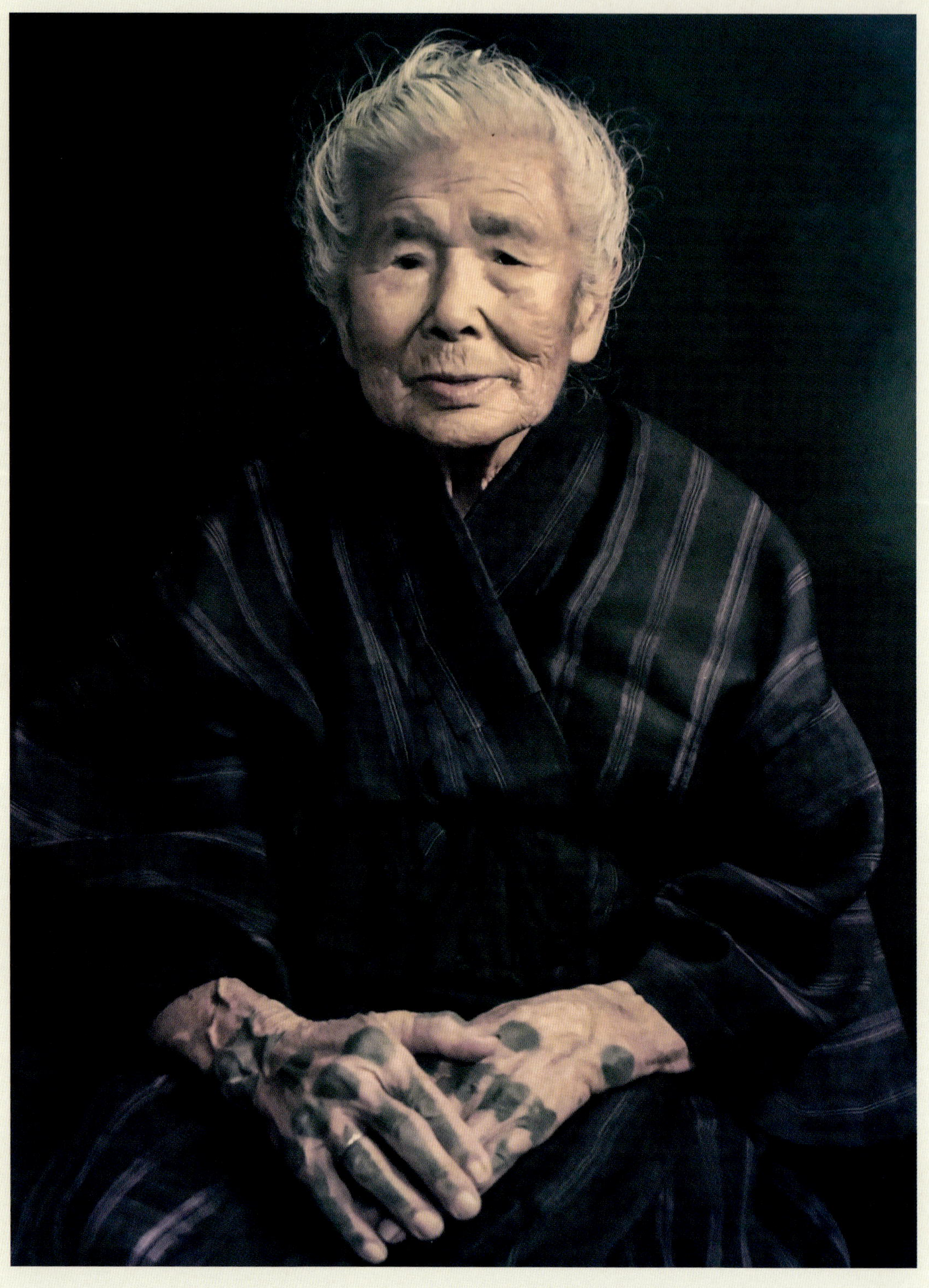

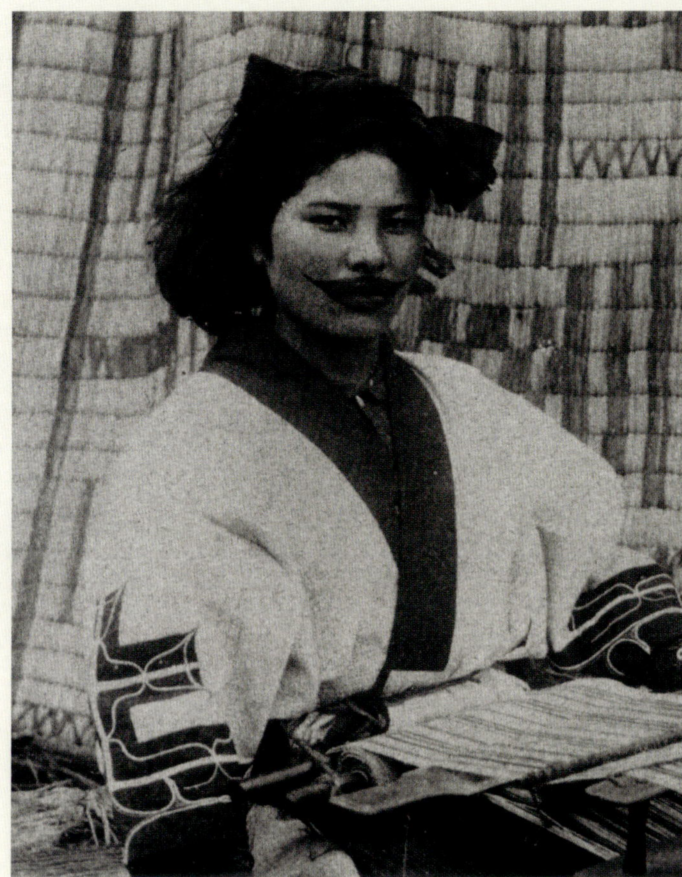

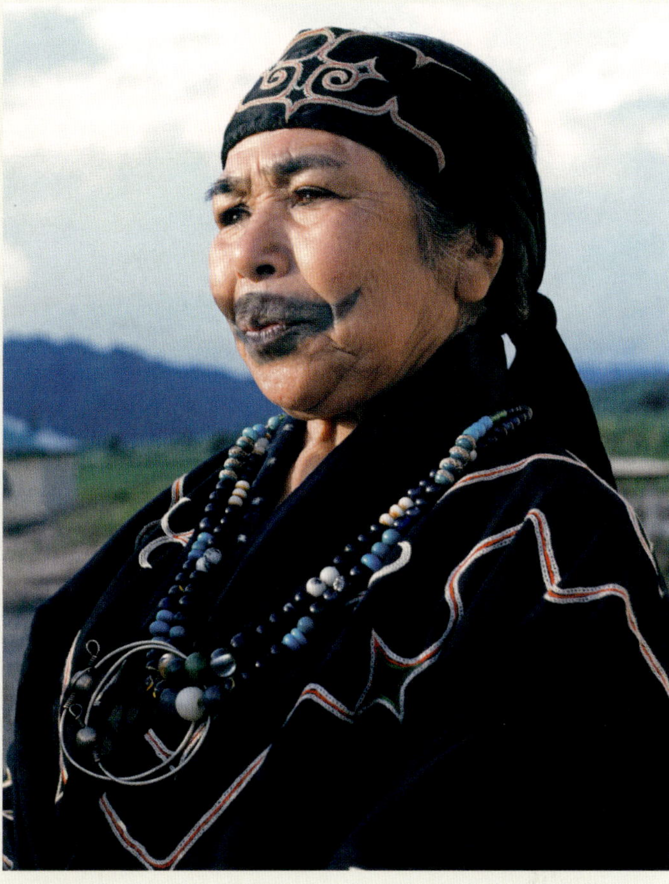

Above Tattooed Ainu woman at the loom, Hokkaido, 1901.

Above right Ainu elder with incised facial tattoos, 1962. The Ainu were officially recognized as an Indigenous people of Japan in 2019.

or eighteen, she was usually fully tattooed, since it was customary to complete the tattooing process before marriage.

The first incisions on the upper lip were delicate and small, gradually expanding over three sessions until the tattoo encircled the entire mouth, taking on the graceful shape of a crescent moon. The design's edges were as varied as the regions themselves: flaring upward in central and southern Hokkaido, curving downward in northern Hokkaido, running parallel to the mouth corners among the Chikabumi Ainu, or simply tracing a complete circle around the mouth in the Kuril Islands and parts of Sakhalin Island and northern Hokkaido. These intricate designs served as a regional mark of identity, enabling others to "read" a woman's origins and cultural heritage through her facial tattoos.

Therapeutic Tattoos of Japan

Before 1920, the Ryukyuans and Ainu engaged in the practice of therapeutic tattooing, often placing these marks over aching limbs or injury sites.

Ainu woman with partially completed mouth tattoo, halted by Japanese bans in the late nineteenth century, 1962.

Around 1890, anatomist Yoshikiyo Koganei journeyed to Kutcharo village in Kushiro Province, Hokkaido, where he met an adult man with a striking 1¼ in. (3 cm) blue line along the back of his left thumb. He also encountered another man and a boy with a cross marking the same location. This cruciform pattern, Koganei noted, sometimes appeared on the outside of an upper arm too.

In Ishikari Province, Koganei observed women adorned with various forms of "medicinal" tattooing. One woman bore "two blue stripes on the thorax at the level of the third rib and four such stripes on the forehead."[21] Koganei wrote of these tattoos: "Such abnormally tattooed areas have arisen from the fact that bad blood has been extracted through skin incisions to strengthen the body [or relieve head or joint pain], and afterward soot has been rubbed in to stop the bleeding . . . They are therefore not to be regarded as decorations."[22]

The British Anglican missionary John Batchelor documented other instances of Ainu therapeutic tattooing, called *pashka-oingara* or "looking over the tattoo."[23] He observed: "When the eyes of old women are growing dim and they are becoming blind, they should re-tattoo their mouths and hands, that they might see

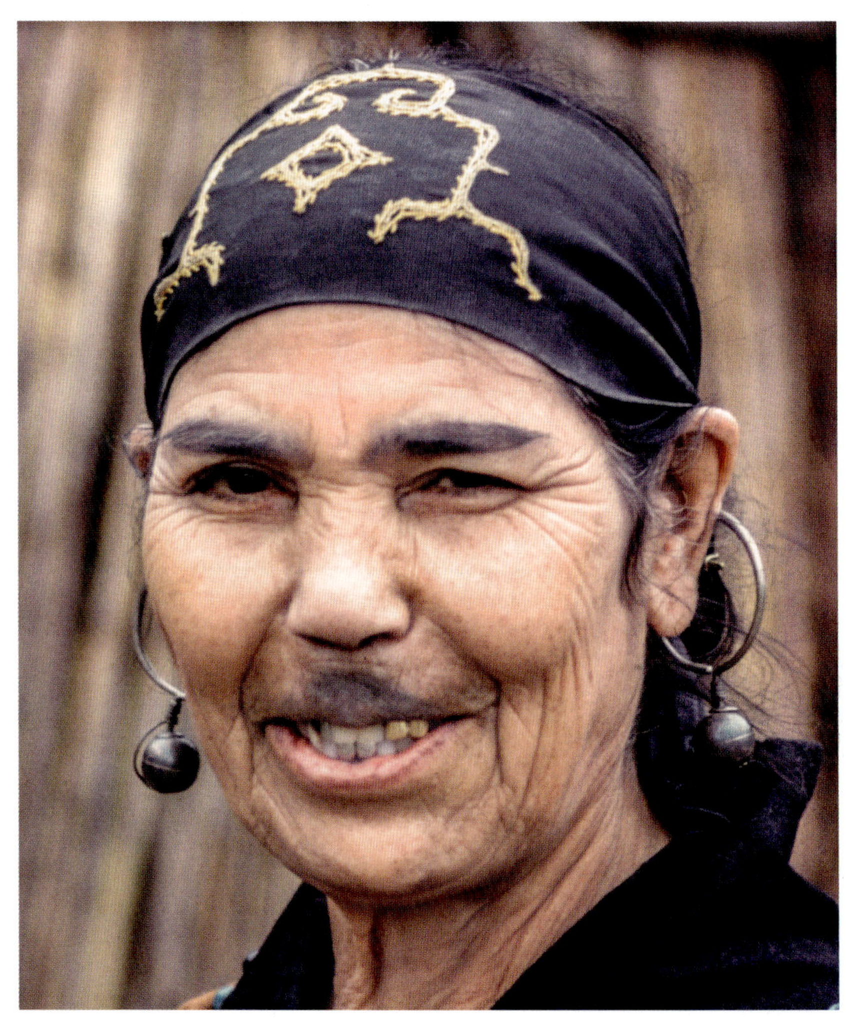

better . . . I am well acquainted with one old lady who actually tattoos herself quite frequently, in order to strengthen her eyesight."[24]

In the 1930s, the anatomist and anthropologist Sakuzaemon Kodama encountered Ainu women who possessed various forms of medicinal skin markings cut into their skin. These tattoos, often consisting of rows of irregular lines, were placed on the injured body parts, such as the back, upper arms, and shoulders, to cure rheumatism, swelling, and pain. One remarkable therapeutic tattooing case involved Taka Hosoda, an eighty-seven-year-old woman from Otofuke village. At the age of fourteen, she was thrown from a horse, suffering a severe injury to her right shoulder. Her aunt, utilizing traditional methods, made a series of incisions, including a swastika pattern, on the injured shoulder. Miraculously, after this procedure, Hosoda's pain vanished, and the "bad blood" was believed to have been released from her body, bringing her relief and healing.[25]

In his travels, American writer and ethnologist William H. Furness noted the presence of crisscross markings on the legs, arms, and shoulders of Ryukyuan men and women. These intricate designs were believed to cure rheumatism, a common ailment.[26] Among the women, swastika designs were also seen in their arm tattoos, although these particular patterns were not associated with medicinal purposes.

German anthropologist Edmund Simon witnessed similar curative tattooing practices on Okinawa in the early 1900s.[27] One woman he observed had three sets of three thick parallel lines tattooed on the back of her knee, just above the calf. Another woman bore intricate tattoos around her right heel, with six squares arranged in two vertical rows on the instep and six oval tattoos forming a circle below the ankle.

This therapeutic tattooing practice endured well into the twentieth century in the Ryukyus. Around 1950, American anthropologist

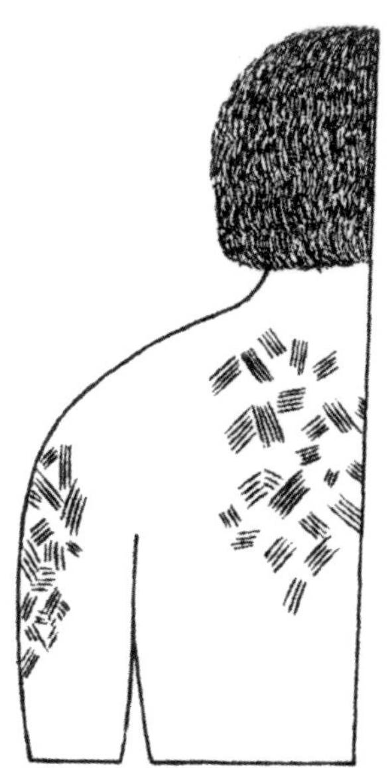

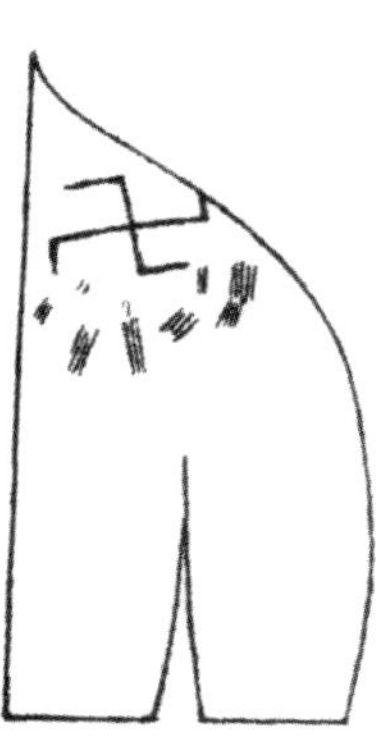

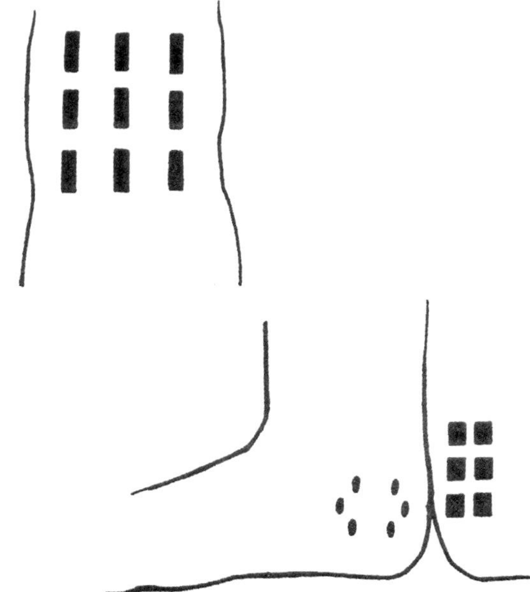

Right Medicinal tattooing patterns seen on Ainu women in 1935. The women who possessed these tattoos stated they were cured after the tattoo application. At the time of their tattooing (twenty-four and fourteen years of age), both were residents of villages in the Tokachi Province of Hokkaido.

Far right Therapeutic tattooing seen on the leg and heel of an Okinawan woman.

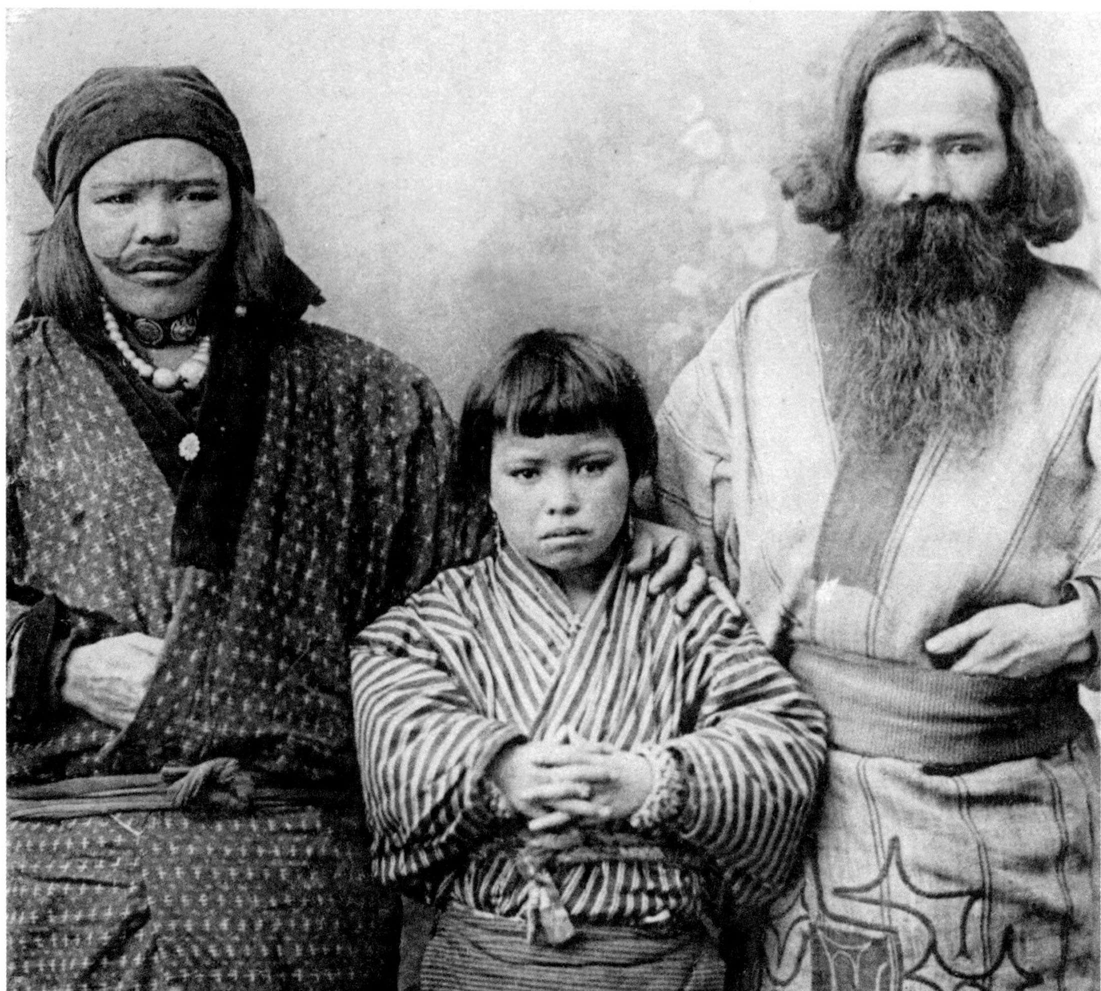

Ainu family, *ca*. 1920. Although this postcard does not provide the village location, the line tattooed between the eyebrows of the woman was not therapeutic and instead a distinctive identifier that she was from the West Iburi district of Hokkaido.

Clarence Glacken observed that medicinal tattooing was still prevalent among Okinawan elders.[28] These tattoos often featured sets of blue spots and circles of blue dots made from indigo ink, strategically placed on the back of the neck, the shoulder, or the upper back. This was a testament to the enduring belief in the healing power of tattoos.

In 1995, anthropologist Yoshimi Yamamoto reported that in the Yaeyama Islands, therapeutic tattoos were typically administered by *yabuu*, male practitioners skilled in aspects of Chinese medicine. These tattoos were created using Chinese ink mixed with sake or the local spirit *awamori*, enhancing their medicinal potency.[29] Occasionally, *yuta*, or female shamans, also performed tattooing for various injuries, demonstrating the gender-inclusive nature of this healing practice.

The ailments treated by these therapeutic tattoos were diverse, ranging from hot flashes, migraine headaches, and back pain to sciatica, sprains, and general joint pain. This practice was similar to tattoo-acupuncture documented in other parts of the world and

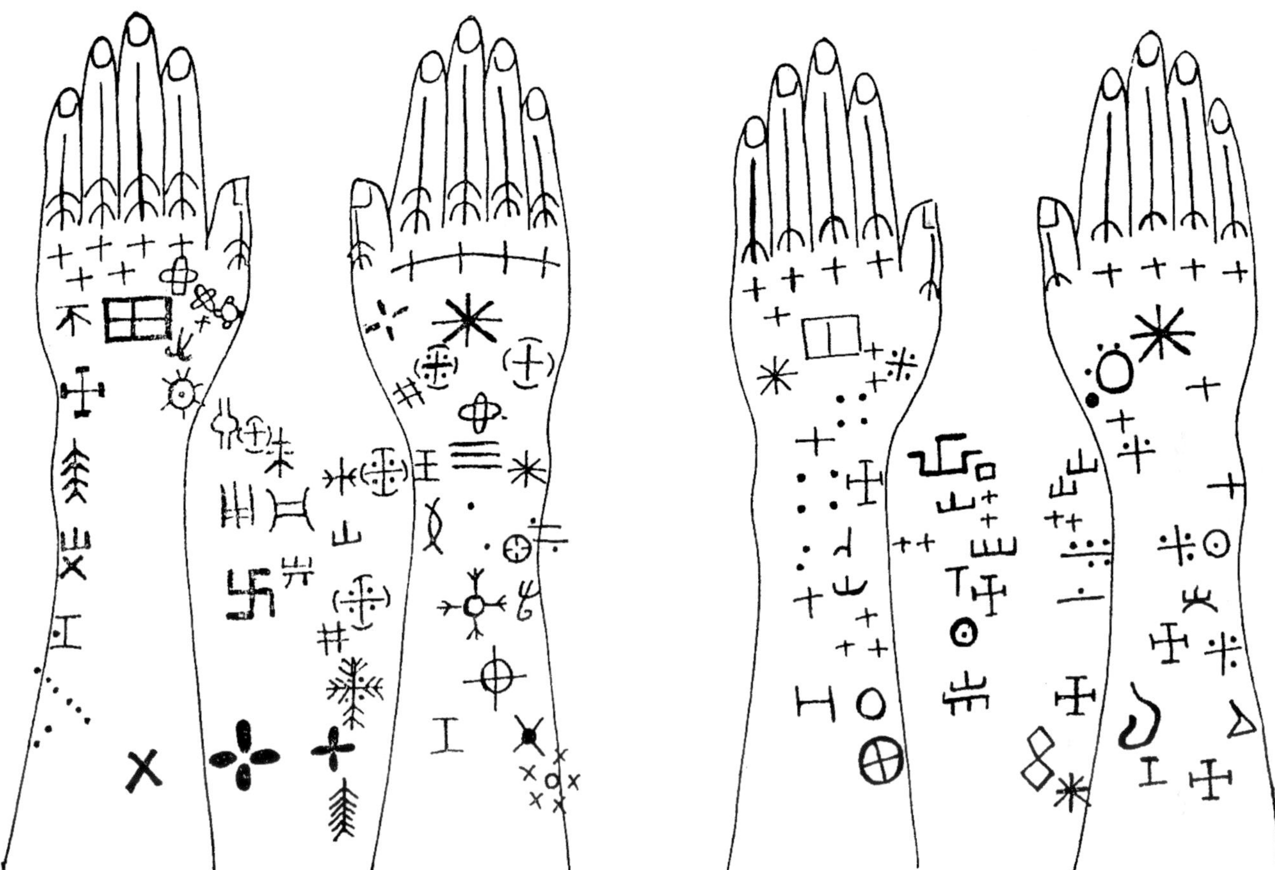

Women's tattoo patterns of Minnajima Island, *ca*. 1930. Although the swastika pattern is featured as a primary tattoo motif on several Ryukyuan islands, it has not been recorded if the symbol carried medicinal value as it did for the Ainu.

where it was revered as a universal remedy.[30] According to Glacken, these tattoos were particularly effective in alleviating neuralgia, inflammation of the joints, neck pain, rheumatism, and general soreness of the back or shoulder.[31]

These accounts suggest a fascinating intersection between traditional healing practices and body art among the Ryukyuans and Ainu. While these tattoos were therapeutic, the ethnographic record is rather silent regarding how such practices were perceived locally within their cultural contexts. Did these communities see a clear boundary between medical treatment and ritualistic or symbolic body modification? Furthermore, how did these practices compare with other traditional healing methods across regions and eras? Understanding these perspectives encourages a deeper reflection on the complex role of tattoos in human history, extending beyond mere decoration to encompass Indigenous epistemologies of health, spirituality, and well-being.

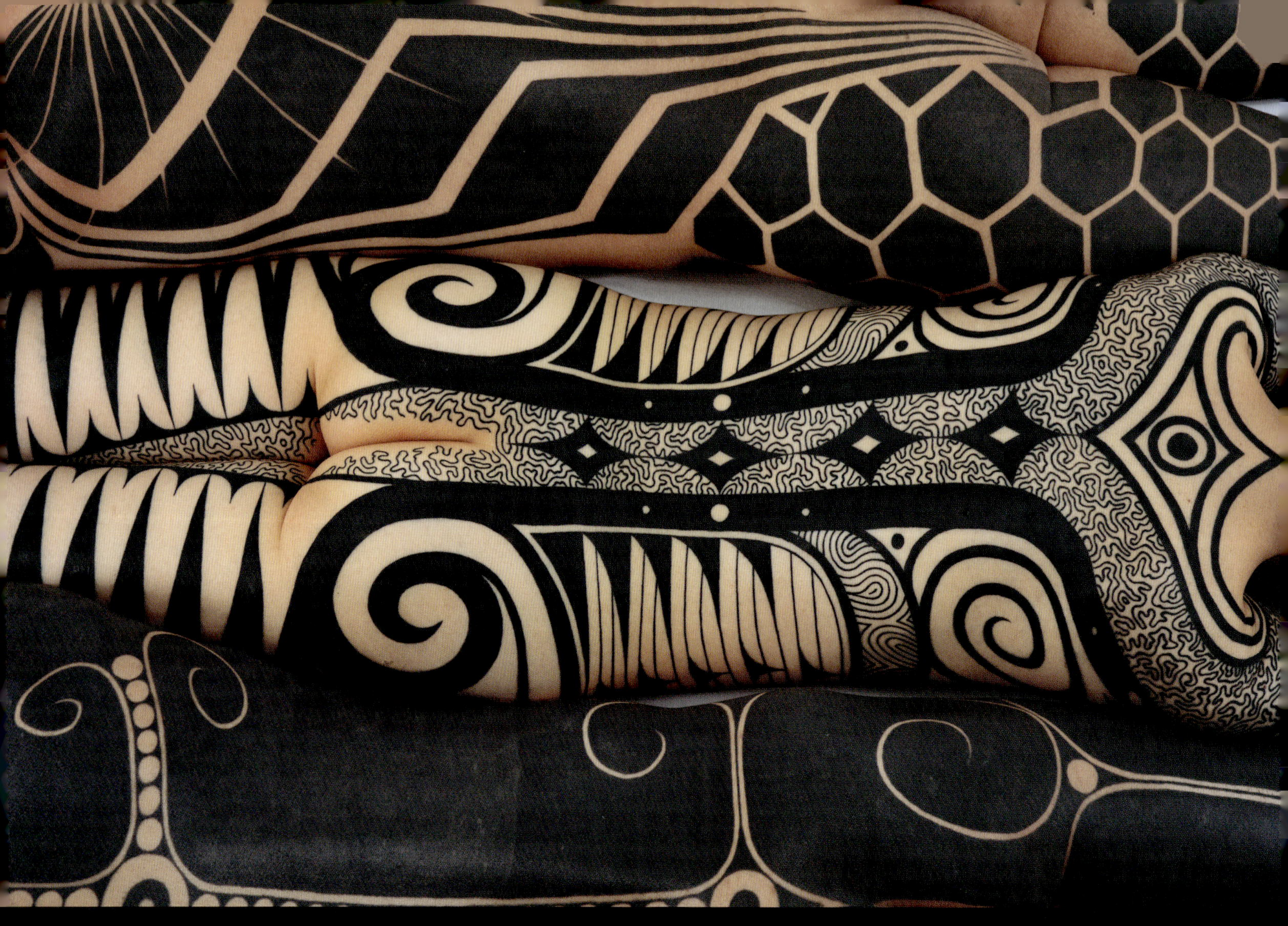

Taku Oshima: Japan's Blackwork Master

Opposite *Jōmon Project* bodysuits by Taku Oshima, 2022.

Right *Dogū* dating to the Final Jōmon Period, 1000–300 BCE. The Jōmon were a prehistoric people that inhabited Japan as early as 16,000 years ago. Jōmon artisans created ceramic figurines called *dogū* that were probably used for protection against illness, infertility, and spirits.

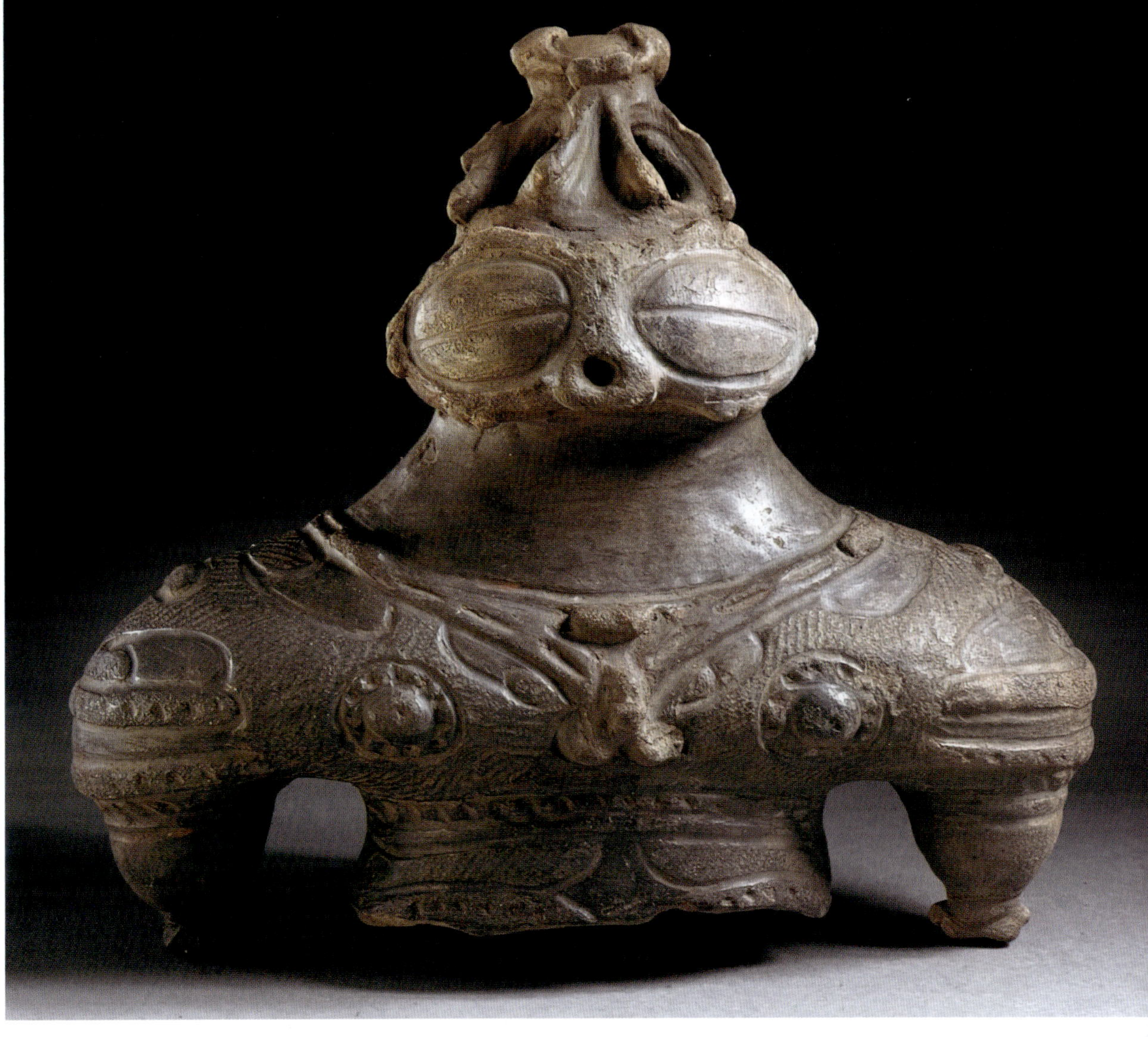

Among the iconic artifacts of prehistoric Jōmon culture are the intricate *dogū*, ceramic figurines primarily depicting the female form, crafted by the Jōmon people from around 12,000 to 300 BCE. These enigmatic figures, with complex surface decorations, have long sparked debate among scholars. Do these markings represent tattoos, body paint, or scarification? While their true nature remains uncertain, their striking designs have inspired contemporary tattoo artist Taku Oshima to channel their spiritual essence into his bold blackwork tattoos.

Blackwork tattooing, produced exclusively with monochromatic pigment, has been a cornerstone of Indigenous tattoo cultures for millennia. This aesthetic has evolved into a contemporary art form that bridges the gap between ancient tribal and neo-tribal practices. Blackwork tattoos are celebrated for their versatility, featuring an array of designs including black lines, spirals, zigzags, dots, bold geometric planes, and sacred geometry. Modern blackwork tattoos are renowned for their purity, skillful use of negative space, and unconventional layouts that embrace the human form, creating patterns that are now larger, darker, and more intricate than ever before.

Tokyo-based Oshima exemplifies the power and potential of blackwork with his captivating neo-tribal designs. Oshima's work is a testament to the endless creative possibilities within the monochromatic palette, igniting the visual senses with designs that resonate on profound and spiritual levels. His tattoos are not merely body art but are deeply influenced by the ancient *dogū*, embodying a timeless connection between past and present, tradition and innovation.

Through his artistry, Oshima breathes new life into the ancient spirit of the Jōmon *dogū*, transforming their enigmatic markings into contemporary expressions of identity and spirituality. His work stands as a bold statement within the world of modern tattooing, a fusion of historical reverence and avant-garde creativity

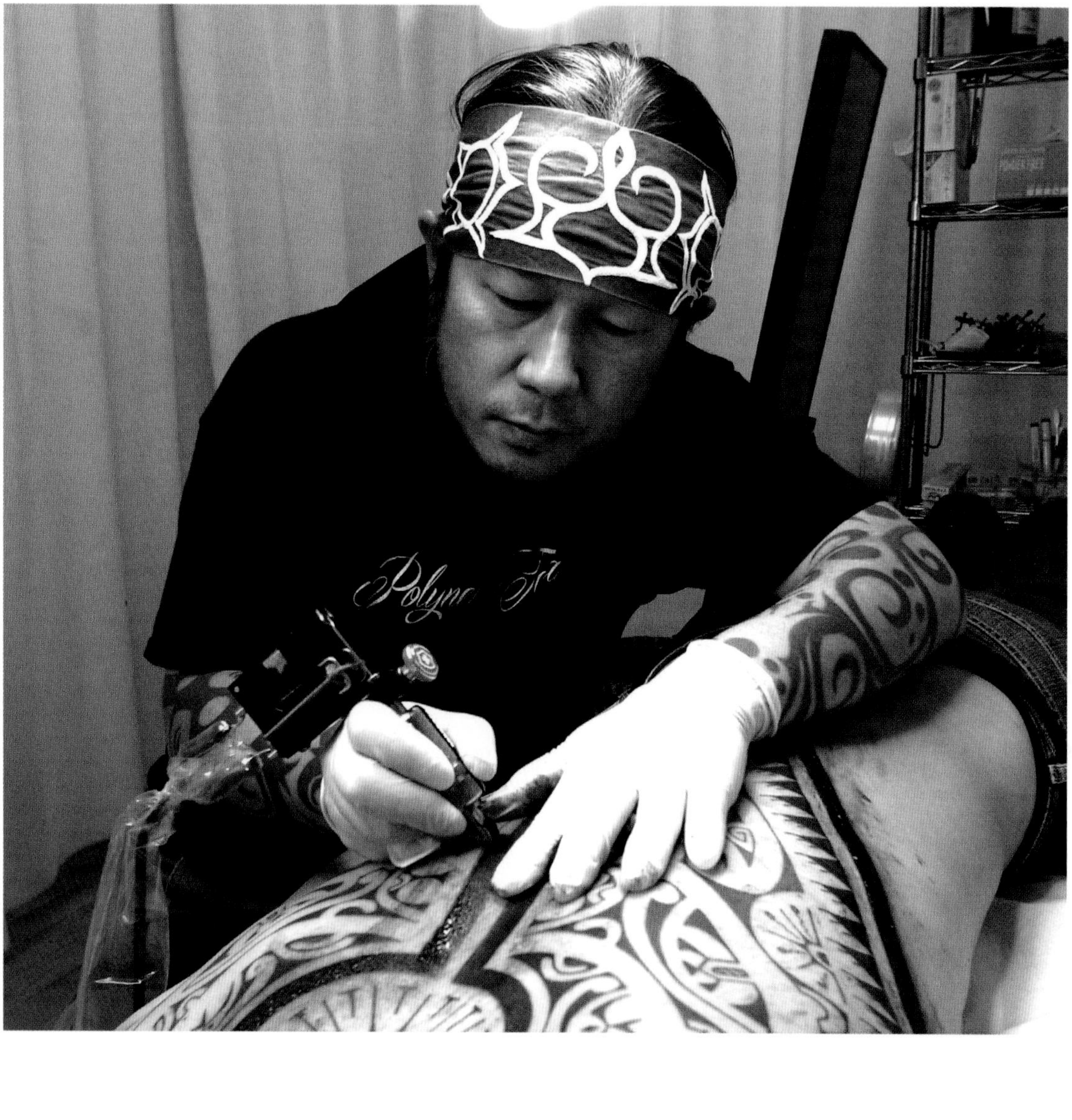

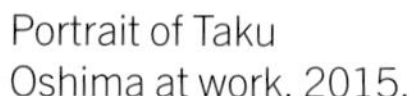

Portrait of Taku Oshima at work, 2015.

that captures the essence of human expression in its most primal and powerful form.

Oshima, a seasoned tattoo artist with a quarter-century of experience, originally pursued anthropology at university before dedicating himself entirely to the art of tattooing. His journey into the world of tattoos began in the vibrant, eclectic atmosphere of Goa, India, in the mid-1990s. From there, Oshima embarked on a seven-year odyssey as a nomadic artist, traveling the globe and honing his craft. This journey allowed him to cultivate a unique style free from the influence of the traditional Japanese *irezumi* school, known for its colorful and realistic portraits of heroes, dragons, and legendary beings.

Oshima's artistic inclinations gravitated early on toward tribal aesthetics. He was particularly captivated by the intricate designs of Indian *mehndi* (henna) and the bold, spiritual patterns of Indigenous Borneo tattoos. These early influences were marked by their graceful, black-ink designs that spoke to a deep, spiritual connection with their cultural roots.

As his travels continued, Oshima's sources of inspiration broadened. He drew upon the rich tattooing traditions of Polynesia, including the Marquesan and Māori styles, known for their striking and symbolic patterns. He also explored the artistry of Native North American cultures, particularly the Northwest Coast, where tattoos are deeply intertwined with local geography, clan crests, and oral history. Southeast Asia offered further inspiration, with the intricate and meaningful Indigenous designs from Taiwan, Indonesia, and the

Jōmon Project backpieces by Taku Oshima, 2022.

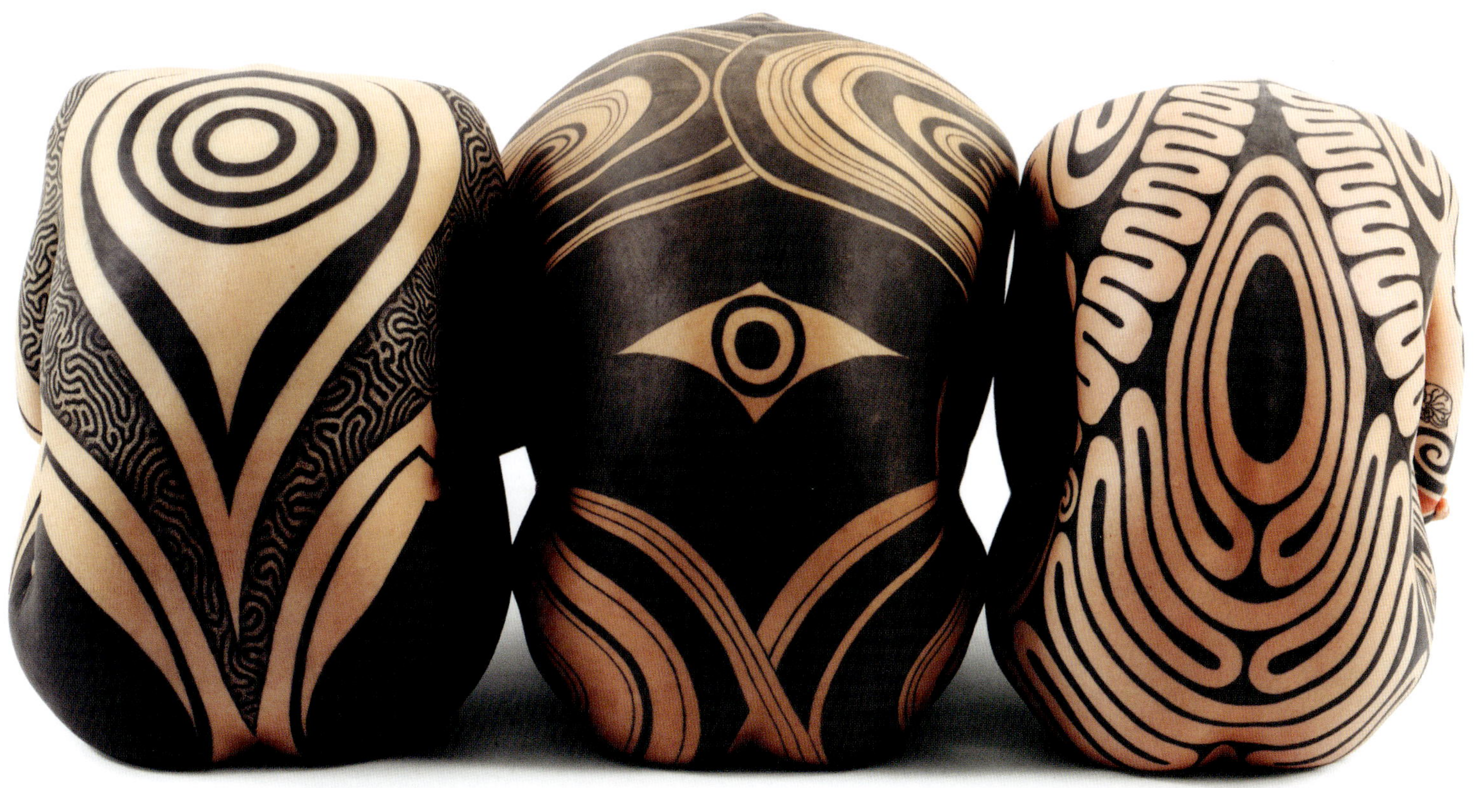

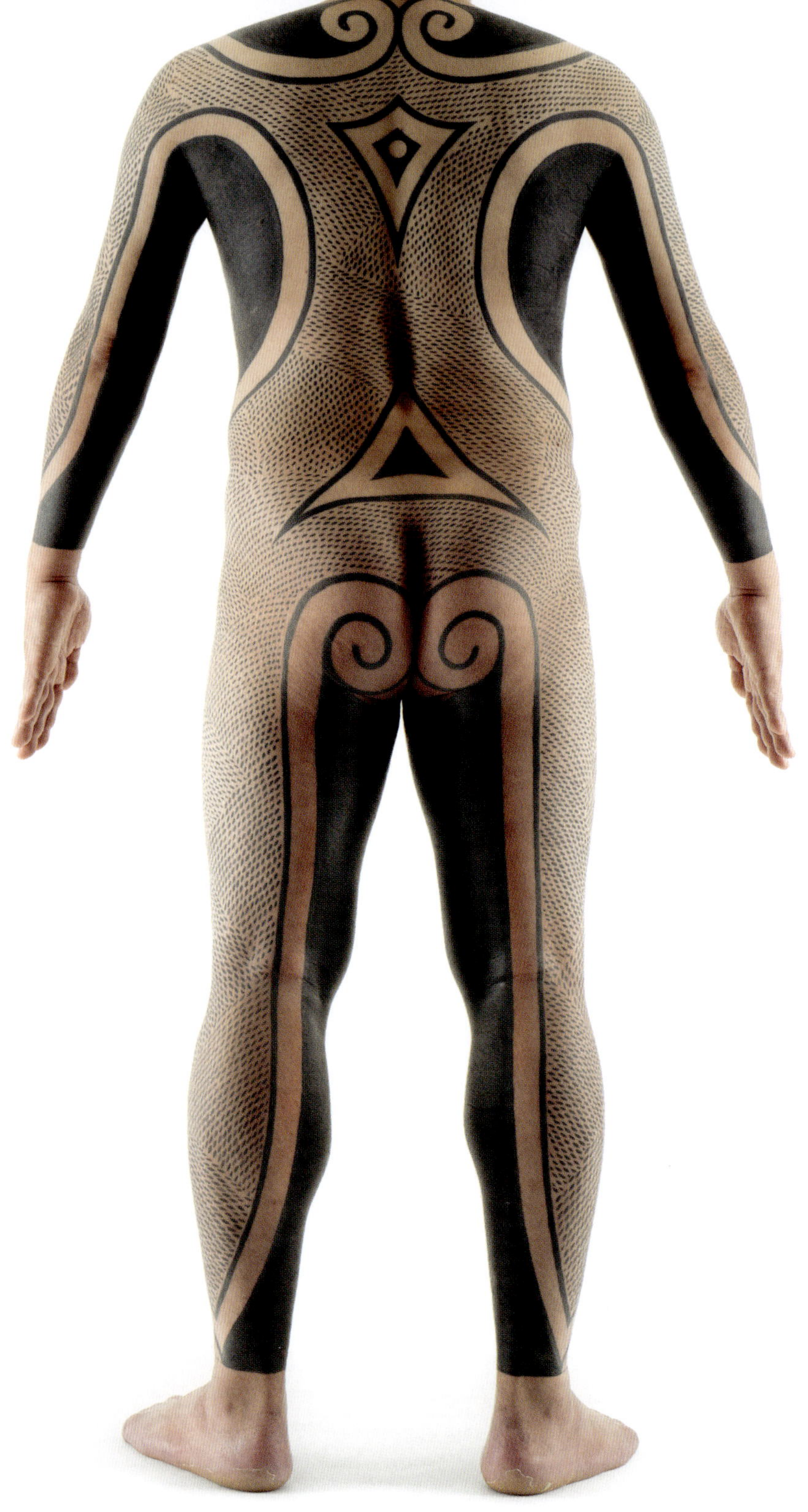

Philippines. Pre-Columbian art from the Maya and Aztec civilizations introduced Oshima to another layer of historical depth and symbolism.

Oshima's fascination with Indigenous Japanese art forms, such as those of the Jōmon, Ainu, and Ryukyuan peoples, brought his journey full circle, connecting him back to his own cultural heritage. These ancient styles, with their mysterious and evocative motifs, provided a rich tapestry of inspiration that Oshima wove into his own work.

In several interviews, Oshima shared his sources of inspiration. "For me, tattooing is a spiritual act, but I don't mean this in the sense that it is an initiation rite, as in tribal societies," he said. "Rather, it's more an act of affirming an already existing identity, it's like deciding to show off the invisible thing which is your soul. I truly believe this."[32]

He also expressed to me his love for Indigenous tattoos, ideally preferring larger pieces. Although tribal tattooing was not very popular in Japan until recently, more Japanese people are now gravitating toward these ancient designs.

However, Oshima faced challenges in aligning his artistic vision with client desires. "I felt like a Sumo wrestler," he explained, referring to his struggle to create large, black, tribally inspired artworks. He desired to produce entire human canvases or at least large works visible from a distance.

In 2016, Oshima's dreams began to take tangible form through the creation of the *Jōmon Project*, a groundbreaking tattoo art series in collaboration with writer and photographer Ryoichi "Keroppy" Maeda. For years prior, Oshima had been urging his clients to join him in reviving the long-lost tattoo patterns of Indigenous Japanese cultures – the intricate designs of the Ryukyuan, Ainu, and prehistoric Jōmon peoples. His pioneering efforts yielded stunning Jōmon-styled tattoos inspired by the enigmatic patterns found on ancient *dogū* ceramic sculptures. Oshima proclaimed, "I want people around the world to become aware of these incredibly beautiful tattooing styles that only recently have been rediscovered."

The *Jōmon Project* is more than a mere revival; it is a visionary endeavor to resurrect and celebrate the ancient art of Japanese tattoo culture and introduce it to a global audience. Oshima's ambition through this project is twofold: to reconstruct and honor the ancient tattooing traditions and to innovate and evolve these practices into new forms of modern body art.

The intricate patterns and designs, rooted in millennia-old traditions, are given new life through Oshima's skilled hands. His tattoos, that push the boundaries of modern blackwork, serve as a bridge between the past and the future, merging ancient artistry with contemporary techniques and designs to create something entirely new and profoundly meaningful. Each piece he creates is a testament to his global journey, an intricate dance of lines and patterns on skin that capture and tell stories of tradition and timeless beauty.

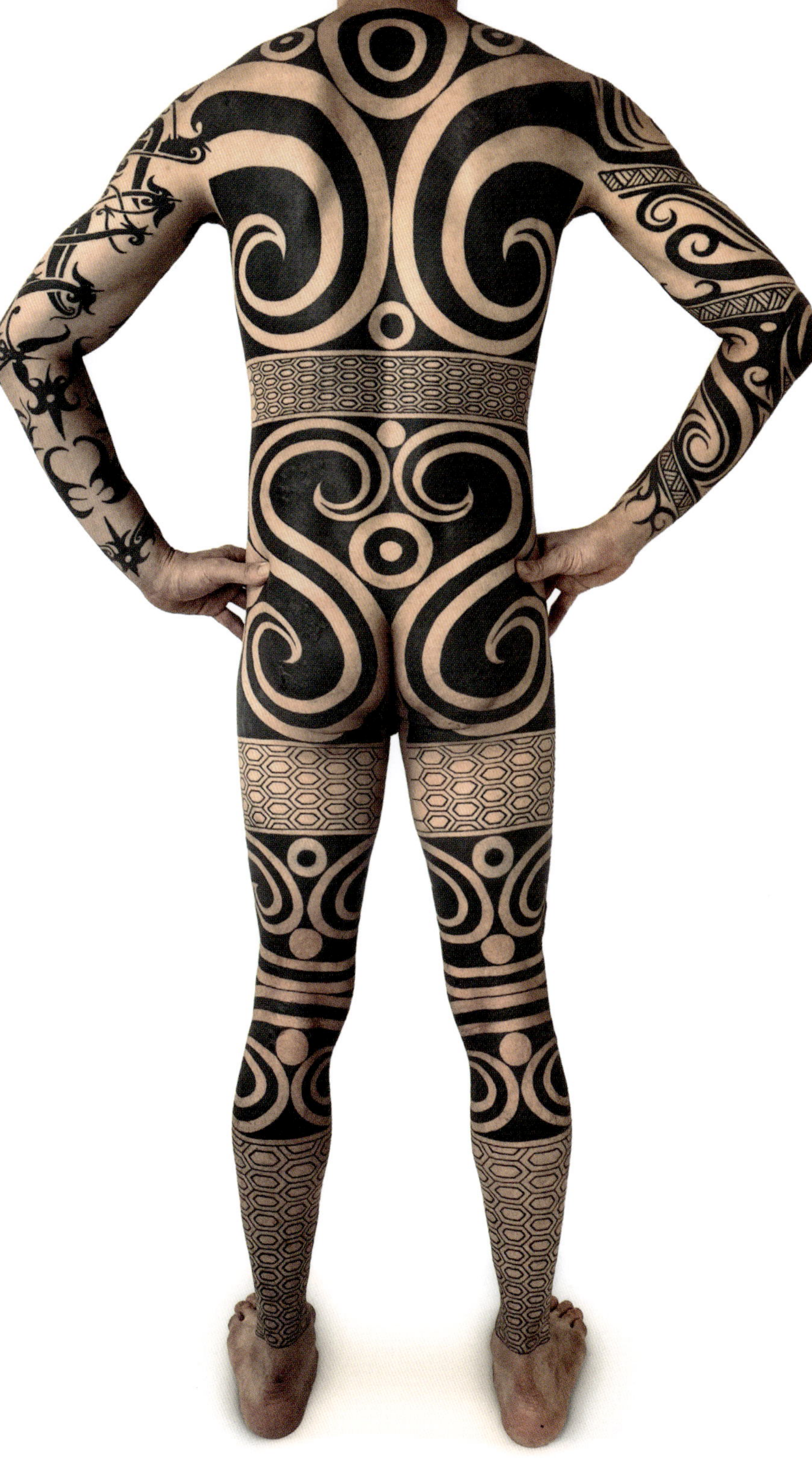

Opposite and right *Jōmon Project* backpieces by Oshima, 2022.

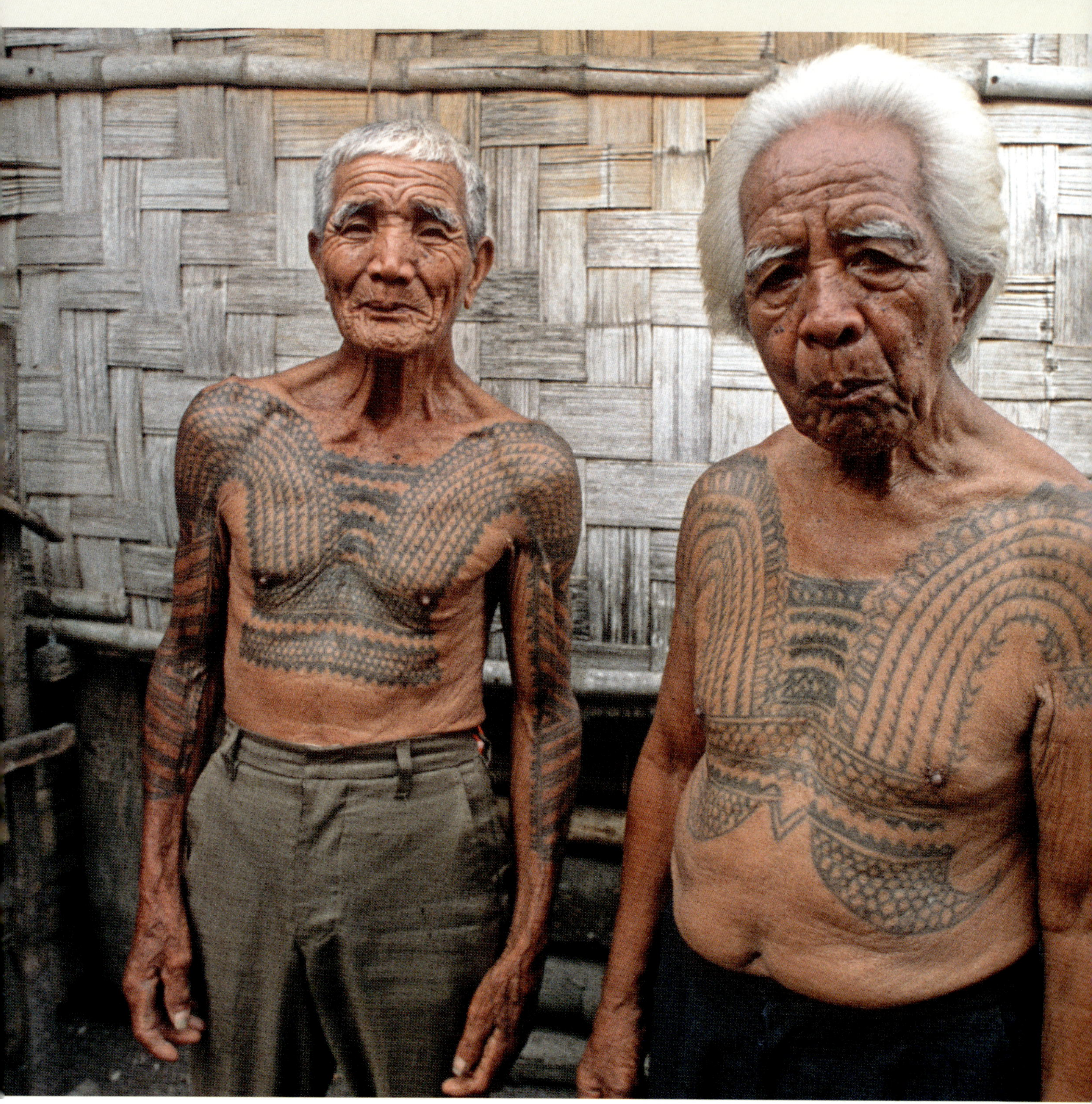

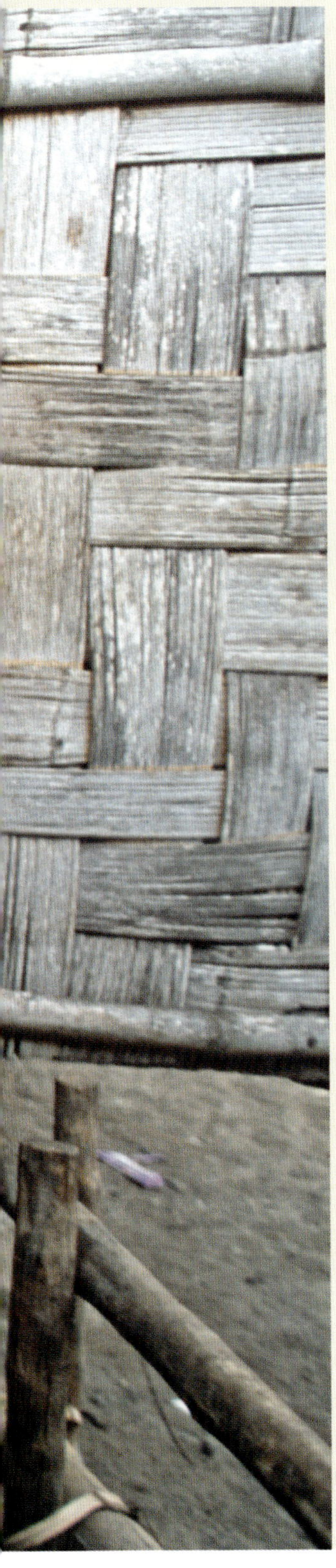

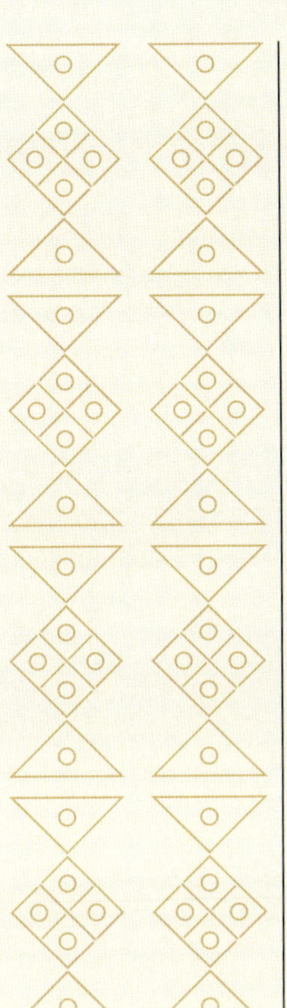

6

TATTOOS OF SOUTHEAST AND MAINLAND ASIA

One hundred years ago, Indigenous tattooists working across Asia marked human skin with tattoos to signal rites of passage, social status (e.g., warriors and aristocrats), tribal and clan identity, therapeutic treatment (e.g., sprains or joint injuries), and spiritual beliefs about the afterlife. A variety of techniques were employed, including hand-poking, hand-tapping, and incision tattooing.[1]

Kalinga *mengor* and war captain Jaime Alos with fellow warrior Maymayao Sagangab of Dananao village, northern Philippines, 2008.

In the northern Philippines, Taiwan, Borneo, parts of China and Northwest India, female tattooists usually created tattoos for both men and women via the technique of hand-tapping. Tattoo pigments were organic and, generally speaking, derived from charred resins, plants, and wood to form soot that was mixed with water or other liquid substances. The tattooing process was often ritualized and offerings to deities, ancestors, and spirits were performed to help safeguard the health of the tattoo client.[2] Various taboos were also observed, especially while the tattoo client healed, and certain foods or liquids were restricted during this period. Payments to the tattooer ranged from foodstuffs, tools, currency, or labor in the tattooist's agricultural fields.

By the early-twentieth century, however, tribal tattooing culture in Asia began to fade with the advances of Christian missionaries and acculturative policies of governmental agents. Today, only a few thousand Indigenous elders carry the marks of their ancestors, which in former times helped guarantee one's safe passage into the hereafter.

Philippines

The mountainous region of northern Luzon perhaps featured more tattooing cultures than any other area in the Philippines. Until the present day, many forms of traditional tattooing here have survived longer than in other regions of the country because of its remoteness and warrior tribes who successfully defended their ancestral homelands from foreign invaders, like the colonial Spanish. Here, among the Bontok, Kalinga, Ifugao, Ibaloy, Isneg, and other peoples, tattooing was intimately related to one's social status, and especially to a man's exploits on the battlefield. For example, warriors typically earned the right to a tattoo only after slaying an enemy and taking their head. This sacred act was believed necessary to increase the fertility of the land and ensure good harvests, among other things.[3]

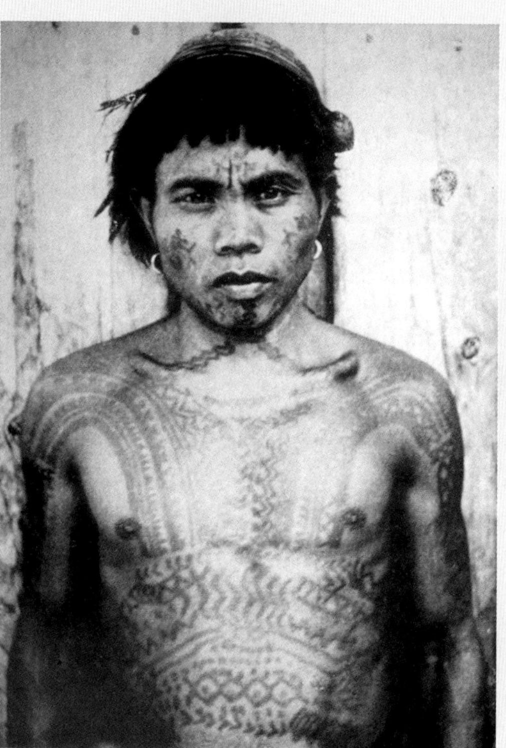

Bontok warrior, northern Philippines, *ca*. 1900.

The tribes of this region recognized several kinds of tattoo, and very often the designs worn by a man were directly related to the number of human heads he had taken in hand-to-hand combat. The *chaklag* chest tattoo indicated that a Bontok man had taken at least one head.[4] When an Isneg man had killed one or more enemies, he was allowed to have a special design, called *andóri*, tattooed on the inside of one or both of his forearms.[5]

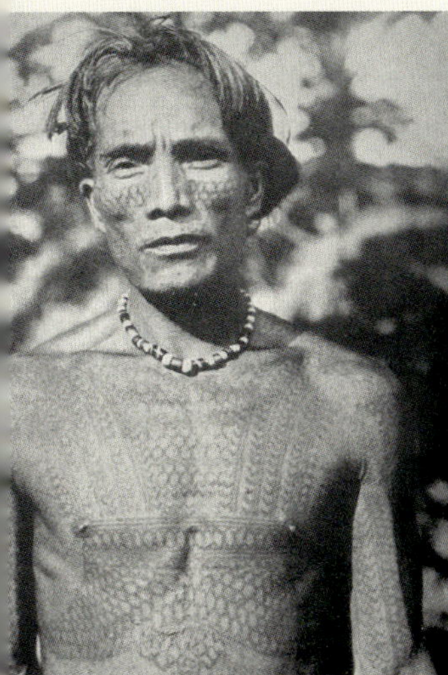

Above Veteran Kalinga warrior chieftain of Balatok village displaying facial markings and other motifs associated with *mengor* status, northern Philippines, 1905.

Right Kalinga *mengor* Candido Baliyao of Lubo village, 2008.

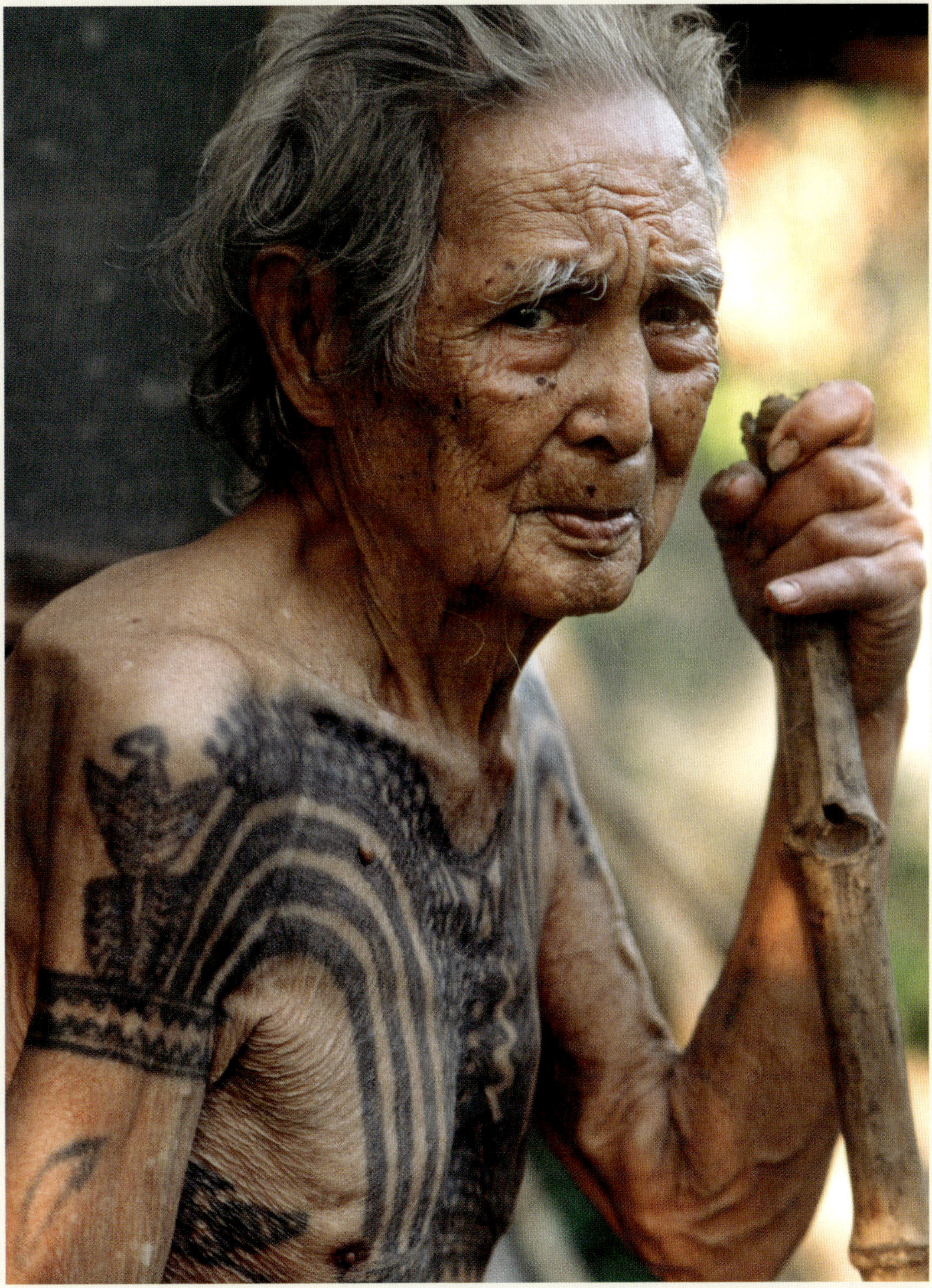

Kalinga elder Gannao Oggay pounding rice in Buscalan village, 2007.

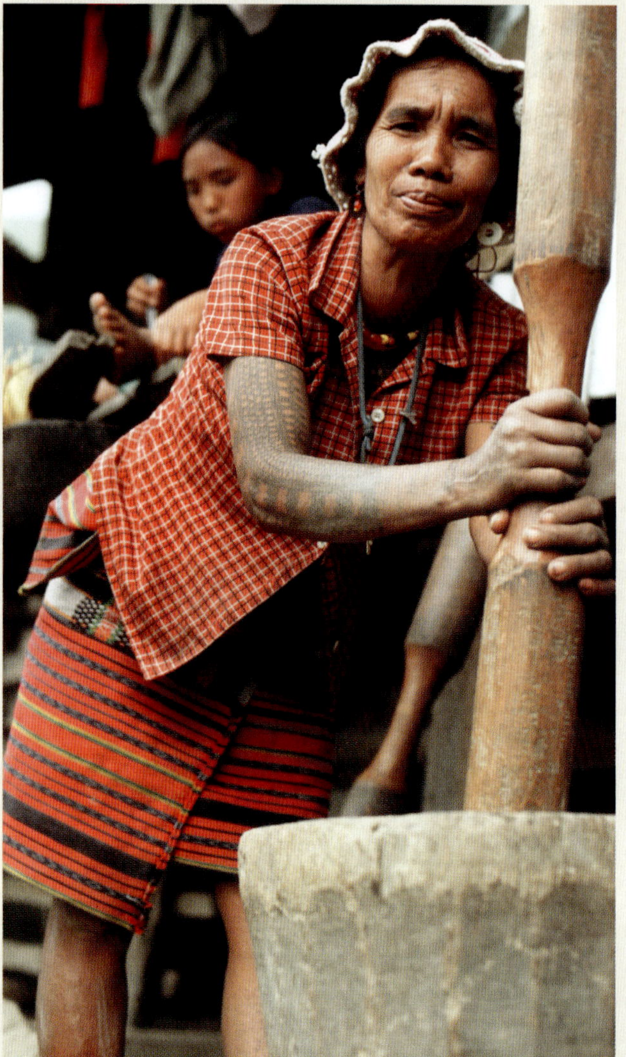

Among the Kalinga, the bravest of warriors, known as *mengor*, earned intricate *batok* (tattoos) on their arms and faces as symbols of their prowess in battle. These elaborate tattoos often featured designs inspired by the scales of centipedes or pythons and included *bikking* (chest designs) that abstractly represented the outstretched wings of the predatory Philippine eagle (*Pithecophaga jefferyi*).[6] In some villages, the curving baselines of the *bikking* served as a tally of the number of enemies the warrior had slain. Kalinga men who displayed exceptional bravery on the battlefield were also adorned with *dakag*, linear markings on their backs, and anthropomorphic and geometric designs on their ribcages. Additional tattoos behind their ears recorded the number of battles they had fought.[7] The most revered "war captains" bore *sinaksak'od*, horn-like motifs projecting outward above their navels, marking their distinguished status and fearsome reputation.

Tattooists celebrated the transition of girls into womanhood by adorning them with exquisite and intricate designs. These stunning patterns were meticulously crafted using hand-tapping tools tipped with the delicate yet razor-sharp thorns of pomelo, lemon, or orange trees. Kalinga oral histories stated that women should be tattooed to increase their fertility, and the wives of warriors wore special tattoos to note the status of their husbands. Female tattoos were inspired by nature and everyday objects: rice bundles, rice terrace steps, bamboo shelves, woven grass mats, ferns, spiders, a star or moon, and snake or centipede scales were used. The latter two designs predominate in Kalinga tattooing because of their significance in oral history. They were "friends of the warriors" because of the powerful omens they once delivered on the warpath.

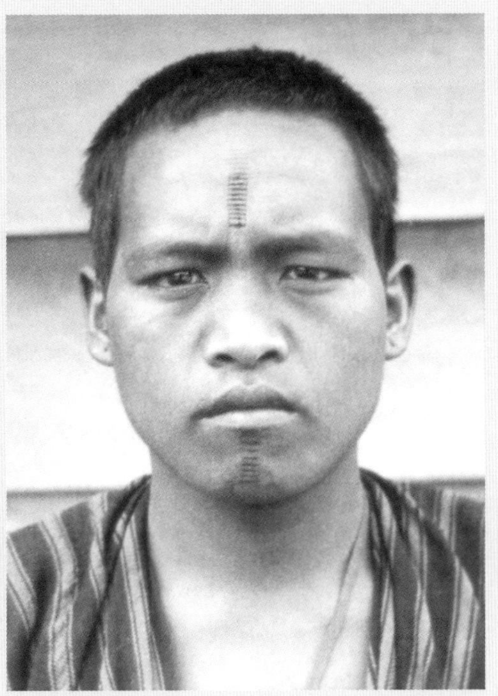

Tattooed Atayal warrior, *ca.* 1900. His tribal forehead markings consist of a single band of tattooing that are "braced" by lines on either side.

Taiwan

Just as great tribal warriors in the Philippines were tattooed to mark their achievements in headhunting, so too were those of the Atayal of northern Taiwan who tattooed until the early twentieth century.[8] Here, amidst the rain-soaked Central Mountain Range, tattooing and headhunting were two traditional customs considered indispensable to human existence. According to Atayal elders, tattoos represented the teachings of the ancestors and were part of the customary laws and protocols of the people. If a person did not follow these rules, it was believed the ancestral spirits might inflict personal or collective (community) misfortune.

Atayal boys embarked on their journey to become a proper member of society at the age of six or seven, receiving their first tattoos on their foreheads. These horizontal lines, varying in width and spacing, served as a unique tribal or subtribal identifiers. Some tribes framed these lines to create a ladder-like pattern, while others segmented them into one, two, or three distinct sections.

Chin tattoos held a deeper significance, symbolizing adulthood and warrior status. These marks were not easily earned; boys had to prove their mettle through life-threatening tests.[9] Mastery of hunting, farming, and family care were essential, but the ultimate rite of passage was participation in a successful war party that captured one or more enemy heads.[10] Only upon completing these formidable tasks could a boy earn his chin tattoos and be recognized as a *tayan*, a "true" or "real" man, in Atayal society. With these markings, a man gained the right to marry,[11] and great warriors who had claimed numerous heads were honored with chest tattoos.

Girls, too, bore tattoos as symbols of tribal or subtribal affiliation, with forehead tattoos marking their membership. Mastery of weaving allowed them to earn intricate cheek tattoos, as a "real woman" was defined by her weaving skills.[12] A popular rhomboid weaving pattern, representing the protective "eyes of the ancestors," was often incorporated into these cheek tattoos. Exceptional weavers or those who created new patterns were further distinguished with tattoos on their chests, hands, and legs,[13] mirroring the chest tattoos of great warriors.

Atayal tattoo artists, revered women of high virtue, typically inherited their craft from their mothers or aunts, though some honed their skills through apprenticeship. The expense of a woman's facial tattooing, often requiring multiple sessions to achieve the desired color and beauty, could exceed the cost of a girl's wedding dowry.[14]

Tattooing operations took place in a small hut or in the shadow of a barn-like structure, away from the living quarters. Most tattooing was done in winter, since the cold weather was believed to aid healing. The tattoo pattern was first delicately stenciled on the face using a feather, twig, grass stem, string, or chopstick. The designs were then hand-tapped into the skin with tools tipped with locally available citrus thorns, such as orange or tangerine, bound to an instrument resembling a toothbrush. This tool featured four to sixteen needles arranged in rows and fastened to a wooden baton.[15] A single piece of wood served as the hammer to tap the tattoo instrument, and a rattan or bamboo splint was used to scrape away the blood.

Until the early twentieth century, among the Paiwan of southern Taiwan,[16] tattooing was a profound symbol of social status and leadership. Distinctive motifs were reserved exclusively for ruling chiefs and their families, signifying their high rank. Warriors could earn the right to be tattooed, but only with the explicit permission of village chiefs. Commoners, on the other hand, could only bear motifs corresponding to their social stratum if they purchased this privilege from the ruling family—a luxury few

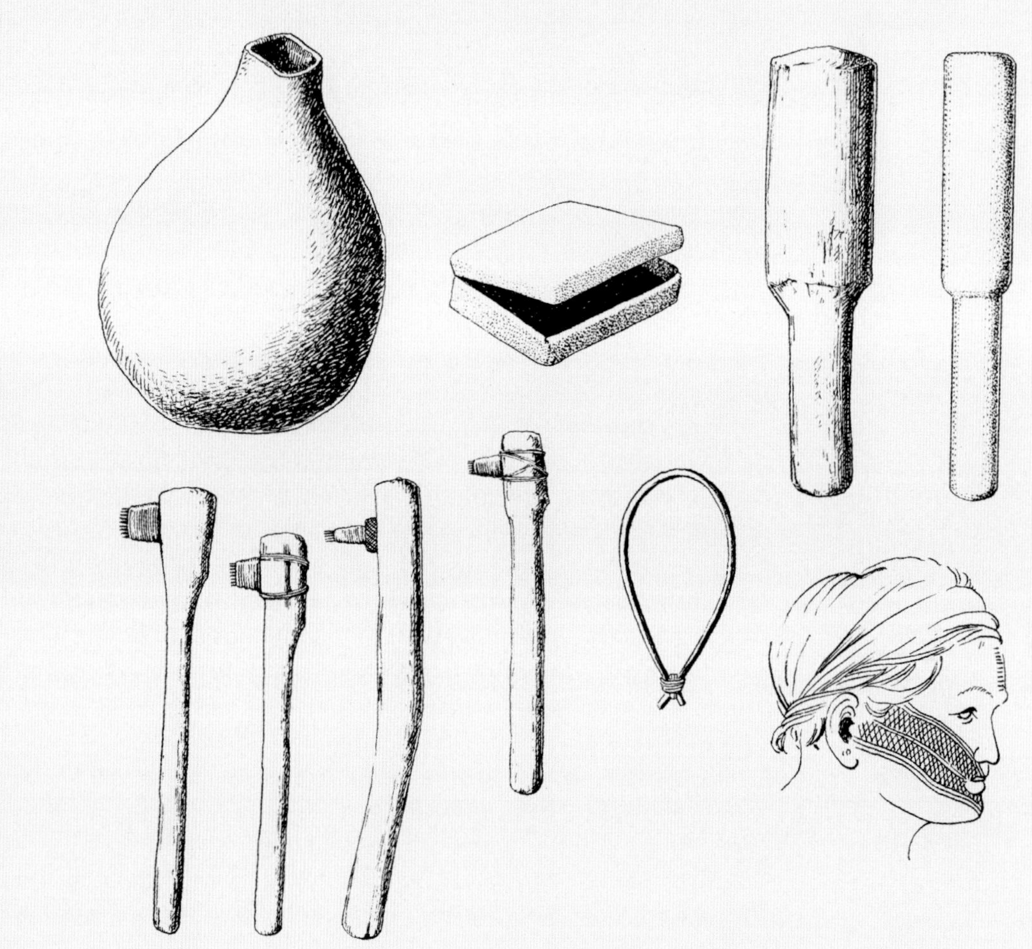

Atayal tattooing tools, some tipped with thirteen, seven, or five needles, *ca.* 1930s.

Tattooed Atayal woman smoking a pipe, *ca*. 1950.

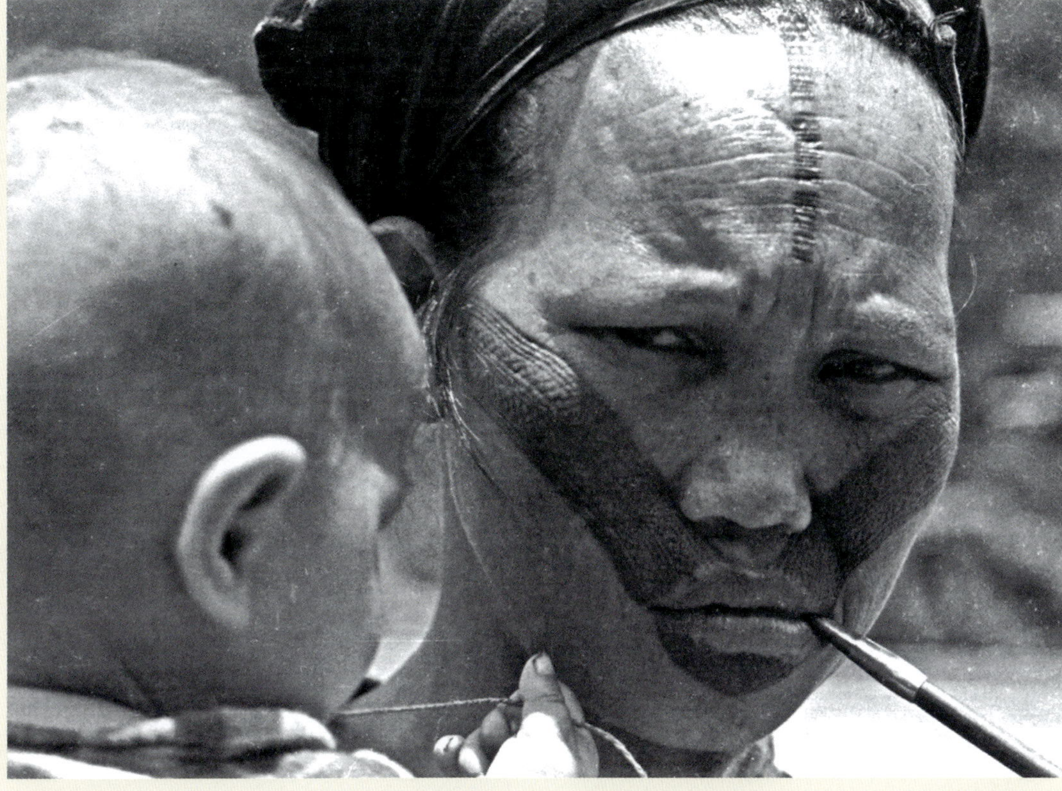

Below Atayal tattooist at work, *ca*. 1935.

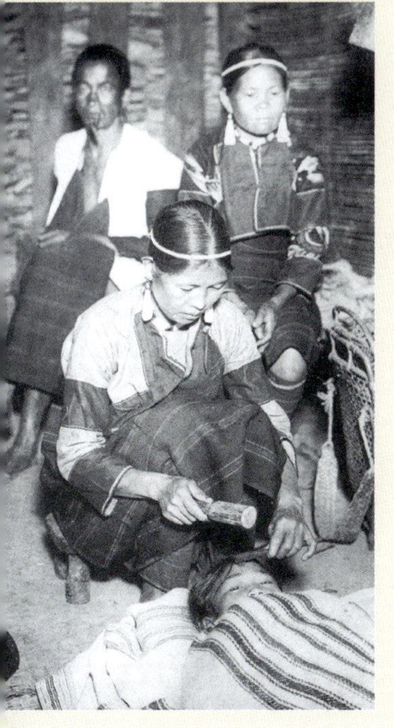

could afford. Tattoos were honors bestowed by the village leadership. When a person reached the appropriate age for or earned the right to a tattoo through feats of bravery or warrior exploits, the village chief would send an envoy to the family, inquiring if their son or daughter wished to be marked with the revered tattoos.

Paiwan tattoo artists, predominantly women, often inherited their esteemed occupation through their family lineage. Each village boasted one or more tattoo artists, mostly from noble families, although commoners could buy the right to become tattooers.[17] The hand-tapping technique used by these artists differed from those in northern Taiwan. Tattoo needles were crafted by binding steel needles with linen thread to a bamboo stick about 15¾ inches (40 cm) in length. Before the advent of steel needles, artists used two or three mountain orange or pomelo thorns. A small knife with a wooden handle was employed to tap the needled tool into the skin, using a sooty pigment to create the intricate designs.

On the appointed day, the tattooist would perform a sacred ritual at the gate of the recipient's house, seeking ancestral blessings. A sample Paiwan prayer might be: "We ask your help, ancestors, before the operation. Please let the patterns be tattooed like a wild cat's skin, black and straight."[18] Offerings of meat were made to the ancestral spirits of the village,[19] invoking their protection for the tattooist against the malevolent spirits drawn by the flowing blood during the tattooing process.[20]

Chief Jigals Salapits of Gulou village, Laiyi Township, Pingtung county, Taiwan, 1955.

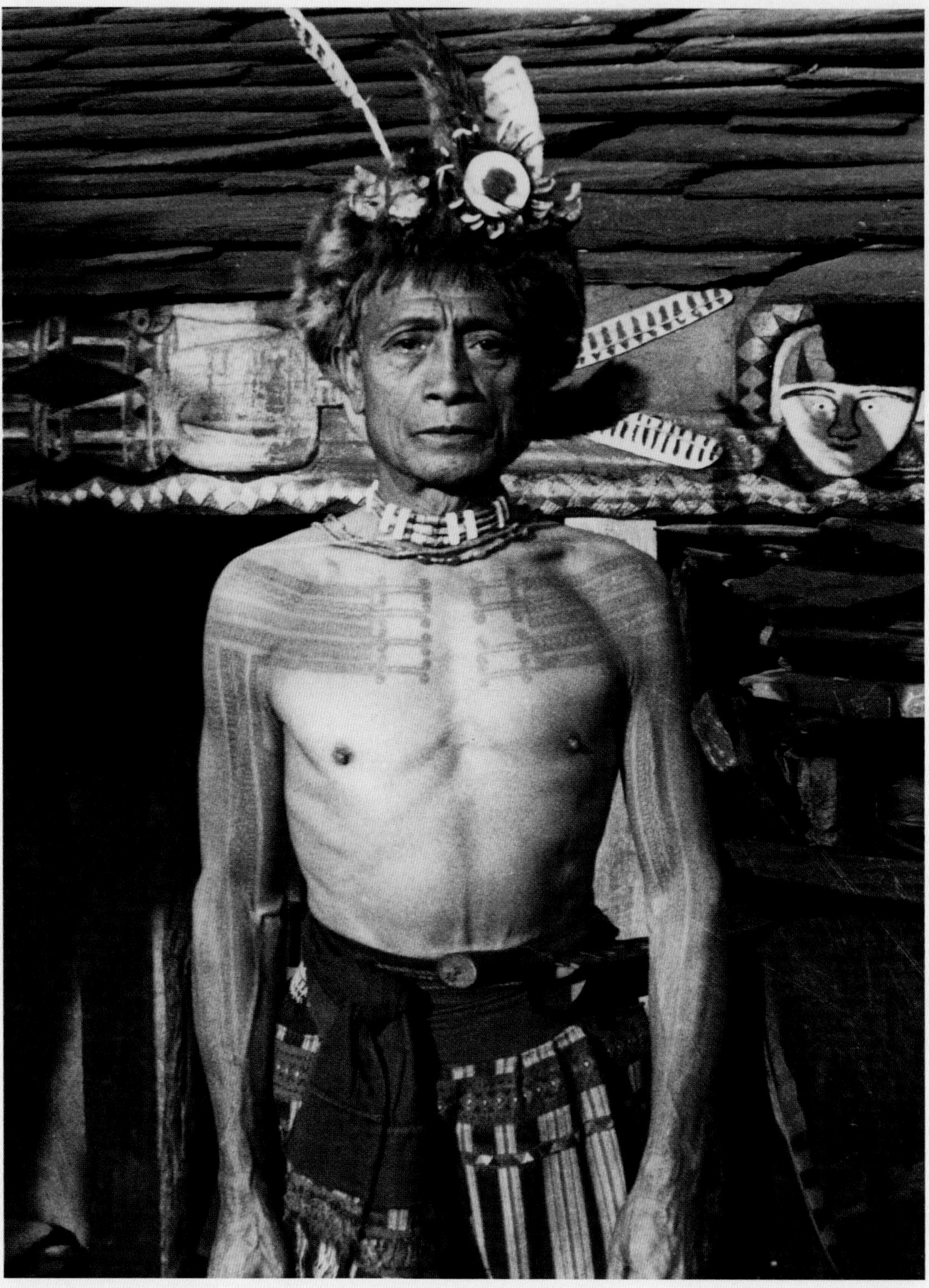

Right Male and female tattoos of the Paiwan, *ca*. 1935.

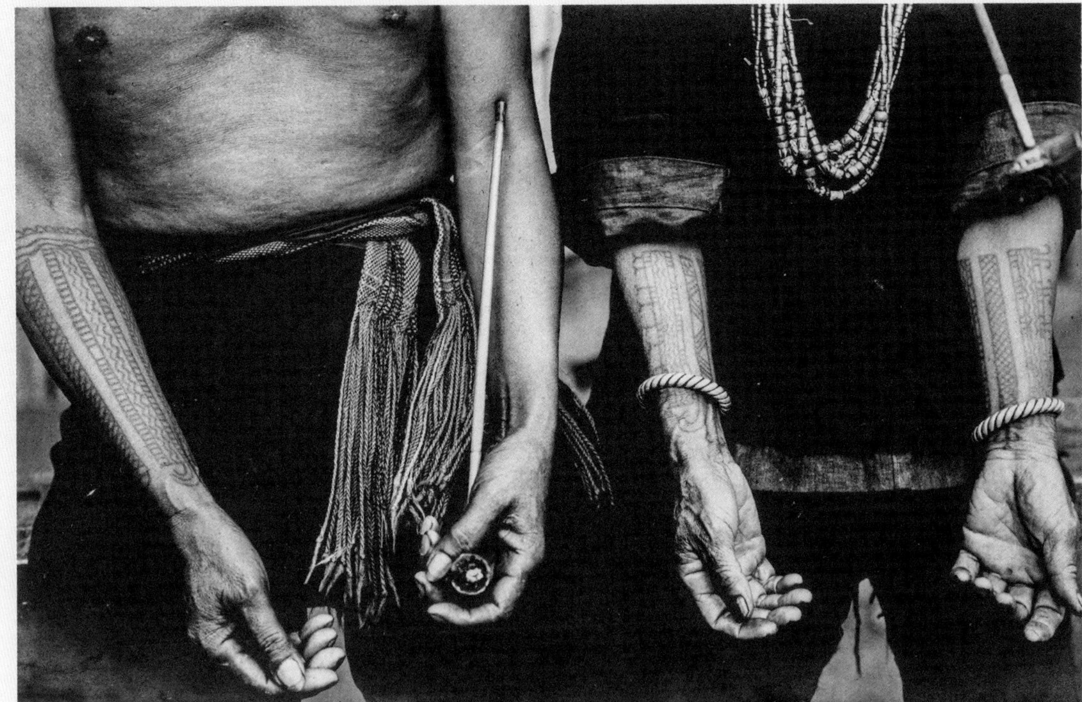

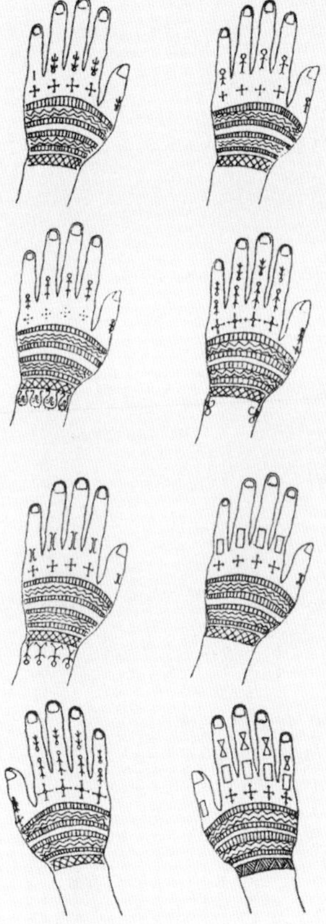

Above Patterns of Paiwan hand tattooing, from the villages of Parirayan, Tokubul, Timor, Kabianan and Chalaabus, 1930s.

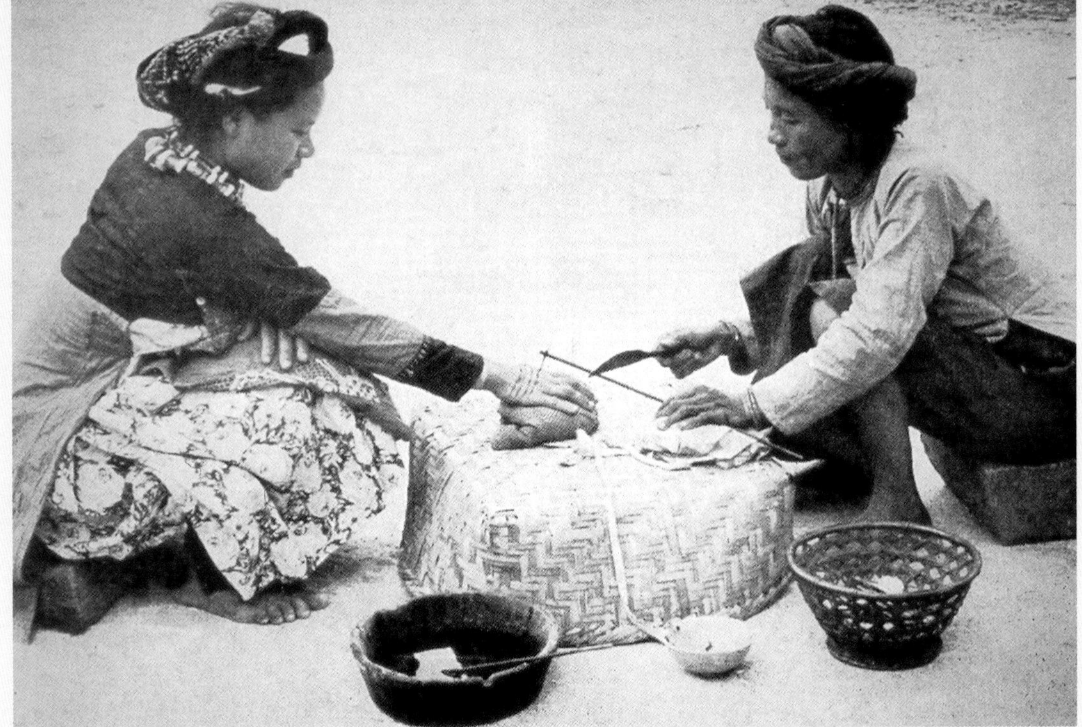

Right Female Paiwan tattooist demonstrating her profession, 1955.

Borneo

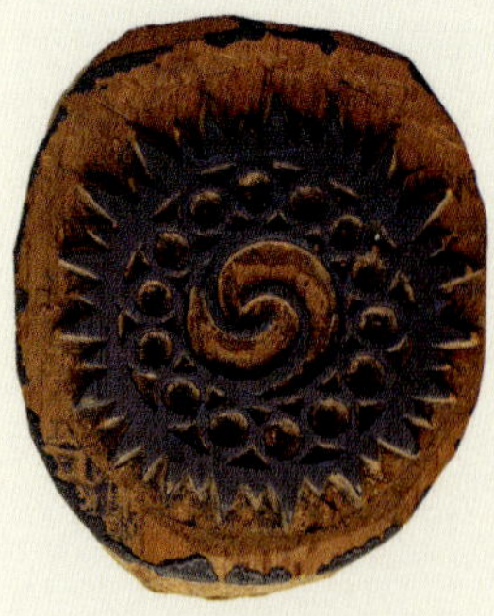

Kayan *klingé* (tattoo stencil block), *ca.* 1898.

On the island of Borneo, the art of tribal tattooing reached its zenith before the dawn of the twentieth century, particularly among the Dayak and Orang Ulu peoples. The term Dayak, meaning "interior" or "inland" person, and Orang Ulu, or "upriver people," encompass various Indigenous groups native to Borneo.

Among these groups, the Iban stand out for their elaborate full-body tattoos. Traditionally, Iban tattooists were men who often worked under the guidance of spirit helpers. These spirits provided them with magical charms to enhance their skills and the potency of their designs, communicating through dreams to reveal the locations of these charms.

Iban tattooing was intricately linked to the concept of *bejalai*, or a journey abroad. According to Iban *adat* (customary law), men could only receive tattoos during *bejalai*.[21] These journeys took Iban men through dense forests in search of trade goods, to confront enemies, or to visit relatives or unmarried women in other communities. To commemorate these travels, men often acquired *pantang* (body tattoos). Warriors, in particular, could earn *tegulun*, or special tattoos on their fingers and hands, to signify their success in taking enemy heads during combat.[22]

The motifs of Iban tattoos were initially carved by men into wooden blocks or bone stencils and then stamped onto the skin. Inspired by nature, these patterns featured designs such as spirals, eggplant flowers, prawns, scorpions, dragon-dogs, crabs,

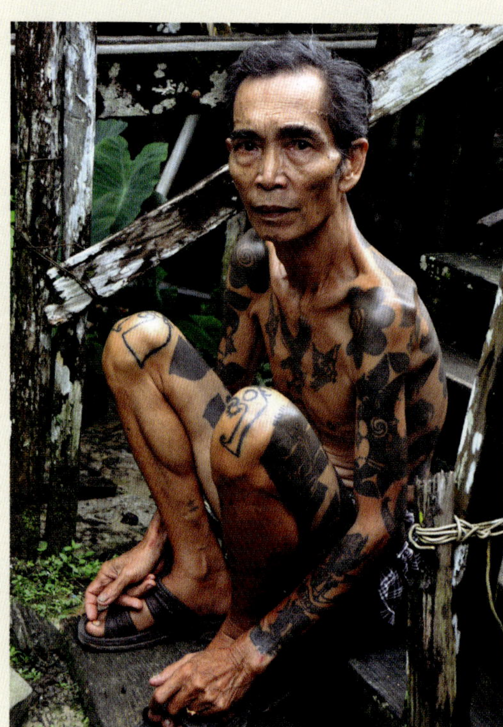

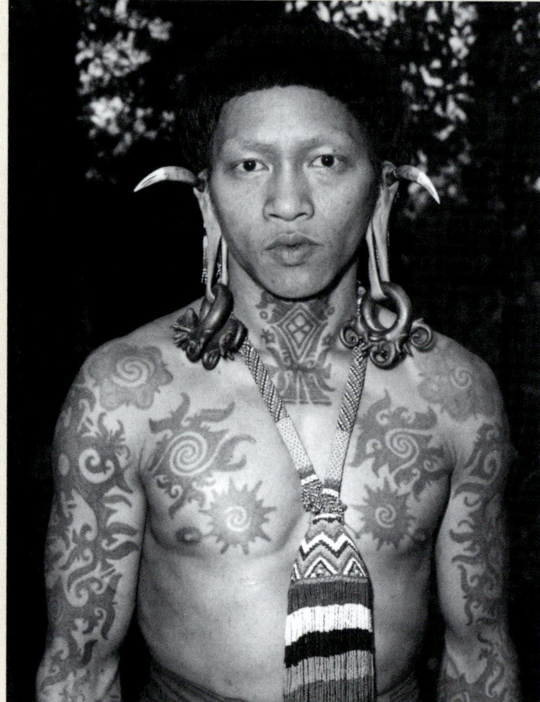

Right The late headman of the Skrang River Iban Penghulu Legan Anak Narok of Entalau longhouse, Sarawak, 2011.

Far right Ninyang Inang with tattoo patterns of the Punan Busang, *ca.* 1955. Also known as the Punan Vuhang, both men and women tattooed.

frogs, and centipedes. Some motifs were believed to possess apotropaic (protective) or other magical powers, adding a layer of spiritual significance to the intricate artistry. These symbols were so powerful that when a man died his deceased ancestors could see them in *Sebayan*, the Land of the Dead.

Unlike the Iban, Kayan tattooists living in Borneo were always female and women were more heavily tattooed than men. Kayan society was highly stratified and female aristocrats were allowed to receive specific tattoo patterns because of their high social status. Tattooists worked under the tutelage and protection of two spirits, who were invoked before any new tattoo pattern was initiated.[23] The prayer announced to the spirit the particular design that was to be applied and asked for the client to feel little pain and the tattooist to make beautiful designs.

Kayan tattooists worked with one or more female assistants, especially as it was necessary to have a skin stretcher before the intricate designs were tapped into the skin. Kayan women were extensively tattooed on their hands, arms, feet, and legs. One of the most powerful tattoo motifs was the *lukut*, or bead design, resembling a starburst or star. This tattoo was worn on the knuckles, wrists, or forearms and was believed to keep the soul from wandering away from its human host.

Tattooing among the Kayan and related tribes (e.g., Kenyah) was universal. They believed that designs acted as "torches" after death, leading them through the darkness of the afterlife to the longhouses of their beloved ancestors.[24]

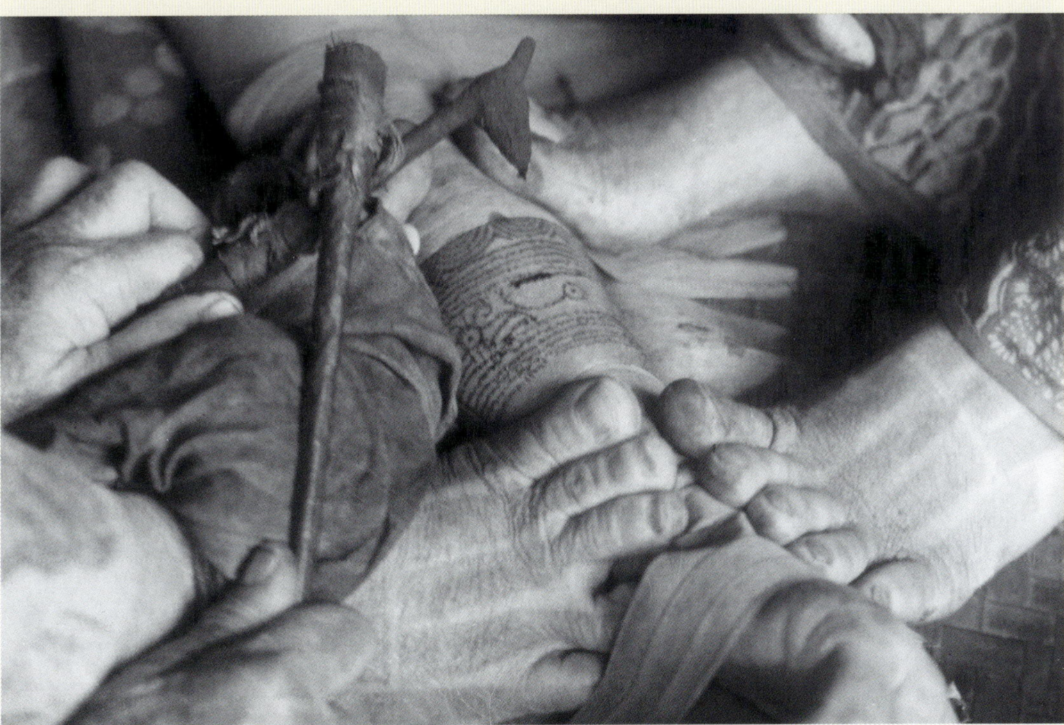

Kayan tattooist and her assistant at work, Long Jegan, Sarawak, 1956.

Spiritual Tattoos of Indonesia

The Mentawai of Siberut Island in Indonesia are some of the most profusely tattooed Indigenous people living today. The tattooing customs of the Mentawai are closely connected to their religious beliefs and their concept of the soul.

Traditionally, tattoos were applied by a designated tattooist, usually a *sikerei* (shaman) or "one who has magic power,"[25] at specific stages in life. But, with missionary activity beginning in the nineteenth century and aggressive government campaigns launched in the 1950s to modernize the Mentawai, cultural practices like tattooing were largely forbidden and gradually abandoned. Today, only a handful of clan members living in remote interior communities bear the tattoos of their ancestors.

The spiritual beliefs of the Mentawai are deeply rooted in the quest for harmony between the human soul and the spirits that govern their world. Central to this quest is the principle of caring for one's soul through the art of body beautification.[26] Men and women who neglect their appearance, failing to adorn themselves with intricate tattoos, vibrant beads, and fragrant flowers, risk becoming unappealing to their souls.[27] In such instances, the soul may choose to abandon its human host, either wandering aimlessly nearby or retreating to the ancestral realm—a departure believed to result in the individual's death. This profound belief highlights the intricate relationship between the Mentawai people, their tattoos, and spirituality, where the act of beautification becomes a lifeline, a vivid testament to the unity of body and spirit.

Mentawai shaman Aman Bereta tattooing Aman Ipai. Buttui, Siberut Island, 2007.

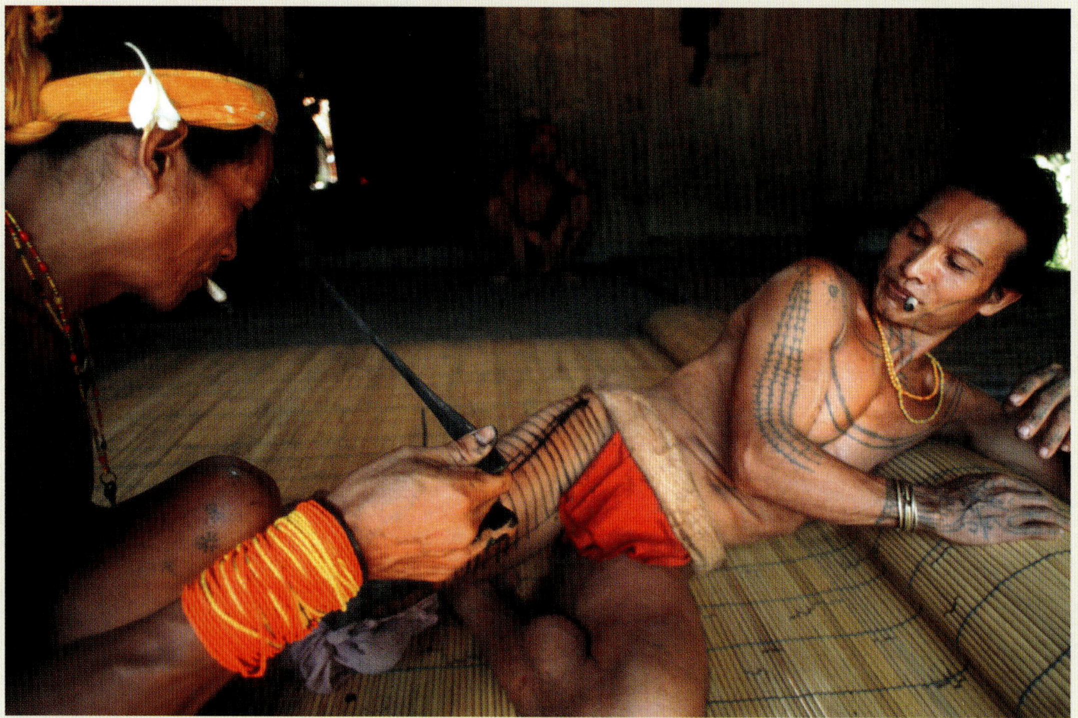

Mentawai shaman with ornaments of beautification, Siberut Island, 2007.

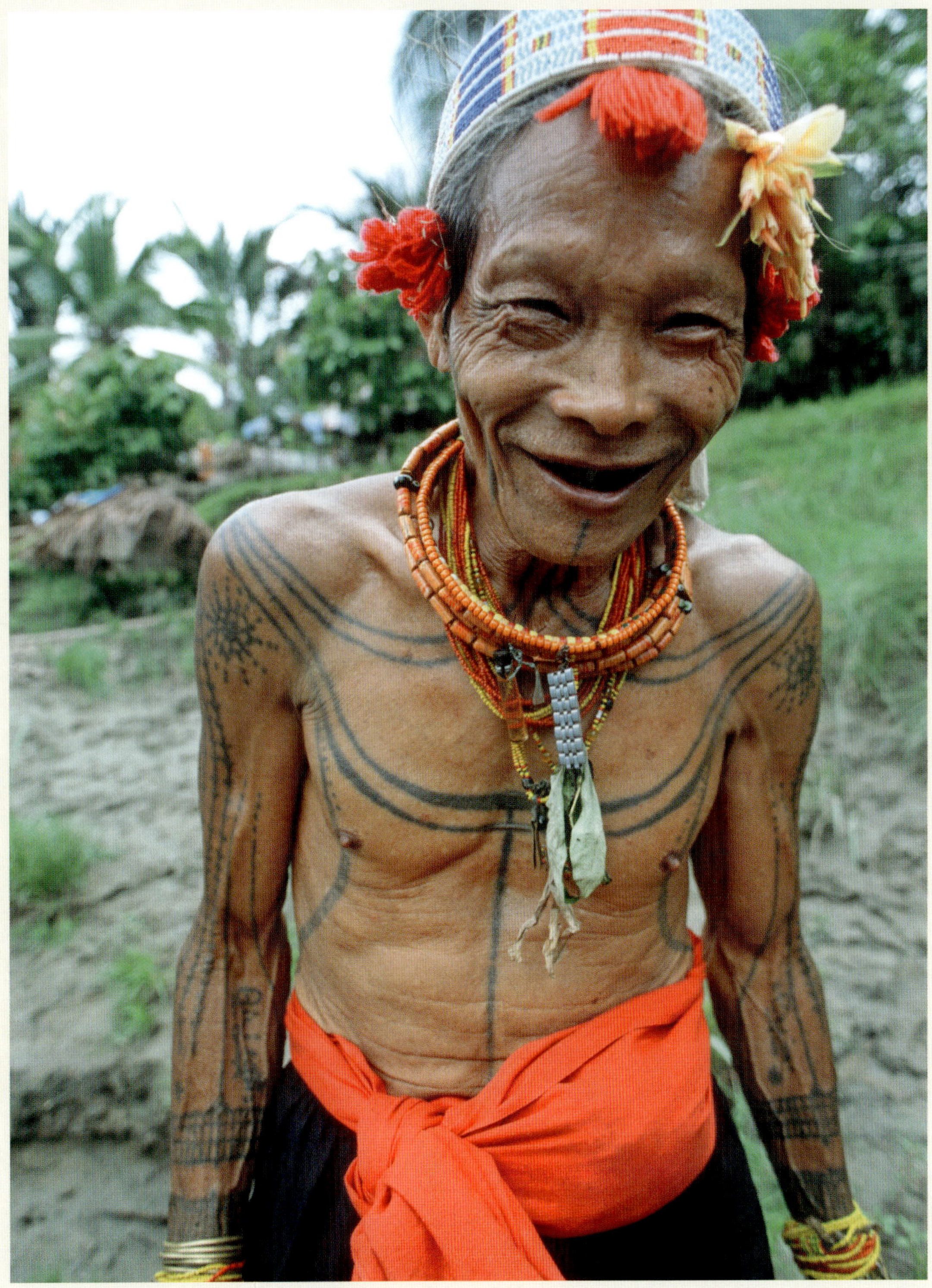

Apart from spiritual beautification, Mentawai tattooing fulfills other functions. Several Mentawai shamans stated that their ancestors would only be able to recognize them in the afterlife because of their tattooing. Other shamans reported that their spirit guides would not recognize them without a full complement of body tattooing. Some men wear crucifix-like crab tattoos on their forearms. Crabs are invoked by Mentawai shamans during healing and other rites because they are believed to live forever; they can discard their old exoskeletons and obtain new ones, or regenerate severed limbs.[28]

Mentawai tattoos can also distinguish people regionally, a kind of zip code on the skin's surface, because the subtle variations of a person's tattoos tell you where a man or woman is from.

In some regions of Siberut Island, the intricate body tattoos of specific clans are believed to represent the tree of life or the sago palm, a tree vital for producing the Mentawai's staple foods. For instance, stripes on men's upper thighs symbolize the veins and trunk of the sago; long, dotted lines running down their arms represent the prickly fronds of its branches; patterns on the hands and ankles mimic the bark or roots; and curved lines on the chest signify the sago flower.[29] Some Mentawai elders believe that the tree of life must be tattooed on every shaman, as being part of this sacred tree is thought to prevent death.

Different Mentawai clans offer unique interpretations of their tattoos. Barbed tattoos running down the arms represent the thorny fronds of the rattan palm. Rosettes tattooed on the shoulders of both men and women symbolize the power of the tattoo to repel evil, like raindrops bouncing off a flower.[30] Abstract bead tattoos on the chest, wrists, and backs of the hands symbolically bind a person's soul, keeping it close to the body. Small marks on men's inner thighs and the tops of their feet, resembling chicken

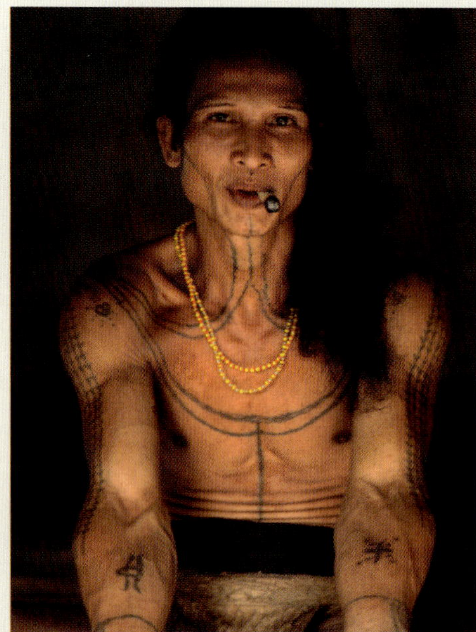

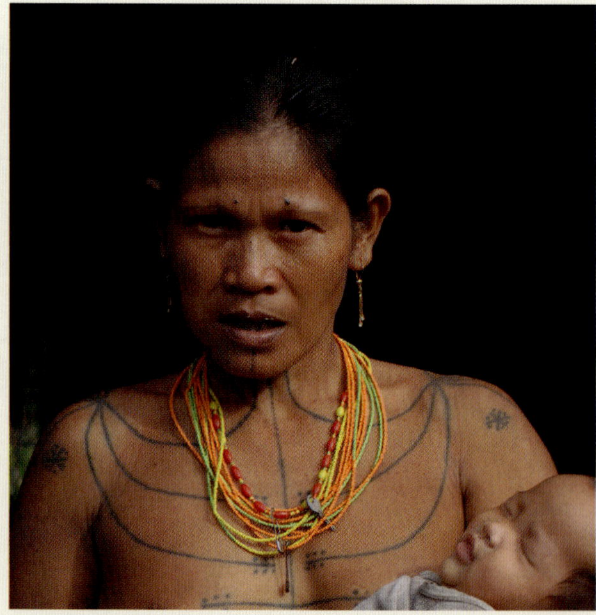

Right Aman Ipai of Buttui, Siberut Island, 2007. He has many tattoos, including a crucifix-like crab tattooed on his forearm. He bears two rosettes on his shoulders, symbolizing that evil will bounce off his body like raindrops from a flower.

Far right Mentawai mother and child, Buttui, Siberut Island, 2011.

feet, actually depict dog paws, serving as sympathetic magic to help the tattooed men run as fast as their hunting companions.[31]

In essence, these elaborate Mentawai tattoo designs tell a story, connecting the wearer to the natural world and the mystical forces that shape its existence, ensuring an individual's place within the sacred cycle of life and death.

Seram

Although there were many other tattooing traditions across the Indonesian archipelago (e.g., Sulawesi, Lesser Sunda Islands, Timor, Timor-Leste), one of the least known revolved around the secretive Kakean initiation society of Seram Island in the Maluku Islands. Prior to the early twentieth century, *masau* or male initiates of the Alune and Wemale tribes were secluded in a *tutué* ("spirit house") where they were taught how to become proper men.[32] To commemorate the event, each initiate was tattooed with their respective clan marking upon their faces. If these men participated in future Kakean rites, they might receive additional tattoos on their bodies depending on the role they played in the initiation. Men who were successful headhunters might also acquire special tattoos that demarcated their social rank.

Maloine or young women who assisted Kakean initiates (e.g., bringing them food during the seclusion period, provided gifts at the conclusion of the rite, etc.) also earned the right to receive a tattoo. *Maloine* who participated in subsequent Kakean initiations could add to their collection of tattoos.[33] These tattoos indicated clan membership. Others were perhaps reserved for specific families, but far less is known about female tattooing traditions among the Alune and Wemale.

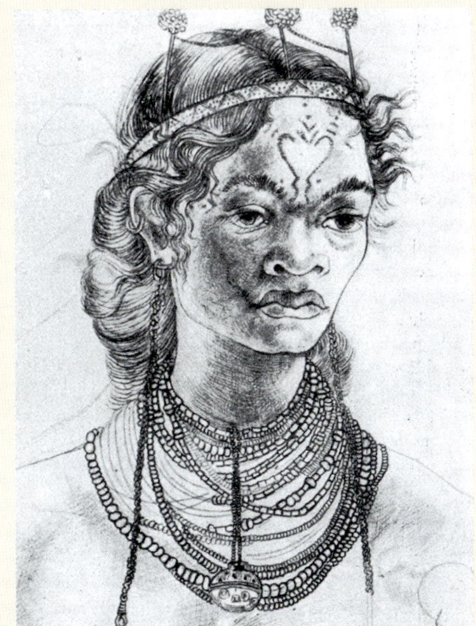

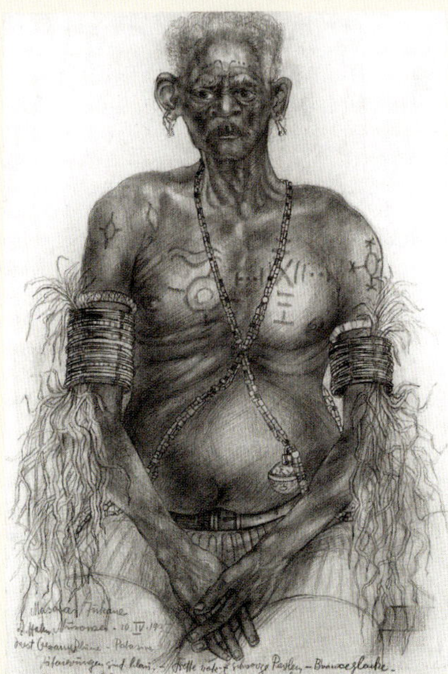

Right Tattooed Wemale woman of Waraloin village, West Seram, 1937. Illustration by Albert Hahn.

Far right Elderly Alune man of Nurwe village in festive attire, West Seram, 1937. Illustration by Albert Hahn.

Tattooed Mummies of the Philippines

The antiquity of the tattooing practice in the northern Philippines can be traced to elaborately tattooed and purposefully mummified human remains aged 700–900 years from upland rock shelters and caves located in Benguet Province, primarily within the municipality of Kabayan.

Tattooed Ibaloy woman from southern Benguet Province, Philippines, 1904.

In the rugged highlands of the northern Philippines, skin marking transcends mere body art, reaching deep into the heart of ancient tradition and cultural identity. Hidden within the secluded rock shelters and caves of Benguet Province, archaeologists have unearthed a remarkable legacy – meticulously mummified human remains, their skin adorned with intricate tattoos that have withstood the passage of time for 700–900 years.[34] These male and female mummies, known as "fire mummies," nestled within wooden coffins carved with motifs that echo the very patterns inked onto their skin, offer an enduring connection to the Indigenous Ibaloy and Kankanaey peoples. These communities, with a history steeped in the practice of *bátek* (tattooing), carried on this sacred art form until the early twentieth century.

These "fire mummies" were preserved through a unique process of smoking over a low fire. This method enhanced tissue dehydration, inhibited fat decay, and created an antimicrobial barrier to prevent bacterial growth and insect infestation.[35] Following this, an embalming "juice" made from local plants – including guava (*Psidium guajava*), *diwdiw* (*Ficus septica*), *patani* (*Phaseolus lunatus*), *duming* (*Dolichos lablab*), and *besodak/sopedak* (*Embelia philippinensis*) – was applied.[36] To further mummify the internal organs, tobacco smoke was blown into the mouth of the deceased.

Once the mummification process was complete, the body and its ornate coffin were transported to their final resting place in the mountains. These sacred sites are believed by the Ibaloy to be the abode of the *kaapuan* (ancestral spirits).[37] This intricate blend of embalming practice and ritual not only preserved the physical form but also honored the spiritual journey, ensuring that the mummified individuals remained connected to their ancestral heritage and the mystical realms of their forebears.

Mount Timbac, a sacred burial site perched at 8,907 feet (2,715 meters) above sea level, faces northeast to greet the rising sun. The Ibaloy people believe that the *kalaching* (soul) "awakens" in the afterlife, welcomed by ancestors and merging with the deities beyond the *duvong* (earth-world).[38] American

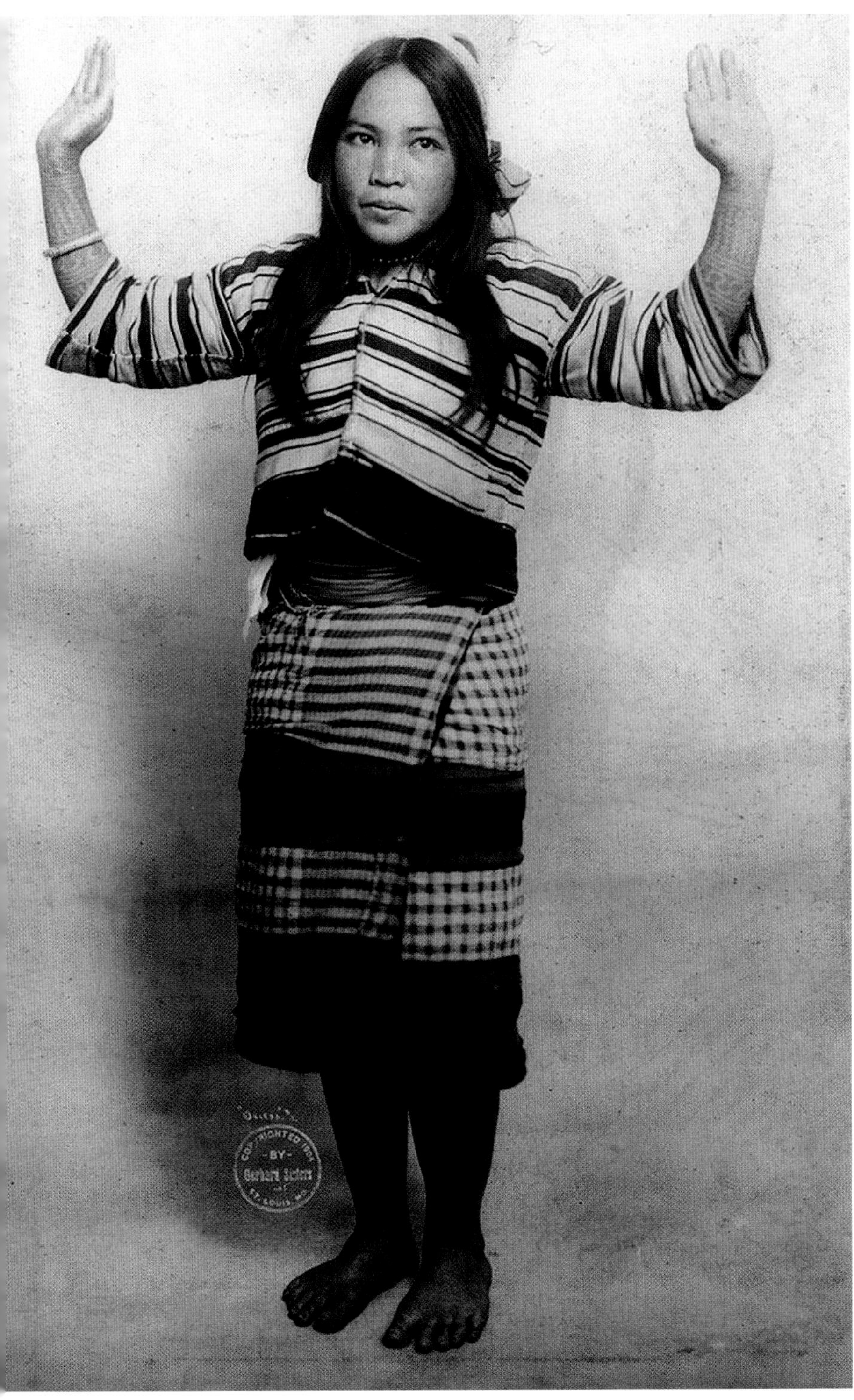

anthropologist Claude Russell Moss, who lived among the Ibaloy and Kankanaey for over a decade in the early twentieth century, observed that the sun was revered as the most powerful deity. Invoked during ordeals and rituals, the sun was considered "the god of justice and the supreme ruler" of all.[39]

Solar motifs were central to both prehistoric and historic Ibaloy and Kankanaey tattoo traditions. These designs adorned the backs of the hands of ancient male mummies found in the Benguet rock shelters, including the legendary demigod, Apo Anno (1100–1300 CE).[40] In the early twentieth century, several writers noted these tattoos on both men and women. Frederic Sawyer, a British engineer who resided in Luzon in the late nineteenth century, documented the prevalence of tattooing among the tribes of the Cordillera Central, including the Ibaloy and Kankanaey. He described sun tattoos, inked in indigo blue, adorning the backs of hands – a common motif in central Benguet, where the sun was worshipped. Alongside these solar symbols were patterns of straight and curved lines tattooed on the chest and arms.[41]

About twenty years before Frederic Sawyer's observations, the German traveler Hans Meyer documented the full-body tattoos of an Ibaloy warrior and the elaborate arm tattoos of a Kankanaey man from Banaao village near Mount Data. Both groups proudly displayed the iconic solar disk tattoos on the backs of men's hands. These intricate tattoos included geometric patterns – lines, bands, zigzags, chevrons, triangles – and figurative motifs, such as centipedes, serpents, scorpions, lizards, deer, dogs, and anthropomorphs, representing omen creatures or earthly manifestations of deities.[42]

Meyer observed that in Banaao village, full-body tattoos were typically found on older

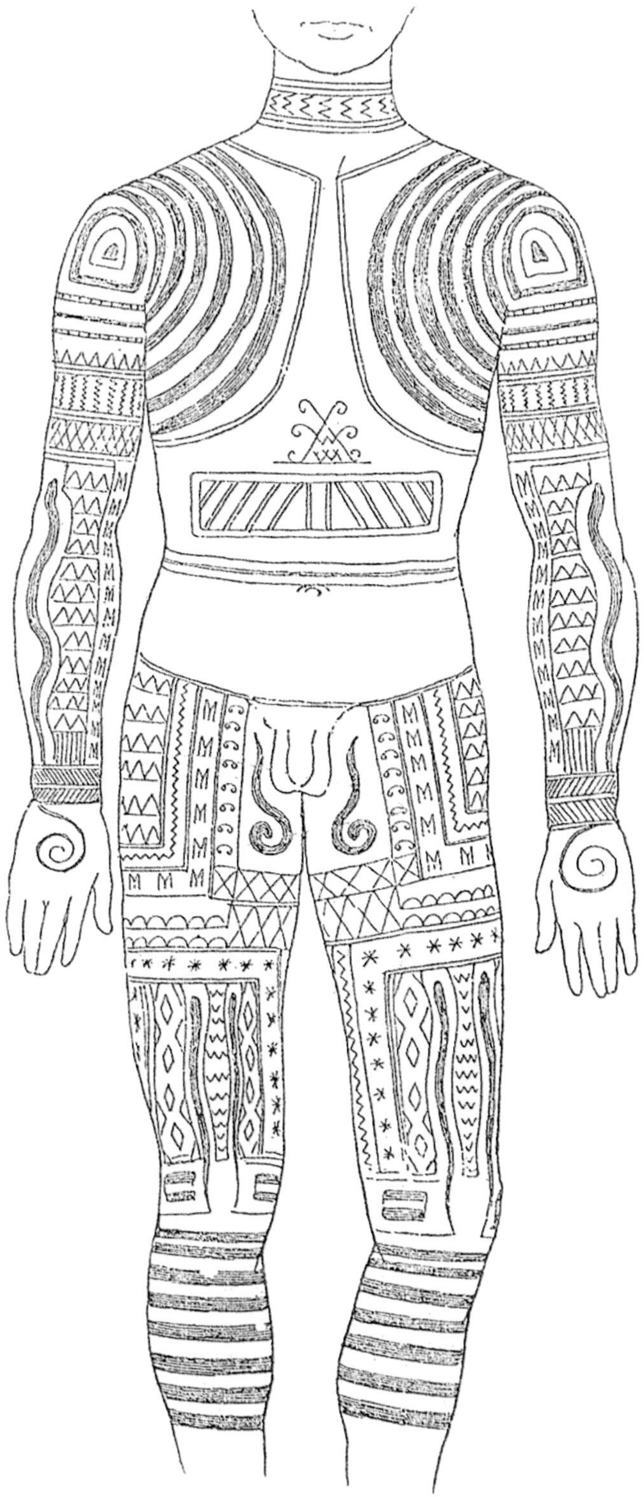

Hans Meyer's detailed illustration of *burik* (tattoos) in the northern Philippines, 1882. *Burik* is also the name of a tattoo design found on the body and translated as "spotted." The tattoos are composed of figurative (man, lizard, snake, and scorpion) and geometric (lines, circles, stripes, and zigzags) designs. Similar figurative patterns are found on the thighs and buttocks, while the chest, back, and legs display parallel stripes, making the body look like "a sailor's striped jacket and the legs like Tyrolean stockings."

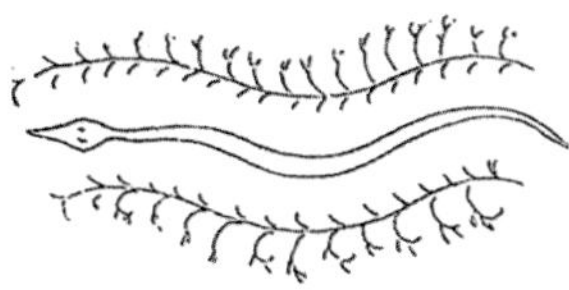

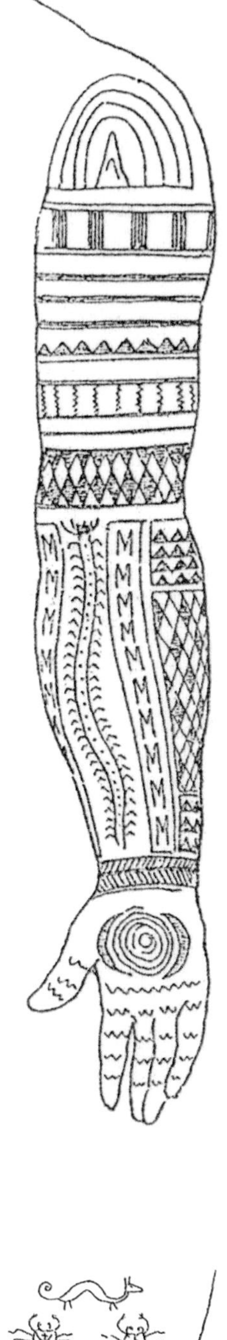

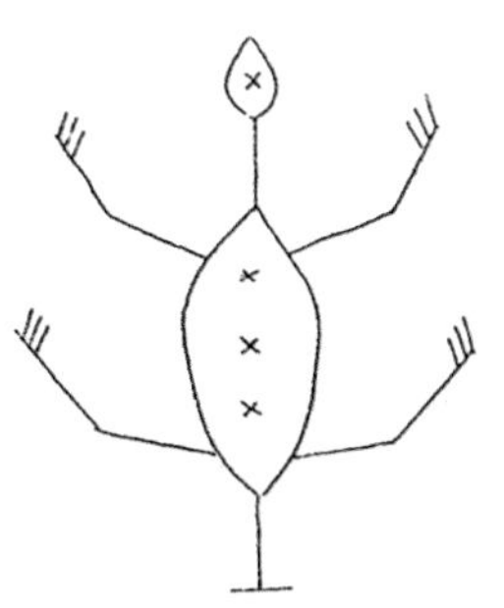

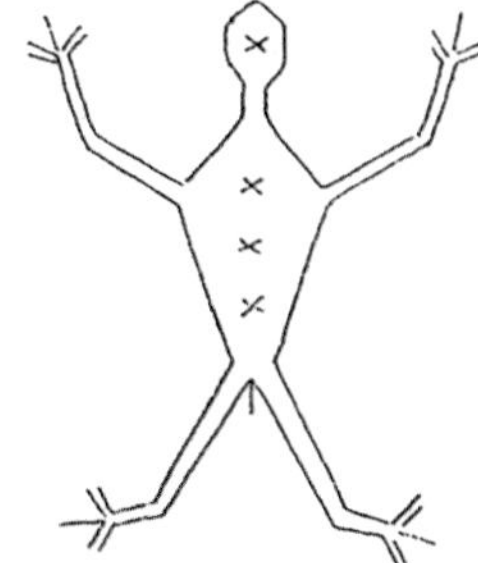

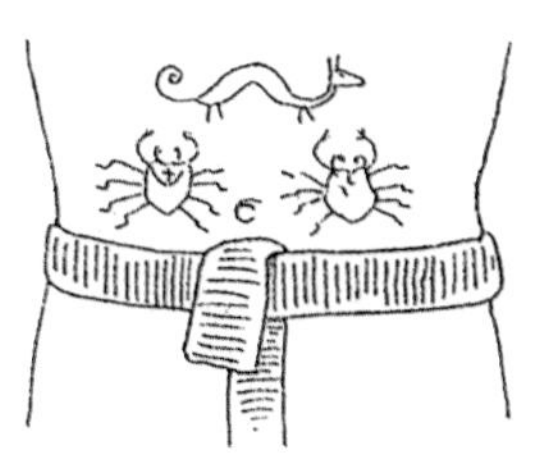

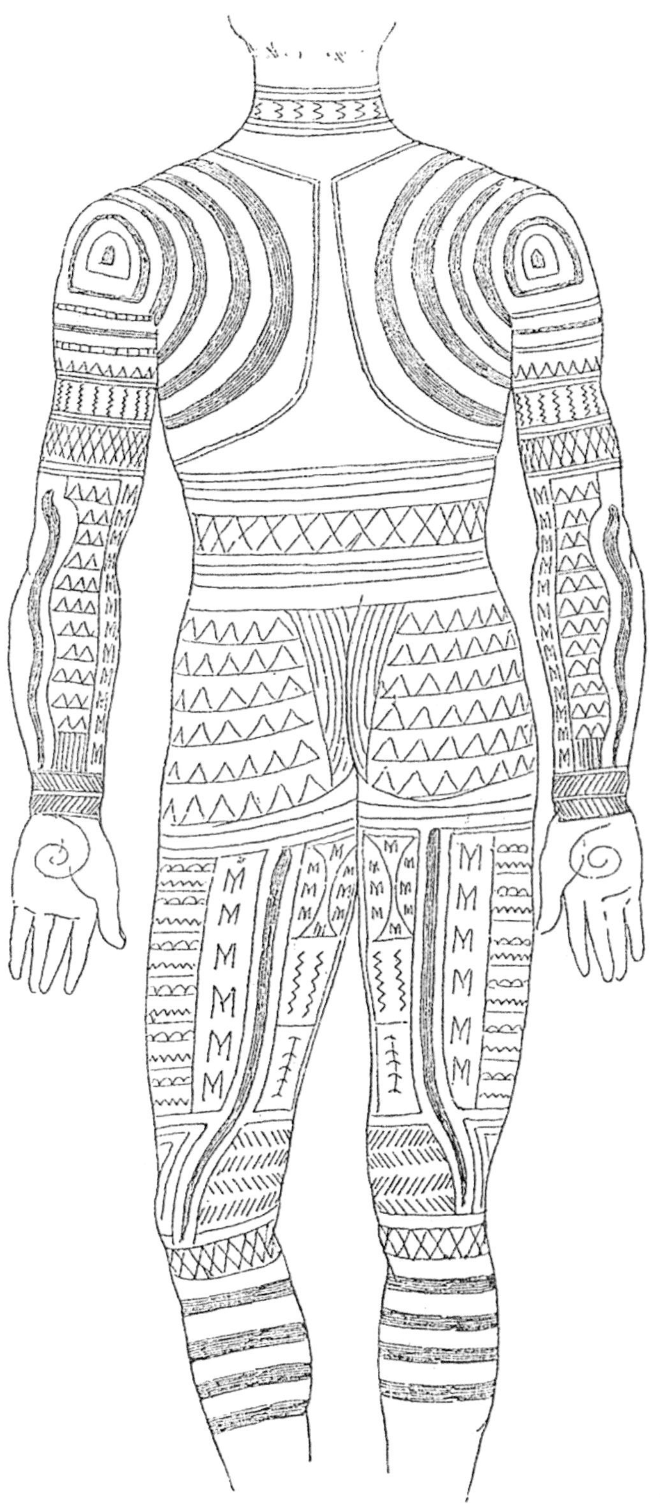

men, while younger men bore minimal arm tattoos, a spiral or circular sun image on the back of the hand, and parallel rings around their calves.[43] This incomplete tattooing among the youth was likely due to their not yet having proven themselves in battle, as taking another human life was a prerequisite for receiving warrior chest tattoos among the Kalinga, Bontok, and other Cordilleran groups.[44]

Meyer also noted the impact of Spanish "pacification" on the Kankanaey villages, leading to a decline in traditional tattooing practices. By the time Moss lived among the Ibaloy and Kankanaey in the early twentieth century, full-body male tattooing had largely faded into memory, with some villages having abandoned the practice for over a decade.[45]

This historical tapestry of Indigenous Philippine body art, intertwined with cultural rites and warrior traditions, illustrates a tattoo heritage slowly fading under the influence of external forces. The once vibrant symbols of Cordilleran identity and spiritual connection are now remnants of bygone era where each mark told a story of valor, belief, and belonging.

Kenyah Tattoos of Borneo

One hundred years ago, Kenyah women's tattooing, much like neighboring Kayan skin marking (see page 167), was ubiquitous. Both groups wore elaborate and spiritually significant tattoos, symbols of their social status until the practice waned in the early twentieth century. Although distinctions can be made, Kenyah tattoo motifs often mirrored those of the Kayan in form, and their tattooists, like their Kayan counterparts, operated under the guidance of a tattoo deity or spirit. This divine presence was invoked to enter their basket of tattooing tools through offerings of old pearls and *kawit* (charms).[46]

Before beginning a tattooing session, the tattooist would recite a prayer to her spiritual guide, seeking blessings for her work, minimal pain for her client, and ideal conditions for tattooing – strong light and cool temperatures.[47] In some Kenyah groups, such as the Leppo' Tau of Long Nawang in Kalimantan, the chief's daughter had to be tattooed first. However, if she passed away, other girls in the community could then be marked.[48]

A Kenyah woman's social status was evident from her tattoo patterns. Poi Mirang Pai, a noblewoman of the Uma Bakah clan, explained to me that only women of her status could wear anthropomorphic tattoos representing the face and body of Bungan Malan, the Kenyah Goddess of Creation. These sacred motifs adorned her legs, arms, and hands. Commoners and slaves were forbidden from wearing these designs, facing severe punishment or even death if they attempted to do so. This is because only women of high rank possessed the

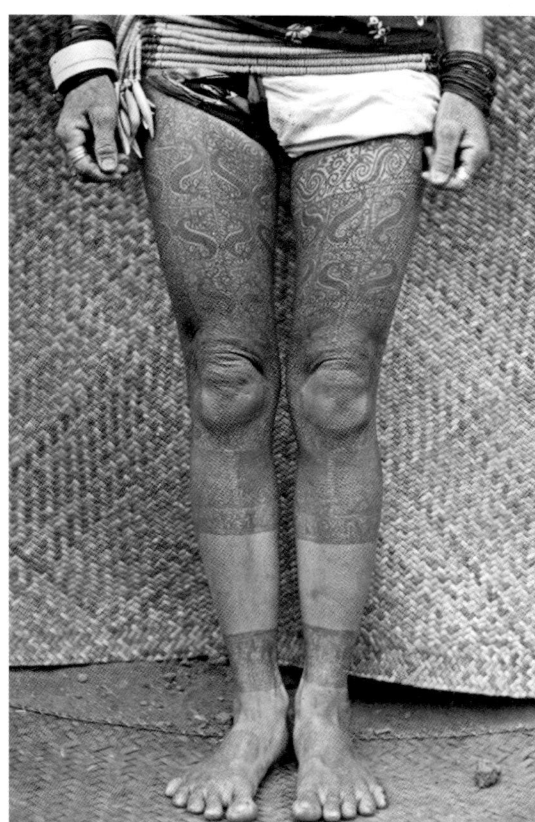

Left and opposite Front and profile views of high-ranking Kenyah woman of Long Nawang, Kalimantan, with *aso'* motifs and other designs reserved for her status, 1932.

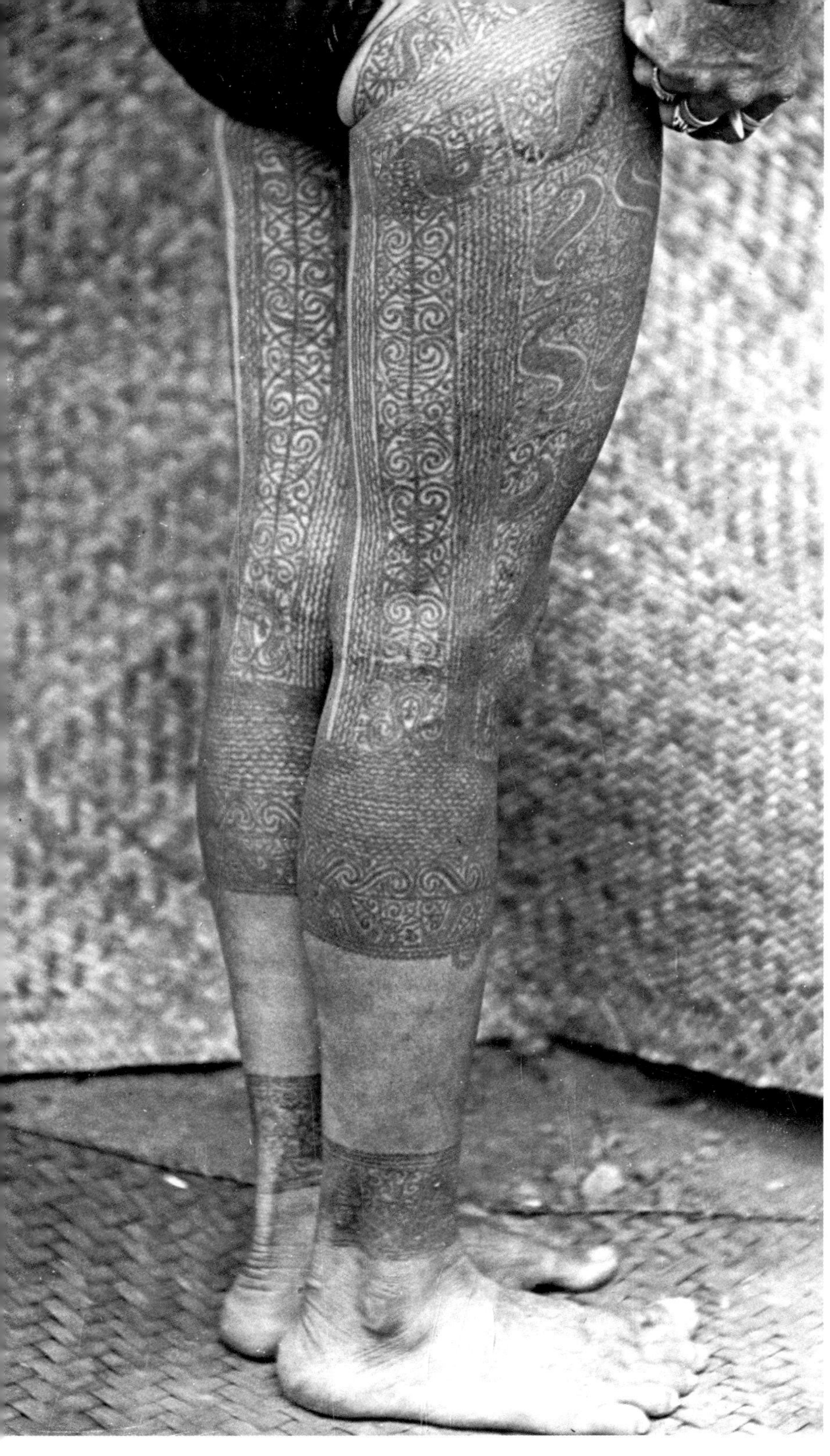

spiritual fortitude to resist the negative magic associated with these designs, as aristocrats were considered closer to the spirit world.[49]

Aspects of Kenyah leg patterning were unique among the Indigenous peoples of Sarawak. Namely, progressive bands were hand-tapped on the lower legs with each band speaking volumes about one's social status. Members of the royal family, like Poi Mirang Pai, proudly displayed five bands, while lesser nobility bore four to two bands, reflecting their rank within the hierarchy.[50]

These exquisite tattoos extended up the thighs to the pubis, composed of delicate, symmetrically balanced tendril-like elements. Each design represented the vibrant plant, animal, and spiritual life of the surrounding rain forest. Motifs included the majestic hornbill, the mythical *aso'* (dragon-dog), and the sacred tree of life.

Tattooing could not commence if the man of the household was away, adhering to the customs of the time. During the tattooing ceremonies, male family members donned bark cloth and remained confined to a longhouse.[51] This attire, made from the paper mulberry tree, was traditionally worn during coming-of-age and mourning rituals, symbolizing a transition from an old life to a new beginning. Once the tattooing was completed, the men would shed their bark-cloth garments for new clothes, marking the end of the ritual.

One of the most significant Kenyah tattoo gatherings took place at the expansive Long Nawang longhouse complex on the upper Kayan River in Kalimantan.[52] Here, female tattooing was indelibly linked to headhunting and the grand nine-day Mamat Festival, where the *bali akang* (spirits of courage) were invoked to shield the community from illness and danger. The festival included various purification rituals and numerous sacrifices.

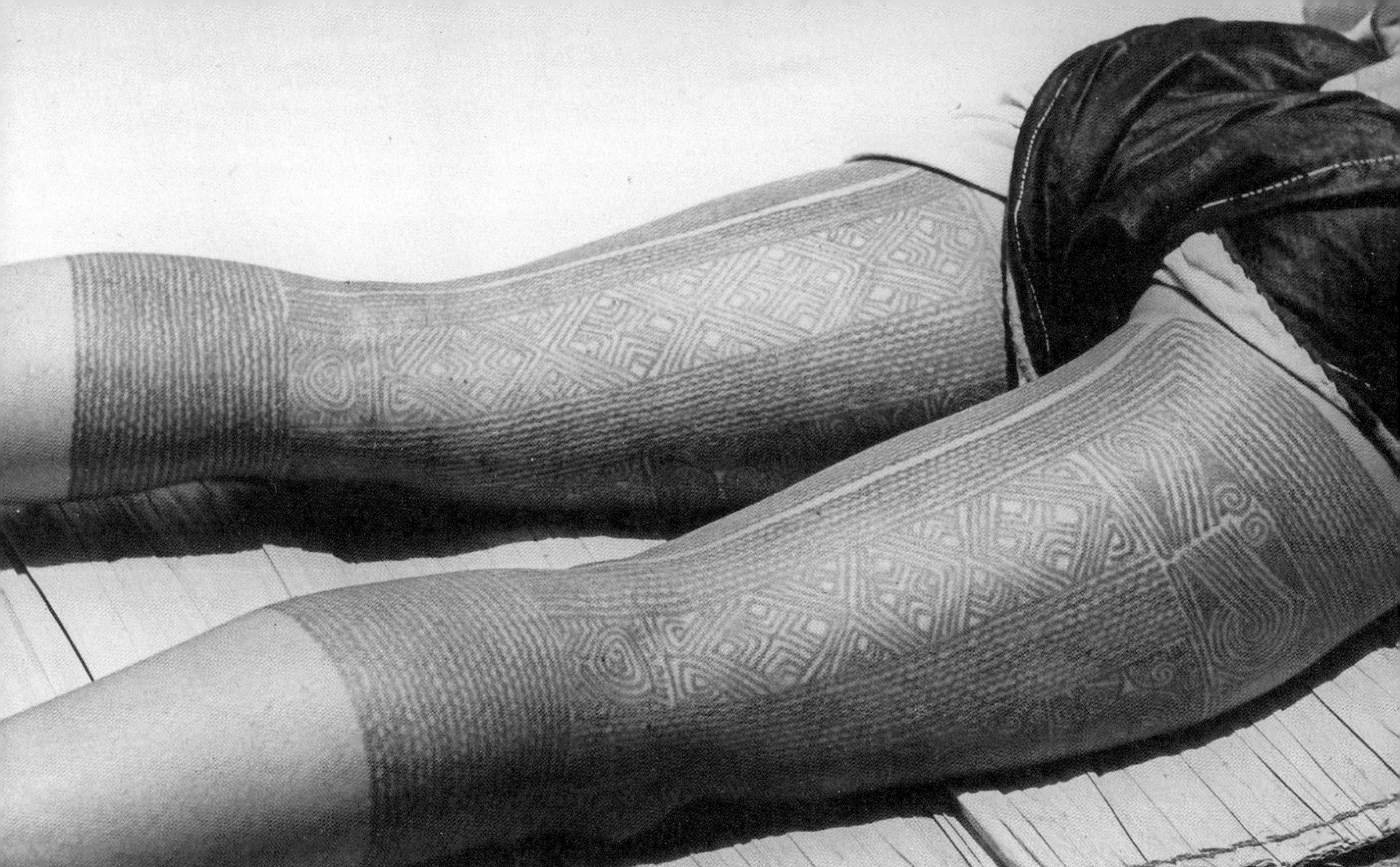

High-ranking Kenyah woman, with apotropaic ancestral face (back of knee) and assorted geometric motifs, Kalimantan, 1932.

The heads of recently slain enemies, believed to have a cleansing effect on humanity, were prominently featured.[53] These grisly trophies were thought to transfer courage to the male attendees, imbuing them with the valor of the fallen foes.[54]

Women were excluded from Mamat activities because the spirits of courage were not attracted to them. Instead, women were associated with *bali leang* and *bali kadjang*, spirits believed to induce fear and lethargy.[55] Consequently, women's tattooing was permitted only once every six to ten years, at the conclusion of a major Mamat, when purification rituals could neutralize the supposed harmful magic of female tattooing.[56] The tattooing process took place in small huts away from the festival to prevent weakening the spirits of courage.[57] During the healing period, tattooed women were in a taboo state and could not feed themselves, relying on a friend to help them recover.

Sometimes, Long Nawang women obtained their tattoos outside of the Mamat by traveling to neighboring tribes, such as the Ma Koelit, renowned for their tattooing skills. After healing for a month or more, they returned to Long Nawang and had to offer a pig and a sword to the ruling chiefs to "cool" them down.[58] A feast was then held to cleanse the men and longhouses from the "harmful magic of the women."[59]

The late Poi Mirang Pai, a Kenyah aristocrat and one of the last fully tattooed members of the royal family of the Uma Bakah clans, Sarawak, 2011. She bears various tattooing motifs (arms, hands, legs, feet) reserved for her lofty social status, including the face of Bungan Malan, the Goddess of Creation.

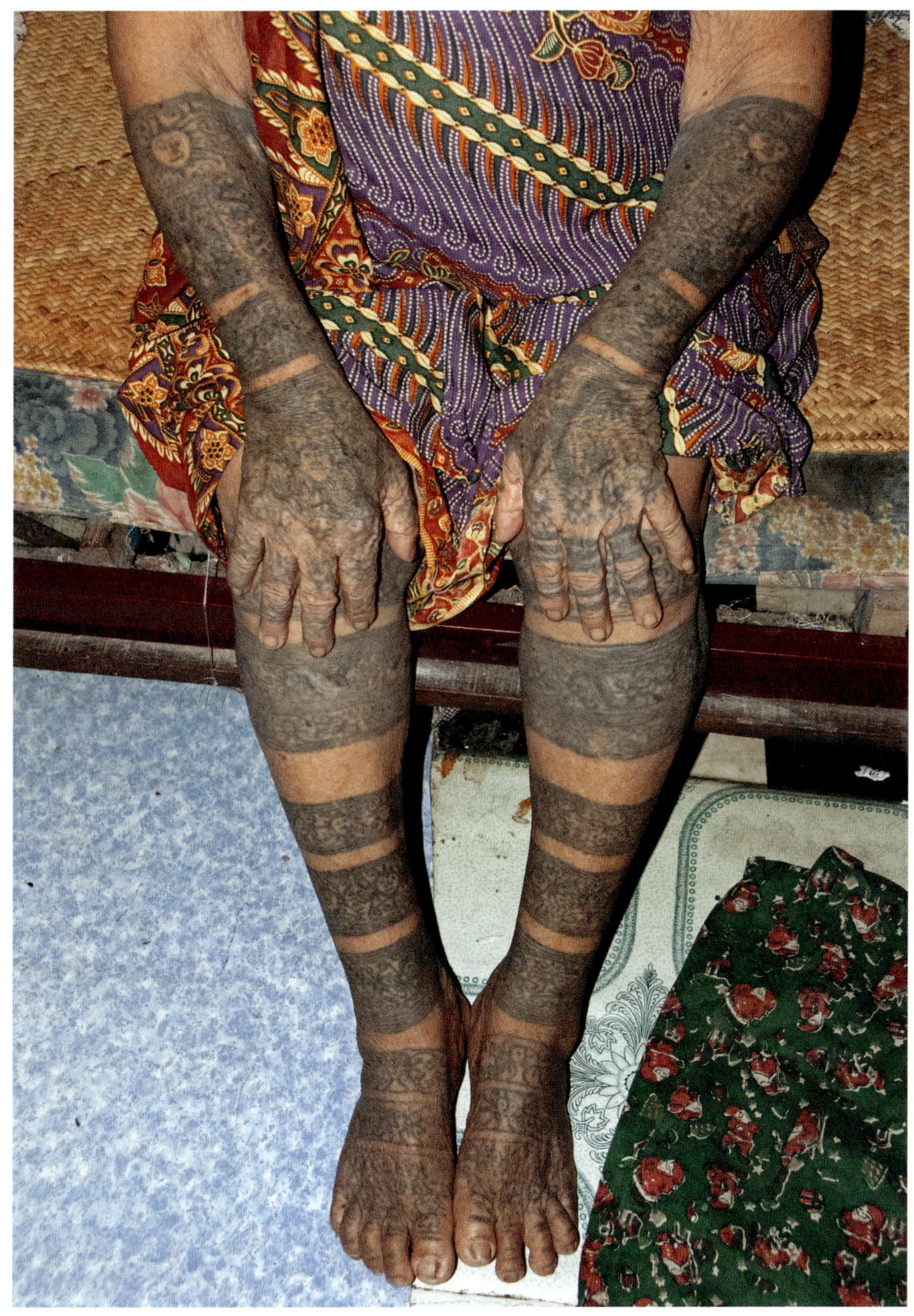

Marks for the Afterlife: Tattoos of Timor and Rote (South Indonesia)

The custom of tattooing totem animals on the body has been vividly chronicled among the Indigenous peoples of Timor and the neighboring islands of Sumba and Rote. In the nineteenth century these tattoos – featuring depictions of animals, floral designs, and objects from material culture – served myriad purposes. Dr. Johann Gerard Friedrich Riedel, an early twentieth-century Dutch civil servant, marveled at how the Dawan people of West Timor used these tattoos as property marks or "brands," meticulously delineating territorial boundaries, family lands, specific trees, animals, and even textiles.[60]

Women's tattooing marked the arms, hands, legs, thighs, torso, and chin with motifs such as radiant solar patterns, blazing fire, and fire-making tools. These designs possessed a mystical apotropaic power, repelling the malevolent *nitu* (evil spirits) and safeguarding women during pregnancies by invoking heat, which evil spirits abhorred, and summoning the protective gaze of Usi-Neno, the Lord Sun, guardian of the hereafter.

In the spiritual realm of the Dawan afterlife, the connection between heat and tattoos takes on an almost mythic significance. Indonesian author Fransisco Jacob,[61] who recently delved into the fading *lunat* (tattooing) traditions of the Dawan, revealed that tattoos were bartered for fire in the

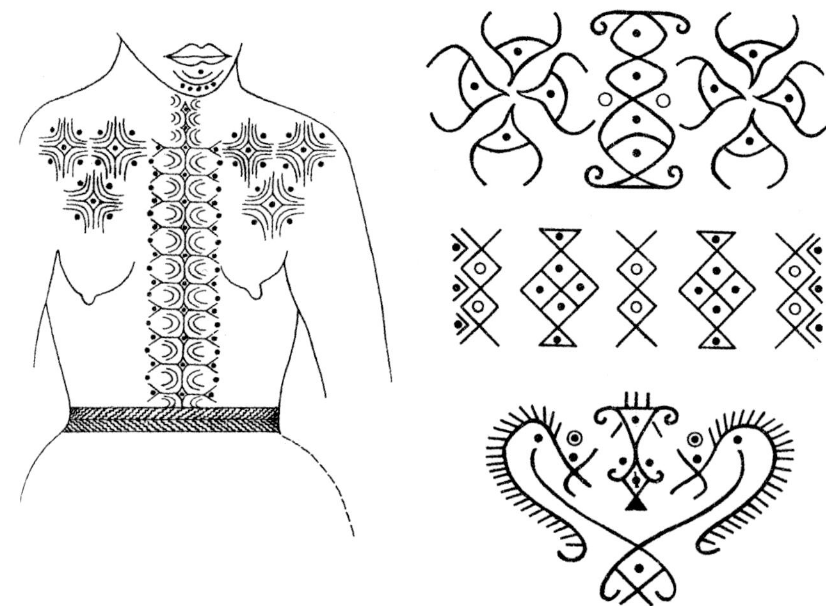

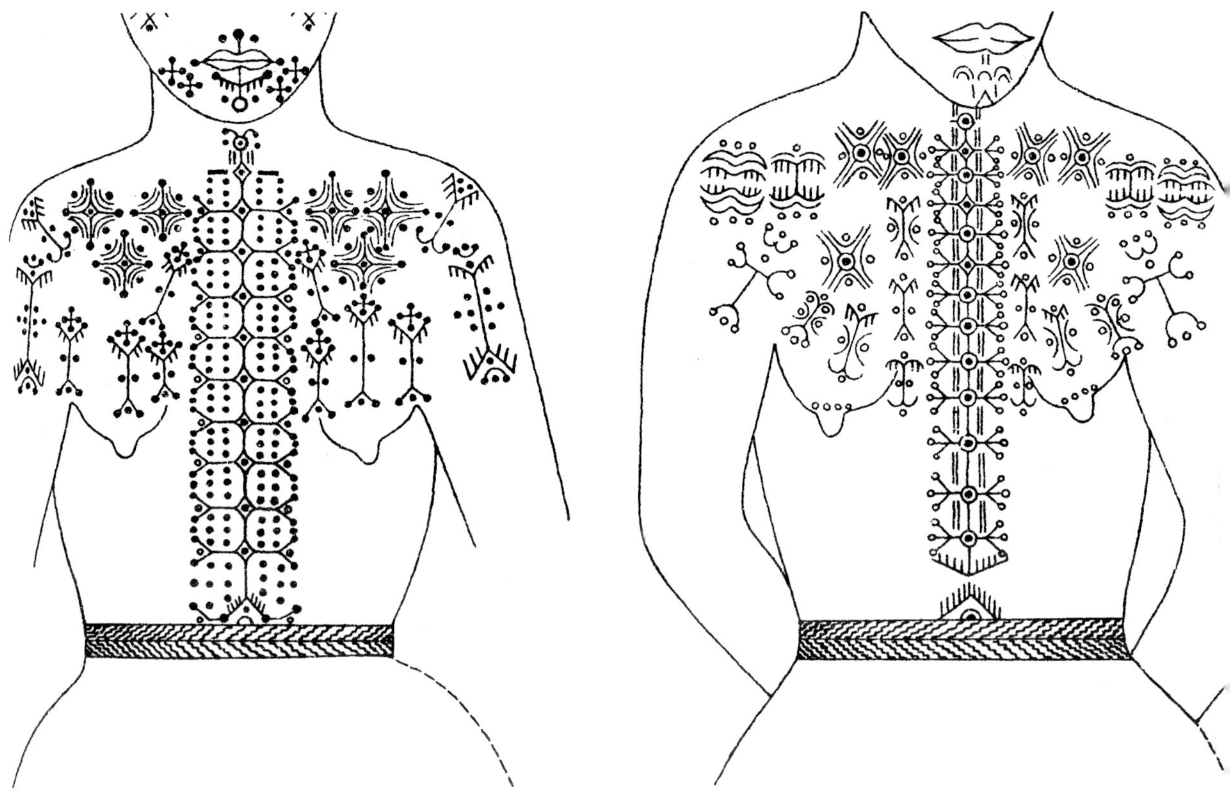

Opposite and right
Female body tattooing patterns, Timor Leste, *ca*. 1900. The "fire-making tool" was a primary tattoo motif placed on either breast. Riedel believed the motif was a fertility emblem.

afterworld. The Dawan envision that upon death, the *smanaf* (soul) embarks on a journey to the *pah nitu* (ancestors) through the shadowy passage of Mount Mutis. This path, cloaked in impenetrable darkness, requires the soul to possess fire for illumination, a precious resource obtained by trading one's body tattoos.[62] Fire is essential not just for light but also for cooking and warmth in the cold afterlife.

Dutch missionary-ethnographer Albert C. Kruyt, who chronicled the oral histories of tattooed Timorese elders in 1920, painted an even more vivid picture of this fiery exchange.[63] He described how a tattooed woman, upon her celestial arrival, was guided to Usi-Neno, the Heavenly Lord Sun, who judged her worthiness to reside in the afterworld. Clutching a piece of wood, the soul awaited Usi-Neno's divine spark, ignited with a piece of iron. In a sacred transaction, the tattoos on her forearm were exchanged for this life-giving fire, while the rest of her tattoos remained intact, preserving her identity for future celestial exchanges.

The fear of facing death without tattoos was so immense that even young children, barely three or four years old, received small, dotted tattoos on their forearms, resembling a simple cross.[64] Just one dot was enough to purchase fire in the afterlife, additional dots served as a reserve for future needs. Without these sacred markings, a soul was doomed to become a "servant" to a tattooed soul.[65]

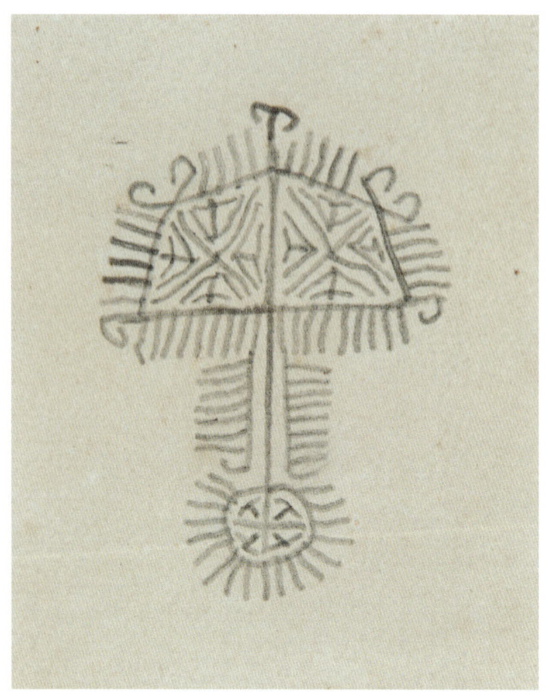

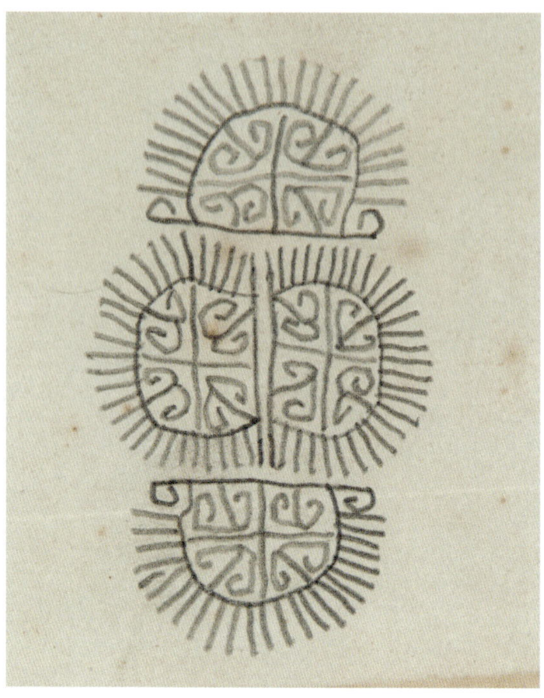

Left Two tattoo motifs from the 388-page pattern book of female Tetun tattooist Raboe, West Timor, before 1862.

Opposite Tattooed Rindi elder, Sumba Island, 1980.

On the neighboring island of Rote, the practice of *balatete* (tattooing) was deeply intertwined with beliefs about the afterlife until it was abandoned in the early twentieth century. Female *manbalatetes* (tattooists) hand-tapped intricate local patterns – stars, animals, cruciforms with dots, and floral and geometric designs – onto the arms, legs, and sometimes the chests of men and women using tree thorns.[66] According to Dutch missionary F. H. van de Wetering, tattoos in Rote served as currency for food exchanges in the afterlife with Mani Daè, or Bei Daè, the Lord of the Ground.[67]

In West Timor, a local proverb asserted that female tattooing and tooth filing were essential in "making" women in the eyes of ancestors and the community.[68] The arduous process of tattooing the cheeks, chin, breast, and abdomen down to the navel signified a woman's holiness, vigilance, and her status as a "wife" of the tribe, showcasing her strength and endurance. Local informants expressed the belief that, as the body grows larger with age, more tattoos were needed to buy food for the "bigger" body in the afterlife.[69]

Tattooing in West Timor was an art performed by skilled women. The tattoo pattern was first stenciled on the skin using a liquid pigment made from charred leaves and tree resin. In some regions, the ink was derived from soot mixed with sugarcane juice and honey.[70] A thorn from the kaffir lime tree was attached at a right angle to a wooden baton and hand-tapped into the skin. The leaves of the thorn apple (*Datura metel* L.) were used to help heal the wounds.[71]

The timing of tattooing varied regionally. In some areas, it occurred before the corn harvest and rainy season, while in others, it coincided with summer or funerals. Apart from the "fire markings" applied to young children, girls received more substantial tattoos at the onset of puberty. They were not tattooed during their

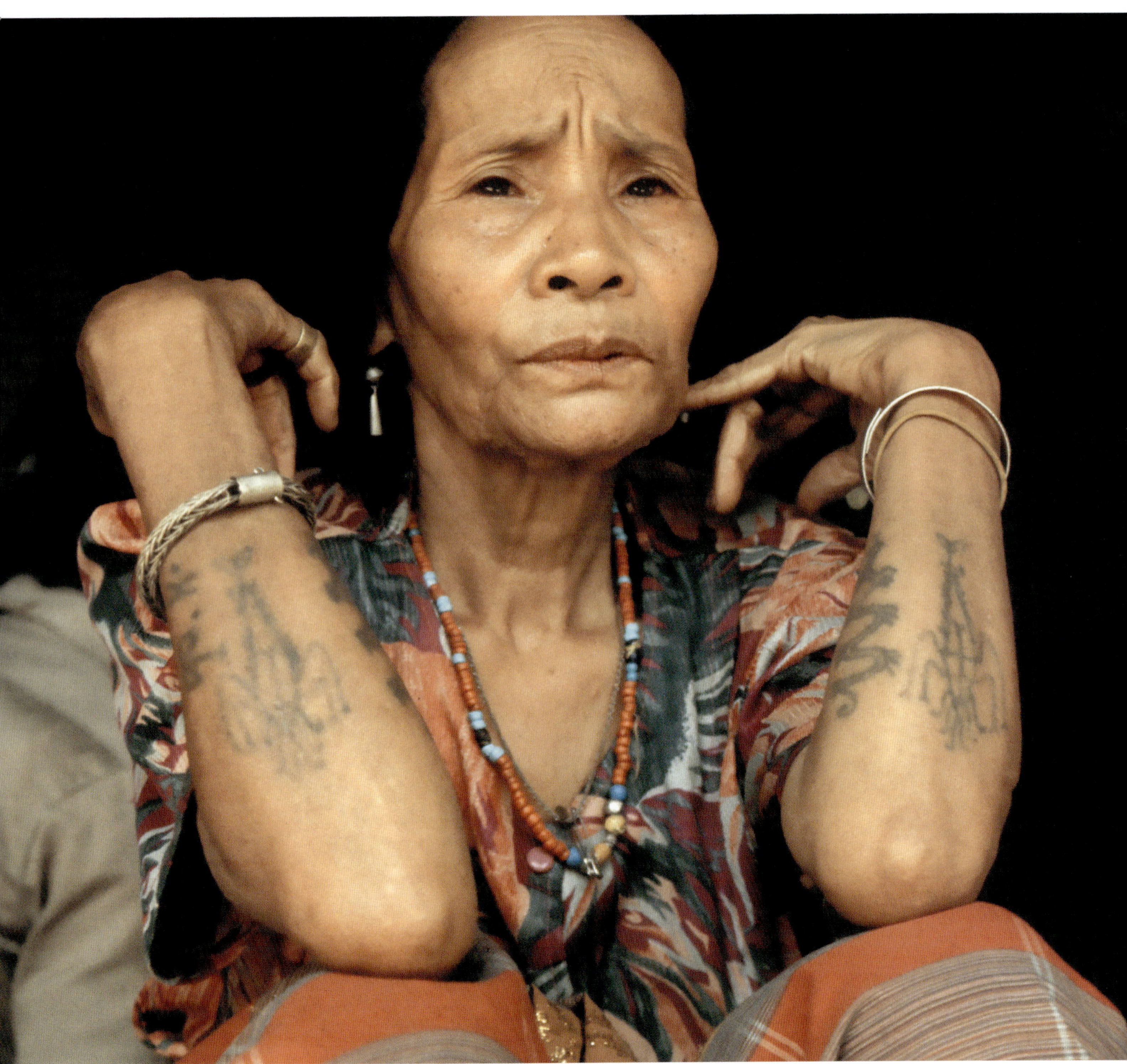

menses, as it was believed the blood from the wounds might flow uncontrollably. Pregnant women were prohibited from receiving tattoos to avoid blinding their newborns. After a woman had children, she typically did not receive more tattoos, as she was considered too "old."[72]

In the North Amanatun District, tattooing was timed with the agricultural calendar, specifically before the corn harvest and rainy season, as it was believed wounds would not heal properly outside this period.[73] In South Amanatun, Dawan elders revealed that tattooing was performed in summer while a deceased community member lay in state,[74] contradicting Kruyt's account that tattooing was forbidden if a dead person's body remained unburied, as that "angered" its spirit.[75]

In Timor-Leste, Tetun men and women of Suai Loro village received tattoos during funerals. Entire families gathered, and the ancestral spirits were invoked by the *lia nain*, a traditional leader and spokesperson knowledgeable in village law, history, and the names of the dead.[76]

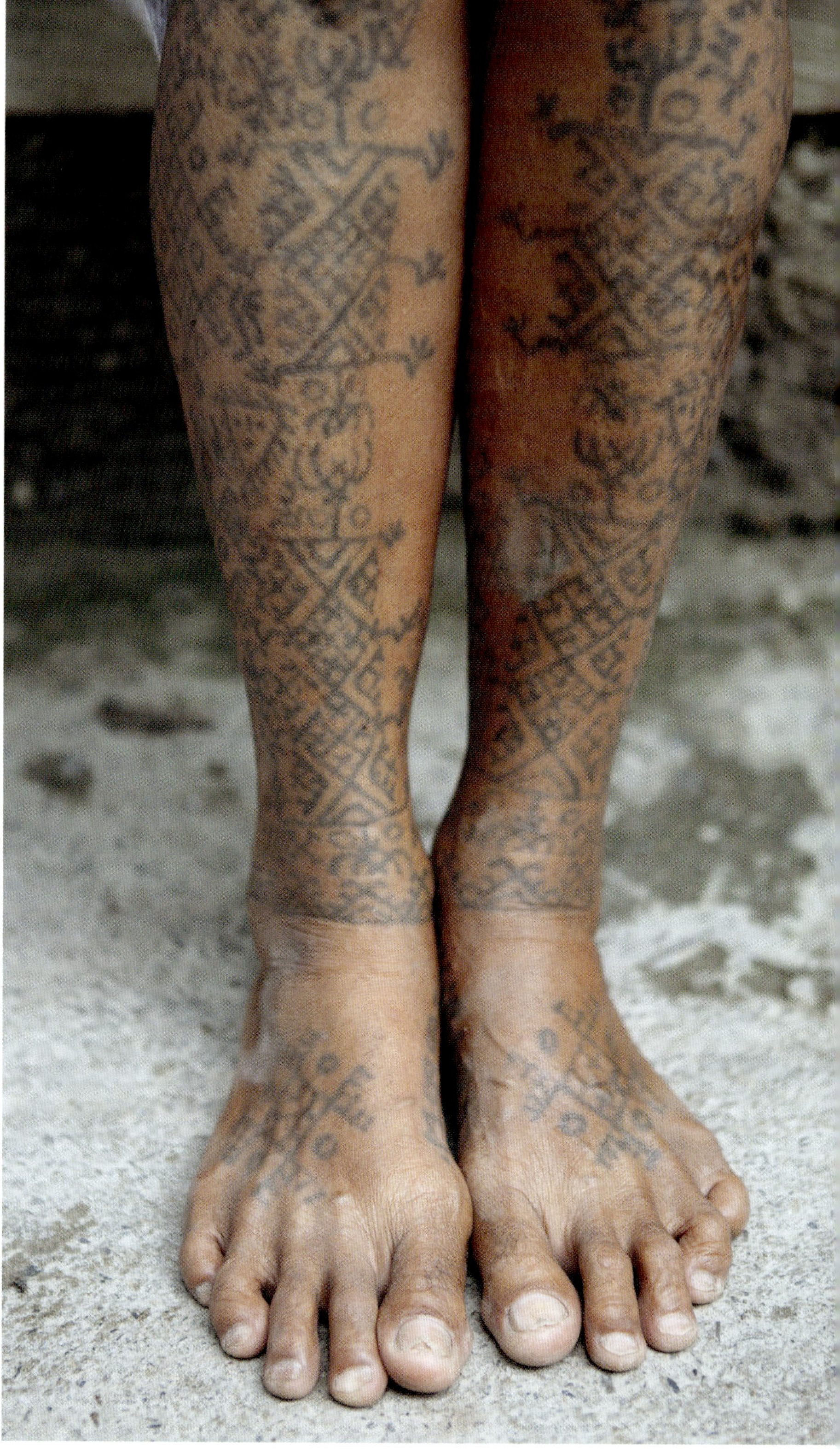

Opposite and right
Tattooed Wehali elder with symbols on her shins and calves representing her family's *uma lulik* or "sacred house," Timor Leste, *ca*. 2002.

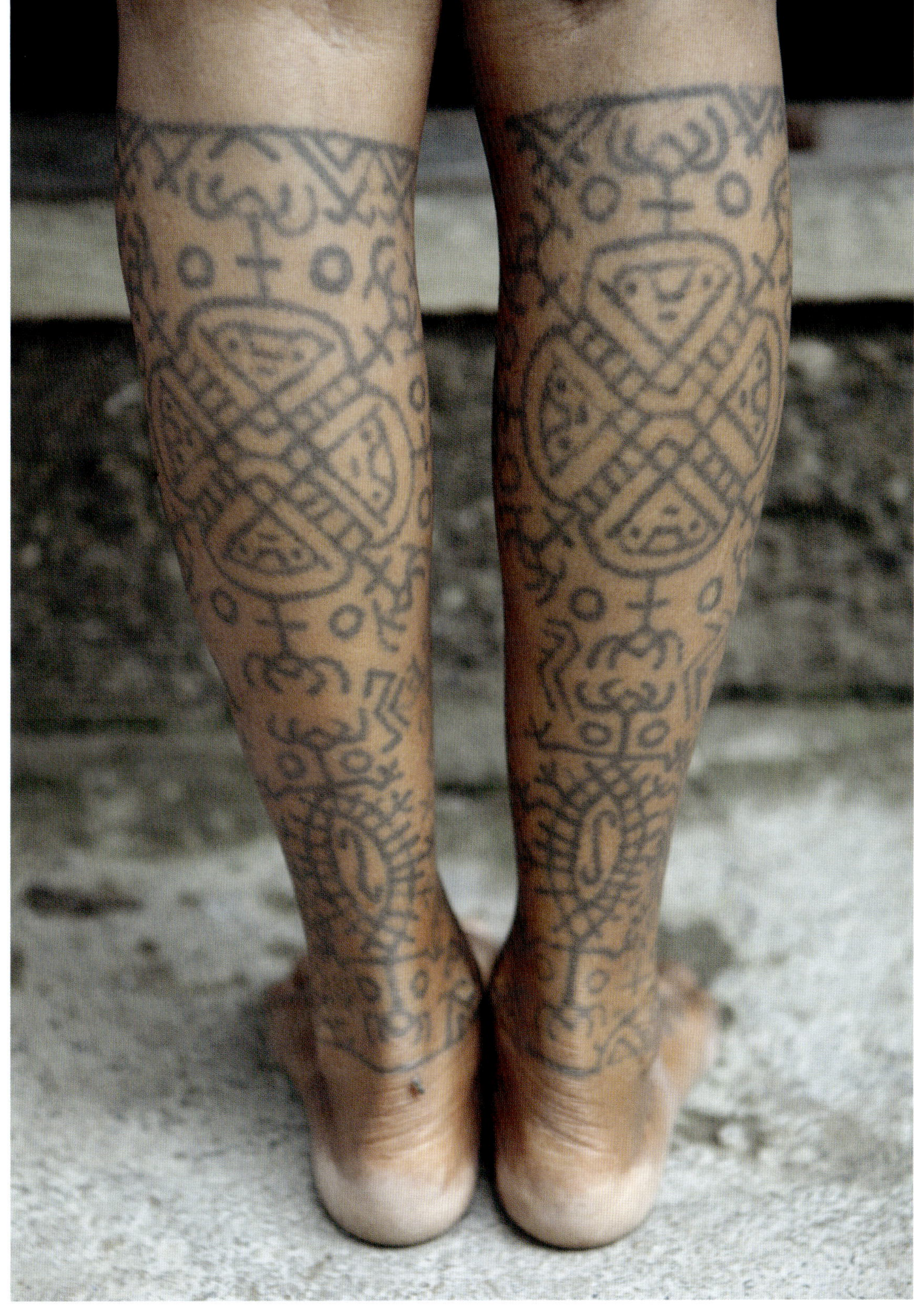

Chin Tattoos of Myanmar

Myanmar is home to the largest group of facially tattooed Indigenous women in Asia – the Chin. These Tibeto-Burmese people are divided into fifty-three ethnic subgroups, speaking over forty different languages and dialects.[77]

Opposite The oldest published depiction of a tattooed Chin woman, *ca*. 1795.

Below Daw Kau Tu, a tattooed woman of the Laytu Chin, Oakken village, Myanmar, 2005.

Perhaps the first historical account of Chin facial tattooing came from British diplomat Michael Symes in 1795, who described the intricate designs of women as "segments of circles" covering the entire face. He found these tattoos "truly hideous" as an "unaccustomed beholder," yet he couldn't deny their intricate artistry.[78]

Until recently, the specific patterns of each Chin group practicing facial tattooing were neither well-researched nor documented. The number of different facial tattoo patterns among the Southern Chin remained a mystery, shrouded in cultural and artistic diversity yet to be fully unveiled.[79]

Myanmar- and Thailand-based photographer and writer Jen Uwe Parkitny has devoted more than two decades to meticulously documenting these mesmerizing tattoo patterns, uncovering and cataloging thirteen distinct group and subgroup designs. His tireless work, akin to that of an intrepid explorer charting unknown territories, has unveiled a hidden tapestry of cultural tattoo artistry. Through his lens and pen, Parkitny has immortalized the intricate beauty and profound significance of these

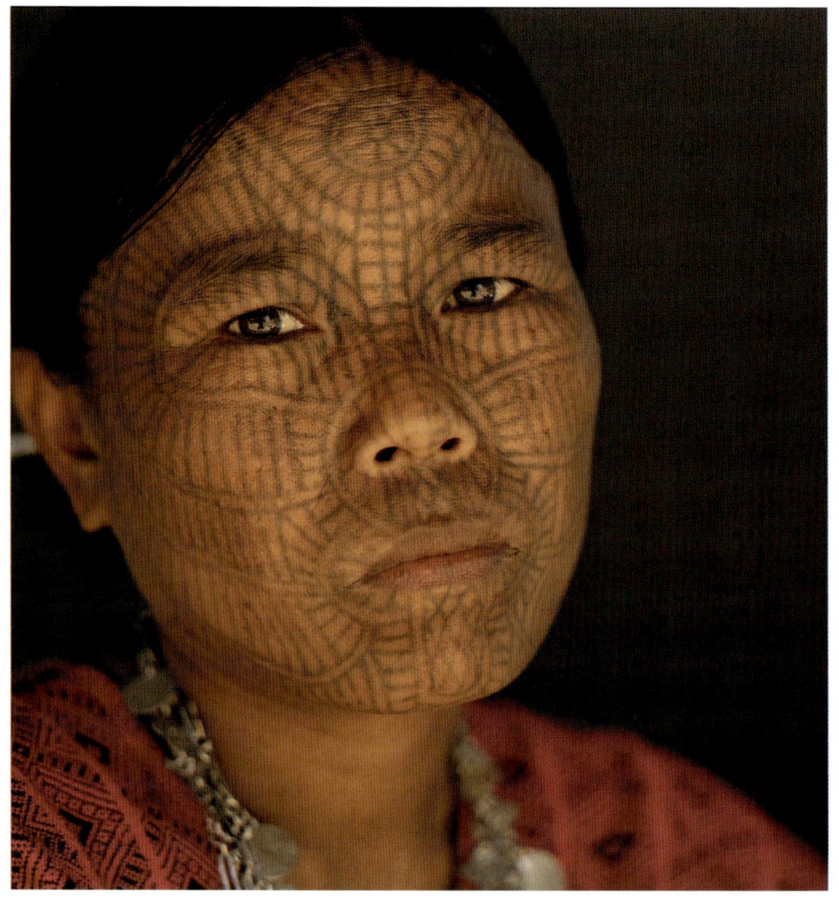

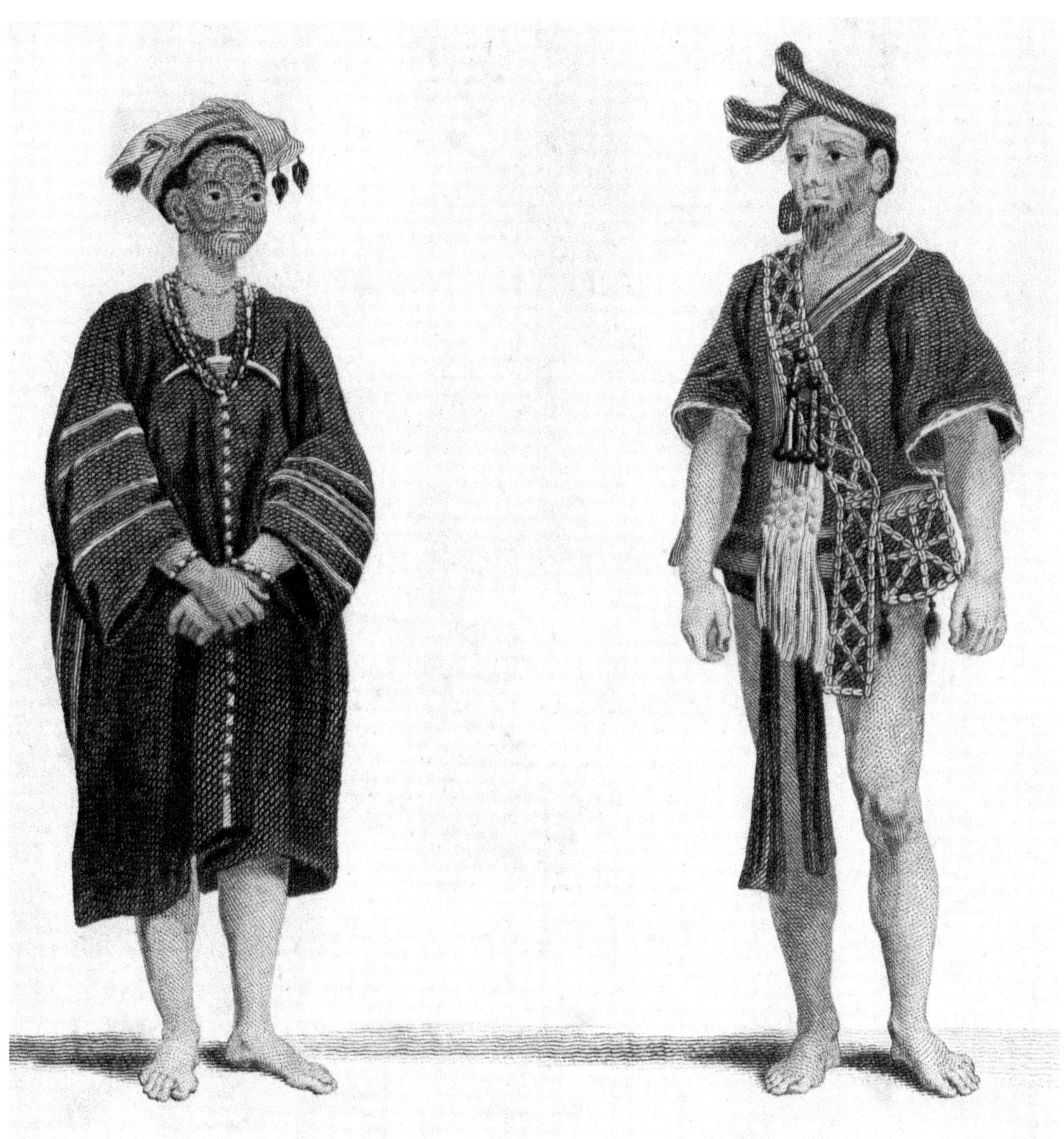

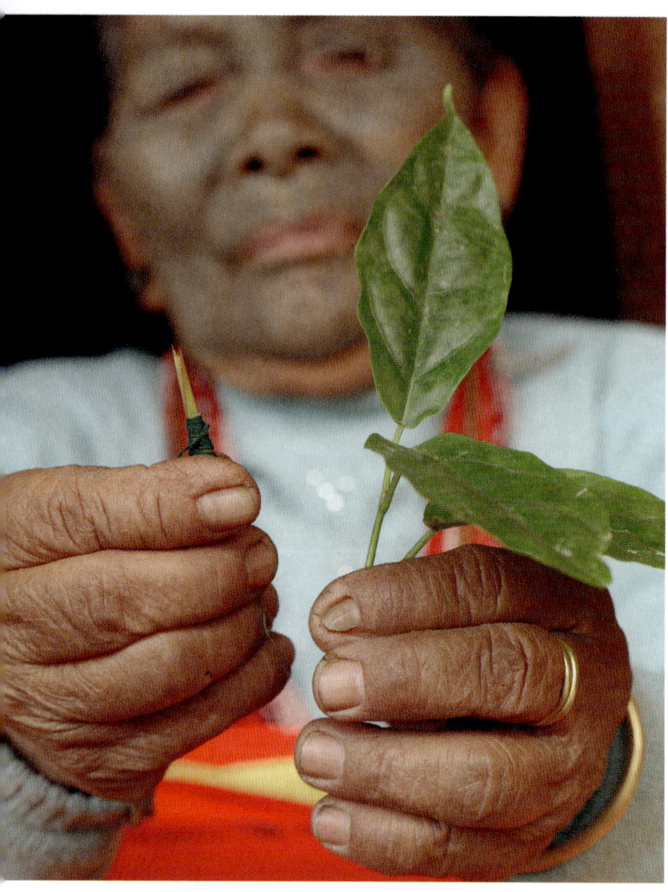

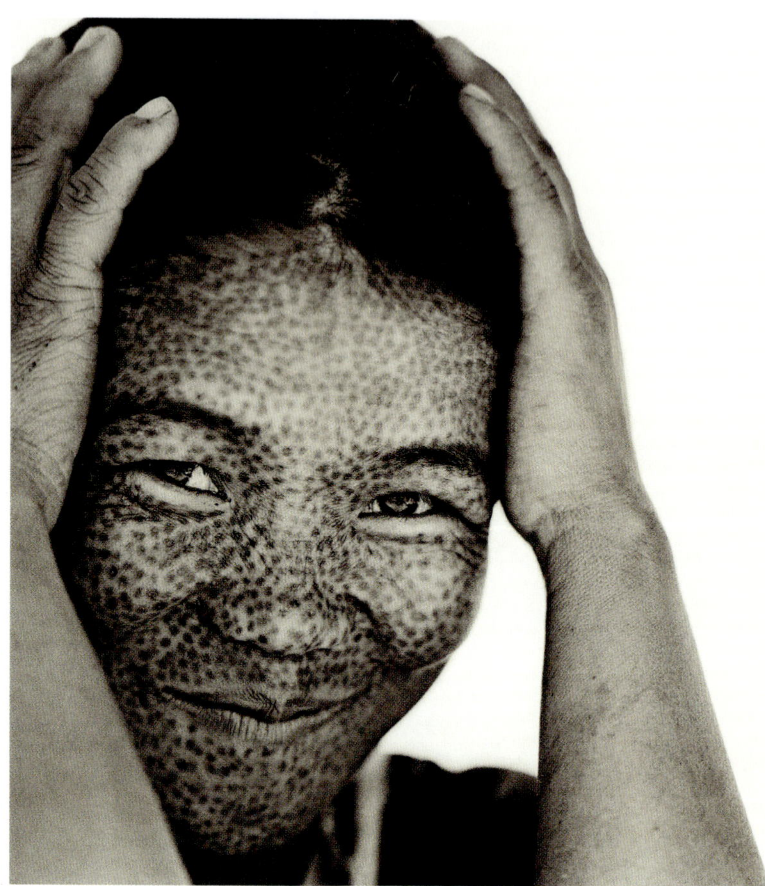

ancient traditions, preserving them for future generations to marvel at and study.

Among the Laytu Chin, three primary tattoo patterns exist, each with subtle variations that distinguish clan members and establish socio-kinship identities. These unique markings are ancient emblems of belonging, fiercely guarded and exclusive to each clan. Copying these revered patterns was an act of ultimate betrayal, one so grave that undoubtedly "would have meant war."[80] Every tattoo was customized and meticulously crafted to harmonize with the unique contours and features of each woman's face.[81]

Chin tattoo masters, revered and well-compensated artisans, could be either male or female. A full facial tattoo by Yindu masters commanded a payment of "five arrows, one cotton blanket, one glass beads necklace, one basket of raw cotton, and one cotton ball."[82] Ubtu tattooists in the Magway Division received currency for their work.[83]

The Southern Chin mountain groups, such as the M'Khan (M'Kan), Mün (Ng'men, Muun), Yindu Dai (Zindu), N'Gha (Ya), Hmoye (Nghmoye), Matu, and Ubtu (Uppu, Ubun), display relatively simple tattoo designs. These range from clusters of dots (M'Khan, Matu,

Above left Yindu Dai elder of Hlaing Doh village displaying items used to make tattooing tools and pigment, 2014.

Above Tribal member Daw Lee Mana possesses the dotted tattoos of her tribe, the Matu Chin, Matupi, Myanmar, 2005.

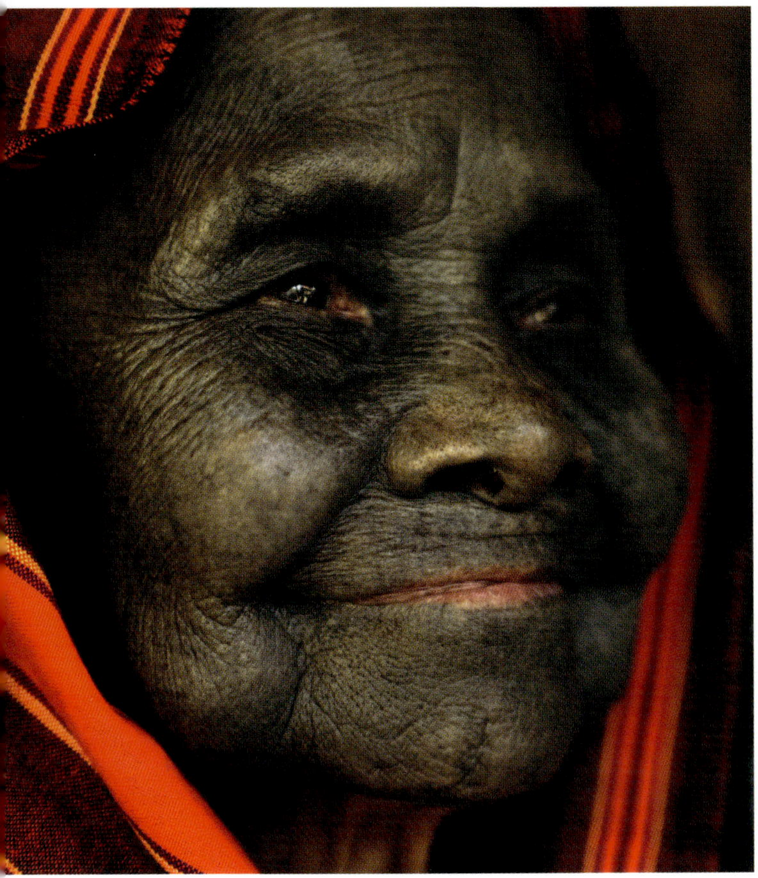

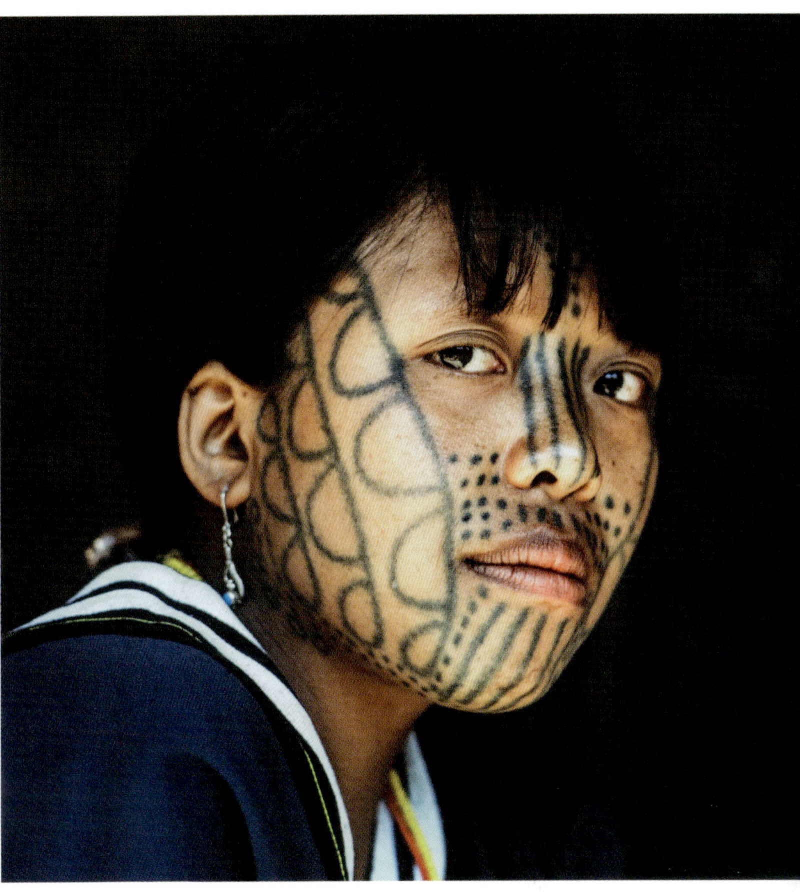

Above Tattooed Ubtu Chin elder, Salin, Myanmar, 2014.

Above right Mün Chin tribal member Ma Ning Li, Chador village, Myanmar, 2002.

Hmoye) and interrupted vertical lines with dots (Yindu Dai and N'Gha), to half-circles, vertical lines, and a Y-post-shaped rune on the forehead (Mün). Some, like the Ubtu, eschewed patterns entirely, opting instead for completely blackened faces. In contrast, the intricate designs of the Southern Chin hill groups, or "Highland Chin," paled in comparison to the elaborate tattoos of the Lemro River groups, such as the Laytu, Sunghtu, and Sutu (Sone-glai).

Among these, Laytu Chin women, nicknamed "spider women," dazzled with their tattoos resembling a spider web intricately spanning their entire faces. These complex designs were meticulously crafted using rattan thorns bound together – four for the forehead and three for the rest of the face. The ink, a concoction of soot, water, and vine sap, brought these elaborate designs to life.

For Yindu and Hmoye women, tattooing sessions could span several years, resulting in pattern breaks and irregularities indicating the work of multiple artists or various stages of completion.[84] Some women, possessing an extraordinary tolerance for pain, chose to complete their facial tattoos in a single, grueling session.[85]

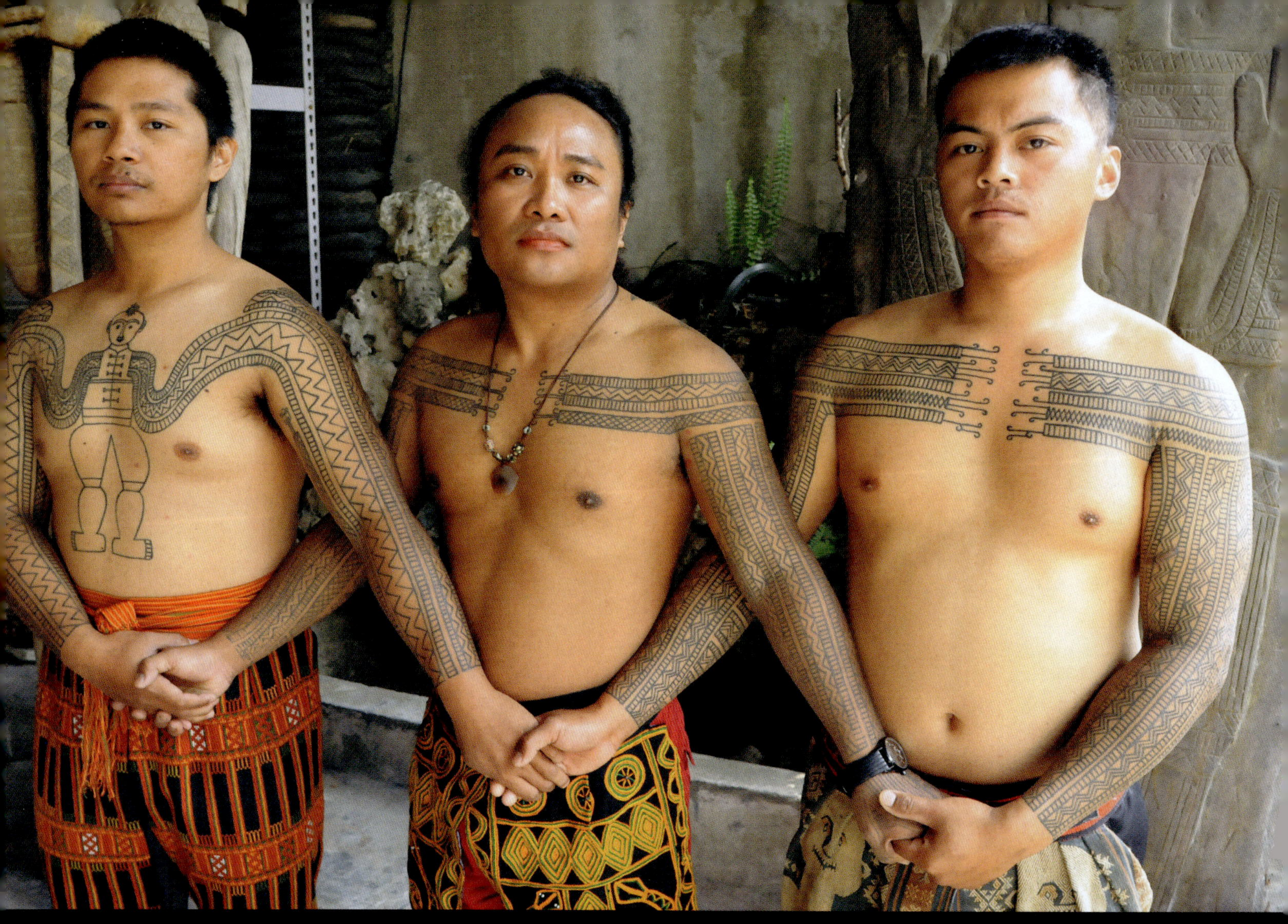

Paiwan Tattoo Artist: Cudjuy Patjidres

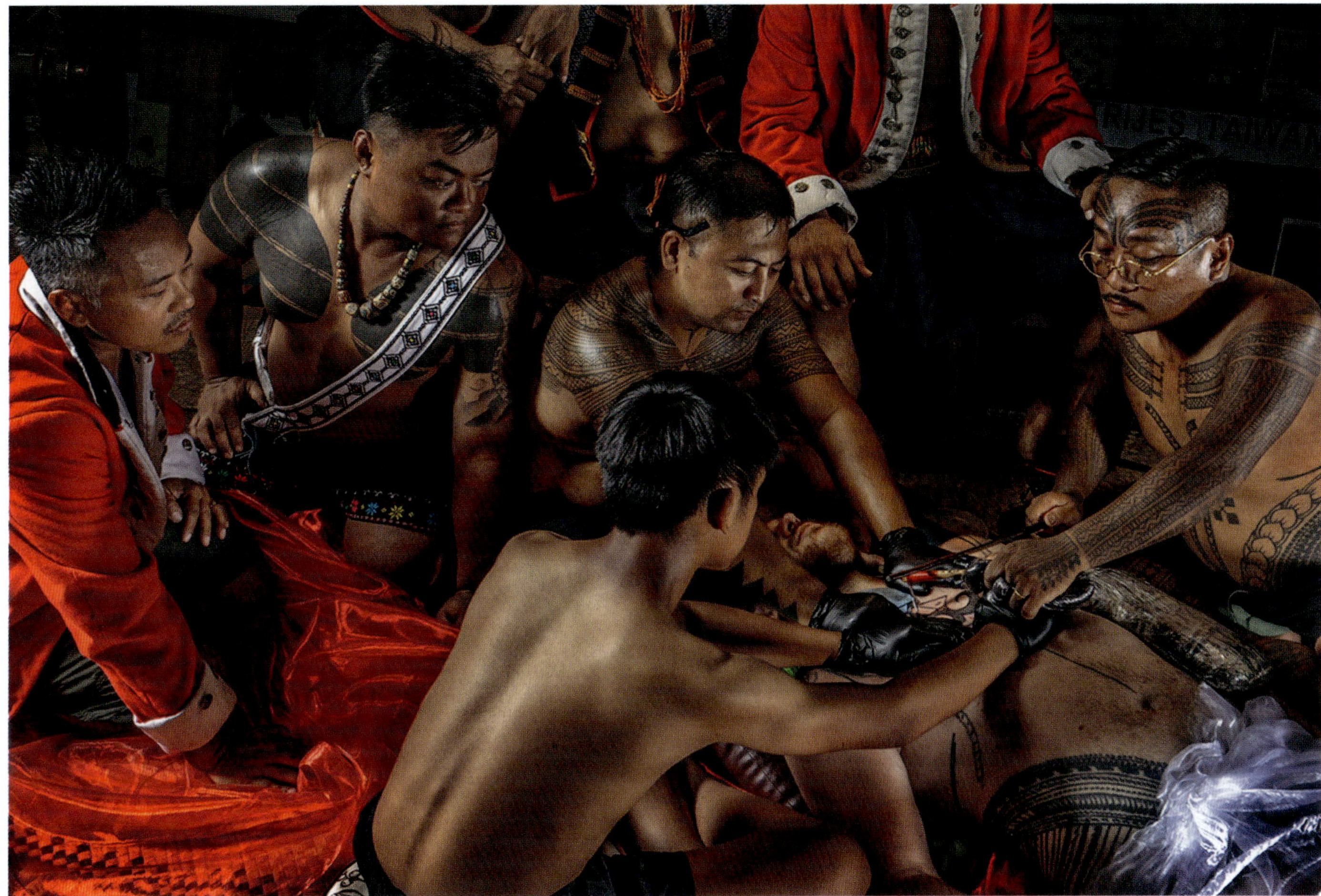

Opposite Tattoo bearers of the Paiwan tribe, Pingtung County, Taiwan, 2016. Pictured here are nobleman Kuljelje Kalivuan, tattoo artist Cudjuy Patjidres (center), and future chief Cangal.

Above New Zealand visual artist Greg Semu, who is of Sāmoan heritage, created *The Anatomy of a Tattoo Lesson* (2024), featuring tattoo artist Cudjuy Patjidres.

About a decade ago, Paiwan tattoo artist Cudjuy Patjidres, hailing from Taitung County in southeastern Taiwan, embarked on a mission to resurrect the ancient tattooing practices of his tribe, infusing new life into the art for both men and women. With a blend of reverence and innovation, he has crafted stunning bodysuits for noblemen and aristocratic women, drawing from traditional designs and family oral histories. Additionally, he has created tattoos for individuals outside the Paiwan nobility, broadening the reach of this cultural revival. For men, the designs are predominantly inspired by the sacred hundred-pace pit viper, reflecting its movements and body parts, embodying the spirit protector of the tribe. For women, Patjidres employs a rich mosaic of patterns including the sun, door, millet pounder/mortar and pestle, anthropomorphs, and the hundred-pace viper.[86]

Initially, Patjidres used a machine for tattooing but has since mastered the traditional Paiwan hand-tapping tools. He now showcases this ancient technique at cultural events, museums, and international tattoo conventions, employing it for clients who seek an authentic experience. When I first met

Patjidres in Taiwan in 2016, I inquired if he knew of other Paiwan tattoo artists. "There are others from my tribe working in Western-style shops in the cities," he replied. "They sometimes create tattoos based on Paiwan designs, but they often make mistakes with the traditional patterns because they haven't done the research and don't know the rituals."[87]

Patjidres holds the ancient rituals of Paiwan tattooing in high regard. Before commencing a new tattoo, he performs a sacred ceremony, offering a ceremonial drink to the ancestral spirit of his village. "I face the direction of our sacred mountain and offer the spirit this drink of alcohol," he said. This ritualistic gesture underscores his deep respect for tradition and his commitment to preserving the tattooing legacy of the Paiwan people.

I also asked why the revival of Paiwan tattooing was so important to him. "I don't want to see this ancient tradition disappear in the future," he explained. "I want to preserve this aspect of Paiwan culture and not let it slip through our fingers. I feel a responsibility to bring it back since my grandfather Jiaxuban was tattooed, and he encouraged people to have tattoos. I also have the support of the elders, which is very important to me."[88]

One of Patjidres's noble clients, Kuljelje Kalivuan, boasts a bodysuit tattoo that celebrates a legendary family ancestor. Kalivuan explained, "The central figure is from an ancient story that belongs to my family. There was a powerful man who took two huge pieces of slate from the mountaintop and leapt into the valley below. There, he established the chiefly lineage of my family. He is our ancestral hero, and that is why he is immortalized on my body."[89]

In 2014, Patjidres completed a full-body tattoo for Cangal, a future chief of the Gulou Paiwan tribe, whose family is royalty. Before the session, he had to discuss the tattoo patterns with the tribe's leader. After finalizing the drawing of the bodysuit, Patjidres received approval from the tribal head to begin tattooing. Due to Cangal's high social status, a special offering to the ancestral spirit of his tribe was made. A pig was dedicated and sacrificed, with the meat distributed to relatives and community members.

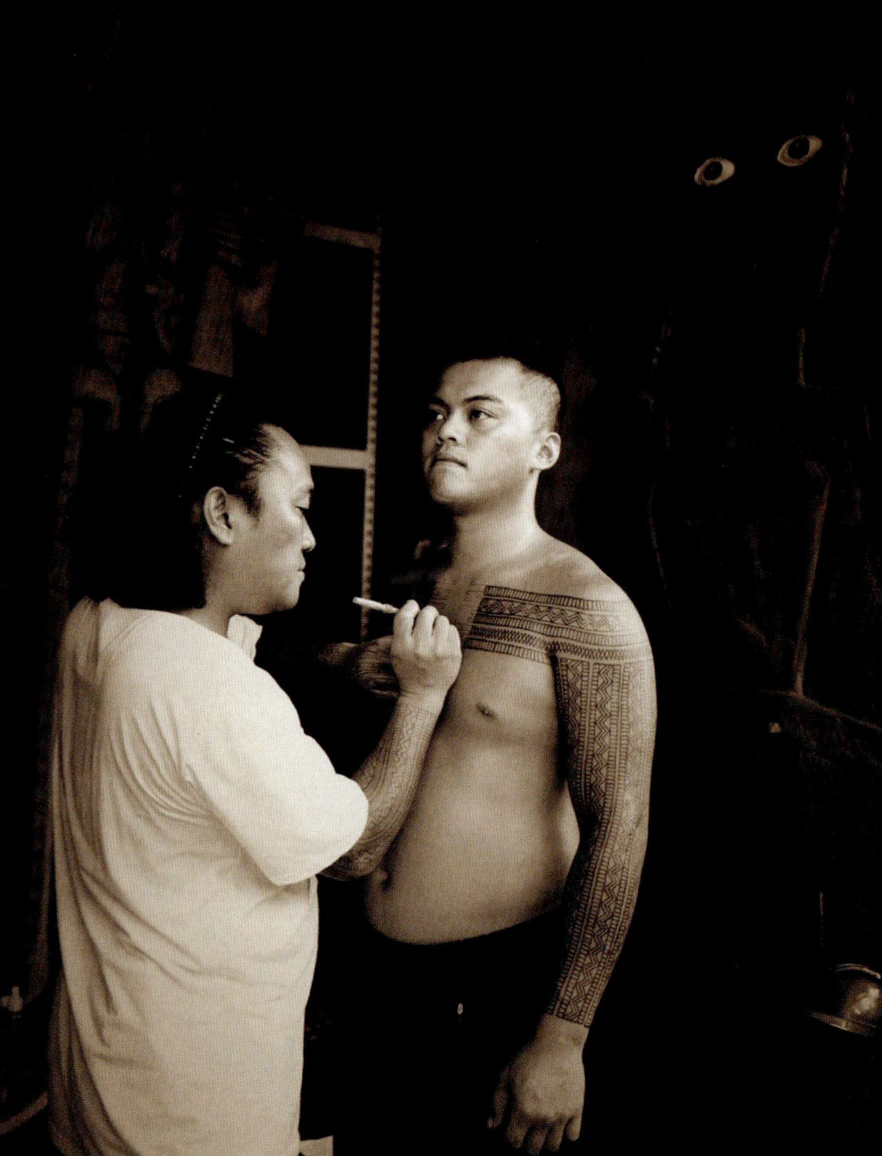

Patjidres stenciling a tattoo design on the chest of Cangal, 2014.

In 2018, the National Taiwan Museum produced a captivating mini-documentary on Patjidres's life, titled *Images from My Dreams*, directed by Huang Huang-ju.[90] The film features the inspiring story of Amby Lindaw from the Xinxing Paiwan Community. Though not from a noble family, Lindaw desired a contemporary version of a traditional Paiwan tattoo on his leg to honor his father. "This tattoo is in memory of my father," he explained. "Due to a car accident, his left leg had to be amputated. He was a hunter, and having his leg amputated did not cause him to become miserable. On the contrary, he continued to live as he did before. He went into the mountains and hunted, [and] this spirit is worth learning from," Lindaw said. He chose the pattern of the hundred-pace pit viper, the ancestral spirit protector of the Paiwan people, for his tattoo.

These vivid narratives, hand-tapped into skin, capture the essence of Paiwan heritage. From Kuljelje Kalivuan's homage to an ancestral hero to Amby Lindaw's tribute to his father's resilience, each tattoo tells a story of courage, legacy, and the enduring spirit of the Paiwan people. Through his artistry, Patjidres has become a modern-day storyteller, preserving the indelible heritage of his culture one tattoo at a time.

Below Cangal, a future chief of the Paiwan Gulou tribe, 2016. "I am aware that I am a member of a high-class family, an important family," he said. "I want to show that I am responsible, so I experienced the pain to get these traditional marks."

Below right Back tattoos of Cudjuy Patjidres, 2016. The hundred-pace pit viper dominates the overall composition.

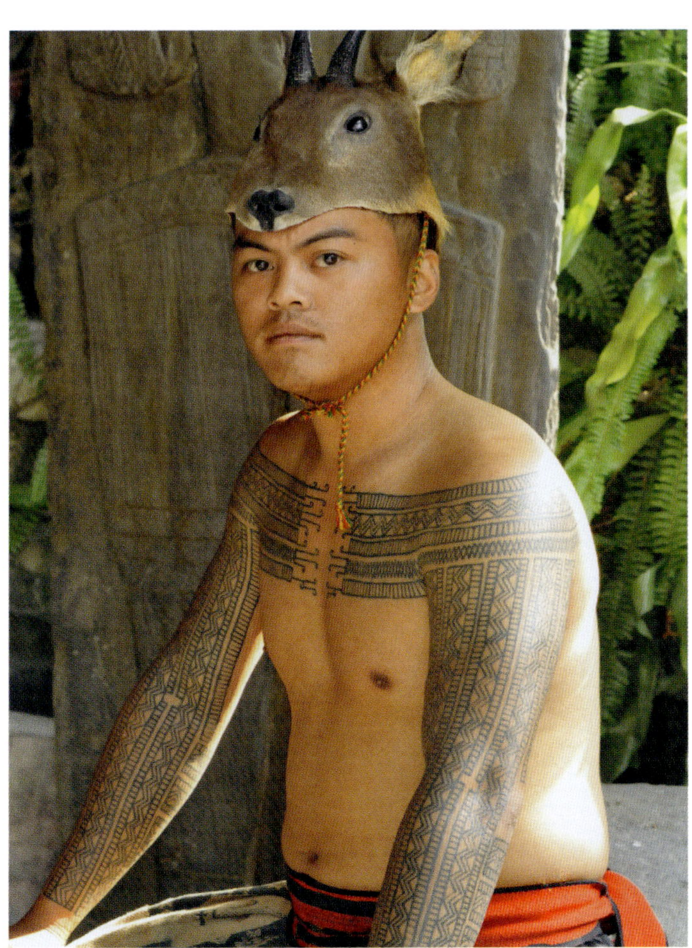

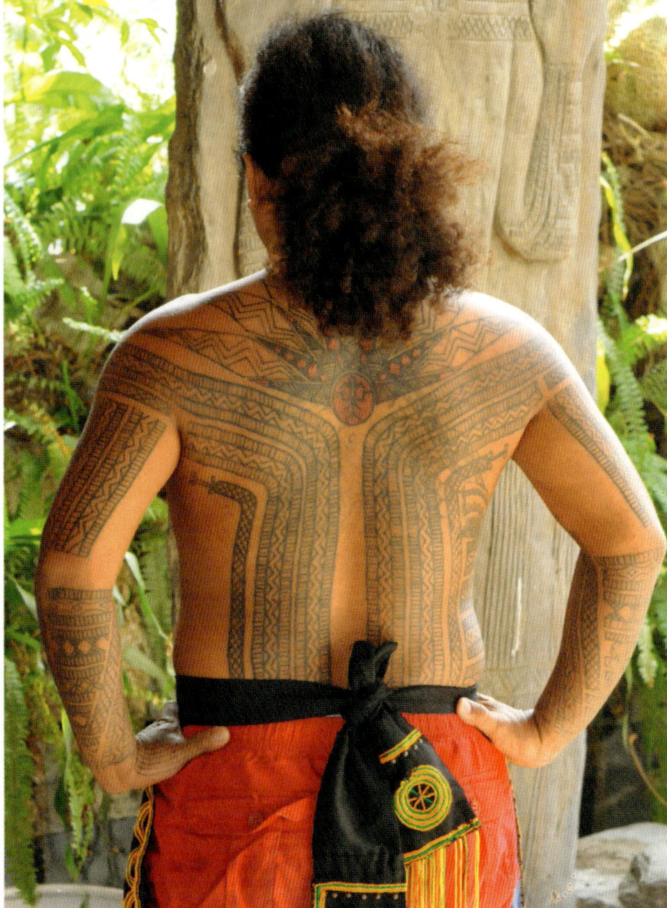

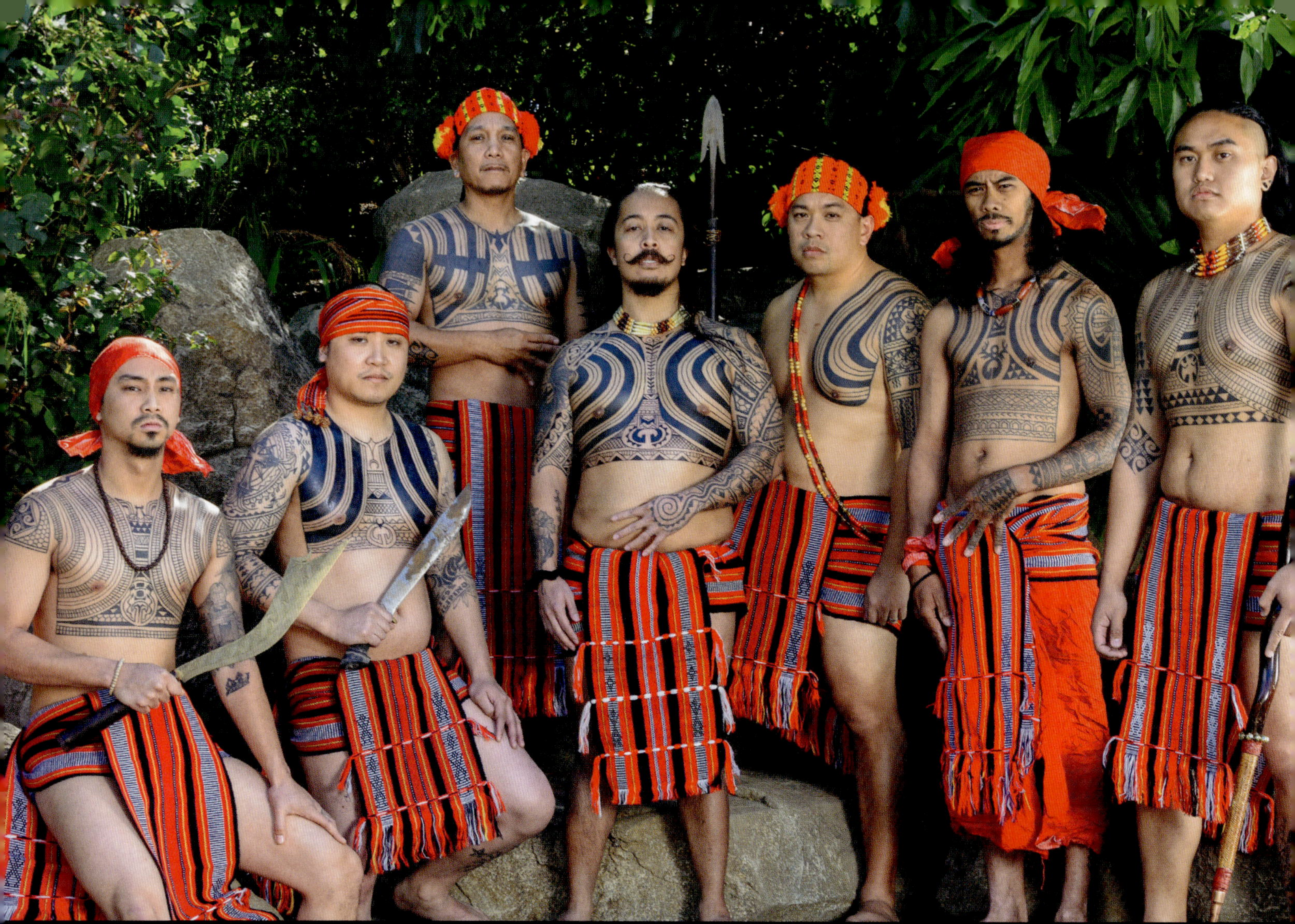

Elle Festin: Mark of the Four Waves Tribe

Opposite Mark of the Four Waves tribe members, Orange County, California, 2014. *Left to right:* Timothy Cross, Iam Ordaz, Vince Bantilles, Jordan Lumaquin, Ryan Mallari, Bub Enay, and Kimo Demingoy, each wearing Ibaloy-inspired tattoo designs.

Right Elle Festin, tattoo artist and cofounder of the Mark of the Four Waves tribe, Orange County, California, 2014. The tribe is a worldwide contemporary group dedicated to preserving Indigenous Filipino tattooing.

In the late 1990s, a visionary Filipino-American tattoo researcher named Elle Festin co-founded the Mark of the Four Waves tribe (Tatak Ng Apat Na Alon). Born from the hearts of a small band of diasporic Filipinos in Orange County, California, the tribe sought to resurrect the ancient and sacred tattooing traditions of the Philippines. The name "Mark of the Four Waves" pays homage to the epic waves of immigrants who shaped the archipelago's vibrant and multifaceted culture: the Afro-Asiatic Aeta, the Malayo-Polynesians, the Indians and Arabs, and, finally, the Spanish.[91]

As the years passed, Festin transformed into a tattoo artist and the tribe swelled from a close-knit circle into a global movement, boasting hundreds of members scattered across continents and major American cities. This diverse brotherhood and sisterhood includes professors, doctors, nurses, chefs, police officers, musicians, soldiers, firemen, and IT professionals, all united by an indomitable spirit and their striking, intricate blackwork tattoos. These powerful symbols of identity and heritage are meticulously crafted by Festin, his talented wife Zel, and their team of skilled artists at Spiritual Journey Tattoo, a haven of tattoo artistry they established in Stanton, California, in 2011.

Born on the Philippine island of Mindoro, Festin is not just a tattoo artist; he is a master of contemporary ink, wielding hand-poking and hand-tapping tools with the precision of a time-traveling artisan. For Festin, these handcrafted tattoos are sacred tributes to the Indigenous trailblazers of this ancient art form. "Each tap or poke is like a whisper from another time or place," he observes. "We want to pay our deepest respects to those tribal artists who came before us, and that is why we give it proper ceremony and ritual when using these kinds of implements. Otherwise, the practice of tattooing will be like an empty vessel, hollow and without meaning, and I will never let that happen now that the Philippine tattoo revival is underway."[92]

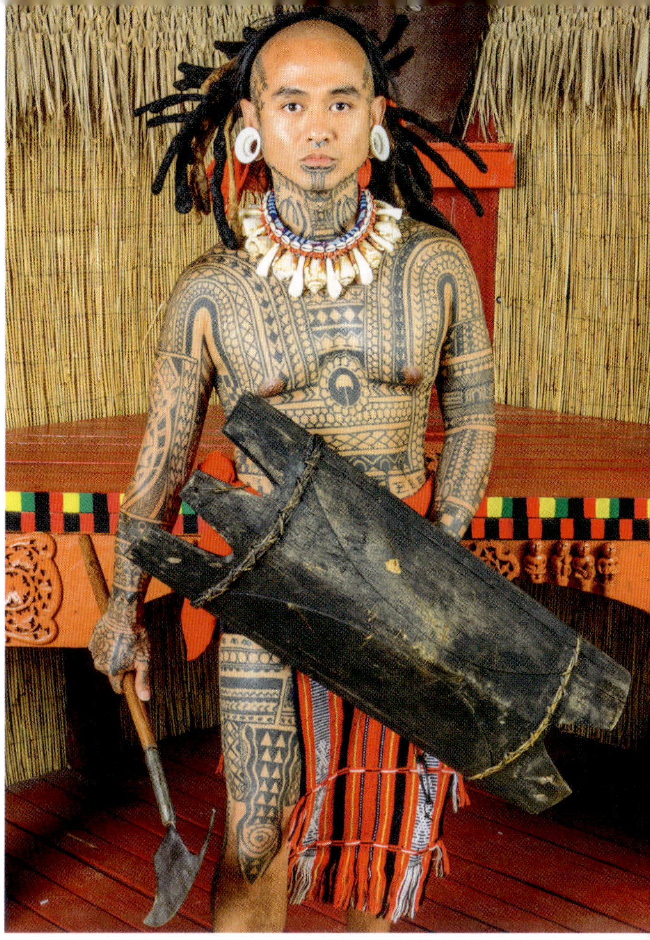

Tina Astudillo-Ash, a dedicated member of the Mark of the Four Waves tribe, echoes Festin's passion. "They have become a part of my extended family. These are people who I respect, admire, and strive to make proud through my contributions to the group," she shares.[93] Her son Joseph, who began an apprenticeship with Festin in 2018, is now carrying forward this legacy, tattooing the next generation of tribe members at Spiritual Journey.

While tattoo artists across the Philippines are rekindling various Indigenous tattooing aesthetics and practices,[94] the Mark of the Four Waves tribe ignited this global revival.

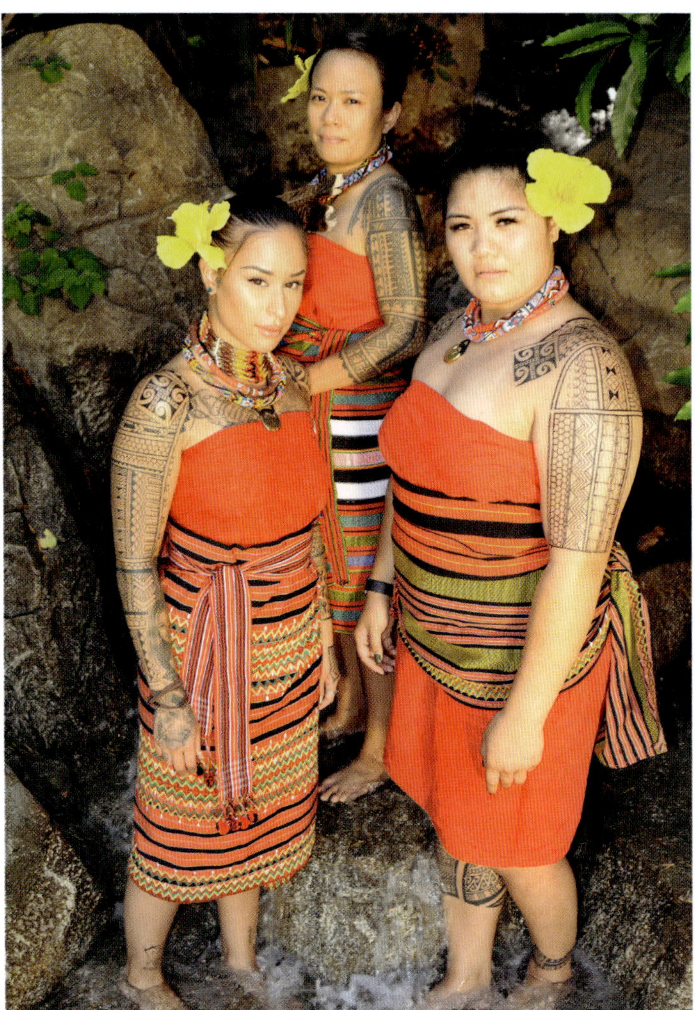

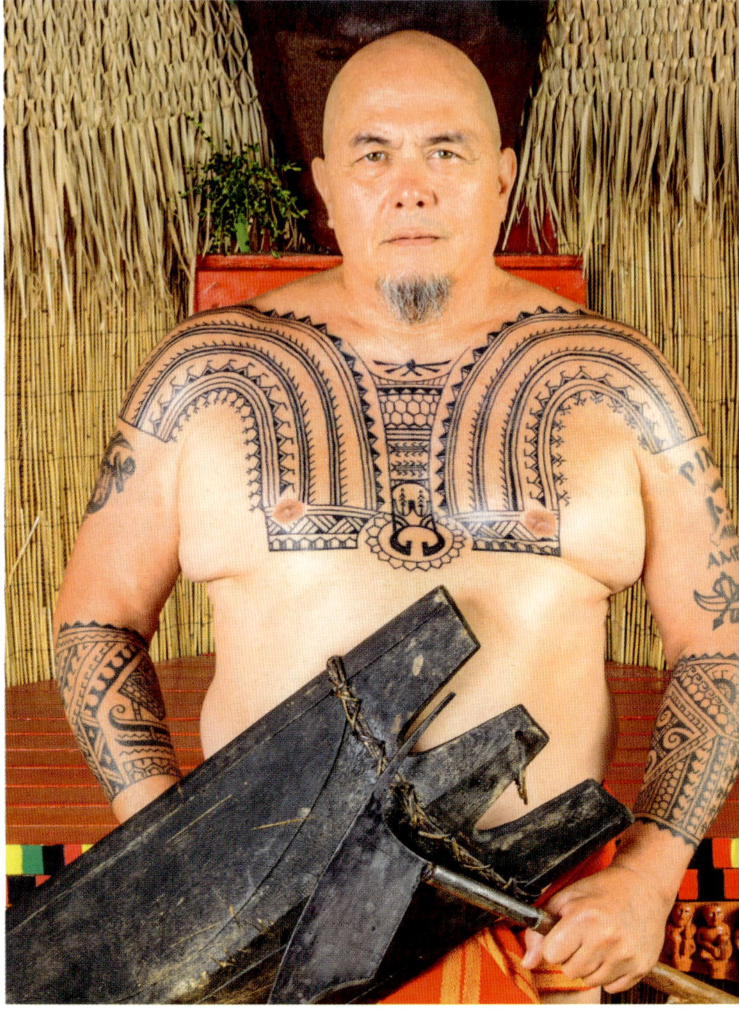

Above Mark of the Four Waves tribe members Sampaguita Jay, Jazmine Atienza, and Hannah Perez, Orange County, California, 2017. Jay and Atienza also tattoo for the tribe.

Above right Larry Alcantra, Seattle, Washington, 2015. Alcantra's tattoos pay homage to his Filipino roots and honor his military service and accomplishments.

They are the heartbeat behind the resurgence of traditional Philippine tattoo artistry, drawing inspiration from the bold and beautiful designs of Indigenous groups such as the Kalinga, Bontok, Visayans, Ibaloy, Manobo, and Ifugao – tribes that many members proudly call their ancestors.

Tribe member Ryan Mallari, whose lineage traces to Benguet Province – the land of the Philippines' legendary tattooed mummies – wears his heritage like a badge of honor through his tattoos. His grandmother, a revered traditional healer, performed sacred curing rituals for their community. "The Ibaloy-inspired tattoos that I wear are an affirmation of that connection and link me to those traditions [that are now] long lost, lost because of cultural assimilation and the colonization of our traditions and heritage by outsiders," he declared. "The breaking of skin and imprinting of the culture of my ancestors is my own personal revolt against time, forgetfulness, assimilation, and irreverence that would have those traditions disappear. Without a doubt,

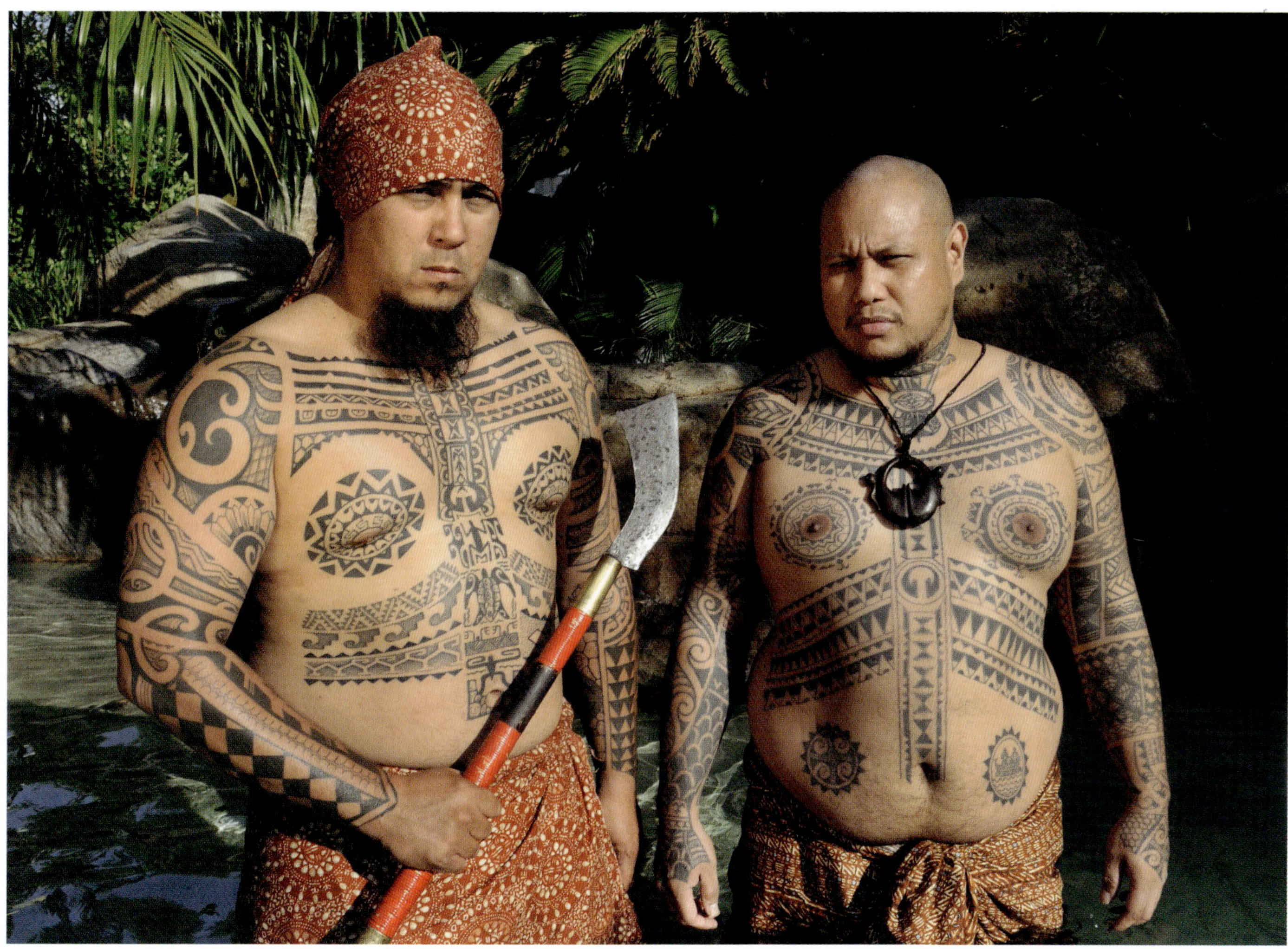

Mark of the Four Waves tribe members Martin Barikuda and Shawn "Crushy" Canete proudly wear the new generation of Filipino tattoo, Anaheim, California, 2014.

these tattoos are for my children and those yet to come."

Today, both new and seasoned tribe members flock to Festin and Spiritual Journey not only for their transformative tattoos but also to immerse themselves in the rich tapestry of Indigenous Philippine design aesthetics, cultural heritage, and history. Festin has curated an impressive collection of rare and ancient reference materials, including books, photographs, and artifacts, which his clients delve into to create bespoke tattoo designs.

The tattoos worn by tribe members are profoundly personal, each one a unique embodiment of ancestral and individual significance. They transcend mere fashion statements; copying another's design is considered a grave disrespect. These tattoos are etched with deep meaning, defining who you are and permanently inscribing your personal history into your very skin.

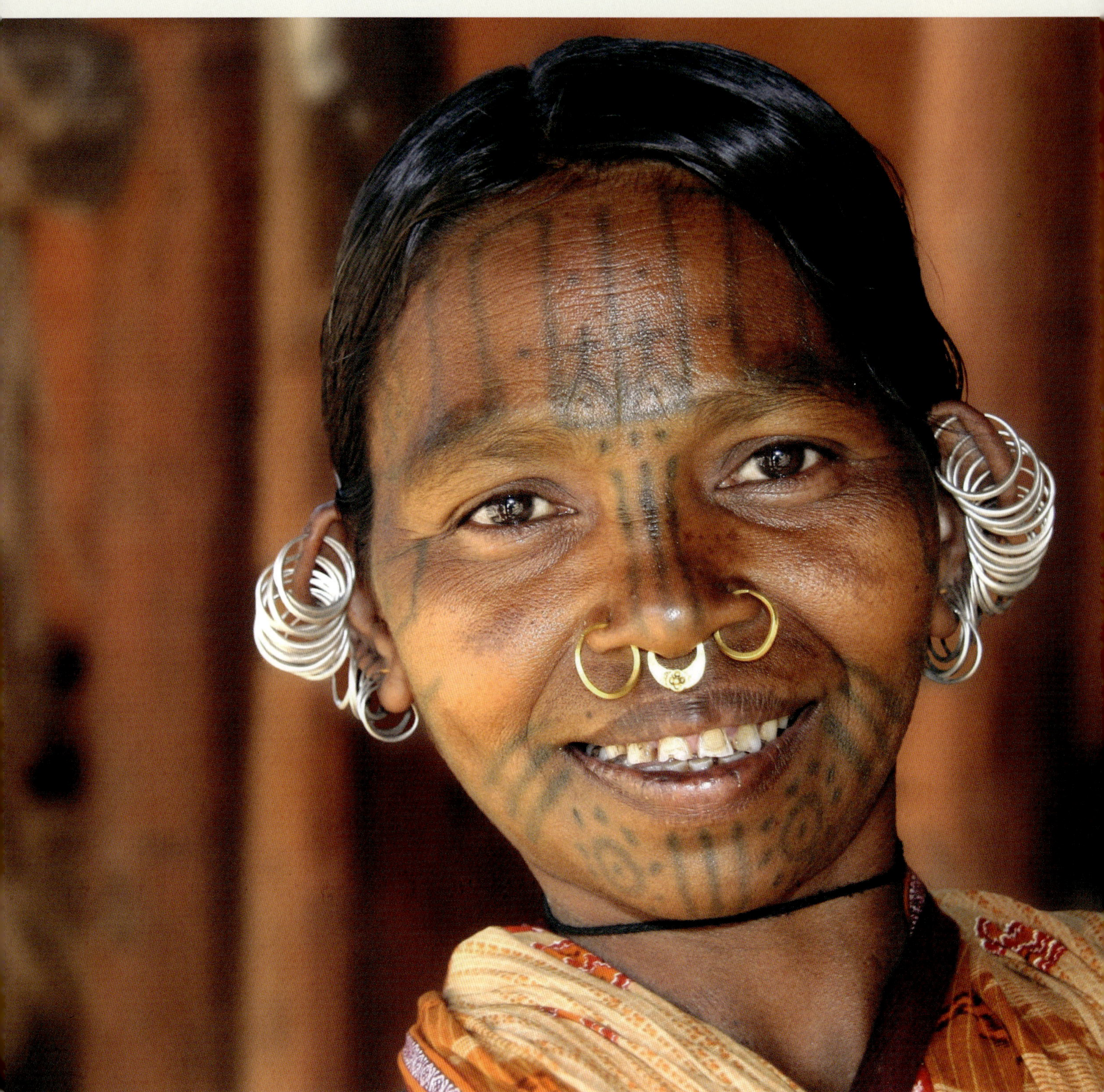

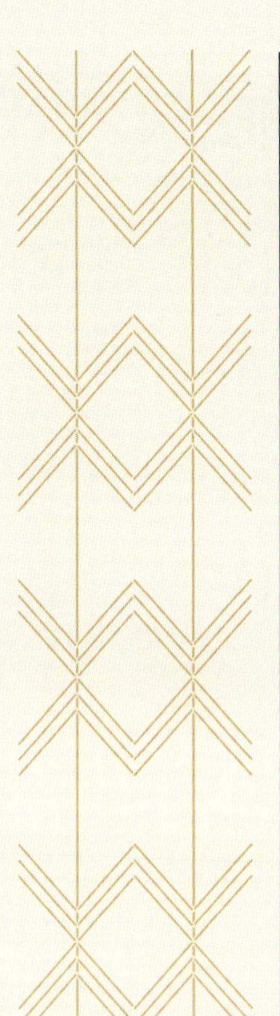

7

INDIA, LAND OF ETERNAL INK

For hundreds, if not thousands, of years, India has maintained a rich cultural tattooing tradition spanning the entire length and breadth of the country.[1] From the dense, rain-soaked mountain forests of Arunachal Pradesh and Nagaland in the northeast to the dry deserts of Kutch in Gujarat on the Pakistan border in the far west, tattoos have not only served to beautify the human body but to also carry it into the afterlife.

Tattooed Kutia Khond woman, Orissa, 2005.

Portrait of Satiya Bai of Samnapur village, Mandla district of Madhya Pradesh, 2018. The tattoo on her forehead is the mark of being a Baiga woman.

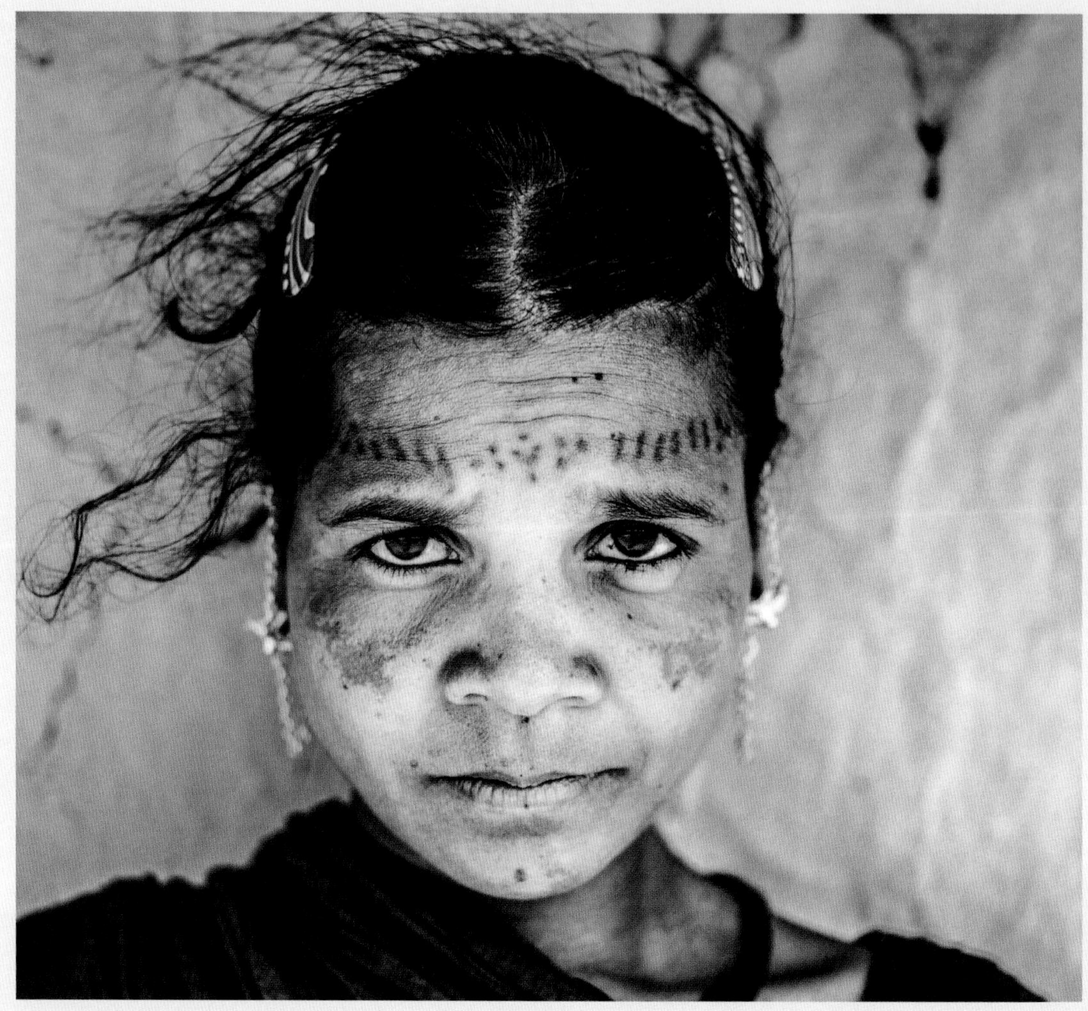

Madhya Pradesh

One hundred years ago in Madhya Pradesh men and women of the Khonds (also Kondh) and Baiga were heavily tattooed, though the custom among men was already dying out. Baiga men formerly wore markings on the back of the hand and forearms, and sometimes they were tattooed on painful areas of the body to cure rheumatism.[2]

Today, women among both groups continue to be tattooed by professional tattooers who ply their client's bodies at fairs and weekly bazaars with electric machines operated by dry cell batteries. Traditionally, however, tattoos were hand-poked into the skin with pigments consisting of the juice of the bhilawan tree (*Semicarpus anacardium*) or a concoction of the cast and burnt skin of a snake (the Indian cobra being preferred) mixed with black *til* (*Sesamum indicum*) and some *ramtilla* (*Guzotia abyssinica*) oil.[3] The skin was pricked with a needle and additional juice rubbed into the wound. After

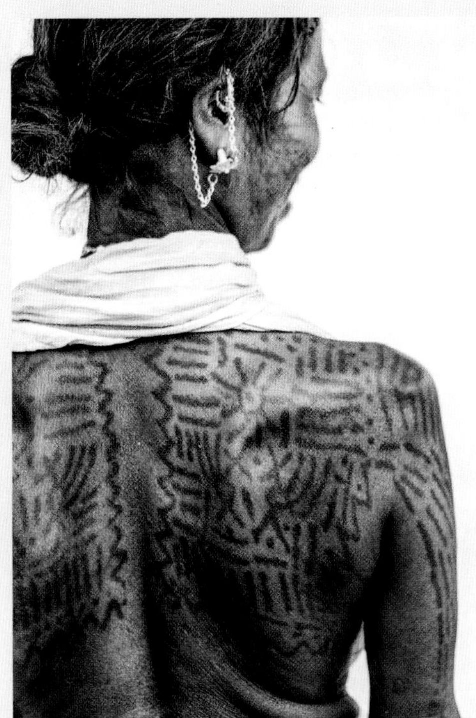

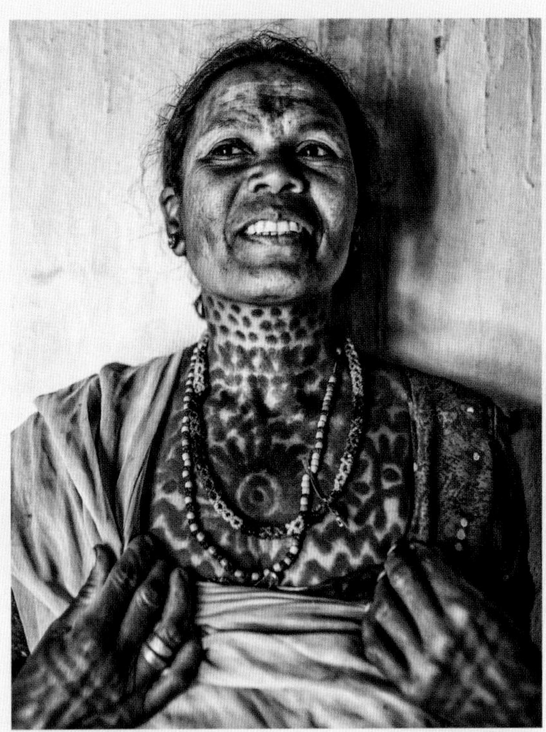

Right Baiga back tattooing, Mandla district of Madhya Pradesh, 2018. Baiga women are elaborately tattooed, with patterns on their backs, legs, and arms. The motifs are inspired by nature and depict birds, animals, rivers, mountains, and celestial objects.

Far right Portrait of tattooed Baiga woman Tihro Bai, Mandla district of Madhya Pradesh, 2018. Her neck and chest were tattooed only after she gave birth. The sun is strategically placed in the center of the chest, while the triangular lines are an interpretation of water.

the design was completed, it was washed with cow-dung water or soap-nut liquid. The soap-nut water provided a cooling effect and decreased the pain.[4]

The traditional pricking process was extremely painful, and one elder commented: "we don't give them any drugs. It hurts for seven or eight days and swells up. Then it gets right, and they find they have something that no one will ever take away from them."[5] If a girl screamed during her tattoo session, old women or boys might laugh at her and say, "If you cannot bear *godan* (tattooing), how will you endure *chodan* (intercourse)?"[6]

For the Baiga female tattoos were and continue to be considered a form of sexual expression and a powerful sexual stimulant. A Baiga man speaking in the 1930s said, "When she is well tattooed, then our sinful eyes declare her beautiful. A light-colored girl needs it; how lovely she looks when she wears bangles that match the line of tattooing!"[7]

When a Baiga woman was asked about the significance of her tattoos around 1935, she replied: "Desire! If you buy bangles, they will break. But if you are tattooed, it will last forever."[8] Another said they are like "a jacket that can never be taken off. These marks are the only things that are certain to go with us to the grave and beyond it."

There is also a Baiga belief that a woman's tattoos served functions in the afterlife. On the back appears the figure *dhandha* which is comprised of six dots joined together by lines. One elder stated, "after death Bhagavan [the supreme being] takes everything from us, but if there is one *dhandha* he can't solve [it's like a riddle], then he has to put that mark on the child into whose body the *jīv* [soul] would be reincarnated."[9]

Baiga men were traditionally forbidden from witnessing the tattooing operation. Tattooed girls or women had to undergo a two-day period of seclusion whereupon they were covered with turmeric and oil and then bathed. If a man witnessed the rite, or if a Baiga girl failed to receive her markings, it was believed that Bhagavan, the supreme deity, would dig holes all over the woman's body with an iron bar after death.[10]

Baiga women interviewed in the 1990s said that their tattoos also prevented arthritis, made them immune to weather changes, prevented poisonous substances from affecting them, and increased their ability to fight blood-related disorders.[11]

Mer tattoo motifs, *ca*. 1950.

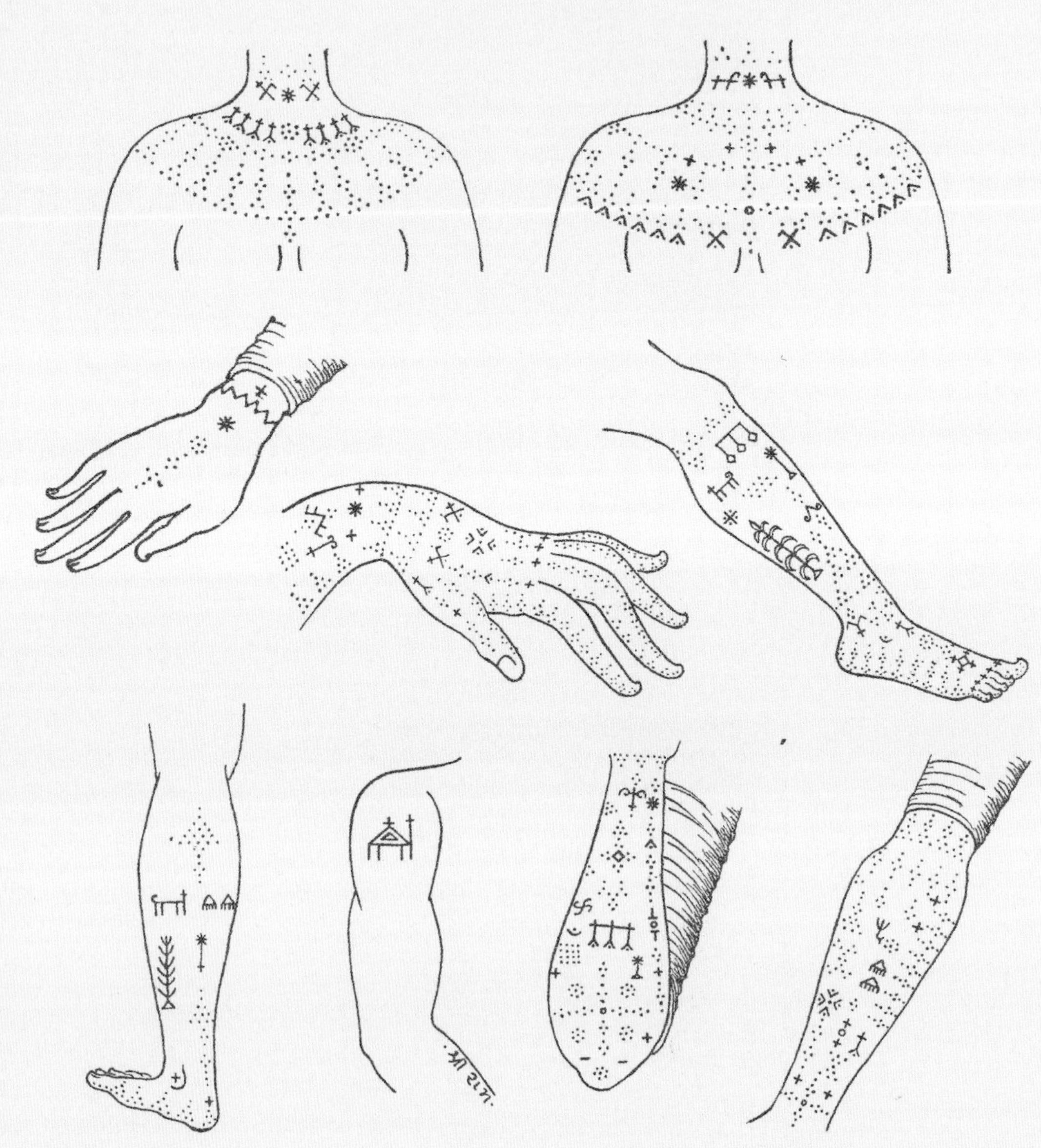

Tattooed Mer woman, Junagadh, 2016.

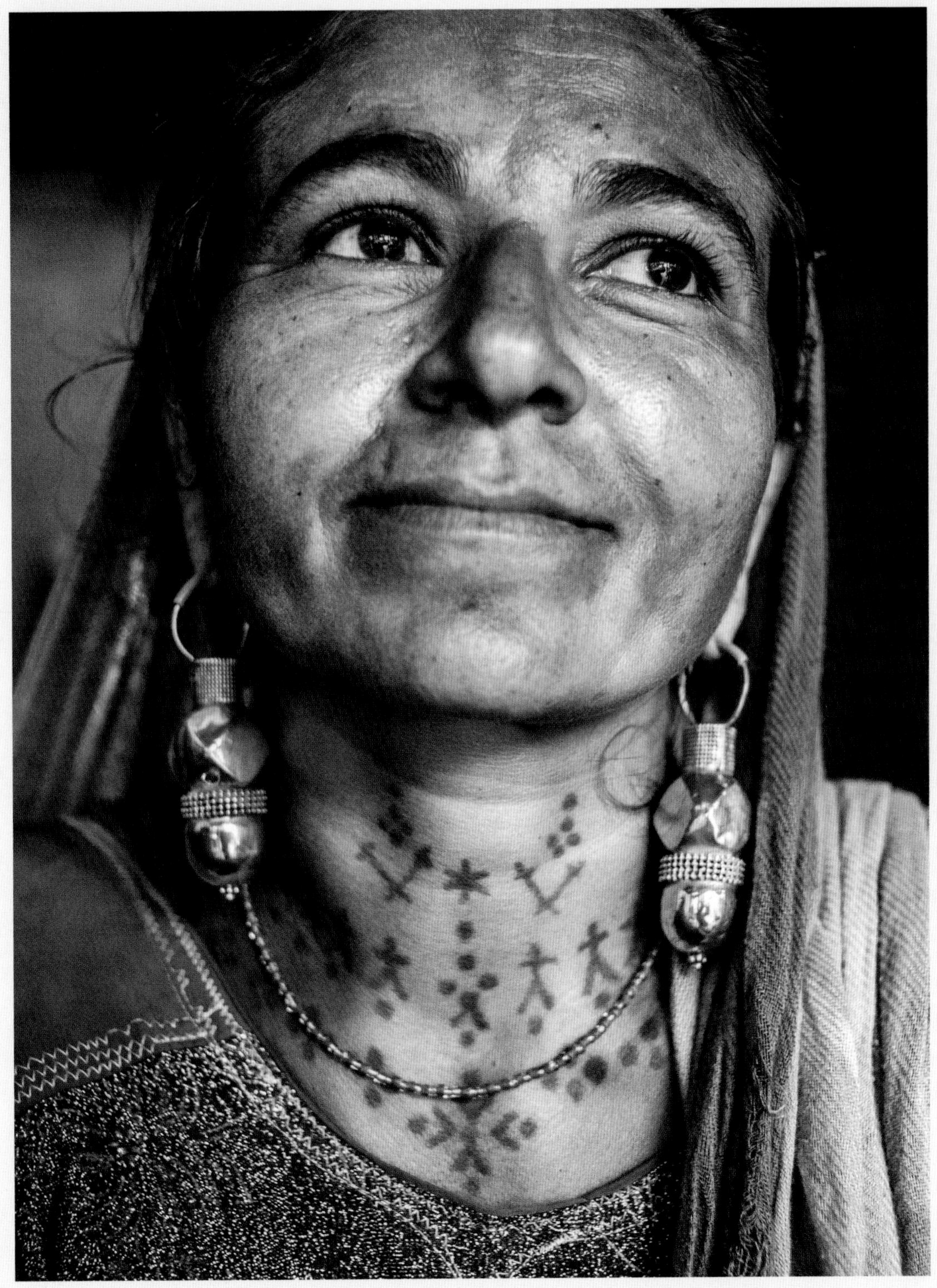

Tattooed Ramnami men, Chhattisgarh, 2014. The Ramnami are a Hindu sect founded in the 1890s who worship the god Ram, an avatar of Vishnu. Because they belonged to the lowest caste, they were not allowed to pray in temples. In turn, they transformed their bodies into temples through tattooing the word "Ram" on the surfaces of their bodies as a sign of devotion.

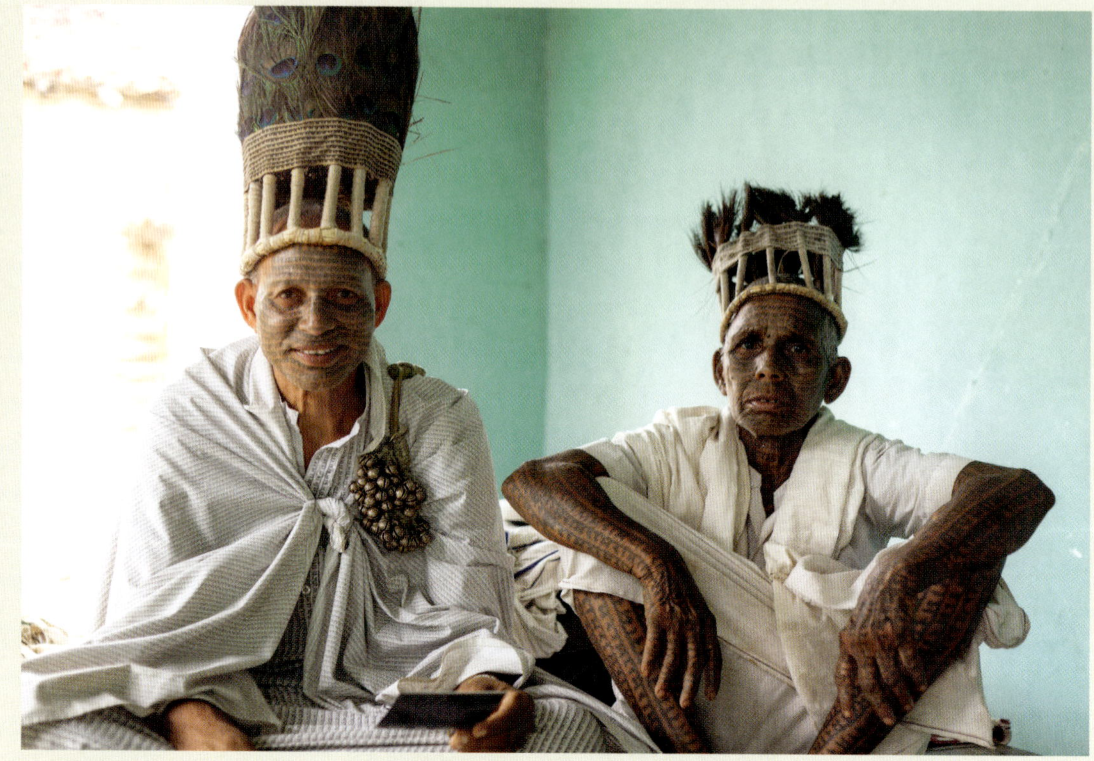

Gujarat

In Gujarat, the agrarian Mer believe that tattoos, not prosperity or wealth, are the only substantive things that accompany them into the afterlife. A Mer proverb relates: "We may be deprived of all things of this world, but nobody has the power to remove the tattoo marks."[12]

The tattoo motifs preferred by the Mers have a close relation to secular and religious subjects of devotion. Designs include holy men, the feet of Rama or Lakshmi, women carrying water in pitchers on their head, Shravana carrying his parents on a lath to centers of pilgrimage, popular gods like Rama, Krishna, and Hanuman, and a host of symbols drawn from the natural world.

Although the Mer tattooing tradition is fading, girls were usually tattooed by experienced female tattooists when they were about seven or eight years old.[13] The hands and feet were marked first, then the neck and breast. The Indigenous instrument used in tattooing was a reed stick with two or three needles inserted at one end in such a way that only a tiny fraction of the points remained visible. The needled points were dipped into a prepared pigment of soot and cow's urine or soot and the juice of the leaves of the *tulsi* plant—sometimes water in which the bark of *biyān* or *sisam* (*Dalbergia lotifolia*) had been mixed with turmeric was used.[14] The first type of pigment provided a blue-black color while the second produced a green hue. Red pigment (mercury

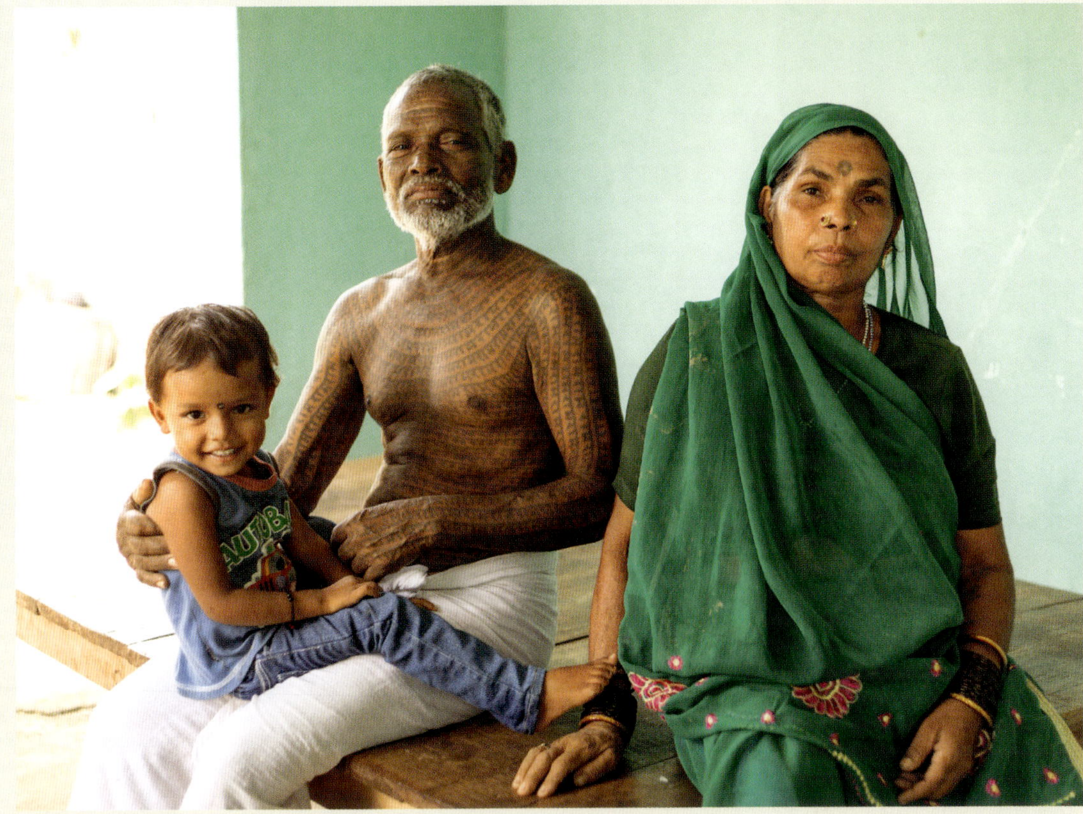

Portrait of a Ramnami family, 2014.

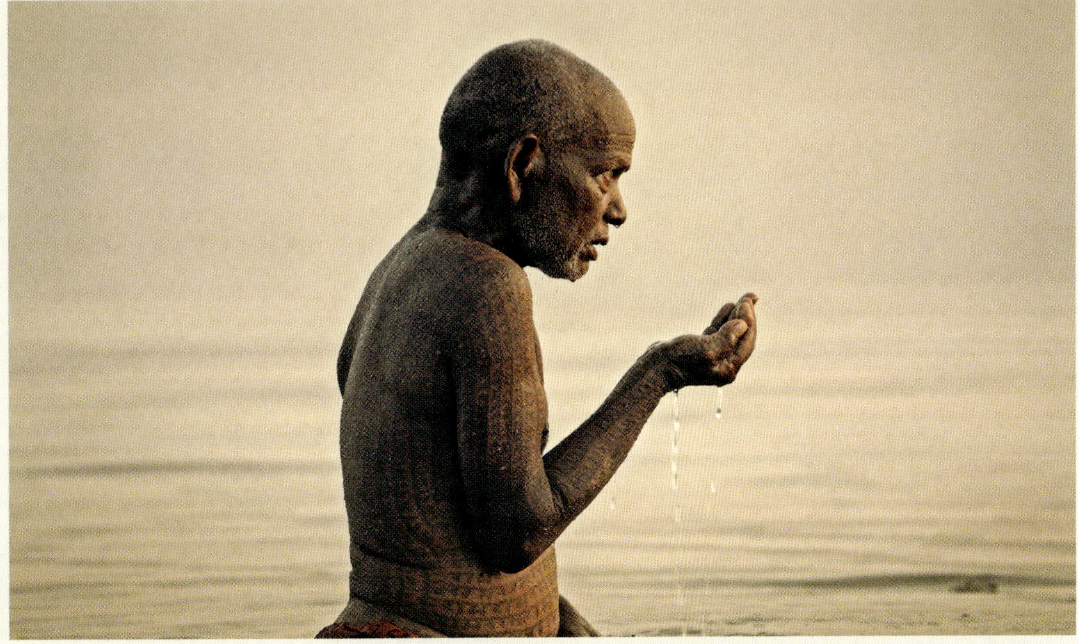

Portrait of tattooed Ramnami elder bathing, 2022. Today, individuals who possess full body tattoos are mostly in their sixties and seventies. Younger generations no longer desire the tattoos of their elders because of discrimination and inability to find work.

Tattooed Rabari woman, Junaghad, 2016. For hundreds of years the Rabari practiced tattooing for decorative, religious, and therapeutic purposes. Today, however, younger women are receiving fewer tattoos. As one woman explained, "We are now city people, and tattoos are old-fashioned."

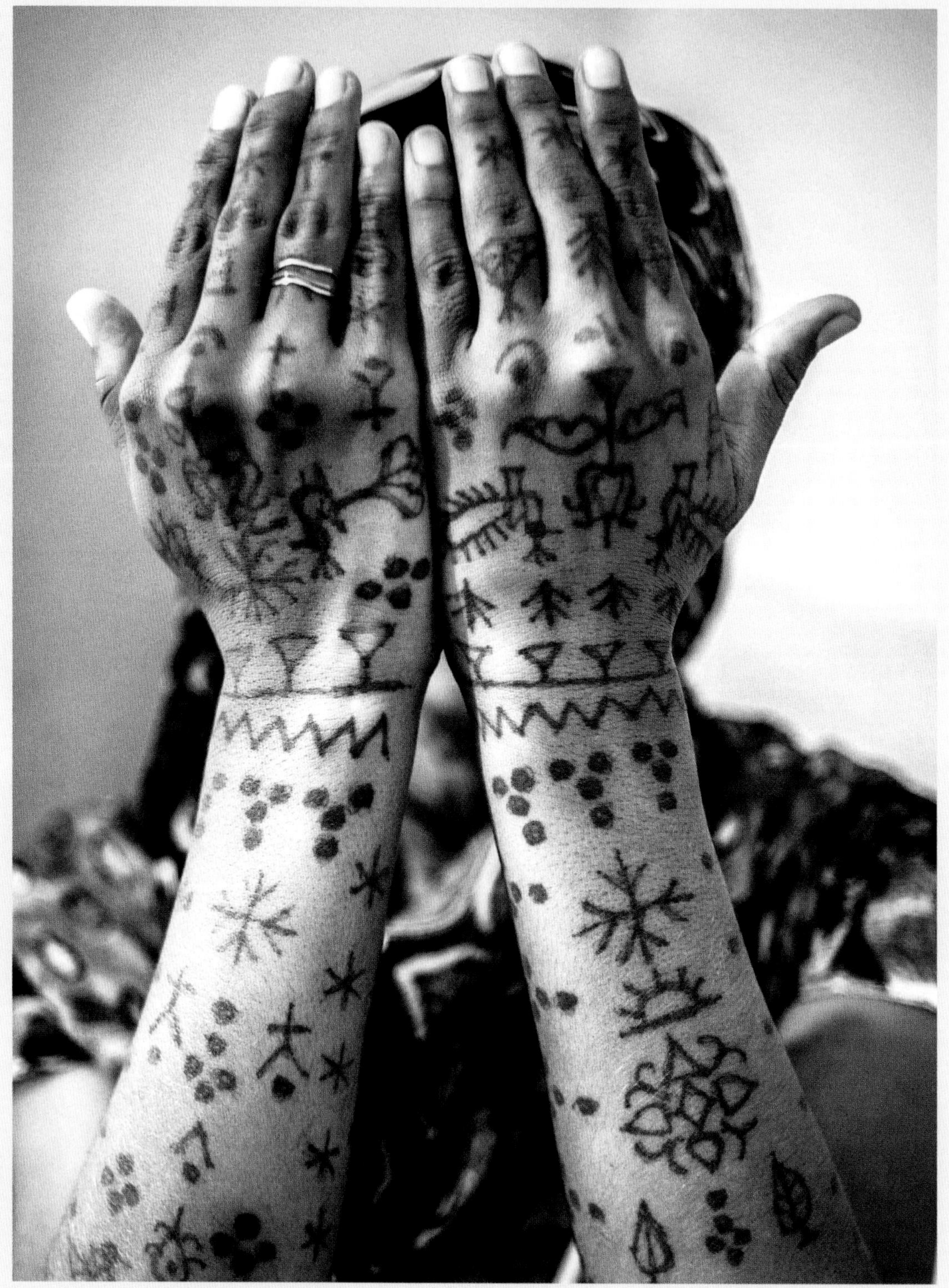

Tattooed Rabari women, Junaghad, 2016. Like the Mer, the Rabari of the Kutch district on India's northwest coast near the Pakistan border continue to tattoo to this day.

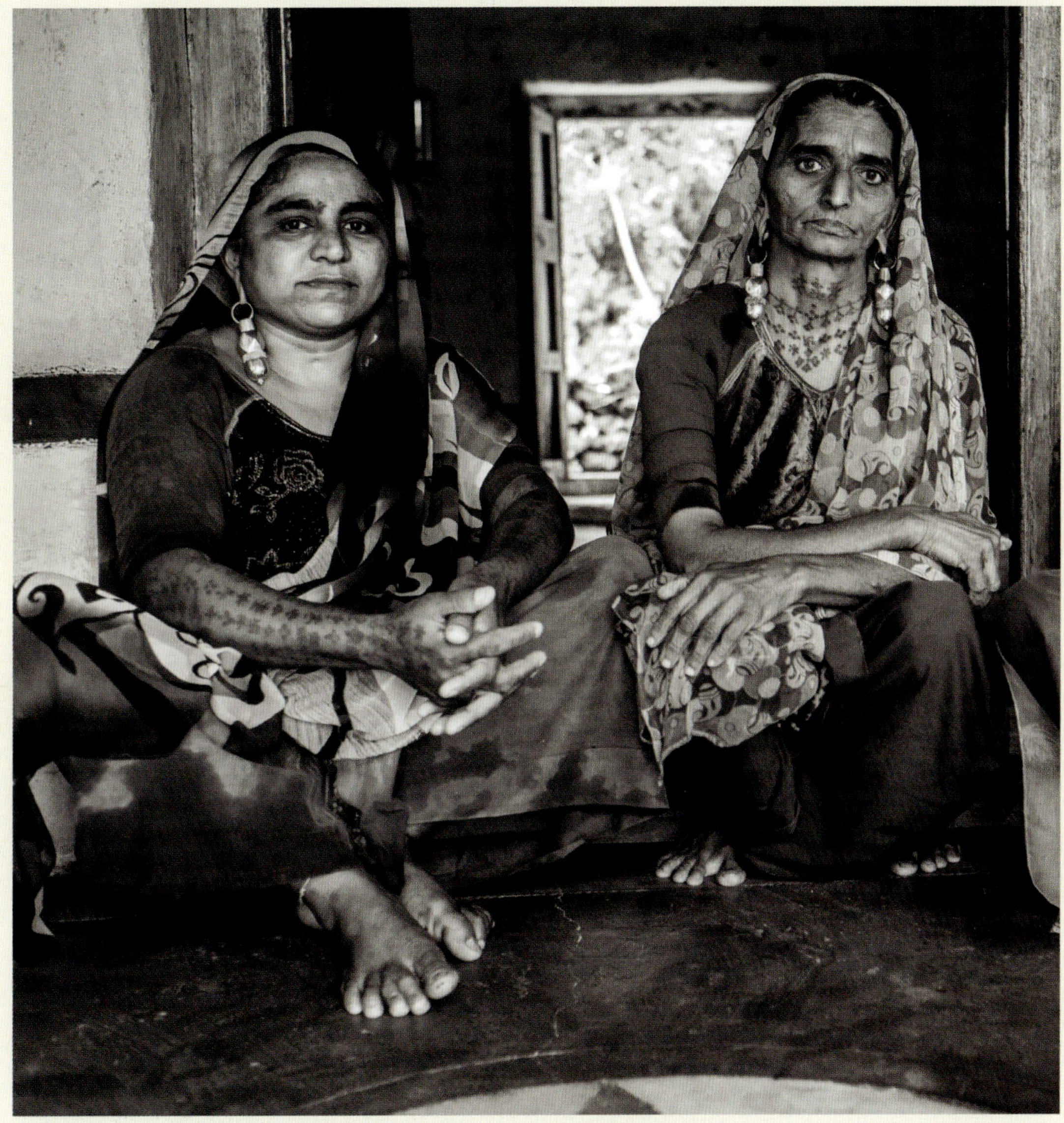

oxide) has also been reported to have been used by some. These pigments were pricked into the stretched skin at least seven or eight times to form the desired tattoo.

Perhaps the most favored tattooed design was the *hānsali* that encompasses the neck and moves downward toward the breasts.[15] Its name is derived from a silver necklace that is thick in the middle and coiled at both ends. More specifically, the *hānsali* tattoo begins at the neck with a flower-motif in the center adjoined by peacocks on either side. It is followed below by the *lādu* (sweet meat) or *bājoth* (pedestal) figure, on either side of which occur rows of four or five holy men. These human figures are supposed to protect the chastity of the tattooed woman.

Naga Regions

On the other side of the Indian subcontinent, high-up in the mountainous regions of northeast India and northwest Myanmar, various Naga tribes continue to wear elaborate tattoos across their faces and bodies. However, these elders represent the last generation of tattooed Naga, and within a generation many forms of Naga tattooing will cease to exist.

For both men and women, Naga tattoos were invariably produced by female practitioners through the technique of hand-tapping. Tattoo pigments were organic and typically derived from charred tree resins mixed with water or rice beer.

Women's leg and facial tattoos often denoted the clan, tribe, and/or family an individual belonged to. Men also bore ethnic markers, but those who had taken human life and heads in war were entitled to bold facial, neck, or other tattoos denoting their status in Naga society.[16] Men and women of aristocratic status possessed special tattoos that could not be worn by others.

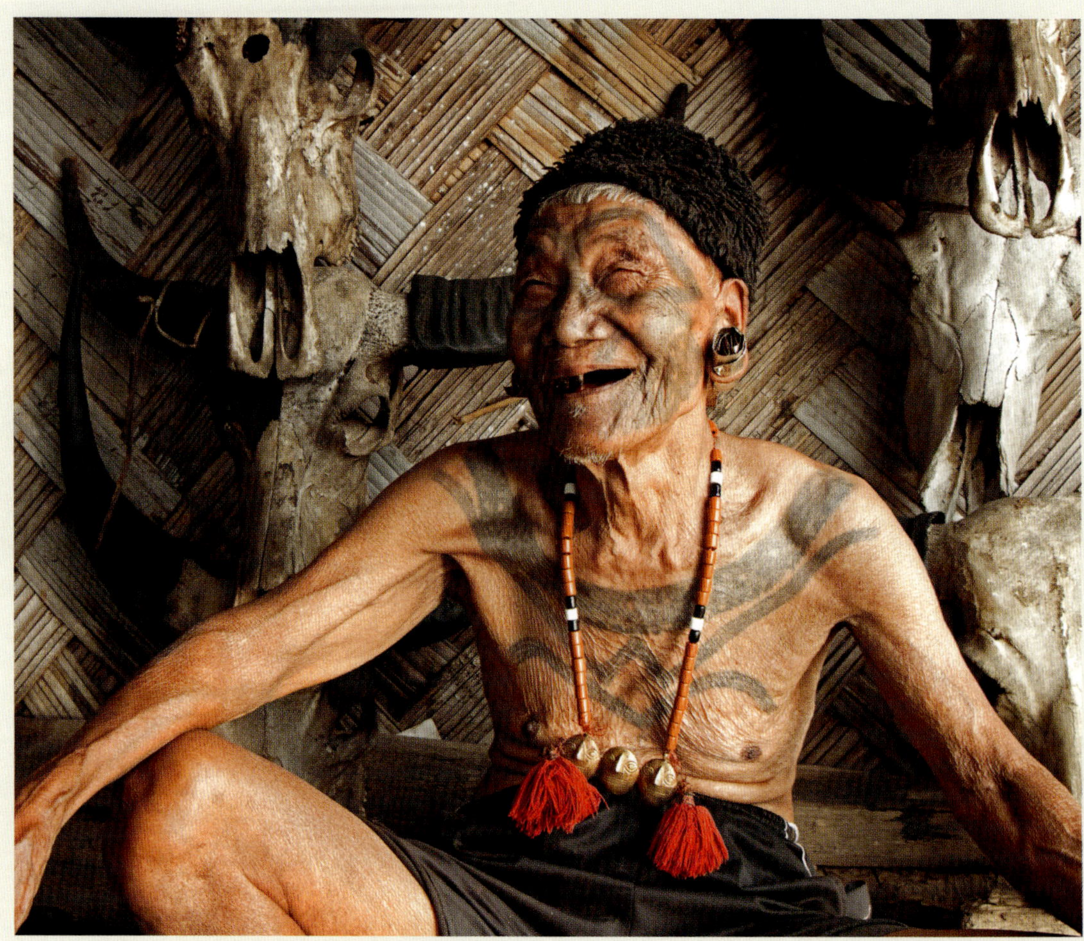

Konyak elder Nokging Wangnao of Hungphoi village, Nagaland, 2018. Due to headhunting bans imposed by the Indian government in the 1950s, the Indigenous Naga people retraditionalized their cultural practices to allow their men to receive the warrior tattoos of their ancestors.

Right Tattooed Lazu Naga woman, Arunachai Pradesh, India, 2006.

Far right Lainong woman, Lahe town, northwest Myanmar, 2014. Perhaps the most common tattoos for Naga women were those related to marking their life stages. Facial tattoos were usually the first marks placed upon an individual.

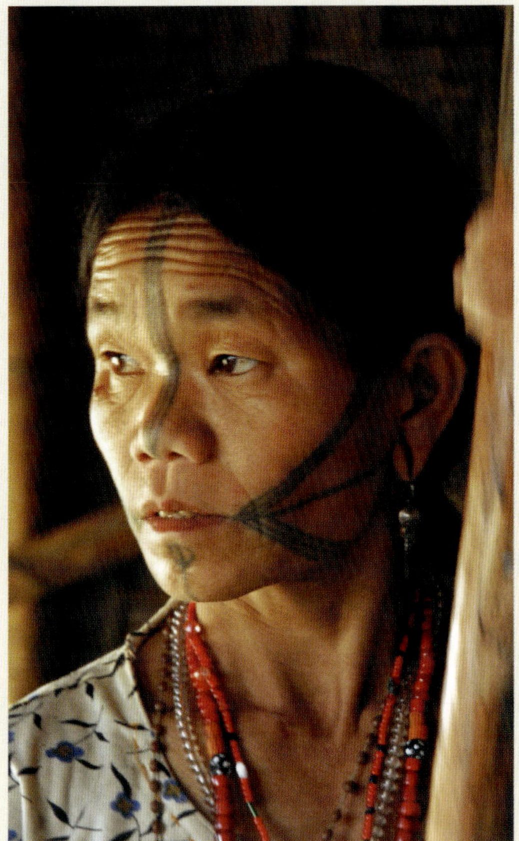

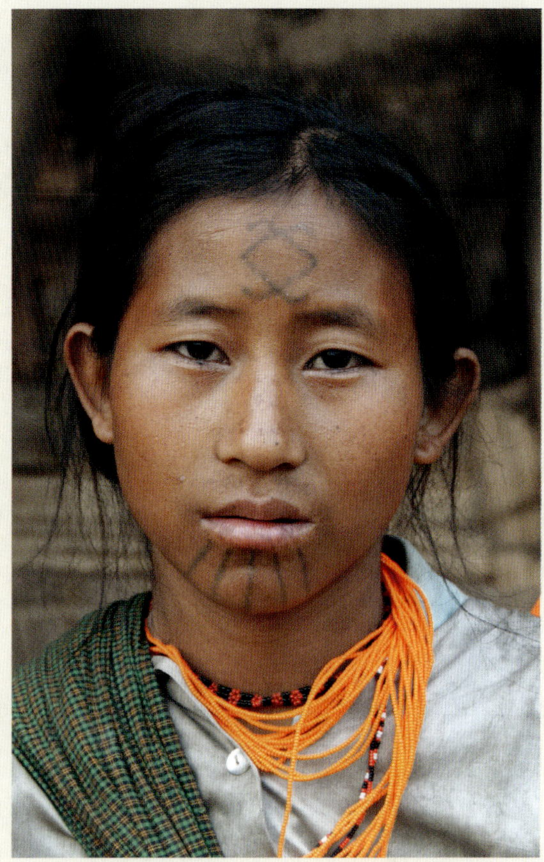

Perhaps the most common tattoos for Naga women were those marking their life stages, which took various forms across the Naga universe. Facial tattoos were usually the first marks placed upon an individual around the age of seven. In some Naga communities, facial tattooing was not a tradition, and a young woman's first tattoos were instead applied to her navel or calves. Facial tattoos, particularly those on the forehead, held significant importance for the afterlife because they ensured that the deceased could travel there to meet their ancestors.[17] These tattoos could also be exchanged for provisions in the afterworld. If a Lainong, Khiamniungan, Makuri, Chang, or Pounyu Naga girl passed away without these tattoos, they were posthumously stenciled onto her skin.

Among the Chen Naga, male members of three aristocratic families could have distinctive back tattoos linked to their spirit companions and guides—the tiger. These "tiger-spirit" men, when dreaming, could perceive the world through the senses of their tiger companion, experiencing what their animals counterpart encountered.[18] During armed conflicts, warrior chiefs with tiger-spirit tattoos could track enemy movements through their tiger allies, adopting tiger-like traits and becoming nearly invincible in combat.

Marks of Identity: Naga Women's Leg Tattoos

Prior to the influx of missionaries in the late nineteenth and early twentieth century, Naga women of northeast India and northwest Myanmar possessed a diversity of leg tattoos, and sometimes these marks displayed very subtle variations within a village or village group.

Naga women's permanent markings typically identified the bearer's particular clan and/or Naga subtribe. Other differences, especially in the linework or design of a leg or thigh tattoo, might also have identified the social class of the wearer.

For instance, female members of Konyak and Wancho ruling chiefs' families adorned their legs with special designs resembling diamonds or lozenges, carefully placed over the tibia or shin. Moreover, the daughters of Wancho chiefs may have also acquired eight small dots arranged in two rows atop the lines tattooed on their thighs, a unique marker of their high birth and status. Among the Chen Naga, diamond shapes tattooed onto the calves signified a woman's noble lineage, underscoring her esteemed place within the social hierarchy.

Leg tattoos were often complemented by distinctive shoulder tattoos featuring checkered designs of diamonds or lozenges,

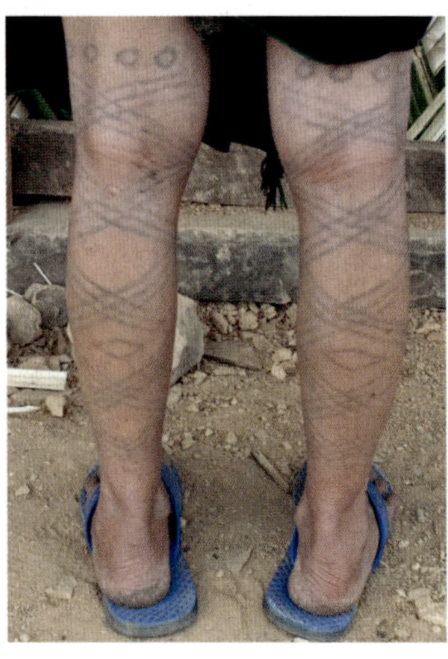

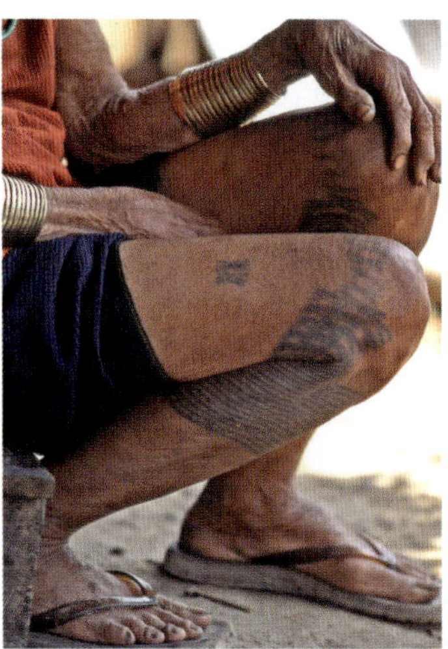

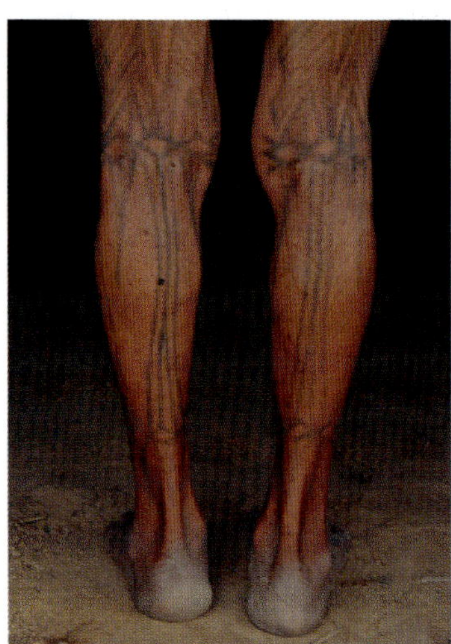

Far left Chen Naga aristocrats bear special tattoos on each of their calves (i.e., a single diamond motif), like this noblewoman of Yan Khone village, Myanmar.

Center left The Konyak Naga *anghya* (queen) of Wanching village, Nagaland, showing the *naopai* or "cradling the baby" XX tattoo on her upper thigh.

Left Leg tattoos of Konyak Naga elder Monyu Langmei of Kenjenshu village, Nagaland.

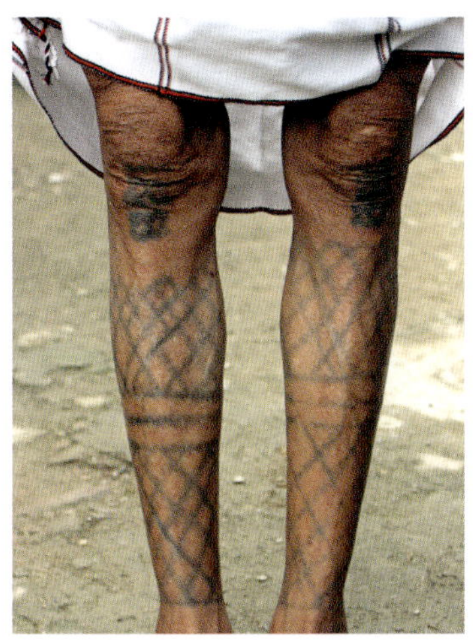

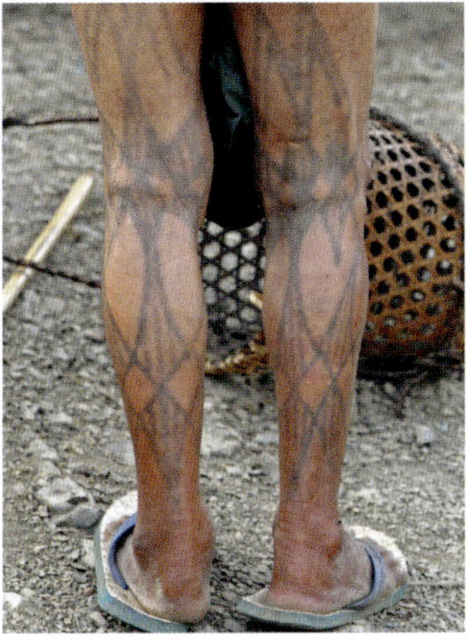

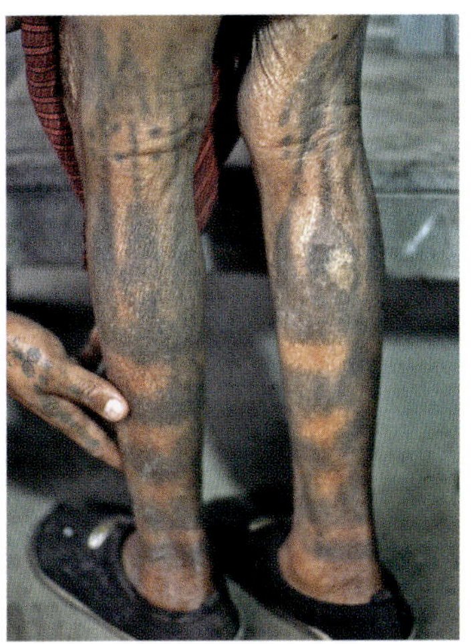

Far left Leg tattoos of Tsakiuchi Thongru, a Sangtam Naga aristocrat of Phelungre village, Nagaland. The XXX markings below her kneecaps are important for the afterlife: A guardian spirit, "Jerepi," inspected women, and if they did not possess these markings, it devoured their spirit.

Center left Leg tattoos of Konyak Naga elder Monyu from Jakphang village. These markings are regional indicators for a specific group of villages.

Left Ao Naga women's leg tattooing identifies the linguistic group of the bearer. These tattoos differentiated individuals of the Chungli, Mongsen, and Changki divisions. Pictured here is an Ao elder of the Chungli group, Nagaland.

further emphasizing elite status. Other bodily design elements, including tattooed geometric lines terminating in /\/\/\ or XXX patterns on the navel, shins, and legs stood as powerful emblems of aristocratic status and noble heritage for the Wancho and select Konyak Naga groups.

Some female tattoos also served to communicate other aspects of local culture. After the birth of a Konyak or Wancho woman's first child, two small XXs were placed on her right thigh. This practice, as explained by Konyak elder Ngipen of Totok Chingnyu village, was believed to "ensure fertility."[19] The local term for this tattoo was *naopai*, meaning "cradling the baby," as a newborn's head often rested on this tattooed mark during nursing.

Among the Sangtam Naga, women often wore XXX markings just below their kneecaps. When a woman entered the afterlife, a guardian spirit named Jerepi looked for these markings. If the individual did not bear this tattoo, her soul was devoured by the spirit.

The tattoos of Naga women illustrate the deep cultural intertwining of body art with significant life milestones and the perpetuation of lineage. These tattoos were living records of aristocracy, motherhood, and cultural identity, and Naga tattoo bearers wore their ancestral marks with pride and purpose. Today, the legacy of these tattoos lives on among the last generation of traditional tattoo bearers and serves as a vivid reminder of the Naga's unique and once ubiquitous skin-marking tradition.

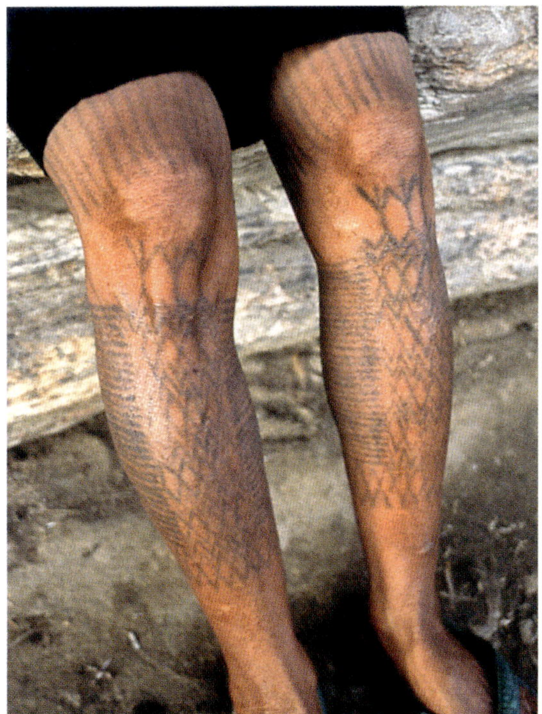

Left Phekhaw Wangcha, a Wancho Naga queen and former tattooist of Nianu village, Arunachal Pradesh, 2008. She wears special tattoo leg motifs consisting of various XXX, diamond, and Y-form patterns that only women of her social status can own.

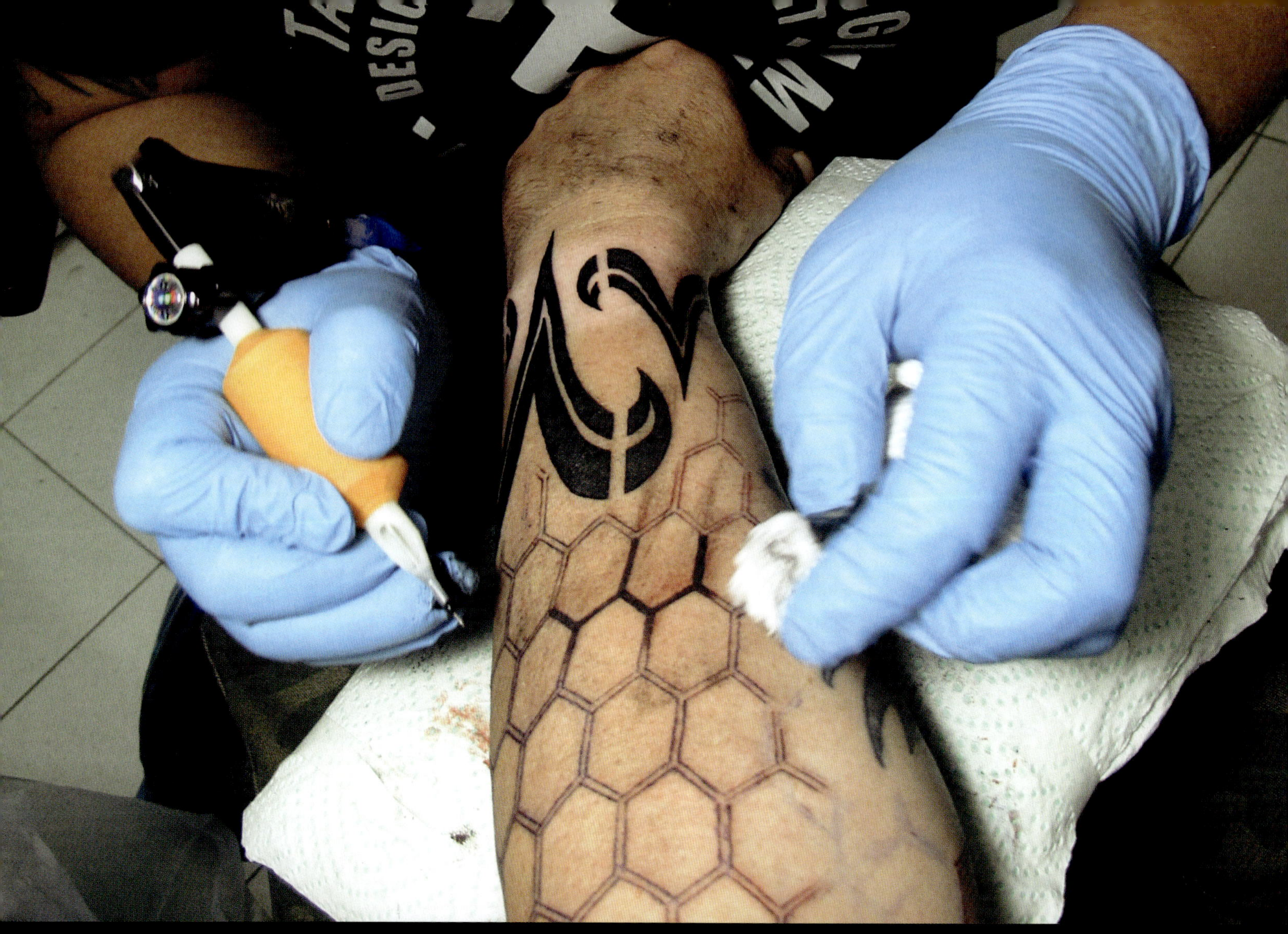

Mo Naga: Reinvigorating Naga Tattoo Traditions

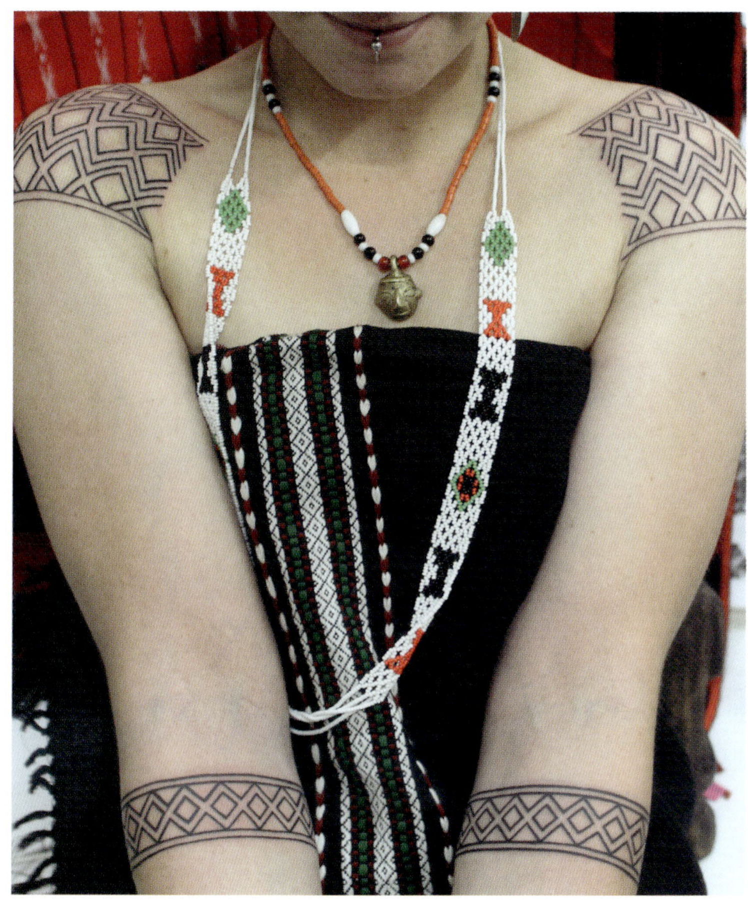

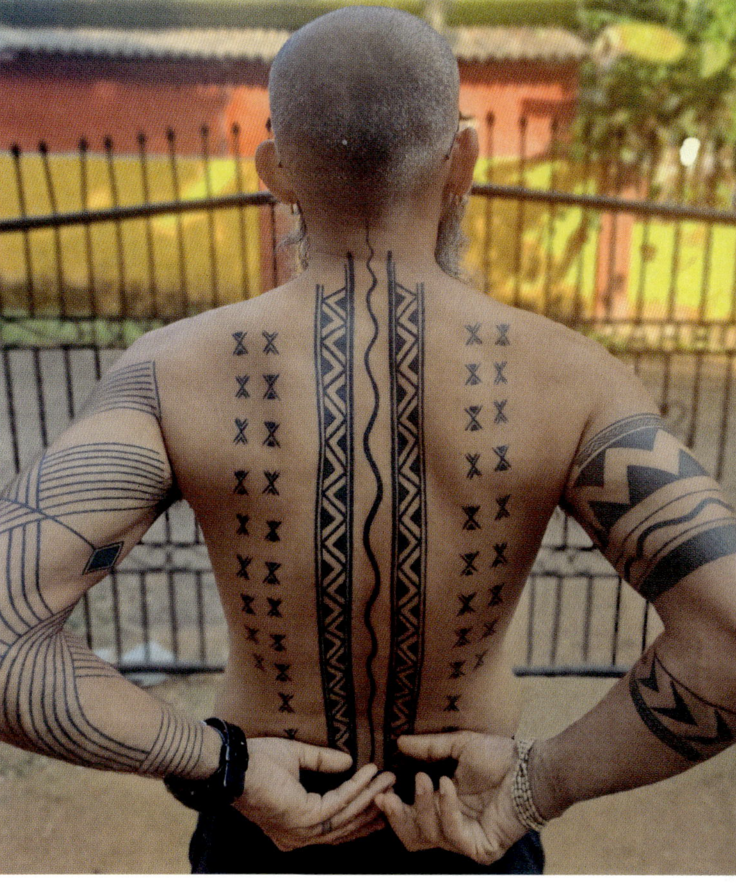

Opposite Mo Naga at work, 2015. For more than fifteen years, the artist has worked to revive Naga tattooing practices and iconography through contemporary renditions of traditional patterns.

Above Neo-Naga shoulder and forearm tattoos, 2014.

Above right Neo-Naga backpiece, 2021.

For more than fifteen years Moranngam Khaling, better known as Mo Naga, has been on a passionate quest to revive the Naga tattooing tradition, a practice that was nearly obliterated by the Baptist Church and subsequently faded from the collective memory of younger generations of Naga in the twentieth and twenty-first centuries. A visionary Uipo Naga tattoo artist from Manipur in northeastern India, Mo Naga initially trained as a fashion designer at the prestigious National Institute of Fashion Technology in Hyderabad. It was here, in 2004, that his journey into the world of tattooing began.

Widely celebrated in the Indian media for his bold, contemporary, and geometric tattoo artistry, his work has captivated both Naga and non-Naga clients. His dynamic creations fuse traditional Naga tattoo patterns with other artistic influences drawn from aspects of Naga material culture. These include the rich tapestry of Naga textile designs, sculptural forms, intricate beadwork, and ritual artifacts, such as painted human skulls and *mithun* (bovine) horns.[20]

After establishing a client base, Mo Naga opened a series of tattoo studios, including a tattooing school in India's northeastern state of Assam, near the Naga heartland, where he taught basic design, tattoo machine mechanics, clinical hygiene, and sterilization practices, among other offerings.

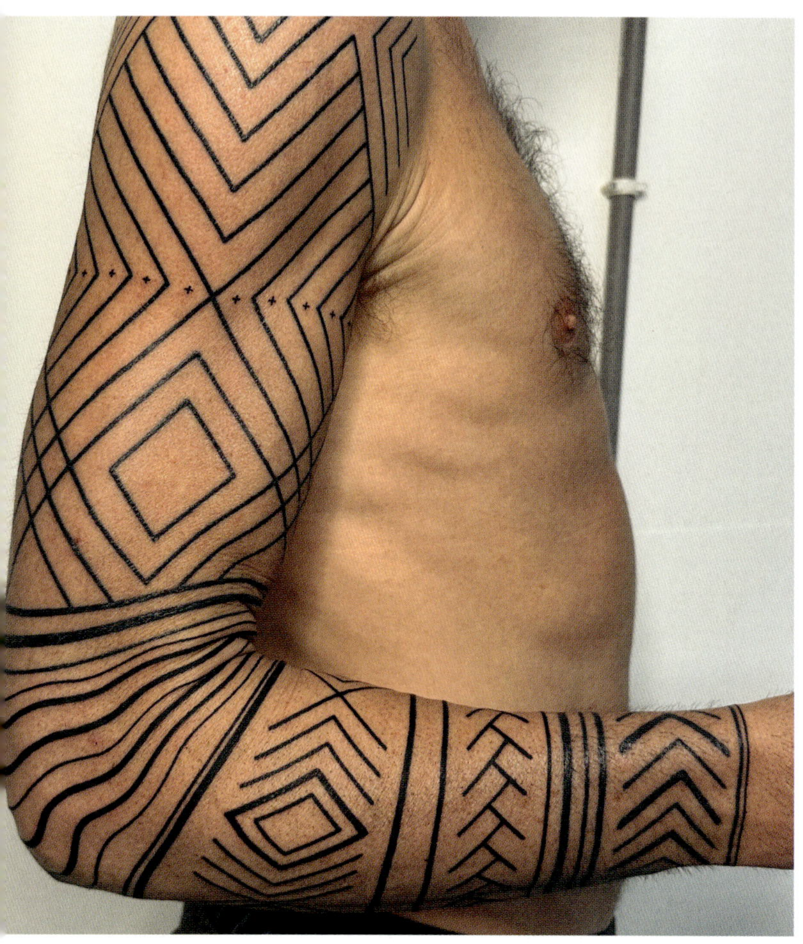

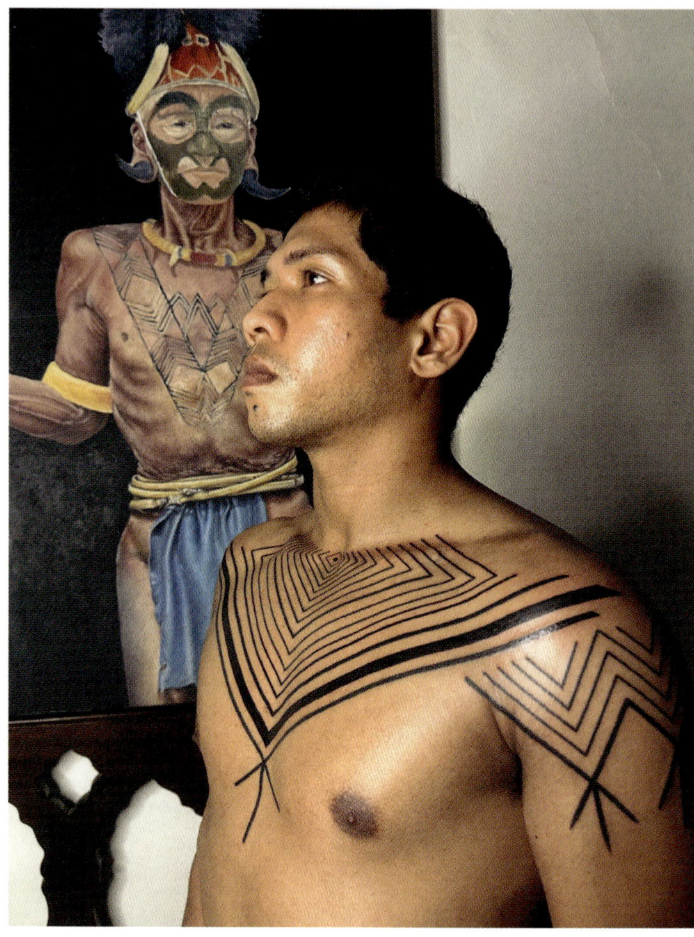

Above Neo-Naga arm tattoos, 2023.

Above right Hand-poked Neo-Naga chest and shoulder tattoos, 2023.

Subsequently, he moved his tattoo-operating base to Dimapur, the capital of Nagaland state, then back to his home village of Tengnoupal, in Manipur.

When asked about the iconography he tattoos on his clients, especially those with Naga roots, Mo Naga emphasized his avoidance of Western tattoo designs, as they are foreign to Naga culture. "If we can develop tattoo designs inspired by our local Indigenous art and heritage, tattooing will become more meaningful and more acceptable to them," he explained. "In this way, it can be reclaimed and revived."[21]

In my interviews with the artist, Mo Naga elaborated on the distinction between Western and Naga tattoos, noting that both serve as a language, telling stories about the person or community they come from. "They are a language, an expression, and they talk about the people, their journey, their beliefs, and their community and way of life. They are based on aesthetics that developed over time, so I do not differentiate between them," he shared. "But . . . if we look at them from a design standpoint, there are differences and similarities. Naga tattoos are prominently inspired by nature, and the aesthetics of the designs are built around that. Just as Western tattoos are built around an environment that is an expression of that community."[22]

Right Hand-poked Neo-Naga back tattoos, 2023.

Far right Neo-Naga tattoos inspired by male Ao Naga textile patterns on arm and traditional tattoo motifs on chest, 2017–23.

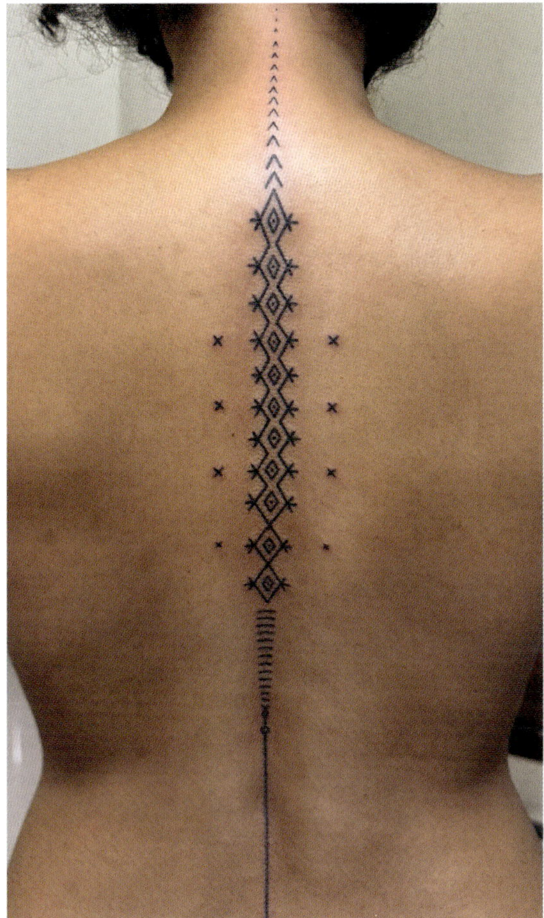

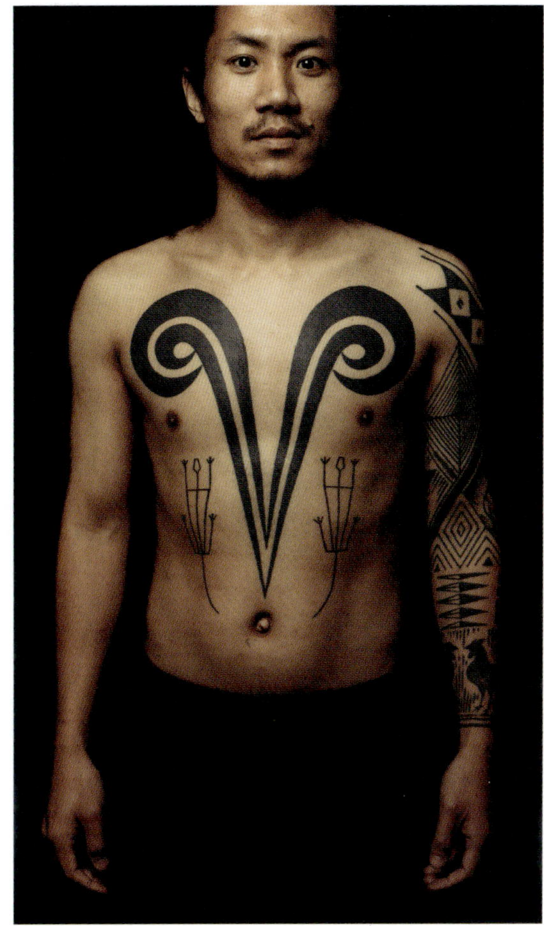

In the Naga tradition, tattoos were not mere fashion statements but profound symbols of life achievements, marking rites of passage and victories in combat. Mo Naga believes that crafting "a new line" of neo-Naga tattoos for the Naga people will help preserve this endangered ancestral practice. "Naga warriors may not be headhunting anymore and receiving tattoos for valor, but the relevance of those designs should not be lost," he explained. "Even now, a Naga person can still get a tattoo in accordance with their achievements, just like their ancestors did. In this way, we can preserve our tattoo culture and ensure that the noble way of our Naga forefathers does not fade from memory."[23]

Mo Naga's dedication to reclaiming and revitalizing the ancient art of Naga tattooing is not just about preserving a fading tradition but about breathing new life into it. He seamlessly blends the old with the new, infusing traditional motifs with contemporary flair. His work is a vibrant celebration of Naga heritage, a living canvas that tells stories of identity, culture, and ancestral wisdom. Through his art, Mo Naga continues to inspire a renaissance, ensuring that the legacy of Naga tattooing is not only remembered but also revered and reinvented for future generations.

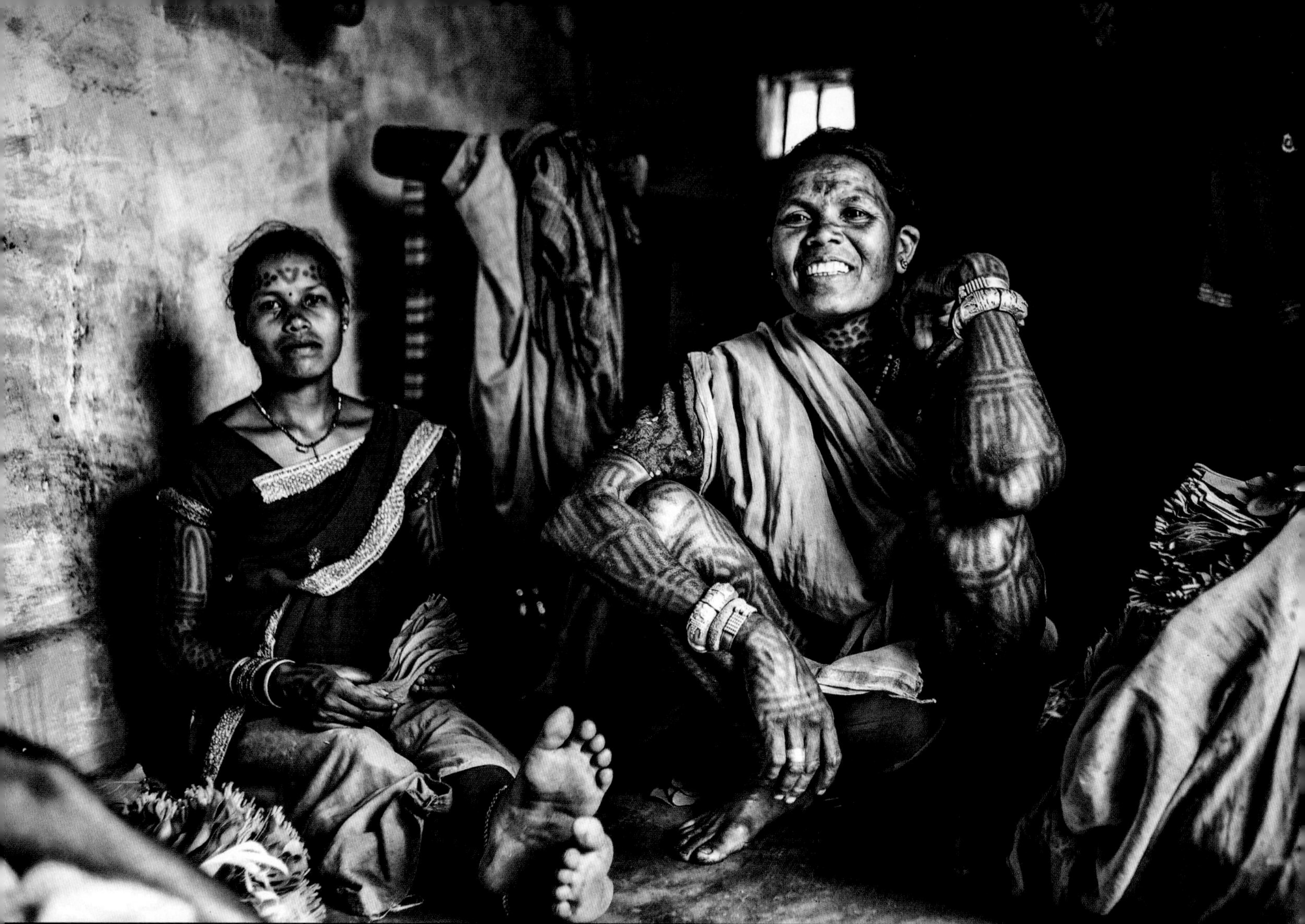

Shatabdi Chakrabarti: Capturing India's Indigenous Tattooing Traditions

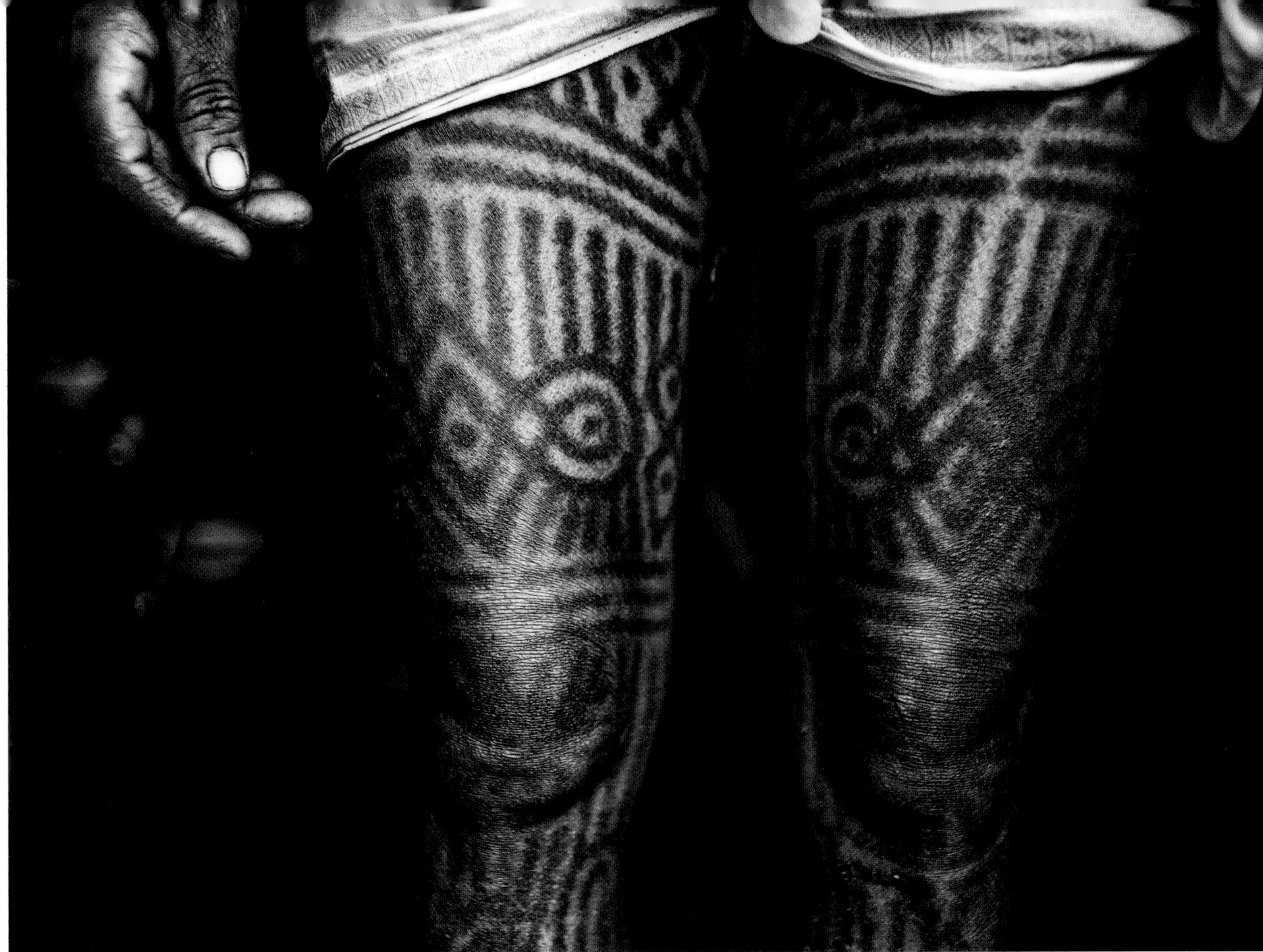

Opposite Tattooed Baiga women Tihro Bai and her daughter-in-law Ramphali, Ranjara village in Dhindhori district, 2018.

Above Baiga woman with tattooed knees and legs, 2018. The sun is an important motif for the Baigas since it depicts the life source. This motif finds a strategic placement on the knees due to the shape of the body part.

For more than fifteen years, professional photographer Shatabdi Chakrabarti has documented the vanishing traditions of Indigenous tattoo culture across India. As a heavily tattooed creative artist, her interest in tattoos inspired her to delve deep into these local practices with projects focusing on the tattoos of the Apatani (Arunachal Pradesh), the Baiga (Madhya Pradesh, Jharkhand, Chhattisgarh), Rabari and Mer (Gujarat), and more recently the Santhal, Oraon, Malhar, Kurmi and Bediya (Jharkhand), among others.

In India, tattooed tribespeople can be found across the length and breadth of the country. In the subcontinent, Indigenous communities employed tattoos not only as forms of adornments, but also for magical, religious, and sociocultural aspects encompassing identity and social standing, among other things.

"Human life can be summed up as a continuous quest for self-identity, and individual identity is necessary for inclusion into peer groups, because humans are social animals and we need to be a part of a larger

Forearm tattoos of Santhal elder Chumman Hemram, Bihar state, 2021. Santhal women have elaborate tattoos on their forearms depicting natural elements and everyday objects. A mango tree and a stylized hair accessory can be seen in this image. The motifs are used for beautification and represent abundance.

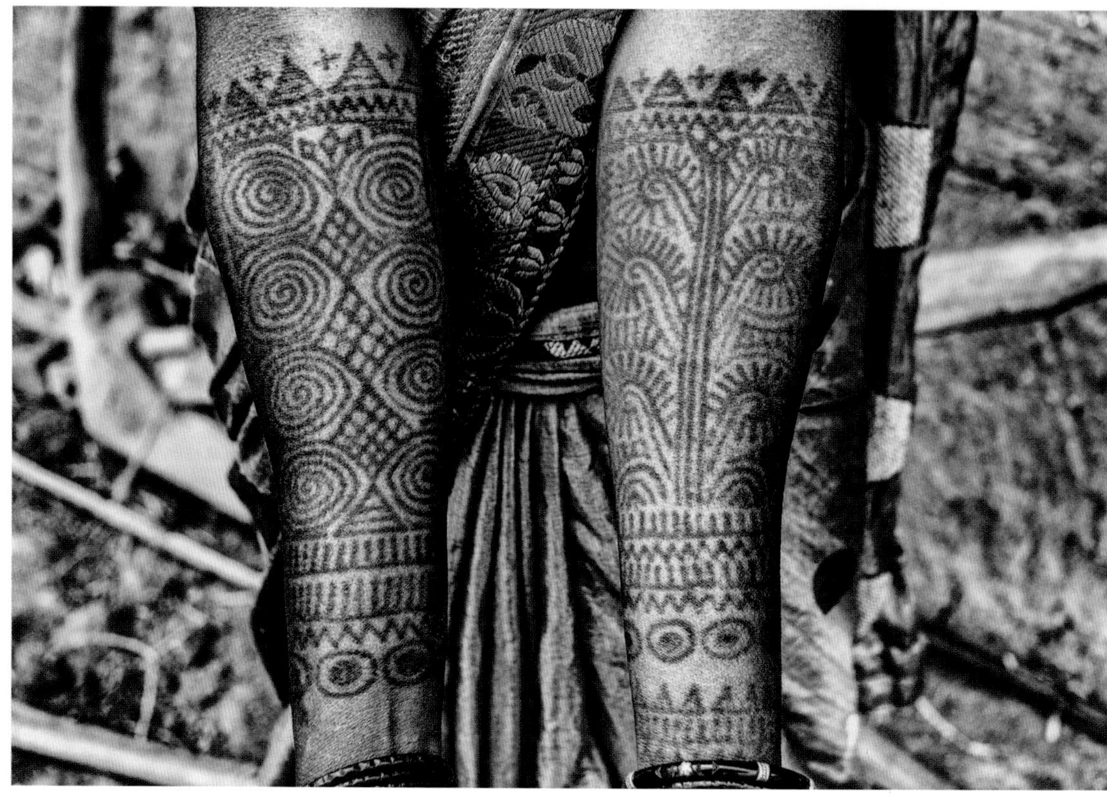

community to survive," Chakrabarti explained. "For these reasons, human cultures have, since prehistoric times, created visual markers that tell stories of the self and of communities these marked bodies belong to."[24]

According to Chakrabarti, the need for visual markers was perhaps the reason why humans first started scarring, piercing, and tattooing their bodies. "As civilizations became more complex and diverse, the body modification and tattooing culture expanded its role to suit a wide range of purposes. For example, over time tattooing transcended from being purely semantic to serving spiritual and aesthetic purposes," she said. "In turn, tattoos were deployed as markers denoting rites of passage, symbols of birth status and social rank, iconography related to religion and spirituality, insignia of victory in hunting and battle, displays of sexual virility and fertility, protective talismans for love and luck, and much more, especially in India."[25]

In recent decades, however, these once powerful markers of identity and culture have begun to disappear from view. Migration from rural communities to urban centers (for work and education), the influx of Christian missionaries to central India, and Saffronization (the right-wing policy that seeks to implement a Hindu nationalist agenda that undermines Indigenous ideologies) have each played important roles. Widely looked upon as an uncivilized and primitive custom in contrast to the modern, cultured, and sophisticated lifestyles in India's cities, tribal tattooing practice has been suppressed and tattoo bearers face increasing discrimination.

Apatani woman with facial tattoos and traditional nose plugs, Ziro Valley, Arunachal Pradesh, 2016. Today, tattooing is no longer practiced, and the youngest generation of tattoo bearers are in their sixties.

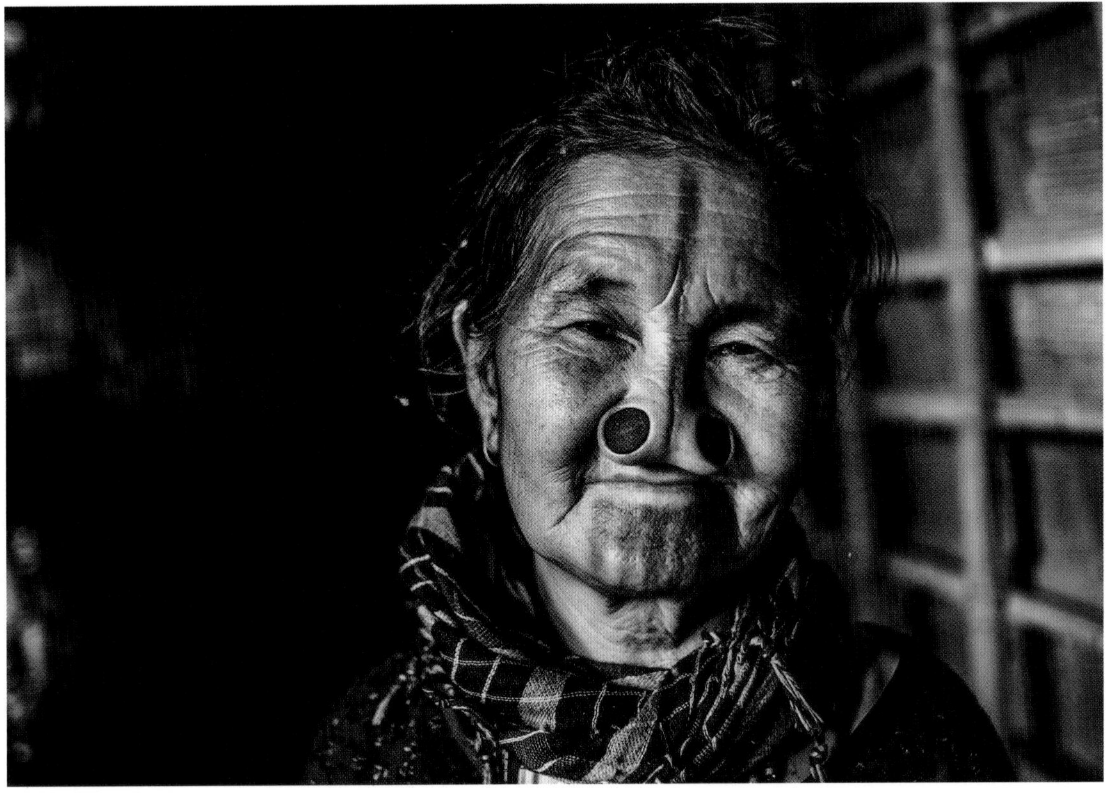

"The decline of the tattooing culture among the tribal groups is not a reflection of the overall culture of tattooing in India," Chakrabarti observed. "With increasing urbanization, tattooing has gained popularity amongst the young population as a form of self-expression. In the urban space, tattoos are associated with being a 'rebel' and being 'cool.' This has created a binary where traditional tattooing is looked down upon as something 'uncultured' and 'primitive' – terms which are derogatory toward the art form and its carriers," she revealed. "This is ironic, because unlike modern tattooing which is largely individualistic, Indigenous tattoos are rooted in collective memory, origin myths, local religious beliefs, folklore, ancestor worship, representation of the natural environment, etc., which carry significant value for the people who wear them because they hold a shared language and meaning."[26]

As for the future, Chakrabarti shared that she will continue to document these important aspects of India's cultural heritage and history because capturing the essence of these ancient tattoos and the voices of their bearers will be a lifelong journey. Eventually she plans to publish a book on her tattoo documentation work.

"I am deeply connected to this work because, for me, it's about documenting a shared history and a disappearing art form and cultural practice," she said. "Every time I visit a far-flung village or a hamlet in the forests in search of the tattooed tribal elders, there is an instant connection because of the motifs imprinted on our skins. Even when there is a language barrier, we understand each other through the ink on our bodies."[27]

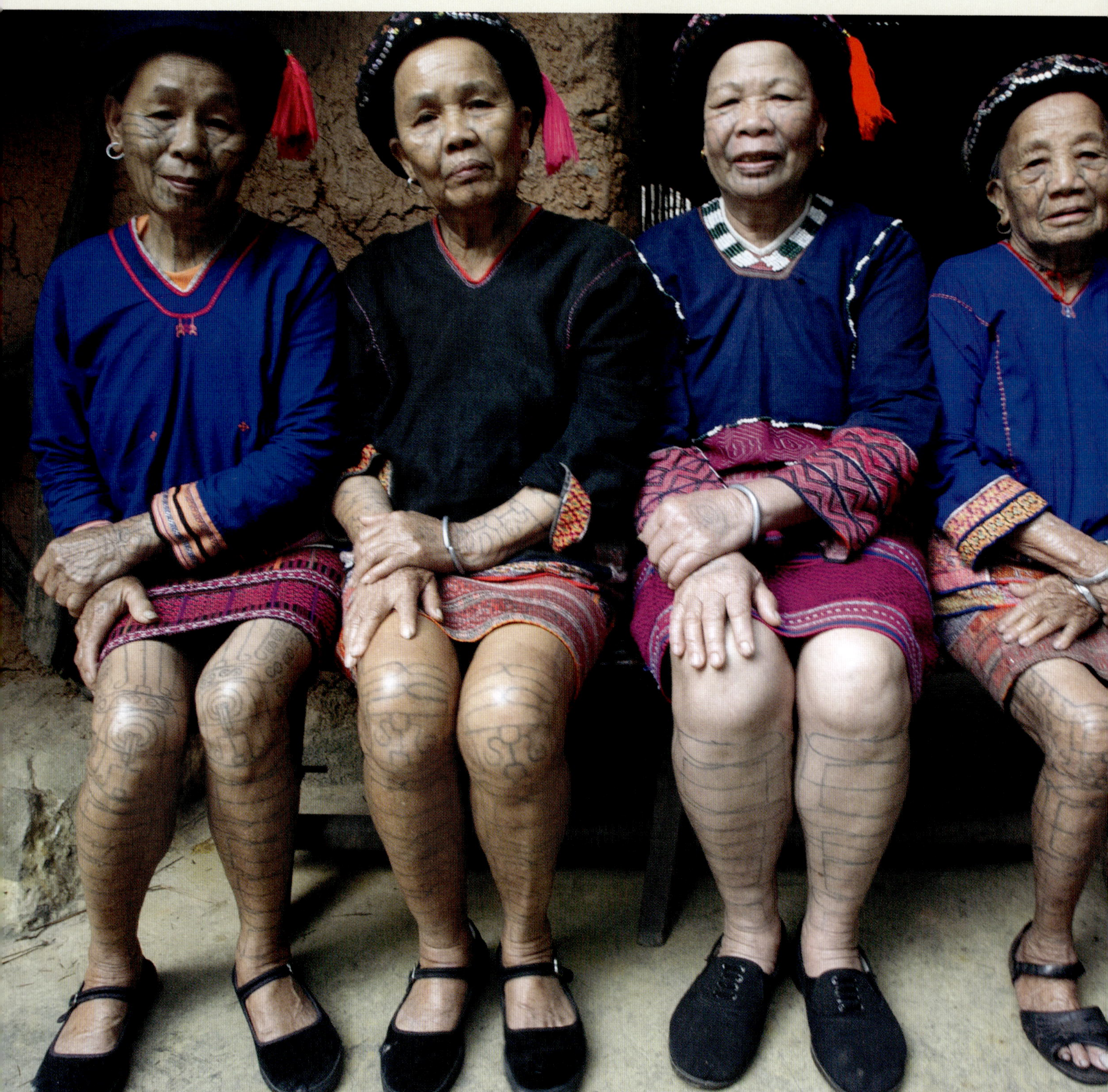

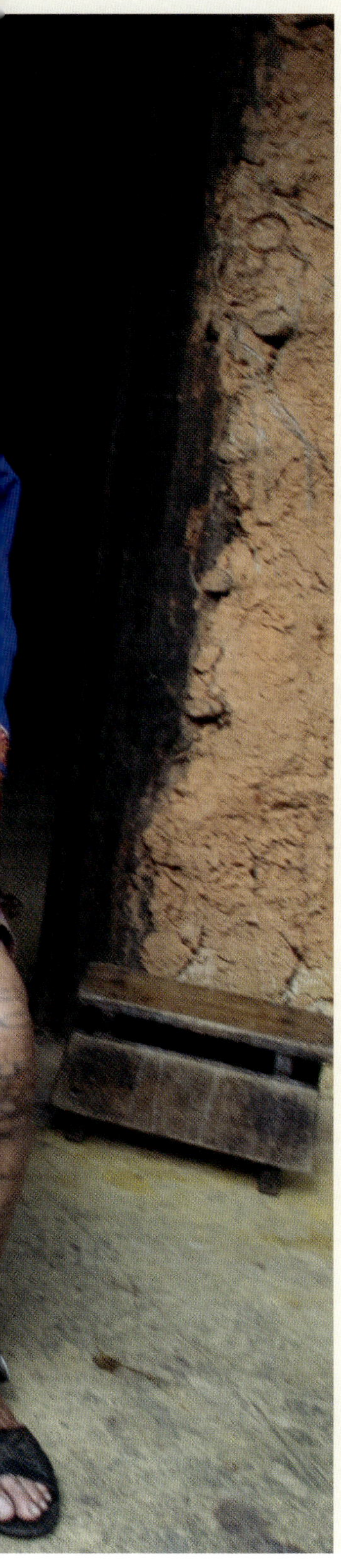

8

TATTOOS OF CHINA AND SIBERIA

The entry of the word *wen* or "tattoo" into the history of China extends back to the Han Dynasty (206 BCE–220 CE). Although there are several other terms associated with the practice of tattooing the body like *mo* ("to ink"), *lou shen* ("to engrave the body"), *xiu mian* ("to embroider the face") among others, it is widely accepted that *wen* is the most appropriate historical term for two reasons.[1] Because the word is used more frequently than the others in ancient texts and, more importantly, because the original character meaning "to pattern" or "to write" is believed to symbolize an anthropomorph or individual, perhaps a northern Indigenous "barbarian," with a tattooed chest.[2]

Four tattooed Run elders of Baisha County, Hainan Island, China, 2001.

China possesses an ancient heritage of tattooing traditions and technology that spans millennia. Beginning with the Majiayao culture (3300–2000 BCE) of northern China, we discover tantalizing glimpses of body art praxis through highly decorated prehistoric mortuary urns and other ceramic vessels. These artifacts often feature human heads adorned with chin, nose, and other facial skin markings resembling tattoos, vividly painted in intricate patterns.[3]

These ancient depictions bear an uncanny resemblance to the ethnographic traditions of female facial tattooing still practiced in regions such as southwest China, Myanmar, northwest India, and Siberia.[4] The continuity of these designs across time and space speaks to an ancient and unbroken tradition of facial marking across the centuries.

These painted figures, with their detailed facial markings, not only serve as a testament to the artistic prowess of the Majiayao culture but they also whisper stories of ancestors who likely marked their skin with symbols of identity, protection, and belonging, echoing the rituals and beliefs that continue in various Indigenous Asian and Siberian communities today.

Notwithstanding, in Chinese antiquity, tattoo was typically associated by the ruling Han elite as a "primitive" and "barbaric" practice reserved for ethnic minorities and other foreigners.[5] The Han considered themselves to be the only "real" Chinese people and all others as *man* or *yi*—tribal "primitives" who cut, scarred, or tattooed their skins with permanent marks. In other words, if you were not Han, you were "uncivilized" and perhaps even considered to be an "enemy" of the state, like the inhabitants of *Wo* in Japan, who in the third century CE were said to "tattoo their faces and bodies."[6]

Later texts clearly state that the only form of tattoo acceptable in Chinese society is that reserved as punishment for robbery, adultery, and other grave offenses. In fact, the sixth–seventh century CE text *Han shu* ("Treatise on Punishment") relates that there were 500 crimes punishable by tattoo.[7] The term used in that text is *mo zui* ("ink crimes") and tattoo was often combined with exile, "ensuring that the defiled person was removed as far as possible from law-abiding, civilized people."

The religious beliefs of this early era through the twentieth century also dictated that tattooing was immoral and negative. This is because popular Confucian principles generally discouraged any kind of permanent body modification since filial conduct maintained that one's body should remain as it was given to them by their parents. Some scholars have also suggested that the Buddhist idea of reincarnation may have also contributed to the tradition of keeping the body pure.

These negative connotations continued down through the centuries, and with the establishment of the People's Republic of China in 1949 the Communist government implemented policies of *pochu mixin* ("eradicating superstitions") and *yifengyisu* ("changing prevailing customs and transforming social traditions").[8] These laws were aimed at China's fifty-six ethnic minority groups and ultimately began to alter cultural institutions like tattooing, which began to gradually disappear among those peoples who practiced the indelible custom, including the Li of Hainan Island and the Drung of Yunnan.

Drung elder Dang Muxi of Longyuan village, Dulongjiang Township, China, 2002. The fee for her tattooing included a pot of wine, a large bowl, and sack of grain.

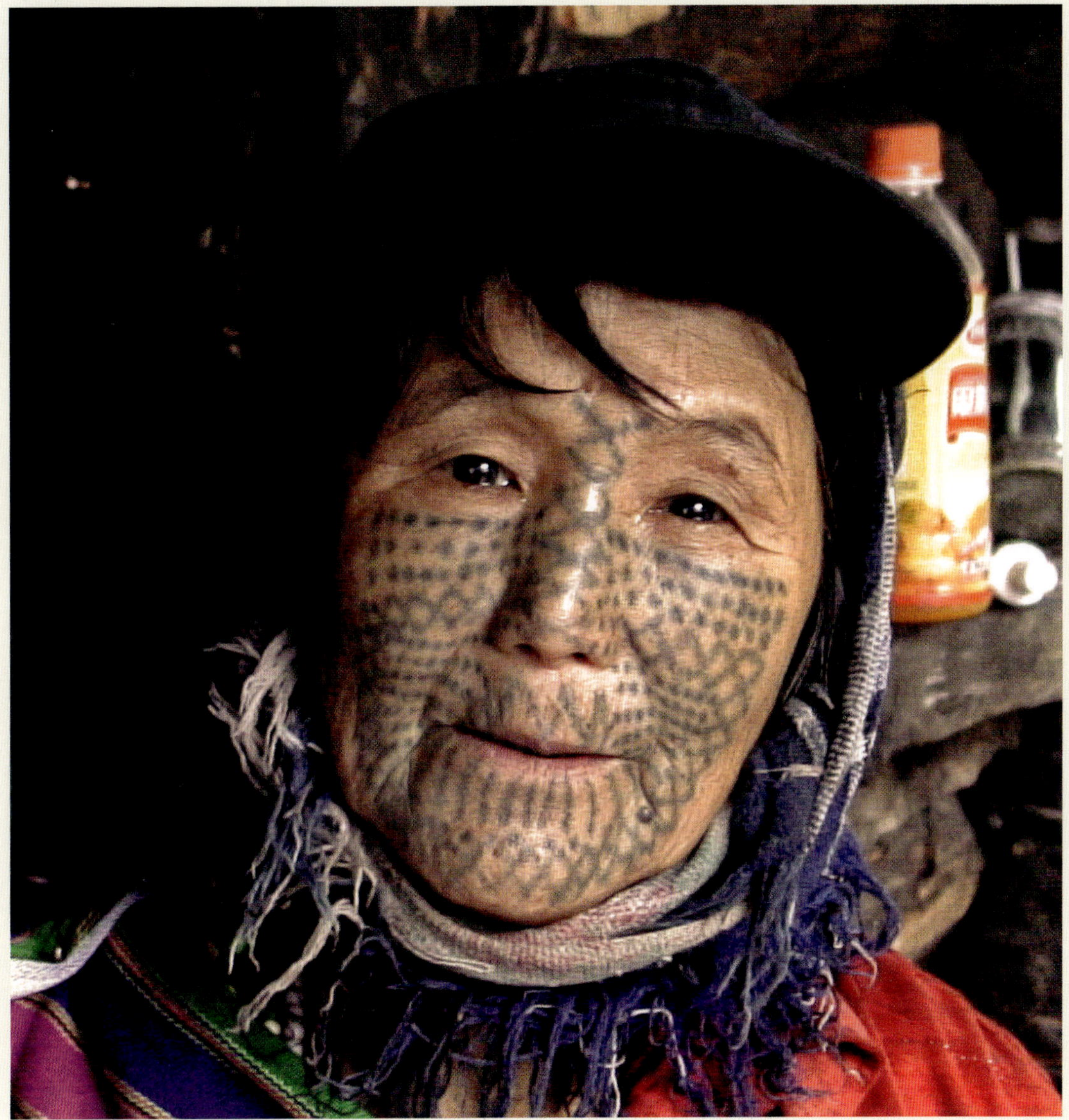

Drung Women of Yunnan

In a remote corner of Yunnan Province in southwestern China, *bāktūq* or facial tattooing was once widespread among women of the Drung (also Dulong or Trung) people until the establishment of the People's Republic of China. The Chinese government banned Drung tattooing in the mid-1960s, labeling it "primitive" and "superstitious"[9] in an effort to transition all ethnic minorities to socialism.

For centuries before this prohibition, the origins of these tattoos were steeped in legends. Several early writers suggested that elders tattooed women's faces as a form

Drung elder Li Wensi of Xiongdang village, Dulongjiang Township, China, 2002.

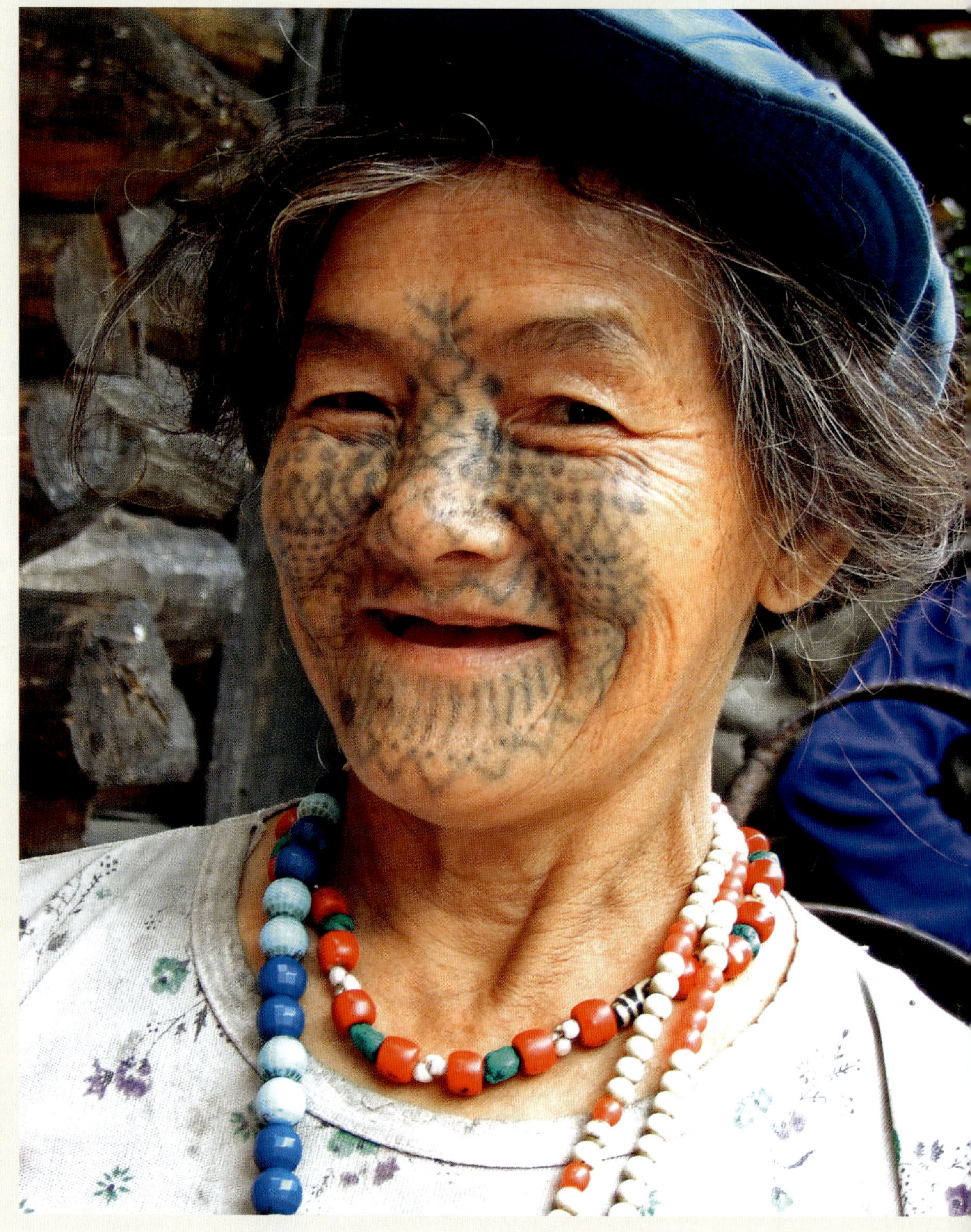

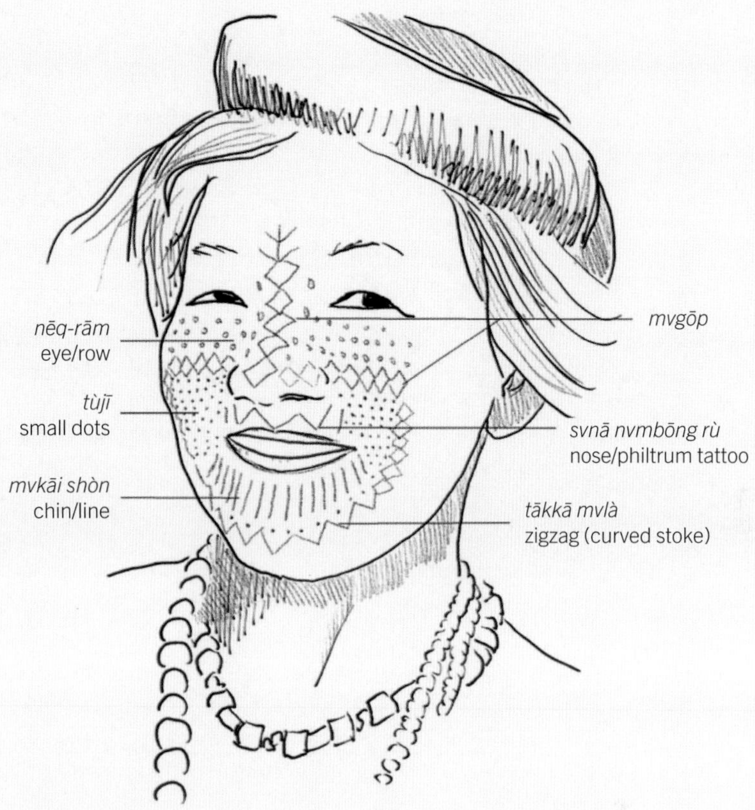

Drung tattoo terminology. Illustration by Stéphane Gros.

of "disfigurement" to deter the once-powerful Tibetan slave traders and other enemies from abducting the fair "maidens" of the mountains.[10] More recent theories propose that these dark-blue markings discouraged Drung women from being enticed by the allure of modern city life, as tattoos in China are often associated with outcasts and criminals. However, these hypotheses are incorrect. Young women were tattooed in their early teens at puberty with unique and "beautiful" designs that were distinctive to their home region and possibly indicated clan affiliation or family group through subtle variations in the overall design.[11]

Despite the tattoo ban, the 2003 Chinese census recorded that sixty-five tattooed Drung women still resided in the mountains above the isolated Dulongjiang River near Tibet. Much of this region, lying 13,100 ft (4,000 m) above sea level, is usually cut off from the outside world for at least six months each year due to heavy snowfall. Currently, fewer than forty tattooed Drung women remain, the youngest of whom were tattooed in the early 1960s. The rest are between seventy and one hundred years old.

The pointillinear facial tattoos resemble a winged insect, with the body and antennae extending upward along the bridge of the nose to the forehead, and the wings spread across the cheeks and face. Some Drung women have noted that they were tattooed with an actual "butterfly" pattern because it is beautiful and associated with the afterlife.

Elders explained that the souls of deceased women were believed to transform into various butterfly species, and without their facial markings, they would become lost in the afterworld and not reunite with their ancestors.[12] Consequently, collecting butterflies was forbidden, and it was considered a bad omen if one flew into a household.[13]

The tattooing process was complex and painful. After a stencil was created, skilled women, typically a relative (i.e., one's mother, older cousin, or aunt), performed the tattooing using the hand-tapping technique. The design was punctured into the skin with bamboo needles or local thorny brambles dipped in a sooty ink made of pitch pine, water, and sometimes mixed with the tattooist's saliva.[14] Tattooing began on the chin, followed by the cheeks and nose. The operation could last seven or eight hours, and women were advised not to wash their wounds for several days to ensure the pattern remained intact. Payment for the tattooist ranged from a basket of taro, bread, or grain alcohol or utilitarian items like a knife.

It was crucial to compensate the tattooist before the procedure, because it was believed that the tattooer might lose her sight if the transaction was not completed.[15] For example, the tattoo client needed to provide an *akpeù* (retribution) or *tvpeù* (compensation) in kind, usually consisting of various feminine goods.[16] Similarly, Drung women who acted as midwives faced the same risk of their vision being affected after childbirth if they had not received their compensation.

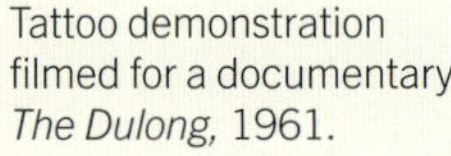
Tattoo demonstration filmed for a documentary *The Dulong,* 1961.

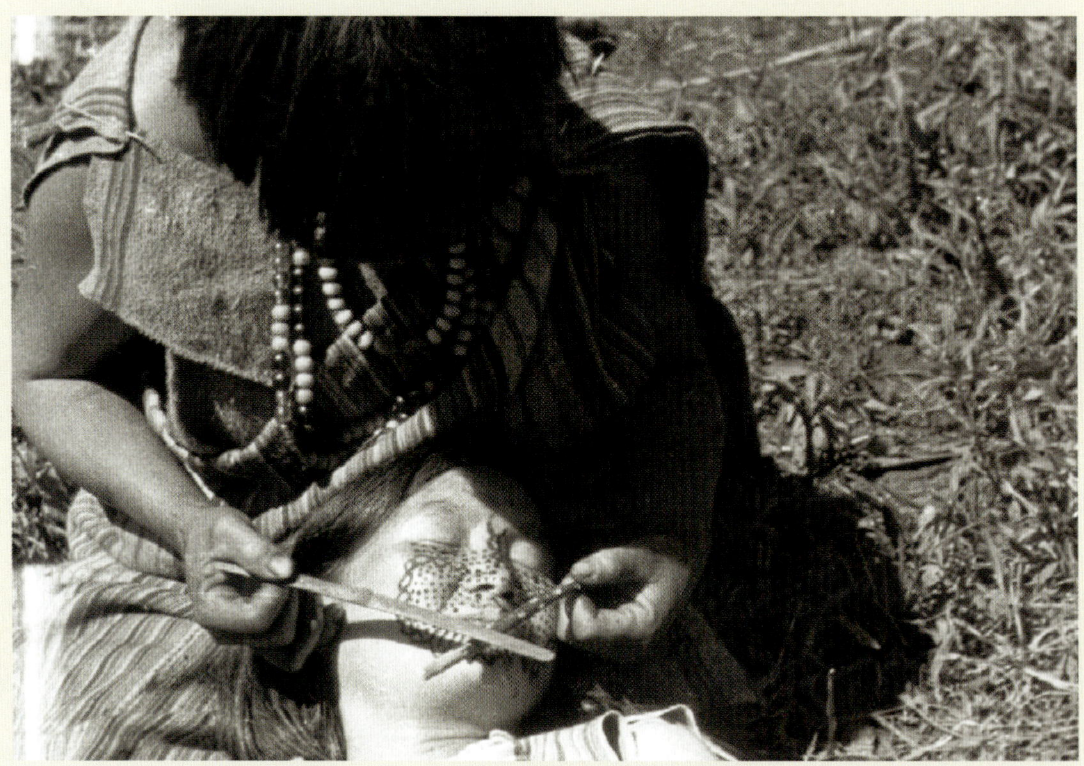

In the Drung lexicon, vision embodies a potent and formidable power. The eyes are seen as conduits of mutual influence and exchanges of forces, acting as windows to the soul and channels of unseen energies. The *nēq kù*, or "envious eye," is a piercing gaze that conveys jealousy, its intensity capable of stirring turmoil and unrest. Conversely, the *nēq mvdàm*, or "full eye," radiates satisfaction and contentment, its serene gaze fostering harmony and well-being.

These expressions of vision focus human desire through the power of the gaze, suggesting that such sight can wield significant effects on individuals, households, and entire communities.[17] The envious eye can cast shadows of envy and strife, while the full eye can illuminate and uplift. In this way, the Drung belief in the power of vision underscores a deep understanding of the gaze's dual nature—capable of both harm and healing, destruction and creation. It is a reminder that the eyes, as windows to our inner selves, can influence the world around us in profound and mysterious ways.

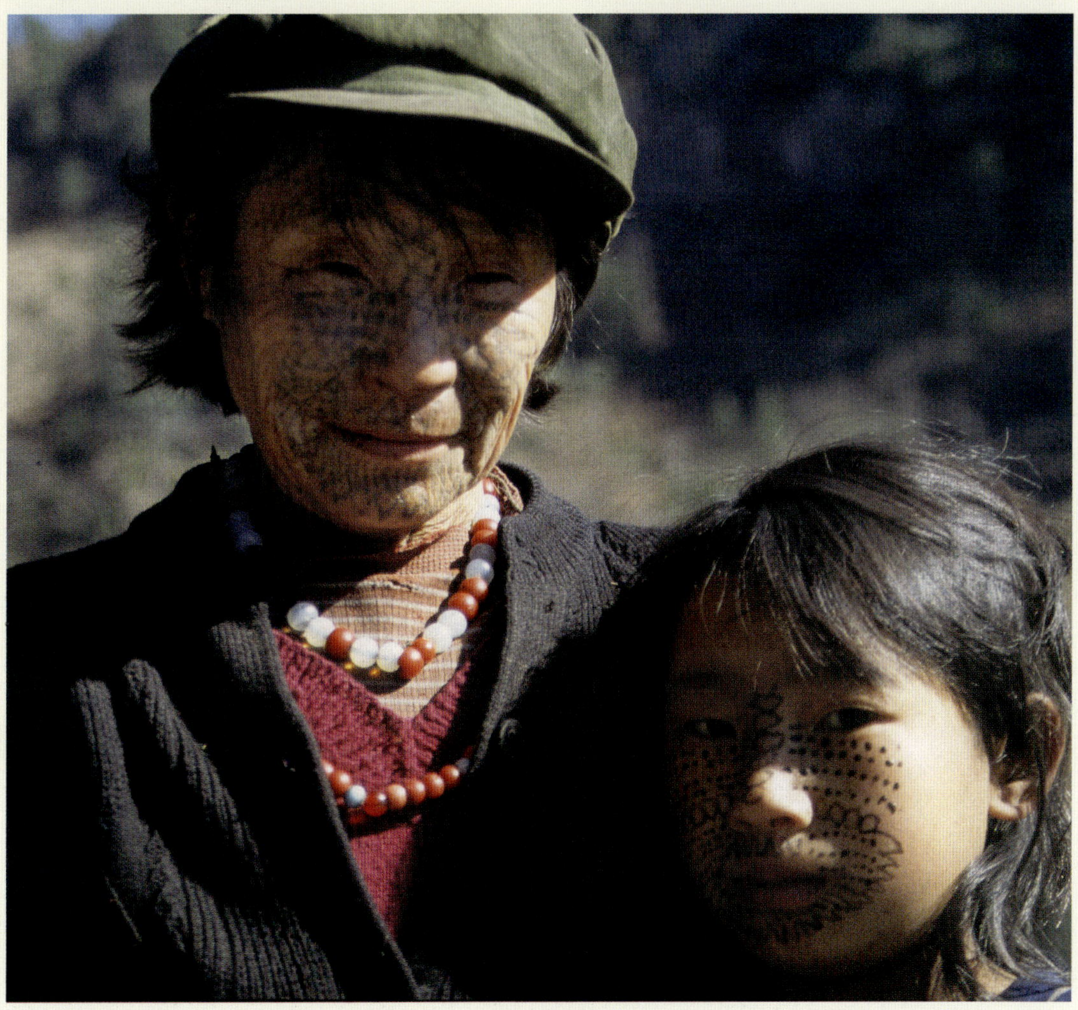

Tshineng, a former Drung *rū sō* (one who "knows how to prick"), stands with her granddaughter Tsemu, Dizhengdang (Zungdam) village, China, 2003. The stencil on the girl's face was simply applied to demonstrate a traditional pattern and was not part of an actual tattoo in process.

Tattooed Run Li elder of Baisha county, Hainan Island, China, 2008.

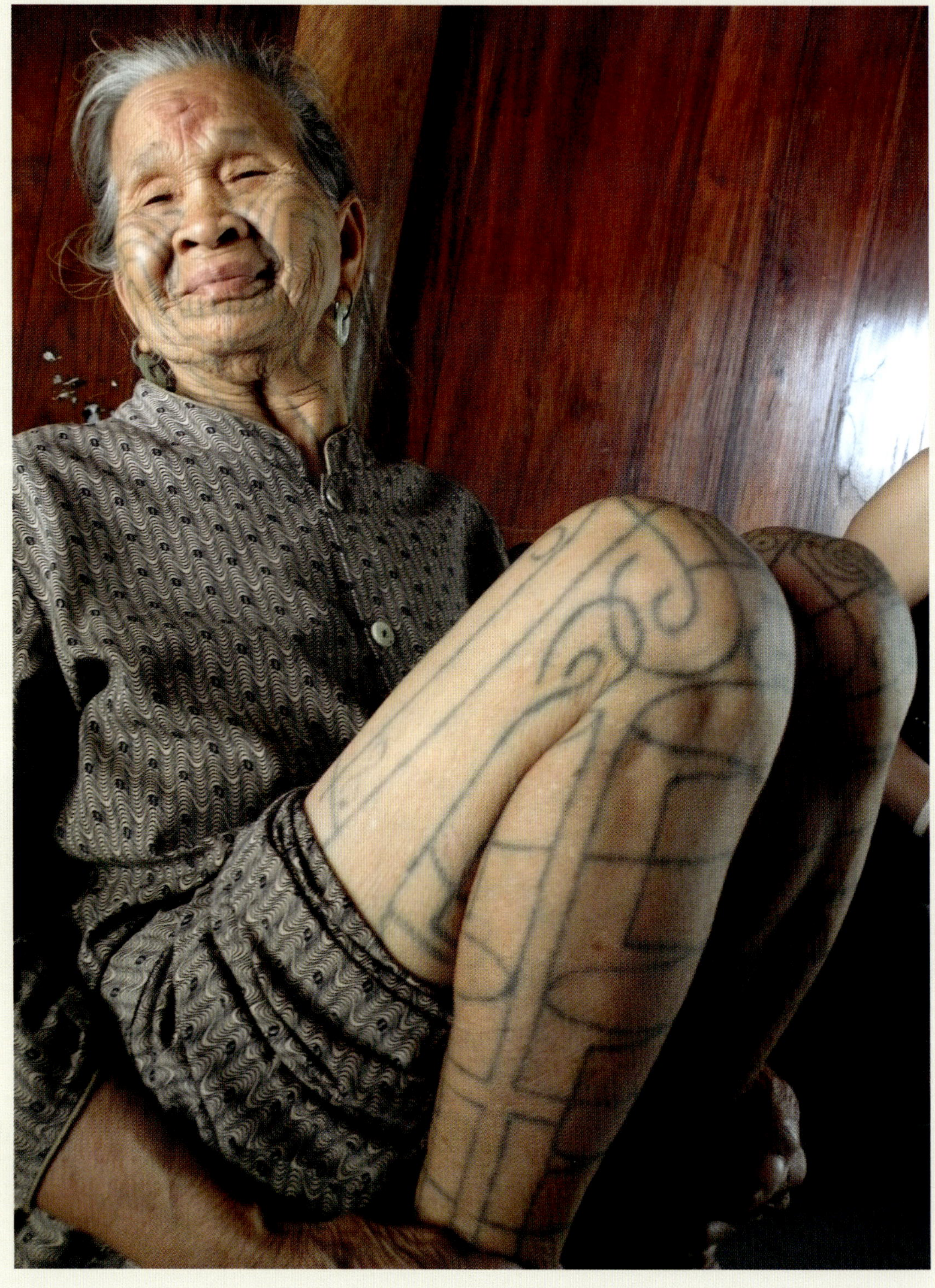

The Li of Hainan Island

Lying some 650 miles (1,050 km) southeast of Drung territory, Hainan Island is home to several ancient Indigenous tattooing traditions. The Li people, comprised of five tribes (Qi, Ha, Run, Sai, and Meifu), are believed to have lived on Hainan for more than 2,500 years and early Chinese chronicles document that tattooing has long been part of their unique culture.

Tattooing was an integral practice among all Li groups, with women far more frequently receiving these intricate skin markings than men. While men typically bore therapeutic tattoos to alleviate ailments like sprains and joint pain—with three blue rings around their wrists or small cruciforms on their hands or body[18]—the true artistry and cultural depth of tattooing flourished in the markings of Li women. Each tattoo was a tribute to their heritage, with designs and motifs varying between Li tribes and even among families. These variations were not merely aesthetic but served as indelible identifiers, allowing one to trace a woman's lineage back to specific villages and clans with just a glance at her facial patterns.

The creation of these tattoos was a sacred ritual, beginning with the preparation of the ink itself. Tattoo pigments were derived from an alchemical mix of plants, including the charred seeds of the "castor oil plant" (*Ricinus communis*), castor bean plant (*Jatropha curcus*), coconut palm, and charred lentil greens. These ingredients were meticulously mixed with water and soot from the bottom of a cooking pot, transforming humble elements into a liquid capable of helping transport the soul into the afterlife.[19]

Before the first mark was made, the tattooist, revered as a spiritual conduit, would utter a solemn prayer to the ancestors. The air would be thick with the scent of offerings, as the tattooist invoked the protective spirits: "Oh [spirits of the] ancestors! We offer the pig's head; We offer honey wine; We offer rice. Eating and drinking have been arranged, these offerings are delicacies, and please enjoy! Today is an auspicious day, a descendant came to tattoo. Oh [spirits of the] ancestors, we ask you to bless us for success, we ask you to bless us for peace. We ask you to bless us for beauty!"

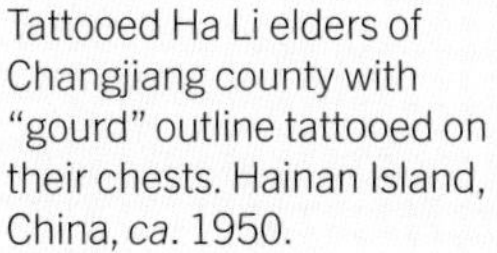

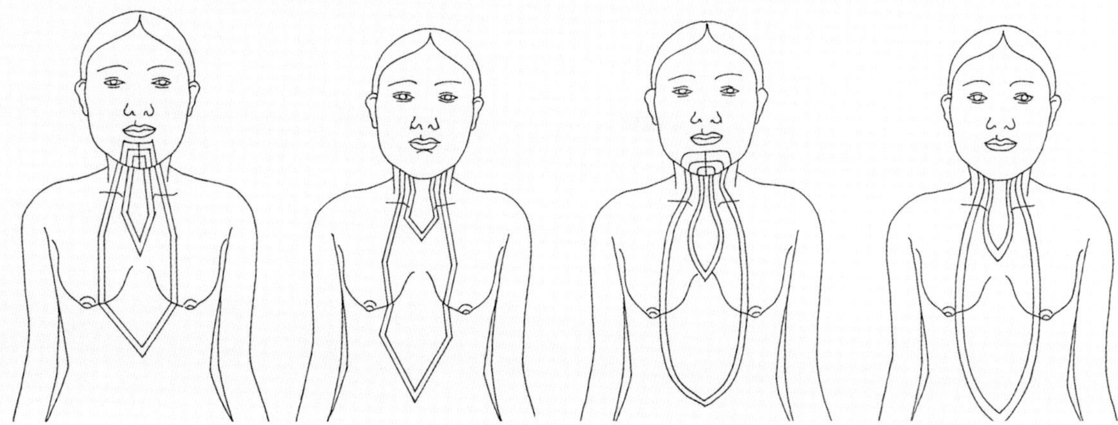

Tattooed Ha Li elders of Changjiang county with "gourd" outline tattooed on their chests. Hainan Island, China, *ca*. 1950.

Below Illustrations of Run Li women's tattooing for legs. Hainan Island, China, *ca*. 1932.

Below right Illustrations of Run Li women's tattooing for arms. Hainan Island, China, *ca*. 1932.

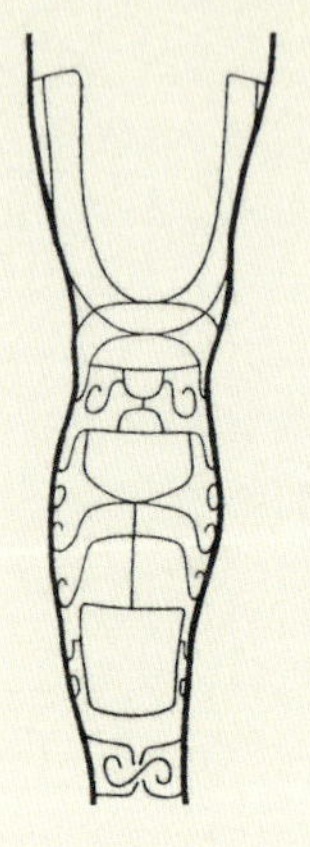

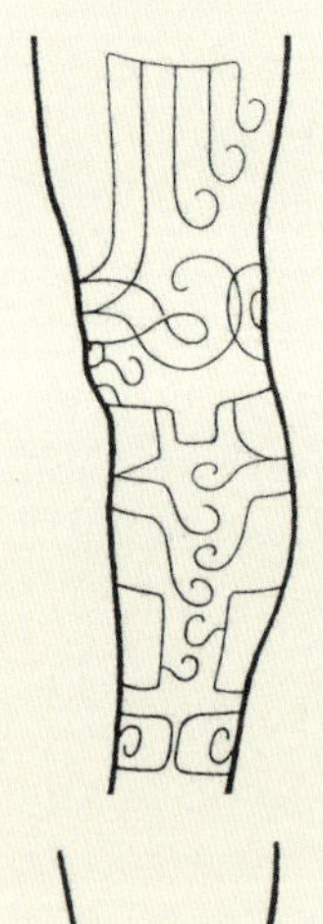

This ritual was much more than a mere formality; it was a deeply spiritual act that infused the tattoo with divine protection and ancestral blessings. Each mark was a prayer, a plea for prosperity, peace, and beauty, etched into the flesh with reverence and care.

In the animistic world of the Li people, tattooing was a powerful shield against the supernatural and a living tribute to cultural lore. Some Qi women bore branched cruciform-shaped "spider" tattoos on their knees, shins, or calves, to ensnare or ward off evil spirits.[20] For the Meifu and Run women, tattoos took the forms of frogs and turtles, emblazoned upon their arms, legs, and especially their chests. These amphibious and reptilian symbols were deeply embedded in Li cosmology, playing crucial roles in agricultural rites and weather prognostication. Frogs symbolized fertility and were revered for their remarkable reproductive success and were a prayer for many children and bountiful blessings. They were also admired for their mystical ability to summon rain. As creatures that transitioned between worlds—from tadpole to amphibian—they were believed to be "transporters of souls," guiding spirits between realms.[21] If a woman passed away without a frog tattoo, it was traced upon her body to ensure that she would be recognized by the ancestors in the afterlife.[22]

Although only traces of these captivating tattoos can be seen today, Ha women once proudly displayed an elaborate blend of anthropomorphic and figurative tattoos on their shins. Ha women also showcased intricate hand tattoos, where single, double, or quadruple concentric rings mingled with dots, circles, and coin-shaped motifs. These symbolic tattoos were sacred clan markers, interweaving the women's identities with their ancient lineage and cultural heritage.

Although women possessed frog, turtle, and anthropomorphic tattoos, oral history recounts that the origin of Li tattooing was in some way connected to beautiful birds: "The progenitor of the Li had a daughter, whose mother died shortly after the birth of this child. Whereupon a hoopoe bird (*Upupa epops*) fed the child with grains. In remembrance, the Li women still tattoo themselves in order to appear to be as colorful as birds. Perhaps, the tattoos should represent the pattern on the wings of the hoopoes."[23]

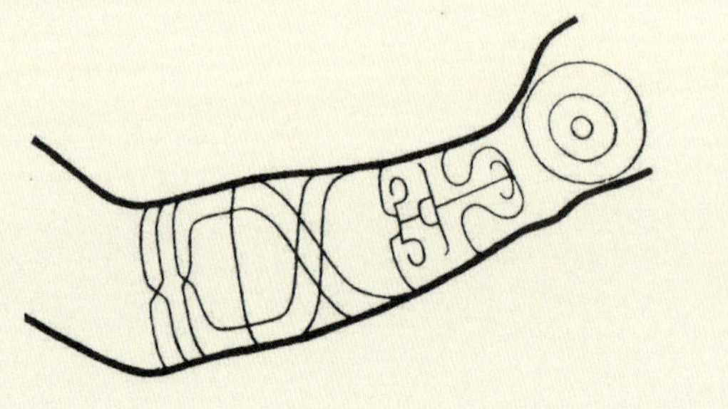

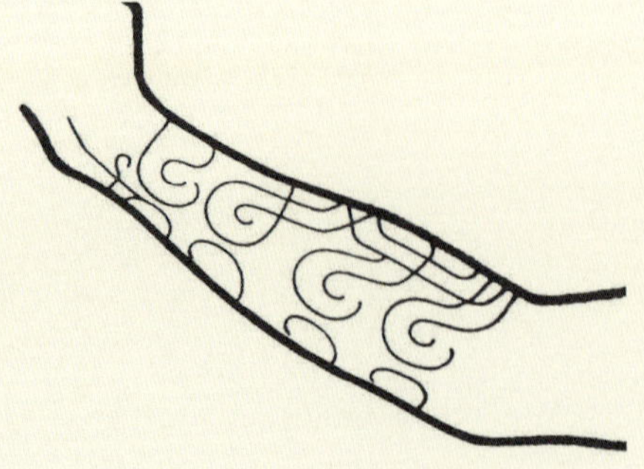

Tattooed Meifu elder of Changjian County with turtle motifs on shins, forearms, and chest. Hainan Island, China, 2010.

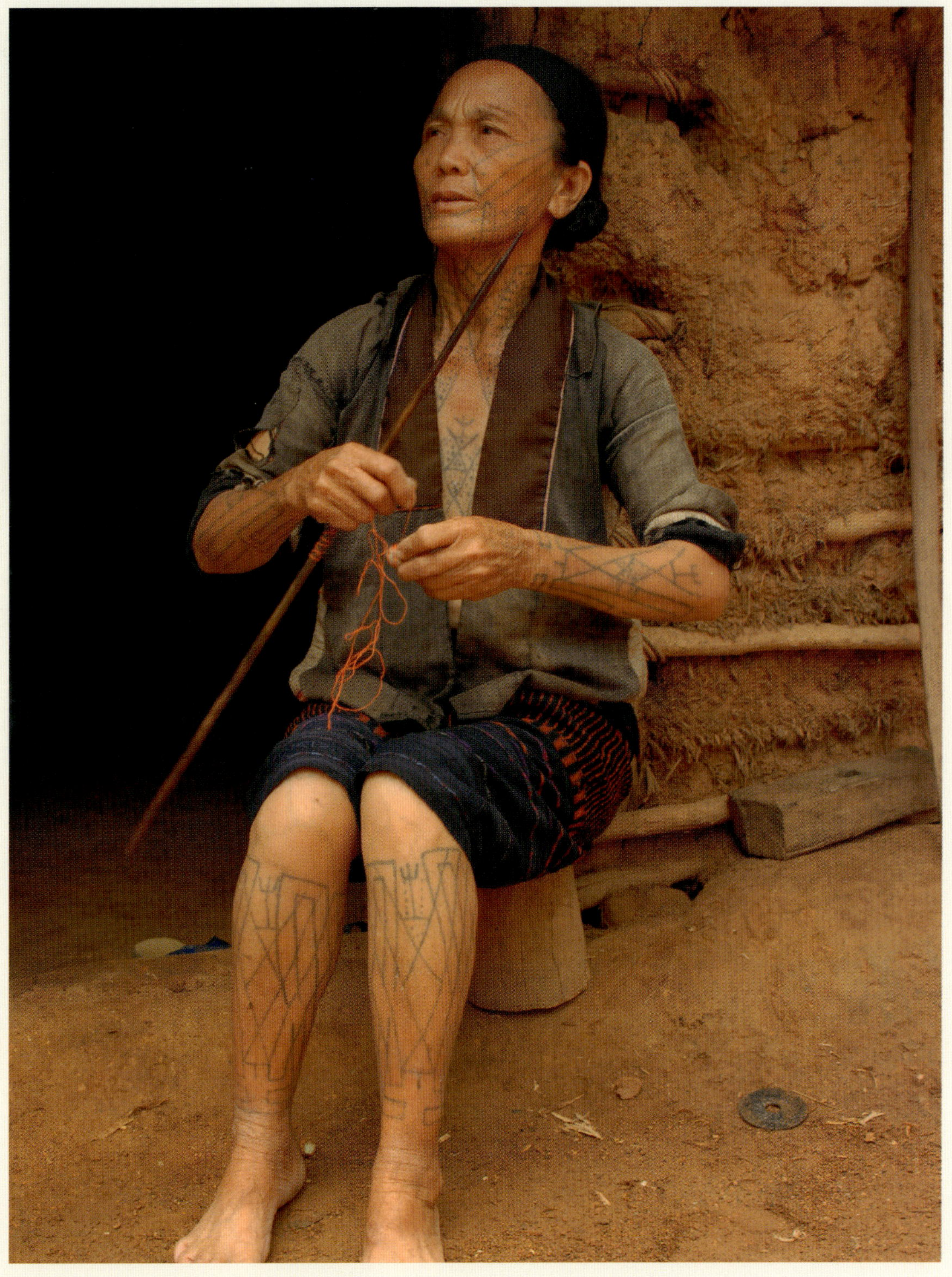

Tattooed Mummies of China and the Siberian Steppes

Since the late 1970s, hundreds of mummies with purported Caucasian features have been discovered in the Tarim Basin, northwest China, and some bear evidence of a highly evolved tattoo culture.

Although their origins have been obscured by time, recent DNA evidence suggests that these individuals represent an ancient Asian population that was genetically isolated, despite extensive cultural interactions in the region.[24]

From the standpoint of their tattooing, however, we know very little outside of the intricate designs adorning many of their desiccated bodies. This is partly due to lack of access to the tattooed mummies, lack of documentation in the press and scientific community, and perhaps even disinterest in the ancient tradition within China itself.

What is known is that some of the earliest tattoos date to the second century BCE and depict solar motifs and other designs on the backs of the hand and around the wrist. Not surprisingly, similar heliolatrous designs have been found at rock art sites across Central and South Asia, and on the horse bridles of neighboring nomadic pastoralists, including the Scythians who worshipped the sun and were heavily tattooed. Solar motifs also appear on the 3,800-year-old "Cherchen man" mummy from the Zaghunluq cemetery in the Tarim Basin, applied as body paint after he died.[25]

One 3,500-year-old blonde female mummy from the Tarim Basin is adorned with an incredibly intricate latticework of tattoos on the back of her hand, which some scholars believe is a form of text. Shaped like a backward "S" in series, and juxtaposed with other alphabetiform symbols, this indelible calligraphy resembles early Chinese characters. The ancient woman is also tattooed on her forehead with a series of circular designs that, to date, have not been deciphered.[26]

The Scythians, a primarily Indo-European people, were one of a number of tribes of early nomadic warrior horsemen (including the Sarmatians, Yuezhi, and Xiongnu) whose realm stretched across the steppes from Greece to Persia to China and southern Siberia and Mongolia between the ninth and second centuries BCE. Through tribal alliances and intermarriages with other groups, they encapsulated several ethnicities, but each tribe shared a common culture bred in the saddle.

At the beginning of the eighteenth century, Scythian grave-goods reached the Russian Imperial Court and were proof of a highly sophisticated culture where skilled craftspeople created complex works in gold, silver, and other precious materials. Then, in the early to mid-twentieth century, large barrows in the Pazyryk Valley of the Altai Mountains, which

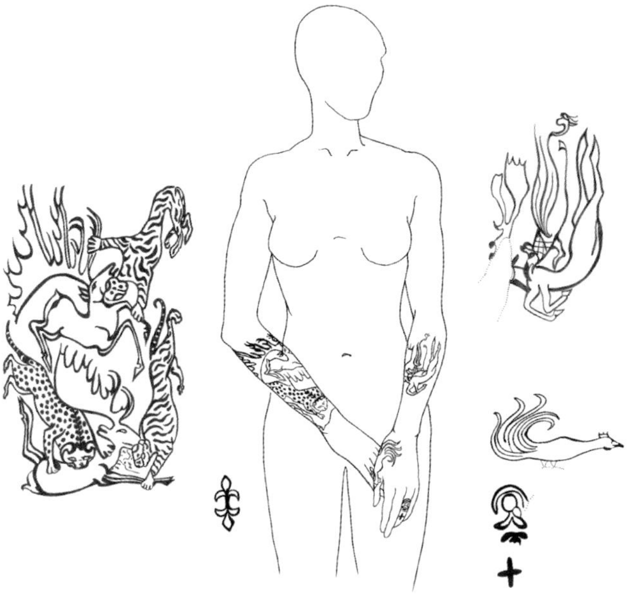

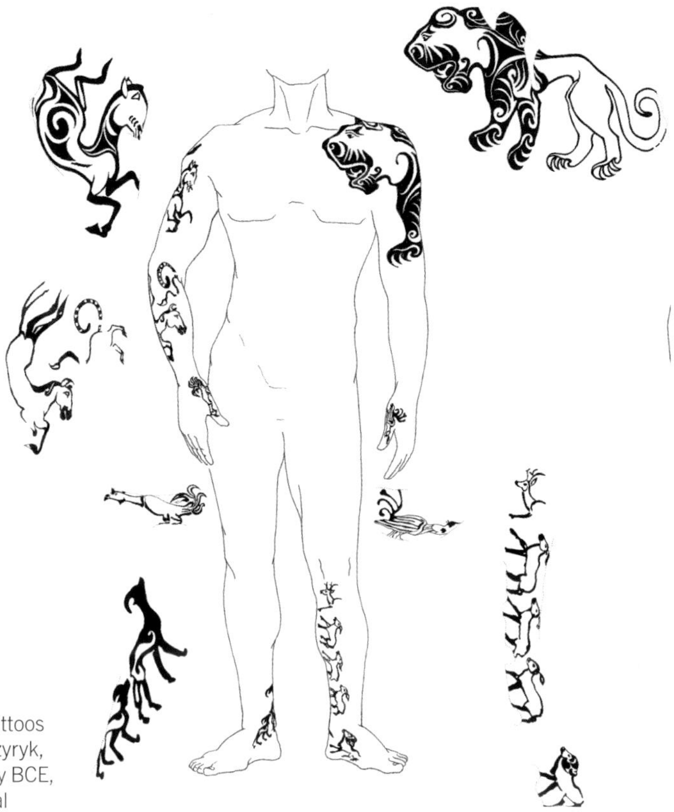

Above Tattoos of a Scythian noblewoman buried at Pazyryk, Russia,fourth century BCE, include a raptor, two tigers and a leopard attacking a deer.

Above right Tattoos on the body of a Pazyryk chieftain from Pazyryk, Russia, fourth century BCE, depict a feline predator, a horse, and birds.

Below Zoomorphic tattoos on a woman from Pazyryk, Russia, fourth century BCE, portray a mythological griffon and an argali sheep.

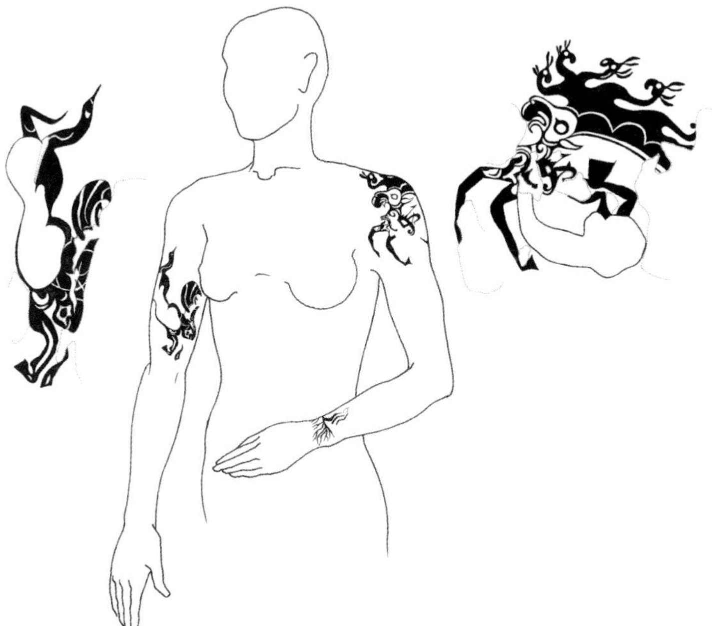

are situated about 450 miles (725 km) north of the Tarim Basin, were uncovered by Russian archaeologist Sergei Rudenko. The barrows contained the mummified bodies of heavily tattooed high-ranking individuals, including a high-ranking man whose torso and extremities were covered with a menagerie of zoomorphic images, including griffons, winged lions, and eagle-headed stags that mirrored the utilitarian art produced by his people. All the mummified Scythian bodies examined thus far display physical evidence of heavy falls, including this Pazyryk chieftain; a series of fourteen dotted tattoos appear on his lower back and six on his right ankle, which are suggestive of a medicinal therapy akin to acupuncture.[27]

Tattoos of the Li People of Hainan Island, China

For more than two decades, Hainan-based photographer Hu Yaling has embarked on a tireless journey across Li country, capturing the essence of their rich cultural heritage. Her lens has documented the beauty of their festivals and the distinctive elegance of their traditional dress. Yet, it is the tattooed elders of the Li people who have truly captured her heart and focus.

Yaling's extensive archive boasts hundreds of portraits of tattooed individuals. Despite her exhaustive efforts and numerous interviews with the elders about their tattoos, Yaling admits, "[t]hey have not been completely deciphered, and their meanings have not been clarified."[28] She emphasizes the need for more research to record these living tattoo symbols in detail, as Li tattooing has not been practiced for decades and is gradually fading away. "Thousands of years of ancient culture have left behind their memories on human skin, and this is what inspired me to photograph as many elders as possible," she explains.[29] Her work is not just a collection of images but a race against time to preserve the visual remnants of a profound cultural legacy.

In her portraits, the lines and patterns of the tattoos tell stories of identity, heritage, and tradition. Each mark is a fragment of history, a piece of a larger narrative that speaks of the Li people's connection to their ancestors and their way of life. Yaling's photography is a

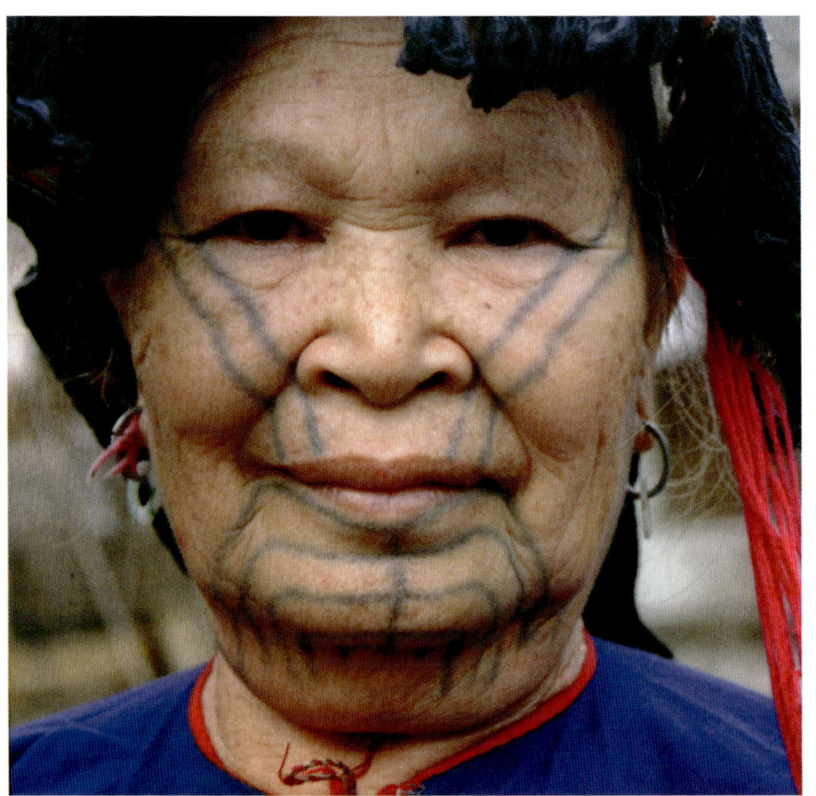

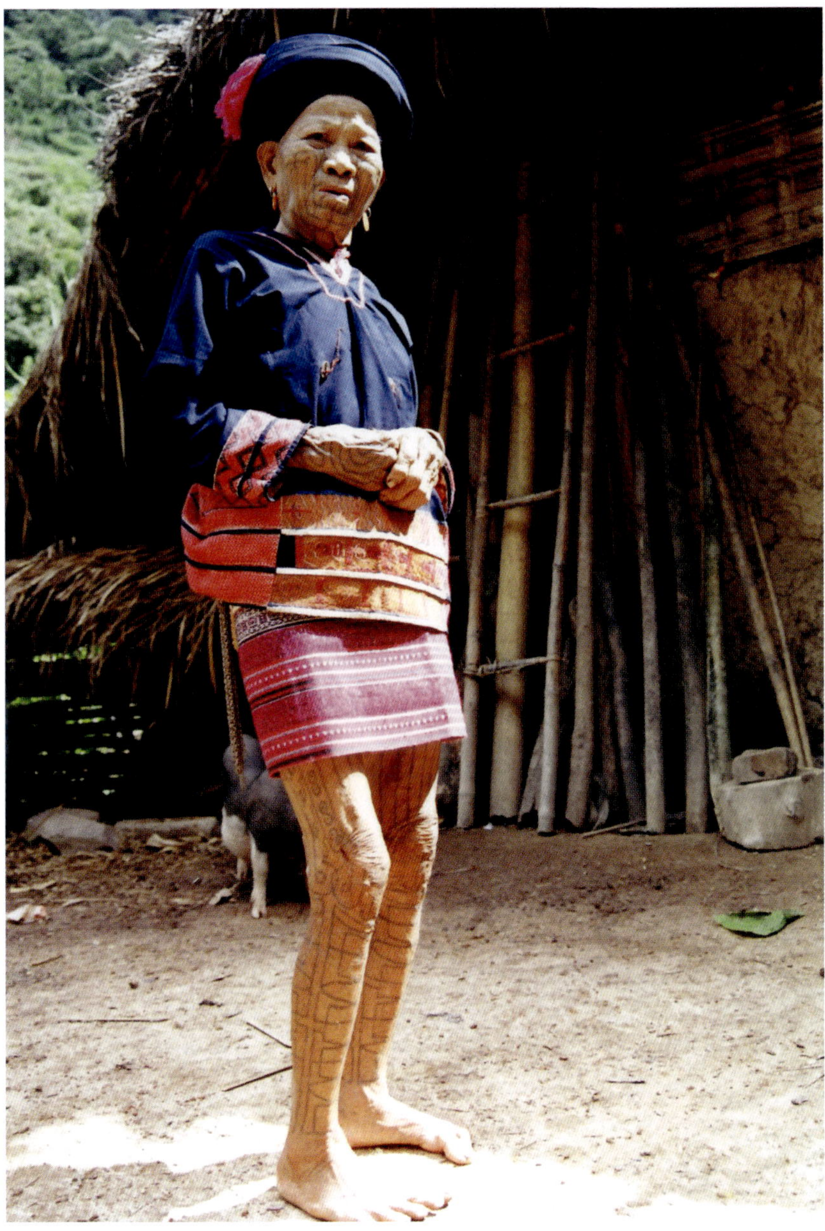

Opposite Tattooed Li woman of the Qi group, Jiaxi village, 2001.

Above Tattooed Run elder of Baisha County with hand and leg tattooing, 2001.

beacon, illuminating the intricate and often cryptic beauty of these tattoos, and calling for a deeper understanding and appreciation of this fading art. Through her lens, the world glimpses the indelible marks of time and culture, urging us to remember and honor the stories inscribed on the skin of the Li elders now and onward into the future.

To date there are very few English- or foreign-language monographs on the culture of the Li, let alone on their tattooing practices.[30] Notwithstanding, all Li groups (Qi, Ha, Run, Sai, and Meifu) tattooed,[31] and the practice was more common among women, although men received therapeutic tattoos (see page 229).[32] Additional male tattoos have been documented for the Run and Meifu, with the majority of these worn by Meifu men. Although many specific details were not provided, the meanings and motifs for Meifu men included tattoos depicting agricultural tools, tattoos for longevity,[33] and tattoos that enabled the ancestors to identify the bearer in the afterlife.

In the 1930s, Bernard Clark,[34] writing for *National Geographic* magazine, observed that a woman's tattoos in Li culture served as a detailed map of her village, social standing, and identity, much like the intricate patterns of their woven textiles. By the 1940s, interviews with Li women revealed that their tattoos were not just a mark of beauty but also a crucial means of ensuring recognition by their ancestors in the afterlife.[35]

Li tattoos were a rite of passage signaling a woman's eligibility for marriage, with all her tattoos completed before her betrothal. This significant milestone was traditionally celebrated with an elaborate puberty ceremony held in the village center. The actual tattooing took place during the cooler months of fall (October to December) within the privacy of the family home, with strict

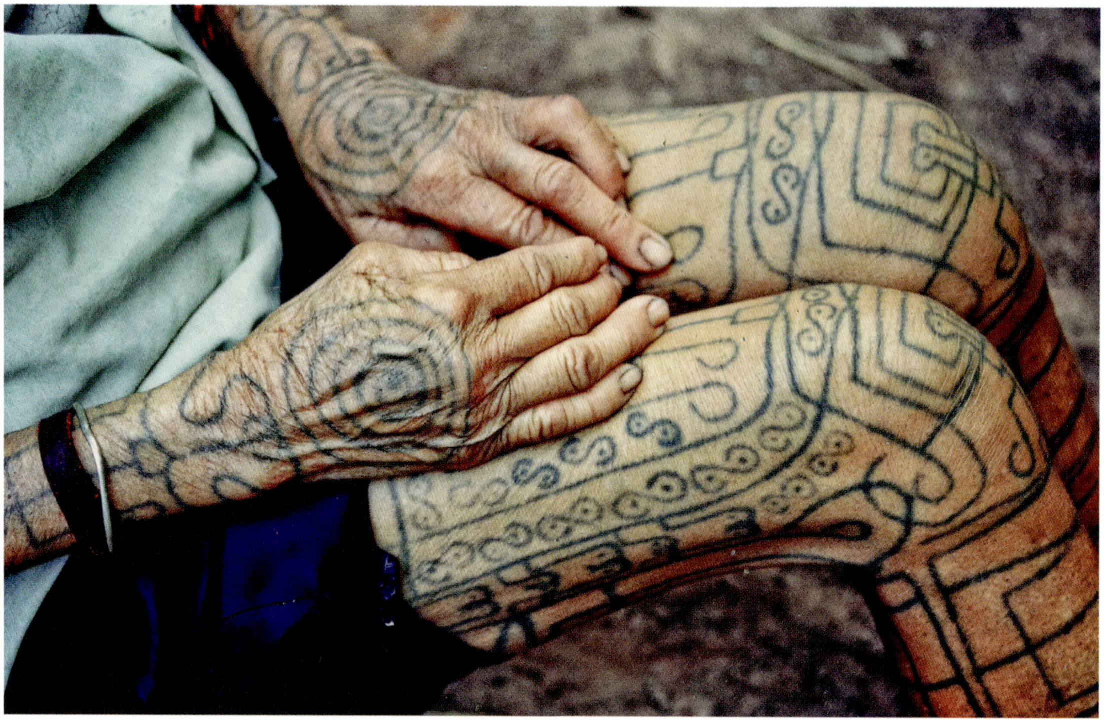

Close-up of Run leg and hand tattoos, Baisha County, 2001.

prohibitions on men viewing the process. Additionally, young women could not be tattooed during menstruation, adhering to cultural taboos.

Following the tattooing session, certain restrictions had to be observed: the newly tattooed girl remained secluded at home for a short period and was forbidden from eating papaya or pickled cabbage, to prevent her tattoos from becoming blurred (i.e., "blown out") or infected. The Li meticulously recorded time using twelve zodiac signs, distinguishing auspicious from inauspicious days. Tattooing was performed on one of three auspicious days (ox, pig, and dragon) during the week, preferably in the morning before noon when daylight was "strong" and "the human spirit was at its best."[36]

Before the tattooing began, intricate motifs were delicately stenciled onto the skin using a feather, twig, grass stem, string, or even a chopstick in some villages. The actual tattooing process was a precise and rhythmic art, where patterns were hand-tapped into the skin using one or more red or white rattan thorns, carefully chosen depending on the design. To ensure sharpness and prevent the thorns from drying out, the rattan stem holding them was soaked in water the day before the tattooing ritual.[37]

A transformative milestone awaited every Run teenage girl. At about the age of thirteen or fourteen, an elder woman, often unconnected by blood, would initiate a sacred rite of passage by first marking the nape of her neck. Over the next four or five days, the girl's face and throat would become a canvas for more intricate tattoos.[38] This metamorphic journey continued over the ensuing three years, with her chest, arms, legs, and thighs becoming gradually marked. If a family death occurred during this period, the tattooing

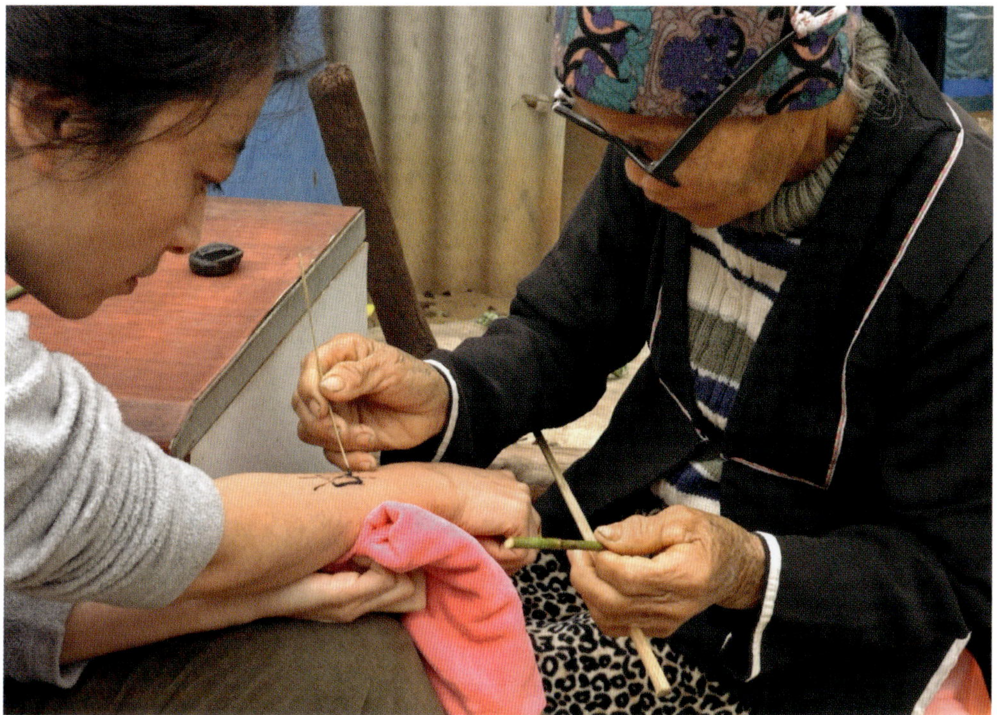

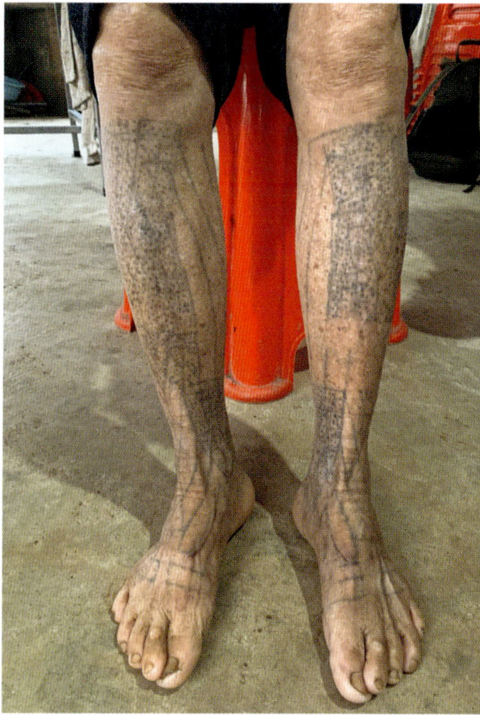

Above Nonagenarian Meifu Li tattoo artist Fu LianMei of Baobai village tattooing documentary filmmaker Emily Shen, 2022.

Above right Close-up photo of Meifu tattoo artist Fu LianMei's shins with frog and dotted motifs, 2001.

was paused until associated mortuary rituals were performed.

The Meifu people observed a similar processual practice to the Run, while the Ha and Qi groups developed a rather unique style of facial tattoos. This aesthetic featured pairs of lines just below or above the corners of the eyes, extending gracefully down the face to the throat. Subtle variations in these facial designs served as unique identifiers for specific villages and clans.

In the early 1940s, Japanese naval employee Kunio Odaka made a fascinating observation among the Qi people. He noted that if a woman married into another clan and passed away, her soul would embark on a spiritual journey back to her mother's home. There, her ancestors, recognizing her unique and intricate facial tattoos, would welcome her with open arms. These identifying marks served as a bridge between worlds, ensuring that the woman's soul found its rightful place among her kin.[39]

For the Ha, the tattoo lines extended down the torso, creating an intricate pattern across the breast and outlining an oval "gourd" motif around the sternum.[40] This design continued downward to the belly and encircled the navel.

For the Li people, each mark, each line, told a story of identity, lineage, and belonging. The tattoos were a living, breathing map of one's heritage, ensuring that even in death, the individual's spirit could be recognized and welcomed by their beloved ancestors.

Tamga Tattoos of Siberia

Numerous Indigenous nomadic cultures of Eurasia employed identifying emblems of a particular tribe, clan or family called *tamgas* through classical antiquity and the Middle Ages.

Tamgas perhaps evolved from simple animal brands and property marks into dynastic signs more than 2,000 years ago.[41] One of the earliest *tamgas*, a square jade ink stamp, dates to the Warring States Period in China (475–221 BCE) and was used by nomadic Xiongnu rulers as a seal of office.[42]

The Indigenous Nenets and Khanty of Siberia once applied *tamga* tattoos to their bodies, but according to archaeologist Sergei Rudenko (working at the beginning of the twentieth century) they began to disappear in the 1920s. *Tamga* tattoos were usually placed on the forearm, back of the hand, and legs and feet of men and women. A primary *tamga* mark represented the wagtail, or "soul carrier bird," which after death was believed to carry a person's soul to its proper place in the afterlife.[43]

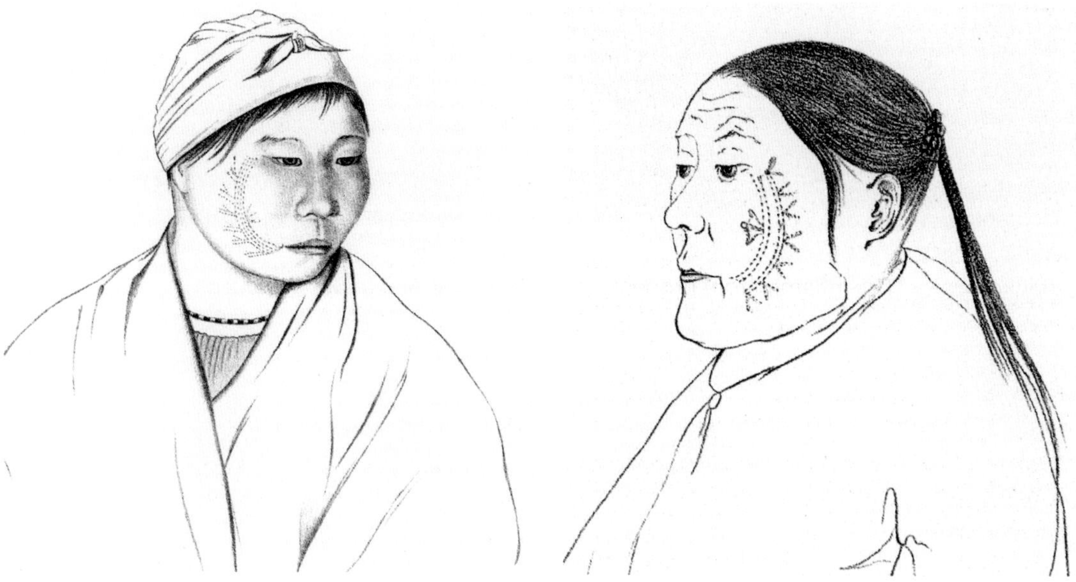

Facial tattooing of Tungus women, Siberia, *ca*. 1870.

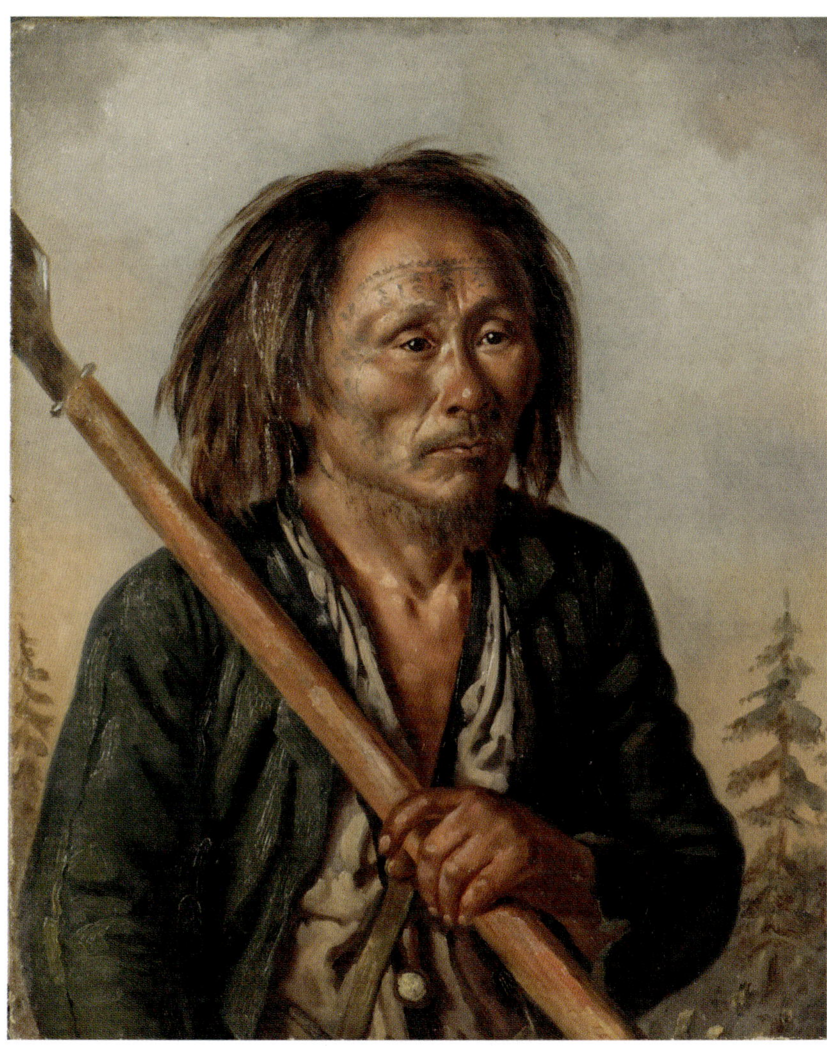

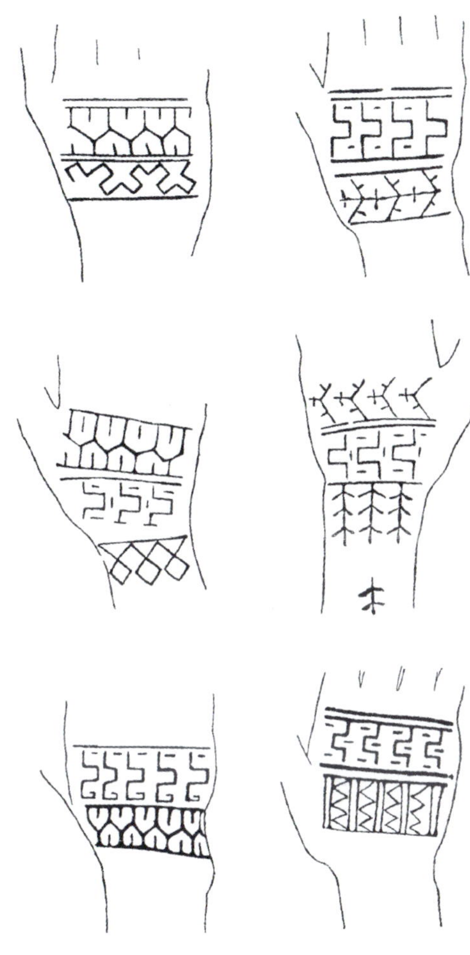

Above Portrait of a tattooed Tungus man, 1850. Painting by Carl Peter Mazer.

Above right Khanty (Ostyak) *tamgas* and other tattoo patterns for the hand, *ca.* 1920.

Apart from these markings, other Nenets and Khanty motifs were therapeutic, relieving rheumatism, aching joints, and broken limbs. Rudenko wrote: "The inflammatory process that accompanies tattoo, distracts the pain and even, in their opinion, heals. Therefore, we found tattoo more often in the area of the joints of the hands, less often shoulders and legs. Medical tattoos appeared in the form of a series of patterned bands," he explained, but some individuals also had *tamga* patterns hand-poked over the injured area.[44]

Earlier travelers to Siberia (during the middle and end of the nineteenth century), like the Russian biologist Nikolai Sorokin, Estonian zoologist Alexander Theodor von Middendorff, and German botanist Johann Georg Gmelin, also described "totemic" *tamga* tattooing among the Tungus and Yakuts that denoted the individual belonged to a certain family as well as medicinal tattooing for joint pain.[45]

Tattoos of Chukotka

The Chukotka Peninsula is the easternmost peninsula of Asia. The antiquity of tattooing here reaches back to 500 BCE, if not earlier. Objects of material culture, namely anthropomorphic ivory "dolls" of men and women produced by members of the Old Bering Sea, Punuk, and later cultures, bear tattoo patterns that were worn by several Indigenous peoples into the historic period.

Prior to the early twentieth century, tattooing was practiced by the Chukchi, Maritime Chukchi, Siberian Yupiit, and Kerek people of Chukotka and was most common among women.[46] As a general rule tattoo artists were respected elderly women because their extensive training as skin seamstresses (parkas, pants, boots, hide boat covers, mammal-skin tent covers, etc.) facilitated the need for precision when applying tattoos to human skin, especially since tattoos were usually stitched into the face, arms, and other body parts. Tattoo designs, which often delineated the tribal identity, clan, or family of the tattooed, were usually made freehand, but in some instances a rough outline was first sketched upon the area of application.

Tattooing an individual in the traditional manner required extensive knowledge of animal products, pigments, and natural substances suitable for indelible marking.[47] Lampblack or soot was the primary pigment used to darken the sinew thread for stitching because it was believed to be highly efficacious against "spirits."[48] However, fine dark graphite was also used, because it was considered to be the

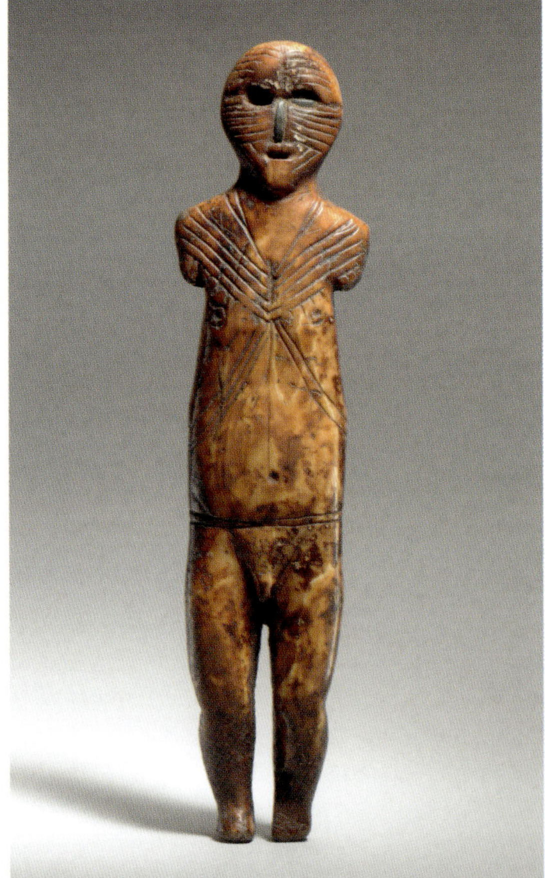

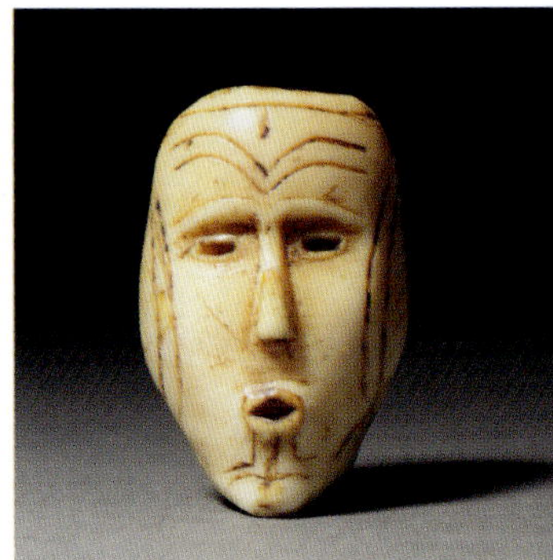

Above Punuk culture ivory doll head, St. Lawrence Island, Alaska, *ca*. 500-1000 CE.

Left Female Old Bering Sea ivory figurine with inlaid jade nose and eye and extensive facial tattooing, St. Lawrence Island, Alaska, *ca*. 100-300 CE.

Lantern slide of a Siberian Yupik woman skin-stitching her client on a polar bear skin at Ungaziq (Indian Point) village, Chukotka, 1901.

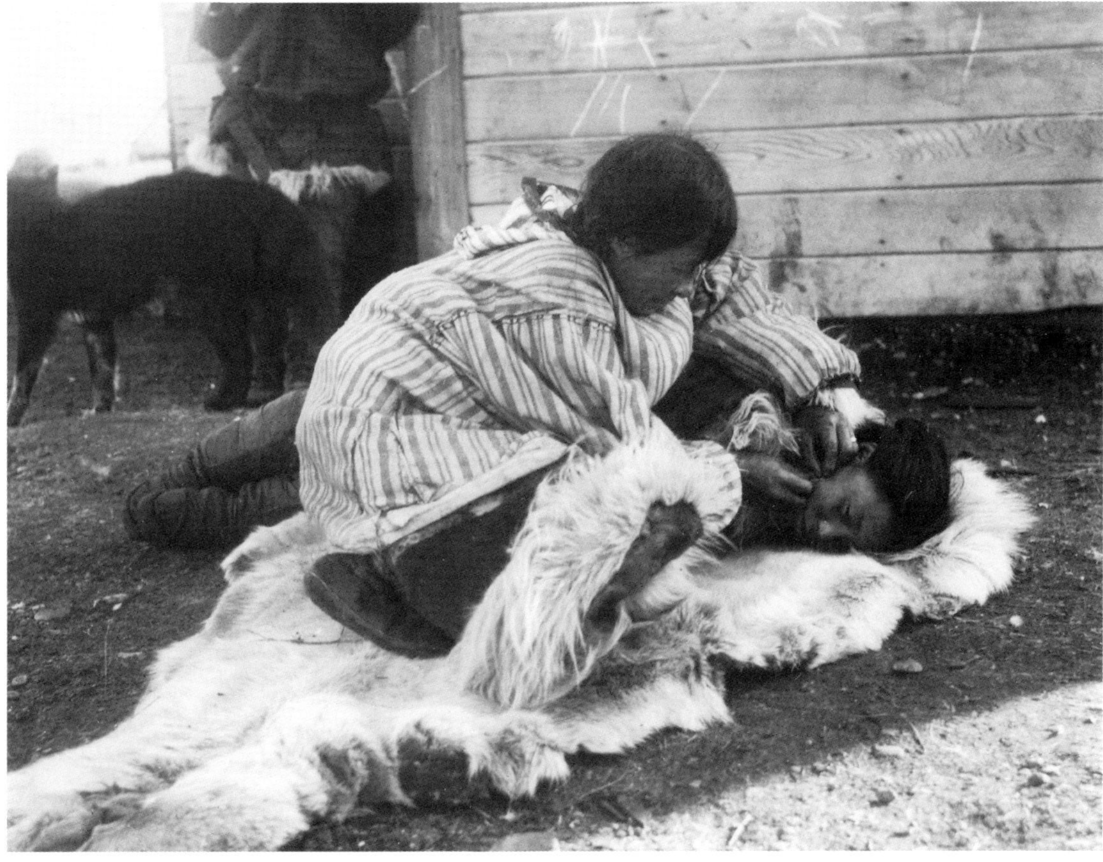

"stone spirit" that safeguarded humankind from evil spirits and the sicknesses they carried.[49] These black pigments were mixed with human urine because it was also believed to possess apotropaic properties. On a practical level, urine was utilized because of its high ammonia content, and helped reduce the scabbing of a new tattoo and promoted healing.[50]

Tattooing needles were originally made from slivers of bone, but with the arrival of trade goods in the eighteenth century the Indigenous coastal peoples of Chukotka began using steel needles, which were stored in a small bag of seal intestine. The sinew thread used for tattooing usually came from reindeer tendons and sometimes from the tendons of sea mammals, like bowhead or gray whales.[51]

Apart from clan and family patterns, prior to the arrival of missionaries in the late nineteenth century, tattoos carried other functions, including those related to spiritual concepts, therapeutic medicine, and markings that recorded individual life achievements. Among the Siberian Yupiit and their Yupik neighbors inhabiting St. Lawrence Island, Alaska, stick-like anthropomorphic forms of tattoo recalled an ancestral spiritual presence and could be understood to function as the conduit for a visiting spiritual entity to the world of the living.[52] These so-called "guardian" spirits (see page 57) could be harnessed by the possessor to protect them

Right Polly Apeyeka of Savoonga, St. Lawrence Island, Alaska, *ca*. 1930. Although illustrations exist, this is perhaps the only known photograph depicting *yugaaq* guardian tattoos.

Far right Tattooed Chukchi woman, Chukotka, 1901. She possessed three lines on each cheek that were believed to function as fertility charms and horseshoe-shaped tattoos near the corners of her mouth that altered her identity to confuse and repel the spirits of disease.

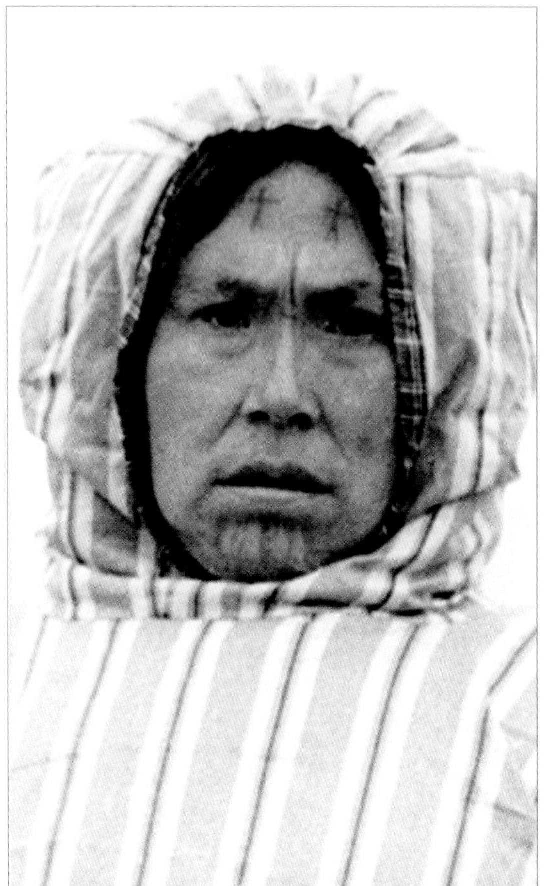

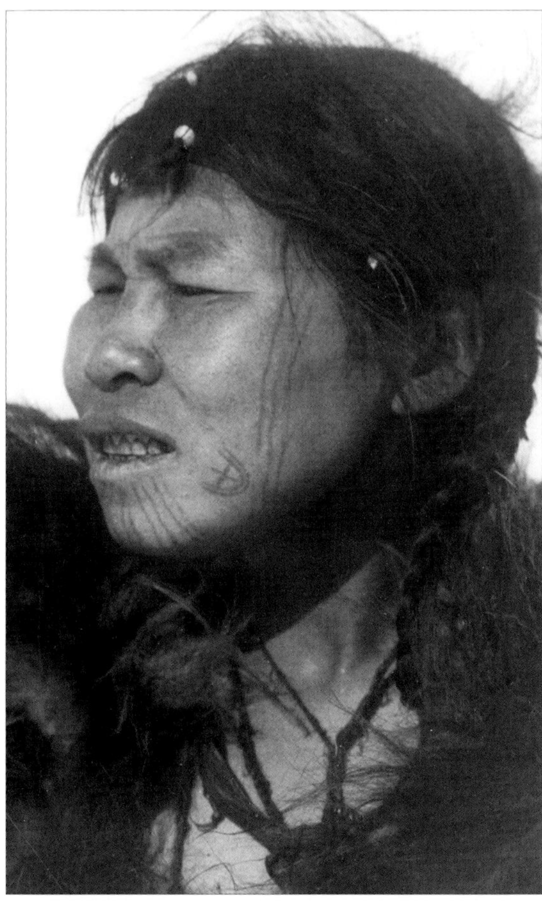

from evil spirits associated with land and sea, future disasters, the spirits of strangers (which were regarded as dangerous), the spirits of the dead, and the spirits associated with unknown areas where a person had not previously traveled.[53] Among the Chukchi, nineteenth-century writers described warriors who were tattooed with stick-like figures on their shoulders in the hopes of capturing the soul of their victim(s), thus transforming it into a kind of supernatural assistant "or even cause it to become part of himself."[54]

In coastal Chukotka and around Bering Strait, boys and girls were also variably marked by tattooists beneath the lip with circles or sometimes concentric lunettes, or at both corners of the mouth with angled cruciform elements to disguise the wearer from disease-bearing spirits.[55] Small squares in front of the ears indicated the wearer was subject to periodic headaches, which the marks were supposed to relieve. Various other tattoos might be placed across the seat of an injury to relieve joint pain, above or beside the eyes to treat vision problems, and other small marks over the sternum for heart or chest pain.[56]

Exceptional men were tattooed in Chukotka and Bering Strait for extreme feats of bravery in war and success in dispatching dangerous game animals, like polar bears and whales, which were considered equivalent to

Facial tattoos of St. Lawrence Island Yupik elder Anna Aghtuqaayak of Gambell village, Alaska, 1997.

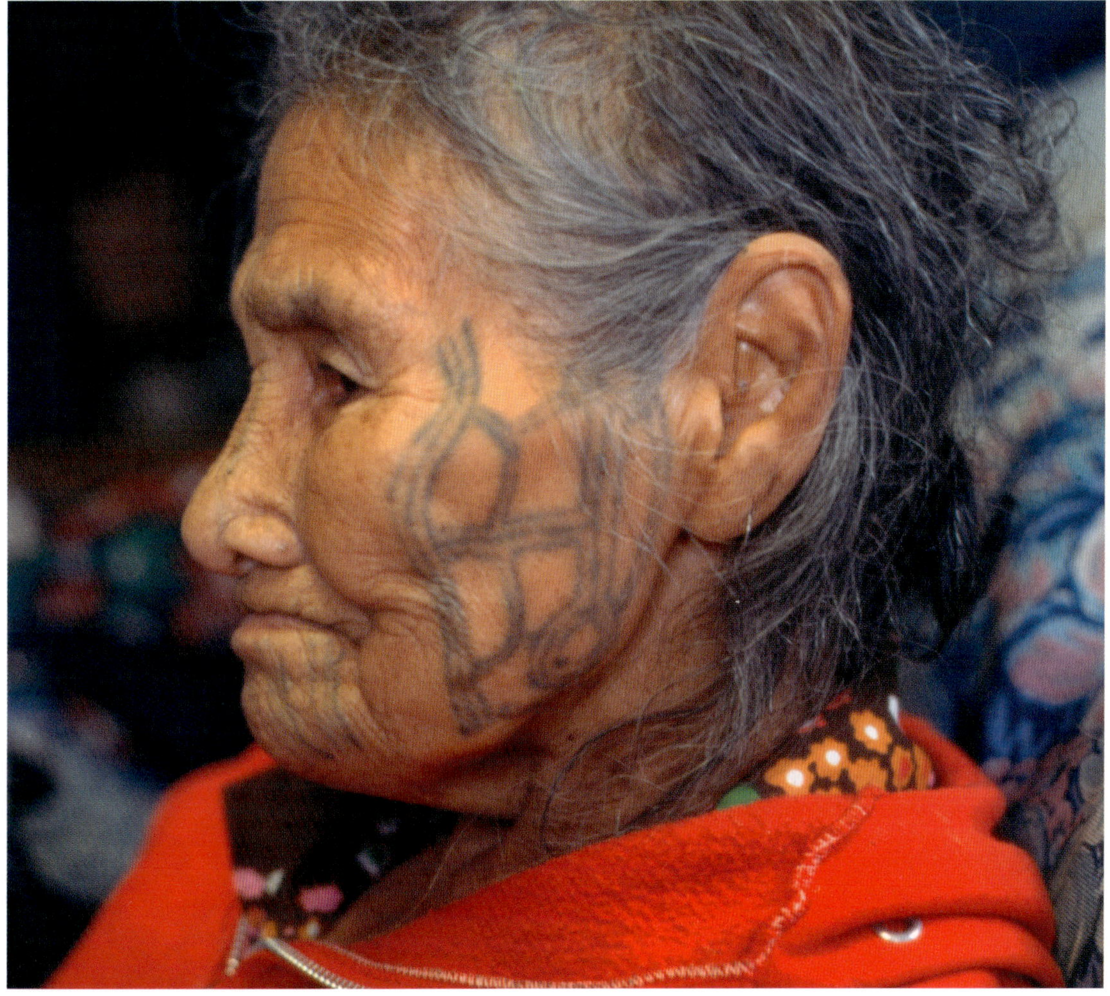

humans.[57] For example, Chukchi men received unspecified forms of facial tattooing "for an act of prowess or success, such as killing a bear, capturing a whale . . . and in war time for the death of an enemy."[58] In other areas around Bering Strait, successful warriors might possess two small lines over the bridge of the nose indicating they had killed another man.[59] Moreover, whaleboat captains and harpooners wore facial tattoos comprised of many indistinct lines or whale flukes at the corners of their mouths; the latter might also be shared by the wives and daughters of the hunter.[60] The former markings either resembled a broad band across each cheek from the corners of the mouth toward the ear or a tattooed line that began at the inner angle of the eye and moved downward across the cheek.[61] In both cases, a new line was added for every whale struck with the harpoon, and the markings formed a tally. Interestingly, each of these tattoo (tally) motifs, as well as marks crossing the bridge of the nose, are present on the faces of prehistoric male ivory figurines, demonstrating 2,000 or more years of continuity in Bering Strait tattooing practice.[62]

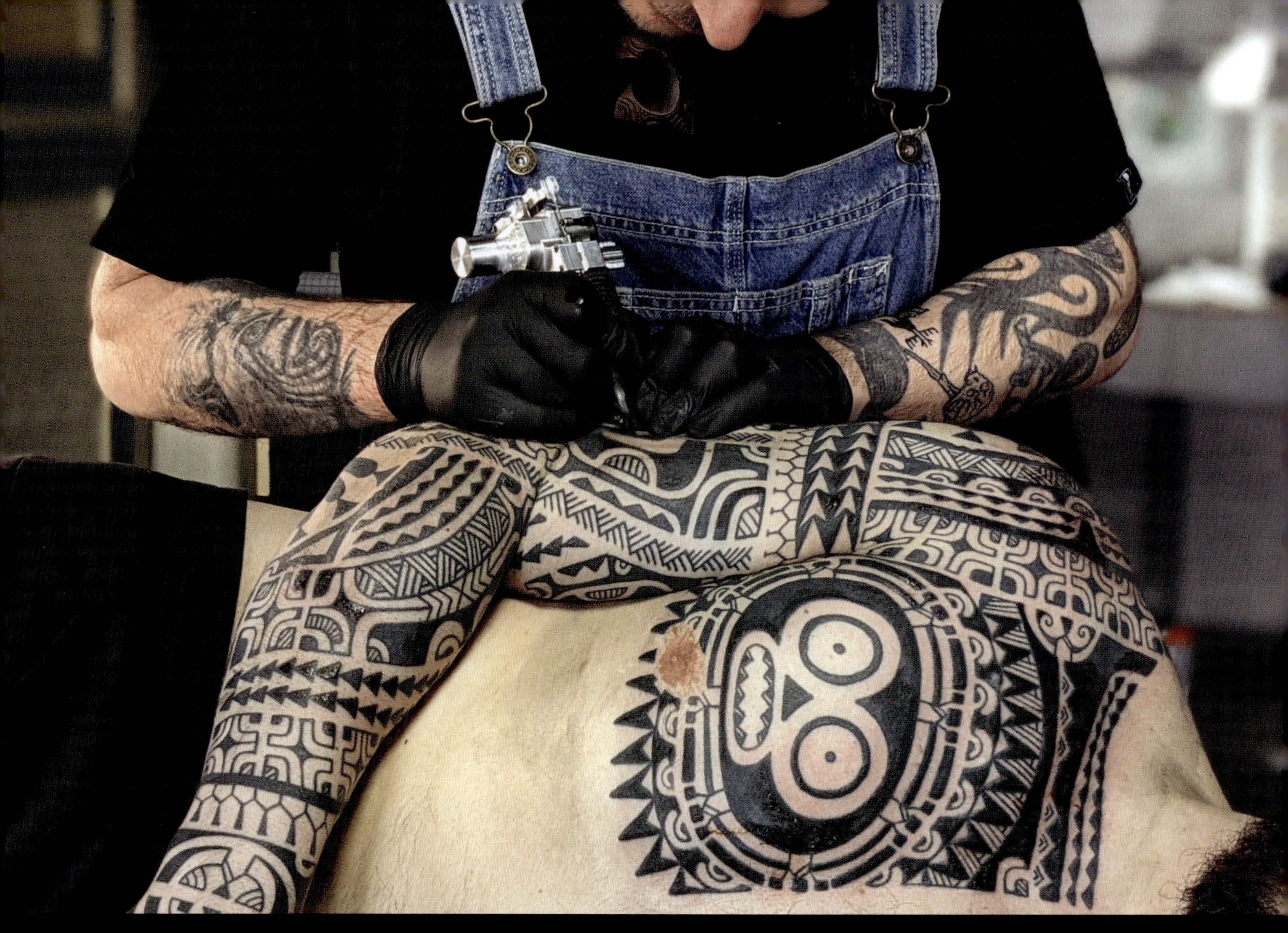

Dmitry Babakhin and the Chukchi Tattoo Revival

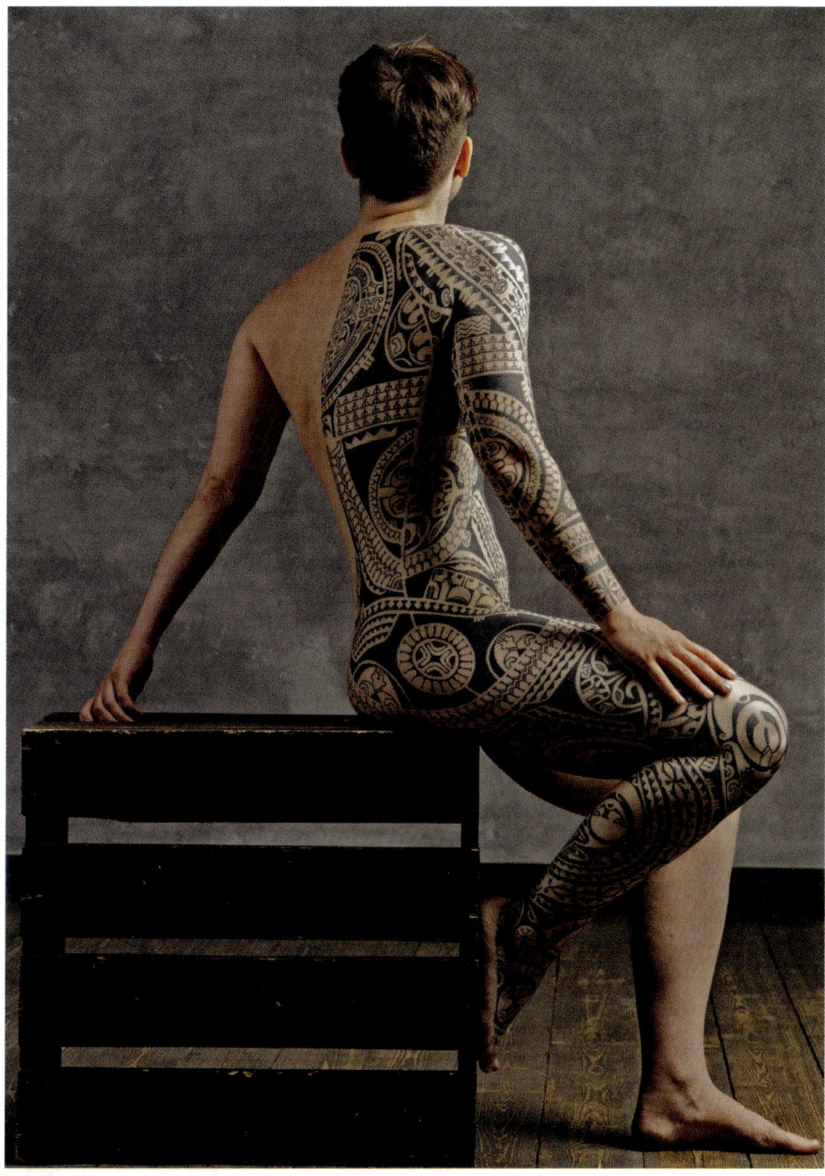

Opposite Dmitry Babakhin at work, St. Petersburg, 2023.

Above Marquesan-inspired full-body tattoos, 2019. By Dmitry Babakhin.

Currently based in Munich, Germany, Russian-born Dmitry Babakhin has been inspired by Polynesian and Indigenous tattoo cultures from an early age.

While in the Russian Navy he began tattooing clients onboard ships and was particularly drawn to the aesthetics of Polynesian and specifically Marquesan tattooing. Although St. Petersburg is far away from Polynesia, it is home to the Hermitage and Kunstkamera museums that house remarkable collections of Polynesian and Indigenous art, much of which was collected by Russian explorers and mariners who sailed to every corner of the habitable world. Babakhin also draws inspiration from his private collection of Polynesian objects, photographs, and rare books, which he acquires from art and antique dealers in Europe.

Although Babakhin does not create his customized tattoos through the traditional Polynesian hand-tapping technique, his artistry is highly acclaimed and his colleagues have voted him Artist of the Year for the Polynesian Tattoo Awards. Babakhin's expertise stems not only from his technical abilities but also from knowing how to read bodily contours and accentuate them with artistically rendered tribal blackwork patterns.

Recently, Babakhin was invited to help film a short documentary on the disappearing tradition of tattooing among the Chukchi who inhabit the farthest eastern point of Asia near the Bering Sea. Here, he captured several portraits of the last generation of Chukchi tattoo bearers who were all marked with needle-and-thread in the 1930s. About the same time, Chukchi language and literature instructor Zoya Toure, who was born in the village of Lorino on the Chukotka Peninsula and teaches at the Institute of the Peoples of the North (Институт Народов Севера) in St. Petersburg, was preparing a learning module

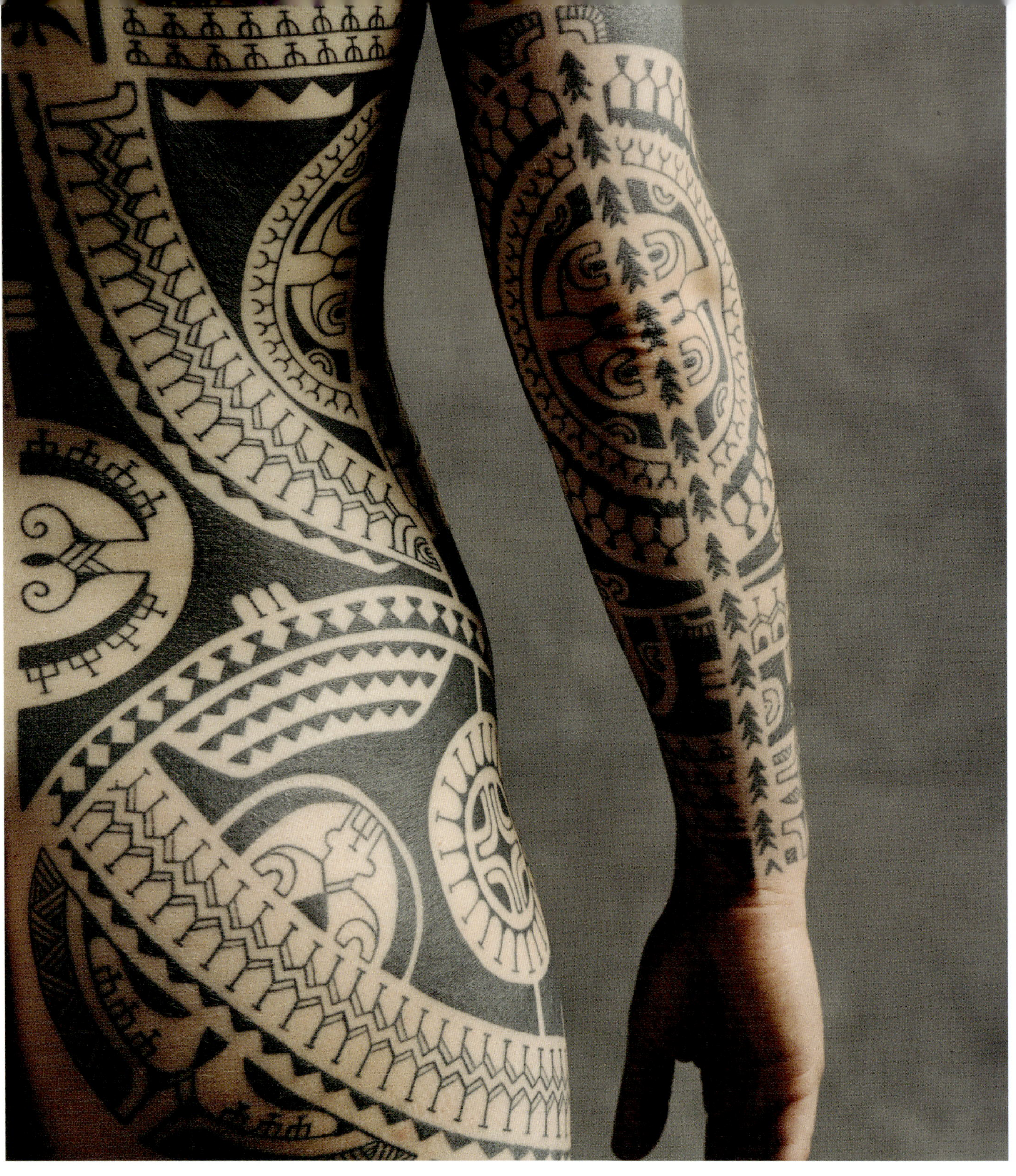

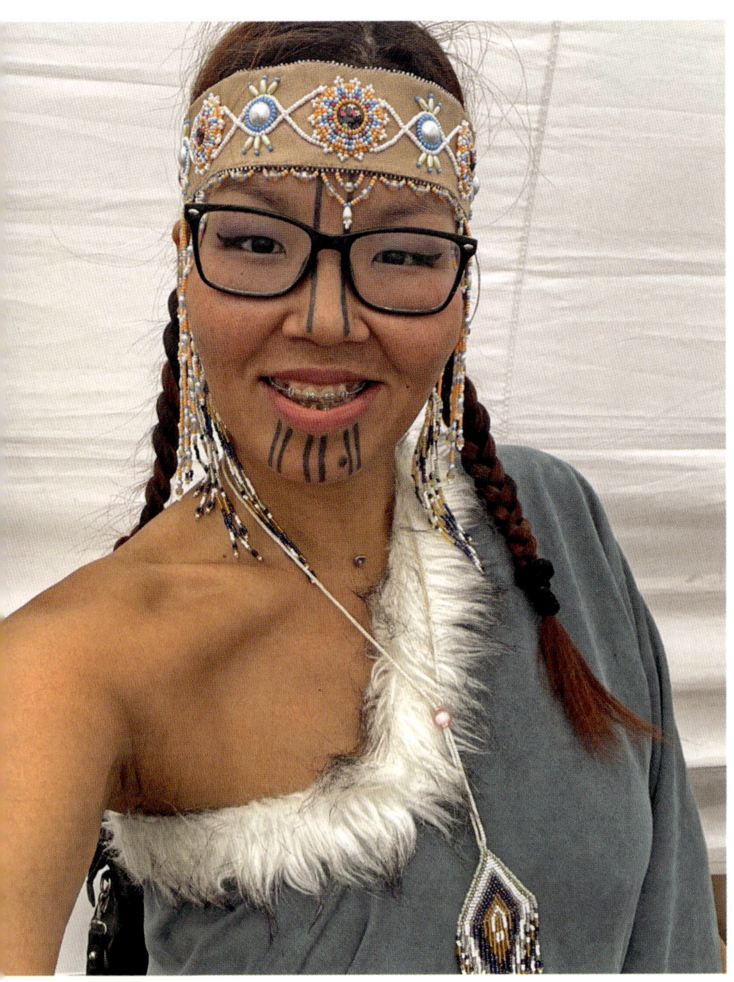

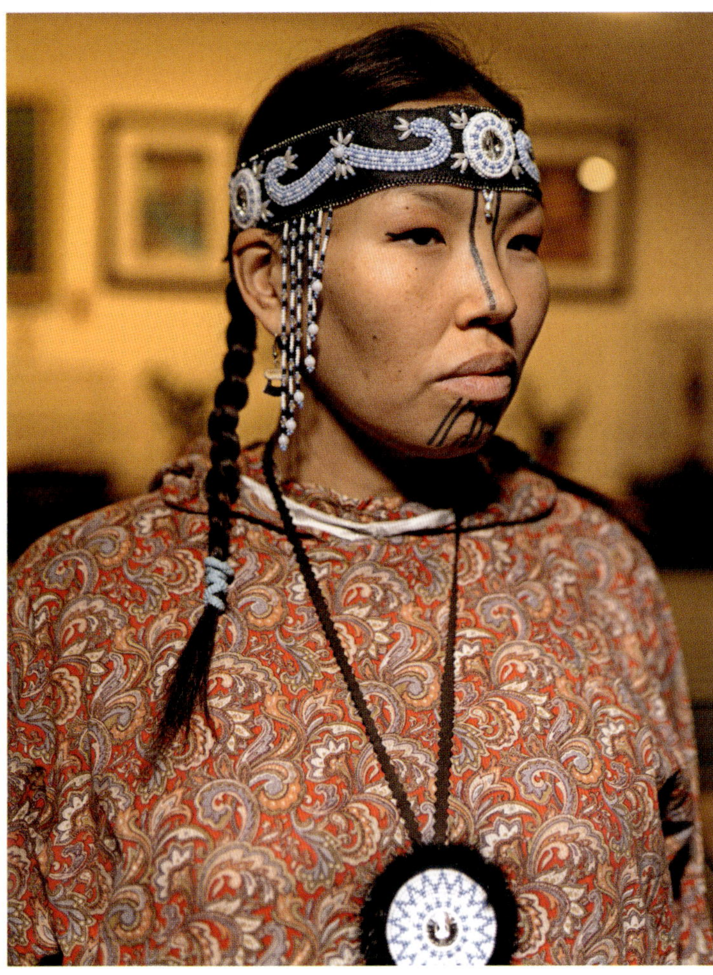

Opposite Marquesan-inspired full-body tattoo, 2019, by Dmitry Babakhin.

Above and above right Portraits of Zoya Toure with traditional Chukchi facial tattoos, 2023. Just before her birthday in September 2022, Toure decided it was time to receive the marks of her ancestors in Dmitry Babakhin's St. Petersburg studio and gallery *Mata Hoata*. These are the first Chukchi facial tattoos given in more than ninety years.

on her people's tattooing traditions for the Instagram page (@chukchi.language) she manages. In her research for this project, she came across Babakhin's tattooing work and was astonished that he happened to live in the same city.

As a child, Toure grew up with women from her grandmother's generation that possessed facial tattoos and she always had a desire to receive one herself, but her mother forbade it. "So my dream remained unfulfilled until I moved to St. Petersburg, began teaching at the university, and started speaking with Dima [Dmitry]," she says.[63]

"He told me, 'Only you can revive this tradition, and you will inspire your people!' And yes, this did influence my decision, but I also wanted to pay tribute to my Chukchi culture," she explains. "For me as a teacher, my tattoos allow me to tell others about my ancestors, my people, and how to be more present in the world. These tattoos also marked a transition in my life from one stage to the next, and now I truly feel I am stronger and more beautiful because they are a personification of my inner core, and permanently root me to my culture."

Conclusion

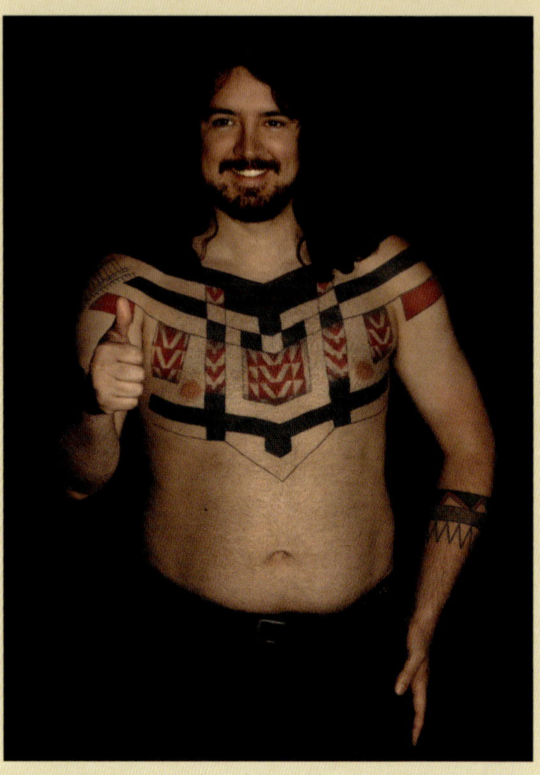

Cody Tolmie is a participant of the Nlaka'pamux *Blackwork Project* that seeks to embrace and revive the ancient tattooing practices of Interior Salish peoples. Tattooing by Dion Kaszas, 2022.

With *Indigenous Tattoo Traditions*, my intention was to open a window onto one of the world's most vibrant yet misinterpreted mediums of human expression. I have argued that this inscriptive practice can be understood as a kind of visual language, binding individuals to a collective history rendered corporeally on the skin. However, to consider Indigenous tattooing as a language-like practice requires us to decolonize our thought and engage with Native epistemologies of knowing, thinking, being, and especially writing itself.

The Akimel O'otham (Pima) writer Pauline Alvarez suggests that marking the skin with Indigenous tattoos is textual in nature because it "imprint[s] our knowledge on us. Reflected in the knowledge involved in tattooing are the immeasurable amounts of knowledge rooted in our connections to [our] land and communit[ies]"[1] – connections that are constantly evolving based on time and place.

Today, Indigenous tattoos encompass art, social activism, politics, media, and fashion, and allow individuals to reclaim and heal their bodies and selves while also helping to build communities and solidarity. For the Indigenous peoples featured in this book, tattoos have been and remain deeply integrated into social and cultural frameworks, expressing the stories, beliefs, ideas, knowledge, and aspirations of those who make and wear them. In essence, tattoos constitute an Indigenous epistemology, emphasizing the development of an individual through specific rites, protocols, and standards. Recounting the words of Māori scholar Ngahuia Te Awekotuku, skin marking is "about who we are, whom we come from, where we are going, and how we choose to get there. And it is about for always, forever."

For Nlaka'pamux tattoo artist Dion Kaszas and other contemporary Indigenous tattoo practitioners, tattooing also transforms the effects of colonization on Indigenous tattooing practices. As they work to reclaim the signs, values, and performances of their ancestral skin markings, they confront the past and themselves to celebrate what is achievable now and what is to come in the future. "Yes, we, as Indigenous peoples . . . have been through wave after wave of colonial attempts to erase us out of existence," writes Kaszas.

Josh Wikiriwhi's facial *tā moko* speaks to his roles in his community, as a teacher of the Māori language and as a martial artist in traditional Māori weaponry. He is a strong leader and role model among his Ngāti Whātua people. His *tā moko* is a reclamation of the art form and a revival of its social relevance in the modern world. Tattooing by Turumakina Duley, 2023.

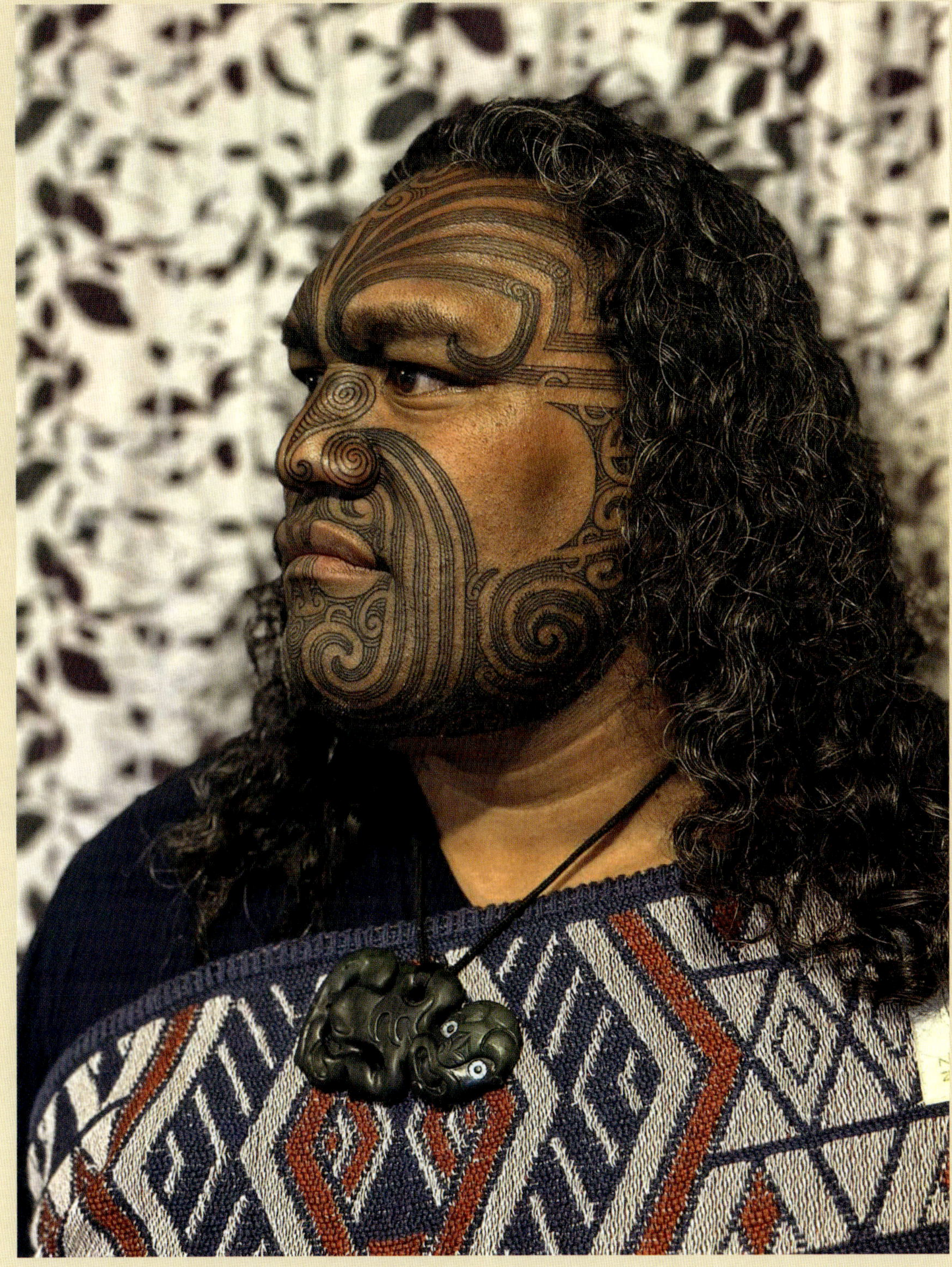

Stacey Fayant tattooing her daughter Lilla Fayant, 2024.

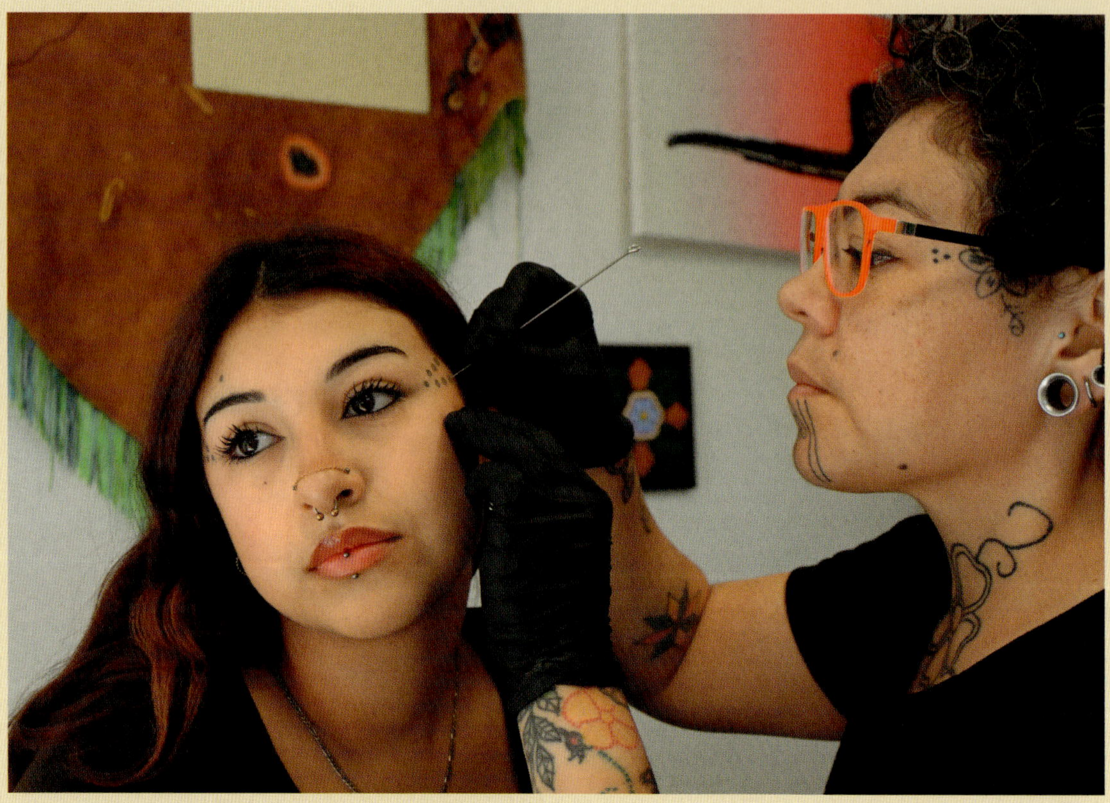

"Every embodied ancestral mark that I do reminds me that this work changes us. We are constantly reminded that we endured these traumatic events [and] as we continue to gain strength, confidence, and balance physically, mentally, emotionally, and spiritually, our tattoos will continue to be read as beacons of resilience of the ancestors who prayed us into existence."[2]

Indeed, the perseverance of Indigenous tattooing underscores the autonomy and self-determination of the men and women who create and receive tattoos today. The capacity to adapt, recover, survive, reclaim, transform, innovate, and reimagine reflects a legacy that I view as a language of continuity and resilience. Kaszas's brother-in-law, Wes Wilson, a member of the Nlaka'pamux community and photographer, shares his thoughts: "I think it's important for us to continue this history. It's like, we're [(re)]writing history on our skin, right? Wherever we go . . . we take that with us and we talk about it and we tell them what it means and how we did it. That's like our ancestors writing these stories on the rocks forever."[3]

From the hands of the ancestors to those at the forefront of contemporary tattooing practice, Indigenous tattoo making continues to be a tool for retaining and transmitting knowledge. It also enables bearers to be visible to other Indigenous people by asserting cultural pride and taking control of how they represent themselves to the world. In her self-published book *People With Face Tattoos Make Me Heal*, Métis, Nêhiyaw, and Salteaux

Right Mohorangi Peckham-Tukaokao bears a new *peha* (torso-to-thigh tattoo) that in ancestral times was part of a warrior's rite of passage and signified a warrior of rank. At once a *taonga* or highly prized possession, it fosters a connection to Māori *whenua* (land) and the *toto ariki* (chiefly bloodlines). Tattooing by Turumakina Duley, 2023.

Far right Mark of the Four Waves tribe member and tattoo artist Kristine Angeles wears hand-poked tattoos inspired by the Agusan Manobo people of Mindanao, the Philippines, 2023. She is one of the first individuals to bear neo-Manobo full-body tattoos. Tattooing by Elle Festin, 2024.

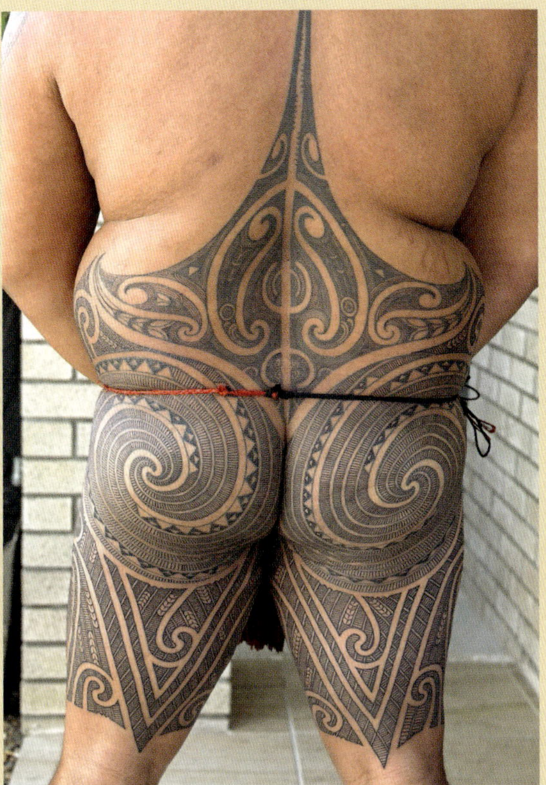

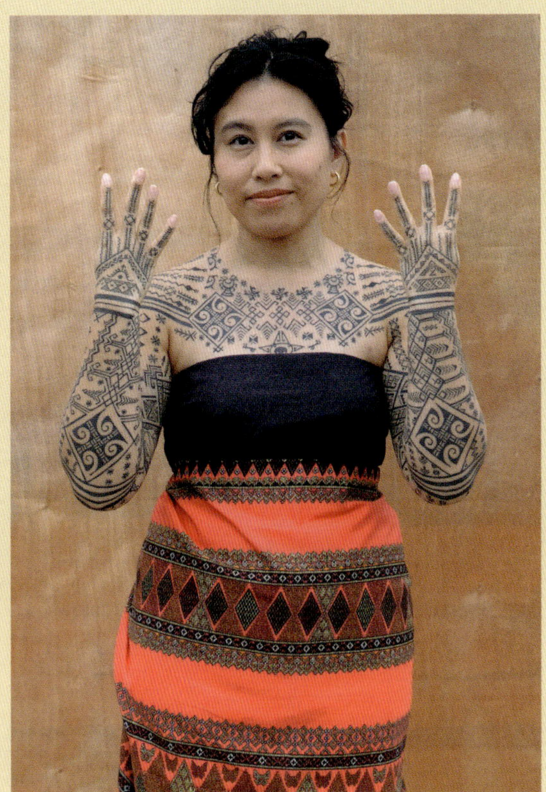

skin-marker Stacey Michelle Fayant reflects on how tattooing helped her reconnect with her true self: "These tattoos have not cured the trauma and racism I have encountered in my life, but they actively heal me, they heal me every day, every time someone sees them, every time I see myself in the mirror. These tattoos have shown me how to take back space, how to reach out and be present, be together with people. These tattoos are sacred, I am sacred."[4]

This book honors the accomplishments and contributions of Indigenous tattoo practitioners like Stacey, as well as past generations of tattooists, by celebrating their impact on the history and culture of tattooing. The significance of Indigenous tattoo art and practice cannot be overstated. These deeply felt practices are cultural expressions that highlight the great diversity of the world's artistic heritage and emphasize its importance. I have provided glimpses into both past and present generations of tattooing, showcasing a variety of cultural tattoo styles that embody traditional and contemporary strands of artistic innovation, inclusivity, community-based practices, and tattooing as a form of liberation.

As a narrative art form of the skin, and as an engagement with the body and the cultures it represents, Indigenous tattooing remains a compelling, visceral, visible, and textual reality that will continue to express complex identities and global histories of humanity for generations to come.

Endnotes

Introduction

1 More specifically, I am referencing the "Tattoo Pacific" column which appeared in the inaugural (1982) and subsequent issues.
2 Deter-Wolf and Krutak (2017).
3 Krutak (2007, 2013a, 2019a, 2020).
4 This term is derived from the Omaha and Osage languages.
5 Alvarsson (2012: 411, 413).
6 Tregear (1891: 486).
7 Te Awekotuku (1997).
8 van Gulik (1982: 188).
9 Batchelor (1901); Hilger (1971); Honda (2000); Krutak (2007); Munro (1963).
10 Ming-Chieh [Taligu] (2013: 13).
11 Ho (1960); Krutak (2024a).
12 Bachner (2014).
13 Reed (2000: 12, fn. 27).
14 Kaszas (2024); Krutak (2007, 2024a).
15 Some of these tools are quite ancient, including 2,700-year-old human and animal bone combs used for hand-tapping in Tonga (Clark and Langley, 2020).
16 Krutak (2016a: 73).
17 Krutak (2008).
18 Wardwell (1994: 212).

Chapter 1

1 Friedman (2017).
2 Deter-Wolf et al. (2016).
3 Austin and Gobeil (2017).
4 Cola Alberich (1949).
5 Kapchan (1993: 6–8); Searight (1984 II, 190–93).
6 Gobert (1956); Herber (1946); Legey (1926).
7 Searight (1984 II: 195, 235).
8 Bourdieu (1990: 246–47).
9 Searight (1984 II: 142–43).
10 Searight (1984 I: 67–68).
11 Gobert (1924: 63); Roth (1905: 130); Smeaton (1937).
12 Field (1958: 68).
13 Smeaton (1937: 54–55).
14 Smeaton (1937: 59–60).
15 Today, many tattooed Kurdish elders live in and around the town of Viranşehir, Turkey. Author Ahmet Yavuklu has captured the essence and beauty of these tattoos in his recent book (2021) *Ancient Footprints. Tattoo (Daq): History Engraved on the Body*. Several photographs from this work are presented in this chapter.
16 Field (1958).
17 Izady (1992: 249).
18 Field (1958: 19).
19 Cola Alberich (1949).
20 Field (1958: 19).
21 Krutak (2007, 2017a).
22 Mountain peoples of Dagestan continue to bear similar tattoos that had perceived healing properties, enhanced female fertility, and marked rites of passage (Chenciner et al. 2006).
23 Durham (1929: 104); Krutak (2007: 46; 2017a: 151).
24 Laukien (2001: 26); Truhelka (1896).
25 Turalija (2011).
26 Durham (1929: 104); Truhelka (1896: 497).
27 Beckwith (1983: 508).
28 Beckwith (1983: 509).
29 Bovin (2001).
30 Fisch (1991/92); Young (1967: 11).
31 Fisch (1991/92: 63).
32 Fisch (1991/92: 51).
33 Köhler (1973: 226).
34 Bleek (1929: 114).
35 Krutak (2008).
36 Throughout this text, drawings and diagrams have been used in place of documentary photographs of mummified remains, out of respect for the subjects and communities from which they originate.
37 Friedman (2017); Friedman et al. (2018).
38 Petrie (1930: pl. 24).
39 Morris (2011: 83, fig. 5).
40 Morris (2011: 74).
41 Anokhina (2020: 36); Morris (2011: 82–83).
42 To see a color photograph of this object, please visit: https://pushkinmuseum.art/data/fonds/ancient_east/1_1_a/1_1_a_3627/index.php?lang=en.
43 Anokhina (2020: 36).
44 Lotus blossoms have been documented as graffiti on the floor of the Hathor temple at Deir el-Medina (Austin and Gobeil, 2017: 32), and a singular bloom appears as a "tattoo" on the back of the neck of a painted Middle Kingdom ceramic female figurine from Lisht (Keimer 1948, pl. XIV, no. 2). This sculpture bears a series of diamond-shaped lozenge patterns across its abdomen, thighs, and buttocks, characteristic of tattoos found on mummified human remains.
45 Strandberg (2009:134–35, 138–40).
46 A New Kingdom fresco from Deir el-Medina portrays a nude dancing woman bearing only a necklace and two Bes figures painted in blue-black on her thighs (see Vandier d'Abbadie, 1938: pl. III).
47 Austin and Arnette (2022). In this article, the authors reveal that a previously undescribed New Kingdom female mummy from the Deir el-Medina site bears a partially preserved composite symmetrical tattoo on its lower back (i.e., waistline) that includes two standing Bes figures.
48 Collection of the Rijksmuseum van Oudheden (AD 14).
49 Collection of the Brooklyn Museum (60.27.1).
50 Dasen (1993).
51 Drewal (1988: 84).
52 Ibid.
53 Ibid.
54 Drewal (1988: 88).
55 Faleti (1977: 24–25).
56 Prince (1960: 73).
57 Drewal (1988: 96, fn. 4).
58 Sabater i Pi and Sabater i Coca (1992: 243).
59 Sabater i Pi and Sabater i Coca (1992: 240).
60 Tessmann (1913: 199).
61 Tessmann (1913: 199–200).
62 Tessmann (1913: 200).
63 Sabater i Pi and Sabater i Coca (1992: 245).
64 Trilles (1912: 618).
65 Trilles (1912: 621).
66 Yavuklu (2021: n.p.).
67 The interview material presented here is based on personal communications with the artist in August 2023.
68 The interview material presented here is based on personal communications with the artist in August 2023.
69 Renault (2017).
70 Durham (1929); Petrić (1973, 1976); Truhelka (1896).

Chapter 2

1 Due to editorial considerations and space constraints, many Native North American Tribal Nations have been excluded from this chapter. For more information, please see Krutak (2014a).
2 Therapeutic tattoos typically consisted of small marks placed at bodily joints or beside the eyes to help cure vision problems (see Krutak, 2019a).
3 Krutak (2007, 2009).
4 Gifford (1933: 277).
5 Taylor and Wallace (1947: 5). The Halchidhoma of Arizona also maintained a similar belief (see

Spier 1933: 102).

6 Krutak (2013b: 161).

7 La Flesche (1939: 138, 395).

8 This "pointed" star is the Morning Star, and "its use is said to be of some help to the wearer, through the supernatural power of the star itself" (Skinner 1926: 269). When personified complimentary pairs of visible bodies like the sun (male) and stars (female) were combined together in ritual practices like tattooing, a procreative relationship was implied. See Krutak (2013b) for a detailed look into Great Plains tattooing practices, symbolic associations, and cosmological implications.

9 Fletcher and La Flesche (1911: 505); Rice (1988: 105–106).

10 Fortune (1932: 148).

11 Fletcher and La Flesche (1911: 203).

12 Whitman (1937: 73).

13 Whitman (1937: 73–74, fn. 3).

14 Bailey (2010); Skinner (1915a).

15 Kinietz (1965: 251–253).

16 For a more thorough discussion of Pacific Northwest guardian spirits and guardian tattoos please see Krutak (2012). For information on the *manitou* complex and associated tattooing traditions of the Great Lakes and Eastern Woodlands see Krutak (2013c).

17 Kinietz (1965: 289).

18 Krutak (2013c).

19 Krutak (2013c: 115).

20 Krutak (2013c).

21 See Krutak (2013c: 103) and Meachum (2007: 68).

22 Other Northwest Coast tribal peoples tattooed crests upon their bodies, but due to space constraints I only focus on the Haida and Tlingit.

23 Historic Haida and Tlingit tattooing tools resemble miniature versions of Japanese *tebori* hand-poking tools. However, the old Tlingit term for tattooing is *kuy-kay-chul*, meaning "sewing on the body" (Emmons 1991: 254).

24 During times of war, crest objects were frequently alienated and were sometimes forcefully taken to satisfy a liability. In other instances, crests were simply exchanged with a rival group in payment of a lingering debt.

25 Crests tattoos were also embodied with sympathetic magic. One Haida woman interviewed in 1860 told a naval officer: "a halibut [crest], laid open with the face of the chief of her tribe drawn on the tail, would protect her and her kin from drowning at sea" (Poole 1872: 311).

26 Krutak (2007: 141).

27 Olson (1967: 69).

28 Krutak (2013b: 113, 149, 157).

29 Skinner (1915b: 754).

30 Skinner (1915b: 753).

31 Bowers (1965: 280).

32 Denig (1930: 592).

33 La Flesche (1921: 208).

34 Krutak (2013b: 157).

35 Tattoos on the Great Plains were created by men who wielded sacred tattoo bundles. For an in-depth study of these supernaturally charged objects, see Krutak (2013b).

36 La Flesche (1921: 248–249).

37 Deter-Wolf et al. (2021); Gillreath-Brown et al. (2019).

38 Densmore (1928); Hilger (1960); Hoffman (1888); Krutak (1999, 2013a, 2014a, 2016a, 2018); Piombino-Mascali and Krutak (2020); Skinner (1921); Smith (1923).

39 Skinner (1926: 270); Swan (1886: 72–73).

40 Krutak (2013b, 2014a).

41 Krutak (2014a); La Flesche (1916: 281).

42 Krutak (2013b, 2014a: 153–63).

43 Krutak (2017c); VanStone (1959: 20–21).

44 St. Lawrence Island men and women typically wore stick-like *yugaaq* tattoos on their foreheads, although they were also applied to the hands, neck, or aching joints (Krutak 2019a: 105). They represented a powerful ancestor or other sentient being who protected the possessor from evil spirits associated with the land and sea, the spirits of the evil dead, evil spirits associated with unknown areas where one had not previously traveled, and spirits who plagued humankind with disorders of the nervous system, among other ailments (e.g., rheumatism) (Krutak 2017c: 275–76; 2019a: 105). The *yugaaq* of a new mother was also believed to protect infants from evil influences. For illustrations and photographic imagery of these tattoos, see Bogoras (1904–909: 343) and Krutak (2014a: 35, figs. 37–38, 2019a: 275, fig. 18.5).

45 Tein (1994: 119).

46 cf. Tein (1994: 119).

47 Collins (1930: 130).

48 VanStone (1959: 20).

49 Geist and Rainey (1936: 34).

50 Collins (n.d.: n.p.).

51 Keim (1969: 143–44).

52 Krutak (2014a: 21–28).

53 Krutak (2017c).

54 Krutak (2009: 203).

55 Hollowell (2009: 281).

56 Linn and Lee (1999: 15).

57 St. Lawrence Island Yupik men who survived dangerous events while hunting (i.e., stranded on ice flows) recounted they were tattooed with anthropomorphic stick-like figurines on their bodies, presumably to give thanks to ancestral personages who saved their lives (Moore 1923: 345). Regarding charm belts, Chukchi men in Siberia continue to employ them today and they are called *ka'mak'-lu'u* ("wooden face"); the Koryak also used these "spirit faces" (Bogoras 1904–909: 341). Chukchi men say they provide them with the body or appearance of an evil spirit (*kele*, pl. *ke'let*). In turn, the latter recognizes the charm holder as a fellow spirit and leaves them unmolested (see Krutak 2019a: 105–107).

58 Bogoras (1904–909: 341; 353–56).

59 Tein (1994: 121).

60 Krutak (2017b: 210).

61 Kaszas (2018: 15).

62 Kaszas (2024).

63 Kaszas (2018: 9,12).

64 Krutak (2016b).

65 Krutak (2014a, 2017b).

66 One example of a Greenland Inuit hand-poking tool is housed in the Musée du Quai Branly, Paris (71.1930.12.38).

67 In East Greenland, *Kagierneq* is used.

68 There are only a few scattered historical records concerning male tattooing in Greenland. Among the Ammassalimniut of East Greenland, male hunters were seldom tattooed, only "having a few lines on their arms and wrists 'to enable them to harpoon well,'" (Holm 1914: 29), a practice observed in other regions of the Arctic (Krutak, 2003, 2014a). Other accounts centered on the Ammassalimniut relate that men might also bear an amuletic mark between the eyebrows, as in the case of one hunter who was tattooed "in order to prevent a shark he had once harpooned from recognizing and pursuing him" in the future (Thalbitzer 1914: 608). Other writers have observed that West Greenland Inuit men might have received dotted tattoo forms for wrist pain (Rosing 1998:160).

69 Pikilak (2022b).

Chapter 3

1 Deter-Wolf et al. (2016).

2 Allison (1996: 127); Allison et al. (1981: 220).

3 Allison et al. (1981: 221).

4 Deter-Wolf et al. (2024a).

5 Krutak (2007, 2014a, 2024b).

6 Alva and Donnan (1994); Cordry-Collins (2001); Proulx (1996); Silverman and Proulx (2002).

7 Proulx (2001: 121).

8 Cordry-Collins (1996: 190).

9 Ubbelohde-Doering (1967).

10 Williams (2006).

11 Alva and Donnan (1994).

12 Deter-Wolf et al. (2024b); Erikson (1999); Fabius (2013).

13 Barreda (2007: 242).

14 By the mid-twentieth century, tattooing had largely been abandoned by the Munduruku, Apiaká, Matsés, and Marubo.

15 Erikson (1990: 53).

16 Erikson (1999: 396).
17 Horton (1948: 281); Murphy (1958: 12).
18 Yvinec (2014: 34).
19 Ibid.
20 Ibid.
21 Krutak (2012:80); Nimuendajú (1948: 319).
22 Krutak (2012: 80).
23 Prior to the Second World War, German-Brazilian anthropologist Curt Nimuendajú conducted field research with Tukuna of the Putomayo River region of Brazil. According to one of his Indigenous informants, the Tukuna formerly practiced tattooing but this tradition was borrowed from a neighboring tribe, the Yumana, that had become extinct in the nineteenth century. These people, however, wore an oval tattoo pattern surrounding the mouth, with ramifications of the design extending to the ears. The Tukuna elder explained that members of the macaw clans (there were two, with one derived from *Ara ararauna* and the other possibly *Ara maracana*) formerly tattooed the cheeks in imitation of the feather markings of macaws. The lines of the design were first drawn in by charred *cicantã* resin obtained from *Protium heptaphyllum* and were then punctured with a needle (Nimuendajú. 1952: 39). Another informant told Nimuendajú that "those who were learned" had the figure of a crayfish, *caranguejo*, and a scorpion tattooed on the forearm or on the back of the hand, and that the pigment came from the juice of a plant called *bu'rë* (Nimuendajú 1952: 39, 42).

The scorpion also finds prominence in other Indigenous tattooing traditions of the Amazon. Among the Akawaio of British Guiana, who once practiced both hand-poking and incision tattooing, the *kansök* (scorpion's tail) pattern was placed on the face of young women at the rite of puberty with additional patterns being added from that time through marriage (Butt 1961: 149–50). These tattoos, among others, worked as "women's charms," because they were believed to enable tattooed women to make sweet, fermented drinks and particularly foodstuffs, especially the staple food cassava bread. Men also received the pattern around their mouths, but the pigment was derived from charred plant roots that were believed to provide hunting success because specific plants attracted prey. 25 Krutak (2007: 203).
24 Matos (2012: 4).
25 Welper (2009: 33).
26 Other scholars have recorded that a guardian spirit of the afterlife inspects individuals who journey along the "Path of Danger." If the soul of the dead does not possess the tattoo, s/he will not be allowed to travel to the *maloca* (large communal house) of their ancestors (Mellati 1986: 8).
27 Welper (2009: 33).
28 Allison (1996); Allison et. al (1981); Barreda (2007); Cagigao et al. (2013); Gill-Frerking et al. (2013); Krutak (2007, 2013a); Pabst et al. (2010).
29 See Arroyo (2017); Castillo et al. (2016); Donnan (2001, 2003); Donnan and McClelland (1999); Lau (2017).
30 Krutak (2007, 2010, 2012, 2014a, 2024b).
31 Ceramics and textiles of the period also carry similar scenes.
32 For more information on the iconography of Ancient Andean tattooing appearing on mummies, see Deter-Wolf et al. (2024b).
33 Krutak (2007).
34 Barreda (2007); Bourget (2001ab); Prieto et al. (2019); Verano (2001).
35 Donnan (1996: 137–39); Joyce (1908: 17–18); Krutak (2007).
36 Donnan (1996: 137).
37 Deter-Wolf et al. (2024b).
38 The catalog number for this object is 99.161.2. Another "tattooed" Chimú wooden mirror shaped in the form of a human hand is illustrated in Topic (1990: 158, fig. 10).
39 This iconography also appears on woven fabrics and ceramic vessels. For more information, see Arroyo (2017), Reiss and Stübel (1880), and Ruiz Estrada (1990).
40 See Krutak (2007: 193); Pabst et al. (2010: 3257, fig. 1).
41 Alva and Donnan (1994: 139); Cordry-Collins (1992); Salazar-Burger and Burger (1982).
42 According to Arenas (2004: 251), tattooing was progressively abandoned in the 1940s and during the 1970s and 1980s it was only possible to see tattoos on elderly people.
43 Fock (1982: 18, 23–25).
44 Alvarsson (2012: 413). For a listing of other pigment and needle sources, see Arenas 2004 (253: tables 1 and 2).
45 Rosen (1924: 75).
46 Frič (1918: 53).
47 Alvarsson (2012: 413).
48 Furlong (1938: 24–25).
49 Grubb (1911: 125); Karsten (1926): 272-273..
50 Dalostto (2010: 40).
51 Dozens of ethnographic accounts describing the Indigenous tattooing traditions of South American peoples, including those on the Kayabí, document that *genipapo* (or *jagua* as it is known in Spanish) was the source of tattooing pigment. Indeed, the substance is widely used in body-painting traditions because once it contacts human skin it remains there for a period of several weeks before it disappears. Thus, I believe there is a certain level of misinformation that was and continues to be reported by researchers regarding the actual tattoo pigments of Amazonian and even Pre-Columbian peoples (i.e., Moche and Chimú) (see Deter-Wolf et al. 2024b and Krutak 2012). I was certainly astonished when I discovered that the Kayabí's tattoo pigment was derived from resin extracted from a tree and not *genipapo* itself.

That being said *genipapo* juice is virtually indistinguishable from the prepared tattoo resin of the *ipau-ip* tree. When I visited the Kayabí, I learned that only one elderly man named Tiwit – who was born and tattooed in the traditional Kayabí homeland of the Rio dos Peixes region – could identify the *ipau-ip* tree when his people migrated to the Xingu in the early 1960s. The reason for this is that the tree is extremely rare in the Xingu, and by the time of the Kayabí migrations, most men and women had not received tattoos in nearly twenty years.

Chapter 4

1 Fieldwork for the PNG section of this chapter was conducted in 2011. Due to editorial considerations, this chapter does not include the Polynesian cultures of Fiji, Tonga, Tahiti, Hawai`i, Rapa Nui (Easter Island), and outlying islands.
2 Ambrose (2007, 2012); Anderson (2014); Furey (2017); Kirch (1997, 2000).
3 Ryan (1970).
4 Coastal Papua men typically displayed chest, arm, or back tattooing related to their exploits in combat (see Krutak 2007). Men among the inland Managalase were tattooed all over their bodies with patterns associated with complex initiation rituals (see Chapter 4 and Krutak 2013d). For more details on these tattooing traditions among women, see Krutak (2014b).
5 Barton (1918). Across Oceania, centipede and frigate bird designs are widely used across Pacific tattooing cultures. For details, see Krutak (2007).
6 It was taboo for men to witness the tattooing, otherwise it was believed a girl's wounds would not heal; also, no person was allowed to view the girls as their tattoos healed. Tattoo recipients were also tabooed from certain foods. One Korafe woman named Daphne told the author that fish with spines, hot food, and crabs were forbidden. Maisin informants stated that if crabs or spiny fish were eaten, an unpleasant feeling would overcome the tattoo recipient during their tattooing – a feeling likened to bony creatures crawling across the face. A type of plant medicine (*uwgha*, Korafe; *bua kain*, Maisin) was applied to heal the wounds (Barker and Tietjen 1990).
7 Te Awekotuku (2007).
8 Te Awekotuku (1997).
9 Simmons (1984: 186).
10 Petelo (1991).
11 Krämer (1903).
12 Krämer (1903: 65); Mallon and Galliot (2017).

13 von den Steinen (1925).
14 Handy (1922).
15 Ibid.
16 Thomas (1995).
17 Lemma (2010: 184).
18 Putzi (2006: 14)
19 DeMello (2000: 47).
20 Sturtevant (1980).
21 Ellis (2008:189).
22 Scutt and Gotch (1974: 152).
23 Barnes (2006: 39) citing Scutt and Gotch.
24 See Kotondo (1928).
25 My journey to Managalase country would not have been possible without the assistance of journalist David Lornie. I remain grateful for his assistance and support.
26 Noble (1978: 908).
27 Fuamoli (2024).
28 Krutak (2017e: 190).
29 This quote is excerpted from a March 4, 2022, interview with the author.
30 Krutak (2017e: 191).
31 *Fiji Sun* (online), September 18, 2015.
32 December 9, 2023, personal communication with the author.
33 Ibid.
34 Ibid.
35 February 11, 2022, personal communication with the author.
36 Te Awekotuku (2006: 135).
37 Te Awekotuku (2007: 147).
38 cf. Kerekere (2024).

Chapter 5

1 Arutiunov (1999: 31); Ishida (1999: 56); Jinam et al. (2012); Jinam et al. (2015).
2 Edwards (2014: 47).
3 According to Criminal Code Number 428, Article 9, published in newspapers in 1899, fines varied from ten *sen* to one *yen* (Ryūkyū News Report 1899 cited in Nakijin Village Board of Education 1983: 42).
4 Hilger (1971: 150).
5 Iha ([1919] 2000: 270) cited by Barske (2013: 84).
6 Obara (1962: 62).
7 Hilger (1971: 151).
8 Honda (2000: 140).
9 Nakijin Village Board of Education (1983); Obara (1962).
10 Lebra (1966).
11 Krutak (2007).
12 In the Nakijin village area of Okinawa, a similar term, *hajicji-ayaa* or "aunt that makes tattoos," was used (Nakijin Village Board of Education 1983: 19, fn. 16). This term serves as a sign of respect or affection for elder females who might not be blood relatives of the tattoo client.
13 Nakijin Village Board of Education (1983: 18).
14 Obara (1962: 51).
15 Nakijin Village Board of Education (1983).
16 Obara (1962: 46); Yamamoto (1996: 90).
17 Keira and Keira (1999: 235).
18 Munro (1963: 118).
19 Ohnuki-Tierney (1976: 136, 2014: 65, 219, fn. 9); Philippi (1979: 192, fn. 3).
20 Hilger (1971: 152).
21 Koganei (1894: 264).
22 Ibid.
23 Batchelor (1901: 23).
24 Ibid.
25 Kodama (1970: 124).
26 Furness (1899: 11).
27 Simon (1914: 135).
28 Glacken (1955).
29 Yamamoto (1995).
30 Field (1958); Krutak (1999, 2013a, 2015a, 2019a); Pabst et al. (2010); Piombino-Mascali and Krutak (2020); Samadelli et al. (2015).
31 Glacken (1955: 236).
32 Krutak (2024a).

Chapter 6

1 Aspects of this chapter have been covered in the author's 2024 book *Tattoo Traditions of Asia: Ancient and Contemporary Expressions of Identity* (University of Hawai`i Press).
2 The act of tattooing was ritualized across Asia because flowing blood was believed to attract evil spirits lurking in the vicinity.
3 This belief has been recorded for the Kalinga and Kankanaey (De Raedt 1996: 170–71; Folkmar 1962 [1906]: 21; Vanoverbergh 1929: fn. 11, 189). Hoskins (1996) provides other ethnographic examples for headhunting societies outside of the Philippines. See Krutak (2010) for more information on the Kalinga headhunting complex and its relationship to tattooing.
4 Jenks (1905: 172).
5 Isneg warriors may have had their daughter's forearms tattooed with these designs, instead of their own (Vanoverbergh, 1929: 229).
6 Krutak (2012: 142).
7 Men and women of Luzon wore additional markings, typically small lines or dots, which were believed to have therapeutic benefits and were applied over goiters, tumors, and varicose veins.
8 Other northern tribes, such as the Seediq, Truku, and Saisiyat, also practiced tattooing, but I am unable to elaborate on these traditions due to space limitations.
9 Vadan et al. (2008: 87).
10 Vadan et al. (2008: 10).
11 Ma (1998: 61).
12 Rau (1992: 224).
13 Ho (1960: 10).
14 Vadan et al. (2008: 81).
15 Chi-Lu (1968: 247).
16 Tattooing was practiced by southern tribes like the Puyuma, Bunun, Rukai, but I cannot cover them here due to space limitations.
17 Ho (1960).
18 Ho (1960: 22).
19 The gender of these entities was not specified.
20 Krutak (2016c).
21 Freeman (1967: 335).
22 Hose and Shelford (1906: 66–67); Richards (1997: 375).
23 Krutak (2014c: 191).
24 Hose and Shelford (1906: 67).
25 Loeb (1929: 66).
26 Krutak (2012).
27 Schefold (1992).
28 Krutak (2012).
29 Henley (2001: 93).
30 Lindsay (1992: 61).
31 Krutak (2008: 47).
32 Jensen (1948: 89).
33 Jensen (1948).
34 Beckett et al. (2017); Picpican (2003); Salvador-Amores (2017). As mentioned in Chapter 1, out of respect for the Indigenous individuals and communities referenced, I will not include photographs of the tattooed human remains discussed in this section.
35 Beckett, Lohmann, and Bernstein (2011); Beckett et al. (2017).
36 Piombino-Mascali et al. (2017: 63).
37 Beckett et al. (2017: 27).
38 Salvador-Amores (2017: 46).
39 Moss (1920a: 281).
40 Krutak (2024a).
41 Sawyer (1900: 255).
42 Krutak (2010: 116); Moss (1920a: 243, 288; 1920b: 351); Vanoverbergh (1972: 123).
43 Meyer (1885: 514).
44 Krutak (2010). Scott (in Meyer [1890] 1975: 67n11) noted that calf tattoos and incomplete tattooing might indicate that young men had not yet engaged in battle. The French scientist Antoine-Alfred Marche, who visited the Kankanaey region in the late eighteenth century, encountered serpentine and flora-form tattoos on men. He remarked: "As one becomes richer and more powerful, the designs increase" (Marche [1887] 1970: 115).
45 Moss (1920a).
46 Nieuwenhuis (1904: 452).
47 Thomas (1968: 219).
48 Hose and Shelford (1906: 77).
49 Mashman (1989: 218).
50 Thomas (1968).
51 Nieuwenhuis (1904: 453).

52 Elshout (1926).

53 Rodney Needham (1976: 75), discussing Kenyah headhunting, stated that trophy heads signified the favor of *bali akang*, suggesting that without this spiritual support, headhunting would not be successful. He added, "Men in particular are dependent on these spirits, and it is thanks to this spiritual support that they are able to protect themselves, their womenfolk, and their children from possible attacks by other longhouses or tribes." Jacob M. Elshout (1926: 216) also emphasized the power of trophy heads, noting, "A fresh head is the best means for the strengthening of the sick and the old people and indeed of everyone's soul in the village. Everybody benefits from it and hence the Kenyah says: 'We become stronger through it.'"

54 Tillema (1937: 96).

55 Elshout (1926: 284).

56 Tillema (1989: 168).

57 Elshout (1926: 282).

58 Elshout (1926: 403). Coolness is linked to good health.

59 Tillema (1989: 168).

60 Riedel (1907: 181).

61 Jacob (2021: 59).

62 In the Dawan village of Haulasi, a fire is lit under a deceased person's bed for four days, serving as a guide for the souls to cross into the afterlife. After this period, the soul can exchange its body with the Creator for fire (Gual et al. 2019: 165).

63 Kruyt (1923: 385).

64 In East Sumba, Rindi children received a simple cross tattoo on their forearms. Forth (1981) noted that Rindi tattoos were exchanged for fire in the afterlife, though he did not clarify if the child's first skin marks (i.e., cruciform) were related to this belief.

65 Kruyt (1923: 385).

66 Kruyt (1921: 292). On Rote Island, payment for tattoos might include rice, betel nuts, tobacco, dried fish, or meat, while wealthy individuals might offer a pig, sheep, or goat (van de Wetering 1924: 24–25).

67 Van de Wetering (1924: 23).

68 Riedel (1907: 182–83).

69 Van de Wetering (1924: 24).

70 Kruyt (1923: 386).

71 Van de Wetering (1924: 25) described the preparation of *kadek* (tattooing pigment) in detail: The tattooist scrapes soot residue from the exterior of a rice cooking pot and mixes it with the juice of the thorn apple fruit. Lontar palm sugar is then added to the mixture, which is thoroughly stirred and left to sit for two days before use. If the rice pot is new, soot from a charred Java olive (*Sterculia foetida*) tree, locally known as the Nitas tree, is captured on a hanging rice pot.

72 Kruyt (1923: 386).

73 Jacob (2021: 59).

74 Jacob (2021: 58).

75 Kruyt (1923 :387).

76 Kaviani (2015).

77 This section is paraphrased, abbreviated, and revised after Parkitny (2024).

78 Symes (1800: 446).

79 Parkitny (2007, 2010, 2017).

80 Parkitny (2010: 19).

81 Parkitny (2010: 12).

82 Parkitny (2017: 30).

83 Most Ubtu groups resided on the plains, near Burmese populations, and consequently adopted coin and paper currencies early on.

84 Sherman and Sherman (1922).

85 A Laytu woman informed Parkitny (2010) that during the tattooing process, girls were occasionally wrapped in a braided mat to restrict their movement.

86 Krutak (2016c).

87 Krutak (2016c: 57).

88 Ibid.

89 Ibid.

90 Huang-ju (2018).

91 Krutak (2010).

92 Krutak (2014c).

93 Krutak (2010: 295–96).

94 See Salvador-Amores (2012, 2017).

Chapter 7

1 Due to space constraints and editorial considerations, this chapter does not cover the tattooing traditions of many other Indian tribes. For more information, please see Fischer and Shah (1973), Guillerme (2016), Gupte (1902), Iyer (1935), Rao (1946), Rose (1902), Rubin (1988), Thurston (1898, 1906), among others.

2 Elwin (1939: 19).

3 Ibid; Fuchs (1968: 64).

4 Soap-nuts are also strung on a thread and placed around the necks of small children in the belief that this device helps them cut their teeth and protects them from evil spirits.

5 Elwin (1939: 22).

6 Elwin (1939: 22, 1991: 79).

7 Elwin (1939: 18–19).

8 Elwin (1939: 19).

9 Ibid.

10 Elwin (1939: 22).

11 Gupta (1999).

12 Trivedi (1952: 125).

13 Traditionally, tattoo artists were paid in grain. As the Mer moved towards mechanized tattooing in recent decades, tattoos are now increasingly made by men with tattoo machines and transactions are in cash (Rubin 1988).

14 Trivedi (1952: 124–25).

15 Trivedi (1952: 124).

16 Krutak (2020).

17 Mills (1926); Saul (2005).

18 Krutak (2020, 2022).

19 Krutak (2024).

20 Krutak (2015b, 2020).

21 Krutak (2015b: 301).

22 Krutak (2020: 200).

23 Krutak (2015b: 303).

24 Chakrabarti (2021).

25 Ibid.

26 Ibid.

27 Chakrabarti, personal communication with the author, December 11, 2023.

Chapter 8

1 Reed (2000: 3).

2 Reed (2000: 12, fn. 27); van Gulik (1982: 5).

3 Palmgren (1934: pl. 19); Priewe (2017).

4 Krutak (2014a, 2017d).

5 Lei (2009: 102).

6 van Gulik (1982: 247).

7 Reed (2000: 16).

8 Mu (1996: 109–10).

9 This section is paraphrased, abbreviated, and revised after Gros (2024); Gros (2021, 2024).

10 Gros (2012, 2021).

11 See Jin (2006). Drung writer Luo Rongfen (1995: 12) shared the tale of a tattooed elder who was marked at thirteen by a tattooist named Mujinnan. Mujinnan assured the girl's mother, "After being tattooed, your girl will be able to dispel evil and call down a blessing."

12 Jin (2006).

13 Rongfen (1995).

14 Gros (2021, 2024); McCabe (2008).

15 For a similar exploration of beliefs among the Pantaron Manobo of the Philippines and the Kayan of Borneo, see Krutak (2024a).

16 Gros (2024).

17 Gros (2024).

18 Odaka (1950: 24); Xianjun (2016: 41).

19 Xianjun (2016: 181).

20 Xianjun (2016: 142, fig. 3.17).

21 Chinalai (2004:248).

22 Shunai and Simin (2010: 87).

23 Stübel (1937: 36).

24 Mallory and Mair (2000).

25 Mallory and Mair (2000: pl. VII-VIII).

26 Mallory and Mair (2000).

27 Krutak (1999, 2013a, 2019a); Piombino-Mascali and Krutak (2020).

28 Hu Yaling, personal communication, December 23, 2022.

29 Ibid.

30 Krutak (2024a).

31 The Sai also practiced tattooing in the past, but these traditions had vanished by the mid-twentieth century (Tian Fu, 2010: 7).

32 Odaka (1950: 24); Xianjun (2016: 41). In the past, Meifu boys who were the sole male children in their families occasionally had figurative tattoos on their chest. The motifs featured a tiger head with a moon below it, and the Chinese characters 求安 ("seeking peace") between them. A *daoishi,* or Taoist monk, would stencil these symbols onto the skin, which were then hand-tapped by a female tattooist. It was believed that those with such tattoos sought peace in all their pursuits (Hu Yaling, personal communication, December 12, 2021).

33 Among these designs, the "fishtail" pattern stands out. One Meifu male elder with this tattoo claimed it improved his ability to catch fish and swim more effectively (Xianjun 2016: 205).

34 Clark (1938: 407).

35 Odaka (1950: 24). It has been documented that if a Li woman was not accepted by her ancestors, she would become a "homeless and wild ghost" (Xueping 2001: 199).

36 Tian Fu (2010: 8).

37 Xianjun (2016: 179).

38 Odaka (1950: 24).

39 Shaogong (2016: 41).

40 In Taoist traditions, the bottle gourd has long held profound significance in China. In oral histories and symbolic representations, gourds were used as charms for longevity and healing, among other purposes (Reed 2000: 35, fn. 88).

41 Krutak (2019b).

42 Tezcan (2010: 384).

43 Rudenko (1929).

44 Rudenko (1929: 16).

45 Sorokin (1873: 17); Titova (1978); von Middendorff (1875: 1461). On the Chukotka Peninsula of easternmost Asia, Siberian Yupik and Maritime Chukchi boys and girls received often complex family and clan tattoo designs on their faces that were stitched into the skin by female practitioners (Krutak 2007, 2014; Rudenko 1949).

46 Krutak (1998, 2000, 2023).

47 Krutak (1998: 22–27).

48 Bogoras (1904–909: 298).

49 Hughes (1959: 90).

50 Krutak (2014a: 35).

51 Krutak (1998: 23).

52 Krutak (1998: 37).

53 Krutak (2014a: 35–36).

54 Bogoras (1904–909: 342–43).

55 Krutak (2009: 194).

56 Anderson and Eells (1935: 175); Sverdup (1978 [1938]: 162–63).

57 Gordon (1906); Murdoch (1892).

58 Hooper (1853: 37).

59 Murdoch (1892: 139).

60 Gordon (1906: pl. IX); Murdoch (1892: 139).

61 Krutak (2009, 2014a, 2017c); Wardwell (1986: 47, pl. 26, 67, pl. 63).

62 Sometimes great whalers also bore body tattoos, including individual fluke tail tattoos that came to mark the chest or forearms; each tale representing a kill (Murdoch, 1892: 139).

63 Zoya Toure, personal communication, November 8, 2023.

Conclusion

1 Alvarez (2020: 164).

2 Kaszas (2024: n.p.)

3 Kaszas (2024: n.p.)

4 Fayant (2023: n.p.)

Bibliography

Abouda, Mohand. 2000. *Aouchem: La Mémoire À Fleur de Peau* [Aouchem: Memory on Edge]. Paris: Noir Sur Blanc Editions.

Allison, J. Marvin. 1996. "Early Mummies from Coastal Peru and Chile." In*The Man in Ice*, vol. 3, *Human Mummies, A Global Survey of Their Status and the Techniques of Conservation*, edited by K. Spindler, H. Wilfring, E. Rastbichler-Zissernig, D. zur Nedden, and H. Nothdurfter, 125–30. Vienna: Springer.

Allison, J. Marvin, Lawrence Lindberg, Calogero Santoro, and Guillermo Foracci. 1981. "Tatuajes y Pintura Corporal de Los Indigenas Precolumbinos de Peru y Chile [Tattoos and Body Painting of the Pre-Columbian Indians of Peru and Chile]." *Chungara*, 7: 218–25.

Alva, Walter, and Christopher B. Donnan. 1994. *Royal Tombs of Sipán*. Los Angeles: UCLA Fowler Museum of Cultural History.

Alvarez, Pauline. 2020. "Indigenous (Re) inscription: Transmission of Cultural Knowledge(s) through Tattoos as Resistance." In *Tattoo Histories: Transcultural Perspectives on the Narratives, Practices, and Representations of Tattooing*, edited by S. Kloß, 157–75. New York & London: Routledge.

Alvarsson, Jan-Åke. 2012. *Etnografía 'Weenhayek, Volumen 3. Belleza y Utilidad: La Cultura Material* [Ethnography 'Weenhayek, Volume 3. Beauty and Utility: Material Culture Material]. Uppsala: Universidad de Uppsala.

Ambrose, Wal. 2007. "The Implements of Lapita Ceramic Stamped Ornamentation." In *Oceanic Explorations: Lapita and Western Pacific Settlement*, edited by S. Bedford, C. Sand, and S. P. Connaughton, 213–21. Canberra: Terra Australis 26, ANU E Press. 2012 "Oceanic Tattooing and the Implied Lapita Ceramic Connection." *Journal of Pacific Archaeology* 3, no. 1: 1–21.

Ammitzbøll, T., M. Bencard, J. Bodenhoff, et al. 1991. "Clothing." In *The Greenland Mummies*, edited by J.P.H. Hansen, J. Meldgaard, and J., Nordqvist, 116–149. Washington, DC: Smithsonian Institution Press.

Anderson, Atholl. 2014. "Ancient Origins, 3000 B.C.–A.D. 1300." In *Tangata Whenua, an Illustrated History*, edited by A. Anderson, J. Binney, and A. Harris, 16–41. Wellington: Bridget Williams Books.

Anderson, H. Dewey, and Wallace C. Eells. 1935. *Alaska Natives: A Survey of Their Sociological and Educational Status*. Stanford: University of Stanford Press.

Anokhina, Evgenia. 2020. "Татуировки В Древнем Египте [Tattooing in Ancient Egypt]." In *TATY* [*TATTOO*], 32–37. Moscow and Paris: Pushkin State Museum of Fine Arts and Musée du quai Branly.

Arenas, Pastor. 2004. "Los vegetales en el arte del tatuaje de los indígenas del Gran Chaco [Vegetables in the tattoo art of the indigenous people of the Gran Chaco]." In *Los mundos de abajo y los mundos de arriba. Individuo y sociedad en las tierras bajas, en los Andes y más allá*, edited by M. S. Cipolletti, 249–74. Quito: Abya Yala.

Arroyo, Victor H. A. 2017. "Rastreo y análisis comparative de la presencia del tatuaje en el antiguo Perú: Una aproximación a través de la colección de cerámica del MNAAHP [Tracking and Comparative Analysis of the Presence of Tattooing in Ancient Peru: An Approach Through the Ceramic Collection of the MNAAHP]." *International Journal of South American Archaeology* 11: 45-57.

Arutiunov, Sergei A. 1999. "Ainu Origin Theories." In *Ainu: Spirit of a Northern People*, edited by W. W. Fitzhugh and C. O. Dubreuil, 29–31. Washington, DC and Seattle: Arctic Studies Center, National Museum of Natural History and University of Washington Press.

Austin, Anne, and Marie-Lys Arnette. 2022. "Of Ink and Clay: Tattooed Mummified Human Remains and Female Figurines from Deir el-Medina." *The Journal of Egyptian Archaeology* 108, no. 1–2: 63–80.

Austin, Anne, and Cédric Gobeil. 2017. "Embodying the Divine: A Tattooed Female Mummy from Deir el-Medina." *Bulletin de L'Institut Français D'Archéologie Orientale* 116, 23–36. Cairo.

Bachner, Andrea. 2014. *Beyond Sinology: Chinese Writing and the Scripts of Culture*. New York: Columbia University Press.

Bailey, Garrick A. 2010. *Traditions of the Osage: Stories Collected and Translated by Francis La Flesche*, edited by G. Bailey. Albuquerque: University of New Mexico Press.

Barker, John, and Anne Marie Tietjen. 1990. "Women's Facial Tattooing Among the Maisin of Oro Province, Papua New Guinea: The Changing Significance of an Ancient Custom." *Oceania* 60, no. 3: 217–34.

Barkova, Ludmila L. and Svetlana V. Pankova. 2006. "Tatuirovki na mumijakh iz Pazyrykskikh kurganov v infrakrasnykh luchakh [Tattoos on the Mummies from the Pazyryk Burial Mounds in the Infrared Rays]." *Vestnik Istorii, Literatuty, Iskusstva* 3: 31-42.

Barnes, Geraldine. 2006. "Curiosity, Wonder, and William Dampier's Painted Prince." *Journal for Early Modern Cultural Studies* 6, no. 1: 31–50.

Barreda, Elías Mujica, ed. 2007. *El Brujo: Huaca Cao, Centro Ceremonial Moche en el Valle de Chicama/Huaca Cao, A Moche Ceremonial Center in the Chicama Valley.* Lima: Fundación Wiese.

Barske, Valerie H. 2013. "Visualizing Priestesses or Performing Prostitutes? Ifa Fuyū's Depictions of Okinawan Women, 1913–1943." *Studies on Asia* 3, no. 1: 65–91.

Barton, Francis R. 1918. "Tattooing in South Eastern New Guinea." *Journal of the Royal Anthropological Institute of Great Britain and Ireland* 48: 22–79.

Barton, Roy F. 1930. *The Half-Way Sun: Life Among the Headhunters of the Philippines.* New York: Brewer & Warren Inc.

Batchelor, John. 1901. *The Ainu and Their Folk-Lore*. London: The Religious Tract Society. 1927 *Ainu Life and Lore: Echoes of a Departing Race*. Tokyo: Kyobunkan.

Beckett, Ronald G., Gerald J. Conlogue, Orlando V. Abinion, Analyn Salvador-Amores, and Dario Piombino-Mascali. 2017. "Human Mummification Practices Among the Ibaloy of Kabayan, North Luzon, the Philippines." *Papers on Anthropology* 25, no. 2: 24–37.

Beckett, Ronald G., Ulla Lohmann, and Josh Bernstein. 2011. "A Field Report on the Mummification Practices of the Anga of Koke Village, Central Highlands, Papua New Guinea." *Yearbook of Mummy Studies* 1: 11–17.

Beckwith, Carol. 1983. "Niger's Wodaabe: 'People of the Taboo.'" *National Geographic* 164, no. 4: 483-509.

Blackburn, Mark. 1999. *Tattoos from Paradise: Traditional Polynesian Patterns*. Atglen, PA: Schiffer Publishing.

Bleek, Dorothea F. 1929. "Bushmen of Central Angola." *Bantu Studies* 3, no. 1: 105-125.

Bogoras, Waldemar. 1904–09. *The Chukchee*. Publications of Jesup North Pacific Expedition 7; Memoirs of the American Museum of Natural History 11. New York.

Bourdieu, Pierre. 1990. *The Logic of Practice*. Stanford University Press: Stanford.

Bourget, Steve. 2001a. "Rituals of Sacrifice: Its Practices and at Huaca de la Luna and Its Representation in Moche Iconography." In *Moche Art and Archaeology in Ancient Peru*, edited by J. Pillsbury, 89-109. Washington, DC: National Gallery of Art. 2001b "Children and Ancestors: Ritual Practices at the Moche Site of Huaca de la Luna, North Coast of Peru." In *Ritual Sacrifice in Ancient Peru*, edited by E.P. Benson and A. Cook, 93-118. Austin: University of Texas Press.

Bovin, Mette. (2001). *Nomads Who Cultivate Beauty: Wodaabe Dances and Visual Arts of Niger*. Uppsala: Nodiska Afrikainstitutet.

Bowers, Alfred W. 1965. Hidatsa Social and Ceremonial Organization. *Bureau of American Ethnology Bulletin* 194. Washington, DC: Smithsonian Institution, U.S. Government Printing Office.

Butt, Audrey J. 1961. "Symbolism and Ritual Among the Akawaio of British Guiana." *New West Indian Guide* 41(1):141–161.

Cagigao, Elsa T., Ann Peters, Mellisa Lund, and Alberto Ayarza. 2013. "Body Modification at Paracas Necropolis, South Coast of Peru, ca. 2000 BP." In *Tattoos and Body Modifications in Antiquity: Proceedings of the Sessions at the EAA Annual Meetings in The Hague and Oslo 2010/11*, edited by P. Della Casa and C. Witt, 49-58. Zurich Studies in Archaeology 9. Chronos-Verlag: Zurich.

Castillo, Luis Jaime, Cecilia Pardo, and Julio Rucabado. 2016. *Moche y sus vecinos: Reconstruyendo identidades* [Moche and Its Neighbors: Reconstructing Identities]. Lima: Museo de Arte de Lima.

Chakrabarti, Shatabdi. 2021. "Traditions on Skin: Tattoo Making Among Baiga Women." *Sahapedia.* Accessed November 19, 2023. https://map.sahapedia.org/gallery/Traditions-on-Skin:-Tattoo-making-among-Baiga-Women-/11025.

Chan, Henry. 2007. "Survival in the Rainforest: Change and Resilience Among the Punan Vuhang of Eastern Sarawak, Malaysia." PhD diss., University of Helsinki.

Chenciner, Robert, Gabib Ismailov, and Magomedkhan Magomedkhanov. 2006. *Tattooed Mountain Women and Spoon Boxes of Daghestan*. London: Bennett & Bloom.

Chi-Lu, Chen. 1968. *Material Culture of the Formosan Aborigines*. Taipei: The Taiwan Museum.

Chinalai, Lee J. 2004. "Dragon Covers – Mysterious Aberrations of the Li." *Textile Society of America Symposium Proceedings* 454: 242–51.

Choris, Louis. 1822. *Voyage pittoresque autour du monde, avec des portraits de sauvages d'Amérique, d'Asie, d'Afrique, et des îles du Grand Océan* [Picturesque Voyage around the World, with Indigenous Portraits from America, Asia, Africa, and the Islands of the Great Ocean] . . . Paris: Firmin Didot.

Clark, Bernard. 1938. "Among the Big Knot Lois of Hainan." *National Geographic Magazine* 74, no. 3: 391–418.

Clark, Geoffrey and Michelle C. Langley. 2020. "Ancient Tattooing in Polynesia." *The Journal of Island and Coastal Archaeology* 15, no. 3: 407–20.

Cola Alberich, Julio. 1949. *Amuletos y tatuajes marroquíes* [Amulets and Tattoos of Morocco]. Instituto de Estudios Africanos.

Collins, Henry B. n.d. St. Lawrence Island Notes on Miscellaneous Ethnological Data . . . Field Notes from the H. B. Collins Collection, Box 108. National Anthropological Archives, Smithsonian Institution, Suitland, Maryland. 1930 Notebook A. Field Notes from the H. B. Collins Collection, Box 45, fldr. 83. National Anthropological Archives, Smithsonian Institution, Suitland, Maryland.

Coon, Carleton S. 1931. *Tribes of the Rif*. Peabody Museum of Harvard University: Cambridge.

Cordry-Collins, Alana. 1992. "Archaism or Continuing Tradition: The Decapitator Theme in Cupinesque and Moche Iconography." *Latin American Antiquity* 3, no. 3: 206-220. 1996 "Lambayeque." In *Andean Art at Dumbarton Oaks*, vol. 1, edited by E. H. Boone, 189–222. Washington, DC: Dumbarton Oaks. 2001 "Blood and the Moon Priestesses: Spondylus Shells in Moche Ceremony." *Ritual Sacrifice in Ancient Peru*, edited by E. P. Benson and A. Cook, 35–54. Austin: University of Texas Press.

Cowan, James. 1921. "Maori Tattooing Survivals: Some Notes on *Moko*." *Journal of the Polynesian Society* 30, no. 120: 241–45.

Dalostto, Flavio. 2010. *Historia sagrada del pueblo qom en el país chaqueño* [Sacred History of the Qom people of Chaco Country]. Tomo I. Santa Fe: Ediciones del Hombre Negro Atrapasoles.

Dasen, Véronique. 1993. *Dwarfs in Ancient Egypt and Greece.* Clarendon Press: Oxford.

DeMello, Margo. 2000. *Bodies of Inscription: A Cultural History of the Modern Tattoo Community*. Durham: Duke University Press.

Denig, Edwin T. 1930. "Indian Tribes of the Upper Missouri." In *46th Annual Report of the Bureau of American Ethnology [for] 1928–1929*, edited by J.N.B. Hewitt, 375–628. Washington, DC: Smithsonian Institution, U.S. Government Printing Office.

Densmore, Francis. 1928. Uses of Plants by the Chippewa Indians. In *44th Annual Report of the Bureau of American Ethnology for the Years 1926-1927*, 275–397. Washington: Government Printing Office.

De Raedt, Jules. 1996. "Buaya Headhunting and Its Ritual: Notes from a Headhunting Feast in Northern Luzon." In *Headhunting and the Social Imagination in Southeast Asia*, 167–83. Stanford: Stanford University Press.

Deter-Wolf, Aaron, Benoît Robitaille, Lars Krutak, and Sebastien Galliot. 2016. "The World's Oldest Tattoos." *Journal of Archaeological Science: Reports*. 5: 19–24.

Deter-Wolf, Aaron, Benoît Robitaille, Rhoda Fromme, Robin Gerst, and Danny Riday. 2024a. "Pre-Columbian Tattooing Methods on the Peruvian Central Coast." *Andean Past 14*: 335-366.

Deter-Wolf, Aaron, and Lars Krutak. 2017. "Introduction." In *Ancient Ink: The Archaeology of Tattooing*, edited by L. Krutak and A. Deter-Wolf, 1–8. Seattle: University of Washington Press.

Deter-Wolf, Aaron, Tanya M. Peres, and Steven Karacic. 2021. "Ancient Native American Bone Tattooing Tools and Pigments: Evidence from Central Tennessee." *Journal of Archaeological Science: Reports* 37.

Deter-Wolf, Madison Auten, Benoît Robitaille, and Daniel Riday. 2024b. "Ancient Andean Tattooing: New Perspectives from North American Museum Collections." In *Oxford Handbook on the Archaeology and Anthropology of Body Modification*, edited by F. D'Errico and F. Manni. New York: Oxford University Press.

Donnan, Christopher B. 1996. "Moche." In *Andean Art at Dumbarton Oaks*, vol. 1, edited by E. H. Boone, 123-162. Washington, DC: Dumbarton Oaks. 2001 "Moche Ceramic Portraits." In *Moche Art and Archaeology in Ancient Peru*, edited by J. Pillsbury, 126-139. Washington, DC: National Gallery of Art. 2003 *Moche Portraits from Ancient Peru*. Austin: University of Texas Press.

Donnan, Christopher B. and Donna McClelland. 1999. *Moche Fineline Painting: Its Evolution and Its Artists*. Los Angeles: Fowler Museum of Cultural History, University of California.

Dorsey, George A. 1898. "A Cruise Among Haida and Tlingit Villages About Dixon's Entrance." *Appleton's Popular Science Monthly* 53: 1–15.

Drewal, Henry J. 1988. "Beauty and Being: Aesthetics and Ontology in Yoruba Body Art." In *Marks of the Civilization: Artistic Transformations of the Human* Body, edited by A. Rubin, 83–96. Los Angeles: UCLA Museum of Cultural History.

Durham, Mary E. 1929. *Some Tribal Origins and Laws and Customs of the Balkans*. Macmillan Co.: New York.

Edwards, James Rhys. 2014. *Between Two Worlds: A Social History of Okinawan Musical Drama*. PhD diss., University of California Los Angeles, Department of Musicology, Los Angeles.

Ellis, Juniper. 2008. *Tattooing the World: Pacific Designs in Print & Skin*. New York: Columbia University Press.

Elshout, J. M. 1926. *De Kenja-Dayaks uit het Apo-Kajan-gebied: Bijdragen tot de Kennis van Centraal-Borneo* [The Kenyah Dayaks of the Apo Kayan Region: Contributions to the Knowledge of Central Borneo]. The Hague: Martinus Nijhoff.

Elwin, Verrier. 1939. *The Baiga*. London: John Murray.

Emmons, George T. 1991. The Tlingit Indians. *Anthropological Papers of the American Museum of Natural History* 70, edited by F. de Laguna. Seattle: University of Washington Press.

Emory, William H. 1857. *Report on the United States and Mexican Boundary Survey Made Under the Direction of the Secretary of the Interior*, vol. 1. Washington, DC: Cornelius Wendell.

Erikson, Philippe. 1990. "Near Beer of the Amazon." *Natural History* 99, no. 8: 52–61. 1999 *El Sello de los antepasados: marcado del cuerpo y demarcacíon étnica entre los matis de la Amazonía* [The Seal of the Ancestors: Body Marking and Ethnic Demarcation Among the Matis of the Amazon]. Quito: Abya-Yala.

Fabius, Carine. 2013. *Jagua, A Journey Into Body Art from the Amazon*. Los Angeles: Kouraj Press

Faleti, Adebayo 1977. "Yoruba Facial Marks." *Gangan* 7: 22–27.

Fayant, Stacey M. 2023. *People With Face Tattoos Make Me Heal: Stories About Our Indigenous Face Tattoos*. Self-published.

Field, Henry. 1958. "Body-Marking in Southwestern Asia." *Papers of the Peabody Museum of Archaeology and Ethnology, Harvard University* 45, no. 1.

Fiji Sun (online). 2015. "Artists Meet To Revive Fijian Art Of Tattooing." September 18. Accessed December 3, 2023. https://fijisun.com.fj/2015/09/18/artists-meet-to-revive-fijian-art-of-tattooing/

Fisch, Maria. 1991/92. "Tattoos and Cicatrizations among the Namibian Peoples." *Namibia Scientific Society* 43: 49-69.

Fischer, Eberhard, and Haku Shah. 1973. "Tatauieren in Kutch [Tattooing in Kutch]." *Ethnologische Zeitschrift Zurich* 11: 105–29.

Fletcher, Alice C. and Francis La Flesche. 1911. "The Omaha Tribe." In *27th Annual Report of the Bureau of American Ethnology [for] 1905–'06*, 17–672. Washington, DC: Smithsonian Institution, U.S. Government Printing Office.

Fock, Niels. 1982. "History of Mataco Folk Literature and Research." In *Folk Literature of the Mataco* Indians, edited by J. Wilbert and K. Simoneau, 1–33. Los Angeles: UCLA Latin American Studies.

Folkmar, Daniel K. 1962 [1906]. Social Institutions of the Tinglayan Igorot. *Sagada Social Studies* 12. Sagada: Sagada Social Studies.

Forth, Gregory L. 1981. *Rindi: An Ethnographic Study of a Traditional Domain in Eastern Sumba*. Verhandelingen van het Koninklijk Instituut voor Taal-, Land- en Volkenkunde 93. The Hague: Martinus Nijhoff.

Fortune, Reo F. 1932. Omaha Secret Societies. *Columbia University Contributions to Anthropology* 14. New York.

Francillon, Gérard. 1967. Some Matriarchic Aspects of the Social Structure of the Southern Tetun of Middle Timor. PhD diss., The Australian National University, Canberra.

Freeman, Derek. 1967. "Shaman and Incubus." *Psychoanalytic Study of Society* 4: 315–44.

Frič, Alberto V. 1918. *Mezi Indiany* [Among Indians]. Prague.

Friedman, Renée. 2017. "New Tattoos from Ancient Egypt: Defining Marks of Culture." In *Ancient Ink: The Archaeology of Tattooing*, edited by L. Krutak and A. Deter-Wolf, 11–36. Seattle: University of Washington Press.

Friedman, Renée, Daniel Antoine, Sahra Talamo, Paula J. Reimar, John H. Taylor, Barbara Wills, and Marcello A. Mannino. 2018. "Natural Mummies from Predynastic Egypt Reveal the World's Earliest Figural Tattoos." *Journal of Archaeological Science* 92: 116–25.

Fuamoli, Sose. 2024. "'A Woman's Practice First:' Julia Mageau Gray on Revitalising Melanesian Tattoo Traditions." Australian Broadcast Corporation (ABC) Pacific. https://www.abc.net.au/pacific/programs/nesia-daily/julia-mageau/103287472.

Fuchs, Stephan. 1968. *The Gond and Bhumia of Eastern Mandla*. Bombay: New Literature Publishing House.

Fukui, Yoshimaro. 1814. *Ezo No Shimabumi* [Traversing Ezo Island].

Furey, Louise. 2017. "Archaeological Evidence for Tattooing in Polynesia and Micronesia." In *Ancient Ink: The Archaeology of Tattooing*, edited by L. Krutak and A. Deter-Wolf, 159–84. Seattle: University of Washington Press.

Furlong, Guillermo. 1939. *Entre Los Abipones del Chaco: Según Noticias de los Misioneros Jesuitas Martin Dobrizhoffer, Domingo Muriel, José Brigniel, Joaquín Camaño, José Jolis, Pedro Juan Andreu, José Cardiel y Vicente Olcina* [Among the Abipón of the Chaco: According to Missionary Reports of the Jesuits Martin Dobrizhoffer, Domingo Muriel, José Brigniel, Joaquín Camaño, José Jolis, Pedro Juan Andreu, José Cardiel and Vicente Olcina]. Buenos Aires.

Furness, William H. 1899. "Life in the Luchu Islands." *Bulletin of the Free Museum of Science and Art* 1, vol. 2: 1–28. Philadelphia: University of Pennsylvania.

Gallois, Dominique Tilkin. 1992. "Arte iconográfica Waiãpi [Iconographic Art of the Wajãpi]." In *Grafismo Indígena: Estudios de Anthropologia Estética*, edited by L. Vidal, 209–203. São Paulo: Studio Nobel.

Galvin, Rev. A. D. 1974. "Headhunting – Fact or Fiction?" *Brunei Museum Journal* 3, no. 3: 16–142.

Geist, Otto W., and Froelich G. Rainey. 1936. *Archaeological Excavations at Kukulik, St. Lawrence Island, Alaska.* Miscellaneous Publications of the University of Alaska 2. Government Printing Office: Washington, D.C.

Gifford, Edward W. 1933. "The Cocopa." *University of California Publications in American Archaeology and Ethnology* 31, no. 5: 257–334. Berkeley: University of California Press.

Gill-Frerking, Heather, Anna Maria Begerock, and Willfried Rosendahl. 2013. "Interpreting the Tattoos on a 700-year-old Mummy from South America." In *Tattoos and Body Modifications in Antiquity: Proceedings of the Sessions at the Annual Meetings of the European Association of Archaeologists in The Hague and Oslo, 2010/11*, edited by P. Della Casa and C. Witt, 59-66. Zurich Studies in Archaeology 9. Zurich: Chronos-Verlag.

Gillreath-Brown, Andrew, Aaron Deter-Wolf, Karen R. Adams, Valerie Lynch-Holm, Samantha Fulgham, Shannon Tushingham, William D. Lipe, and R. G. Matson. 2019. "Redefining the Age of Tattooing in Western North America: A 2000–year–old Artifact from Utah." *Journal of Archaeological Science: Reports* 24: 1064–75.

Glacken, Clarence J. 1955. *The Great Loochoo: A Study of Okinawan Village Life.* Berkeley: University of California Press.

Glück, Leopold. 1894. "Die Tätowirung der Haut bei den Katholiken Bosniens und der Hercegovina [Skin Tattooing Among the Catholics of Bosnia and Herzegovina]." *Wissenschaftliche Mitteilungen aus Bosniens und der Herzegowina* 2: 455–62.

Gobert, E. 1924. "Notes sur les tatouages des indigénes tunisiens [Notes on the Indigenous tattoos of Tunisia]." *L'Anthropologie* 34: 57–90. 1956 "Remarques sur les tatouages nord-africains [Notes on North African Tattoos]." *Revue Africaine* 100: 446–49.

Gordon, George B. 1906. "Notes on the Western Eskimo." *Transactions of the Department of Archaeology, Free Museum of Science and Art* 2, no. 1: 69–101.

Gros, Stéphane. 2012. *La Part manquante:* Échanges *et pouvoirs chez les Drung du Yunnan* [The Missing Share: Exchange and Power Among the Drung of Yunnan]. Nanterre, France: Société d'ethnologie. 2021 "Fertile Tattoos: Play, Embodiment, and the Transition to Womanhood in Drung Female Facial Tattooing." *Asian Ethnology* 80, no. 2: 319–41. 2024 "Drung Female Tattooing in Southwest China." In *Tattoo Traditions of Asia: Ancient and Contemporary Expressions of Identity*, edited by L. Krutak, 335–44. Honolulu: University of Hawai'i Press.

Grubb, Wilfrid B. 1911. *An Unknown People in an Unknown Land; An Account of the Life and Customs of the Lengua Indians of the Paraguayan Chaco, with Adventures and Experiences Met with During Twenty Years Pioneering and Exploration amongst Them.* Philadelphia: J.B. Lippincott Company.

Grünberg, Georg. 2004. *Os Kaiabi do Brasil Central: História e Etnografia* [The Kayabí of Central Brazil: History and Ethnography]. São Paulo: Instituto Socioambiental.

Gual, Yoseph A., Fransiska D. Setyaningsih, and Primus P. Bolaer. 2019. "Tattoo Tradisional Masyarakat Dea Haulasi Kecamatan Miomafo Kabupaten Timor Tengah Utara [Traditional Tattoo of the Dea Haulasi Community, Miomafo District, North Central Timor Regency]." *Jurnal Pendidikan dan Kebudayaan Missio* 11, no. 1: 160–78.

Guanghai, Yang (dir.). 1961. *Dulongzu* [The Dulong]. Historical and Ethnographical Film Series, 52 mins.

Guillerme, Stéphane. 2016. *Tribal Tattoo Designs from India.* Self-published. Amazon Kindle.

Gupta, Ruby. 1999. "Significance of Tattooing Among the Baigas." *The Tribune*. April 25. Accessed October 1, 2021. https://www.tribuneindia.com/1999/99apr25/sunday/head2.htm

Gupte, B. A. 1902. "Notes on Female Tattoo Designs in India." *The Indian Antiquary* 33: 293–97. July.

Handy, Willowdean C. 1922. *Tattooing in the Marquesas*. Bernice Bishop Museum Bulletin 1. Honolulu.

Hardy, Don E., ed. 1982. *TattooTime: New Tribalism.* Honolulu, HI: Hardy Marks Publications.

Harrington, Mark. 1913. "A Visit to the Otoe Indians." *The Museum Journal, University of Pennsylvania* 4, no. 3: 107–13.

Hata, Awagimaru. 1799. Ezotō kikan [*Wonders of Ezo Island*]. Self-published.

Henley, Thom. 2001. *Living Legend of the Mentawai*. Victoria: Baan Thom Publishing.

Herber, J. 1946 "Les tatouages de la face chez la Marocaine [Moroccan Face Tattoos]." *Hespéris* 33, no. 3–4: 323–51. 1949 "Les tatouages du cou, de la poitrine et du genou chez la Marocaine [Moroccan Neck, Chest and Knee Tattoos]." *Hespéris* 36, no. 3–4: 333–46.

Hilger, M. Inez. 1960. "Some Early Customs of the Menomini Indians." *Journal de la Société des Américanistes* 49: 45–68. 1971 *Together with the Ainu: A Vanishing People*. Norman: University of Oklahoma Press.

Ho, John Ting-Jui. 1960. "A Study on Tattooing Customs Among the Formosan Aborigines." *Bulletin of the Department of Archaeology and Anthropology* 15: 1–48.

Hoffman, Walter J. 1888. "Pictography and Shamanistic Rites of the Ojibwa." *American Anthropologist* 1, no. 3: 209–30.

Hollowell, Julie. 2009. "Ancient Ivories in a Global World." In *Gifts from the Ancestors: Ancient Ivories of Bering Strait*, edited by W. F. Fitzhugh, J. Hollowell, and A. L. Crowell, 252–89. Princeton and New Haven: Princeton University Art Museum and Yale University Press.

Holm, Gustav F. 1914. "Ethnological Sketch of the Angmagsalik Eskimo." *Meddelelser om Grønland* 39, no. 1: 3–147. Copenhagen.

Honda, Katsuichi. 2000. *Harukor: An Ainu Woman's Tale*. Trans. K. Selden. Berkeley: University of California Press.

Hooper, William H. 1853. *Ten Months Among the Tents of the Tuski with Incidents of an Arctic Boat Expedition in Search of Sir John Franklin as Far as the Mackenzie River, and Cape Bathurst*. London: John Murray.

Hornblower, George. 1929. "Predynastic Figures of Women and Their Successors." *The Journal of Egyptian Archaeology* 15: 29-47.

Horton, Donald. 1948. "The Mundurucu." In *Handbook of South American Indians*, edited by J. H. Steward, vol. 3, *The Tropical Forest Tribes*, 271–82. Washington, DC: U.S. Government Printing Office.

Hose, Charles, and Robert Shelford. 1906. "Materials for a Study of Tatu in Borneo." *The Journal of the Anthropological Institute of Great Britain and Ireland* 36: 60–91.

Hoskins, Janet. 1996. "Introduction: Headhunting as Practice and as a Trope." In *Headhunting and the Social Imagination in Southeast Asia*, edited by J. Hoskins, 1–49. Stanford: Stanford University Press.

Huang-ju, Huang (dir.). 2018. *Images from My Dreams: The Story of Tattoo Artist Cudjuy Patjidres.* Taipei: National Taiwan Museum. 8:46 mins.

Hughes, Charles. 1959. "Translation of I. K. Voblov's 'Eskimo Ceremonies.'" *Anthropological Papers of the University of Alaska* 7, no. 2: 71–90.

Iha, Fuyū. (1919) 2000. *Okinawa josei-shi* [Okinawa Women's History]. Naha: Ozawa Shoten.

Ishida, Hajime. 1999. "Ancient People of the North Pacific Rim: Ainu Biological Relationships with Their Neighbors." In *Ainu: Spirit of a Northern People*, edited by W. W. Fitzhugh and C. O. Dubreuil, 52–56. Washington, DC and Seattle: Arctic Studies Center, National Museum of Natural History and University of Washington Press.

Iyer, D.B.L.K.A. 1935. *The Mysore Tribes and Castes*. Vol. 1. Mysore: The Mysore University.

Izady, Mehrdad R. 1992. *The Kurds: A Concise Handbook*. London: Crane Russak.

Jacob, Fransisco de Ch. Anugerah. 2021. "Lunat: Tato Tradisional Masyarakat Dawan di Timor Barat Lunat: The Traditional Tattoo of the Dawan Peoples in West Timor." *Anthropos: Jurnal Antropologi Social dan Budaya* 7, no. 1: 54–66.

Jenks, Albert E. 1905. *The Bontoc Igorot*. Manila: Philippine Islands Ethnological Survey.

Jensen, Adolf E. 1948. *Die Drei Ströme: Züge aus dem Geistigen und Religiösen Leben der Wemale, Einem Primitiv-Volk in den Molukken* [The Three Rivers: Traits from the Spiritual and Religious Life of the Wemale, a Primitive People in the Moluccas]. Leipzig: Otto Harrassowitz.

Jin, Chen R., ed. 2006. Imprints of History: The Last Face Tattooed Women. Beijing: China Travel & Tourism Press.

Jinam, Timothy, Hideaki Kanzawa-Kiriyama, Ituro Inoue, Katsushi Tokunaga, Keiichi Omoto, and Naruya Saitou. 2015. "Unique Characteristics of the Ainu Population in Northern Japan." *Journal of Human Genetics* 60: 565–71.

Jinam, Timothy, Nao Nishida, Momoki Hirai, Shoji Kawamura, Hiroki Oota, Kazuo Umetsu, Ryosuke Kimura, Jun Ohashi, Atsushi Tajima, Toshimichi Yamamoto, Hideyuki Tanabe, Shuhei Mano, Yumiko Suto, Tadashi Kaname, Kenji Naritomi, Kumiko Yanagil, Norio Niikawa, Keiichi Omoto, Katsushi Tokunaga, and Naruya Saitou. 2012. "The History of Human Populations in the Japanese Archipelago Inferred from Genome-wide SNP Data with a Special Reference to the Ainu and the Ryukyuan Populations." *Journal of Human Genetics* 57: 787–95.

Joyce, Thomas. 1908. "The Southern Limit of Inlaid and Incrusted Work in Ancient Peru." *American Anthropologist* 19: 16-23.

Kapchan, Deborah. 1993. "Moroccan Women's Body Signs." In Bodylore, edited by K. Young, 3–35. Knoxville: University of Tennessee Press.

Karsten, Rafael. 1926. *Civilization of the South American Indians: With Special Reference to Magic and Religion*. London: Kegan Paul.

Kaszas, Dion. 2018. "Echoes of the Ancestors: Inherited Knowledge and Responsibilities." In *Body Language: Reawakening Cultural Tattooing of the Northwest*," edited by B. Carter and D. Kaszas, 7–27. Vancouver: Bill Reid Gallery of Northwest Coast Art.

Kaszas, Dion. 2024 (in press). "Nlaka'pamux Skin Markings (British Columbia, Canada): Past Significance and Current Efforts to Document, Preserve, and Update Its Ancestral Meaning." In *The Oxford Handbook of the Archaeology and Anthropology of Body Modification*, edited by F. Manni and F. d'Errico. Oxford: Oxford University Press.

Kaviani, Fareed. 2015. "Tattooing Timor." *The 4th Wall*. https://www.the4thwall.net/blog/2015/11/19/guest-article-tattooing-timor-by-thomas-henning-dedicated-to-the-dilli-collective. Accessed October 1, 2021.

Keim, Charles J. 1969. *Aghvook, White Eskimo: Otto Geist and Alaskan Archaeology*. University of Alaska Press: Fairbanks.

Keimer, Louis. 1948. *Remarques sur le tatouage dans le Égypte ancienne* [Notes on Tattooing in Ancient Egypt]. Mémoires de L'Institut D'Égypte. Imprimerie de L'Institut Français D'Archéologie Orientale: Le Caire.

Keira, Mitsunori, and Tomoko Keira. 1999. "Village Work: Seasons and Gender Roles." In *Ainu: Spirit of a Northern People*, edited by W. W. Fitzhugh and C. O. Dubreuil, 234–39. Washington DC, and Seattle: Arctic Studies Center, National Museum of Natural History and University of Washington Press.

Kerekere, Elizabeth. 2024. "Te Whare Takatāpui – Reclaiming the Spaces of Our Ancestors." In *Honouring Our Ancestors: Takatāpui, Two-Spirit and Indigenous LGBTQI+ Well-being*, edited by A. Green and L. Pihama, 73–96. Wellington: Te Herenga Waka University Press, Victoria University of Wellington.

Kinietz, W. Vernon. 1965. *The Indians of the Western Great Lakes, 1615–1760*. Ann Arbor: University of Michigan Press.

Kirch, Patrick, V. 1997. *The Lapita People: Ancestors of the Oceanic World*. Oxford: Blackwell Publishers. 2000 *On the Road of the Winds: An Archaeological History of the Pacific Islands Before European Contact*. Berkeley: University of California Press.

Kodama, Sakuzaemon. 1970. *Ainu: Historical and Anthropological Studies*. Sapporo: Hokkaido University School of Medicine.

Koganei, Yoshikiyo. 1894. *Beiträge zur physichen Anthropologie der Aino. II. Untersuchungen am Lebended* [Contributions to the Physical Anthropology of the Ainu. II. Investigations of the Living]. Mittheilungen aus der Medicinischen Facultät der Kaiserlich-Japanischen Universität. Tokyo: Verlag der Kaiserlichen Universität.

Köhler, Oswin. 1973. "Die rituelle Jagd bei den Kxoé-Buschmannforschung von Mutsiku [The Ritual Hunt among the Kxoé Bushmen from Mutsiku]." *Festschrift zum 65. Geburstag von H. Petri*, 215-257. Köln & Wien: Böhlau Verlag.

Kotondo, Hasebe. 1928. "The Tattooing of the Western Micronesians." *The Journal of the Anthropological Society of Tokyo* 43, no. 483–94: 129–52.

Krämer, Augustin. 1903. *Die Samoa-Inseln: Entwurf Einer Monographie mit Besonderer Berücksichtigung Deutsch-Samoas. Band II: Ethnographie* [The Samoa Islands: An Outline of a Monograph with a Particular Consideration of German Samoa. Vol. 2: Ethnography]. Stuttgart: E. Schweizerbartsche Verlagsbuchhandlung.

Krutak, Lars. 1998. *One Stitch at a Time: Ivalu* and *Sivuqaq* [St. Lawrence Island] *Tattoo*. Unpublished Master's Thesis, University of Alaska, Fairbanks, AK. 1999 "St. Lawrence Island Joint-Tattooing: Spiritual/Medicinal Functions and Inter-Continental Possibilities." *Études/Inuit/Studies* 23, no. 1–2: 229–52. 2000 "The Arctic." In *Tattoo History: A Source Book*, edited by S. Gilbert, 172–85. New York: Juno Books. 2003 *Uglalghii Keluk Unguvalleghmun: Many Stitches for Life. History of St. Lawrence Island Yupik Tattoo*. Unpublished Manuscript. 101 pp. Author's Possession. 2007 *The Tattoo Arts of Tribal Women*. Bennett & Bloom: London. 2008 "*Titi*: Spirit Tattoos of the Mentawai Shaman." *Skin and Ink: The Tattoo Magazine* 35: 38–49. July. 2009 "Of Human Skin and Ivory Spirits: Tattooing and Carving in Bering Strait." In *Gifts from the Ancestors: Ancient Ivories of Bering Strait*, edited by W. F. Fitzhugh, J. Hollowell, and A. L. Crowell, 190–203. New Haven and London: Yale University Press. 2010 *Kalinga Tattoo: Ancient and Modern Expressions of the Tribal*. Aschaffenburg: Edition Reuss. 2012 *Magical Tattoos and Scarification: Spiritual Skin. Wisdom. Healing. Shamanic Power. Protection*. Aschaffenburg: Edition Reuss. 2013a "The Power to Cure: A Brief History of Therapeutic Tattooing." In *Tattoos and Body Modifications in Antiquity: Proceedings of the Sessions at the EAA Annual Meetings in The Hague and Oslo, 2010/11*, edited by P. Della Casa and C.

Witt, 27–34. Zurich Studies in Archaeology 9. Zurich: Chronos-Verlag. 2013b "The Art of Enchantment: Corporeal Marking and Tattooing Bundles of the Great Plains." In *Drawing with Great Needles: Ancient Tattoo Traditions of North America*, edited by A. Deter-Wolf and C. Diaz-Granados, 131–73. Austin: University of Texas Press. 2013c "Tattoos, Totem Marks, and War Clubs: Projecting Power through Visual Symbolism in Northern Woodlands Culture." In *Drawing with Great Needles: Ancient Tattoo Traditions of North America*, edited by A. Deter-Wolf and C. Diaz-Granados, 95–130. Austin: University of Texas Press. 2013d "Die Tattoos der Managalase-Stammes auf Papua-Neuguinea [The Tattoos of the Managalase Tribe of Papua New Guinea]." *TätowierMagazin* 1: 118–22. 2014a *Tattoo Traditions of Native North America: Ancient and Contemporary Expressions of Identity.* Arnhem, Netherlands: LM Publishers. 2014b "The Bold and Beautiful: Women's Tattoos of Coastal Papua New Guinea." *Ink Fashion* 8: 16–23. 2014c "Tribal Tattoos of Indonesia: An Ancestral Art." In *TATTOO*, edited by S. Galliot, P. Bagot, Anne & Julien, 188–92. Paris and Arles: Musée du Quai Branly/ Actes Sud. 2015a "The Cultural Heritage of Tattooing: A Brief History." In *Tattooed Skin and Health*, edited by J. Serup, N. Kluger, and W. Baumler, 1–5. *Current Problems in Dermatology* 48. Basel: Karger. 2015b "Mo Naga." In *The World Atlas of Tattoo,* edited by A. F. Friedman, 300–303. New Haven, CT: Yale University Press. 2016a "Indelible Grace: In Asia, Tattooing Traditions Abide as Both Prayer and Protection." *El Palacio* 121, no. 2: 64–73. 2016b "Marked for Life: An Indigenous Tattoo Reawakening." *First American Art Magazine* 13: 30–37. Winter. 2016c "Taïwan: Renaissance du Tatouage Paiwan [Taiwan: Paiwan Tattoo Renaissance]." *Rise Tattoo Magazine* 52–7. August–September. 2017a "Balkan Ink: Europe's Oldest Living Tattoo Tradition." In *Ancient Ink: The Archaeology of Tattooing*, edited by L. Krutak and A. Deter-Wolf, 150–158. Seattle: University of Washington Press. 2017b "Native North American Tattoo Revival." In *Ancient Ink: The Archaeology of Tattooing*, edited by L. Krutak and A. Deter-Wolf, 210–214. Seattle: University of Washington Press. 2017c "Sacrificing the Sacred: Tattooed Prehistoric Ivory Figures of St. Lawrence Island, Alaska." In *Ancient Ink: The Archaeology of Tattooing*, edited by L. Krutak and A. Deter-Wolf, 262–85. Seattle: University of Washington Press. 2017d "The Visual Language of Facial Tattooing." In *Marked for Life: Myanmar's Chin Women and Their Facial Tattoos,* edited by J. U. Parkitny, 14–19. Bielefeld/Berlin: Kerber. 2017e "Reading Between Our Lines: Tattooing in Papua New Guinea." In *Ancient Ink: The Archaeology of* Tattooing, edited by L. Krutak and A. Deter-Wolf, 185–192. Seattle: University of Washington Press. 2017f "Reviving Tribal Tattoo Traditions in the Philippines." In *Ancient Ink: The Archaeology of Tattooing,* edited by L. Krutak and A. Deter-Wolf, 56–61. Seattle: University of Washington Press. 2018 "They Last A Lifetime – And Beyond: Tattoos and Ageing." In *Grey is the New Pink: Moments of Ageing*, edited by A. Pawlik, 154–164. Bielefeld/Berlin: Kerber. 2019a "Therapeutic Tattooing in the Arctic: Ethnographic, Archaeological, and Ontological Frameworks of Analysis." *International Journal of Paleopathology* 25: 99–109. 2019b "Ink." In *The SAS Encyclopedia of Archaeological Sciences*, edited by S. López Varela, 942–45. New York: John Wiley & Sons. 2020 "Sacred Skin: Tattooing, Memory, and Identity Among the Naga of India." In *Tattoo: Transcultural Perspectives on the Narratives, Practices, and Representations of Tattooing*, edited by S. Kloß, 191–217. New York: Routledge. 2022 "*Hüh tu pu* / To Mark with Tattoo: Chen Naga Tiger-Spirit Tattoos and Indigenous Ontologies in Northeast India." In *Tattooed Bodies: Theorizing Body Inscription across Disciplines and Cultures*, edited by J. Martell and E. Larsen, 91–116. Cham: Palgrave Macmillan. 2023 "Tattoos of the Kerek People." Accessed October 28, 2023. https://www.larskrutak.com/tattoos-of-the-kerek-people/. 2024a *Tattoo Traditions of Asia: Ancient and Contemporary Expressions of Identity*. Honolulu: University of Hawai'i Press. 2024b "One Mark at a Time: Ethnographic Notes on Tattooing." In *The Oxford Handbook on the Archaeology and Anthropology of Body Modification*, edited by F. Manni and F. d'Errico. Oxford: Oxford University Press.

Kruyt, Albert C. 1921. "De Roteneezen [The Rotese]." *Tijdschrift voor Indische Taal-, Land- en Volkenkunde* 40: 266–344. 1923 "De Timoreezen [The Timorese]." *Bijdragen tot de Taal-, Land- en Volkenkunde* 79, no. 1: 347–490.

La Flesche, Francis. 1916. "Right and Left in Osage Ceremonies." In *Holmes Anniversary Volume: Anthropological Essays*, 278–87. Washington, DC: J. W. Bryan Press. 1919 "Researches Among the Osage." *Smithsonian Miscellaneous Collections* 70, no. 2: 110–13. 1921 "The Osage Tribe: Rite of Chiefs; Sayings of the Ancient Men." In *36th Annual Report of the Bureau of American Ethnology [for] 1914–'15*, 37-604. Washington, DC: Smithsonian Institution, Government Printing Office. 1939 War Ceremony and Peace Ceremony of the Osage Indians. *Bureau of American Ethnology Bulletin* 101. Washington, DC: Smithsonian Institution, U.S. Government Printing Office.

Lau, George F. 2017. "South America – Andes." In *The Oxford Handbook of Prehistoric Figurines*, edited by T. Insoll, 391-416. Oxford: Oxford University Press.

Laukien, Michael. 2001. "Catholic Tattoos in Bosnia." *Skin and Ink,* no. 3: 24–28. March. 2010 "Letter from Barabaig." *Skin and Ink,* no. 4: 26–28. April.

Lebra, William P. 1966. *Okinawan Religion: Belief, Ritual, and Social Structure*. Honolulu: University of Hawai'i Press.

Legey, Doctoreses (Françoise). 1926 *Contes et legends du Maroc: recueillis à Marrakech* [Tales and Legends of Morocco: Collected in Marrakech]. Publicaciones de l'Institut des hautes études marocaines v. 16. E. Leroux: Paris.

Lei, Daphne P. 2009. "The Blood-Stained Text in Translation: Tattooing, Bodily Writing, and Performance of Chinese Virtue." *Anthropological Quarterly* 82, no. 1: 99–128.

Lemma, Alessandra. 2010. *Under the Skin: A Psychoanalytic Study of Body Modification*. London: Routledge.

Lindsay, Charles. 1992. *Mentawai Shaman: Keeper of the Rainforest.* New York: Aperture.

Linn, Angela J. and Molly Lee. 1999 "Intimates and Effigies: Dolls and Human Figurines in Alaska Native Cultures." In *Not Just a Pretty Face: Dolls and Human Figurines in Alaska Native* Cultures, edited by M. Lee, 3–48. Fairbanks: University of Alaska Museum.

Loeb, Edwin M. 1929. "Shaman and Seer." *American Anthropologist* 31: 60–84.

Ma, Tengue. 1998. Tai ya zu wen mian tu pu [*Atayal Facial Tattoo*]. Taipei.

Mallery, Garrick. 1894. "Picture-Writing of the American Indians." In *10th Annual Report of the Bureau of American Ethnology for the Years 1888–'89*, 1–822. Washington, DC: Government Printing Office.

Mallon, Sean. 2018. "Tattooing: A Hidden History." In *Tatau: A History of Sāmoan Tattooing*, edited by S. Mallon and S. Galliot, 72–73. Honolulu: University of Hawai'i Press.

Mallon, Sean, and Sébastien Galliot. 2017. *Tatau: A History of Sāmoan Tattooing*. Honolulu: University of Hawai`i Press.

Mallory, J. P. and Victor H. Mair. 2000. *The Tarim Mummies: Ancient China and the Mystery of the Earliest Peoples from the West*. London: Thames and Hudson.

Marche, Alfred. (1887) 1970. *Luçon et Palaouan: Six années de voyages aux Philippines* [Luzon and Palawan: Six Years of Journeys in the Philippines]. Paris: Librarie Hachette.

Mashman, Valerie. 1989. "Ethnic Arts and Society – An Orang Ulu Study." *Sarawak Museum Journal* 40, no. 61: 215–30.

Matos, Beatriz de Almeida. 2012. "Guerra e Aliança: a política entre os Matses [War and Alliance: Politics Among the Matsés]." Paper presented at the 28th Brazilian Anthropology Meeting, July 2–5, 2012, 1–19. São Paulo, Brazil.

McCabe, Michael. 2008. "Tattooed Women of Yunnan, China." *Skin and Ink*, no.39: 64–74.

Meachum, Scott. 2007. "'Markes Upon Their Clubhamers': Interpreting Pictography on Eastern War Clubs." In *Three Centuries of Woodlands Indian Art*, edited by J.C.H. King and C. F. Feest, 67–74. Vienna: ZKF Publishers.

Métraux, Alfred. 1946. "Indians of the Gran Chaco: Ethnography of the Gran Chaco." In *Handbook of South American Indians*, edited by J. H. Steward, vol. 1, *The Marginal Tribes*, 197–370. Washington, DC: U.S. Government Printing Office.

Meyer, Hans. 1885. *Eine Weltreise: Plaudereien aus einer zweijährigen Erdumseglung* [A Journey around the World: Stories from Circumnavigating the World for Two Years]. Leipzig: Verlag des Bibliographischen Instituts. (1890) 1975. "A Trip to the Igorots in the Interior." In German Travelers in the Cordillera, 1860–1890, translated and annotated by W. H. Scott. Manila: Filipiniana Book Guild.

Mills, James P. 1926. *The Ao Nagas*. London: Macmillan & Co.

Ming-Chieh, Chou (Lulji Taligu). 2013. *A Catalogue of Hand Tatoos [sic] at the Puljetji Village of Paiwan: The Writings on the Hand (Vecik Izua ta Lima)*. Majia: Taiwan Indigenous Peoples Culture Park.

Moore, Riley D. 1923. "Social Life of the Eskimos of St. Lawrence Island." *American Anthropologist* 25, no. 3: 339–75.

Morris, Ellen F. 2011. "Paddle Dolls and Performance." *Journal of the American Research Center in Egypt* 47: 73–103.

Moss, Claude R. 1920a. "Nabaloi Law and Ritual." *University of California Publications in American Archaeology and Ethnology* 15, no. 3: 207–342. 1920b. "Kankanay Ceremonies." *University of California Publications in American Archaeology and Ethnology* 15, no. 4: 343–84.

Mu, Yang. 1996. "Music Loss Among the Ethnic Minorities in China – A Comparison of the Li and Hui Peoples." *Asian Music* 27, no. 1: 103–30.

Munro, Neil Gordon. 1963. *Ainu Creed and Cult*, edited by B. Z. Seligman. New York: Columbia University Press.

Murdoch, John. 1892. "Ethnological Results of the Point Barrow Expedition." In *9th Annual Report of the Bureau of American Ethnology for the Years 1887–1888*, 19–441. Washington, DC.

Murphy, Robert F. 1958. *Mundurucú Religion*. Berkeley: University of California Press.

Nakijin Village Board of Education. 1983. *Nakijin no Haritotsu* (*Pajichi*): *Kieyuku Shūzoku* [Nakijin Tattoo (*Pajichi*): Disappearing Customs]. Nakijin, Okinawa Prefecture: Nakijinmura bunkazai chōsa hōkoku-sho dai 7-shū.

Needham, Rodney. 1976. "Skulls and Causality." *Man* 11, no. 1: 71–88.

Nieuwenhuis, Anton. W. 1900. *In Centraal Borneo* [In Central Borneo]. Leiden: E. J. Brill. 1904 *Quer durch Borneo* [Across Dutch Borneo]. Leiden: E. J. Brill.

Nimuendajú, Curt. 1948. "The Cayabi, Tapanyuna, and Apiaca." In *Handbook of South American Indians*, vol. 3, *The Tropical Forest Tribes*, 307–20. Washington, DC: U.S. Government Printing Office. 1952 *The Tukuna*, edited by R. H. Lowie, translated by W. D. Hohenthal. *University of California Publications in American Archaeology and Ethnology* 45. Berkeley.

Noble, Philip D. 1978, "Tattoos of the Managalasi People of Northern Papua." *Anthropos* 73, no. 5–6: 904–908.

Oakdale, Suzanne. 2005. *I Foresee My Life: The Ritual Performance of Autobiography in an Amazonian Community*. Lincoln. University of Nebraska Press.

Obara, Kazuo. 1962. *Nantō irezumikō* [On Tattoos of the Southern Islands]. Tokyo: Chikuma Shobō.

Odaka, Kunio. 1950. *Economic Organization of the Li Tribes of Hainan Island*, translated by M. Hane. New Haven: Yale University, Southeast Asia Studies, Translation Series.

Ohnuki-Tierney, Emiko. 1976. "Regional Variations in Ainu Culture." *American Ethnologist* 3, no. 2: 297–329. 2014 *Illness and Healing Among the Sakhalin Ainu: A Symbolic Interpretation*. Cambridge: Cambridge University Press.

Olson, Ronald L. 1967. Social Structure and Social Life of the Tlingit in Alaska. *University of California Anthropological Records* 26. Berkeley.

Oppenheim, Victor. 1936. "Sobre os restos da Cultura Neolítica dos Índios 'Panos' do Alto Amazonas [About the Remains of the Neolithic Culture of the 'Panos' Indians of the High Amazon]." *Anais da Academia Brasileira de Ciências* 8: 311–14.

Pabst, Maria A., Ilse Letofsky-Pabst, Maximilian Moser, Konrad Spindler, Elisabeth Bock, Peter Wilhelm, Leopold Dorfer, Jochen B. Geigl, Martina Auer, Michael R. Speicher, and Ferdinand Hofer. 2010. "Different Staining Substances Were Used in Decorative and Therapeutic Tattoos in a 1,000-Year-Old Peruvian Mummy." *Journal of Archaeological Science* 37, no. 12: 3256–62.

Pacific Island Management, Production + Ideas (PIMPI). 2015. "Fiji Forever." https://pimpiknows.com/category/the-veiqia-project/.

Palmgren, Nils. 1934. "Kansu Mortuary Urns of the Pan Shan and Ma Chang Groups." *Palaeontologica Sinica,* series D, vol. 3, facs. 1.

Parkitny, Jens Uwe. 2007. *Bloodfaces. Through the Lens: Chin Women of Myanmar.* Singapore: Flame of the Forest: Singapore. 2010 *Im Porträt: Gesichtstatauierungen der Chin-Frauen in Birma/Chin Women of Burma and Their Facial Tattoos: A Portrait.* Munich, Germany: Staatliches Museum für Völkerkunde. 2017 *Marked for Life: Myanmar's Chin Women and Their Facial Tattoos*. Bielefeld: Kerber Verlag. 2024 "Facial Tattoos of the Southern Chin of Myanmar." In *Tattoo Traditions of Asia: Ancient and Contemporary Expressions of Identity*, edited by L. Krutak. Honolulu: University of Hawai`i Press.

Petelo, Su'a Sulu'ape. 1991. "A Tattoo Chief of Samoa" In *Tattoo Time: Art from the Heart*, edited by Don E. Hardy, 102–109. Honolulu: Hardy Marks Publications.

Petrić, Mario. 1973 Običaj tatauiranja kod balkanskih naroda: Karakteristike, uloga i porijeklo [Tattooing Custom of the Balkan Peoples: Characteristics, Role and Origin]. Doktorska disertacija, Univerzitet u Sarajevu, Filozofski fakultet, Sarajevu. [PhD diss., University of Sarajevo, Department of Philosophy, Sarajevo]. 1976 O pitanju porijekla običaja tatauiranja kod balkanskih naroda [On the Issue of Tattoo Origins in the Balkan Nations]. *Glasnik Etnografskog Muzeja u Beogradu* 39–40: 219–37.

Petrie, W. M. Flinders. 1930. *Antaeopolis: The Tombs of Qau*. British School of Archaeology in Egypt. London.

Philippi, Donald L. 1979. *Songs of Gods, Songs of Humans: The Epic Tradition of the Ainu*. Princeton: Princeton University Press.

Picpican, Isikias. 2003. *The Igorot Mummies: A Socio-Cultural and Historical Treatise*. Quezon City, Philippines: Rex Bookstore.

Pikilak, Paninnguaq. 2021. *Talloqut: A Story from West Greenland*, illustrated by Michelle Simpson. Iqaluit, Nunavut, and Toronto: Inhabit Education Books, Inc. 2022a *Pivik Learns from Takannaaluk*, illustrated by Hannah Barrett. Iqaluit, Nunavut, and Toronto: Inhabit Education Books, Inc. 2022b "Tunniit: A Guide to Inuit Tattoos in Greenland." *Visit Greenland*, November 23, 2022. Accessed November 6, 2023. https://visitgreenland.com/articles/a-guide-to-inuit-tattoos-in-greenland/

Piombino-Mascali, Dario, and Lars Krutak. 2020. "Therapeutic Tattoos and Ancient Mummies: The Case of the Iceman." In *Purposeful Pain: The Bioarchaeology of Intentional Suffering*, edited by S. G. Sheridan and L. A. Gregoricka, 119–136. Cham: Springer.

Piombino-Mascali, Dario, Ronald G. Beckett, Orlando V. Abinion, and Dong Hoon Shin. 2017. "The Mummification Process Among the 'Fire Mummies' of Kabayan: A Paleohistological Note." In *Ancient Ink: The Archaeology of Tattooing*, edited by L. Krutak and A. Deter-Wolf, 62–65. Seattle: University of Washington Press.

Poole, Francis. 1872. *Queen Charlotte Islands: A Narrative of Discovery and Adventure in the North Pacific*, edited by J. W. Lyndon. London: Hurst and Blackett.

Prieto, Gabriel, John W. Verano, Nicolas Goepfert, Douglas Kennett, Jeffrey Quilter, Steven LeBlanc, Lars Fehren-Schmitz, Jannine Forst, Mellisa Lund, Brittany Dement, Elise Dufour, Olivier Tombret, Melina Calmon, Davette Gadison, and Khrystyne Tschinkel. 2019. "A Mass Sacrifice of Children and Camelids at the Huanchaquito-Las Llamas Site, Moche Valley, Peru." *Plos One* 14, no. 3: e0211691. https://doi.org/10.1371/journal.pone.0211691

Priewe, Sascha. 2017. "Prehistoric Figurines in China." In *The Oxford Handbook of Prehistoric Figurines,* edited by Timothy Insoll, 469–92. Oxford: Oxford University Press.

Prince, R. 1960. "Curse, Invocation and Mental Health Among the Yoruba." *Canadian Psychiatric Association Journal* 5: 65–79.

Proulx, Donald A. 1996. "Nasca." In *Andean Art at Dumbarton Oaks*, vol 1., edited by E. H. Boone, 107–22. Washington, DC: Dumbarton Oaks. 2001 "Ritual Uses of Trophy Heads in Ancient Nasca Society." In *Ritual Sacrifice in Ancient Peru*, edited by E.P. Benson and A. Cook, 119–36. Austin: University of Texas Press.

Putzi, Jennifer. 2006. *Identifying Marks: Race, Gender and the Marked Body in Nineteenth-Century America*. Athens: University of Georgia Press.

Rao, C. H. 1946. "Note on Tattooing in India and Burma." *Anthropos* 37: 175–79.

Rau, Der-Hwa Victoria. 1992. A Grammar of Atayal. PhD diss., Cornell University, Department of Linguistics, Ithaca, New York.

Reed, Carrie E. 2000. "Early Chinese Tattoo." *Sino-Platonic Papers* 103: 1–52.

Reiss, Wilhelm and Alphons Stübel. 1880. *The Necropolis of Ancón in Perú,* vol. 1. Translated by Augustus H. Kean. Berlin: A. Asher & Co.

Renault, Luc. 2017. "What to Make of the Prehistory of Tattooing in Europe?" In *Ancient Ink: The Archaeology of Tattooing*, edited by L. Krutak and A. Deter-Wolf, 243–61. Seattle: University of Washington Press.

Rice, Florence C. 1988. "A 100–Year-Old Ponca Ceremonial Drum." *The Chronicles of Oklahoma* 66, no. 1: 105–109.

Richards, Anthony. 1997. *An Iban-English Dictionary*. Kuala Lumpur: Oxford University Press.

Riedel, Johann G. F. 1907. "Prohibitieve teekens en Tatuage-vormen op het eiland Timor [Prohibitive Signs and Tattoo Forms on the Island of Timor]." *Tijdschrift voor Indische Taal-, Land- en Volkenkunde* 49:181–187.

Rongfen, Luo. 1995. *Face-Tattooed Women in Nature: The Dulongs*. Kunming: Yunnan Education Publishing House.

Rose, H. A. 1902. "Note on Female Tattooing in the Panjab." *The Indian Antiquary* 33: 297–98. July.

Rosen, Eric von. 1924. *Popular Account of Archaeological Research during the Swedish Chaco-Cordillera-Expedition, 1901-1902*. Stockholm: C. E. Fritze.

Rosing, Jens. 1998. "Fortællinger om inua [Tales of Inua]." *Tidsskriftet Grønland* 5: 155–74.

Roth, Henry L. 1905. "Tatu in Tunis." *Man* 72–73: 129–31.

Rubin, Arnold. 1988. "Tattoo Trends in Gujarat." In *Marks of Civilization*, edited by A. Rubin, 141–53. Los Angeles: UCLA Museum of Cultural History.

Rudenko, Sergei I. 1929. "Graficheskoye iskusstvo ostyakov i vogulov [Graphic Art of Ostyaks and Voguls]." *Materialy po etnografii Rossii* 4, no. 2: 13–40. 1949 "Tatuirovka aziatskikh eskimosov." *Sovetskaia Etnografiia* 14: 149–54.

Ruiz Estrada, Arturo. 1990. "El Hombre Tatuado de Huacho [The Tattooed Man of Huacho]." *Los Especiales de Huacho* 1, no.3: 6-7.

Russell, Robert V. and Rai B. H. Lāl (1916). *The Tribes and Castes of the Central Provinces of India*. Vol. 3. London: Macmillan and Co.

Ryan, Dawn. 1970. *Rural and Urban Villages: A Bi-Local Social System in Papua*. PhD diss., University of Hawai'i, Honolulu.

Ryūzō, Torii. 1990. *The Torii Ryūzō Photographic Record of East Asian Photography*. Vol. 3. Tokyo: University Museum.

Sabater i Pi, J. y J.O.S i Coca. 1992. *Els Tatuatges dels Fang de l'Àfrica Occidental: Art, simbolisme I biologia en una manifestació artistic poc coneguda* [Fang Tattoos of West Africa: Art, Symbolism and Biology in a Little-known Artistic Manifestation]. Barcelona: Ajuntament de Barcelona, Treballs del Museu Etnològic/1.

Salazar-Burger, Lucy and Richard L. Burger. 1982. "La araña en la iconografía del Horizonte Temprano en la costa norte del Perú [The Spider in the Iconography of the Early Horizon on the North Coast of Peru]." *Beiträge zur Allgemeinen und Vergleichenden Archäologie* 4: 213-252.

Salvador-Amores, Analyn. 2012. "The Recontextualization of Burik (Traditional Tattoos) of Kabayan Mummies in Benguet to Contemporary Practices." *Humanities Diliman* 9, no. 1: 55–94. 2017 "*Burik:* Tattoos of the Ibaloy Mummies of Benguet, North Luzon, Philippines." In *Ancient Ink: The Archaeology of Tattooing,* edited by L. Krutak and A. Deter-Wolf, 37–55. Seattle: University of Washington Press.

Samadelli, Marco, Marcello Melis, Matteo Miccoli, Eduard Egarter Vigl, and Albert R. Zink. 2015. "Complete Mapping of the Tattoos of the 5300–year–old Tyrolean Iceman." *Journal of Cultural Heritage* 16, no. 5: 753–58.

Saul, Jamie. 2005. *The Naga of Burma: Their Festivals, Customs and Way of Life.* Bangkok: Orchid Press.

Sawyer, Frederic Henry Read. 1900. *The Inhabitants of the Philippines.* New York: Charles Scribner's Sons.

Schefold, Reimar. 1992. "Shamans on Siberut: Mediators Between the Worlds." In *Mentawai Shaman: Keeper of the Rain Forest*, 105–117, edited by C. Lindsey. New York: Aperture.

Schmidt, Max. 1942. "Los Kayabís en Matto-Grosso (Brazil) [The Kayabís in Mato Grosso (Brazil)]" *Revista de la Sociedad Científica del Paraguay* 5, no. 6: 1–34.

Scutt, Ronald and Christopher Gotch. 1974. *Skin Deep: The Mystery of Tattooing.* London: Peter Davies.

Searight, Susan. 1984. *The Use and Function of Tattooing on Moroccan Women.* 3 vols. Human Relations Area Files: New Haven.

Shaogong, Han, ed. 2016. *Hainan dao lizu de shehui zuzhi he jingji zuzhi* [Social Organization and Economic Organization of the Li Nationality in Hainan Island. By Kenji Okada and Kunio Odaka]. Translated by Jin Shan. Haikou, China: Hainan Publishing.

Sherman, Lucian, and Christine Sherman. 1922. *Im Stromgebiet des Irrawaddy, Birma und seine Frauenwelt* [In the Irrawaddy River Basin, Burma's Women World]. Munich, Germany: Schloss.

Shibatani, Masayoshi. 1990. *The Languages of Japan.* Cambridge: Cambridge University Press.

Shunai, Zhang, and Wu Simin. 2010. "Research on Frog Pattern in Li Brocade." *International Journal of Costume Culture* 13, no. 2: 82–87.

Silverman, Helaine and Donald A. Proulx, 2002. *The Nasca*. Malden, Mass.: Blackwell. Simmons, David R. 1984. "Catalogue." In *Te Maori*, edited by S. M. Mead, 176–235.

Simon, Edmund M. H. 1914. *Beiträge zur Kenntnis der Riukiu-Inseln* [Contributions to Knowledge of the Ryukyu Islands]. Leipzig: R. Voitländers.

Skinner, Alanson B. 1915a. "Societies of the Iowa." *American Museum of Natural History Anthropological Papers* 11, no. 9: 679–740. 1915b "Kansa Organizations." *American Museum of Natural History Anthropological Papers* 11, no. 9: 741–75. 1921 *Material Culture of the Menomini.* New York: Museum of the American Indian, Heye Foundation. 1926 "Ethnology of the Ioway Indians." *Bulletin of the Public Museum of the City of Milwaukee* 5, no. 4: 181–352.

Smeaton, Winnifred. 1937. "Tattooing Among the Arabs of Iraq." *American Anthropologist* 39: 53–61.

Smith, Huron H. 1923. "Ethnobotany of the Menomini Indians." *Bulletin of the Public Museum of the City of Milwaukee* 4, no. 1: 1–174.

Sorokin, Nikolai V. 1873. *Puteshestvie k vogulam: Otchet, predstavlennyi otdelu antropologii i etnografii pri kazanskom obshchestve estestvoispytatelei* [Travel to the Voguls: Report, presented to the Department of Anthropology and Ethnography at the Kazan Association of Explorers]. T. III, No. 4. Kazan: Kazanskii universitet.

Spier, Leslie. 1933. *Yuman Tribes of the Gila River.* Chicago: University of Chicago Press.

Strandberg, Åsa. 2009. *The Gazelle in Ancient Egyptian Art: Image and Meaning.* Uppsala Studies in Egyptology 6. Department of Archaeology and Ancient History, Uppsala University, Uppsala.

Stübel, Hans. 1937. *Die Li Stämme der Insel Hainan: Ein Betrag zur Volkskunde Südchinas* [The Li Tribes of Hainan Island: A Contribution to the Folklore of Southern China]. Berlin: Klinkhardt & Bierman.

Sturtevant, William C. 1980. "The First Inuit Depiction by Europeans." *Études/Inuit/ Studies* 4, no. 1–2: 47–49.

Sverdup, Harald U. 1978 [1938]. *Among the Tundra People.* San Diego: Scripps Institution of Oceanography, University of California, San Diego.

Swan, James G. 1874. "The Haidah Indians of Queen Charlotte's Islands, British Columbia: With a Brief Description of Their Carvings, Tattoo Designs, etc." In *Smithsonian Contributions to Knowledge*, 1–15. Washington, DC. 1886 "Tattoo Marks of the Haida Indians of Queen Charlotte Islands, BC, and the Prince of Wales Archipelago, Alaska." In *Fourth Annual Report of the Bureau of American Ethnology for the Years 1882–1883*, 66–73. Washington, DC: U.S. Government Printing Office.

Symes, Michael. 1800. *An Account of an Embassy to the Kingdom of Ava.* London: Nicol.

Taylor, Edith, and William J. Wallace. 1947. "Mohave Tattooing and Face-Painting." *Southwest Museum Leaflets* 20: 1–13.

Te Awekotuku, Ngahuia. 1997. "*Tā Moko:* Māori Tattoo." In *Goldie*, edited by R. Blackley, 109–114. Auckland: Auckland Art Gallery Toi o Tāmaki. 2007 *Mau Moko: The World of Māori Tattoo.* London: Penguin.

Tein, Tassan S. 1994. "Shamans of the Siberian Eskimos." *Arctic Anthropology* 31, no. 1: 117–25.

Tessmann, Günther. 1913. *Die Pangwe: Völkerkundliche Monographie eines west-afrikanischen Negerstammes . . .* [The Pangwe: Ethnological Monograph of a West African Negro Tribe]. Berlin: E. Wasmuth.

Tezcan, Mehmet. 2010. "Tamgas Among the Turks in the Middle Ages: Their Role as Legal Signs, and Some Related Terms." In *Traditional Marking Systems: A Preliminary Survey*, edited by J. E. Pim, S. A. Yatsenko, and O. T. Perrin, 371–92. London: Dunkling.

Thalbitzer, William. 1914. "Ethnographical Collections from East Greenland (Angmagsalik and Nualik) Made by G. Holm, G. Amdrup and J. Petersen and Described by W. Thalbitzer." *The Ammasalik Eskimo* 1, no. 7. *Meddelelser om Grønland* 39, no. 1: 319–755. Copenhagen.

Thomas, Nicholas. 1995. *Oceanic Art.* London: Thames and Hudson.

Thomas, Sharon. 1968. "Women's Tattoos of the Upper Rejang." *Sarawak Museum Journal* 16: 209–34.

Thurston, Edgar. 1898. "Note on Tattooing." *Madras Government Museum Bulletin* 2, no. 2: 115–19. 1906 *Ethnographic Notes in Southern India.* Madras: Government Press.

Tian Fu, Cheng, ed. 2010. Li zu wen shen xin tan [*Discoveries of Li Tattoos*]. Beijing, China: Federation of Literary and Art Publishing House.

Tillema, Hendrik F. 1936a. "The Subtleties of Tattooing." *Nederlandsch-Indië Oud en Nieuw. Yearbook 1936:* 197–200. 1936b "Vom Tätowieren [From Tattooing]." *Die Umschau* 40, no. 10: 190–92. 1937 "The Kenya Dayak and His Magic." *Nederlandsch-Indië Oud en Nieuw* 22: 95–98. 1989 *A Journey Among the Peoples of Central Borneo in Word and Picture*, edited by V. T. King. Singapore: Oxford University Press.

Titova, Z. D. 1978. "Materialy I.G. Gmelina o Tungusakh XVIII Veka [J. G. Gmelin's Materials On the Tungus of the 18th Century]." *Sovetskaia etnografiia,* no. 1: 59–71.

Topic, John R. 1990. "Craft Production in the Kingdom of Chimor." In *The Northern Dynasties: Kinship and Statecraft in Chimor*, edited by M. E. Moseley and A. Cordry-Collins, 145-176. Washington, DC: Dumbarton Oaks Research Library and Collection.

Touchette, Joseph I. 1931. "The Manners, Customs, and Economic Activity of the Chaouian Berbers of Algeria." (Unpublished manuscript. On file in the John Wesley Powell Library of Anthropology, Smithsonian Institution, Washington, DC).

Tregear, Edward. 1891. *The Maori-Polynesian Comparative Dictionary*. Wellington: Lyon and Blair.

Trilles, R. P. 1912. *Le totemisme chez les fang* [Totemism Among the Fang]. Münster: Biblio. Anthrop.

Trivedi, Harshad R. 1952. "The Mers of Saurashtra: A Study of Their Tattoo Marks." *Maharaja Sayajirao University Journal* 1, no. 2: 121–31.

Truhelka, Ćiro. 1896. "Die Tätowirung bei den Katholiken Bosniens und der Hercegovina [The Practice of Tattooing Among the Catholics of Bosnia and Herzegovina]." *Wissenschaftliche Mitteiulungen aus Bosniens und der Herzogovina* 4: 493–508.

Turalija, Tea. 2011. *Traditional Croatian Tattooing in Bosnia and Herzogovina*. Unpublished manuscript in possession of author, Kupres, Bosnia.

Tuttle, Lyle, ed. *The Tattoo Historian*. San Franciso, CA: The Tattoo Art Museum.

Ubbelohde-Doering, Heinrich. 1967. *On the Royal Highways of the Inca*. New York: Frederick A. Praeger.

Vadan, Youbas, Wei Dao, and Yuma Dada, eds. 2008. Tai ya au wun mian chi lao kou shu li shih ji ying siang ji lu cheng guo bao gao [*Study on Atayal Tattoo Patterns, Oral History, and History Research Report*]. Tai'an Township, Miaoli County, Taiwan: Sheba National Park Administration, Conservation Research Report.

Vale, V., and Andrea Juno, eds. 1989. *Modern Primitives: An Investigation of Contemporary Adornment and Ritual*. San Francisco, CA: RE/Search Publications.

van de Wetering, F. H. 1924. "Het Tatoueeren op Rote [Tattooing on Rote]." *Bijdragen tot de Taal-, Land- en Volkenkunde* 80, no. 1: 23–32.

van Gulik, Willem R. 1982. *Irezumi: The Pattern of Dermography in Japan*. Leiden: E. J. Brill.

Vandier d'Abbadie, J. 1938. "Une fresque civile de Deir el Médina [A Civil Fresco from Deir el Médina]." *Revue d'Égyptologie* 3: 27–35.

Vanoverbergh, Maurice. 1929. *Dress and Adornment in the Mountain Province of Luzon, Philippine Islands*. Washington, DC: Catholic Anthropological Conference. 1972 "Kankanay Religion (Northern Luzon, Philippines)." *Anthropos* 67: 72–128.

VanStone, James. 1959. "Carved Human Figures from St. Lawrence Island, Alaska." *Anthropological Papers of the University of Alaska* 2, no. 1: 18–29.

Verano, John W. 2001. "War and Death in the Moche World: Osteological Evidence and Visual Discourse." In *Moche Art and Archaeology in Ancient Peru*, edited by J. Pillsbury, 111-125. Washington, DC: National Gallery of Art.

von den Steinen, Karl. 1925. Die Marquesaner und Ihre Kunst: Vol. 1. Tatuierung [*The Marquesans and Their Art: Vol. 1. Tattooing*.] Berlin: Dietrich Reimer.

von Middendorff, Alexander T. von. 1875. *Reise in den äussersten Norden und Osten Sibiriens,* Band IV [Travel to the Far North and East of Siberia, vol. 4]. St. Petersburg: Buchdruckerei der Kaiserlichen Akademie der Wissenschaften.

von Spix, Johann B. and Karl F. Phil. von Martius. 1823–1831. *Reise in Brasilien . . . 1817 bis 1820* [Voyage in Brazil . . . 1817 to 1820]. Atlas. München: Gedruckt M. Lindauer.

Wardwell, Allen. 1986. *Ancient Eskimo Ivories of the Bering Strait*. New York: Hudson Hills Press. 1994 *Island Ancestors: Oceanic Art from the Masco Collection*. Seattle: University of Washington Press.

Welper, Elena M. 2009. *O mundo de João Tuxaua: (Trans)formação do povo Marubo* [The world of João Tuxaua: (Trans)formation of the Marubo people]. PhD diss. Social Anthropology. Rio de Janeiro: Universidade Federal do Rio de Janeiro.

Wendt, Maualaivao Albert. 2018. "Tatauing the Post-Colonial Body." In *Tatau: A History of Sāmoan* Tattooing, edited by S. Mallon and S. Galliot, 154–55. Honolulu: University of Hawai'i Press.

Westermarck, Edward. 1926. *Ritual and Belief in Morocco*. 2 vols. Macmillan and Company, Ltd.: London.

Whitman, William. 1937. The Oto. *Columbia University Contributions to Anthropology* 28. New York.

Wied-Neuwied, Prinz Maximilian de. 1840–1843. *Voyage dans l'intérieur de l'Amérique du Nord, Exécuté pendant les Années 1832, 1833 et 1834* [Voyage to the Interior of North America, Executed during the Years 1832, 1833 and 1834]. Chez Arthus Bertrand: Paris.

Williams, A. R. 2006. "Mystery of the Tattooed Mummy." *National Geographic* 209, no. 6: 70–83.

Worchester, Dean. 1912. "Head-Hunters of Northern Luzon." *National Geographic Magazine* 23, no. 9: 833–930.

Xianjun, Wang. 2016. Li zu wen shen: Hai nan dao li zu de dun huang bi hua [*Li Nationality Tattoo: Dunhuang Murals of Li Nationality on Hainan Island*]. Beijing: National Publishing House.

Xueping, Wang, ed. 2001. *Li zu chuan tong wen hua* [Traditional Culture of the Li Group]. Beijing: Xinhua.

Yaling, Hu. 2012. *The Li and Miao Villages in Hainan*. Haikou, China: Hainan Publishing House.

Yamamoto, Yoshimi. 1995. "Yaeyama, Okinawa no irezumi ni tsuite – toku ni kekkon to minkan ryoho ni kanren suru [On the Tattooing Among the Yaeyama, Okinawa – Especially Related to Marriage and Folk Medicine]." *Seiji-gaku kenkyū ronshū* 2: 41–63. 1996 "Mon'yō no sekai-kan ichi Okinawashotō no irezumi ni kansuru ichikōsatsu [A Cosmology of Tattooing: A Study of Tattooing in Okinawan Islands]." *Seiji-gaku kenkyū ronshū* 3: 85–118.

Yamashiro, Hiroaki, and Isao Namihira. 2020. *Hajichi: Ryukyu no kioku* [*Hajichi*: Memories of Ryukyu]. Tokyo: Kōbunken.

Yavuklu, Ahmet. 2021. *Ancient Footprints. Tattoo (Daq): History Engraved on the Body, Viranşehir/Kadim İsler. Bedene Naksedilen Tarih: Daq (Dövme), Viranşehir*. Viranşehir Government Press.

Young, Allan. 1967. "Varieties of Amhara Graphic Art." *Expedition* 9, no. 4: 2-11.

Yvinec, Cédric. 2014. "Temporal Dimensions of Selfhood: Theories of Person Among the Suruí of Rondônia (Brazilian Amazon)." *The Journal of the Royal Anthropological Institute* 20, no. 1: 20–37.

Zhang, F., C. Ning, A. Scott, et al. 2021. "The Genomic Origins of the Bronze Age Tarim Basin Mummies." *Nature* 599: 256–61.

Zining, Li, and Wu Bailu, eds. 2015. *MaSpalaw (hui niangjia): Taiboguan Saixiazu wenwu fanxiang tezhan tulu* [MaSpalaw (Return to Mother's Home): Catalogue of the Saixia Cultural Relics Returning to Hometown Special Exhibit at the National Taiwan Museum]. Taipei: Guoli Taiwan Bowuguan.

Index

Image Credits

Every effort has been made to trace all copyright owners, but if any have been inadvertently overlooked the publishers would be pleased to make the necessary arrangements at the first opportunity.

Key: top = t; bottom = b; left = l; right = r; m = middle

1 Melissa Pizović / @melpzvc. **2** Dmitry Babakhin / @babakhintatau. **10** National Anthropological Archives, Smithsonian Institution (T13408). **11** © Keri Oberly. **12** Japanese Rare Book Collection, Library of Congress. **13** Sarawak Museum Archives. **14** © Lars Krutak. **16** © Michael Zomer / www.patternsof.life. **18t** Metropolitan Museum, New York (08.200.18). **18b** After Herber (1949: pl. IV-V). **19** © Michael Zomer / www.patternsof.life. **20** © Michael Zomer / www.patternsof.life. **21t** Collection of the author. **21b** After Field (1958: figs. 12, 20, 36). **22** © Laura Strachan. **23t** Ahmet Yavuklu. **23b** After Field (1958: fig. 16). **24t** Ahmet Yavuklu. **24r** Ahmet Yavuklu. **24l** © Jordi Zaragozà Anglès. **24b** After Field (1958: figs. 4, 12). **25t** After Glück (1894: 456, fig. 68). **25m** After Truhelka (1896: 505, fig. 1). **25b** After Durham (1929: 105). **26tl** After Truhelka (1896: 505, fig. 69). **26tr** After Truhelka (1896: 505, fig. 70). **26bl** © Tanja Kanceljak. **26br** © TTM. **27bl** © Jordi Zaragozà Anglès. **27br** © Jordi Zaragozà Anglès. **28t** © Eliot Elisofon / National Museum of African Art (EEPA EECL 2558). **28b** © Joan Riera / @lastplacestravel. **29l** © Jordi Zaragozà Anglès. **29r** © Jordi Zaragozà Anglès. **30l** © Lluis Font. **30r** © Kathy Gerber. **31t** © Jordi Zaragozà Anglès. **31b** © Jordi Zaragozà Anglès. **32** Original drawings after Hornblower (1929) and revised by Claire Thorne. After Friedman (2017: 19, fig. 1.05). **33l** RMN-Grand Palais / Christian Dècamps / RMN-GP / Dist. Foto SCALA, Florence. **33r** The Metropolitan Museum of Art, New York (31.3.35). **34t** National Museum of Antiquities, Leiden. **34b** © Genevra Kornbluth. **35t** After Keimer (1948: 41, fig. 39). **35b** After Friedman (2017: 23, fig, 1.7b). **36** © Henry Drewal. National Museum of African Art (EEPA D09086). **37l** © Edith Scharffenberg. **37r** © Jordi Zaragozà Anglès. **38** © Rheinisches Bildarchiv Cologne. Rautenstrauch-Joest-Museum – Kulturen der Welt (48860). **39t** After Tessmann (1913: 200, pl. 152). **39b** After Sabater i Pi and Sabater i Coca (1992: 88). Original illustration from the Jordi Sabater Pi Fund, CRAI Fine Arts Library, Barcelona University. **40l** Photography by Vincent Girier Dufournier. Courtesy of Galerie Bernard Dulon, Paris. **40r** After Tessmann (1913: 265, pl. 218). **41t** After Sabater i Pi and Sabater i Coca (1992: 164). Original illustration from the Jordi Sabater. Pi Fund, CRAI Fine Arts Library, Barcelona University. **41b** After Sabater i Pi and Sabater i Coca (1992: 186). Original illustration from the Jordi Sabater. Pi Fund, CRAI Fine Arts Library, Barcelona University. **42** Elu / Rojda Orhan @deq.ttt. **43r** Elu / Rojda Orhan @deq.ttt. **43l** © Benjamin Au / IG @benjamin_museo. **44-45** Elu / Rojda Orhan @deq.ttt. **46-47** Melissa Pizović / @melpzvc. **48-49** Melissa Pizović / @melpzvc. **50** Library and Archives Canada/National Film Board of Canada fonds/ e011176882. **52l** Metropolitan Museum, New York (1991.228.2). Gift of Dorothy Elowitch, 1991. **52r** Library and Archives Canada/Collection Joseph-Elzéar Bernier/ c001499. **53** Photograph by Edward S. Curtis. Courtesy Library of Congress. **54t** After Taylor and Wallace (1947: 2, fig. 1). **54b** Department of Anthropology, Smithsonian Institution (E217935). © Lars Krutak. **55l** After La Flesche (1919: 113, fig. 119). **55t** Photograph by Edward S. Curtis. Courtesy Library of Congress. **56l** After Fletcher and La Flesche (1911: fig. 105). **56r** Smithsonian American Art Museum, Gift of Mrs. Joseph Harrison, Jr. (1985.66.96). **57l** Courtesy of the Library of Congress. **57r** See Krutak (2014: 181). **58** After Krutak (2014a: 193). **59l** After Dorsey (1898: 5). **59r** After Swan (1874: pl. 4). **60** After Wied-Neuwied (1840–1843: vig. 22). **61l** After Wied-Neuwied (1840–1843: tab. 24). **61r** National Anthropological Archives, Smithsonian Institution (T13408). **62** After Deter-Wolf et al. (2021). **63t** After Gillreath-Brown et al. (2019). **63tr** After Harrington (1913: 110–11). **63b** Courtesy of the Division of Anthropology, American Museum of Natural History (50.1/6643 A-E). **64** Edmund Carpenter Collection, Rock Foundation, New York (A7958). **65** Donald Ellis Gallery, New York and Vancouver. **66** Princeton University Art Museum, the Lloyd E. Cotsen, Class of 1950 Eskimo Bone and Ivory Carving Collection (1997-106). **67l** Collection of Perry J. Lewis and Basha Lewis. **67r** Edmund Carpenter Collection, Rock Foundation, New York (A7753). **68** © Toonasa Tseke. **69l** © Billie Jean Gabriel. **69r** © Dion Kaszas. **70l** © Lars Krutak. **70r** © Wynne Taylor. **71** © Steven Recalma. **72-73** © Aningaaq Rosing Carlsen. **74-75** © Paninnguaq Pikilak. **76** © Philippe Erikson. **78** Collection Museo Oro del Perú. **79bl** After Ubbelohde-Doering (1967: 30, fig. 5). **79br** After Allison et. al (1981: 234). **80t** After Pabst et al. (2010: 3257). **80b** After Barreda (2007: 242). **81** After von Spix and von Martius (1823–31). **82** © Dan James Pantone Dobbratz. **83l** Archives of the Academy of Sciences, St. Petersburg, Russia. **83r** After von Spix and von Martius (1823–1831). **84tl** After von Spix and von Martius (1823–1831). **84tm** After von Spix and von Martius (1823–1831). **84tr** After von Spix and von Martius (1823–1831). **85t** © Lars Krutak. **85bl** Archives of the Academy of Sciences, St. Petersburg, Russia. **85br** Stock Connection Blue / Alamy Stock Photo. **86** Craig Stennett / Getty Images. **87** Dmitry Babakhin / @babakhintatau. **88** Dmitry Babakhin / @babakhintatau. **91** Dumbarton Oaks, Pre-Columbian Collection, Washington, D.C. **92l** © Dan Dennehy. Minneapolis Institute of Art, Ethel Morrison Van Derlip Fund (99.161.2). **92m** © Dan Dennehy. Minneapolis Institute of Art, Ethel Morrison Van Derlip Fund (99.161.2). **92b** See Krutak (2007: 190). **93** The Metropolitan Museum of Art, New York (1978.412.219). **94** Courtesy of the Museum of World Culture, Göteborg. **95l** See Krutak (2007: 212). **95r** After Métraux (1946: 281, fig. 31). **96** Collection of Zisterzienserstift Zwettl, Stiftsbibliothek. **97l** See Krutak (2007: 216). **97r** See Krutak (2007: 212). **98-99** © Lars Krutak. **100** © Lars Krutak. **102** © Lars Krutak. **103t** © Lars Krutak. **103l** After Schmidt (1942: fig. 34). **103r** Archives of the Academy of Sciences, St. Petersburg, Russia. **104t** After Schmidt (1942: fig. 34). **104b** © Lars Krutak. **105** © Lars Krutak. **106** Collection of Dmitry Babakhin, Mata Hoata Tattoo Gallery. **108t** © Lars Krutak. **108b** Collection of the author. **109** © Lars Krutak. **110** Collection of the author. **111l** © Museum of New Zealand Te Papa Tongarewa (OL000135). **111r** Collection National Park Service. **112** Photograph by Thomas Andrew. **113** Collection of Dmitry Babakhin, Mata Hoata Tattoo Gallery. **114r** Collection of Dmitry Babakhin, Mata Hoata Tattoo Gallery. **114l** Collection of Daniel Blau, Munich. **115t** Photo Scala, Florence/bpk, Bildagentur fuer Kunst, Kultur und Geschichte, Berlin. **115b** After von den Steinen (1925: 106, pl. 56). **116** Collection State Library of New South Wales, Australia. **117l** © The Trustees of the British Museum. **117r** IanDagnall Computing / Alamy Stock Photo. **118** After Sturtevant (1980). **119l** After Kotondo (1928). **120r** Collection of the author. **121** © Lars Krutak. **122l** Drawings after Noble (1978: 904). **122-123** © Lars Krutak. **124-129** © Julia Mage'au Gray. **130** © Hekewaru Nathan. **131-135** Courtesy of the artist. **136** Michele and Tom Grimm / Alamy Stock Photo. **138** Collection of the author. **139l** After Simon (1914: 138–39, 141). **139r** Japanese Rare Book Collection, Library of Congress. **140l** Department of Anthropology, Smithsonian Institution (E150715). **140r** Collection of the Penn Museum, Philadelphia (21436-37). **141** After Obara (1962). **141** After Obara (1962). **142t** After Furness (1899: 10, fig. 3). **142b** After Obara (1962: 98). **143** © Hiroaki Yamashiro. **144** © Tube Photo Studio. **145l** National Anthropological Archives, Smithsonian Institution (04754600). **145r** Michele and Tom Grimm / Alamy Stock Photo. **146** Michele and Tom Grimm / Alamy Stock Photo. **147bl** After Kodama (1970: 123, fig. 49). **147br** After Simon (1914: 135). **148** Collection of the author. **149** After Obara (1962: 147). **150** © Ryoichi Keroppy Maeda / IG @keroppymaeda. **151** Photo by Heritage Art/Heritage Images via Getty Images. **152** © Taku Oshima. **153** © Ryoichi Keroppy Maeda / IG @keroppymaeda. **154-155** © Ryoichi Keroppy Maeda / IG @keroppymaeda. **156** © Lars Krutak. **158** After Barton (1930: pl. VII). **159tl** After Worchester (1912: 859). **159r** © Lars Krutak. **160** © Lars Krutak. **161** Courtesy University Museum, The University of Tokyo. **162** After Chi-Lu (1968: 248, fig. 87). **163l** Collection of the author. **163r** Collection of the author. **164** Courtesy National Taiwan University, Department of Anthropology (A1638-1). **165l** After Ho (1960: pl. IV). **165t** Collection of the author. **165b** After Ho (1960: pl. VII). **166l** Wereldmuseum Leiden and Amsterdam (RV-1219-183). **166m** © Lars Krutak. **166r** Photograph by Tom Harrison. © Sarawak Museum Department, Kuching. **167** © Sarawak Museum Archives. **168** © Lars Krutak. **169** © Lars Krutak. **170l** © Lars Krutak. **170r** © Tomasz Madej. **171l** After Jensen (1948: 112, fig. 14). **172r** Frobenius-Institut, Frankfurt am Main. **173** Collection of Elle Festin. **174-175** After Meyer (1885: 512-514). **176-177** Photograph by Hendrik Tillema. Collection Leiden University Library (KITLV 173835–36). **178** Photograph by Hendrik Tillema. Collection Leiden University Library (KITLV 173508). **179** © Lars Krutak. **180-181** After Riedel (1907). **182** National Museum of Ethnology, Leiden (inv. 26–37). **183** Photograph by Michael Barak. Collection Tropenmuseum (TM-20018330), National Museum of World Cultures. **184** © Bernadino Soares. **185** © Bernadino Soares. **186** © Jens Uwe Parkitny. **187** After Symes (1800). **188-189** © Jens Uwe Parkitny. **190** © Lars Krutak. **191** © Greg Semu. **192** © Angusan / Laiyi Indigenous Museum. **193** © Lars Krutak. **194-195** © Joe Ash. **196l** © Lars Krutak. **196r** © Joe Ash. **197** © Lars Krutak. **198-201** © Shatabdi Chakrabarti. **202** After Trivedi (1952: fig. 29). **203** © Shatabdi Chakrabarti. **204, 205t** © Maellyn MacIntosh. **205b** © Michael Zomer / www.patternsof.life. **206-207** © Shatabdi Chakrabarti. **208** © Lars Krutak. **209l** © Jonathan Derksen. **209r** © Lars Krutak. **210** © Lars Krutak. **211tl** © Mo Naga. **211 ©** Lars Krutak. **212** © Stéphane Guillerme. **213-215** © Mo Naga. **216-219** © Shatabdi Chakrabarti. **220** © Hu Yaling. **223-224** © Kisen Wang. **225-227** Stéphane Gros. **228** © Thomas Murray and Wenhua Liu. **229** After Tian Fu (2010: 177). **230** After Stübel (1937). **231** © Hu Yaling. **233** After Barkova and Pankova (2006). **234-236** © Hu Yaling. **237** © Emily Shen. **238** After von Middendorff (1875, pl. IX). **239l** Photograph by Erik Cornelius. Collection of the National Museum, Stockholm (NM 7055). **239r** After Rudenko (1929: 18). **240l** Photography by David Heald. Edmund Carpenter Collection, Rock Foundation, New York (A8360). **240r** Photography by David Heald. Edmund Carpenter Collection, Rock Foundation, New York (A8035). **241** Photography by Waldemar Bogoras. American Museum of Natural History (N-22323). **242l** Photograph by Leuman Waugh. National Museum of the American Indian (N42762). **242r** Photograph by Waldemar Bogoras. American Museum of Natural History (N-2459). **243** © Lars Krutak. **244-246** © Dmitry Babakhin / @babakhintatau. **247** © Zoya Toure. **248** © Billy Jean Gabriel. **249** © Turumakina Duley. **250** © Jason Hipfner. **251l** © Turumakina Duley. **251r** © Elle Festin / @spiritualjourneytattoo.